Turkey
a travel survival kit

Turkey – a travel survival kit
1st edition

Published by
Lonely Planet Publications
PO Box 88, South Yarra, Victoria 3141, Australia
PO Box 2001A, Berkeley, California, USA 94702

Printed by
Colorcraft, Hong Kong

Photographs by
Tom Brosnahan

Design by
Graham Imeson

First published
July 1985

(To Read: Lord Kinross "Atatürk": The Rebirth of a Nation)
London—Weidenfied & Nicholson 1964

Mark Twain — Innocents Abroad

Philip Glazebrook Journey to Kars

National Library of Australia
Cataloguing-in-publication entry

Brosnahan, Tom.
Turkey – a travel survival kit

Includes index.
ISBN 0 908086 45 8

1. Turkey – Description and travel – 1960 – Guide-books. I. Title.

915.61'0438

Tom Brosnahan was born and raised in Pennsylvania, went to college in Boston, then set out on the road. His first two years in Turkey, during which he learned to speak fluent Turkish, were spent as a US Peace Corps Volunteer. He studied Middle Eastern history and the Ottoman Turkish language for eight years, but abandoned the writing of his Ph.D. dissertation in favour of travelling and writing guidebooks. So far his twenty books for various poublishers have sold over two million copies in twelve languages. *Turkey – a travel surival kit* is the result of seven years' experience and travel in the country.

Dedication:
For my Mother and Father,
this one too.

Bu otel aile' için mi?
Is this hotel for ladies?

Guidebooks in Turkey — Pub. Redhouse

Introduction

In the minds of most western visitors, the mention of Turkey conjures up vague visions of oriental splendor and decadence, mystery and intrigue. Once in the country, this romantic but shallow stereotype is quickly dumped in favour of a look at the real thing. For sixty years the Turkish Republic has been working to put its imperial past behind it (while preserving the best parts for posterity), and has done remarkably well. Turkey today is a modern, secular and western-oriented country with a vigorous economy. Its people are disarmingly friendly to foreign visitors, the cuisine is outstanding, the cities like vast outdoor museums, the countryside often like a national park.

The visions of oriental splendor originated at least partly from reality. In the last years of the decadent Ottoman Empire, the entire Middle East ruled by the Turkish sultan was up for grabs, and the western powers did whatever they could to gain advantage. This included putting pressure on the sultan by portraying him in the western press as little better than a monster. This negative image built easily on the notion of the 'terrible Turk' left from the days, in the 1600s, when Ottoman armies threatened the gates of Vienna, and thus all of central Europe.

By contrast with this European stereotype, Muslim tourists coming to Turkey today from the Arab countries formerly subject to the sultanate, have a view of Istanbul as the glittering imperial capital, fount of culture and seat of the last Caliph of Islam. Istanbul is to an easterner what Rome is to a westerner.

Turks themselves are proud of their imperial past. Not the last, decadent centuries, but the times of Mehmet the Conqueror and Süleyman the Magnificent, when the Turkish Empire was the richest, most powerful, most civilized state in the world. And they are fascinated by the depth of history in their homeland, the progression of kingdoms and empires which fostered a dozen great cultures: Hittite, Hellenic, Hellenistic, Roman, Christian, Byzantine, Seljuk, Ottoman and more. But Turks harbour no romantic visions of reclaiming past glories or territories. Kemal Atatürk, founder of the modern republic, set forth the plan in no uncertain terms: preserve the high culture of the past, but get on with the work of the future.

Turkey's past is simply incredible. In fact, the world's oldest 'city' was discovered here, at Çatal Höyük (7500 BC). The Hittite Empire, little known in the west, rivalled that of ancient Egypt, and left behind breathtaking works of art. The the heartland of ancient Greek culture is actually in Turkey, including cities such as Troy, Pergamum, Ephesus, Miletus and Halicarnassus. Most Turkish cities have a Roman past, and all have a Byzantine one, too. The Seljuk Turkish Empire could boast of men like Omar Khayyam; and Celaleddin Rumi, called 'Mevlana,' the poet, mystic, and founder of the order of Whirling Dervishes.

When you've had your day's dose of history and culture, you can head out to the beach. At Side, on the Mediterranean coast, the Roman ruins are right *on* the beach. Or have dinner at a little fish restaurant on the shores of the Bosphorus. Or sit in a shady tea garden for a little *keyf*. Order a tiny, tulip-shaped glass of hearty Turkish tea (for about 5c), enjoy the pleasant surroundings, think over the day's good times, and let it all come together: that's *keyf*. There's no adequate translation; pleasure, contentment, positive outlook, relaxation? It's all part of a normal day in Turkey.

PLANNING WHERE TO GO

Any itinerary is an expression of interest, energy, time and money. Here are some suggestions to help you plan your travels in Turkey.

Less than a week (3-5 days) Istanbul, with an overnight trip to Iznik and Bursa, or Troy and the Dardanelles.

The basic one-week (7-9 day) itinerary Istanbul (2 nights), Bursa (1), Dardanelles and Troy (1), Bergama, İzmir and Kuşadası (2) with excursions to Ephesus, Priene, Miletus, Didyma; return to Istanbul (1). Spend any extra time in Istanbul.

Two weeks Add an excursion from Kuşadası via Afrodisias to Pamukkale/Hierapolis (1-2 nights); also take a loop excursion to Ankara, Konya and Cappad-ocia. Visit the Hittite cities. If you have time left over, spend a day or two on the Turquoise Coast (Antalya, Side, Alanya).

Three weeks Add a yacht cruise or coastal highway excursion from Kuşadası south to Bodrum, Marmaris, Fethiye, Kaş, Finike, Kemer and Antalya; or (second-best), an excursion along the Black Sea coast.

Eastern tour A 10-14 day tour for mid-May to mid-October only: a circuit beginning in Ankara or Cappadocia going to Adiyaman (Nemrut Dağı), Diyarbakir, Bingöl, Van, Doğubayazit (Mount Ararat), Erzurum, Kars, Artvin, Hopa, Rize, Trabzon, Samsun, Amasya, and return to Ankara via Boğaz-kale and Hattuşaş.

Everything You can see an awful lot of the country if you spend six weeks.

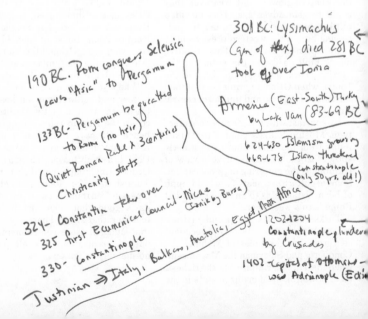

190 BC. Rome conquers Seleucia leaves "Asia" to Pergamum

133 BC - Pergamum bequeathed to Rome (no heir) (Quiet Roman Rule & 3 centuries) Christianity starts

324 - Constantin takes over
325 first Ecumenical Council - Nicae (Iznik by Bursa)
330 - Constantinople
Justinian ⇒ Italy, Balkans, Anatolia, Egypt, North Africa

301 BC: Lysimachus (gen of Alex) died 281 BC took over Ionia

Armenia (East-South) Turkey by Lake Van (83-69 BC

624-630 Islamism growing
669-678 Islam threatened Constantinople (only 50 yrs. old!)

1202-1204 Constantinople plundered by Crusades

1402 capital of Ottomans was Adrianople (Edir

Facts about the Country

HISTORY

Turkey's history is astoundingly long – almost 10,000 years. Before giving a summary, here is a table so you can keep the various periods in the right place:

7500 BC: Earliest known inhabitants; Çatal Höyük. *Stone Age*

5000 BC: Stone-and-Copper Age; settlement at Hacilar.

2600 to 1900 BC: Old Bronze Age; Proto-Hittite Empire.

1900 to 1300 BC: Hittite Empire.

1250 BC: Trojan War.

1200 to 600 BC: Phrygian and Mysian invasions, followed by the great period of Hellenic civilization; Yassi Hoyük; Midas and Croesus; Kingdoms of Ionia, Lycia, Lydia, Caria, Pamphylia; Empire of Urartu. *Coins*

550 BC: Cyrus of Persia invades Anatolia.

334 BC: Conquest by Alexander (the Great) of Macedon. *(died 323 BC.)*

279 BC: Celts, or Gauls, invade and set up Galatia. *(capital = Ankara)*

250 BC: Rise of the Kingdom of Pergamum. *– Library + Asclepium (Medicine)*

129 BC: Rome establishes the Province of Asia, with its capital at Ephesus.

47 to 57 AD: St Paul's trips in Anatolia.

330 AD: Constantine dedicates the 'New Rome' of Constantinople.

527 to 565: Reign of Justinian, greatest Byzantine emperor. *(Sancta Sophia)*

570 to 622: Muhammed's birth; revelation of the Kuran; flight to Medina ('Hegira').

1037 to 1109: Empire of the Great Seljuk Turks, based in Iran.

1071 to 1243: Seljuk Sultanate of Rum, based in Konya. *Jeladin Rumi (Mevlana), Whirling Dervish*

1000s to 1200s: Age of the Crusades.

1288: Birth of the Ottoman Empire, near Bursa. *1326 - Ottomans took Bursa (capital)*

1453: Conquest of Constantinople by Mehmet II.

1520 to 1566: Reign of Sultan Süleyman

1830 Greek Independence – Ottoman (and Fr + GBr)
1853-1856 - Crimean War - (over protecting the Orthodox) against Russians

the Magnificent, the great age of the Ottoman Empire. *- Constantinople + Jerusalem, to Vienna*

1876 to 1909: Reign of Sultan Abdul Hamid, last of the powerful sultans. *1908 - Constitution, 1909 - Coup*

1923: Proclamation of the Turkish Republic. *1920-1922 war of Independence -*

1938: Death of Atatürk. *[Turkey sided c germany +] WWI*

1919 - Greek tries to take Smyrne (Izmir)

Earliest Times *1924 - Constitution*

The Mediterranean region was inhabited as early as 7500 BC, during Paleolithic, or Old Stone Age, times. By 7000 BC a Neolithic (New Stone Age) city had grown up at what's now called Çatal Höyök, 60 km south-east of Konya. These early Anatolians developed fine wall paintings, statuettes, domestic architecture and pottery. Artifacts from the site, including the wall paintings, are in Ankara's Museum of Anatolian Civilizations.

The Chalcolithic (Stone-and-Copper Age) period saw the building of a city at Hacilar (HA-juh-LAHR), near Burdur, in about 5000 BC. The pottery here was of finer quality, and copper implements, rather than stone or clay, were used.

Hittites: The Bronze Age

The Old Bronze Age (2600-1900 BC) was the time when Anatolian man first developed cities of substantial size. An indigenous people now named the Proto-Hittites, or Hatti, built cities at Nesa, or Kanesh (today's Kültepe), and Alaca Höyük. The first known ruler of Kanesh was King Zipani (circa 2300 BC), according to Akkadian texts. You can visit the archaeological site near Kültepe, 21 km northeast of Kayseri. As for Alaca Höyük, 36 km from Boğazkale (see below), it was perhaps the most important pre-Hittite city, and it may have been the first Hittite capital.

The Hittites, a people of Indo-European language, overran this area and established themselves as a ruling class over the local people during the Middle Bronze Age (1900-1600 BC). They took over existing cities, and built a magnificent capital at Hattusas (Boğazkale), 212 km east of Ankara near Sungurlu. The early Hittite Kingdom (1600-1500 BC) was replaced by the greater Hittite Empire (1450-1200 BC). They captured Syria from the Egyptians (1380-1316), clashed with the great Ramesis II (1298), and meanwhile developed a wonderful culture. Their graceful pottery, ironwork ornaments and implements, gold jewellery and figurines now fill a large section of the Museum of Anatolian Civilizations in Ankara. The striking site of Boğazkale (bo-AHZ-kahl-eh), set in dramatic country-side, is worth a visit, as is the religious centre of Yazilikaya nearby. The Hittite religion was based upon worship of a sun goddess and a storm god.

The Hittite Empire was weakened in its final period by the cities of Assuwa ('Asia'), subject principalities along the Aegean coast, which included the city of Troy. The Trojans were attacked by Achaean Greeks in 1250 – the Trojan War – which gave the Hittites a break. But the *coup-de-grace* came with a massive invasion of 'Sea Peoples' from various Greek islands and city-states. Driven from their homelands by the invading Dorians, the Sea Peoples flocked into Anatolia by way of the Aegean coast, and the Hittite state survived for a few centuries longer in the south-eastern Taurus mountains, but the great empire was dead.

Phrygians, Urartians, Lydians and Others

With the Hittite decline, smaller states filled the power vacuum. About 1200 BC the Phrygians and Mysians, of Indo-European stock, invaded Anatolia from Thrace and settled at Gordium (Yassi Höyük), 106 km south-west of Ankara. This Hittite city became the Phrygian capital (circa 800 BC). A huge Hittite cemetery and a royal Phrygian tomb still exist at the site. King Midas (circa 715 BC), he of the golden touch, is Phrygia's most famous son.

At the same time (after 1200 BC), the Aegean coast was populated with a mixture of native peoples and Greek invaders. The region around İzmir became Ionia, with numerous cities. To the south was Caria, between modern Milas and Fethiye, a mountainous region whose people were great traders. The Carians sided with the Trojans during the Trojan War. When the Dorians arrived, they brought some Greek culture to Caria, which the great Carian king, Mausolus, developed even further. His tomb, the Mausoleum, was among the Seven Wonders of the Ancient World. Of his capital city, Halicarnassus (modern Bodrum), little remains.

Further east from Caria was Lycia, a kingdom stretching from Fethiye to Antalya; and Pamphylia, the land east of Antalya.

As the centuries passed, a great city grew up at Sardis, 60 km east of İzmir. Called Lydia, it dominated most of Ionia and clashed with Phrygia. Lydia is famous not only for Sardis, but also for a great invention: coinage. It's also famous for a king who was the world's first great coin collector: King Croesus. Lydia's primacy lasted only from 680 to 547 BC, at which date Persian invaders overran everybody.

Meanwhile, out east on the shores of salty Lake Van, yet another kingdom and culture arose. Not much is known about the Urartians who founded the Kingdom of Van (860-612 BC), except that they left interesting ruins and vast, bewildering cuneiform inscriptions in the massive Rock of Van just outside the modern town.

The Cimmerians invaded Anatolia from the west, conquered Phrygia and challenged Lydia, then settled down to take their place as yet one more ingredient in the great mulligan stew of Anatolian people. The stew was simmering nicely, but in 547 BC the Persians brought it to a boil. Though the Ionian cities survived the invasion and lived on under Persina rule, the great period of Hellenic culture was winding down. Ionia, with its important cities of Phocaea (Foça, FO-chah, north of İzmir), Teos, Ephesus, Priene and Miletus, and Aeolia centred on Smyrna (İzmir), had contributed a great deal to ancient culture, from the graceful scrolled capitals of Ionic columns to Thales of Miletus, the first recorded philosopher in the west. While the great city of Athens was relatively unimportant, the Ionian cities were laying the foundations of Hellenic civilization. It is ironic that the same Persian invasion which curtailed Ionia's culture was what caused that of Athens to flourish. On reaching Athens, the Persians were overextended. By meeting the Persian challenge, Athens grew powerful and influential, taking the lead in the further progress of Hellenic culture.

Cyrus & Alexander

Cyrus, Emperor of Persia (550-530 BC), swept into Anatolia from the east, conquering everybody and everything. Though he subjected the cities of the

Aegean coast to his rule, this was not easy. The independent-minded citizens gave him and his successors trouble for the next two centuries.

The Persian conquerors were conquered by Alexander the Great, who stormed out of Macedon, crossed the Hellespont (Dardanelles) in 334 BC, and within a few years had conquered the entire Middle East from Greece to India. Alexander, so it is said, was frustrated in untying the Gordian knot at Gordium (Yassi Höyük), so he cut it with his sword. It seems he did the right thing, as the domination of Asia – which he was supposed to gain by untying the knot – came to be his in record time. His sword-blow proved that he was an impetuous young man. But then, if you're going to conquer the known world in time to die at the age of 33, you've got to make a few short cuts.

Alexander's effects on Anatolia were profound. He was the first of many rulers who would attempt to meld western and eastern cultures (the Byzantines and the

Alexander the Great

died : Age 33

Ottomans followed suit). Upon his death in 323 BC, in Babylon, his empire was divided up among his generals in a flurry of civil wars. Lysimachus claimed western and central Anatolia after winning the battle of Ipsus (301 BC), and he set his mark on the Ionian cities. Many Hellenistic buildings went up by his orders. Ancient Smyrna was abandoned, and a brand-new city built several kilometres away, where the modern city stands. But the civil wars continued, and Lysimachus was slain by Seleucus (King of Seleucid lands, 305-280 BC), another of Alexander's generals, at the Battle of Corupedium (281 BC). Though Seleucus was in turn slain by Ptolemy Ceraunus, the kingdom of the Seleucids was to rule a great part of the Middle East for the next century, based in Antioch (Antakya).

Meanwhile, the next crowd of invaders, Celts or Gauls this time, was storming through Macedonia on its way to Anatolia (279 BC) to establish the Kingdom of Galatia. The Galatians made Ancyra (Ankara) their capital, and subjected the Aegean cities to their rule. The foundations of parts of the citadel in Ankara date from Galatian times.

While the Galatians ruled western Anatolia, Mithridates I had become king of Pontus, a state based on Trebizond (Trabzon) on the eastern Black Sea coast. At its height, the Pontic kingdom extended all the way to Cappadocia in central Anatolia.

Still other small kingdoms flourished at this time, between 300 and 200 BC. A leader named Prusias founded the Kingdom of Bithynia, and gave his name to the chief city: Prusa (Bursa). Nicaea (Iznik) was also of great importance. And in southeastern Anatolia, an Armenian kingdom grew up, centred on the town of Van. The Armenians, a Phrygian tribe, settled around Lake Van after the decline of Urartian power. A fellow named Ardvates (ruled 317-284 BC), a Persian satrap (vice-regent) under the Seleucids, broke away from the Seleucid kingdom to found

the short-lived Kingdom of Armenia. The Seleucids later regained control, but lost it again as Armenia was split into two kingdoms, Greater and Lesser Armenia. Reunited in 94 BC under Tigranes I, the Kingdom of Armenia became very powerful for a short period (83-69 BC). Armenia finally fell to the Roman legions not long afterwards.

But the most impressive and powerful of Anatolia's many kingdoms at this time was Pergamum. Gaining tremendous power around 250 BC, the Pergamene king picked the right side to be on, siding with Rome early in the game. With Roman help, Pergamum threw off Seleucid rule and went on to challenge both King Prusias of Bithynia (186 BC) and King Pharnaces I of Pontus (183 BC). The kings of Pergamum were great warriors, governors, and also mad patrons of the arts, assembling an enormous library which rivalled that of Alexandria. The Asclepium, or medical centre, at Pergamum was flourishing at this time, and continued to flourish for centuries, under Rome. Greatest of Pergamene kings was Eumenes II (197-159 BC), who ruled an enormous empire stretching from the Dardanelles to the Taurus mountains near Syria. He was responsible for building much of what's left on Pergamum's acropolis, including the grand library.

Roman Times

The Romans took Anatolia almost by default. The various Anatolian kings couldn't refrain from picking away at Roman holdings and causing other sorts of irritation, so finally the legions marched in and took over. Defeating Antiochus III, King of Seleucia, at Magnesia (Manisa, near İzmir) in 190 BC, the Romans were content for the time being to leave 'Asia' (Anatolia) in the hands of the kings of Pergamum. But the last king, dying without an heir, bequeathed his kingdom to Rome (133 BC). In 129 BC, the Romans established the Province of Asia, with its capital at Ephesus.

An interesting postscript to this period is the story of Commagene. This small and rather unimportant little kingdom in central Anatolia, near Adiyaman, left few marks on history. But the one notable reminder of Commagene is very notable indeed: atop Nemrut Dağı (NEHM-root dah-uh, Mt Nimrod), Mithridates I and his son Antiochus I (62-32 BC) built an astounding memorial. Their mammoth cone-shaped funerary mound is framed by twin temples filled with huge stone statues portraying themselves and the gods and goddesses who were their 'peers'. A visit to Nemrut Dağı, from the nearby town of Kahta, is one of the highpoints of a visit to Turkey.

Roman rule brought relative peace and prosperity to Anatolia for almost three centuries, and provided the perfect conditions for the spread of a brand-new, world-class religion.

Early Christianity

Christianity began in Roman Palestine (Judea), but its foremost proponent, St Paul, came from Tarsus in Cilicia, in what is now southern Turkey. Paul took advantage of the excellent Roman road system to spread Jesus's teachings. When the Romans drove the Jews out of Judea in 70 AD, Christian members of this Diaspora may have made their way to the numerous small Christian congregations in the Roman province of Asia (Anatolia).

On his first journey in about 47-49 AD, Paul went to Antioch (Antakya), Seleucia (Silifke), and along the southern coast through Pamphylia (Side, Antalya) and up into the mountains. First stop was Antioch-in-Pisidia, today called Yalvac, near Aksehir. Next he went to Iconium (Konya), the chief city in Galatia; Paul had written an important 'Letter to the Galatians' which is now the ninth book of the New Testament.

From Iconium, Paul tramped to Lystra, 25 miles south, and Derbe, nearby. Then it was back to Attaleia (Antalya) to catch a boat for Antioch.

Paul's second journey took him to some of these same cities, and later north-west to the district of Mysia where Troy (Truva) is located; then into Macedonia.

His third trip (53-57) took in many of these same places, including Ancyra (Ankara), Smyrna (İzmir), and Adramyttium (Edremit). On the way back he stopped in Ephesus, capital of Roman Asia and one of the greatest cities of the time. Here he ran into trouble, because his teachings were ruining the market for silver effigies of the local favourite goddess, Cybele/Diana. The silversmiths led a riot, and Paul's companions were hustled into the great theatre for a sort of kangaroo court. Luckily, the authorities kept order: there was free speech in Ephesus; Paul and his companions had broken no laws; they were permitted to go freely. Later in this third journey, Paul stopped in Miletus.

Paul got his last glimpses of Anatolia as he was being taken to Rome as a prisoner, for trial on charges of inciting a riot in Jerusalem (59-60). He changed ships at Myra (Demre); further west, he was supposed to land at Cnidos, at the tip of the peninsula west of Marmaris, but stormy seas prevented this.

Other saints played a role in the life of Roman Asia as well. Tradition has it that St John retired to Ephesus to write the fourth gospel near the end of his life, and that he brought Jesus's mother with him. John was buried atop a hill in what is now the town of Selçuk, near Ephesus. The great, now ruined, basilica of St John marks the site. As for Mary, she is said to have retired to a mountaintop cottage near Ephesus. The small chapel at Meryemana ('Mother Mary') is the site of a mass to celebrate her Assumption into heaven on 15 August.

The **Seven Churches of the Revelation** were the Seven Churches of Asia: Ephesus (Efes), Smyrna (İzmir), Pergamum (Bergama), Sardis (Sart, east of İzmir), Philadelphia (Alasehir), Laodicea (Goncali, between Denizli and Pamukkale), and Thyatira (Aksehir). 'Church' here of course meant 'congregation', so don't go to these sites looking for the ruins of seven buildings.

The New Rome

Christianity was a struggling faith during the centuries of Roman rule. By 250 AD, the faith had grown strong enough, and Roman rule so unsteady, that the Roman emperor Decius decreed a general persecution of Christians. Not only this, but the empire was falling to pieces. Goths attacked the Aegean cities with fleets, and later invaded Anatolia. The Persian Empire again threatened from the east. Diocletian (284-305) restored the empire somewhat, but continued the persecutions.

When Diocletian abdicated, Constantine battled for succession, which he won in 324. He united the empire, declared equal rights for all religions, and called the first Ecumenical Council to meet at Nicaea (Iznik, near Bursa) in 325.

Meanwhile, Constantine was building a great city on the site of Hellenic Byzantium. In 330 he dedicated it as New Rome, to be his capital city. The city came to be called Constantinople. The emperor died seven years after its founding, in Nicomedia (Izmit), east of his capital. On his deathbed, he adopted Christianity.

Justinian

While the barbarians of Europe were sweeping down on weakened Rome, the eastern capital grew in wealth and strength. Emperor Justinian (527-565) brought the Eastern Roman, or Byzantine, empire to its greatest strength. He reconquered Italy, the Balkans, Anatolia, Egypt and North Africa, and further embellished Constantinople with great buildings. His personal triumph was the Church of the Holy Wisdom, or Sancta Sophia, which remained the most splendid church in Christendom for almost a thousand years, at which time it became the most splendid mosque.

Justinian's successors were generally good, but not good enough, and the empire's conquests couldn't be maintained. Besides, something quite momentous was happening in Arabia.

The Birth of Islam

Five years after the death of Justinian, Muhammed was born in Mecca. In 612 or so, while meditating, he heard the voice of God command him to 'recite'. Muhammed was to become the Messenger of God, communicating His holy word to men. The written record of these recitations, collected after Muhammed's death into a book by his family and followers, is the Kuran.

The people of Mecca didn't take to Muhammed's preaching at once; in fact, they forced him to leave Mecca, says tradition, in 622. This 'flight' (*hijra*, or 'hegira') is the starting-point for the Muslim lunar calendar.

Setting up housekeeping in Medina, Muhammed organized a religious commonwealth which over ten years became so powerful that it could challenge and conquer Mecca (624-630). Before Muhammed died two years later, the *Muslims* (adherents of *Islam*, 'submission to God's will') had begun the conquest of other Arab tribes.

The story of militant Islam is one of history's most astounding tales. Fifty years after the Prophet's ignominious flight from Mecca, the armies of Islam were threatening the walls of Constantinople (669-678), having conquered everything and everybody from there to Mecca, plus Persia and Egypt. The Arabic Muslim empires that followed these conquests were among the world's greatest political, social and cultural achievements.

Muhammed was succeeded by 'caliphs', or deputies, whose job it was to oversee the welfare of the Muslim commonwealth. His close companions got the job first, then his son Ali. After that, two great dynasties emerged. The Umayyads (661-750) based their empire in Damascus; the Abbasids (750-1100) in Baghdad. Both continually challenged the power and status of Byzantium.

The Coming of the Turks

The history of the Turks as excellent soldiers goes back at least to the reign of the Abbasid Caliph Al-Mutasim (833-842). This ruler formed an army of Turkish captives and mercenaries that became the empire's strength, and also its undoing. Later caliphs found that their protectors had become their masters, and the Turkish 'praetorian guard' raised or toppled caliphs as it chose.

The Seljuk Empire

The first great Turkish state to rule Anatolia was the Great Seljuk Turkish Empire (1037-1109), based in Persia (Iran). Coming from Central Asia, the Turks captured Baghdad (1055). In 1071, Seljuk armies decisively defeated the Byzantines at Manzikert (Malazgirt), taking the Byzantine emperor as a prisoner. The Seljuks then took over most of Anatolia, and established a provincial capital at Nicaea/Iznik. Their domains now included today's Turkey, Iran and Iraq. Their empire developed a distinctive culture, with especially beautiful architecture and design; the Great Seljuks also produced Omar Khayyam (died 1123). But politically the Great Seljuk Empire declined quickly, in the style of Alexander the Great's, with various pieces being taken by generals.

But a remnant of the Seljuk empire lived on in Anatolia, based in Iconium (Konya). Called the Seljuk Sultanate of Rum ('Rome', meaning Roman Asia), it continued to flourish, producing great art and great thinkers until overrun by the Mongol hordes in 1243. Jelaleddin Rumi, or 'Mevlana', founder of the Mevlevi (Whirling) Dervish order, is perhaps the Sultanate of Rum's outstanding thinker.

The Crusades

These 'Holy Wars', designed to provide work for the lesser nobles and riff-raff of Europe, proved disastrous for the Byzantine emperors. Although a combined Byzantine and Crusader army captured Nicaea (Iznik) from the Seljuks in 1097, the Crusaders were mostly an unhelpful, unruly bunch. The Fourth Crusade (1202-1204) saw European ragtag armies invade and plunder Christian Constantinople. This was the first and most horrible defeat for the great city, and it was carried out by 'friendly' armies.

Having barely recovered from the ravages of the Crusades, the Byzantines were greeted with a new and greater threat: the Ottomans.

The Birth of the Ottoman Empire

Byzantine weakness left a power vacuum which was filled by bands of Turks fleeing from the Mongols. Guerilla units, each led by a warlord, took over parts of the Aegean and Marmara coasts. The Turks who moved into Bithynia, around Bursa, were followers of a man named Ertugrul. His son, Osman, founded (in about 1288) a principality which was to grow into the *Osmanli* (Ottoman) empire.

The Ottomans took Bursa in 1326. It

Sultan Mehmet II

Mehmet the Conqueror

served them well as their first capital city. But they were vigorous and ambitious, and by 1402 they moved the capital to Adrianople (Edirne) because it was easier to rule their Balkan conquests from there. Constantinople was still in Byzantine hands.

The Turkish advance spread rapidly to both east and west, despite some setbacks. By 1452, under Mehmet the Conqueror, they were strong enough to think of taking Constantinople, capital of eastern Christendom. They took it in 1453. Mehmet's reign (1451-1481) began the great era of Ottoman power.

Süleyman the Magnificent

The height of Ottoman glory was under Sultan Süleyman the Magnificent (1520-1566). Called 'The Lawgiver' by the Turks, he beautified Istanbul, rebuilt Jerusalem, and expanded Ottoman power to the gates of Vienna (1529). The Ottoman fleet under Barbaros Hayrettin Pasha seemed invincible. But by 1585 the empire had begun its long and celebrated decline. Most of the sultans after Süleyman were incapable of great rule. Luckily for the empire, there were very competent and talented men to serve as Grand Vezirs, ruling the empire in the sultans' stead.

The Later Empire

By 1699, Europeans no longer feared an invasion by the 'terrible Turk'. The empire was still vast and powerful, but it had lost its momentum, and was rapidly dropping behind the west in terms of social, military, scientific and material progress. In the 19th century, several sultans undertook important reforms. Selim III, for instance, revised taxation, commerce, and the military. But the Janissaries and other conservative elements resisted the new measures strongly, and sometimes violently. It was tough to teach an old culture new tricks.

Affected by the new currents of ethnic nationalism, the subject peoples of the

Süleyman the Magnificent
The Lawgiver

empire revolted. They had lived side-by-side with Turks for centuries, ruled over by their heads of communities (Chief Rabbi, Patriarch, etc) who were responsible to the sultan. But decline and misrule made nationalism very appealing. The Greeks gained independence in 1830; the Serbs, Bulgarians, Rumanians, Albanians, and Arabs would all seek their independence soon after.

As the empire broke up, the European powers (England, France, Italy, Germany, Russia) hovered in readiness to colonize or annex the pieces. They used religion as a reason for pressure or control, saying that it was their duty to protect the Catholic, Protestant, or Orthodox subjects from misrule and anarchy. The Holy Places in Palestine were a favourite target, and each power tried to obtain a foothold here for colonization later.

The Russian Empire took control of Ottoman Rumania in 1853, and then put pressure on the Turks to grant them powers over all Ottoman Orthodox subjects.

The Russian Emperor would 'protect' all the sultan's orthodox subjects. The result of this pressure was the Crimean War (1853-56), with Britain and France fighting on the side of the Ottomans against the Russians.

More reforms were proposed and carried out in the Ottoman Empire, in an attempt to 'catch up' several centuries in a few years. The last powerful ruler, Abdul Hamid II (1876-1909), was put on the throne by Mithat Pasha, who also proclaimed a constitution in 1876. But the new sultan did away with Mithat Pasha and the constitution both, and established his own absolute rule.

Despite Abdul Hamid's harsh methods, the empire continued to disintegrate, with nationalist insurrections in Crete, Armenia, Bulgaria, Macedonia and other parts of the empire. The situation only got worse. The Young Turk movement for western-style reforms gained enough power by 1908 to force the restoration of the constitution. In 1909, the Young Turk-led Ottoman Parliament deposed Abdul Hamid and put his weak brother on the throne.

In its last years, though a sultan still sat on the throne, the Ottoman Empire was ruled by three members of the Committee of Union and Progress named Talat, Enver and Jemal. Their rule was vigorous, but harsh and misguided, and only worsened an already hopeless situation. When World War I broke out, they sided with Germany and the Central Powers. The Central Powers were defeated, the Ottoman Empire along with them.

The victorious Allies had been planning, since the beginning of the war, how they would carve up the Ottoman Empire. They even promised certain lands to several different peoples or factions in order to get their support for the war effort. With the end of the war, the promises came due. Having promised more than they could pay, the Allies decided on the dismemberment of Anatolia itself in order to get more land with which

to pay 'claims'. The Turks were about to be wiped off the map. As for the last sultans, they were under the control and occupation of the Allies in Istanbul, and thought only of their own skins.

The Turkish Republic

The situation looked very bleak for the Turks as their armies were being disbanded and their country taken under the control of the powers. But a catastrophe turned things around.

Ever since independence in 1831, the Greeks had entertained the *Megali Idea* ('Great Plan') of a new Greek empire encompassing all the lands which had once had Greek influence – the refounding of Byzantium, in a way. During World War I, the Allies had offered Greece the Ottoman city of Smyrna. King Constantine declined for various reasons, even though his prime minister, Venizelos, wanted to accept. After the war, however, Alexander became king, Venizelos became prime minister again, and Britain encouraged the Greeks to go ahead. On 15 May 1919, they did.

The Turks, depressed and hopeless over the occupation of their country and the powerlessness of the sultan, couldn't take this: a former subject people capturing an Ottoman city, and pushing inland with great speed and ferocity. Even before the Greek invasion, an Ottoman general named Mustafa Kemal had decided that a new government must take over the destiny of the Turks from the powerless sultan. He had begun organizing resistance on 19 May 1919. The Greek invasion was just the shock needed to galvanize the people and lead them to his way of thinking.

The Turkish War of Independence lasted from 1920 to 1922. In September 1921 the Greeks very nearly reached Ankara, the nationalist headquarters, but in desperate fighting the Turks held them off. A year later, the Turks began their counter-offensive and drove the Greeks back to İzmir by 9 September 1922.

Victory in the bitterly-fought war made Mustafa Kemal even more a national hero. He was now fully in command of the fate of the Turks. The sultanate was abolished and after it, the Ottoman Empire. A Turkish republic was born, based in Anatolia and eastern Thrace. The treaties of World War I, which had taken everything the Turks had, were renegotiated. Venizelos even came to terms with Kemal, signing a treaty in 1930.

Atatürk's Reforms

Mustafa Kemal undertook the job of completely remaking a society. After the republic was declared in 1923, a constitution was adopted (1924); polygamy was abolished and the fez, mark of Ottoman backwardness, was prohibited (1925); new, western-style law codes were instituted, and civil (not religious) marriage was required (1926); Islam was removed as the state religion, and the Arabic alphabet was replaced by a modified Latin one (1928). In 1930, Constantinople officially became Istanbul, and other city names were officially Turkified (Angora = Ankara, Smyrna = İzmir, Adrianople = Edirne, etc). Women obtained the right to vote and serve in parliament in 1934.

In 1935, Mustafa Kemal sponsored one of the most curious laws of modern times. Up to this time, Muslims had only one, given name. Family names were purely optional. So he decided that all Turks should choose a family name, and they did. He himself chose Atatürk, or 'Father Turk', and officially became Kemal Atatürk.

Atatürk lived and directed the country's destiny until 10 November 1938. He saw World War II coming, and was anxious that Turkey stay out of it. His friend and successor as president of the republic, Ismet İnönü, succeeded in preserving a precarious neutrality. Ankara became a hotbed of Allied-Axis spying, but the Turks stayed out of the conflict.

Recent Years

In the beginning years, Atatürk's Republican Peoples' Party was the only political party allowed. But between 1946 and 1950 true democracy was instituted, and the opposition Democratic Party won the election in 1950.

By 1960 the Democratic Party had acquired so much power that the democratic system was threatened. The army, charged by Atatürk to protect democracy and the constitution, stepped in and brought various Democratic Party leaders to trial on charges of violating the constitution. The popular Peron-like party leader, Adnan Menderes, was executed. Elections were held in 1961.

In 1970 there was a gentlemanly coup d'etat again because the successor to the Democratic Party had overreached its bounds. A high-ranking officer entered the national broadcasting headquarters, read a short message, and the government fell.

Things went well for years until political infighting and civil unrest brought the country to a virtual halt in 1980. On the left side of the political spectrum, foreign communist elements pumped in arms and money for destabilization; on the right side, fanatic religious elements and a neo-Nazi party caused havoc. In the centre, the two major parties were deadlocked so badly in parliament that for months they couldn't even elect a parliamentary president. The economy was in bad shape, inflation was 130% per year, the lawmakers were not making laws, crime in the streets by the fringe elements of left and right was epidemic. The military stepped in on 12 September 1980, much to the relief of the man in the street, and began to straighten things out.

The constitution was rewritten so as to avoid parliamentary impasses. In a plebiscite, it was approved overwhelmingly by the people. The immensely popular head of the military government, General Kenan Evren, was elected to be the country's new president. He resigned his military commission to take over his civilian duties, much as Atatürk had done;

because of his role in saving the country from a desparate situation, many people regard him as a 'second Atatürk'. Under the interim Consultative Assembly and National Security Council, laws stalemated for years were passed. The old political leaders responsible for disruption were tried (if they had committed crimes), or excluded from political life. The indictment against the head of the now-outlawed neo-Nazi party ran to nearly 1000 pages. He was convicted.

In 1983, elections under the new constitution were held, and the party less favoured by the military caretakers won. The new prime minister was Turgut Ozal, a former world banker and economist. Under the new government, Turkey will continue on the course it has pursued since Atatürk: a persistent drive towards an industrialized western economy. How successful this will be is, like many small countries who pursue such a course, more in the hands of world banks and world markets than in the efforts of the countries themselves.

ATATÜRK

It won't take you long to discover the national hero, Kemal Atatürk. Though he died on 10 November 1938, his picture is everywhere, a bust or statue (preferably equestrian) is in every park, quotations from his speeches and writings are everywhere. He is almost synonymous with the Turkish Republic.

Without knowing Turkish history, it's easy to discount such hero-worship. One assumes that it is official policy meant to support the regime in power. But Atatürk is different. He is not Lenin, preserved in wax; or George Washington, all but forgotten; or King Arthur, mostly legendary. It is not official policy that keeps his fame alive, but real popular affection.

The best popular account of his life and times is Lord Kinross's *Ataturk: The Rebirth of a Nation* (London: Weidenfeld and Nicholson, 1964). As portrayed by Kinross, Atatürk is a man of great intelligence and even greater energy and daring, possessed by the idea of giving his people a new lease on life. Like all too few people, he had the capability of realizing his obsession almost single-handed. His achievement in turning a backward empire into a forward-looking nation-state was taken as a model by Nasser, the shahs of Iran, and other Islamic leaders. None had the same degree of success, however.

In 1881, a boy named Mustafa was born into the family of a minor Turkish bureaucrat living in Salonika, now Thessaloniki, but at that time a city in Ottoman Macedonia. Mustafa was smart, and a hard worker in school. His mathematics teacher was so impressed that he gave him the nickname *Kemal* (excellence). The name Mustafa Kemal stuck with him as he went through a military academy and the War College, and even as he pursued his duties as an officer.

He served with distinction, and acquired a reputation as something of a hothead, perhaps because his commanders were

Kemal Atatürk

mustafa Kemal

not as bold as he was. By the time of the Gallipoli battle in World War I, he was a promising Lieutenant Colonel of infantry.

The defence of Gallipoli, which saved the capital from British conquest (until the end of the war, at least), was a personal triumph for Mustafa Kemal. His strategic and tactical genius came into full play; his commanders had little to do but approve his suggestions; he led with utter disregard for his own safety. A vastly superior British force (mostly Anzacs) was driven away, and Mustafa Kemal became an Ottoman folk hero.

Though he was promoted to the rank of *paşa* ('pasha', general), the powers-that-be wanted to keep him under control. They saw him as a 'dangerous element', and they were right.

When the war was lost, the empire on the verge of being disarmed and dismembered, Mustafa Kemal Pasha began his revolution. He held meetings and congresses to rally the people, began to establish democratic institutions, and held off several invading armies, all at the same time and with severely limited resources. There was no one in the world ready, willing or able to help the Turkish nation, except the virtually powerless, brand-new government of the Soviet Union, which was suffering similar pressure from the western powers. And the only hope in the world that the Turks had was this one man. Several times the whole effort almost collapsed, and many of his friends and advisors were ready to ride out of Ankara for their lives. But Kemal never flinched, and was always ready to dare the worst.

Given the situation, it is almost miraculous that he won, but he did. He was fortunate – as was his country – that he lived fifteen years into the republican era, introducing reforms and directing the country's progress with incredible foresight. Most importantly, he gave Turks a new, positive image of themselves. The western image of the Ottoman Turk – decadent, sombre, ignorant and incompetent – was based on a little truth and a lot of politics, but also on religious grounds: Turks were not Christian, and therefore unworthy. Atatürk replaced the Ottoman Turk with a new person who was European and modern in outlook.

Atatürk was the right man at the right time, certainly. But the historical record is clear: without this particular man, there is no way Turkey could be what it is today. Rather, it might almost have ceased to exist; at the least, it would be like one of its Islamic neighbours, with less material and social progress, and no real grounding in democratic traditions. The Turks look around them at their Islamic neighbours and thank their lucky stars they had Atatürk.

This all means something to the visitor. There is a law against defaming the national hero, as you might imagine. More importantly, he is still held in the highest regard by the people. You won't see cartoons or caricatures in the newspapers, as you might of Kennedy, or Churchill, or de Gaulle; and no one mentions him in jest. The battle was just too close, and he did too much, for it ever to be anything but a very serious matter. There are still many people who knew him personally, or saw him, or fought under his command. So keep it in mind: Atatürk is a serious matter to the Turks, and for good reasons.

GEOGRAPHY, WEATHER & CLIMATE

Most first-time visitors come to Turkey expecting to find deserts, palm trees, camel caravans, etc. In fact, the country is geographically diverse, with snow-capped mountains, rolling steppe, broad rivers, verdant coasts and rich agricultural valleys.

Distances

It is big: the distance by road from Edirne, on the Bulgarian border, to Kars on the Russian one, is over 1700 km. From the Black Sea shore to the Mediterranean is almost 1000 km. Now, 1000 km on flat ground might take only one very long day to drive but Turkey has many mountain ranges which can lengthen travel times considerably.

Turkey is located between 35° and 42° north latitude, and 25° and 44° east longitude. It has borders with Bulgaria, Greece, Iran, Iraq, Syria, and the Soviet Union. Coastline totals almost 8400 km; the Aegean coastline alone is 2800 km long. As for mountains, the highest is Aĝri Daĝi (Mt Ararat) at 5165 metres (17,275 ft). Uludaĝ (Mt Olympus) near Bursa, is 2543 metres (8343 ft). Under the empire, snow and ice could be taken from Uludaĝ, sailed across the Sea of Marmara, and presented to the sultan in Istanbul to cool his drinks.

Climatic Regions
Going from west to east, here's how you will find the Turkish topography.

Marmara
This region includes eastern Thrace from Edirne to Istanbul, rolling steppeland and low hills, good for grazing, some farming, and industry. The peninsula of Gelibolu (Gallipoli) forms the north shore of the Çanakkale Boĝazi (Dardanelles, Hellespont). On the southern shore of the Sea of Marmara are low hills and higher mountains (including Uludaĝ). The land is very rich, excellent for raising fruits such as grapes, peaches and apricots. Average air temperature is 14° C; rainfall about 670 mm; this is Turkey's most humid region, with an annual average of 73% humidity.

Aegean
A region of fertile plains and river valleys, low hills and not-so-low mountains. The ancient river Meander, now called the Menderes, is a good example of the Aegean's rivers. When you see it from the heights of ruined Priene you'll know where the word 'meander' comes from. For travelling, the Aegean region presents constantly changing views of olive, fig and fruit orchards on hillsides; broad tobacco and sunflower fields. The average sea water temperature in İzmir, in July, is 26° C; the average air temperature is 17° C; the lowest air temperature of the year would be about –8° C, the highest about 43° C.

Mediterranean
The Mediterranean coast is mountainous without much beach between Fethiye and Antalya, but then opens up into a fertile plain between Antalya and Alanya before going to mountains again. All along the south coast, mountains loom to the north. The great Taurus (Toros) range stretches all the way from Alanya east to Adana. Temperatures at Antalya are a few degrees warmer than at İzmir.

Central Anatolia
The Turkish heartland, is a vast high plateau broken by mountain ranges, some with snow-capped peaks. The land is mostly rolling steppe, though, good for growing wheat, and for grazing sheep. Ankara's elevation is 900 metres above sea level; average temperature is 11°C; lowest is –25°C; highest is 40°C. In summer, Ankara is hot and dry; in winter, chilly and often damp. Late spring and early autumn are perfect.

Black Sea
The coast, 1700 km long, has a climate you might not expect in this part of the world. Rainfall is two to three times the national average, and temperatures are moderate (about 14° C average). You will see hazelnut groves, cherry orchards and tobacco fields. The economy depends very heavily on hazelnuts; the root word of 'cherry' is the Turkish kiraz, and this is where they came from; the cattle on the outskirts of every town provide milk, cream and butter that is famous throughout Turkey. At the eastern end of the Black Sea coast, the mountains come right down to the sea, and the slopes are covered with tea plantations. Rainfall and humidity are highest here. The Black sea coast is like central Europe, but pleasantly warmer.

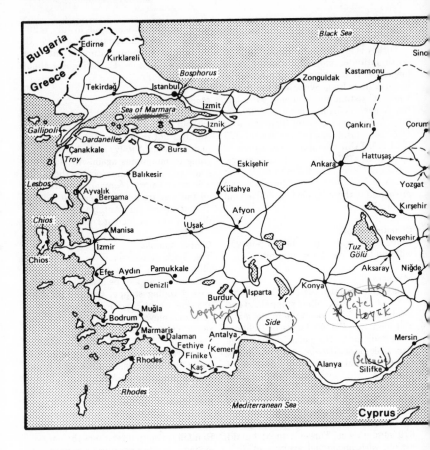

South-east Anatolia

This region is dry (382 mm per year) and hot (average 16° C). The land is rolling steppe with rock outcrops. The major rivers are the Tigris (*Dicle*) and the Euphrates (*Firat*), both of which spring in Turkey.

Eastern Anatolia

A mountainous and somewhat forbidding zone, but wildly beautiful like no other region in Turkey. The average temperature is a cool 9°C, but varying between a hot 38° and a daunting −43°. Rainfall is about average in Turkey, about 560 mm. It's chilly out here except from June through September. The people are not as rich as in other regions, but they do well enough grazing sheep, raising wheat and a few other crops.

When to Visit

Spring and autumn are the best, roughly from April through June and September through November. The climate is perfect on the Aegean and Mediterranean coasts then, and in Istanbul. It's cooler in Central Anatolia, but not unpleasantly. There is

very little rain between May and October.

The best months for water sports are, of course, the warmest: July and August. But the water is just right in May, June, September and October too.

In the hottest months on the coasts you may have to take a siesta during the heat of the day between noon and 3 pm. Get up early in the morning, clamber around the local ruins, then after lunch and a siesta come out again for *piyasa vakti*, 'promenade time', when everyone strolls by the sea, sits in a cafe, and watches the sunset.

If you plan a trip to eastern Turkey, do it in July and August. Don't venture into the east before May or after September, as there will still be lots of snow around, perhaps even closing roads and mountain passes.

What to Wear
For high summer, roughly July through mid-September, you'll need light cotton summer clothes, and a light sweater or jacket for the evenings or to wear up on the Central Anatolian plateau. You won't need rain gear at all, except perhaps on the Black Sea coast.

In spring and autumn, summer clothing will still be right but the evenings will be cooler. If you plan to travel extensively in Central Anatolia (Ankara, Konya, Cappadocia, Nemrut Dağı), pack a heavier sweater and perhaps a light raincoat.

Winter wear – December through March – is woollens and raingear. Though it doesn't get really cold along the Mediterranean, it does get damp, rainy and chilly everywhere. Istanbul and İzmir get dustings of snow; Ankara gets more.

Formality vs informality. How does one dress in a Muslim country? In this one, you dress pretty much as you would for Europe. In high summer, no one will really expect men to have a coat and tie, even when visiting a government official. For the rest of the year, Turks tend to dress formally in formal situations such as at the office or in a good restaurant or nightclub, but informally at other times. Neat and tidy dress is still admired here. Tatty or careless clothes, a sign of nonchalance or independence in other societies, are looked upon as tatty or careless in Turkey.

Anyone can visit a Turkish mosque so long as they look presentable. Your clothes must be neat. No shorts or sleeveless shirts on either men or women; women require skirts of a modest length (knees), and a headscarf. Before you enter a working mosque, that is, one with carpets on its floor, remove your shoes to protect the carpets from soil. Muslims pray on the carpets, so they need to be kept clean.

FESTIVALS & HOLIDAYS

The official Turkish calendar is the western, Gregorian one as in Europe. But religious festivals, some of which are public holidays, are celebrated according to the *Hicri* (HIJ-ree), Muslim lunar calendar. As the lunar calendar is about eleven days shorter than the Gregorian, the Muslim festivals arrive that many days earlier each year.

Actual dates for Muslim religious festivals are not completely systematic. Rather, they are proclaimed by Muslim authorities after the appropriate astronomical observations and calculations have been made. But to help you know what's going on the approximate dates of all major festivals for the near future are listed at the end of this section. No matter what month or year you visit Turkey, you can see at once when a lunar-calendar festival will be held.

Muslim days, like Jewish ones, begin at sundown. Thus a Friday holiday will begin Thursday at sunset and last until Friday sunset. For major religious holidays there is also a half-day vacation for 'preparation', called *arife* (ah-ree-FEH), preceding the start of a festival, and thus shops and offices will close about noon, and the festival begin at sunset.

Friday is the Muslim Sabbath, but it is not a holiday. Mosques and baths will be crowded, especially Friday morning. But the day of rest, a secular one, is Sunday.

Only two religious holidays are public holidays: *Şeker Bayrami* and *Kurban Bayrami*.

Festivals

Regaip Kandili According to the lunar calendar, Regaip Kandili is the first Friday in the month of *Recep*, the traditional date for the conception of the Prophet Muhammad. Mosques are illuminated and special foods prepared. You'll see packets of small, sweetish *simit* bread rings, wrapped in coloured paper, for sale on the streets.

Mirac Kandili The 26th of the month of *Recep*, Mirac Kandili celebrates Muhammad's miraculous nocturnal journey from Mecca to Jerusalem and to heaven, astride a winged horse named *Burak*. Mosques are illuminated and special foods eaten.

Berat Kandili The 'sacred night' between the 14th and 15th of the month of *Şaban*, it has various meanings in different countries, like Hallowe'en (All Saints, Day of the Dead). Mosque illuminations, special foods.

Ramazan The Holy Month, called Ramadan in other Muslim countries, it is similar in some ways to Lent. For the thirty days of Ramazan a good Muslim lets *nothing* pass his lips during daylight hours: not eating, drinking, smoking, or even licking a postage stamp. A cannon shot, and radio announcer these days, signals the end of the fast at sunset. The fast is broken traditionally with flat *pide* bread if possible. Lavish dinners are given, and may last far into the night. Before dawn, drummers circulate through town to awaken the faithful so they can eat before sunrise. Ramazan can be an ordeal when it falls during the long, hot days of summer (as it does now); *Ramazan kafasi* ('Ramazan head', meaning irritability) can cause arguments to break out. Restaurants may be closed till nightfall, and in conservative towns it's bad form for anyone – non-Muslims included – to smoke, munch snacks or sip drinks in plain view. Business hours may change, and be shorter. As non-Muslims, it's understood that you get to eat and drink when you like, and in the big cities you'll find lots of non-fasting Muslims right beside you, but it's best to be discreet and to maintain a polite low visibility. The fasting of Ramazan is a worthy, sacred act, and a blessing to Muslims. Pregnant women, the infirm, and travellers are excused, according to the Kuran, if they feel they cannot keep the fast.

Kadir Gecesi The 27th day of the Holy Month of Ramazan is the 'Night of Power', when the Kuran was revealed and Muhammad was appointed to be the Messenger of God. His duty was to communicate the Word of God to the world. Mosque illuminations, special prayers and foods celebrate the day.

Şeker Bayrami Also called Ramazan Bayrami, Id es-Segir or Id el-Adha, this is a three-day festival at the end of Ramazan. *Şeker* (shek-EHR) is sugar or candy, and it's traditional during the days of this festival for children to go door-to-door asking for sweet treats. Muslims exchange greeting cards, and pay social calls. Everybody enjoys drinking lots of tea in broad daylight after fasting for Ramazan. The festival is a three-day national holiday when banks and offices are closed. Hotels, buses, trains and airplanes are heavily booked.

Kurban Bayrami The most important religious and secular holiday of the year, Kurban Bayrami (koor-BAHN, sacrifice) is equivalent in importance to Christmas in Christian countries. Traditional date for its beginning is the 10th day of the month of Zilhicce.

The festival commemorates Abraham's near-sacrifice of Issac on Mt Moriah (Genesis 22; Kuran, Sura 37). If you remember the story, God orders Abraham to take Isaac, the son of his old age, up to Mt Moriah and sacrifice him. Abraham takes Isaac up the mountain and lays him on the altar, but at the last moment God stops Abraham, congratulates him on his faithfulness, and orders him to sacrifice instead a ram caught in a nearby bush.

Following the tradition today, 2½ million rams get their's on Kurban Bayrami in Turkey each year. For days beforehand you'll see herds of sheep parading through streets or gathered in markets. Every head of household who can afford a sheep buys one and takes it home. Right after the early morning prayers on the actual day of Bayram, the head of household slits the sheep's throat. It's then flayed and butchered, and family and friends immediately cook up a feast. A sizeable portion of the meat is distributed to the needy, and the skin is often donated to a charity; the charity sells it to a leather products company. Lots of people take to the road, going home to parents or friends. Everybody exchanges greeting cards. At some point, you'll probably be invited to share in the festivities.

Kurban Bayrami is a four-day national holiday which you must plan for. Banks will be closed for a full week, though one or two branches will stay open in the big cities to serve foreigners. Transportation will be packed, and hotel rooms, particularly in resort areas, at a premium.

Mevlid-i Nebi The 12th of Rebi ul-evvel is the anniversary of the Prophet's birth (in about 570 AD). Special prayers and foods, mosque illuminations.

THE CALENDAR
January
All month Camel wrestling at various locations in the province of Aydin, south of İzmir.

1 January New Year's Day is a public holiday. Decorations in shops, exchanges of gifts and greeting cards, make it a kind of surrogate Christmas, good for business.

15-16 January Camel-wrestling Festival, in the village of Selcuk, next to Ephesus, south of İzmir.

February
In February, it rains almost everywhere, and is chilly and cheerless. The only fun to be had is indoors, or at the ski slopes on Uludağ, near Bursa. Another ski resort is in the Beydaglari mountains near Antalya.

March
Regaip Kandili (see above) occurs 24-25 March 1985; and 13-14 March 1986.

April
The movement of the lunar calendar now makes April a time of *kandil* festivals (see above). Miraç Kandili is on 17-18 April 1985; and 6-7 April 1986. Berat Kandili is 24-25 April 1986.

20-30 April Manisa Powergum Festival, when a traditional remedy called *Mesir macunu* or *Kuvvet macunu* ('power-gum'), said to restore health, youth and potency, is brewed in Manisa, near İzmir.

23 April The big national holiday is National Sovereignty Day, when the first Grand National Assembly, or republican parliament, met in Ankara in 1920; it's also Children's Day.

Late April to early May Tulip Festival in Emirgân, the Bosphorus suburb of Istanbul.

May
May begins the tourist season in earnest, and also includes important civil and religious holidays. Sound and light shows begin at the Blue Mosque in Istanbul, and last until October.

In Konya, the javelin-throwing game of *cirit* (jirid), played on horseback, takes place every Saturday and Sunday until October.

Religious holidays Berat Kandili is 5-6 May 1985. The Holy Month of Ramazan is 21 May to 20 June 1985; 10 May to 9 June 1986.

First week Şelcuk Ephesus Festival of Culture and Art at Şelcuk, south of İzmir; folk dances, concerts, exhibits, some in the Great Theatre at Ephesus.

19 May Youth and Sports Day, held to commemorate Atatürk's birthday (1881).

29 May In Istanbul there are celebrations remembering the conquest of the city from Byzantium in 1453.

Last week Festival of Pergamum at Bergama – drama in the ancient theatre, folk dancing and craft exhibits.

June
Sound and light shows take place at the Blue Mosque in Istanbul all month.

If you stay in Turkey the entire month, you're sure to encounter some part of Ramazan during the month. *Kadir Gecesi*, a *kandil* festival (see above), occurs on 16-17 June 1985, and 5-6 June 1985. The important festival and public holiday of Seker Bayrami is 21-23 June 1985; and 10-12 June 1986.

First week
The International Mediterranean Festival takes place in İzmir usually at this time.

4-5 June Traditional Rosegrowing Competition at Konya, when roses grown in the region are judged.

7-13 June Music and Art Festival at Marmaris – musical performances, folk dances, exhibitions.

Second week There's the Traditional Kirkpinar Oiled Wrestling Competition at Edirne, and also the Festival of Troy at Çanakkale, on the Dardanelles near Troy.

Late June to mid-July The world-class Istanbul International Festival, with top performers in the arts and special exhibitions, takes place in Istanbul.

July

In Istanbul, sound and light at the Blue Mosque continues, as does the Istanbul Festival. These are the two highlights of the month.

1 July The first day of the month is *Denizcilik Günü* (Navy Day), when seamen, ships and various maritime pursuits are celebrated. It commemorates the day when Turkey regained the right to operate its own ships along its own shores. (Under the empire, this right of *cabotage* had been granted under the Capitulations exclusively to foreign shipping companies.) You'll see decorations, hear speeches, and share in a moment of silence (except for ships' sirens and car horns) at 10 am. No public holiday, though.

5-10 July Nasreddin Hoca Celebrations, in honour of the semi-legendary humorous master of Turkish folklore legends and tales; in Aksehir.

7-12 July At Bursa, the Folklore and Music Festival is one of Turkey's best folk dancing events of the year; the Bursa Fair (trade and tourism) starts about the same time.

29-31 July Music, Folklore and Water Sports Festival in Foça, north of İzmir.

August

In Istanbul, sound and light continues at the Blue Mosque. Similar shows begin at the Anitkabir, Atatürk's Mausoleum, in Ankara.

Kurban Bayrami, the most important holiday of the year, falls on 27-28 August 1985; 16-17 August 1986. Remember, this is a four-day holiday. The country will probably close down during 27-31 August 1985, and 16-20 August 1986; in later years, about eleven days earlier each year.

15 August A special mass celebrates the Assumption of the Virgin Mary, at the House of the Virgin Mary (Meryemana), near Ephesus. The Catholic Archbishop of İzmir says mass.

15-18 August Çanakkale Troy Festival at Çanakkale, near Troy – folk dances, music, tours of Mt Ida and Troy.

20 August to 20 September The biggest festival is the İzmir International Fair; for a month the city's hotels are packed and transportation is crowded. The fair has amusements, cultural and commercial-industrial displays.

26 August Armed Forces Day, with speeches and parades.

30 August Zafer Bayrami (zah-FEHR, Victory), commemorating the decisive victory at Dumlupinar of the republican armies over the invading Greek army during Turkey's War of Independence in 1922. Several foreign countries, including Greece, invaded Anatolia after World War I. Towns and cities celebrate their own *kurtuluş günü* (koor-too-LOOSH gew-new, Day of Liberation) on the appropriate date when Atatürk's armies drove out the Greeks during July and August 1922.

September

Sound and light shows continue at the Blue Mosque in Istanbul and at the Anitkabir in Ankara. The İzmir Fair goes on until 20 September.

1-9 September Bodrum Culture and Art Week, Turkish classical music concerts in Bodrum Castle, art exhibits, and water sports shows.

2-4 September Kirşehir Ahi Evran Crafts and Folklore Festival at Kirsehir, when the products of Turkish handicrafts are displayed and modelled in shows.

9 September In Izmir it's *Kurtuluş Günü*, or Liberation Day. In 1922, Atatürk's armies pushed the Greek invaders into the sea. Lots of parades, speeches and flags.

11-12 September Çorum Hittite Festival, craft shows, musical performances, tours of Hittite archaeological sites at Çorum, near Ankara.

15-18 September Cappadocia Tourism Festival, a grape harvest and folklore festival highlighting the 'fairy chimneys' and underground cities of Cappadocia.

15 September to 5 October Textile and Fashion Fair at Mersin – fashion shows, handicrafts exhibitions, musical and folk-dancing performances.

22-30 September Konya hosts performances by the Whirling Dervish order, based here. On the 24th there's a culinary contest.

26-29 September At Diyarbakir, the Watermelon Festival. One year when I attended, everybody was disappointed because the prize-winning watermelon weighed in at a mere 32 kilograms. Bad year, they said. No rain.

October

Sound and light shows are supposed to continue in Istanbul at the Blue Mosque, but check in advance.

1-9 October Film and Art Festival in Antalya, with a competition for best Turkish film of the year; other exhibits.

21-29 October Turkish Troubadors' Week at Konya – bards who continue the traditional poetic forms hold contests in repartee, free-form composition, and riddles.

29 October Cumhuriyet Bayrami (joom-hoor-ee-YEHT, Republic Day), commemorating the proclamation of the republic by Atatürk in 1923; big holiday, lots of parades and speeches.

November

10 November is the most important day of the month, the day Atatürk died in 1938. At precisely 9.05 am, the moment of his death, the entire country comes to a screeching halt for a moment of silence. Literally everything stops in its tracks (you should too), just for a moment. Car horns and sirens blare. In schools, in the newspapers (whose normally red mastheads are all in black on this day), on radio and television, the national hero's life and accomplishments are reviewed.

The Prophet Muhammad's birthday, *Mevlid-i Nebi*, falls on 24-25 November 1985; and 14-15 November 1986; *kandil*-like celebrations and illuminations.

December

All month Camel wrestling at various locations in the province of Aydin, south of İzmir.

6-8 September St Nicholas Festival, when commemorative ceremonies are held in the 4th-century church of St Nicholas, the original Santa Claus, in Demre, near Antalya.

14-17 December (approx) The Mevlana Festival, honouring Celaleddin Rumi, the great poet and mystic who founded the Mevlevi order of Whirling Dervishes, is held in Konya. Hotel space is tight, so try to pin down a room in advance, or be prepared to take a room below your normal standard.

RELIGION

The Turkish people are 99% Muslim. There is a tiny Turkish Orthodox patriarchate. A small community of Sephardic Jews, descendants of those who were driven out of Spain by the Inquisition and welcomed into the Ottoman Empire, exists in Istanbul. There are groups of Greek Orthodox, Armenian Orthodox, Byzantine Catholic, Armenian Roman Catholic, Armenian Protestant, and a few even smaller sects. But all of these non-Muslim groups make up less than 1% of the population, so to talk about Turkish religion is to talk about Islam.

The story of Islam's founding is covered in the History section.

The basic beliefs of Islam are these: God (Allah) created the world and every-

A verse of the Kuran

thing in it pretty much according to the Biblical account. In fact, the Bible is a sacred book to Muslims. Adam, Noah, Abraham, Moses and Jesus were prophets. Their teachings and revelations are accepted by Muslims, except for Jesus's divinity and his status as savior. Jews and Christians are called 'People of the Book', meaning those with a revealed religion that preceded Islam. The Kuran prohibits enslavement of any People of the Book. Jewish prophets and wise men, Christian saints and martyrs, are all accepted as holy men in Islam.

But Islam is the perfection of this earlier tradition. Though Moses and Jesus were great prophets, Muhammed was the greatest and last, *the* Prophet. To him, God communicated his final revelation, and entrusted him to communicate it to the world. Muhammed is not a savior, nor is he divine. He is God's messenger, deliverer of the final, definitive message.

Muslims do not worship Muhammed, only God. In fact, *muslim* in Arabic means, 'One who has submitted (to God's will)'; *islam* is 'submission (to God's will)'. It's all summed up in the phrase called out from the minaret five times a day, and said at the beginning of Muslim prayers: 'There is no god but God, and Muhammed is his Prophet.'

God's revelations to Muhammed are contained in the *Kuran-i Kerim*, the Holy Kuran. Muhammed, who couldn't read or write, recited the *suras* (verses or chapters) of the Kuran in an inspired state. They were written down by followers, and are still regarded as the most beautiful, melodic and poetic work in Arabic literature, sacred or profane. The Kuran, being sacred, cannot be translated. It exists truly only in Arabic.

Ideally, Islam is a commonwealth, a theocracy, in which the religious law of the Kuran is the only law – there is no secular law. Courts are religious courts. In Turkey and several other Muslim countries, this belief has been replaced by secular law codes.

To be a Muslim, one need only submit in one's heart to God's will, and say, 'There is no god but God, and Muhammed is his Prophet'. Basic religious duties are simple, and few in number:

- One must say, understand and believe, 'There is no god but God, and Muhammed is His Prophet'.

- One must pray five times a day: at dawn, at noon, at mid-afternoon, at dusk, and after dark.

- One must give alms to the poor.

- One must keep the fast of Ramazan, if capable of doing so.

- One must make a pilgrimage to Mecca once during one's life, if possible.

Muslim prayers are set rituals. Before praying, a Muslim must wash hands and arms, feet and ankles, head and neck in running water; if no water is available, in clean sand; if there's no sand, the motions will suffice. Then he must cover his head, face Mecca and perform a precise series of gestures and genuflexions. If he deviates from the pattern, he must begin again.

In daily life, a Muslim must not touch or eat pork, or drink wine (interpreted as any alcoholic beverage), and must refrain from fraud, usury, slander, and gambling. No sort of image can be revered or worshipped in any way.

Islam has been split into many factions and sects since the time of Muhammed. Islamic theology has become very elaborate and complex. But these tenets are still the basic ones, the ones shared by all Muslims.

LANGUAGE

Turkish is the dominant language in the Turkic language group which also includes such less-than-famous tongues as Kirghiz, Kazakh and Azerbaijani. Once thought to be related to Finnish and Hungarian, the Turkic languages are now seen as comprising their own unique language group. You can find people who speak Turkish, in one form or another, from Belgrade, Yugoslavia all the way to Sinkiang, China.

In 1928, Atatürk did away with the Arabic alphabet and adopted a Latin-based alphabet much better suited to easy learning and correct pronunciation. He also instituted a language reform to purge Turkish of abstruse Arabic and Persian borrowings, to rationalize and simplify it. The result is a logical, systematic and expressive language which has only one irregular noun (*su*, water), one irregular verb (*etmek*, to be), and no genders.

Word order and verb formation are very different from the Indo-European languages', which makes Turkish somewhat difficult to learn at first, despite its elegant simplicity. Verbs, for example, consist of a root plus any number of modifying suffixes. Verbs can be so complex that they constitute whole sentences in themselves, though this is rare. The standard blow-your-mind example is, *afyonkarahisarlılaştıramadıklarımızdanmıymuştunuz?* 'Weren't you one of those people whom we tried – unsuccessfully – to make to resemble the citizens of Afyonkarahisar?' It's not the sort of word you see every day.

Turks don't expect any foreigner to know Turkish, but if you can manage a few words you'll delight them. For their part, they'll try whatever foreign words they know, usually English or German, but some French. In this guide I've written the necessary Turkish words into the text wherever possible, so that you won't be at a loss for words. For a full collection of words, see the Turkish Language Guide section at the back of this book.

You may be approached by university students or school children wanting to practise their English. The approach is usually what it's purported to be, although if you're a good looking young woman and he's a good looking young Turkish man, he'll figure (naturally), why stop at English? Alas, foreign men are very rarely approached by good looking Turkish women for English practice or anything else.

If you want to be 'fluent' as a first-time speaker of Turkish, pick up *Turkish for*

Travellers by Berlitz. More than just a phrase book, it describes and explains cultural nuances on matters such as dining, shopping and meeting people, and provides all the words and sentences you'll ever need.

LOCAL CUSTOMS & TRADITIONS

Under the Ottoman Empire (1300s to 1923), Turkish etiquette was highly organized and very formal. Every encounter among people turned into a mini-ceremony full of the flowery 'romance of the East'. Though the Turks have adapted to the informality of 20th-century life, you'll still notice vestiges of this courtly state of mind. Were you to learn Turkish, you'd find dozens of polite phrases – actually rigid formulas – to be repeated on cue in many daily situations. Some are listed in the language section at the back of this book. Pull out one of these at the proper moment, and the Turks will love it.

Turks are very understanding of foreigners' different customs, but if you want to behave in accordance with local feelings, use all the politeness words you can muster, at all times. This can get laborious, and even Turks complain about how one can't even get out the door without five minutes of politenesses. But even the complainers still say them.

Also note these things: don't point your finger directly towards any person. Don't show the sole of your foot or shoe towards any person (ie, so they can see it). Don't blow your nose openly in public, especially in a restaurant; instead, turn or leave the room and blow quietly. Don't pick your teeth openly, but cover your mouth with your hand. Don't do a lot of kissing or hugging with a person of the opposite sex in public. All of these actions are considered rude and offensive.

Mosque Etiquette

Always remove your shoes before stepping on a mosque's carpets, or on the clean area just in front of the mosque door. This is not a religious law, just a practical one.

Worshippers kneel and touch their foreheads to the carpets, and they like to keep them clean. If there are no carpets, as in a saint's tomb, you can walk right in with your shoes on.

Wear modest clothes when visiting mosques, as you would when visiting a church. No tatty blue jeans, no shorts on men or women, no weird gear. Women should have head, arms and shoulders covered, and modest dresses or skirts, preferably to the knees. At some of the most-visited mosques, attendants will lend you long robes if your clothing doesn't meet a minimum standard. The loan of the robe is free, though the attendant will probably indicate where you can give a donation to the mosque. If you donate, chances are that the money actually will go to the mosque.

Visiting Turkish mosques is generally very easy. There are no hard and fast rules, however. Though most times no one will give you any trouble, now and then there may be a stickler for propriety guarding the door.

Avoid entering mosques at prayer time, (ie., at the call to prayer – dawn, noon, mid-afternoon, dusk, and evening) or 20 minutes thereafter. Avoid visiting mosques at all on Fridays, especially morning and noontime. Friday is the Muslim holy day.

When you're inside a mosque, even if it is not prayer time, there will usually be several people praying. Don't disturb them in any way; don't take flash photos; don't walk directly in front of them.

Everybody will love you if you drop some money into the 'Donations' box.

Body Language

Turks say 'yes' (*evet*, eh-VEHT) by nodding the head forward and down.

To say 'no' (*hayır*, HAH-yuhr), nod your head up and back, lifting your eyebrows at the same time. Or just raise your eyebrows: that's 'no'.

Another way of saying 'no' is *yok* (YOHK), literally 'It doesn't exist (here)', or 'We don't have any (of it)'. Same head upward, raised eyebrows.

Remember, when a Turk seems to be giving you an arch look, he's only saying 'no'. He may also make the sound 'tsk', which also means 'no'. There are lots of ways to say 'no' in Turkish.

By contrast, wagging your head from side to side doesn't mean 'no' in Turkish; it means 'I don't understand'. So if a Turk asks you, 'Are you looking for the bus to Ankara?' and you shake your head, he'll assume you don't understand English, and will probably ask you the same question again, this time in German.

There are other signs that can cause confusion, especially when you're out shopping. For instance, if you want to indicate length ('I want a fish this big'), don't hold your hands apart at the desired length, but hold out your arm and place a flat hand on it, measuring from your fingertips to the hand. Thus, if you want a pretty big fish, you must 'chop' your arm with your other hand at about the elbow.

Height is indicated by holding a flat hand the desired distance above the floor or some other flat surface such as a counter or table top.

If someone – a shopkeeper or restaurant waiter, for instance – wants to show you the stockroom or the kitchen, he'll signal 'Come on, follow me' by waving his hand downward and toward himself in a scooping motion. Waggling an upright finger would never occur to him, except perhaps as a vaguely obscene gesture.

Facts for the Visitor

ACCOMMODATION
Hotels
Istanbul has a Hilton, a Sheraton and two Etap hotels. Ankara has the Büyük Ankara Oteli (Grand Ankara Hotel). These few top-class luxury places charge 'international' prices of, say, $115 to $150 for a double room. Somehow they get away with it, and always seem to be busy. Rates on package deals, and group rates, are down in the $75 to $80 range for the same room, however.

Luckily, Turkey has lots of less luxurious hotels, which are modern, comfortable but not overly fancy. There are many smaller, plainer, much cheaper hotels and pensions.

In almost every city you'll visit, including many cities in eastern Turkey, you will be able to find a clean, fairly modern room with twin beds, and private bath or shower, for $15 to $20 per night ($7.50 to $10 per person). The small, bare hotels and the pensions can cost as little as $5 for a double room without private bath ($2.50 per person). There are seaside hotels and motels, right on the beach, which charge $20 or $25 double. In general, then, the lodging situation is very good.

Hostels
With hotels and pensions so cheap, few people stay at hostels. The youth hostel system is not really necessary in Turkey. Hostels, when they exist, tend to be extremely basic, intended for low-budget Turkish students from the provinces who are attending university classes.

The Ministry of Youth Affairs and Sports operates a number of hostels and camps in Istanbul, Ankara, İzmir, Bolu, Çanakkale and Bursa. Hostel arrangements change from season to season and year to year. Ask at a Tourism Information Office, or at Gençtur Tourism and Travel Agency, Ltd., Yerebatan Cad. 15/3, Sultanahmet, Istanbul (tel 528 0734). Genctur works closely with the Ministry of Youth Affairs and Sports.

Choosing a Hotel
Here are some points to watch. Don't judge a hotel by its facade. Look at the rooms. I've never had a desk clerk refuse to show me a room. Next, prices should be posted prominently at the reception desk. Usually there is very little fiddling around in this regard. Prices are posted, and charged as they should be.

In some cities, and particularly in summer, there may be temporary water problems. Water may be cut off for several hours at a time, though many hotels have roof tanks which do away with this problem. As for hot water, it's often difficult to find in summer in the cheaper hotels. Many of these have only a single furnace for both hot water and central heating, and they really don't want to run that furnace in summer. Since the summers are warm, even hot, this doesn't present much of a problem. Early spring and late fall are another matter, though. Every desk clerk will say, 'Yes, we have hot water', but when you try to take a shower, the new facts will be, 'Ah, the furnace just this minute broke down!'

Believe it or not, the most dependable hot water is in the cheapest pensions, because in these places the *patron* builds a little fire in the bottom of the hot water tank thirty minutes before your shower appointment, and you bathe in as much steaming water as you want. The extra charge for this luxury is about 50c or 75c. An alternative, fairly dependable hot water method is the *şofben* (SHOHF-behn), or flash heater. This type runs on gas, and flashes into action as soon as you turn on the hot water tap. It's activated by water flow through the hot-water pipe. Obviously, this sort of heater is not dependent on a central furnace, but it does have other problems. Gas pressure must be sufficient to heat the water, which it sometimes is not; and the flow of water must be strong enough to activate the şofben, which it sometimes is not. Often it's a balancing act, keeping flow of water fast enough to activate the heater, yet slow enough to make sure the water is hot. The ideal şofben is one in your bathroom, which you control yourself, hooked up to a full tank of propane, plus lots of water pressure. In any case, any şofben is better than a hotel furnace that's shut down for the summer. If there's no gas, the management can get more. If there's no water pressure now, there probably will be later on.

You should know of a rare but significant danger: if there is a şofben in your bathroom, be sure to leave a window or door open as you use it. They burn up a lot of oxygen, and produce a lot of invisible, odourless carbon dioxide. You must have a source of ventilation.

Electricity may go off for short periods in some locations. This is not much of a problem, however.

Hotel Restaurants These, in general, do not offer good value in Turkey. You may want to have breakfast there for convenience, but most other meals should be taken in independent, local places. There are exceptions, of course, as in those remote towns where the one nice hotel in town also has the one nice restaurant.

If you just don't feel like going out to eat, you can usually have the hotel send a boy to a local restaurant and have the meal brought to your room. Carrying meals, tea, coffee, beverages, etc is done all the time. Tip the boy.

The same boy will gladly run to remedy any little faults in the room, such as burnt-out light bulbs or missing toilet paper, and you needn't tip him then. In the very cheapest places, by the way, you may find no toilet paper. 'Gosh', the owner will say, 'we've just run out'. What he means is that

he can't afford it, even though he's required to have it. Most Turks wash with water, and don't use paper. This is where you're glad you have your own supply, bought in a corner store (ask for *tuvalet kâğıdı*, too-vah-LEHT kyah-uh-duh). And speaking of such matters, the cheapest places may have only the flat 'elephant's feet' type of toilet, where you squat. Most have at least some of the western, sit-down type, though.

Unmarried Couples Unmarried couples sharing rooms usually run into no problems, even though the desk clerk sees the obvious when he takes down the pertinent information from your passports onto the registration form. The cheaper the hotel, the more traditional and conservative its management tends to be. Very simple hotels which are clean and 'proper' want to maintain their reputations. If you look clean and proper, and act that way, there should be no trouble. Lots of allowances are made for odd foreign ways.

Single Women Single women travelling alone or in pairs should look for *aile* (ah-yee-LEH) hotels – hotels where families stay. Men travel much more than do women in Turkey, and many hotels, from moderate to rock-bottom, cater mostly to men on business. No sharp dividing line, no key word in the hotel's name lets you know that one hotel is good and another not-so-good. In principle, every hotel accepts all potential guests. In practice, you may feel uncomfortable in a place which customarily is filled with men; and they may wonder why you're staying there when there are better *aile* hotels nearby. To locate a suitable hotel, look to see if there are matronly types waiting in the lobby, or just ask, *Bu otel aile için mi?* (BOO oh-tehl ah-yee-LEH ee-cheen mee, Is this hotel for families/ladies?) If it's not, the clerk will direct you to a more suitable place nearby.

In any hotel, regardless of price, you'll find a willingness to provide for your needs, a curiosity about your country and your travels, and a desire to be friendly and hospitable. Do your best to break the ice (because the staff won't presume to disturb your privacy). Reach across the cultural and linguistic barriers, and you'll find every Turk anxious to make your stay comfortable and pleasant.

ADDRESSES

Turkish postal adresses are usually written with the name of the main street first, then the minor street and then the number of the building. For example:

Bay Mustafa Adıyok
Geçilmez Sok. Bulunmaz Cık.
Luks Ap. No. 23/14
Tophane
ISTANBUL

In this example, *Bay* means 'Mr', (for 'Mrs' or 'Miss', it's *Bayan*); the next line has the name of a largish street, 'Geçilmez Sokak', followed by the name of a smaller street, alley, mews, or dead end, 'Bulunmaz Çikmazı', which runs off it. The third line has the name of an apartment building, 'Luks Ap'. As for the numbers, the first one, '23', is the street number of the building; the second, '14', is the apartment or office number within the building. The district, 'Tophane', comes next, then the city.

The address can be written more simply when the desired building is on a large, well-known street. For example:

Bay Mustafa Adıyok
Büyük Cad. No. 44/10
Taksim
ISTANBUL

In some cases the district of the city is put at the beginning of the second line, as 'Taksim, Büyük Caddesi No. 44/10'. In any case, you've got to be familiar with the district names to find a certain address.

Turkey does not use postal codes.

BOOKS TO READ

Everyone from St Paul to Mark Twain and Agatha Christie has written about Turkey. It's one of those Middle Eastern countries with an incredibly deep history and culture. You will get far more out of your visit if you read up on the history, the culture and the people before you go.

In a few cases, you might want to carry a specialized guide or history with you on your visit. A list of prominent foreign-language bookstores in Turkey follows this section.

Almanacs

The *Turkish Daily News* (Ankara) publishes the *Turkey Almanac* annually, in English. Its 400-plus large-format pages are packed with statistics and details on the government, the military, the press, trade, agriculture, population, culture, religion, sports – it even includes the musical score of the National Anthem. The price is about $9.

Anthropology

For a good overview of life during the great days of the empire, look for Raphaela Lewis's *Everyday Life in Ottoman Turkey* (London: B.T. Batsford; New York: G.P. Putnam's Sons, 1971; 207 pp., many photographs) in a library. It is not easily found in bookshops these days.

Archaeology

Akurgal, Ekrem, *Ancient Civilizations and Ruins of Turkey*, (Istanbul: Haşet Kitabevi, 1973 and later editions; 390 pp. of text, plus 112 pp. of photographs; about $8), a very detailed and fairly scholarly guide to most of Turkey's ruins 'from Prehistoric Times until the End of the Roman Empire'. Good, readable English translation. This is the best handbook for those with a deep interest in detailed classical archaeology.

George Bean(1903-1977) was the dean of western travel writers on Turkish antiquities. His four books cover the country's greatest wealth of Greek and Roman sites in depth, but in a very readable style. These four works were written as guidebooks to the ruins. They contain plenty of detail, but not so much that the fascination of exploring an ancient city or temple is taken away.

If you'd like to go deeply into a few sites, but not make the investments of time, energy and money necessary to cover the entire coast from Pergamum to Silifke, just buy Bean's *Aegean Turkey*, London: Ernest Benn; New York: W W Norton, 1979; 250 pp, diagrams, photos; about $16). This book covers İzmir and the surrounding region, Pergamum, Aeolis, sites west of İzmir to Sardis, Ephesus, Priene, Miletus, Didyma, Magnesia on the Meander, and Heracleia.

Also by George Bean (and from the same publishers):

Lycian Turkey, (1978; 197 pp., diagrams, maps and photos; about $16). Covers the Turkish coast roughly from Fethiye to Antalya, and its hinterland.

Turkey Beyond the Meander, (1980; 236 pp., maps, diagrams, photographs; about $22). Covers the region south of the Meander (*Menderes*) River, excluding Miletus, Didyma and Heracleia, (which are covered in *Aegean Turkey* but including sites near Bodrum, Pamukkale, Aphrodisias, Marmaris, and to the western outskirts of Fethiye.

Turkey's Southern Shore, (1979; 154 pp., maps, photographs, diagrams; about $20). Overlaps with *Lycian Turkey* a bit; covers eastern Lycia, Pisidia and Pamphylia, which is roughly the coast from Finike east to Silifke.

Besides these archaeological guides, you'll find shorter, locally-produced guides on sale at each site. Most of these include colour photographs (of varying quality). The text, however, is often badly translated, or else doesn't go into much depth.

Biography

Kinross, Lord, *Atatürk, The Rebirth of a Nation* (London: Weidenfeld and Nicolson, 1964 and later; 542 pp., photos). Lord Kinross's biography of Atatürk is essential reading for anyone who wants to understand the formation of the Turkish Republic, and the reverence in which modern Turks hold the Father of modern Turkey. It's well written, and far more exciting than most novels.

Dictionaries and Phrase Books

Several companies publish Turkish-English pocket dictionaries, including Langenscheidt/McGraw-Hill. The most useful thing to have is not a dictionary, but a good phrase book such as Berlitz Publications's *Turkish for Travellers*. Besides lots of phrases and glossaries, this one includes a lot of cultural details and information, menu readers, etc.

For a more detailed dictionary, look to *The Concise Oxford Turkish Dictionary*. Similar in scope, and easier to find in Turkey, is the *Portable Redhouse/ Redhouse Elsözlüğü*; this 500-page work on thin paper was actually intended for Turkish students learning English, but it does the job well when you graduate from the pocket dictionary.

For grammars, there's *Teach Yourself Turkish*, in the popular English series. Longer, more expensive, and far more interesting is Geoffrey L. Lewis's *Turkish Grammar* (London: Oxford U. Press, 1967). You've got to be pretty interested in Turkish (and in grammar) to get this far into it. But if a grammar can be said to read like a novel, this one does.

Fiction

Everybody knows about Agatha Christie's *Murder on the Orient Express*, and so they should. It has some scenes in Turkey itself, though most of the train's journey was through Europe and the Balkans. In any case, it helps to make vivid the 19th century importance of the Turkish Empire.

Guidebooks

This book was written to tell you just about everything you'd need to know on a first or even subsequent trip to Turkey. Other excellent guides exist, however, each with its own special interest.

The excellent French series of Blue Guides published by Hachette has a commendable volume on Turkey, but the latest edition (1978) is in French only. An earlier English translation (1960, 1970) is useful for some detailed archaeological information, and out-of-the-way spots; but the writing now seems stilted, the printing crude, and the practical information far out of date. If you see it in a used bookshop, cheap, you might want to pick it up.

Otherwise, the most interesting guides on Turkey are those published by the Redhouse Press of Istanbul. Founded under the Ottoman Empire as part of an American missionary effort, the Redhouse Press now does an admirable job of publishing dictionaries, guidebooks and general works designed to bridge the gap between the Turkish and English-speaking realms. Some of the Redhouse guides have been translated into German, French and Italian. Though only a few Redhouse books turn up in bookshops outside of Turkey, you'll find them readily within the country itself, in decent editions at moderate prices. A good example of a Redhouse work is *Biblical Sites in Turkey* by Everett C. Blake and Anna G. Edmonds (1982; 200 pp., colour photos, maps; about $4). Other guides cover Istanbul and day-trips from it.

History

Lewis, Bernard, *The Emergence of Modern Turkey*, (London: Oxford U. Press, 1965 and later; 511 pp., maps). This is a scholarly work covering Turkey's history roughly from 1850 to 1950, with a few chapters on the earlier history of the Turks. It tells you just about everything you want to know about how modern Turkey came to be.

Lewis, Geoffrey L., *Turkey*, (London, 1955 and later); a good general introduction to the country, the people and the culture through their history.

Moorhead, Alan, *Gallipoli*; the fascinating story of the battles for the Dardanelles, which figured so significantly in the careers of Atatürk and Winston Churchill.

Travellers' Accounts

The published diaries and accounts of travellers in Turkey provide fascinating glimpses of Ottoman life. One of the more familiar of these is by Mark Twain in his *Innocents Abroad*. Twain accompanied a group of wealthy tourists on a chartered boat which sailed the eastern Mediterranean and Black Seas over a century ago. Many of the things he saw in Istanbul haven't changed much.

A more recent account is Philip Glazebrook's *Journey to Kars* (Atheneum, 1984), which does a slow lap around the country.

BOOKSHOPS

As far as Turks are concerned, their country is part of Europe. Western culture is their culture, and if they learn a foreign language it will be English, French or German. Thus it is easy to find bookshops (*kitabevi*) selling works in these languages.

The major cities all have excellent foreign-language bookshops

Istanbul

Sander Kitabevi has a small branch a few doors north-east of the PTT in Galatasaray, on the same side of Istiklal Caddesi. The main store is at Hâlâskargazi Caddesi 275-277, Osmanbey, north of Taksim Square. Books are in English, French and German.

Alman Kitabevi ('German Bookstore'), Istiklal Cad. 481, Tünel, Beyoglu, has mostly German books.

Haşet Kitabevi (*Hachette*), Istiklal Cad. 469, Tünel, Beyoğlu, has a good selection of French and English books and periodicals.

Redhouse Kitabevi, Riza Pasa Yokuşu, Uzun Çarşı, in the Old City down the hill from the Grand Bazaar, publishes books in English and Turkish, including excellent guides and dictionaries. It has an English-language bookstore as well.

Sahaflar Çarşısı, the used book bazaar, is great fun for browsing. It's just west of the Grand Bazaar across Çadırcılar Caddesi, sandwiched in between that street and the Beyazit Mosque.

The big hotels – Hilton, Sheraton, Etap, Divan – all have little bookshops or newsstands. The one in the Hilton arcade is quite good.

Ankara

Tarhan Kitabevi, Sakarya Caddesi at Atatürk Bulvarı, a few steps north (down the hill) out of Kizilay, is perhaps Turkey's best foreign-language bookstore, with a predominance of books in English, but some in French and German as well. To find it, walk out of Kızılay toward Ulus and the old part of Ankara along Atatürk Bulvarı, and take the first turn on the right (a pedestrian street).

İzmir

There are several foreign-language bookstores on Cumhuriyet Caddesi, or *İkinci Kordon*, the second street in from the waterfront. Look near the NATO headquarters. The Büyük Efes (Grand Ephesus) hotel also has a small shop.

Other Towns

If tourists go there in any numbers, you'll find a news-stand selling international papers and at least some paperback novels, perhaps second-hand.

CONSULATES & EMBASSIES

Istanbul has many palatial consulates left from the days of Ottoman glory, when foreign power built splendid embassy compounds to impress the sultan. The embassies are all now in Ankara, the modern capital. But there are helpful consulates or consular agents in Istanbul, İzmir, Adana and a few other port cities.

If you plan to travel from Turkey to Europe by way of Bulgaria, you'll save time and money by picking up a Bulgarian transit visa in Istanbul or Ankara. In fact, they may not be issuing them at the border. See 'Getting There' for details.

Here is a list of diplomatic missions. To help you find one, use these phrases:

(Name of country) Büyükelçiliği nerede?
(... bew-YEWK-ehl-chee-lee neh-reh-DEH), 'Where is the (...) embassy?'
(Name of country) Konsolosluğu nerede?
(KOHN-sohl-lohs-loo-oo), 'Where is the (...) Consulate?'

Australia (*Avustralya*)
Embassy: Nene Hatun Cad. 83, Gazi Osman Paşa, Ankara, tel 27 53 18.

Austria (*Avusturya*)
Embassy: Atatürk Bulvarı 189, Kavaklıdere, Ankara, tel 25 47 61.
Consulate: Silâhhane Cad. 59/4, Teşvikiye, Şişli, Istanbul, tel 146-3769.

Bulgaria (*Bulgarya*)
Embassy: Atatürk Bulvarı 129, Kavaklıdere, Ankara, tel 26 74 55.
Consulate: Büyükdere Sok. 4, Mecidiyekoy, Istanbul, tel 140-4217.

Canada (*Kanada*)
Embassy: Nene Hatun Cad. 75, Gazi Osman Paşa, Ankara, tel 27 58 03.

Denmark (*Danimarka*)
Embassy: Kırlangıç Sok. 42, Gazi Osman Paşa, Ankara, tel 27 52 58.
Consulate: Silâhhane Cad., İzmir Palas Ap. 31/1, Teşvikiye, Şişli, Istanbul, tel 140-4217.

France (*Fransa*)
Embassy: Paris Cad. 70, Kavaklıdere, Ankara, tel 26 14 80.

Consulate: İstiklal Cad. 8, Taksim, Istanbul, tel 143-4387.

Germany (Federal) (*Federal Almanya*)
Embassy: Atatürk Bulvarı 114, Kavaklıdere, Ankara, tel. 26 54 65.
Consulate: İnönü (Gümüşsuyu) Cad., Ayazpaşa, Taksim, Istanbul, tel 145-0705.

Greece (*Yunanistan*)
Embassy: Şölen Sok. 8, Çankaya, Ankara, tel 39 04 10.
Consulate: Ağahamam Sok., Kuloğlu, Beyoğlu, Istanbul, tel 145-0596.

Iran (*İran*)
Embassy: Tahran Cad. 10, Kavaklıdere, Ankara, tel 27 43 20.
Consulate: Ankara Cad., Cağaloğlu, Istanbul, tel 528-5053.

Israel (*İsrail*)
Embassy: Farabi Sok. 43, Çankaya, Ankara, tel 26 39 04.
Consulate: Büyük Çiftlik Sok., Arif Aras Ap., Teşvikiye, Şişli, Istanbul, tel 146-4125.

Netherlands (*Holanda*)
Embassy: Şehit Ersan Cad. 4, Çankaya, Ankara, tel 27 43 26.
Consulate: İstiklal Cad. 393, Galatasaray, Istanbul, tel 149-5310.

Sweden (*İsveç*)
Embassy: Kâtip Çelebi Sok. 7, Kavaklıdere, Ankara, tel 27 35 44.
Consulate: İstiklal Cad. 497, Tünel, Beyoğlu, Istanbul, tel 143-5770.

Switzerland (*İsvicre*)
Embassy: Atatürk Bulvarı 247, Çankaya, Ankara, tel 27 43 16.
Consulate: Hüsrev Gerede Cad. 75/3, Teşvikiye, Şişli, Istanbul, tel 148-5070.

United Kingdom (*İngiltere, Birleşik Kralliği*)
Embassy: Şehit Ersan Cad. 46/A, Çankaya, Ankara, tel 27 43 10.

Consulate: Meşrutiyet Cad. 26, Galatasaray, Istanbul, tel 149-8874.

United States of America (*Amerikan Birleşik Devletleri*)
Embassy: Atatürk Bulvarı 110, Kavaklıdere, Ankara, tel 26 54 70.
Consulate: Meşrutiyet Cad. 106, Tepebaşı, Beyoğlu, Istanbul, tel 145-3220.

Call before you visit any of these embassies or consulates. Diplomats keep very odd business hours sometimes, and they close up on both Turkish and their own national holidays.

CUSTOMS & IMMIGRATION

Visas
If you have a valid passport, chances are good that you can enter Turkey and stay for three months, no questions asked. Citizens of Australia, Canada, Eire, Japan, New Zealand, the United Kingdom, the United States, and virtually all the countries of western and central Europe have that privilege. Citizens of some other countries – Hong Kong, Jamaica, etc – have it as well.

Don't overstay your visit. If you're going to stay a year, you might want to apply for a residence permit (*Ikamet Tezkeresi*), in which case you will have to show means of support. This means savings, a steady income from outside the country, or legal work within the country. The last is very difficult to find. Most people staying for a shorter period, or who are working without a valid permit (say, as private tutors of English), cross the border into Greece for a day or two every three months rather than bother with the residence permit.

Customs Inspection
Upon entering the country, customs inspection is often very cursory for foreign tourists. Indeed, they may only spot-check, and you may not even have to open your bags.

Arrival A verbal declaration is usually all you need. You can bring in up to 1 kilogram of coffee, 5 litres of liquor, and two cartons (400) of cigarettes. Things of exceptional value (jewellery, unusually expensive electronic or photographic gear, etc) are supposed to be declared, and may be entered in your passport, which guarantees that the goods will be taken out of the country when you leave.

Departure Although it's legal to purchase and sell antiquities in Turkey, it is illegal to export them.

You may export valuables (except antiquities) that have been registered in your passport on entry, or that have been purchased with legally converted money. For souvenirs, the maximum export limit is $1000 of all items combined; if two or more similar items are exported, a licence may be required. Also, you may be required to show proof of exchange transactions for at least these amounts. Save your currency exchange slips, and have them ready for the customs officer in the departure area. He may ask you to turn over to him enough currency exchange slips to cover the amount of the purchases.

Your bags may well be checked when you leave the country, and searching questions asked about whether or not you are taking any antiquities with you. Only true antiquities are off-limits (not the many artful fakes). If you buy a real Roman coin from a shepherd boy at an archaeological site, can you take it home with you? Legally not, but it's not the sort of thing they'll find on you as you go through Turkish customs to leave the country. What happens if you get caught trying to smuggle out a significant piece of ancient statuary? Big trouble.

Only in the matter of carpets is there a difficult 'twilight zone', because carpets are too big to hide, and customs men do have the right to search you as you leave the country. At Yeşilkoy Airport in Istanbul you will pass a customs officer in the Departures area. This is often on a spot-check basis. If you have lots of heavy luggage, you'll probably be checked. And if you have a carpet, the matter of its age will come up. Particularly old and valuable carpets fall under the heading of 'antiquities'. To export such an item, you're supposed to have a statement from the shopkeeper, the local museum, or some other authority stating that the carpet is not an 'antiquity'. It's a bad situation, because your flight is about to leave, the customs officer says you ought to go back into the city and get a statement (which may take days). Bribery is not the way out. What to do? Have some sort of a statement to appease the officer, or do a lot of agreeable sweet-talking. Also, be ready to go back into the city and get the statement, as a last resort.

To avoid any chance of such unpleasantness, get your rug dealer to write something and sign it if the carpet's really old. This should do: *Bu halı/kilim antika değildir, ihraç edilebilirdir*, 'This carpet/kilim is not an antiquity, it may be exported'. Such a statement may not fill the bill legally, but it's some ammunition just in case the customs officer questions your purchase. And it beats the hassle of looking up some museum director and letting him gobble your time. Most likely, you'll have no problem, and the language barrier will work to your benefit. Unless, of course, you really *do* have a rug of museum quality.

Vehicles Automobiles, minibuses, trailers, towed seacraft, motorcycles and bicycles can be brought in for up to three months without a *carnet de passage* or *triptique*. Drivers must have a valid driving licence; an International Driving License is useful, but not normally required. Your own national driver's licence should pass all right. Third-party insurance, such as a 'green card' valid for the entire country (not just for Thrace, or European Turkey), or a Turkish policy purchased at the border, is obligatory.

DANGERS & ANNOYANCES

Turkey is a safe country, relative to most of the world. In the good old days (say, the 1960s) before Turkish workers went to Europe in droves, and political unrest came on the scene, most of the crime in Turkey was of the passionate type: 'You fool around with my sister, I smash your face!'

Well, the workers (and, more significantly, the hangers-on) returned from Europe with a new respect and admiration for western greed. This led to western-style robberies, mostly of houses and apartments. But since 1980 and the clean-up of criminals and fringe political elements, the crime rate has dropped way down again.

Police

One of the reasons Turkey is so safe is martial law. Since the terrible times of the late 1970s, when political extremism made it perilous even to walk along the street, martial law has been instituted to protect 'the man on the street'. The military government of the early 1980s brought law and order, and a breath of relief to normal people. But even under the return to democracy, Turks are wary of the fringe elements. They remember all too well how difficult life was while chaos reigned.

You'll see a lot of soldiers in Turkey. This is partly because of martial law, and partly because soldiers make up the *jandarma* (gendarmerie) force, and partly because Turkey has universal male military service – every man serves, even if he is partly disabled. With all these men in arms, jobs have got to be found for them. Other reasons are: NATO commitments, a border with the Soviet Union (which has tried several times to take land in eastern Turkey), and a long, proud military tradition which began when Turks formed the elite units under the later Arab caliphs in the 10th and 11th centuries.

Here's the rundown on the police forces:

The green-clad officers with white caps, both men and women, are part of a national force (*Polis*, poh-LEES) which controls traffic, patrols highways, and attend to other police duties in cities and towns.

The blue-clad officers are called *Belediye Zabıtası* (Municipal Inspector), or Market Police. These men are the modern expression of an age-old Islamic custom of having special commercial police to make sure a loaf of bread weighs what it should, that 24-carat gold is indeed 24-carats, that scales and balances don't cheat the customer. You'll see them patrolling the markets and bazaars, and if you have a commercial problem, they'll be glad to help. They may not speak much of a foreign language.

Soldiers in the standard Turkish army uniforms may be of three types. Without special insignia, they're regular army. With a red armband bearing the word *Jandarma*, they're gendarmes, whose job is to keep the peace, catch criminals on the run, stop smuggling and the like. If the soldiers have white helmets emblazoned with the letters *As. İz.*, plus pistols in white holsters connected to lanyards around their necks, they're *Askeri İnzibat*, or Military Police. They keep off-duty soldiers in line.

Most of these soldiers are draftees inducted into the enormous Turkish army, put through basic training, and sent out to 'guard' jobs that are usually pretty unexciting. They look ferocious – life in the Turkish army is no joke – but basically they are hometown boys waiting to get out. Every single one of them can tell you the precise number of days he has left to serve. Any request from a foreign tourist for help or directions is received as though it were a marvellous privilege.

Theft

In general the Turks are admirably honest and polite sorts. You are unlikely to get into trouble even in Istanbul, even at night. But the prudent person would take normal precautions. These include keeping track of your wallet or other valuables on crowded buses and trains, and in markets; not leaving valuables in your hotel room, or at least not in view; and not walking into unknown parts of town when nobody else is around.

Actually, the biggest danger of theft is probably in youth hostels and other open accommodation where other foreigners can see what sort of camera you have (and can guess its value pretty accurately), or where you stash your money.

Women Alone

Women must be more careful, as in any Mediterranean country. Turkish social customs dictate that a young woman (say, a high school student) not go to a major shopping street without friends or mother; college-aged women usually stroll with friends; women in the prime look purposeful, ignore catcalls, and don't walk on lonely streets after dark. If you're approached by an eastern Romeo, ignore, ignore, ignore. It's best not to say or do anything.

The key is respectability: if you look and act respectable according to Turkish standards, you'll be able to fend off advances easily. A wedding ring helps. It says, 'I've got an Other Half who doesn't like people to fool with me'. If you must say something, say *Ayıp!* (ah-YUHP), which means 'shameful'. Use it all you want to on young kids. But men may take exception if you call them shameful when they're certain that you'll find their masculine charms irresistible.

Disputes

In general, Turks view foreigners as highly cultured, highly educated and wealthy – despite the truth. This means that you will often be given special consideration, jumped to the head of queues, given the best seat on the bus, etc. In a dispute, if you stay calm, you will generally be given the benefit of the doubt. If it is thought you have powerful friends, you will definitely be given that benefit.

It's difficult to imagine that a dispute involving a foreigner would get to the point of blows, as Turks are slow to anger. Don't let it get there. A Turk rarely sees it necessary to fight, but if he does, he wants to win, *whatever* the cost. Knowing that horrible things could happen, bystanders will pull two quarrelling men apart, even if they've never seen them before. In the case of women travellers in disputes with Turks, you should know that Turkish men feel acutely any insults to their manhood, and will retaliate. Insults can include being shouted at or browbeaten by a woman who is not (in their eyes) unquestionably of a higher social status. If you are definitely very much higher in status, you can yell all you want to. But in general, keep it all formal.

Treason

The battle to form the Turkish Republic out of the ruins of the Ottoman Empire was a very tough one, and every Turk has great respect for the accomplishments of Atatürk and of the republic. There are laws against insulting, defaming or making light of Atatürk, the Turkish flag, the Turkish people, the Turkish republic, etc. These are normal for many European countries. Any difficulty would probably come out of misunderstanding. At the first sign that you've inadvertently been guilty of *lese-majeste*, make your apologies. It may seem a trivial thing to you; but if it's important to someone else, you should apologize. An apology will be readily accepted.

Natural Hazards

Earthquakes Turkey sometimes has very bad ones. But the big quakes only seem to hit every eight or ten years, and the same thing happens in many parts of the world, so it's up to Allah.

Undertow At some of the swimming areas, particularly at the Black Sea near Istanbul, this is a real danger. It can kill you by sweeping you out to sea. There may be no signs warning of the danger. Lifeguards may not be present, or may be untrained, or unequipped (no boat). Don't trust to luck. You can't see undertow, necessarily, or predict where it will be. As in any undertow situation, don't exhaust yourself by trying to swim straight back to the beach, because you'll never make it. Rather, swim to the left or right to escape the undertow area, and make for land in that direction. Undertow is usually a problem only on long stretches of open sea beach with surf. In coves and bays, where waves are broken or diverted by headlands, you probably won't be in danger from undertow.

Wildlife Turkey has mosquitoes, scorpions and snakes. You will not see many of them. But be aware, as you tramp around the ruins of Ephesus or Priene that such beasts do live here, and may be nearby, at least in summer. There are also wild boar and wolves around, though you won't encounter these unless you hike deep into the bush.

Man-Made Annoyances

When you close a door, watch out that your knuckles don't bash into the jamb. This happens frequently.

The first time you flush a toilet, pull the cord *very gently*. If nothing happens, pull harder. Some of the flushers are made of iron and take a good heavy tug; most of the new ones are made of plastic. If you pull on a plastic one the way you do on an iron one, you'll pull the cord right off the toilet.

If you encounter a flat, 'elephant's feet' toilet, stand back when you flush it. If it flushes well, it may get all over your feet.

If your bathroom has a *şofben* (gas-fired flash water heater) in it, make sure there is plenty of ventilation as you use it. The *şofben* uses up a lot of oxygen. In a small room with all the doors and windows closed, you could suffocate taking a long bath.

Give way to cars and trucks in all

situations, even if you have to jump out of the way. The sovereignty of the pedestrian is unrecognized in Turkey. If a car hits you, the driver (if not the courts) will blame you for not getting out of the way. This does not apply in a recognized crosswalk controlled by a traffic officer or a traffic signal. If you've got a 'Walk' light, you've got the right of way. Watch out, all the same.

If you're allergic to cigarette smoke, you may have a hard time of it in Turkey. Though the local cancer prevention society fields a brave effort to stop smoking, this is the land of aromatic Turkish tobacco. Smoking is the national passion. No-smoking areas are virtually unheard of, and would not really be observed if they were, even on planes and trains. Okay, some people don't smoke next to the pumps in gasoline filling stations. But in general, position yourself near a fresh-air source if possible.

Noise is a source of annoyance in cities. As in many third world countries, the noise level in Turkey is frequently high. Choose hotel rooms with noise in mind. Often, rooms in the back of a small hotel, away from the street, are looked upon as less desirable (and therefore cheaper) than the noisier, front-side rooms. Take advantage of this anomaly – get a quieter room for less.

In winter, air pollution is a problem in the big cities. In Ankara it is a very serious problem, rivalling that of Tokyo and Mexico City. The major heating fuel is lignite (soft brown coal) which produces enormous clouds of heavy, choking particles. In summer there is some pollution from autos, but it's not bad. But in winter, especially in Ankara, the air is very bad. If you find your nose running, and your eyes watering and itching, and your head aching, that's the pollution. The heating season lasts from 15 October to 1 April.

ELECTRICITY

Most of it is 220 volts, 50 cycles as in Europe, though sometimes it's not up to full voltage ('brown-out'). However, parts of Beyoğlu in Istanbul, wired by the French over a century ago, are still on 110 volts. If you're staying in a hotel near Taksim or Tepebaşı in Beyoğlu, ask before you plug in. The voltage will probably be marked on the socket/points.

Plugs are of the European variety with two round prongs, but there are two sizes in use. Most common is the small-diameter prong and if you have these, you're in fine shape. The large-diameter, grounded plug as used in Germany and Austria is also in use, and you'll find some outlets (points) of this type. But plugs for these won't fit the small-diameter outlets.

Adapters are not easily available (I've never found one). You've got to rig something up yourself unless you've brought an adapter from Europe and it happens to be the right one. (Adapters for the flat-prong North American-type plugs are sold in many electrical shops. If you have these plugs, and 220 volt appliances, you're unusual and in luck.)

For those who have the good sense to plan ahead, here are the Vital Statistics of the Turkish Plug: prongs 4mm in diameter, and 1.9 cm long; distance from the centre of one prong to the centre of the other is 1.9 cm; distance between the prongs is 1.5 cm. The European grounded plug, by contrast, has prongs 4.5 mm in diameter, 1.9 cm apart from centre to centre, but only 1.4 cm apart.

What to do if you can't adapt? I hesitate to recommend what I do, as I don't want it to result in the electrocution of a valued reader; so I won't recommend, just relate. When my European heater coil won't fit a Turkish socket, and I've got to have that early morning cup of coffee or tea, I loosen the two screws on the outlet's cover plate, pull the outlet gingerly from its circular hole-in-the-wall, touch the plug prongs to the contact wires, and hold still until the water boils. The time it takes to boil depends on the strength of the current that day.

FOOD

It is worth travelling to Turkey just to eat. Turkish cuisine is thought by many to rank with French and Chinese as one of the world's great basic cuisines. If French cuisine is based on ingenuity and originality, and Chinese on quick cooking and interchangeability of ingredients, Turkish cuisine's special genius is excellent, fresh ingredients and careful, even laborious preparation. The ingredients are often very simple, but are harmonized with such care and finesse that the result is incredibly edible. With simple ingredients, it's difficult to cover up bad cooking, so bad cooks don't last long.

Restaurants (*restoran, lokanta*) are everywhere, open early in the morning until late at night. Most are very inexpensive, and although price is always some determinant of quality, often the difference between a $2 meal and a $12 meal is not that great, at least as far as flavour is concerned. Service and ambience are fancier at the higher price.

Breakfast (*Kahvaltı*)

In a hotel or pastry shop, breakfast (*komple kahvaltı*, kohm-PLEH kah-vahl-TUH) consists of fresh, delicious Turkish bread (*ekmek*, ek-MEHK) with jam or honey, butter, black olives, white sheep's milk cheese, and tea (*çay*, CHAH-yee). Sometimes a wedge of processed cheese, like the French 'La Vache Qui Rit', is added, or substituted for the sheep's-milk cheese.

You can always order an egg (*yumurta*, yoo-moor-TAH), soft-boiled (*üç dakikalık*, EWCH dahk-kah-luhk), or hard-boiled (*sert*, SEHRT). Fried eggs are *sahanda yumurta* (sah-hahn-DAH yoo-moor-tah). Sometimes your bread will come *kızartmış* (kuh-zahrt-MUSH, grilled, toasted). This is the standard breakfast for tourists. If you order an egg or another glass of tea, you may be charged a bit extra but hardly enough to break the bank.

Breakfast is not normally included in the hotel room rate, though some hotels do include it. When breakfast is included, the desk clerk will mention it as he quotes the price of the room. *Kahvaltı dahil* (kah-vahl-TUH dah-HEEL) means 'Breakfast is included'.

If Turkish bread and Turkish tea weren't so fresh and so good, this breakfast could get dull after awhile. In any case, there are alternative breakfasts. Turks may have a bowl of hot chicken soup (*tavuk çorbasi*, tah-VOOK chor-bah-suh). If that's not for you, find a place serving *su böreği* (SOO bur-reh-yee), a many-layered noodle-like pastry with white cheese and parsley among the layers, served warm.

Hot, sweetened milk (*sicah süt*, suh-JAHK sewt) is also a traditional breakfast drink, replaced in winter by *sahlep* (sah-LEHP), which is hot, sweetened milk with tasty tapioca-root powder added and cinnamon sprinkled on top.

Bacon is difficult to find as any pork product is forbidden to Muslims.

Turkish coffee (*kahve*, kahh-VEH) is better as an after-dinner drink than a breakfast drink. You may find some places willing to serve you *Amerikan kahvesi (ah-mehr-ee-KAHN kahh-veh-see)*, a less concentrated brew than Turkish coffee. *Fransız kahvesi* (frahn-SUHZ kahh-veh-see, 'French coffee') can be either strong *Amerikan kahvesi* (served black) or it can be coffee-with-milk, which may also be called *sütlü kahve* (sewt-LEW kahh-veh).

Instant coffee, often called *neskafe* (NEHS-kah-feh) or *hazır kahve* (hah-ZUHR kahh-veh), is a rare and very expensive import. It's a good idea to bring a good quantity with you to Turkey. If you don't use it, you'll find it handy as a gift or source of ready cash.

Lunch (*Öğle yemeği*)

The noon meal can be big or small. In summer, many Turks prefer to eat a big meal at noon and a light supper in the evening. You might want to do this, too.

Restaurants in Turkey come in three general varieties.

First there is the familiar place with white tablecloths and waiter service, with a variety of dishes, including grilled meats, seafood, and such things as *musakka*.

Haz'ir yemek Next there is the *hazır yemek* (hah-ZUHR yeh-mehk, 'ready food') restaurant. Although all restaurants offer some 'ready food' dishes prepared in advance, these places specialize in an assortment of dishes, prepared in advance of mealtime and served on demand. They are basically working-class cafeterias, but with waiter service. You pass by a steam table, which is often in the front window of the restaurant to entice passers-by, you make your choices, and a waiter brings them to you.

There will always be soup (*çorba*, CHOR-bah), often *mercimek çorbası* (mehr-jee-MEHK, lentil). *Ezo Gelin çorbası* (EH-zoh GEH-leen) is a variation of lentil soup, with rice and lemon juice. *Domates çorbası* (doh-MAH-tess) is creamy tomato soup. *Şehriye* (SHEH-ree-yeh) is vermicelli soup, made with a chicken stock.

Pilav (pee-LAHV) of some sort will always be available. Plain *pilav* is rice cooked in stock. There may also (or instead) be *bulgur pilav*, cracked bulghur wheat cooked in a tomato stock.

Many of the dishes will be vegetables-and-meat. Most popular are *salçalı köfte* (sahl-chah-LUH kurf-teh), meatballs of lamb stewed in a sauce with vegetables; *patlıcan kebap* (paht-luh-JAHN keh-bahp), eggplant and chunks of lamb; or *orman kebap* (ohr-MAHN keh-bahp), lamb chunks, vegetables and potatoes in broth. *Kuzu haşlama* (koo-ZOO hahsh-lah-mah) is lamb hocks in a stew.

Sometimes grilled meats are available in *hazır yemek* restaurants. *Döner kebap* (durn-NEHR keh-bahp), lamb roasted on a vertical spit and sliced off in thin strips as it cooks, is the closest thing you'll find to a national dish. *Şiş kebap* (SHEESH keh-bahp) is meat only, small pieces of lamb grilled on real charcoal.

Sometimes beer is served in these restaurants; more often, it's not. Decor may be non-existent, and the letters on the front window may only say *Lokanta* (restaurant), but the welcome will be warm and the food delicious, and very cheap.

With your meal you will receive as much fresh bread as you can eat, for a nominal charge. It's easy to 'overeat with your eyes' in these places, especially when the bread is so good. Soup, pilav, a main course, and bread, make for a big meal.

Hazır yemek restaurants prepare most of their daily dishes for the noon meal, and then just keep them heated (one hopes) until suppertime. The best reason to eat a big meal at noon is because that's when it's freshest and best. If you want grilled fish or meat, have it in the evening.

Kebapçı, Köfteci The last sort of restaurant is the *kebapçı* (keh-BAHP-chee) or *köfteçi* (KURF-teh-jee). A *kebapçi* is a man who cooks kebap (roast meat). A *köfteçi* roasts *köfte*, rissoles or meatballs of ground lamb made with savory spices. Though they may have one or two ready-food dishes, kebapcis and koftecis specialize in grilled meat, plus soups, salad, yogurt and perhaps dessert. *Döner kebap* and *şiş kebap* (see above) are the two most common kinds of kebap. *Kuşbaşı* (KOOSH-bah-shuh, 'bird's head') is a smaller and finer lamb shish kebab. *Çöp kebap* (CHURP keh-bahp) is tiny morsels of lamb on split bamboo skewers.

If you want any sort of kebap or kofte well-done, ask for it *iyi pişmiş* (ee-YEE peesh-meesh), or *pişkin* (peesh-KEEN).

Kebapcis can be great fun, especially the ones that are *ocakbaşı* (oh-JAHK bah-shuh), or 'fireside'. Patrons sit around the sides of a long rectangular firepit. The kebapci sits enthroned in the middle, grilling hundreds of small skewers of shish kebab and *şiş köfte* (sheesh KURF-teh), which is köfte wrapped around a flat skewer; *Adana köfte* (ah-DAHN-nah) is the same thing, but spicy-hot. The chef hands them to you as they're done, and you eat them with flat bread, a salad, and perhaps *ayran* (ah-yee-RAHN), a drink of yogurt mixed with spring water.

Büfe & Kuru Yemiş Besides restaurants, Turkey has millions of little snack stands and quick-lunch places known by the name of *büfe* (bew-FEH, buffet). These serve sandwiches, often grilled; puddings; portions of *börek* (bur-REHK, flaky pastry); and perhaps *lahmacun* (LAHH-mah-joon), an Arabic soft pizza made with chopped onion, lamb and tomato sauce. In the bigger büfes in Istanbul, you may have to pay the cashier in advance and get a receipt (*fiş*, FEESH), hand it to the cook, and order your snack. Just tell the cashier 'İkilahmacun', pay, give the *fiş* to the cook, and repeat the order. You'll end up with two of the soft pizzas.

A *Kuru yemiş* (koo-ROO yeh-MEESH) place serves dried fruits and nuts. These places are wonderful! Along Istiklal Caddesi in Istanbul you'll find little kuru yemiş shops selling pistachios (shelled or unshelled), walnuts, hazel nuts, peanuts (salted or unsalted), dried figs and apricots, chocolate, sunflower seeds, and a dozen other good things. Prices are displayed, usually by the kilogram. Order 100 gram (*yüz gram*, YEWZ grahm), which is a good portion, and pay exactly one-tenth of the kilogram price displayed.

Another good place for kuru yemiş is the *Misir Çarşısı*, the Egyptian or Spice Bazaar in Istanbul's Eminönü section. Kuru yemiş shops here will also have *pestil* (pehs-TEEL), fruit which has been dried and pressed into flat, flexible sheets. Odd at first, but delicious. It's relatively cheap, and comes made from apricots (*kayısı*), mulberries (*dut*), and other fruits.

Dinner

The evening meal can be a repeat of lunch, a light supper, or a sumptuous repast. In good weather the setting might be outdoors.

Meze The meal starts with *meze* (MEH-zeh), all sorts of appetizers and hors d'oeuvres. You'll find *börek* (bur-REHK), pastry rolls, cylinders or 'pillows' filled with white cheese and parsley, then deep-fried. There will be olives (*zeytin*), white cheese, *turşu* (toor-SHOO, pickled vegetables), fried potatoes or light potato fritters called *patates köftesi*. The famous stuffed vine leaves (*dolma*) come either hot or cold. The hot ones (*etli*, eht-LEE, 'with meat') have ground lamb in them. The cold ones are made without meat, but 'with olive oil' (*zeytinyağlı*).

Salads The real stars of the meze tray, however, are the salads and purees. These are mystifying at first because they all look about the same: some goo on a plate decorated with bits of carrot, peas, parsley, olives or lemon slices. Here's where you'll need words to understand:

Amerikan salatası: A Russian salad, with mayonnaise, peas, carrots, etc.
Beyin salatası: Sheep's brain salad, usually the whole brain served on lettuce. Food for thought.
Cacik: Yogurt thinned with grated cucumber, then beaten and flavoured with a little garlic and a dash of olive oil.
Çoban salatası: A 'Shepherd's salad', this is a mixed, chopped salad of tomatoes, cucumbers, parsley, olives and peppers (sometimes fiery). If you don't want the peppers, order the salad *bibersiz* (bee-behr-SEEZ). But as the salad was probably chopped up all together at once, this order means some kitchen lackey will attempt to pick out the peppers. He may miss some. Be on guard.
Karisik salata: Same as a *Çoban salatası*.
Patlican salatası: This is pureed eggplant (aubergine), perhaps mixed with yogurt. The best of it has a faintly smokey, almost burnt flavour from the charcoal grilling of the eggplant.
Pilâki: Broad white beans and sliced onions in a light vinegar pickle.
Rus salatası: Russian salad. See *Amerikan salatası*.

Söğüş: Pronounced 'sew-EWSH', this indicates raw salad vegetables such as tomatoes or cucumbers peeled and sliced, but without any sauce or dressing.
Taramasalata: Red caviar, yogurt, garlic and olive oil mixed into a smooth paste. Salty and delicious.
Yeşil salata: Green salad of lettuce, oil and lemon juice or vinegar.

Main courses After the mezes comes the main course. The fish is marvellous all along the coast, especially in the Aegean. Ankara has some excellent fresh fish restaurants, too.

Most popular fish are *palamut* (tunny or bonito), a darkish, full-flavoured baby tuna. *Lüfer* (bluefish), *levrek* (sea bass), *kalkan* (turbot), *pisi* (megrim or brill), and *sardalya* (fresh sardines), are other familiar fish.

Many fish will be grilled (*ızgara*) or fried (*tava*), especially turbot and tunny. Lüfer and levrek are particularly good poached with vegetables (*buğlama*). Fresh sardines are best if deep-fried in a light batter.

If you prefer meat, you can order a *karışık ızgara* (kahr-uh-SHUK uhz-gahr-ah), a mixed grill of lamb. For beef, order *bonfile* (bohn-fee-LEH), a small filet steak with a pat of butter on top. *Kuzu pirzolası* (koo-ZOO peer-zohl-ah-suh) is tiny lamb chops, charcoal grilled.

Besides grilled meats, there are numerous fancy kebaps, often named for the places where they originated. Best of the kebaps is *Bursa kebap* (BOOR-sah), also called *İskender kebap*, since it was invented in the city of Bursa by a chef named İskender (Turkish for Alexander). The kebap is standard *döner* which is spread on a bed of fresh, chopped flat *pide* bread, with a side order of yogurt. After the plate has been brought to your table, a man comes with savory tomato sauce and pours a good helping on top. Then another man comes with browned butter, which goes on top of the sauce. This stuff is addictive.

Of the other fancy kebaps, *Urfa kebap* comes with lots of onions and black pepper; *Adana kebap* is spicy hot, with red pepper the way the Arabs like it (Adana is down near the Syrian border).

Cheese Cheeses are not a strong point in the Turkish kitchen. Though there are some interesting peasant cheeses such as *tulum peynir*, a salty, dry, crumbly goat's milk cheese cured in a goatskin bag, or another dried cheese which looks just like twine, these interesting cheeses rarely make it to the cities, and almost never to restaurant tables. What you'll find is the ubiquitous *beyaz peynir* (bey-AHZ pey-neer), white sheep's milk cheese. To be good, this must be full-fat (*tam yağlı*) and not too salty. You may also find *kaşar peynir* (kah-SHAHR pey-neer), a firm, mild yellow cheese which comes *taze* (tah-ZEH, fresh) or *eski* (ess-KEE, aged). The *eski* is a bit sharper, but not very sharp for all that.

Desserts Turkish desserts tend to be very sweet, soaked in sugar syrup. Many are baked things such as crumpets, cookies (biscuits), or shredded wheat, all in syrup.

Baklava comes in several varieties: *cevizli* is with chopped walnut stuffing; *fıstıklı* is with pistachio nuts; *kaymaklı* is with clotted cream. Sometimes you can order *kuru baklava*, 'dry baklava', which has less syrup. True baklava is made with honey, not syrup, and though the home-made stuff may contain honey, the store-bought stuff rarely does.

As an alternative to sweet desserts, Turkish fruits can't be beat, especially in mid-summer when the melon season starts, and early in winter when the first citrus comes in. *Kavun* is a deliciously sweet, fruity melon. *Karpuz* is watermelon.

The standard unsweetened dessert, available in most restaurants, is *krem karamel* (creme caramel, or flan).

Tea & Coffee The national drink is not really Turkish coffee as you might expect, but *çay* (CHAH-yee) – tea. The Turks drank a lot of coffee as long as they owned Arabia, because the world's first (and best) coffee is said to have come from Yemen. But with the collapse of the Ottoman Empire, coffee became an imported commodity. You can get Turkish coffee anywhere in Turkey, but you'll find yourself drinking a lot more çay.

The tea plantations are along the eastern Black Sea coast, centered on the town of Rize. Turkish tea is hearty and full-flavoured, served in little tulip-shaped glasses which you hold by the rim to avoid burning your fingers. Sugar is added, but never milk. If you want your tea weaker, ask for it *açık* (ah-CHUK, clear); for stronger, darker tea, order *koyu* (koh-YOO, dark). You can get it easily either way because Turkish tea is made by pouring some very strong tea into a glass, then cutting it with water to the desired strength.

The tiny glasses may seem impractical at first. But they assure you of drinking only fresh, hot tea. Few Turks sit down and drink only one glass. For a real tea-drinking and talking session, they'll go to an outdoor tea garden and order a *semaver* (samovar) of tea so they can refill the glasses themselves, without having to call the *çaycı* (CHAH-yee-juh, tea-man).

As for Turkish coffee (*Türk kahvesi*, TEWRK kah-veh-see), it is always brewed up individually, the sugar being added during the brewing. You order it one of four ways:

Sade (sah-DEH) – Plain, without sugar
Az (AHZ) – With a little sugar
Orta (ohr-TAH) – With moderate sugar
Çok şekerli (CHOHK sheh-kehr-LEE) – With lots of sugar

Order *bir kahve, orta* (BEER kah-VEH, ohr-TAH) for the first time, and adjust from there. Remember that the pulverized coffee grounds lurk at the bottom of the cup. Stop drinking before you get to them.

Water Turks are connoisseurs of good water, and stories circulate of old men able to tell which spring it came from just by tasting it. *Menba suyu*, spring water, is served everywhere, even on intercity buses. If you ask for *su* (water), most times you'll get spring water in a capped bottle.

Tap water is supposedly safe to drink, because it is treated. But it's not as tasty as spring water.

Soft Drinks Soft drinks include the usual range of Coca-cola, Pepsi, *Yedihün* ('7-Days', a clear lemon-flavoured soft drink like Seven-Up), *Fruko*, an orange soda, and others. If you just want fizzy water, ask for *soda*. Fizzy mineral water is *maden sodası*.

Fruit juices are a favourite refresher, and can be excellent. These used to be only thick juices full of pulp and flavour, but with the advent of modern marketing you will also find watery, sugared drinks of almost no food value.

Traditional drinks include *ayran* (ah-yee-RAHN), yogurt mixed with spring water and shaken; it's tart, refreshing and healthful. *Şıra* (shur-RAH), unfermented white grape juice, is delicious, but is served in only a few places, and only during the summer. *Boza* is a thick, slightly tangy, very mild-flavoured drink made from fermented millet (like bird seed), served only in winter.

Wine & Beer Good Muslims don't touch alcoholic beverages at all, but Turkey is a modern country in which the strictures of religion are moderated by the 20th-century lifestyle. *Bira* (BEE-rah, beer) is served almost everywhere. Tuborg makes light (*beyaz*) and dark (*siyah*) beer in Turkey under licence. A local company with a European brewmaster is Efes Pilsen, which also makes light and dark. The light is a good, slightly bitter pilsener. *Tekel*, the Turkish State Monopolies company, makes *Tekel Birası* (teh-KEHL bee-rah-suh), a small-bubbled (sort of

flat), mildly-flavoured brew that may be an acquired taste.

Turkish wines are surprisingly good and delightfully cheap. Tekel makes all kinds in all price ranges. *Güzel Marmara* is the cheap white table wine. *Buzbağ* (BOOZ-baah) is a hearty Burgundy-type wine with lots of tannin. Restaurants seem to carry mostly the wines of the two big private firms, *Doluca* (DOHL-oo-jah) and *Kavak-lıdere* (kah-vakh-LUH-deh-reh). You'll find the premium *Villa Doluca* wines, white (*beyaz*) and red (*kırmızı*, KUHR-muh-ZUH) in most places. Kavaklıdere wines include the premium white named *Çankaya*, and the medium range wines named *Kavak* (white), *Dikmen* (red) and *Lâl* (rose).

Among the more popular regional table wines are those under the *Doruk* and *Dimitrakopulo* labels.

Strong Liquor Hard liquor is a government monopoly in Turkey, and what's not made by Tekel is imported by them. Imported stuff tends to be very expensive: ask the price before ordering any drink made with non-Turkish stuff.

The favourite ardent spirit in Turkey is *rakı* (rah-KUH), an anise-flavoured grape brandy similar to the Greek *ouzo*, French *pastis*, and Arab *arrak*. Rakı comes under several labels, all made by Tekel, the standard one being *Yeni Rakı*. It's customary (but not essential) to mix raki with cool water, half and half, and drink it with a meal.

Tekel also makes decent *cin* (JEEN, gin), *votka*, and *kanyak* (kahn-YAHK, brandy). When ordering kanyak, always specify the *beş yıldız* or *kaliteli* ('five-star', or 'quality') stuff. The regular kanyak is heavy, the five-star much lighter.

There is a Tekel *viski* (VEES-kee, whisky) named Ankara. You might try it once.

For after dinner, better restaurants will stock the local sweet fruit brandies, which are okay but nothing special.

HEALTH

You need no special inoculations before entering Turkey, unless you're coming from an endemic or epidemic area. If you want to get preventive shots (tetanus, typhoid, etc.) get cholera too. The chances are small that you'll run into cholera, but it may come in handy when crossing borders. Health officers far removed from the scene may not keep track of which countries have it and which countries do not.

Medical services are well developed in Turkey. Many doctors speak English, French or German, and have studied in Europe or America. Your consulate can recommend a good doctor or dentist.

For minor problems, it's customary to ask at a pharmacy (*eczane*, ej-zahn-NEH) for advice. Sign language usually suffices to communicate symptoms, and the pharmacist will prescribe on the spot. Even 'prescription' drugs are usually sold without a prescription.

Though Turkey manufactures most modern prescription medicines, it's not good to risk running out. If you take a drug regularly, bring a supply. If your medicine is available in Turkey, it will probably be far less expensive here than at home. It may be good to buy a quantity to take home with you. The drug's name may or may not be exactly the same as you're used to, though it may be the same substance.

Food & Water

Turkey is generally a safe country as far as food and water are concerned, but you should take precautions for several reasons.

The first of these is the obvious one: sanitary practices are not ever universally observed, no matter where you are in the world. Whereas most kitchens will be clean and tidy, one or two off the beaten track may not be.

The second reason has to do not with the cleanliness of the food, but with its familiarity. Most people suffer some consequences from drastic change of diet and water, for each area and each cuisine has its own 'normal' bacteria, and its own composition. Some people find it difficult to digest olive oil, or even to stomach pure water that has a high limestone content. Any experienced traveller knows that getting sick from food is mostly a chance thing, but there are still a few things you can do to improve your chances.

First, take the normal travel precautions. Choose dishes that look freshly-prepared and sufficiently hot. You can go into almost any Turkish kitchen (except in the very posh places) for a look at what's cooking. In fact, in most places that's what the staff will suggest, the language barrier being what it is. Except for grilled meats, Turkish dishes tend to be cooked slowly for a long time, just the thing to kill any errant bacteria. But if they don't sell on the day they're cooked, they might be saved. If they are, the oil may congeal and become harder to digest. But most of the time, things are very fresh. As for grilled meats, these may be offered to you medium rare. They'll probably be all right, but if they really look pink, send them back for more cooking (no problem in this). The words you'll need are *biraz daha pişmiş* (beer-ahz da-HAH peesh-meesh, 'cooked a bit more') or *iyi pişmiş* (ee-EE peesh-meesh, 'well done').

Beware of milk products and dishes containing milk that have not been properly refrigerated. Electricity is expensive in Turkey, and many places will scrimp on refrigeration temperature. If you want a rice pudding (*sütlaç*) or some such dish with milk in it, choose a shop that has lots of them in the window, meaning that a batch has been made recently, guaranteeing freshness. In general, choose things from bins, trays, cases, pots, etc that are fairly full rather than almost empty.

As for water, it's not really much of a problem. You'll find it preferable to stick to bottled spring water as much as possible. It's found almost everywhere, and is delicious. You can drink the tap water, but it won't taste as good. In Ankara no one drinks the tap water. At a roadside çeşme (CHESH-meh, fountain or spring), look out for the word içilmez (eech-eel-MEHZ, 'not to be drunk') near the water. If what you see is içilir (eech-eel-LEER, 'drinkable'), then everything's all right. Even if the water is pure, its high limestone content may give some people loose bowels at first. This is nothing serious.

Alternatives to normal water include maden suyu, naturally fizzy mineral water, and maden sodası (or just soda), artificially carbonated mineral water. The latter just has bigger bubbles, and more of them, than the former. Both come from mineral springs, and both are true mineral waters – full of minerals. The taste is not neutral. Some people like it, some don't. It's supposed to be good for you, clean out your kidneys, etc.

Soft drinks, beer and wine are reliably pure, except in rare cases. As for wines, be careful when drinking some of the smaller, lesser-known labels. The winemakers may use chemicals to stop fermentation, and these (such as cobalt chloride, göztaşi) aren't good for you. They give you headaches. You'll have no such trouble with the big names: Doluca, Kavaklıdere, Tekel.

Even though few people get sick from the food, there are cases of salmonella (food poisoning) and hepatitis. The way to combat them is to remain generally strong, well-rested and well-fed, and to avoid eating in places which seem to ignore basic rules of sanitation.

The symptoms for food poisoning are headache, nausea and/or stomach ache, diarrhea, fever and chills. If you get it, go to bed, put as many covers on as possible (stay warm no matter what). Drink lots of fluids, preferably hot tea without sugar or milk. Camomile tea, papatya çay, is a specific against queasy stomach. Some tea houses serve it, herbal markets sell the dried camomile, and in many parts of Turkey you can even pick the fragrant

little daisy-like camomile flowers along the roadside and make the tea yourself.

Until the bout of food poisoning has run its course (24 to 30 hours), drink nothing but plain tea (no milk or sugar), and eat nothing but dry toast or rusks, and maybe a little yogurt. The day after, you'll feel weak, but the symptoms will have passed except perhaps for the diarrhea. If you take it easy and eat only bland, easily-digested foods for a few days, you'll be fine.

In almost every case, the few people who get food poisoning while abroad compound the problem by ignoring it, or continuing to travel or see the sights, or eating whatever is easiest. Medicines, available with or without a prescription from any eczane, can help a serious bout of the illness. But nothing can rebuild your intestinal flora, necessary to good digestion, except time and tender loving care. Most medicines for food poisoning are strong antibiotics. They kill the poisonous bugs (which are short-lived in any case), and they also nuke all the necessary bugs. Thus antibiotics can actually prolong the diarrhea.

As for hepatitis (sarılık, sahr-uh-LUHK), this is a serious viral infection which must be treated carefully. The chief symptoms are fatigue, loss of energy, a yellow cast to the eyes and skin, and odd-coloured brownish urine. If you rest when your body tells you to, you will have no trouble curing yourself. If you push on, the disease can cause serious liver damage, or even be fatal. Being a virus, there is no drug known to combat it. Antibiotics can actually make it worse, even fatal, as they put great stress on the liver (which must detoxify them), which is already overburdened.

If you think you have hepatitis, go to a doctor and get an examination and a blood test. If the diagnosis is positive, go to bed and stay there. Eat only easily-digestible non-fatty foods such as toast, yogurt, cooked fruits and vegetables. Don't drink any alcohol for six months after diagnosis. You will have to figure on at least a week or two of bed rest, then an easy life for several months. The doctor may prescribe vitamins, especially B-complex. If he prescribes any other medicine, go to another doctor. This is no joke.

Doctors, Dentists & Hospitals

You can find excellent doctors and dentists in the big cities. Ankara has a first-rate medical center called *Hacettepe* (hah-JEHT-tehp-peh), plus other hospitals (*hastane*, hahs-tahn-NEH) and clinics (*klinik*, klee-NEEK). Istanbul has several foreign-run hospitals.

American Amiral Bristol Amerikan Hastanesi, Güzelbahçe Sok., Nişantaşı, Istanbul, tel 148-6030.

French Pasteur Fransız Hastanesi, Divan Hotel Arkası (behind the Divan Hotel), Taksim, Istanbul, tel 148-4756; also, La Paix Hastanesi, Büyükdere Caddesi, Şişli, Istanbul, tel. 148-1832.

German Alman Hastanesi, Sıraselviler Caddesi, Taksim, tel 143-5500.

Charges at the foreign hospitals will be higher than at the government-supported Turkish hospitals. All charges will be much less than you're used to at home, unless your country has a public health plan (such as National Health in Britain).

Care in Turkish hospitals is sometimes not of the highest standards in terms of comfort or convenience. But medical care, as always, depends upon the particular staff members (doctors and nurses) involved. These can be quite good or not so good. The lower staff echelons may be low paid and trained on the job. Supplies are not used in great quantities, so you may not find such things as disposable syringes. As a foreigner, you will probably be given the best possible treatment and the greatest consideration.

Toilets

Turkey is rapidly switching over to the western commode toilet. Virtually every hotel above the lowest class, most apartments, many restaurants, train stations and airports have the familiar raised bowl type. But you may also meet with the flat 'elephant's feet' variety, a porcelain or concrete rectangle with two oblong foot-places and a sunken hole. This may be daunting at first, but it is actually the best kind of toilet from a physical standpoint. It is also sanitary, in that only your shod feet contact the vessel – you squat, you don't sit on anything. Using it is not as difficult as you may think. Just make sure all the stuff doesn't fall out of your pockets when you squat. Also, bring your own toilet paper. In the government-rated hotels there will be paper. In public conveniences, if there's no attendant, there will be no paper. There will be a spigot and a can for washing (with a hand). It's a good idea to carry enough paper or tissues with you at all times.

Sometimes the plumbing is not built to take wads of paper, and the management will place a wastepaper basket or can next to the toilet for used paper. Signs in Turkish will plead with you not to throw the paper down the toilet. What you do depends upon your feelings on the matter.

Clean public toilets can be found near the very big tourist attractions such as Topkapı Palace and the Grand Bazaar. In other places, it depends. Look first. Every mosque has a toilet, often very basic, but better than nothing.

INFORMATION

Every Turkish town of any size has a Tourism Information Office run by the Ministry of Culture and Tourism. The ministry's symbol is the fan-like Hittite sun figure, which you will get used to seeing.

A town may also have a municipal tourism office. If you need help and you can't find an office, ask for the *Belediye Sarayı* (behl-eh-DEE-yeh sah-rah-yuh, Town Hall). They'll rummage around for someone who speaks some English, and will do their best to solve your problem.

In Istanbul, there are Tourism Information Offices at Yeşilköy Airport (tel

Hittite sun figure,
symbol of the Turkish Ministry of Culture & Tourism

573-7399, 573-4136), in Sultanahmet Square (tel 522-4903), and two long blocks from Taksim Square in the Hilton Hotel arcade (tel 140-6300, 140-6864).

In İzmir, the Information Office (tel 14-2147) is in a corner of the main post office (PTT) on Cumhuriyet Square; that's the square with the equestrian statue of Atatürk and the Büyük Efes hotel.

In Ankara you can go to the ministry itself. It's on Gazi Mustafa Kemal Bulvarı several blocks west of Kizilay, on the south (left) side of the street. Ask for the *Kültür ve Turizm Bakanlığı*. Telephone is 29 09 65.

Here are the addresses of Turkish Tourism and Information Offices abroad:

Austria
Mahlerstrasse 3, 1010 Wien
tel (0222) 522128

Belgium
Rue d'Arenberg 42
1000 Bruxelles
tel (02) 513-8230, –8239
telex 25973 TURKTA B

Denmark
Vesterbrogade 11A
1620 Kobenhavn V
tel (01) 223100, 228374

France
Champs-Elysees 102
75008 Paris

tel 562-7868, 562-7984
  562-2610
telex 29639 TURKTANIT

Germany (West)
Baselerstrasse 37
D-6000 Frankfurt M1
tel (0611) 233081, –82
telex 141-6628

Karlsplatz 3/1
8000 Munchen 2
tel (089) 594902, 594317
telex 528190 INTO OL

Italy
Piazza della Repubblica 56
00185 Roma
tel 462957, 474-1697
telex 612131 TURKTANIT

Japan
33-6, 2-Chome Jingumae
Shibuya-Ku, Tokyo 150 Telex: 426428
tel (03) 470-6380, 470-5131
telex 402031 CIBNEN-51

Kuwait
Turkish Embassy, P.O. Box 24517
Safat, Kuwait
tel 415954, 415955
telex 496-2920 TURKOF KT

Netherlands
Herengracht 451, 1007 BS Amsterdam
tel (020) 266810
telex 044-12692

Saudi Arabia
Km 6, Medina Rd, Al-Musaidiya St
P.0. Box 6966, Jeddah
tel 54872, –3
telex 402031 CIBNEN-51

Spain
Plaza de Espana
Torre de Madrid, Piso 13, Off. 1-3
Madrid 13
tel 248-7014, 248-7114

Sweden
Kungsgatan 3, 11143 Stockholm
tel (08) 218620

Switzerland
Talstrasse 74, 8001 Zurich
tel (01) 221-0810, –12
telex 045-813752

United Kingdom
49 Conduit St, London W1
tel (01) 734-8681
telex 895-4905 TTIOFC G

United States
821 United Nations Plaza
New York, NY 10017
tel (212) 687-2194
telex 426428

LAUNDRY & DRY CLEANING

There are no coin-operated automatic
laundries in Turkey yet, but laundry
(çamaşır, chahm-mah-SHUR) is a simple
matter. At any hotel or pension, ask at the
reception desk, or just short-circuit it and
ask a staff member (chambermaid).
They'll quickly find someone to do
laundry. Agree on a price in advance. In
hotels, the classier they are, the more
exorbitant their laundry rates. Even so,
the rates are reasonable.

Figure at least a day to get laundry
done. It may be washed in a machine, or by
hand, but it will be dried on a line, not in a
drying machine. In summer, drying takes
no time at all. If you wash out a T-shirt at
10.30 am in İzmir and hang it in the sun,
it'll be dry by 11 am.

By the way, the word çamaşır (laundry)
also means 'underwear' in Turkish.

Dry cleaning shops (kuru temizleme,
koo-ROO tehm-eez-lem-MEH) are found
here and there in the big cities, usually in
the better residential sections or near the
luxury hotels. Service is similar to that in
Europe and America: fast service (an hour
or two) if you're willing to pay 50% more;
otherwise, overnight or two-day service is
normal. Prices are very reasonable.

MONEY

The unit of currency is the Turkish *lira*, or TL, which was called the Turkish pound (LT) in the Ottoman Empire. The lira is supposedly divided into 100 *kuruş* (koo-ROOSH), but inflation has rendered the kurus obsolete. There's talk of a hundred-to-one currency switch, which would bring the kurush back to life. So far it's only talk.

Coins are rare, but you may come across coins of 1, 2½, 5, 10 and 20 liras. Notes (bills) come as 5, 10, 20, 50, 100, 500, 1000, 5000 and 10,000 liras.

The exchange rates are:

US$1	=	TL 410
£1	=	TL 507
A$1	=	TL 355
DM1	=	TL 131

Inflation has been brought down to about 30% per annum, from about 130% before 1980. The exchange rate for hard currency reflects a slow 'creeping' devaluation which offsets this inflation and keeps the actual cost for a foreign tourist gratifyingly low. An adventurous traveller can live quite well on US$10 or $15 a day in Turkey. For $20 to $25 a day, you can live in comfort, and even style, so

long as you don't want to stay at a Hilton or a Sheraton.

Note All costs in this book are given in US dollars.

Changing Money

It is illegal to traffic in foreign currency without a licence in Turkey. Many tourist shops, travel agencies, expensive restaurants and some hotels have licences to accept foreign currency. The rate may not be quite as good as you get at the bank, though all rates (except on the black market) will be pretty close.

Banks are open from 8.30 am till 12 noon, and 1.30 to 5 pm, Monday through Friday. Outside those times it's difficult to change money. Plan ahead. There are currency exchange desks at the major entry points to Turkey by road, air and sea. The rate at the entry-point will be pretty close to the one downtown, so it's a good idea to change some money right as you enter – $25 or $50 at least.

Almost any bank will change money for you. Look for a sign on or near the front door which reads, *Kambiyo – Exchange – Change – Wechsel*, which says it all. In the large cities, big banks have branches everywhere, even within a hundred metres of one another, and exchange facilities may be limited to the more convenient branches. If a bank tells you it can't change your money, don't worry. You won't have to walk very far to reach the next one.

Many banks will post the daily exchange rates for all the major European currencies, plus the Japanese Yen and the US dollar. You'll have no trouble exchanging US dollars, pounds sterling, marks, francs, guilders, kroner, etc. Dollars, marks and sterling seem to go fastest. Eurocheques are readily accepted.

Changing money, either notes or traveller's cheques, can take a little while, anywhere from five to fifteen minutes. It depends upon the bank and how cumbersome its procedures are. Usually a clerk must type up a form with your name and passport number, you must sign it once or twice, it must be countersigned by one or two bank officers, and then a cashier in a glass booth (*vezne*) will give you your money. Always take your passport when changing money. Always be prepared to wait a little while. Be patient. The bank people will often be especially kind to you (particularly in small towns). If the man with the tea tray is circulating, they may invite you to have some tea or coffee (on the bank). Even if the tea-man is not around, they may ask your preference and order some specially for you. When Turkish banks become as efficient as the Swiss, there won't be any smiles and free tea, which is a pity.

Save your currency exchange receipts (*bordro*). You will need them to change back Turkish liras at the end of your stay. Turkish liras are worth a lot less outside the country, so you won't want to take them with you. Also, the customs men at the frontier may ask you to show currency-exchange receipts if you've bought a lot of valuable souvenirs such as carpets. They want to make sure you changed money legally to buy them.

The Black Market

Turkey's black market is not very vigorous, and it is chancy. Currency exchange violations are serious matters. Don't get caught at it. The black market, small though it is, exists because foreign currency is scarce, not because it's undervalued. Thus, if a Turk is going to Europe or America, he is allowed to purchase only about $200 in hard currency to cover expenses while abroad. This makes for very short trips indeed. So just to get a few more dollars, a few people are willing to pay a bit more than the going rate.

In a shop, you may get a better deal if you offer to pay in hard currency. But don't depend on it. The official line will be, 'I have a licence to change money. I'll just take it to the bank. There's no difference in price'. What the shopkeeper actually intends to do with the money is another matter, of course. It doesn't hurt to offer. If he grants a reduction, he can always say, 'Okay, just because I'm fond of Australians/Americans/English/etc'. What he does with the money after you leave the shop is his responsibility.

Travellers' Cheques

No problem in exchanging these for Turkish liras in a bank. The more expensive hotels, restaurants and shops will accept the cheques, as will car rental agencies and travel agencies. Generally, though, it's better to change cheques for Turkish liras in a bank.

Though a wide range of cheques is accepted, the more familiar your cheques are, the better. American Express, Thomas Cook, Eurocheques and the like go quickly. I once changed some Swiss Bankers' Traveller's Cheques with little trouble; the clerk just had to look up the example in her book and compare them.

Credit Cards

Turks are beginning to learn about living on plastic. The big hotels and expensive shops may accept your credit card. Car rental agencies certainly will. But make sure in advance. Not all establishments accept all cards. If you have American Express, Visa, Diners Club and Mastercard/Access/Eurocard, you're probably equipped for any establishment that takes cards. If you only have one or two, ask. Turkish Airlines, for instance, may accept only Mastercard/Access/Eurocard; the State Railways doesn't accept any; a souvenir shop may accept all four.

A shopkeeper may require you to pay the credit card fee of 5% to 7%. He may not see it as a normal cost of business. Any price, whether marked or haggled for, is assumed to be for cash. As he must pay the credit card company a percentage, he may reason that the charge should pass on.

Transferring Money

The speed with which you need to transfer money determines the cost of the transfer.

If you have months, send a letter home, ask them to send a cheque, deposit the cheque in a Turkish bank for clearance, and then wait. Of course, banks can wire money in a matter of a day or two (usually), but this may cost as much as $30 per transfer. Sometimes the fee is a percentage of the amount transferred. Still, if you're in a hurry, you may have to do it.

Though the PTT in Turkey handles postal money orders, I would not recommend this route for anything more than token amounts. The PTT is often difficult to deal with; a bank is better.

Before transferring money, consider these alternatives: some shopkeepers and other businesses will accept a personal cheque in exchange for a purchase. If you have a Turkish friend to countersign a cheque, you may well be able to get cash from a bank. With some credit cards you may be able to get a cash advance on the card from a bank, or use the card as security to cash a cheque at the card's company office. Even if the amount is limited ($100 to $150 per day), it doesn't take many days to build up a substantial sum. A bank may require you to pay a telex charge for a credit card cash advance, but it will not be more than a few dollars.

If it comes to transferring money by bank wire, walk into a large bank, preferably in a large town, find someone who speaks English, and explain the problem. The bank may be able to telex your bank and request the funds, or you may have to call your bank (or a friend) and do it yourself. When the funds arrive at the Turkish bank, take your passport and pick up your money.

Should you want foreign currency, you may find that the bank goes through a maddening, fee-producing exercise: your incoming funds will be converted into Turkish liras, then reconverted to your home currency. The bank pockets the 'spread' between buying and selling currency rates, plus two exchange fees. There may also be a fee for the special service.

TURKEY'S FIRST AND ONLY ENGLISH DAILY

NEWSPAPERS & MAGAZINES

The Turks are great readers of newspapers. The local dailies are produced by up-to-date computerized methods, in full colour. Only a decade ago, Istanbul could boast more than a dozen Turkish-language dailies, two in Greek, one in Armenian, one in French and two in Ladino Spanish (spoken by Jews who came from Spain to the Ottoman Empire in the Middle Ages). As everywhere, the number of dailies is dwindling as the more successful papers grow. *Milliyet*, one of the largest dailies, now has an edition printed in Germany for Turkish workers there, as well as numerous local editions.

Of prime interest to visitors is the Ankara *Daily News*, an English-language daily sold in most Turkish cities where tourists go. It is the cheapest source of English-language news in print. The big international papers such as the *International Herald-Tribune, Le Monde, Die Welt*, etc are on sale in tourist spots as well. They may be a day or two late.

Large-circulation magazines including *Newsweek, Time, Der Spiegel*, and the like are also sold in tourist spots.

If you can't find the foreign publication you want, go to a big hotel's news-stand, or check at a foreign-language bookstore (see above for addresses).

POST & TELECOMMUNICATIONS

Postal and telecommunication service in Turkey are handled by the *PTT* (peh-teh-TEH), which stands for *posta, telefon, telgraf*. Look for the yellow signs with black 'PTT' letters.

Mailboxes (letterboxes) and postal vehicles are yellow as well. Every town has a PTT, usually close to the main square. Go here to buy stamps and telephone tokens, send letters and telegrams, or to make telephone calls (if no other phone is available).

Istanbul's *merkez postahane* (mehr-KEHZ POHS-tah-neh, central post office) is in the section called Eminönü, several blocks west of Sirkeci Railway Station. Go here for *poste restante* mail. If you are having mail sent here, have it addressed this way:

Name
Poste Restante
Merkez Postahane
Eminönü
Istanbul
TURKEY

Convenient PTT branches are located in Taksim, Galatasaray, Aksaray and in the Grand Bazaar.

Mailing Parcels

To mail packages out of the country from Istanbul, or to receive dutiable merchandise, you must go to the special *Paket Postahane* (parcel post office) near Karaköy. You must have your package open for customs inspection, and fight a mountain of the world's most frustrating red tape. You'd be far better off mailing your package from another town or city, even if you have to go out of your way to do so. As there is only one post office in a small town, it also serves as the customs office, and small town clerks are nicer to deal with. Postal clerks in Turkey are as a rule cold and curt, often rude, and sometimes even nasty, though foreigners get better treatment than Turks do. You can't be rude back because there's a law (as in Europe) against 'insulting a public official'.

Telephones

The PTT operates two different telephone systems, the traditional operator type, and automatic ('direct-dial'). Both take a while to use, as there are too few circuits. Improvements are being made. In general, you will find the telephone useful in Turkey.

Telephone tokens For most calls, you'll need a *jeton* (zheh-TOHN, token), or perhaps several. They come in two sizes. The smaller ones (*küçük jeton*, kew-CHEWK zheh-tohn) are for local calls. The larger ones, which cost ten times as much, are for long-distance calls. Buy your jetons at the post office, or from a disabled person outside the post office.

Local calls Once you have your jeton, find a phone. There may be a waiting line. You will find one of four types of phones. The desk phones with a small box attached take big jetons for local calls. These are the ones you find in grocery shops and offices. For the old black wall telephones, don't put the jeton in the slot on top until your party answers. For the newer red or gun-metal grey phones, put the jeton in before you dial; if you don't get through, it will be returned to you.

The new yellow automatic push-button phones have pictographs on them demonstrating their use. These phones are described below.

Long-distance calls For long-distance/trunk calls, you can use the operator-type phones, or automatic phones which take the more expensive 'big' jetons (*büyük jeton*, bew-YEWK zheh-tohn).

With an operator phone, (that is, any phone *except* the yellow push-button models), place the call with the operator, then wait for the operator to ring you back. The call will go through according to the speed which you designate: *normal* (nohr-MAHL) means 'slowest' in this instance; *acele* (ah-jeh-LEH) means twice as fast; *yıldırım* (yuhl-duhr-RUHM) means 'lightning', five times as fast as *normal*. Five times as fast costs five times as much. After you place the call, you wait. This may take a minute or two, or an hour or two. The operator can tell you how long you can expect to wait.

The Automatic system If you use the new automatic system, you first must estimate how much a call will cost to your destination. This is so you have enough big jetons to complete your call. You don't want to get cut off in the middle. Next, find an automatic, push-button phone. It may have a sign above it. *Sehirlerarası* means 'Inter-city'; *Milletlerarası* means 'International'. You'll need to know the city and country codes for the place you're calling.

Note that calling on an automatic phone doesn't necessarily mean that you will get through to your party faster. As the inter-city and international lines are often busy, the person (or persons) on line in front of you at the phone may keep dialling and re-dialling their number until they get an answer. This is inefficient, but they don't want to wait through that long line again. And thus the line gets longer . . .

Anyway, when you finally make it to the

automatic push-button phone, do this: look for the little square red light below the push-buttons. Is it lit? It is? Tough luck – the phone is out of order. But if it's not lit, you can assume that either the red light is burnt out or the phone works. We'll assume the phone works.

One big jeton often gives you one minute of calling within Turkey. Buy lots. You can always trade them in at any post office.

Lift the receiver and deposit one big jeton. Now, look for the little round light in the last box, to the right, of the pictorial instructions above the push-buttons. When this light goes out, push '9'. Then, when you hear the long-distance dial tone, push the buttons for the country and/or city codes, and the local number.

As you talk, watch that little round red light up top, and listen for chimes on the line. Both are indications that it's time to deposit another big jeton. Good luck.

Telegraph

You can send a telegram (*telgraf*, tehl-GHRAHF) from any post office in Turkey. Ask for a *telgraf kâğıdı* (tehl-GHRAHF kyah-uh-duh, telegram form), fill it out, and hand it over. For most foreign countries, there is only one rate of service: fast and expensive. A simple telegram to North America may cost $15, for instance.

If you're sending your wire within Turkey, the clerk will ask you what speed you want it sent. As with the phone service, *normal* is slow, quite slow; *acele* is fast, and twice as expensive; and *yıldırım* (lightening) costs five times as much as *normal*. Remember that the address of the recipient is included in the word-count.

Telex

The larger cities have some post offices with telex (*teleks*, TEHL-eks) machines. If your recipient has a telex machine and number, this can be cheaper than sending a telegram. Write out your message, including the telex number if you have it, find a post office with a machine, and the attendant will send the message, give you a receipt, and also a confirmation copy.

There is a telex machine in the branch post office in Ankara's Kizilay Square.

RADIO & TV

T. R. T., for *Türkiye Radyo ve Televizyon*, controls all broadcasting. It's a quasi-independent establishment modelled on the BBC. Western classical and popular music, along with Turkish classics and pop, are played regularly on both AM (medium-wave) and FM channels. Short news broadcasts in English, French and German are given each morning and evening.

Television is one channel, Turkish only, evenings only, with most of the films dubbed in Turkish.

BBC World Service is often receivable on medium-wave (AM) as well as on short-wave. The Voice of America broadcasts in English on middle-wave, relayed from Rhodes, each morning. The rest of the middle wave band is a wonderful babel of Bulgarian, Romanian, Greek, Hebrew, Arabic, Russian, Persian, Italian and Albanian.

SHOPPING

There is simply no way anyone on earth could travel to Turkey and not find a wonderful souvenir. Here are some tips on what to buy, and how to go about buying it:

Haggling

For the best buy in terms of price and quality, know the market. Spend some time shopping for similar items in various shops, asking prices. Shopkeepers will give you pointers on what makes a good kilim, or carpet, or meerschaum pipe, or alabaster carving. In effect, you're getting a free course in product lore. This is not at all unpleasant, as you will often be invited to have coffee, tea or a soft drink as you talk over the goods and prices.

You can, and should, ask prices if they're not marked, but you should not make a counter-offer unless you are seriously interested in buying. No matter how often the shopkeeper asks you, 'Okay, how much will you pay for it?' No matter how many glasses of tea you've drunk at his expense, don't make a counter offer unless you're seriously interested in buying. If the shopkeeper meets your price, you should buy. It's considered very bad form to haggle over a price, agree, and then not buy.

Some shopkeepers, even in the Haggle Capital of the World (Istanbul's Grand Bazaar), will offer a decent price and say, 'That's my best offer'. Many times they mean it, and they're trying to do you a favour by saving time. How will you know when they are, and when it's just another haggling technique? Only by knowing the market, by having shopped around. Remember, even if he says, 'This is my best offer', you are under no obligation to buy unless you have made a counter-offer, or have said, 'I'll buy it'. It's perfectly acceptable to say a pleasant good-bye and walk out of the shop, even after all that free tea, if you cannot agree on a price. In fact, walking out is one of the best ways to test the authenticity of the shopkeeper's price. If he knows you can surely find the item somewhere else for less, he'll stop you and say, 'Okay, you win, it's yours for what you offered'. And if he doesn't stop you, there's nothing to prevent you from returning in a half-hour and buying the item for what he quoted.

Alabaster

A translucent, fine-grained variety of either gypsum or calcite, alabaster is pretty because of its grain and colour, and because light passes through it. You'll see ash trays, vases, chess sets, bowls, egg cups, even the eggs themselves carved from the stone. Cappadocia is a major producing and carving area, and towns like Urgup and Avanos specialize in it. But in fact you will find it wherever good souvenirs are sold.

Antiques

Turkey harbours a lot of fascinating stuff left over from the empire: vigorous peasant jewellery, waterpipe mouth-pieces carved from amber, old Kurans and illuminated manuscripts, Greek and Roman figurines and coins, tacky furniture in the Ottoman Baroque style. Though it's perfectly legal for a shopkeeper to sell you an antiquity, and legal for you to buy it, it is illegal for you to take it with you out of the country. Turkey is one of those countries with treasure troves of antiquities, some of which are smuggled out of the country and fed into the international contraband art market. It's a dirty business.

Only true antiquities are off-limits, not the many artful fakes.

Carpets & Kilims

Turkey has marvellous carpets and kilims (flat-woven mats) at good prices only half or two-thirds what you'd pay at home. Unless you're willing to research patterns, dyes, knots-per-square-centimeter and so forth, you'll buy what you like for a price that fits your budget.

The very basic examination of a carpet, so that you can look like you know what you're doing, involves the following procedures. Turn a corner over and look at the closeness of the weave. Ask, 'How many knots per square centimeter?' The tighter the weave, the smaller the knots, the higher the quality and durability. Compare the colours on the back with the colours on the front. Spread the nap with your fingers and look to the *bottom* of the carpet's pile. Are the colours more vivid there than on the surface? If so, the surface has faded in the sun considerably. Take a white handkerchief, wet it a bit, and rub it on the top surface of the carpet. Do the colours run? Look at the carpet from one end, then from the other; the colours will be different because the pile always leans one way or the other. Take the carpet out into the sunlight and look at it there.

That's about all you can do without

becoming a rug expert. If you don't trust the dealer's sworn oath that the rug is all wool, or silk, or whatever, ask him to clip a bit of the tassle and burn if for you – if you can recognize the smell of burning silk, or wool, or nylon.

Carpet prices are determined by demand, age, quality, condition, the enthusiasm of the buyer and the debt load of the seller. New carpets can be skillfully 'antiquated', damaged or worn carpets can be rewoven (good work, but expensive), or patched, or even painted. Worn carpets look fairly good until the magic paint washes out. But give the carpet a good going-over, decide if you think it's a good price, and go from there.

Method of payment can be a bargaining point, or a point of contention. Some dealers will take personal cheques, but all prefer cash or travellers' cheques. If you pay with a credit card (and not many shops will have facilities for this), the dealer may require you to pay the fee which the credit card company will charge him, and even the cost of the phone call or telex to check on your credit. If he doesn't require you to pay these charges, it means that you've paid a hefty enough price so that another 6% to 8% doesn't bother him.

If all this seems too much trouble, be advised: it isn't. A good Turkish carpet will easily outlast the human body of its owner, and become an heirloom.

Ceramaics

The best Turkish ceramics were made in Iznik (Nicaea) in the 17th and 18th centuries. İznik tiles from the great days are now museum-pieces, found in museums throughout the world.

Today most of the tile-making is done in Kütahya, a pleasant town with few other redeeming qualities for the tourist. For the very best ceramics, you must go to Kütahya. But souvenir shops will have attractive, hand-made tiles, plates, cups, bowls, etc. They're not really high-fired, so they're vulnerable to breaks and cracks, but they are still attractive.

The real, old İznik tiles qualify as antiquities. If you go to İznik, you will find a reviving tile industry there, on a small scale. Some of the items are quite pretty, and reasonably priced.

Copper

Gleaming copper vessels will greet you in every souvenir shop you peep into. Many are old, sometimes several centuries. Most are handsome, and some are still eminently useful. The new copper ware tends to be of lighter gauge; that's one of the ways you tell new from old. But even the new stuff will have been made by hand.

'See that old copper waterpipe over there?' my friend Alaettin asked me once. We were sitting in his impossibly cluttered, closet-sized shop on Istanbul's Cadircilar Caddesi, just outside the Grand Bazaar. 'It dates from the time of Sultan Ahmet III (1703-1730), and was used by the *Padişah* (sultan) himself. I just finished making it yesterday.'

Alaettin is a master coppersmith, and his pieces might well have graced the sultan's private apartments – except that the sultanate was abolished in 1922. He would charge a hefty price for his fine workmanship, but not for the story. The story was the gift-wrapping, so to speak.

Copper vessels should not be used for cooking or eating unless they are tinned inside; that is, washed with moten tin which covers the toxic copper. If you intend to use a copper vessel, make sure the interior layer of tin is intact, or negotiate to have it tinned (*kalaylamak*). If there is a *kalayciü* shop nearby, ask about the price of the tinning in advance.

Inlaid Wood

Cigarette boxes, chess and *tavla* (backgammon) boards, this and that will be inlaid with different coloured woods, or silver, or mother-of-pearl. It's not the finest work here, but it's pretty good. Make sure there is indeed inlay. These days, alarmingly accurate decals/transfers exist. Also, check the silver: is it silver, or aluminum, or pewter? Is the mother-of-pearl actually daughter-of-polystyrene?

Jewellery

Turkey is a wonderful place to buy jewellery, especially the antique stuff. None of the items sold here may meet your definition of 'chic'. But window-shopping is great fun. Jewellers' Row in any market is a dazzling strip of glittering shop windows filled with gold. Light bulbs, artfully rigged, show it off. In the Grand Bazaar, a blackboard sign hung above Kuyumcular Caddesi ('Street of the Jewellers') bears the daily price for unworked gold of so-many karats. Serious gold-buyers should check out this price, watch carefully as the jeweller weighs the piece in question, and then calculate what part of the price is for gold, and what part for workmanship.

Silver is another matter. There is sterling silver jewellery (look for the hallmark), but nickel silver and pewter-like alloys are much more common. Serious dealers don't try to pass off alloy as silver.

Leather & Suede

On any given *Kurban Bayramı* (Sacrifice Holiday), over 2,500,000 sheep get the axe in Turkey. Add to that the normal day-to-day needs of a cuisine based on mutton and lamb and you have a huge amount of raw material to be made into leather items. Shoes, bags, cushions, jackets, skirts, vests, hat, gloves, trousers and other things are all made from soft leather. This is a big industry in Turkey, particularly in and around the Grand Bazaar. So much leather clothing is turned out that a good deal of it will be badly cut or carelessly made. But there are lots of fine pieces, as well.

The only way to assure youself of a good piece is to examine it carefully, taking time. Try it on just as carefully, see if the sleeves are full enough, if the buttonholes are positioned well, if the collar rubs. If

something is wrong, keep trying others until you find what you want. Made-to-order garments can be excellent, or disappointing, as the same tailor who made the ready-made stuff will make the ordered stuff; and he will be making it fast because the shopkeeper has already impressed you with his 'No problem. I can have it for you tomorrow'. It's better to find something off the rack that fits than to order it, unless you can order without putting down a deposit or committing yourself to buy (this is often possible).

Leather items and clothing are standard tourist stuff, found in all major tourist destinations.

Meerschaum

If you smoke a pipe, you know about meerschaum. For those who don't, meerschaum ('seafoam' in German; *Lületaşı*, LEW-leh-tahsh-uh in Turksih) is a hydrous magnesium silicate, a soft, white, clay-like material which is very porous but heat-resistent. When carved into a pipe, it smokes cool and sweet. Over time, it absorbs residues from the tobacco and turns a nut brown colour. Devoted meerschaum pipe smokers even have special gloves with which to hold the pipe as they smoke, so that oil from their fingers won't sully the fine, even patina of the pipe.

The world's largest and finest beds of meerschaum are found in Turkey, near the city of Eskişehir. Artful carving of the soft stone has always been done, and blocks of meerschaum were exported to be carved abroad as well. These days, however, the export of block meerschaum is prohibited because the government realized that exporting uncarved blocks was the same as exporting the jobs to carve them. So any carved pipe will have been carved in Turkey.

Carving is of a very high quality, and you'll marvel at the artistry of the Eskişehir craftsmen. Pipes portraying turban'd pashas, wizened old men, fair maidens, mythological beasts, and many pipes in geometrical designs will be on view in any souvenir shop. Pipes are not the only thing carved from meerschaum these days. Bracelets, necklaces, pendants, earrings and cigarette holders all appear in souvenir shops.

When buying, look for purity and uniformity in the stone. Carving is often used to cover up flaws in a piece of meerschaum, so do look over it carefully. For pipes, check that the bowl walls are uniform in thickness all around, and that the hole at the bottom of the bowl is centered. Purists buy uncarved, just plain pipe-shaped meerschaum pipes that are simply but perfectly made.

Prices for pipes vary, but should be fairly low. Abroad, meerschaum is an expensive commodity, and pipes are luxury items. Here in Turkey meerschaum is cheap, the services of the carver are low-priced, and nobody smokes pipes. If you can't get the pipe you want for a lot less than half of what you'd pay at home, then you're not working at it hard enough.

SPORTS

Turks are enthusiastic sportsmen. Football (soccer), basketball and wrestling are the favoured sports. Every city of any size has a large football stadium which fills up on match days.

The famous oiled wrestling matches, where brawny strong-men in leather breeches rub themselves down with olive oil and grapple with equally slippery opponents, take place each spring in Edirne. Another purely Turkish sight is the camel-wrestling matches held in the province of Aydin, south of İzmir, in the winter months. Konya is the setting for *cirit* (jirid), the javelin-throwing game played on horseback. See the Festivals & Holidays section for full details.

Water sports are big in Turkey because of the beautiful coasts and beaches. Yachting, rowing, water-skiing, snorkeling, diving (with or without scuba gear) and swimming are well represented.

Mountain-climbing (*dağcılık*, DAAH-juh-LUHK) is practised by a small but enthusiastic number of Turks, and Turkey has plenty of good, high mountains for it.

Turkey is a good country for hunting, from small game to wild boar (there's a boar-hunting festival at Ephesus each spring). However, the Turks are touchy about people bringing guns into the country. Check with a Turkish consulate about regulations and permits for importing a sporting gun.

Skiing is decent on Uludağ, near Bursa, and at a few resorts in the Beydağları mountain range near Antalya. Equipment can be rented at the slopes.

Bicycling has not caught on in Turkey as much as in Europe. Many of the highways have fairly rough surfaces which are not bad for cars and trucks, but a bit bumpy for a bike. The sport may catch on though. Turkey's scenery certainly lends itself to bike touring.

TIME

Turkish time is two hours ahead of Greenwhich Mean Time, all year long, with no change for daylight saving (summer time). At noon in Istanbul the time elsewhere is:

Paris, Rome	11 am
London	10 am
New York	5 am
Los Angeles	2 am
Perth, Hong Kong	7 pm
Sydney	9 pm
Auckland	11 pm

(Note: these times are Standard Times; in places that are on Summer Time, it's one hour later. Also, in November 1984, Turkish Standard Time was put one hour *back* to bring it more in line with the rest of Europe)

TIPPING

Restaurants Most of the tipping you'll do will be in restaurants. Some places will automatically add a service charge (*servis ücreti*) of 10% or 15% to your bill, but this does not absolve you from the tip, oddly enough. The service charge goes either into the *patron*s pocket, or to the maitre d'. Leave 5% to 7% on the table for the waiter.

If service is included, it may say *servis dahil* ('service included') on the bill. Still, a small tip is expected. In any situation, 10% is fine. Only in the fancy foreign-operated hotesl will waiters expect those enormous 15% to 20% American-style tips. In the very plain, basic restaurants, you needn't tip at all, though the price of a soft drink or a cup of coffee is always appreciated.

Hotels In hotels, tip the bellboy who shows you to your room and carries your bags. He'll expect about 4% or 5% of the room price. So if your room costs $15, give about 75c. If a bellboy does any other chores that you ask, a slightly smaller tip is in order.

Taxis Don't tip taxi drivers unless they've done some special service. Turks don't tip taxi drivers. The drivers may look for a tip, but that's only because you're foreigner and foreigners tip taxi drivers. Dolmuş drivers never expect tips.

Hairdressers In barbershops and hair-dressers, pay the fee for the services rendered (which goes to the shop), then about 15% to the person who cut your hair, and smaller tips to the others who provided service, down to the one who brushes stray locks from your clothing as you prepare to leave (5% for that). It will all end up being pretty cheap in any case.

Turkish baths In Turkish baths, there will be fees for the several services, but everyone will expect and await tips. You needn't go overboard in this. Share out about 30% or 35% at most to the assembled staff (and they will be assembled for tips as you depart). In a few of the more heavily-touristed baths in Istanbul the

attendents are insistent. Don't let them browbeat you.

Sleeping cars If you take a sleeping compartment on a train, the porter will come around near the end of the trip, request an official 10% service charge, give you a receipt for it, and will expect a few more percent for himself. If you give him 5% extra, he'll be pleased.

Other situations There are other situations in which a tip is indicated, but that must be handled delicately. For instance, at a remote archaeological site, a local person may unlock the gate and show you around the ruins. He will probably have official admission tickets, which he must sell you. If that's all he does, that's all you pay. But if he goes out of his way to help you, he deserves a tip. He may be reluctant to accept it, and may refuse once or even twice. Try at least three times. He may well need the money, but the rules of politeness require several refusals. If he refuses three times, though, you can assume that he truly wants to help you only for friendship's sake. Don't press further, for this will insult his good intentions.

WEIGHTS & MEASURES
Turkey uses the metric system. For those used to the British/American systems of measurement, the following approximations may help.

A litre is slightly more than a US quart, or about 1¾ imperial pints.
A US gallon is 3.8 litres; an imperial gallon is 4.5 litres.
A kilogram (kg, kilo) is 2.2 pounds; a pound is less than ½ kilogram.
A metre is 39 inches, or just over a yard.
An inch is about 25 mm (2.5 cm), so one cm less than half an inch.
A kilometre (km) is 5/8 of a mile; a mile is 1.6 kilometres.

Temperatures are measured in degrees

Celsius (also called degrees Centigrade). For a quick conversion from Celsius to Fahrenheit, double the Celsius figure and add 30; if you want accuracy and you've got your pocket calculator handy, you can simply mutiply the Celsius by 1.8, and then add 32.

Zero Celsius is freezing point; 20°C is room temperature (68°F), and 40°C is a very hot day (105°F).

Getting There

You can get to Turkey by air, rail, road or sea. Note that if you travel by land you will have to deal with the problem of visas for entry to East European countries. See the section on this at the end of this chapter.

BY AIR

Most international flights arrive at Istanbul airport, the country's busiest, with a big new terminal; other airports are at Ankara, İzmir, Adana (down near the Syrian border), and Antalya and Dalaman (on the southern coast). Most foreign visitors arrive in Istanbul because it has the most flights, and is also the first place tourists want to see. Antalya and Dalaman take most charter flights filled with vacationers headed for the south coast.

Turkish Airlines (*Turk Hava Yollari*, or *THY*; symbol TK) has flights to most major cities in Europe, the Middle East and North Africa. The airlines of these destination countries also fly into and out of Turkey.

Most of the European national airlines have flights to Turkey, often connecting with flights from North America. From New York, KLM's connections are particularly good. Pakistan International Airlines (PIA) has a one-stop service from New York to Istanbul, with the lowest fare.

Bargain Airfares

The very cheapest flights are charters and excursions, of course. The situation on these changes frequently. London is a good place to look into charters to Turkey. You might find something even cheaper to Greece, and then get to Turkey by bus or ferryboat from one of the Greek islands (see below). For instance, there are charters from New York to Athens for $449 round-trip in winter ($249 one way), slightly higher in summer. Call any travel agent and ask about 'air only' charters and

tours. You have the option of buying the whole tour package, or just the 'air portion' (that is, the flight; one-way or round-trip).

At the time of writing, PIA has a summer excursion fare from New York to Istanbul of $700. Olympic has a similarly-priced fare from Boston or New York to Athens or Thessaloniki. The flight between Athens and Istanbul is unduly expensive, but there are Athens – Thessaloniki – Istanbul buses. There's also an incredibly slow train. But presumably you won't be rocketing through Greece, so why not take a ship across the Aegean, ending up at one of the Greek islands close to the Turkish coast. Ferries from Greece to Turkey are explained below.

From Australia there is no direct route by air. Qantas can, however, arrange an economy fare to Ankara, ranging from A$1935 to A$2195, depending upon season etc. There is no discounting.

The cheapest way to get to Turkey from Australia is to fly to Athens, take a boat to one of the islands and then a ferry to the Turkish mainland. This route proves, however, the dictum that the smaller the price the greater the inconvenience.

Air fares in Europe tend to be quite high by American standards. If you have a ticket from the US, say New York to Vienna, the extra fare to Istanbul can cost US$400. Eastern European airlines often have lower fares than western airlines (this helps to make up for their poor reputation for service and reliability), so check travel agents and airline offices for any deals that may be going.

It is also worth investigating some alternative fares, such as 'open-jaw' fares where you fly to one city (eg Vienna) and return from another (eg Istanbul). You have to make separate arrangements for transport between the two cities but the overall savings can be considerable.

There are other alternative fares – a good travel agent should be able to work out the best deal for you.

Turkish Airlines (THY) has an unbeatable, actually incredible, deal for students who qualify. Students under 22 years of age with the International Student Identity Card are granted a 60% reduction on THY's international flights to and from Europe. Between Turkey and Middle Eastern cities, the discount is 50% for students under 26 (55% for Cairo). You may have to provide a photocopy of your student card and passport, so it's best to buy your ticket and nail down that discount in advance. Within Turkey, the student discount is 10%, with no age limit.

Transport to and from the airport is covered within the section on each city.

BY SEA

Without question, the most romantic way to arrive in Turkey is by sea. The panorama of the Old City's skyline, with rows of minarets and bulbous mosque domes rising above the surrounding houses, is an incomparable sight. If you can't arrive by sea, don't despair. A trip on a Bosphorus ferryboat will reveal a similar panorama.

Though steamers still ply the Mediterranean from port to port, eventually turning up at İzmir or Istanbul, schedules are erratic. Sometimes fares are not particularly low, as passenger accommodation tends to be deluxe. The Black Sea Steamship Company, a Soviet outfit, runs cruise ships during the summer months. You can sometimes book a place on one, but prices will be moderate to high, and everything will be in Russian, including the chit-chat of your fellow passengers. The occasional Turkish Maritime Lines' freighter may take passengers at low fares, but this is not dependable, either. Going to Turkey by sea, then, you have three choices.

From Ancona, Italy

Turkish Maritime Lines (*T.C. Denizyollari*, or TML) operates modern, comfortable car-and-passenger ferries from Ancona (Italy) to İzmir, departing Ancona every Saturday morning from June through September, arriving in İzmir on Tuesday morning. Fares for passengers in cabins range from about $160 to $320, breakfast and port taxes included. But there is a 'Pullman' class where you get a reclining seat, costing $100. Students get a 10% reduction on fare only (not meals). If you want lunch and dinner, add $40. Fare for a car is about $136.

From Brindisi, Italy

A Greek company called Libra Maritime runs a schedule of boats and buses connecting Brindisi-Patras-Piraeus-İzmir in 40 hours. The Piraeus-İzmir ferryboat carries cars and passengers, and runs three days per week in the summertime, departing Piraeus on Monday, Wednesday and Friday at 8 pm, and departing İzmir on Tuesday and Thursday at 9 pm, Sunday at 2 pm. The ships are the Atlas III and the Atlas IV. Contact Libra in Piraeus at Plateia Loudovicou 4, (tel (1) 411-7864; in Brindisi at 54 Corso Garibaldi, (tel 21 935, 28 004); Libra's agent in İzmir is International Tourism Service (*Enternasyonal Turizm Servis, Seyahat ve Gemicilik A S*).

From the Greek Islands

Getting to Turkey from one of the Greek islands is fairly painless, but it can start out as a hassle. Greeks are very unwilling to provide information on transport to Turkey. In fact, rumour has it that there is a law forbidding the advertisement of such transport, even though the ferries (and, on the mainland, buses) run regularly and frequently. What this means is that if you are on Lesvos (Mytileni), Chios, Samos, Kos or Rhodes, you'll have to keep asking until you find the one little office that sells tickets. According to the rumour, that one little office is allowed to have one

(1) sign, no larger than a normal piece of typing paper, in its window advertising boats to Turkey. If you simply can't find the place, head down to the harbour and ask. Greek and Turkish boats share the trade and operate almost every day in summer.

The procedure is this: once you've found the ticket office, buy your ticket a day in advance. You'll be asked to turn in your passport the night before the trip. The next day, before you board the boat, you'll get it back. There is no problem in this.

In summer, boats run daily from Rhodes to Marmaris, a nice resort town on the Turkish Mediterranean. There is also daily service from Samos to Kuşadası Service from Lesvos (Mytileni) to Ayvalik, Chios to Çeşme, and Kos to Bodrum may not be every day, but rather several days a week. If you can get together a sufficient group of passengers, they may run a special trip. In spring and autumn, service is less frequent, perhaps only once a week. In winter it is mostly suspended, though a few boats will still run from Rhodes to Marmaris and from Samos to Kuşadası.

The latest twist in the Greek anti-Turkish campaign is a rule that anyone with a Turkish visa will not be admitted to Greece. This means that if you sail over and visit Turkey on more than just a day's excursion, the Greek government won't let you back into Greece. But the Turkish immigration officers seem to be making it easy for tourists by doing what the Israelis did when faced with a similar ultimatum from the Arab countries: if you want to enter Turkey, the Turkish officers will stamp a paper form, which you keep in your passport and then hand in as you leave the country. This seems to work quite well, and the Greek officials are none the wiser.

This was the Greek government's response to a Turkish good-will gesture whereby all visa restrictions were lifted for Greeks who wanted to visit Turkey! And Greeks do visit Turkey: Turkey receives more Greek tourists than it does any other nationality. The Greeks want to spend their money in Turkey, where it buys a lot more; but they want you to spend your money in Greece.

For the return trip from Turkey, by the way, there is no problem in finding the ticket office or in getting information. Huge banners hang on the fronts of travel agencies, advertising (in English) 'BOATS TO GREECE'!

From Famagusta, Cyprus

Other TML ferries run between Famagusta (Magosa, Cyprus) and Mersin (Turkey), a ten-hour trip, operating all year. From October to April, departures are Tuesday and Friday evenings from Mersin, arriving in Famagusta the next morning. In summer (late April through September), departures from Mersin are on Monday, Wednesday and Friday evenings. Return trips from Cyprus, then, depart Tuesday, Thursday and Sunday mornings. The Friday departures from Mersin stop at Famagusta on Saturday, then go on to Latakia, Syria.

Note that the Greek Cypriots may not let you cross into Turkish Cyprus. At the least, they'll tell you it's not possible to cross, and will say it's a Turkish regulation. It's not.

BY RAIL

The Orient Express lives on in special excursion trains, but the fares for these deluxe tours are between $2500 and $5500 one way for packages which include transportation from European points to Istanbul aboard restored railway coaches, with lectures and optional side-trips.

Otherwise, there is daily train service from Europe, but it's not to be taken very seriously. In second-class it is indeed cheap, which is why the cars are usually packed with Turkish 'guest workers' and their families. They want to stash away as much as possible from a stint of hard factory work in Europe, so they don't mind discomfort. But the discomfort can be intense, and long-lived. For instance, you can take a late afternoon train from Venice which reaches Belgrade the next morning; but then you must wait until mid-afternoon to catch an onward train to Istanbul. From Belgrade to Istanbul alone is 26 hours, and thus the entire Venice-Istanbul trip takes a full two days. The *Istanbul Express* from Munich is a bit better, taking only a day and a half; it hauls couchette cars and, between Munich and Belgrade, sleeping cars. All these travel times apply only if the trains are on time, which they rarely are.

You'll find a lot of cigarette smoking in every car.

There is no romance left on this famed Orient Express route. In second-class, you're much more likely to meet with delay, discomfort, unpleasantness, or worse. You may be able to resurrect a bit of romance if you travel first-class, preferably in a sleeping car as far as Belgrade, then in a couchette to Istanbul. Another tip is to get off the train in Edirne, the first stop in Turkey. It's an interesting city, well worth a stop. From Edirne to Istanbul, the train takes at least six hours, but the bus takes less than four.

By Train from Greece

I'm not sure why they still run the train between Athens and Istanbul. Neither country cares much about it. The schedule says that the 1400 km journey takes a day and a half, departing Athens or Istanbul in the evening, arriving in mid-morning about 35 hours later. This schedule (if indeed the train is on time), is about an hour faster than the schedule run in 1908 under the Ottoman Empire. My guess is that the Ottoman train ran on time much more frequently than today's does. The train hauls second-class coaches only.

Don't think you'll cut this excruciating time much by going from Thessaloniki to Istanbul. That trip is still about 25 hours – if it's on time. You'd be well advised to take a bus (see below).

BY ROAD

The construction of good highways between Europe and Turkey has opened the Middle East to all sorts of vehicles. Turkish bus companies operate frequent passenger services. Heavy trucks/lorries from a dozen nations thunder along the major roads on their way to Turkey, Syria, Iran and beyond. And private motorists brave the competition for road space, and the whims of border officials, in return for the adventures and freedoms which a private car trip affords.

By Bus from Europe

The past decade has seen the rise of frequent, fairly comfortable and moderately-priced bus travel along this route. Several Turkish companies operate big Mercedes buses which are at least as comfortable as the now-neglected trains (usually more so), comparable in price, often faster, and perhaps safer. The major discomfort on the trip may be cigarette smoke. There will probably be a good deal of smoking going on for much of the trip.

Bosfor Turizm operates from Paris and Lyon ($80), Geneva, Milan and Venice ($63), departing from Paris on this route Monday evening and arriving in Istanbul around noon on Thursday. From Munich they have an express service which departs each Friday and Sunday at noon and arrives in Istanbul about 48 hours later. Cost is $80, plus $25 to $30 for a hotel the second night. From Vienna, an express service departs Tuesday and Friday evenings, arriving in Istanbul Thursday and Sunday evenings ($63). Bosfor Turizm has sales desks or representatives in the international bus terminals of several European cities; or you can contact them at these addresses:

Istanbul: Mete Caddesi, Taksim, tel 90-(11)-143-2525; telex 24324 IBOS TR.
Munich: Seidlstrasse 2, 8 München 2, tel 49-(89)-59-40-02, or 59-24-96; telex 529388 MBOS.

Paris: Gare Routiere Internationale, 8 place de Stalingrad, 75019 Paris, tel 33-(1)-201-7080 or 205-1210; telex 210192.
Vienna: Argentinierstrasse 67, Sudbahnhof, 1040 Wien, tel 43-(222)-65-06-44; telex 136878 WBOS.

Other Turkish companies ply similar routes, and more are getting into the act all the time. For instance, *Varan* run buses to Istanbul and Ankara from Metz, Nancy, Strasbourg, Colmar and Mulhouse, departing on Saturday; from Zurich (Saturday morning); from Bregenz, Dornbirn and Innsbruck (Saturday); and from Salzburg and Vienna (Monday and Friday). Here are some addresses:

Istanbul: İnönü (Gümüşsuyu) Caddesi 17, Taksim, tel 90-(11)-143-2187 or 144-8457.
Innsbruck: Salurnerstrasse 15 (Tourist Center), tel 43-(6222)-32-58-44.
Salzburg: Bahnhof Vorplatz Kaiserschutzenstrasse 12, tel 43-(6222)-75-068.
Strasbourg: 18 Boul. President Wilson, tel 33-(88)-22-03-87.
Vienna: Südbahnhof Südtirolerplatz 7, tel 43-(222)-65-65-93.
Zurich: Klingenstrasse 9, Zürich 5, tel 41-(1)-44-04-77.

By Bus from Greece

As with the ferryboats, there is a Greek blackout on information about buses to Turkey, and you'll get a lot of answers such as 'They don't run anymore', or 'I never heard of them'. They've been running for years, and they'll continue to run, partly because Greeks love to visit Istanbul and Bursa.

The trip from Athens to Istanbul, which operates at least twice a week, takes 22 to 24 hours, part of that time being spent asleep in a hotel in Thessaloniki. Total cost is about $40. Here are the agencies:

Athens: Rika Tours, Marni 44, Platia Vathis, tel 30-(1)-523-2458, –3686, or –5905; telex 21-9473.

Istanbul: Ast Turizm, Beşir Fuat Caddesi 8, Tepebaşi, tel 90-(11)-144-2006.
Thessaloniki: Simeonidis Tours, 26th October St. No. 14, tel 30-(31)-54-09-71 or 52-14-45.

There may be other companies running this route as well. If you find a good one, write and tell us so that we can tell other readers.

By Bus from Northern Greece

You don't need an international bus to get to Turkey. You can take a Greek bus to the frontier, walk across the border, and catch something to Edirne. I once took a night train from Thessaloniki to Pithion (555 km, 10 hours), then a local bus north, and then walked across at a little-used border crossing point at Kastaneai. On the Turkish side, I called a taxi for the short ride into Edirne. You could just as well take a bus from Thessaloniki to Alexandroupolis, then local buses up into the north-eastern limits of Greece. Get as close to Edirne as possible. From Edirne, there are fast, frequent, comfortable and inexpensive services directly to Istanbul.

By Car

Car ferries (see above) from Italy and Cyprus can shorten driving time considerably. No special documents are required for visits of up to three months. The car will be entered in the driver's passport as imported goods, and must be driven out of the country by the same visitor within the time period allowed. *Do not drive someone else's car into Turkey.* Normally, you cannot rent a car in Europe and include Turkey (or many other East European countries) in your driving plans. If you want to leave your car in Turkey and return for it later, the car must be put under customs seal.

For stays longer than three months, contact the Turkish Touring and Automobile Club (*Türk Turing ve Otomobil Kulübü*), Hâlâskargazi Caddesi 364, Şişli, Istanbul, tel 90-(11)-140-7127.

EAST EUROPEAN VISAS
If you go by rail or road (bus, car, motorcycle, bicycle), you will have to deal with the problem of visas for entry to East European countries.

Yugoslavia Holders of UK, Irish and most European passports need no visa; those from the US, Canada, Australia and New Zealand need a transit visa, good for seven days, obtainable at the border at no cost. Israeli passport holders may run into problems, and may not be granted a visa. South African, Taiwanese and South Korean passport holders will not be granted visas.

Bulgaria You will need a transit visa (good for 48 hours), both on the trip from Europe to Turkey and on the trip back, because the train and the highway pass through Bulgaria. It is about US$8 one-way, US$15 round-trip for the privilege of passing through. Traditionally, transit visas have been granted right at the Bulgarian border, upon payment of the fee. This may be changing, though, so don't depend on it. Get some up-to-date information, or better still, get your visa in advance so as to avoid hassle, delay, and possible refusal. Visas can be obtained from your nearest friendly Bulgarian diplomatic representative at home, or in Europe.

In the US write to: Consular Section, Bulgarian Embassy, 1621 22nd St NW, Washington DC 20008. In the UK: the Bulgarian Legation, 24 Queen's Gate Gardens, London SW7. In Australia: Bulgarian Consulate-General, 4 Karlotta Rd, Doublebay, Sydney (tel 02 3277581).

Passport holders from Scandinavian and East European countries do not need visas for Bulgaria. If you carry a South African passport, you can't get a visa; you must go around Bulgaria, through Greece.

Getting Around

Turkey has an elaborate public transport system, as private cars are still quite expensive items, and Turks love to travel all the time. Even the sleepiest village seems to have minibuses darting in and out through the day, and buses running between Istanbul and Ankara depart every few minutes.

INTER-CITY TRANSPORT

By Air

Turkish Airlines (THY) serve all of Turkey's larger cities. Flights among Istanbul, Ankara and İzmir are very frequent. Students are exempt from the 10% transport tax on domestic flights. Show your ISTC card when you buy your ticket.

By Sea

Turkish Maritime Lines (TML, *Denizyollari*) cruise ships sail along the Black Sea, Aegean and Mediterranean coasts. With the advent of good highways and very frequent, inexpensive, speedy bus service, the coastal trips have become no-frills cruises rather than mere passenger transport. Cabins are few and in great demand, so you may have to make reservations well in advance. The popular overnight car ferry service between Istanbul and İzmir (19 hours) also demands advance reservations, for both car space and cabins. The ferries operate Friday afternoon from Istanbul, Sunday afternoon from İzmir all year. In high summer, extra trips are added on Monday and Wednesday from Istanbul, Tuesday and Thursday from İzmir.

There is still some ship service across the Sea of Marmara from Istanbul to points on the southern Marmara shore. *Denizyollari* ships connect the city with the railhead at Bandirma, where a day train takes passengers onward to İzmir. Mail boats call at a few ports along the coast, finally reaching the Dardanelles. You'll no doubt find the buses speedier, cheaper and more convenient.

If you're headed from Istanbul to Bursa, however, you'll doubtless want to take the enjoyable and very cheap ferryboat across the Marmara and the Bay of Izmit to Yalova, where you catch the bus for Iznik or Bursa. Details on this route are given in the appropriate chapter. There is also a fast, more expensive hydrofoil service between Istanbul's Kabatas dock to Mudanya, from whence buses trundle you the half hour inland to Bursa. There have been many attempts to start an air shuttle service between Bursa and Istanbul. If successful, the airline might wrest passengers from the hydrofoil, leaving the ferryboat as the preferable budget means of transport.

By Rail

The Turkish State Railways (*T.C. Devlet Demiryollari*, or TCDD) run to many parts of the country, on lines laid out by German companies which were supposedly paid by the kilometre. But some new, more direct lines have been laid during the republican era, shortening travel times for the best express trains.

It's not a good idea to plan a train trip all the way across Turkey in one stretch. Turkey is a big country, and the cross-country trains are a lot slower than the bus. The *Vangölü Ekspresi* from Istanbul (Haydarpaşa) to Lake Van (Tatvan), a 1900-km trip, takes almost two full days, for example – and that's an express! Train travel among Ankara, İzmir and Istanbul is another matter, however. The top trains on these lines are a pleasure to ride, whether by night or day. A very comfortable private 1st class sleeping compartment on the nightly all-sleeper *Ankara Ekspresi* between Ankara and Istanbul (Haydarpaşa) might cost about $20 for the 12-hour trip.

Several people sharing a 2nd class sleeping compartment might pay about $14 per person. A simple 1st class seat is much less, and a 2nd class seat very cheap indeed. If there's a dining car, table d'hote meals are surprisingly good, and pretty cheap. Breakfast in the dining car is about $1.

Top trains are:

Mavi Tren (Blue Train): daily 1st class express between Ankara and Istanbul, about 7½ hours; a bit faster than the bus, more expensive, more comfortable.
Boğaziçi Ekspresi: daily all-Pullman 1st class express between Ankara and Istanbul, about 9½ hours; a bit slower than the bus, but more comfortable.
Ege Ekspresi: daily 1st class express between Ankara and İzmir, about 9½ hours, about the same time as the bus, but more comfortable.
Ankara Ekspresi: nightly Ankara-Istanbul 1st class all-sleeping car train, about 12 hours.
Anadolu Ekspresi: nightly Ankara-Istanbul sleeping car, couchette and coach train, about 12 hours.
İzmir Ekspresi: nightly Ankara-İzmir coach and sleeping car train, about 12½ hours.

Whenever you take a train in Turkey, you'd do well to take only *ekspres* or *mototren* trains. Anything else will move very slowly indeed, and will not be all that comfortable. There will be a bus that goes faster and more comfortably, no matter where you're going.

Buying Train Tickets

Most seats on the best trains, and all sleeping compartments, must be reserved. This is done when you buy your ticket. At present, you can only buy tickets in the city from which the train departs; that is, you can't reserve a sleeper from Ankara to İzmir when you're in Istanbul – or even in İzmir. You've got to be in Ankara. Turkish State Railways have yet to install a computerized reservations system.

As the best trains are very popular, particularly the sleeping-car trains, you should make your reservation and buy your ticket as far in advance as possible. A few days usually suffices. If you can't do this, check at the station anyway. There may be cancellations, even at the last minute. I once boarded a night train expecting to sleep in a seat, but I mentioned to the sleeping-car conductors that I preferred a bed. They found me after the train departed, and sold me a vacant compartment left by a no-show.

Weekend trains, from Friday evening through Monday morning, seem to be busiest.

By Bus

Bus and minibus (*dolmuş*, see below) are the most widespread and popular means of transport in Turkey. Buses go literally everywhere, all the time, and at low cost. Highways are good, and usually uncrowded. Bus service runs the gamut from plain and very inexpensive to very comfortable and moderately priced. It is so cheap and convenient that many erstwhile hitchhikers opt for the bus. The eight-hour trip between Istanbul and Ankara might cost $6 to $8, a bit more for the luxury companies.

Most Turkish cities and towns have a central bus terminal called variously *Otogar, Otobüs Terminali, Santral Garaj*, or *Sehir Garaji* ('City Garage'). In this book I'll stick to Otogar. Besides intercity buses, the Otogar usually handles minibuses to outlying districts or villages.

Istanbul has several mammoth garages; Ankara and İzmir have one mammoth apiece. Bus companies aiming at the high-class trade may have their own small, private terminals in other parts of town, to save their privileged patrons the hassle of dealing with large crowds at the main terminal. These are mentioned in the text where necessary.

A few small towns have only a collection of bus line offices rather than a proper garage.

About Bus Travel

A bus trip in Turkey is usually a fairly pleasant experience if it's not too long. Most buses are the Mercedes 0302, big and fairly comfortable. The seat cushions are surprisingly firm though, too firm for comfort on a very long ride. As Turks are great cigarette smokers, you'll encounter a decent amount of smoke on the trip. Passengers in the seats near you will offer you cigarettes as an ice-breaker, hoping to strike up a conversation. There's no stigma in refusing. Say *'Hayir, teşekkür ederim, içmem'* ('No, thank you, I don't smoke') or, if this is a mouthful, just *'Ic'mem'* (eech-MEHM) and a smile. Turks, like most people, think it laudable that someone doesn't smoke (or has given up smoking). Besides, the offer was intended as a politeness, a welcome, and a conversation opener. It serves this purpose whether you smoke or not.

Though your fellow passengers will be careful not to abuse your privacy, they'll also be curious about where you come from, what language you speak, and how you're enjoying the country. Openers may be in German. You can talk as much or as little as you like, though it's polite to exchange at least a few sentences.

Shortly after you head out, the *yardimci* ('assistant') will come through the bus with a bottle of lemon cologne with which to refresh his *sayin yolcular* ('honoured passengers'). He'll squirt some into your cupped hands, which you then rub together, and on your face, and on your hair, ending with a sniff to clear your nasal passages. You may not be used to the custom, but if you ride buses in Turkey much you will get used to it quick, and probably love it.

If you want a bottle of cool spring water at any time during the trip, just signal to the *yardimci*, and ask for *Su, lütfen* ('water, please'). There's no charge.

Stops will be made every hour and a half or so for the toilet, for snacks or meals, and the inevitable *çay* (tea). At some stops boys rush onto the bus selling sweets, nuts, sandwiches and the like, or a waiter

from the tea-house (buses always stop at a tea-house) may come through to take orders. But most people welcome the chance to stretch their legs.

Buying Bus Tickets

Though you can often just walk into an Otogar and buy a ticket for the next bus out, it's wise to plan in advance. At the least, locate the companies, and note the times for your destination, a day in advance. Buses on some routes may fill up, so buying tickets a day in advance is good if you can do it. This is especially important along the south coast, where long-distance bus traffic is less frequent than in the rest of the country.

The word for 'tomorrow', very handy to know when buying bus tickets a day in advance, is *yarın* (YAHR-uhn). Bus departure times will be given in the 24-hour clock, eg 18.30 instead of 6.30 pm.

When you enter an Otogar, you'll see lots of people and baggage, buses and minibuses, plus rows of little ticket offices. Competition on some routes is stiff. In most cases, more than one company will run to your desired destination; the cities and towns served by the company will be written prominently at the company's ticket office. It's a good idea to check several ticket offices, asking when the company's next bus leaves. Hawkers near the entrance to the Otogar will approach you as soon as you enter, asking your destination. Tell them, and they'll lead you to a particular company's ticket office. This is fine, except that this company may or may not have the next departure. A few times I have been sold a ticket for the company's next bus (in two hours) when another company had a bus departing – with seats available – in 40 minutes. Let the hawkers lead you, but then ask around at other companies before you buy.

All seats are reserved, and your ticket will bear specific seat numbers. It's very important that you plan your seat strategy, rather than leaving it up to the ticket

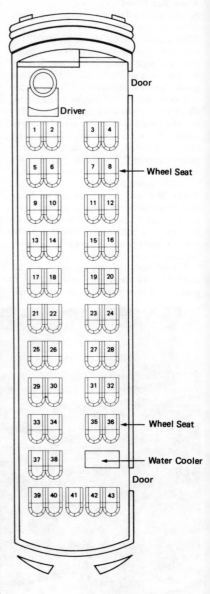

seller. He'll have a chart of the seats in front of him. The ones already taken will be indicated. He should (and usually will) offer the chart to you so you can pick your seats, and may indicate the ones he recommends.

The preferable seats, according to Turkish custom, are in the middle of the bus (that is, not right over the wheels, which can be bumpy), and also on the side which will not get the full sun. On the Mercedes 0302 bus, avoid if possible the front two rows (seats 1-8) and the last three rows (33-43); seats 9-28 are the best, but on the shady side.

Though some buses are now air-con'd, most are not, and in the newer models, ventilation is actually worse than in the older ones, so what side you are on can be important. On a four-hour summer afternoon trip from Ankara to Konya, for instance, you'll roast if you're on the right-hand (western) side of the bus, while the seats on the left side will remain comfortable.

Once you've bought a ticket, getting a refund can be very difficult, though it's possible. Exchanges for other tickets within the same company are easier.

The Dolmuş

Turkish jitney cabs, and some minibuses, are called *dolmuş* (DOHL-moosh, 'filled'). The name comes from the fact that a dolmuş departs as soon as every seat (or nearly every seat) is taken. You can catch a dolmuş from point to point in a city (see below), or from village to village, and in some cases from town to town. Though some minibus routes operate like buses, selling tickets in advance, perhaps even for reserved seats, the true dolmuş does not. Rather, it is parked at the point of departure (a town square, city Otogar, or beach) and waits for the seats to fill up. The dolmuş route may be painted on the side of the minibus, or on a sign posted next to the dolmuş, or in its window; or a hawker may call out the destination.

When the driver is satisfied with the load, he heads off. Fares are collected en route or at the final stop. Often the fare is posted. If it's not, watch what other passengers to your destination are paying and do the same. Though passengers to intermediate stops sometimes pay a partial fare, on other routes the driver (or the law) may require that you pay the full fare. In either case, prices are low, though slightly more than a bus on the same route.

By Car

Driving a car to Turkey is a fine idea, though you can get around perfectly well without one. Turkish highways tend to be good and not madly crowded, though city streets are just the opposite. Parking is a real problem in the large cities.

You don't really need an International Driving Permit while you drive in Turkey. Your home driving licence, unless it's something weird (say, from the Republic of Upper Volta), will be accepted by traffic police officers and by car rental firms. If you'd feel more secure against bureaucratic hassle by carrying an IDP, you can get one through your automobile club at home.

Spare parts for most cars may be available, if not readily so outside the big cities. European models, especially Renaults, Fiats and Mercedes, are preferred, though ingenious Turkish mechanics contrive to keep all manner of huge American models – some half a century old – in daily service.

Rental Cars

Cars may be rented in Istanbul, Ankara, İzmir and Kuşadaşi, Antalya and Adana from the larger international rental firms (Hertz, Avis, National/Europcar, and Dollar/interRent) or from smaller local ones. In Istanbul, Ankara and İzmir/Kuşadaşi, payment by major credit card is easily available. In other areas, ask about payment when you reserve. Most popular rental cars are the Fiat ('Murat') 124 and 131, and the Renault 12.

Total out-of-pocket rental costs for a

week, including fuel, insurance, and 10 percent tax, might be $250 to $300. When you look at a rental company's current price list, keep in mind that the daily or weekly rental charge is only a small portion of what you will actually end up paying. The charge per km normally ends up being higher, per day, than the daily rental charge; and the 10% tax kicks the total even higher. Then there's fuel, which is very expensive by American standards, moderately expensive by European ones.

Motorcycles

Motorcycles and mopeds are becoming more popular in Turkey because they are cheaper than cars to buy and to run. These days, Austrian and German mopeds are the popular items. Motorcycles tend to be large old Czechoslovak Jawa models that make a distinctive hollow putt-putt.

You can bring your motorcycle to Turkey, and have a fine time seeing the country. Spare parts will probably be hard to come by, so bring what you may need, or rely on the boundless ingenuity of Turkish mechanics to find, adapt or make you a part; or else be prepared to call home and have the part flown in, when you will probably have to endure considerable hassles from Customs.

Inter-city Taxis

Inter-city taxis are expensive, but if you must catch a plane, train or bus in town and you're in a village, you may have to use one. Since 1980, municipalities have set intercity (and for that matter, intracity) taxi rates. Before you engage a taxi, ask to see the official rate card, or *tarife* (tah-ree-FEH). If your destination is not on the *tarife*, you've got to strike a bargain. You needn't tip unless the driver has provided some extra service for you.

Hitchhiking

Though long-distance hitchhiking is possible in Turkey, it's not done as much as one might think. The bus and minibus network is so elaborate, and so cheap, that most people opt for that. Private cars are not as plentiful as in Europe, and owners here are not as inclined to pick up hitchers. There are lots of trucks/lorries, and truck drivers are more inclined to stop, but it's customary to offer payment – bus fare, or pretty close – to any commercial driver. So why not take the bus and be comfortable?

Short-distance hitching is completely different, however. As the country is large and vehicles not so plentiful outside the towns, short-distance country hops are the norm. If you need to get from the highway into an archaeological site, you hitch a ride with whatever comes along. Again, private cars are the least amenable, but delivery vans, heavy machinery, oil tankers, farm tractors, etc are all fair game. You should offer to pay for the lift; in most cases your offer will be declined (though appreciated).

Women Hitchhikers

When it comes to women hitchhiking, Turkey is like the rest of the world, perhaps a bit more so: it is done, but you really should not do it, especially alone. Hitching as a couple is fine. Two women hitching together is preferable to each alone. If you're determined to hitch, take the normal precautions: don't accept a ride in a car or truck which is already occupied by more than one man. Look for vehicles which are carrying women and/or children as well as men. Act appreciative and polite, but formal, to the driver who picks you up. Avoid hitching across long, empty spaces, and never hitch at night. As for regional variances, you'll have the easiest time where foreigners and their strange customs are most familiar, naturally. The Aegean coast is the least dangerous. The further east you go, the more misunderstood you'll be.

INTRA-CITY TRANSPORT
Buses

Turkish cities have lots of buses, but they are often crowded to capacity. During rush hours they may fill up at the originating point, and not even stop to pick up passengers en route. There's a problem with fares as well. Most municipal bus systems now work on a ticket system, and you must buy a ticket (*otobus bileti*, or simply *bilet*, 'bee-LEHT'), or a booklet (*karne*, kahr-NEH) of them, at a special ticket kiosk. These kiosks are at major bus terminus or transfer points, but there are not many of them.

What usually happens is that the unsuspecting foreign tourist climbs onto a bus, discovers that money is not accepted for the fare, and a nearby passenger saves the day by handing the tourist a ticket from his own booklet. The tourist offers payment, the Turk declines it. If you intend to use the buses a lot, as in Istanbul, track down a kiosk and buy a *karne* of tickets. The cost is minimal. But if you're just passing through a city, it's obviously better to go through the aforementioned ritual.

The Dolmuş

Besides the inter-city dolmuş system described above, a similar system exists within every town of any size. You'll find yourself using it frequently as it is usually faster, more comfortable, and only slightly more expensive than the bus (and still very cheap). Intra-city dolmuş stops are near major squares, termini or inter-sections, and you'll have to ask, *(Name of destination) dolmuş var mı?* (. . . DOHL-moosh VAHR-muh?) If you're at Sirkeci Railway Station in Istanbul, for instance, and you wanted to get to Taksim Square, you'd ask, *Taksim dolmuş var mı?* Someone would point you to the dolmuş stand, just out the station door and to the right.

Often there is not a direct dolmuş route from where you are to where you're going. Maps of the system don't exist. If your answerer seems to hem and haw, he's probably trying to tell you that you must take one dolmuş to a certain point, and then another.

Once you know a few convenient routes, you'll feel confident about picking up a dolmuş at the curb. In the larger cities, stopping-places are regulated, and marked by signs saying *Dolmuş Indirme Bindirme Yeri* ('Dolmush Boarding and Alighting Place'). You'll see minibuses, old American cars, and new little Turkish-made cars stopping. A true city dolmuş has a solid-colour band, usually yellow or black, painted horizontally around the car just below the windows. But sometimes taxis, with a black-and-yellow checkered band, operate like a dolmuş. You've got to be careful. If you climb into an empty car, the driver might assume (honestly, or for his own benefit) that you want a taxi, and he will charge you the taxi fare. Always ask, *Dolmuş mu?* (dohl-MOOSH moo? 'Is this a dolmuş?') when you climb into an empty car.

You'll get the hang of the dolmuş way of life after only a few days in Turkey, and will find it very useful.

Taxis

The dream of every workingman in Turkey is to get up enough capital to buy a cab and go into business as a taxi driver. The cost of a car is high in Turkey, and cab drivers are members of the economic middle class.

The dream has come true for an awful lot of Turks, however, and the city streets are jammed with taxis which compete for relatively scarce fares. Drivers log far more glasses of tea than they do kilometres. But service in most cities is friendly, efficient, and moderately-priced. In Ankara the taxis have digital meters, and they use them. If yours doesn't, mention it right away by saying, *Saatiniz* (saa-AHT-EE-NEEZ, 'Your meter'). In other cities, meters may not be common, but a *tarife* should be in every car. Ask for it and make sure the price is understood by both parties *before you get into the car*.

None of this strictly applies to Istanbul, which as usual is a world unto itself. Meters are not used, *tarifes* are hard to come by, and haggling over fares is normal. But you can still take taxis. Ask at your hotel what the price should be. If you see a taxi company kiosk, a tiny office with telephone, tables and chairs, teapot, and cabs clustered nearby, hire your taxi there. The organized drivers are less rapacious; they may even show you the office *tarife*. Even so, be sure to settle on a price before you enter the car.

Ferryboats

In Istanbul and İzmir, public transport is augmented with the delightful addition of ferryboats. White with orange trim (the Turkish Maritime Lines' colours), these sturdy craft steam up, down and across the Bosphorus and the Bay of İzmir, providing city dwellers with cheap, convenient transport, views of open water, and (in summer) fresh cool breezes. They are not nostalgic transport toys; they are a real, even vital, part of each city's transport system. You should take the ferry in each city at least once, enjoying the cityscapes that are revealed from the decks, sipping a glass of fresh tea or a soft drink. The ferries can be crowded during rush hour, but there's still lots of air and scenery; and while buses sit trapped in traffic, the ferries glide through the water effortlessly, at speed.

In Istanbul, special ferry sailings on a touristic route are operated daily. There's no better way to see the Bosphorus, and the price for a 2½-hour cruise all the way from Istanbul to the Black Sea is only about $1.

Top: Village family in Karatay
Left: Istanbul craftsman at work on a coffee pot
Right: Entry-way niche in Avanos

Top: Cotton pickers near Side
Left: Back streets of Antalya
Right: A *Çayci* (tea waiter) in his filigree vest

Istanbul

For many centuries this city was the capital of the civilized world. Even though Ankara became the capital of the newly-proclaimed republic in 1922, Istanbul continues to be the Turkish metropolis. It is the largest city (about five million people), the business and cultural centre, the largest port, and the first destination for tourists, Turkish or foreign.

In recent years, Istanbul has yielded some of its pre-eminence to up-and-coming towns such as Ankara, İzmir and Adana. But it is still, without doubt, the heart-beat of the Turkish spirit. For Ankara, the uptempo, modern capital city, Turks feel pride; but it is Istanbul, the well-worn but still glorious metropolis, which they love. Its place in the country's history, folklore, commerce and culture is unchallenged.

The First Glimpse

No matter how you arrive, you'll be impressed. The train skirts the southern coast of the Thracian peninsula, following the city walls until it comes around Seraglio Point and terminates right below Topkapı Palace. The bus comes in along an expressway built on the path of the Roman road, and stops next to the Topkapı (Cannon Gate, not to be confused with the palace of the same name) in the ancient city walls. Flying in on a clear day may reveal the great mosques and palaces, the wide Bosphorus (*Boğaziçi*) and the narrower Golden Horn (*Haliç*), in a wonderful panorama. But nothing beats 'sailing to Byzantium', gliding across the Sea of Marmara, watching the slender minarets and bulbous mosque domes rise on the horizon. Even Mark Twain, who certainly had control of his emotions, waxed rhapsodic on the beauties of arriving by sea, in his *Innocents Abroad*. Even today, when pollution may obscure the view a bit, it's impressive.

Istanbul has grown ferociously in the past decade, and now sprawls westward to the airport, 23 km from the centre, northward half way to the Black Sea, and eastward deep into Anatolia. It is crowded. The Bosphorus, the strait which connects the Black Sea and the Sea of Marmara, is more than a mile wide, and the narrower Golden Horn, a fresh water estuary, also helps to preserve a sense of openness and space. More than that, the Bosphorus provides an uncrowded maritime highway for transport to various sections of the city. For several thousand years before the construction of the Bosphorus Bridge (1973), the only way to go between the European and Asian parts of the city was by boat.

Getting around in the city can be slow at times, but it's always rewarding. Striking panoramas and scenes from Turkish daily life are everywhere.

Istanbul today is interesting as the Turkish metropolis, but nobody visits just for that reason when the city is 3000 years old. The greatest part of the city's fascination comes from its place in history, and from the buildings that remain from ancient times. Without knowing something of its history, a tour of Istanbul's ancient monuments will leave you impressed but bewildered. Here's a quick summary of its past, so that you'll be able to distinguish a hippodrome from a harem.

History

1000 – 657 BC Ancient fishing villages on this site.

657 BC – 330 AD Byzantium, a Greek city-state, later subject to Rome.

330 – 1453 AD Constantinople, the 'New Rome', capital of the Later Roman ('Byzantine') Empire. Reached its height in the 1100s.

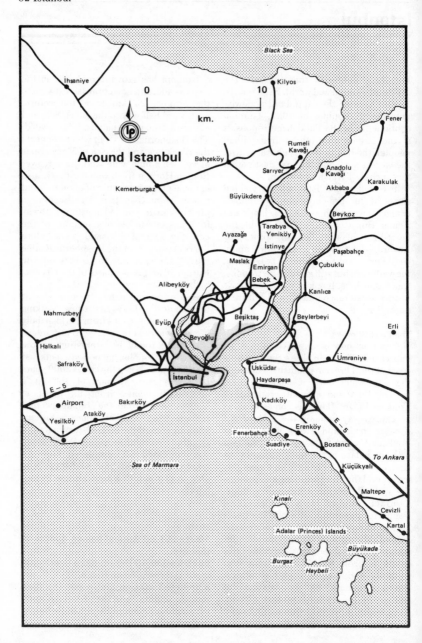

Around Istanbul

1453 – 1922 Istanbul, capital of the Ottoman Turkish Empire, which reached its height in the 1500s.

1922 – Present Ankara becomes the capital of the Turkish Republic, but Istanbul continues to be the country's largest city, largest port, commercial and cultural centre.

Early Times

The earliest settlement, Semistra, was probably around 1000 BC, in the same period as King David and King Solomon ruled in Jerusalem, and a few hundred years after the Trojan War.

This was followed by a fishermen's village named Lygos which occupied Seraglio Point, where Topkapı Palace stands today. Later, about 700 BC, colonists from Megara (near Corinth) in Greece settled at what is now Kadıköy, on the Asian shore of the Bosphorus.

Byzantium

The first settlement to have historic significance was founded by another Megarian colonist, a fellow named Byzas. Before leaving Greece, he asked the oracle at Delphi where he should establish his new colony. The enigmatic answer was, 'Opposite the Blind'. When Byzas and his fellow colonists sailed up the Bosphorus, they noticed the colony on the Asian shore at Chalcedon (Kadıköy). Looking to their left, they noticed the superb natural harbour of the Golden Horn, on the European shore. Thinking, as legend has it, 'Those people in Chalcedon must be blind', they settled on the opposite shore, on the site of Lygos, and named their new city Byzantium. This was in 657 BC.

The legend might as well be true. Istanbul's location, on the waterway linking the Marmara and Black Seas, and on the 'land bridge' linking Europe and Asia, is still of tremendous importance today, 2600 years after the oracle spoke. The Megarian colonists at Kadıköy must certainly have been blind to have missed such a site.

Byzantium submitted willingly to Rome, and fought Rome's battles for centuries, but finally got caught supporting the wrong side in a civil war. The winner, Septimium Severus, razed the city walls and took away its privileges (196 AD). When he relented and rebuilt the city, he named it Augusta Antonina.

Constantinople

Another struggle for control of the Roman Empire determined the city's fate for the next thousand years. Constantine pursued his rival Licinius to Augusta Antonina, then across the Bosphorus to Chrysopolis (Üsküdar). Defeating his rival (324 AD), Constantine solidified his control and declared this city to be 'New Rome'. He laid out a vast new city to serve as capital of his empire, and inaugurated it with much pomp in 330 AD. The place which had been first settled as a fishing village over a thousand years earlier was now the capital of the world, and would remain so for another thousand years, almost.

The Later Roman, or Byzantine, Empire lasted from the re-founding of the city in 330 AD to the Ottoman Turkish conquest in 1453, an impressive 1123 years. A lot remains of ancient Constantinople, and you'll be able to visit churches, palaces, cisterns and the Hippodrome during your stay. In fact, there's more of Constantinople left than anyone knows about. Any sort of excavation reveals streets, mosaics, tunnels, water and sewer systems, houses and public buildings. Construction of a modern building may be held up for months while archaeologists investigate. Re-discovering Byzantium, to a modern developer, is an unmitigated disaster.

Several years ago the telephone company discovered an unknown Byzantine cistern while laying underground telephone lines. As no one came forward with the considerable funds needed to explore and document the site, it was resealed and the telephone lines rerouted.

The Conquest

Westerners usually refer to 'The Fall of Constantinople', whereas to Muslims it was 'The Conquest of Istanbul'. Though the Byzantine Empire had been moribund for several centuries, the Ottomans were quite content to accept tribute from the weak Byzantine emperor as they progressively captured all the lands which surrounded his well-fortified city. By the time of the conquest, the emperor had control over little more than the city itself, and a few territories in Greece.

When Mehmet II, 'the Conquerer' (*Fatih*) came to power in 1451 as a young man, he needed an impressive military victory to solidify his dominance of the powerful noble class. As the Ottomans controlled all of Anatolia and most of the Balkans by this time, it was obvious that the great city should be theirs. Mehmet decided it should be sooner rather than later.

The story of the conquest is thrilling, full of bold strokes and daring exploits, heroism, treachery and intrigue. Mehmet started by readying the two great fortresses on the Bosphorus. Rumeli Hisar, the larger one, on the European side, was built in an incredibly short three months. Anadolu Hisar, the smaller one on the Asian side, had been built a half-century earlier by Yıldırım Beyazıt, so Mehmet had it repaired and brought to readiness. Together they controlled the strait's narrowest point.

The Byzantines had closed the mouth of the Golden Horn with a heavy chain to prevent Ottoman boats from sailing in and attacking the city walls on the north side. In another bold stroke, Mehmet marshalled his boats at a cove (now covered by Dolmabahçe Palace) and had them transported overland on rollers and slides, by night, up the valley (where the Hilton now stands) and down the other side, into the Golden Horn at Kasımpaşa. He caught the Byzantine defenders completely by surprise, and soon had the Golden Horn under control.

The last great obstacle was the mighty bastion of the land walls on the western side. No matter how Mehmet's cannons battered them by day, the Byzantines would rebuild them by night, and the impetuous young sultan would find himself back where he started come daybreak. Then he got an offer. A Hungarian cannon-founder named Urban had come to offer his services to the Byzantine emperor, for the defense of Christendom, to repel the Infidel. But finding that the emperor had no money, he went to Mehmet and offered to make the most enormous cannon ever. Mehmet, who had lots of money, accepted the offer, and the cannon was cast and tested in Edirne. The first shot, which terrified hundred of peasants, sent a huge ball one mile, where it buried itself six feet in the ground. The jubilant sultan had his new toy transported to the front lines and set to firing. A special crew worked hours to ready it for each shot, for every firing wrecked the mount, and the gun had to be cooled with buckets of water as well.

Despite the inevitability of the conquest, the emperor refused surrender terms offered by Mehmet on 23 May, 1453, preferring to wait in hope that Christendom would come and save him. On 28 May, the final attack was begun, and by the evening of the 29th, Mehmet's troops were in control of every quarter. The emperor, Constantine XI Dragases, died in battle fighting on the walls.

Mehmet's triumphant entry into 'the world's greatest city' on the evening of 29 May is commemorated every year in Istanbul. Those parts of the city which did not resist his troops were spared, and their churches guaranteed to them. Those that resisted were sacked for the customary three days, and the churches turned into mosques. As for Sancta Sophia, the greatest church in Christendom (St Peter's in Rome was not begun until 1506), it was converted immediately into a mosque. Mehmet rode into it astride his horse to declare the change.

The Ottoman Centuries

Mehmet the Conqueror began at once to rebuild and repopulate the city. He saw himself as the successor to the glories and powers of Constantine, Justinian and the other great emperors who had reigned here. He built a mosque (Fatih Camii) on one of the city's seven hills, repaired the walls and made Istanbul the administrative, commercial and cultural centre of his growing empire.

Süleyman the Magnificent (1520-1566) was perhaps Istanbul's greatest builder. His mosque, the Süleymaniye (1550), is Turkey's largest. Other sultans added more grand mosques, and in the 19th century, numerous palaces were built along the Bosphorus: Çırağan, Dolmabahçe, Yıldız, Beylerbeyi, Küçük Su.

As the Ottoman Empire grew to include all of the Middle East and North Africa, and half of eastern Europe, Istanbul became a fabulous melting-pot. On its streets and in its bazaars, people spoke Turkish, Greek, Armenia, Ladino, Russian, Arabic, Bulgarian, Rumanian, Albanian, Italian, French, German, English and Maltese. The parade of national costumes was no less varied. But from being the most civilized city on earth in the time of Süleyman, the city and the empire declined. By the 19th century it had lost some of its former glory, though it was still the 'Paris of the East'. Its importance was reaffirmed by the first great international luxury express train ever run, which connected Istanbul with Paris – the famous Orient Express.

Republican Istanbul

Atatürk's campaign for national salvation and independence was directed from Ankara. The founder of the Turkish Republic decided to get away from the imperial memories of Istanbul, and also to set up the new government in a city which could not easily be threatened by gunboats. Robbed of its importance as capital of a vast empire, Istanbul lost a lot of its wealth and glitter. From being the East's most cosmopolitan place, it relaxed into a new role as an important national, more than international, city. But these days it seems to be returning to its former role. More liveable than Cairo or Beirut, more attractive than Tel Aviv, more in touch with the Islamic world than Athens, it may just become a 'world capital' again.

Information & Orientation

It's a daunting prospect to arrive in a strange city of five million people whose language is a complete mystery to you. In general, Turks are extremely friendly and helpful, even amidst the frustrations of a language barrier. It shouldn't take you long to get set up in a suitable hotel.

The Ministry of Culture and Tourism maintains several tourism information offices in the city. Besides the ones at Yeşilköy airport and the Yolcu Salonu (International Maritime Passenger Terminal), there's one right on the Hippodrome in Sultanahmet Square, near the Blue Mosque, Sancta Sophia and Topkapı Palace. In Beyoğlu, the offce is in the Hilton Hotel arcade, just off Cumhuriyet Caddesi. Get to Taksim Square, ask for 'joom-hoor-ee-YEHT jad-dess-see' or simply 'HEEL-tohn oh-tehl-ee', walk two rather long blocks in the direction indicated, and you'll see the Hilton arcade, with the hotel behind it, on the right-hand side of the street.

The City's layout

A glance at the map will show you that Istanbul is divided down the middle, from north to south, by the wide strait of the Bosphorus (*Boğaziçi*, boh-AHZ-ee-chee, 'Inside the throat' in Turkish). The Asian (eastern) half is of less interest to tourists, being mostly bedroom suburbs such as Üsküdar (EU-skeu-dahr, Scutari) and Kadıköy (KAH-duh-keuy). One landmark you'll want to know about is Haydarpaşa İstasyonu ('HIGH'-dahr-pah-shah ee-stahs-yohn-oo), right between Üsküdar and Kadıköy. This is the terminus for Anatolian trains, which means any Turkish

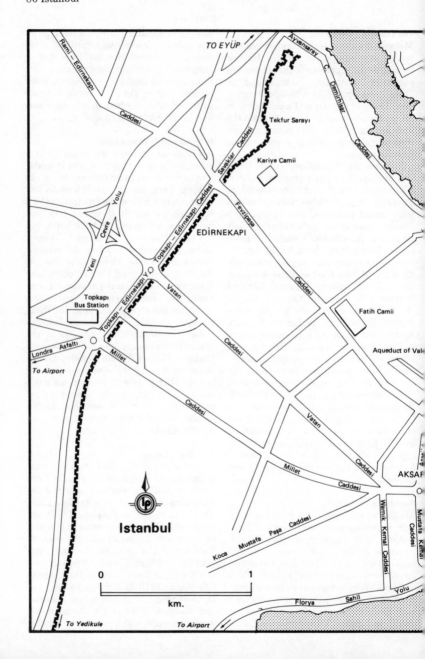

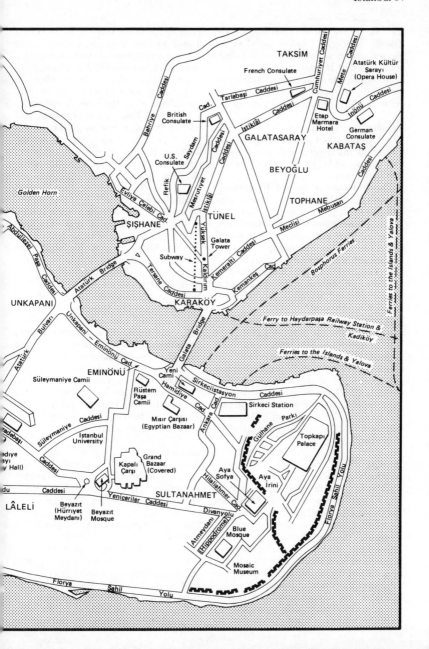

train except for the one from Europe via Edirne. If you're headed for Ankara, Cappodocia, or any point east of Istanbul, you'll board at Haydarpaşa.

Otherwise, the areas of prime attraction for hotels, restaurants, and sightseeing, are in the European portion of the city.

Istanbul, The Old City

The European half of the city is further divided by the Golden Horn into the Old City to the south, and Beyoğlu (BEY-oh-loo) to the north.

The Old City is ancient Byzantium/Constantinople/Istanbul. It's here, from Seraglio Point (*Saray Burnu*) jutting into the Bosphorus to the mammoth land walls some seven km eastward, that you'll find the great palaces and mosques, hippodromes and monumental columns, ancient churches and the Grand Bazaar. The Old City also harbours one of the best areas for inexpensive and moderate hotel choices: Laleli, near Aksaray.

When referring to the Old City, Turks usually mention the name of a particular district such as *Sultanahmet, Aksaray* or *Beyazıt*. They do not say 'Stamboul', as Europeans sometimes do; nor do they use the term 'Old City' because the Turkish for 'old city' (*Eskişehir*) is also the name of a completely different municipality hundreds of kilometres away in Anatolia. Get used to asking for a district, not for 'Stamboul'.

Beyoğlu

North of the Golden Horn is 'Beyoğlu, the Turkish name for the two old cities of Pera and Galata, or roughly all the land from the Golden Horn to Taksim Square. Here is where you'll find the Hilton, the Sheraton and other luxury hotels; airline offices and banks; the European consulates and hospitals; Taksim Square, the very hub of European Istanbul; and the 19th-century palace of Dolmabahçe.

Under the Byzantines, this was a separate city built and inhabited by Genoese traders. Called **Galata** then, it extended from the shore up to the Galata Tower, which still stands, and which now serves as a convenient landmark. Galata is now called Karaköy (KAHR-ah-keuy).

Under the sultans, the non-Muslim European population of Galata spread up the hill and along the ridge, founding the sister city of **Pera**. In modern times, this part of the city has been the fastest growing, and has stretched far beyond the limits of old Galata and Pera. But the name Beyoğlu still refers to just those two old cities.

Galata Bridge

One landmark you will get to know at once is the *Galata Köprüsü* (gahl-AH-TAH KEUP-reu-seu, Galata Bridge). Connecting Karaköy with Eminönü (eh-MEEN-eu-neu), it is Istanbul's jugular vein, always packed with traffic and lively with activity. Views of the Old City, Beyoğlu, the Golden Horn, and the Bosphorus are fantastic from the bridge.

Karaköy and Eminönü, by the way, are the areas from which Bosphorus ferry boats depart. The ferries from Karaköy go exclusively to Haydarpaşa Station and Kadıköy (a lighted signboard tells you which one is the destination); ferries from the Eminönü side go to Üsküdar, the Bosphorus, the Princes' Islands, and Yalova. See below in the Getting Around section for more information.

Arrival by Air

After many years of waiting, the new terminal building is open at Yeşilköy Havaalanı (YESH-eel-keuy HAH-VAH-ahl-ahn-uh), the airport. The Ministry of Culture and Tourism (*Kütür ve Turizm Bakanlığı*) maintains an information office in the Arrivals terminal. They'll be happy to help with questions or problems.

Before you pass through customs, avail yourself of the opportunity to buy duty-free goods if you like. Decent prices, no transcontinental carrying problems.

If you arrive at Istanbul on an international flight, everyone will tell you that the only way to get into town, 23 km away, is by taxi; it's not. By taxi, you buy a fixed-priced ticket before leaving the Arrivals area. On it is the licence number of a particular cab. All you do is exit to the taxi area and show your ticket to the crowd of cab drivers and let your particular driver find you. The cost is $10, worth it only if you have a lot of luggage.

A far cheaper alternative is the airport bus which serves the domestic flights. The catch is that to take advantage of this cheap service ($1.50) you must get to the *İc Hatları* (EECH haat-lahr-uh, Domestic Routes) terminal. Once there, buses leave every half-hour or so, and take you to the Turkish Airlines city terminal in Istanbul's Şişhane quarter, near the Galata Tower. On the way, a stop is made in Aksaray, which is near Laleli and many good budget-priced hotels.

Arrival by Bus

Coming from Europe, your bus will drop you at the Topkapı Otogar, right outside the city walls next to the Topkapı (TOHP-kahp-uh), or Cannon Gate. This is nowhere near Topkapı Palace, which lies seven km to the east, on the Bosphorus. It seems that two gates, at very different places in the city walls, had cannons associated with them.

The better bus lines such as Bosfor Turizm and Varan will provide a *servis arabası* (sehr-VEES ah-rah-bah-suh), or minibus, to take you from the bus station into the city. Both Bosfor Turizm and Varan have their main ticket offices near Taksim Square, so that's where the minibus will end up. But if you ask to be dropped in Aksaray or Laleli, the driver will doubtless oblige.

Coming from Edirne, you get off the bus at Topkapı bus station and, if your bus company doesn't have a servis arabası, you'll have to make your own way into the city. Taxi drivers will be waiting to buttonhole you as you alight. You might want one if your bags are heavy. Otherwise, make your way out of the bus station and

across to the Cannon Gate itself. Just inside the gate (on the other side of the walls from the bus station) is a city bus stop, from which you can catch a bus or a dolmuş to Aksaray. If Aksaray or Laleli is not your final destination, you must change in Aksaray for a bus or dolmuş to Sultanahmet, Eminönü or Taksim.

Bus company ticket offices are found clustered in Laleli on Ordu Caddesi; near Taksim; and near Sirkeci Railroad Station, next to Eminönü.

Arrival by Train

All trains from Europe terminate at Sirkeci (SEER-keh-jee) Station, right next to Eminönü in the shadow of Topkapı Palace. Right outside the station door and across the street you can catch a bus or dolmuş going to Laleli and Aksaray. If you're headed for Taksim, go out the station door and turn right. Over by the little refreshments kiosk is the stop for the dolmuş to Taksim.

The main station door now is a modern structure. But take a look on the north side of the station, facing the Bosphorus: this more ornate facade was the original front of the station, more in keeping with the romantic ideas of what the terminus for the Orient Express should look like.

To continue a train journey deeper into Turkey (meaning Anatolia), you must get to Haydarpaşa Station on the Asian side. The best way is by ferryboat from Karaköy. Cross the Galata Bridge from Eminönü to Karaköy, go to the prominent ferry dock, buy a token, go through the turnstile, and look for the illuminated sign saying *Haydarpaşa*. Some ferries stop both at Haydarpaşa and Kadıköy; but you should be careful not to get a ferry that goes *only* to Kadıköy. If in doubt, just say *Haydarpaşa ya mü?* (To Haydarpaşa?) to anyone while pointing at the boat.

Ferries depart for the station every 15 to 30 minutes; special ferries, timed in sync with departure times of the major expresses, leave Karaköy about a half-hour before express train departure.

Arrival by Ship

Passenger ships dock at Karaköy, near the *Yolcu Salonu* (YOHL-joo sahl-ohn-oo, International Passenger Terminal) on Rıhtım Caddesi. The Ministry of Culture and Tourism has an information office in the terminal, right near the front (street) doors.

The international dock is right next to the Karaköy ferryboat dock and only a hundred metres from Glata Bridge. Bus and dolmuş routes to Taksim pass right in front of the Yolcu Salonu; for those to destinations in the Old City such as Sultanahmet, Laleli and Aksaray, go to the western side of Karaköy Square itself, right at the end of the Galata Bridge. You'll have to find the pedestrian underpass to get to the dolmuş and bus stops.

Some domestic-line ships dock at Kabataş (KA-ba-tash), about two km north of Karaköy on the Bosphorus shore, very near Dolmabahçe Palace and Mosque. As you leave the dock at Kabataş, buses and dolmuşes heading left will be going to Karaköy and the Old City; those travelling right will be going to Taksim, or up the Bosphorus shore.

By Road

The E5 from Europe brings you to Yeşilköy Airport and a bypass heading north and east to cross the Bosphorus Bridge. If you're headed for Aksaray, don't take the bypass, but rather head straight on and you'll end up at Topkapı, the Cannon Gate. Continue straight on through the gate, along Millet Caddesi, and you will end up in Aksaray Square. For Laleli, continue straight through the square and turn left just before the big university buildings on the left. For Taksim, use the flyover in Aksaray Square to turn left and head up Atatürk Bulvarı. Cross the Atatürk Bridge over the Golden Horn, push onward up and up the hill, and you'll join İstiklal Caddesi at the top. İstiklal Caddesi ends in Taksim Square.

If youüre a bit more daring, leave the expressway at the airport, following signs for the *town* of Yeşilköy (not just the airport). You can make your way to the shore of the Sea of Marmara, and drive into the city along the water's edge. You'll pass the city walls near Yedikule, the Fortress of the Seven Towers, and the tower named 'Christ's Postern', which has one foot in the water. The city's southern wall will be on your left as you drive. Across the Bosphorus, the view of Üsküdar, Haydarpaşa and Kadiköy is impressive. You can turn left onto Mustafa Kemal Caddesi for Aksaray and Laleli; or continue on around Seraglio Point to Sirkeci, Eminönü, and the Galata Bridge.

Getting Around

Transport within Istanbul moves slowly. The medieval street patterns do not receive automobiles well, let alone buses. Several conflagrations in the 19th century cleared large areas of the city, and allowed new avenues to be opened. But for these providential disasters, traffic would be even slower.

A subway system has been in the planning for years. But the costs, astronomical in any case, increase dramatically when Istanbul's hilly terrain and water bodies are taken into account. Then there are the Byzantine ruins: every time a Byzantine structure is discovered, construction must be halted and the archaeologists brought in for weeks, perhaps months of study.

By Bus

Istanbul's red-and-beige city buses run most everywhere. Fares are very low, about 15c. Most of them seem to fill to capacity (and beyond) right at the departure point, leaving no room for passengers waiting along the route. It's frustrating to wait five or ten minutes for a bus, only to have it pass right by due to wall-to-wall flesh inside. Even if the driver does stop, is it worth it to jam in? If you're jammed in the middle of the bus when your stop comes, you may not be able to get off. (What you do in this situation is let the driver, and other pasengers, know you must get out by saying, *İnecek var!* (een-eh-JEK vahr), 'I must get out!').

Fares are paid on a ticket system (see the preceding chapter). The route name and number appear on the front of the bus; also on the front, or on the curb side, is a list of stops along the route.

By Dolmuş

The dolmuş and minibus system is preferable to the city buses for several reasons. As a car or minibus has a set number of seats, they are rarely over-crowded, like a bus. It's against the law to carry more than the designated number of passengers. Also, they tend to be faster. Finally, they tend to run on short routes between the major squares, so the tourist unfamiliar with Istanbul's topography can be sure of ending up at the chosen destination. Pluck up your courage and try a dolmuş early on in your stay. Soon you'll find them a great help.

Major dolmuş termini of use to tourists are: Taksim, Karaköy, Eminönü, Sirkeci, and Beyazıt. Sultanahmet, near the majority of Istanbul's most important sights, is not well-served by dolmuş except from Aksaray and Beyazıt. Coming from Galata Bridge, Eminönü and Sirkeci, they tend to pass a few blocks west of Sultanahmet. But a few blocks out is better than walking all the way, so ask for Cağaloğlu (ja-AHL-oh-loo) and you'll be close.

At these major dolmuş termini, look for the rows of cars and lines of people being matched up. If there's no sign indicating your destination, look in the cars' front windows, or ask just by saying the name of your destination. A hawker or driver will point you to the appropriate car.

Here are some rules of dolmuş etiquette. If your stop comes before the final destination, there may be some shuffling to assure that you are sitting right by the door and not way in the back. Also, a woman is expected to choose a side seat, not a middle seat between two men, for

her own comfort and 'protection'. If a man and a woman passenger get into the front of a car, for instance, the man should get in first and sit by the driver (contrary to everything his mother taught him about letting the lady go first), so that the woman is between 'her' man and the door. This is not a gesture against women, but rather the opposite, to show respect for her honour.

The fare should be written on the destination sign, whether it's on a signpost or in the car window. If it's not, watch what other people pay; ask; or hand over a bill large enough to cover the fare but small enough not to anger the driver, who will never have enough change and will not want to change a large bill. Collection of fares will begin after the car starts off, and the driver will juggle and change money as he drives. This thrilling practice costs no extra. Should there be any doubt about fares, or problem in payment, you can always settle up at the last stop.

To signal the driver that you want to get out, say *İnecek var* (een-eh-JEK vahr, 'I must get out'). Other useful words are *durun* (DOOR-oon, 'stop') and *burada* (BOO-rah-dah, 'here').

The Tünel

Istanbul's little underground train is called the *Tünel* (teu-NEHL), which runs between Karaköy, and the southern end of İstiklal Caddesi which is called *Tünel Meydanı* (Tünel Square). Built by French engineers over a century ago, the Tünel allowed European merchants to get from their offices in Galata to their homes in Pera without hiking up the steep hill. The lovely old cars of lacquered wood have been replaced by shiny Paris Metro-type cars with quiet rubber wheels. The fare is about 20c.

There are only two stations on the line, the upper and lower, so there's no getting lost. Buy a token, enter through the turnstile, and board the train. They run every five or ten minutes from early morning until about 10 pm.

Ferryboats

Without doubt the nicest way to go any considerable distance in Istanbul is by ferryboat. You will (and should) use the ferries whenever possible. The alternatives are bus and dolmuş along the coastal roads or across the Bosphorus Bridge. These can be faster, but they will also be less comfortable and more expensive.

The mouth of the Golden Horn by the the Galata Bridge is a seething maelstrom of the sleek white ferries at rush hour. At other times of day, the number of ferries (dozens) and the number of docks (ten) can lead to confusion, but a few bits of information will make it all come clear.

First of all, each dock serves a certain route, though a few routes may overlap. At each dock is a framed copy of the

timetable, or *tarife* (tah-ree-FEH), outlining the service. It's only in turkish, so I'll give you the necessary translations. Each route (*hat* or *hattı*) is designated by the names of the principal stops. IMPORTANT: the tarife has two completely different parts, one for weekdays (*normal günleri*) and saturday (*Cumartesi*), and another for Sunday (*Pazar*) and holidays (*Bayram günleri*). Make sure you're looking at the right part.

The ferryboat to Haydarpaşa Station has already been explained in the section on arrival by train.

If you just want to take a little ride around Seraglio Point (good for photos of Topkapı Palace, Sancta Sophia and the Blue Mosque) and across the Boshorus, catch any boat from Docks 7 or 8 in Karaköy. The trip over to Haydarpaşa or

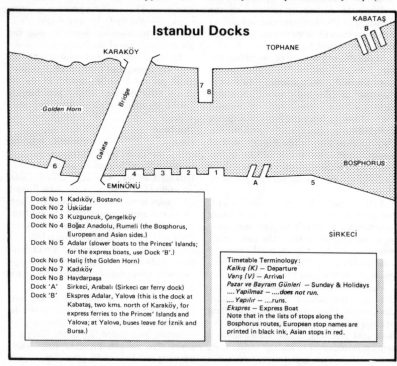

Istanbul Docks

Dock No 1 Kadıköy, Bostancı
Dock No 2 Üsküdar
Dock No 3 Kuzguncuk, Çengelköy
Dock No 4 Boğaz Anadolu, Rumeli (the Bosphorus, European and Asian sides.)
Dock No 5 Adalar (slower boats to the Princes' Islands; for the express boats, use Dock 'B'.)
Dock No 6 Haliç (the Golden Horn)
Dock No 7 Kadıköy
Dock No 8 Haydarpaşa
Dock 'A' Sirkeci, Arabalı (Sirkeci car ferry dock)
Dock 'B' Ekspres Adalar, Yalova (this is the dock at Kabataş, two kms. north of Karaköy, for express ferries to the Princes' Islands and Yalova; at Yalova, buses leave for İznik and Bursa.)

Timetable Terminology:
Kalkış (K) — Departure
Varış (V) — Arrival
Pazar ve Bayram Günleri — Sunday & Holidays
.... *Yapılmaz* — ....*does not run.*
.... *Yapılır* — ....runs.
Ekspres — Express Boat
Note that in the lists of stops along the Bosphorus routes, European stop names are printed in black ink, Asian stops in red.

Kadıköy and back will take about an hour.

Otherwise, the ferry you're most likely to use is the 'Special Touristic Excursion' (*Eminönü - Kavaklar Boğaziçi Özel Gezi Seferleri*) boats up the Bosphorus. These depart Eminönü at about 10.30 am and 1.30 pm each day, and go all the way to Rumeli Kavağı and Anadolu Kavağı, at the Black Sea mouth of the Bosphorus. The entire trip takes about 2½ hours one way. You may want to go only as far as Sarıyer, about two hours' ride, then take a dolmuş back down, stopping at various sights along the way.

On Foot

With an overburdened public transport system, walking can often be faster and more rewarding. The street scenes are never dull, and the views from one hill to the next are often extraordinary. While walking, watch out for broken pavement, bits of pipe sticking a few centimeters out of the pavement, and all manner of other obstacles. Don't expect any car driver to stop for you in any situation. In Turkey, the automobile seems to have the right of way virtually everywhere, and drivers get very annoyed at pedestrians who assert ridiculous and specious rights. It is obvious, isn't it? The automobile, being such a marvellous and expensive machine, should go wherever its driver is capable of taking it, without hindrance. This, at least, is the common belief.

Places to Stay

Istanbul is well provided with hotels in all categories, particularly in the budget and moderate ranges. Hotel clusters in various areas of the city make it easy to find the room you want at an affordable price. If the first hotel you look at is full, there will be another one around the corner, or even right next door.

I have listed hotels in all price ranges, and in Istanbul luxury hotels and super-cheap hostels can often be found side by side.

The letter-and-number in parentheses right after the hotel's name indicate its official Turkish government rating: (HL) is Hotel, Luxury; (H2) is Hotel, Second Class, etc. There are five official classes from (HL) down to (H4); below that, the hotel may be rated by the city government. The Hilton and Sheraton are (HL); a hotel rated (H4) would typically be a modern, respectable little place with quite small but tidy rooms equipped with private showers, a lift, central heat, and at least one or two staff members who know a foreign language.

Generally speaking the best selection of budget-to-moderate rooms is in the quarter named **Laleli**; the lowest-priced hotels and hostels are near **Sultanahmet**, and Istanbul University; and the moderate-to-luxury places are around **Taksim Square** in Beyoğlu.

Places to Stay – Laleli

Laleli (LAA-leh-LEE) is just east of Aksaray, just west of Istanbul University, and north of Ordu Caddesi. It's a pleasant residential and hotel district, with relatively quiet, shady, narrow streets. Several dozen little hotels sit cheek-by-jowl, and a new little place seems to open each year. To the north lies the district named Şehzadebaşı (sheh-ZAH-deh-bosh-uh). It's all one area, really. But some hotels will have Laleli in their address, others will have Şehzadebaşı.

Hotels in this area will rent you a clean, quiet double room with a private shower for $6 to $7 per night single, $9 to $11 double. Off-season, or if you intend to stay for more than just a few days, you can haggle for a reduction. Most will grant it gladly.

Tour groups from a number of European countries use some of the hotels in high summer, as the area is quiet yet convenient. Thus you may find some of them full, and others may be able to rent you a room only until another group arrives.

As everywhere in Turkey, you should inspect the hotel room before you register.

It may be better or worse than the lobby or facade. Also, one room may be better than another. If you don't like what you see, you can look at something else; just ask, *Başka var mı* (BASH-kah VAHR-muh, 'Are there others?').

Start your explorations by walking up Harikzadeler Sokak from Ordu Caddesi. This will take you past several inexpensive hotels, and into the heart of Laleli.

One of the nicer hotels, and about the best value for money, is the *Hotel Barın* (H3) (tel 522 8426 or 526 4440), Fevziye Caddesi 25, Şehzadebaşı, a newer place with 30 rooms. All have showers, some have tubs. Prices are $10 single, $17 double, continental breakfast included. The *Hotel Florida* (H4) (tel 528 1021/22), across the street at Fevziye Caddesi 38, Laleli, has 28 small rooms which go for about single, $15. The *Hotel Doru* (H3) (tel 526 5905 or 527 6928), Gençtürk Caddesi 44, Laleli, a few steps down the street from the aforementioned hotels, is yet another with 25 similar (if small), clean, modern rooms at similar prices.

The little hotels along Harikzadeler Sokak tend to be cheaper than the aforementioned ones, though not quite as comfortable: *Hotel Oran* (H4) (tel 528 5813 or 527 0572), Harikzadeler Sok. 40, 22 rooms with shower, $7 single, $11 double; takes tour groups. *Hotel Neşet* (tel 526 7412 or 522 4474), Harikzadeler Sok, 23, across the street from the Hotel Oran; very similar. *Hotel Ayda* (tel 526 7867), Harikzadeler Sok. 11, is less expensive still: double room with shower for $7 to $8. *Hotel Sırmalı* (tel 520 7642), just off Harikzadeler at Zeynel Kamil Sok. 45, two steps from the Hotel Ömür, is a popular place for foreign backpackers. A bit older than most of the above, it charges $5 single, $9 double for room with shower.

Places to Stay – Nearby Areas

Across Ordu Caddesi from Laleli, to the south, are dozens of other small hotels. In recent years this area has become popular with tourists, students and job-seekers from Iran and the Arab countries south and east of Turkey. Some of the hotels are used to Europeans, but most cater to these other groups.

Places to Stay – Sultanahmet

The Blue Mosque is officially the Mosque of Sultan Ahmet I (*Sultan Ahemt Camii*). It faces the ancient Byzantine Hippodrome, called the *At Maydanı* (Horse Grounds) in Turkish. The mosque has given the square and the quarter its name, which is contracted to *Sultanahmet*.

Around the Hippodrome are grouped the premier sights of Istanbul: Topkapı Palace, Sancta Sophia, the Blue Mosque, the 'Cistern Basilica', and the Hippodrome. There are two hostelries worth considering.

The *Yücelt Y Hostel* (tel 522 4790), Caferiye Sok. 6, Sultanahmet, is literally across the street from the front door of Sancta Sophia. Many years ago it was affiliated with the YMCA. Though the affiliation ended long ago, it keeps a 'Y' in its name to draw the clientele. The Yücelt is where most backpackers head when they arrive in Istanbul, because it has all the things a good tourist hostel should have: double rooms without baths ($8), three-bedded rooms ($13), and dormitories ($2); an inexpensive cafeteria; a laundry room; a bulletin board; public showers and a Turkish bath. The location couldn't be better.

Just past the Yücelt, up the street heading north, is the *Hotel Büyükayasofya* (tel 522 2981), Caferiye Sok. (That name, broken down, is *Büyük Aya Sofya*, 'Great Sancta Sophia'.) There's a restaurant-bar, as well as plain and well-used double rooms for $5 to $6.

In the summer (July and August), several university dormitories open their doors to foreign students. These tend to be extremely basic, and extremely cheap. They're not for all tastes, but if you want to look into one, ask for the latest information from the Tourism Information Office in Sultanahmet, right at the northern end of the Hippodrome next to the bus stop on the main street (called Divan Yolu).

Places to Stay – near Sirkeci Railway Station

Hotels near Sirkeci tend to be noisy, run-down, or off-colour, with a few exceptions. Walk out of the station's main (west) door, turn left, then left again onto Muradiye-Hüdavendigar Caddesi. A block up on the right you'll see Orhaniye Caddesi going up a gentle slope.

The *Küçük Karadeniz Oteli* (tel 522 6300), Orhaniye Caddesi 12, Sirkeci, is new, modern and presentable. Walk up one flight, then there's an elevator. Doubles without bath cost $5 to $7. The *Hotel İpek Palas* (tel 520 9724), Orhaniye Caddesi 9, is all the way up at the end of Orhaniye Caddesi, on the right. In the thirties and forties this 'Silk Palace' was probably a place where traders and business travellers put up for the night. It's seen a lot of use, but the rooms are big, the location good and quiet, and the prices good: $10 for a double with a bath.

Places to Stay – Taksim

In the 19th century, Istanbul's Old City was the Muslim centre, filled with mosques and history. Beyoğlu was where the foreigners lived, bustling with commerce, noisy with telephones, bright with electric light. As the rage for anything western spread through the upper classes, even the sultans succumbed. Abandoning Topkapı, the palace of their ancestors, they built new palaces near Beyoğlu.

Though the city has changed greatly in a century, Beyoğlu is still, generally speaking, the center of European-style living. The airline offices, foreign banks and luxury hotels are all here. The Etap Marmara (formerly the Inter-Continental) hotel is right in Taksim; the Sheraton is a block away, the Hilton two blocks. On the site of the wonderful old Art Deco Park Hotel, a

new ultra-luxurious five-star hotel is being constructed. All these places charge a very un-Turkish $100 to $150 for a double room; that is, they charge international rates.

There are several smaller hotels near Taksim which charge more reasonable rates, but even these sufer from price inflation due to location. They all charge a bit more because they're in the shadow of the Big Boys. A hotel room that costs $15 at a nice little place in Laleli will cost $25 near Taksim.

Before looking for a hotel room near Taksim, ask yourself 'why?' Laleli hotels are more convenient to the major tourist attractions of the Old City, and cheaper. The answer might be that you like the comforts. Taksim hotels tend to have hotter water, more English-speaking staff, little things like notepaper and telephones in the rooms. Some of the moderately-priced hotels have rooms with views of the Bosphorus, and you definitely pay a premium for these (but that view is marvellous). There is also status: Laleli is middle class, Taksim is upper.

Here are tips on staying in or near Taksim, including moderate-priced hotels, and also luxury hotels that charge a good deal less than the 'international' places.

There are two old favourites with tourists in Taksim. *Hotel Keban* (keh-BAHN) (H2) (tel 143 3310, –1, –2, –3), Sıraselviler Cad. 51, Taksim, is just out of Taksim Square near İstiklal Caddesi. Look for the MAKSIM theatre – that's at the beginning of Sıraselviler Caddesi, and the hotel is just a few doors down form it. The Keban has 87 rooms with bath or shower, plus elevators, air-conditioning, barber shop, restaurant, even little refrigerators in some of the rooms. For all this posh stuff you pay $23 double, breakfast included.

The *Dilson Hotel* (DEEL-sohn) (H2) (tel 143 5372,-4,–5), Sıraselviler Cad. 49, Taksim, near the Keban, is very similar. Its 90 rooms are priced at $19 single, $27 double, $33 triple, and $39 for four.

There is a middle ground for those who want the full comforts of a luxury hotel, but who don't want to pay 'international' prices. The *Divan Oteli* (dee-VAHN) (HL) (tel 146 4020), is on Cumhuriyet Caddesi, across from the Sheraton and a block from the Hilton. Founded by Vehbi Koç, Turkey's millionaire industrialist, it was meant as a suitable place for his friends and associates to stay in the days before the big international chain hotels arrived. It is very comfortable, but smaller (96 rooms) than the 400 plus room Hilton or Sheraton. The dining room has a reputation for being among the best restaurants in the city, and reasonably priced compared with the 'international' places. All the comforts and services of a luxury hotel are here; the staff are friendly, expert, and accommodating. Rooms cost $60 single, $75 double, taxes and services included.

The *Etap Istanbul Oteli* (H1) (tel 144 8880), Meşrutiyet Caddesi, Tepebaşi, is right across the street from the Pera Palas, and a few steps from the American Consulate, in Beyoğlu. Don't confuse it with its sister hotel, the Etap Marmara, which is right in Taksim Square. The Etap Istanbul has all the modern conveniences, a good enough location, a splendid view of the Golden Horn, the Old City and the Bosphorus from many of its rooms, and room prices similar to the Divan Oteli. If you take a room with a less spectacular view, you save money. The view from the rooftop swimming pool is best of all.

Places to Stay – Special Places

When Georges Nagelmackers began his renowned *Compagnie Internationale des Wagons-Lits et Grands Express Europeens* in the 1880s, he had a problem. When his pampered passengers debarked in constantinople, the luxury ended, for there was no suitable place for them to stay. So he built a place in Pera (Beyoğlu), and called it the Pera Palace. It opened in the 1890s, advertised as having ' ... a thoroughly healthy situation, being high up and isolated on all four sides', and 'over-looking the Golden Horn and the whole panorama of Stamboul'.

Though it is no longer 'isolated on all four sides', the Pera Palas Oteli (PEH-ra pa-LAHS) H1) (tel 145 2230), Meşrutiyet Cad. 98-100, Tepebaşı (TEP-eh-bash-uh), is still open and thriving. It fills up regularly with tourists looking to relive the great age of Constantinople, and with groups brought in by travel agents. The guest rooms are very large by modern standards; the bathrooms are larger than most modern hotel bedrooms. It is a worthy place.

It used to be fairly cheap, too. But the management has discovered what foreigners will pay for nostalgia (a lot), and has upped the prices accordingly. Even so, if you want nostalgia, the Pera Palas has it, and so you'll probably be happy to pay $36 single, $48 double, $110 for the Royal Suite (HRH Boris of Bulgaria slept here . . .). The Pera Palas has 120 rooms with high ceilings, period (more or less) furnishings, and bathrooms to match. Some rooms have views of the Golden Horn. The hotel is right next door to the American Consulate, and three blocks from the British consulate, in Beyoğlu's Tepebaşı quarter. Best way to get there is by dolmuş from Taksim; you may have to use a dolmuş that goes past Tepebaşı (say, to Aksaray), and pay the full fare. You can catch a bus along Tarlabaşı Caddesi (TAHR-la-bash-uh) just out of Taksim, but it will be packed. Coming from Karaköy, take the Tünel to the top station and walk the several blocks to the hotel.

Food

In Istanbul you will eat some of the best meals of your life, no matter whether you eat in a simple workingman's cafeteria or in a luxury restaurant. The quality and nutrition will be very high, the price will be ridiculously low.

It is not at all unusual to find several Turkish men involved in a passionate, even heated discussion over recipes. Though this passion for food does not fit

Top: The Mosque of Sultan Ahmet III (Blue Mosque), Istanbul
Left: The Grand Bazaar (Kürkçüler Çarşısı), Istanbul
Right: A hazy view of the Golden Horn

Top: Sancta Sophia, Istanbul
Bottom: A spice merchant in the Egyptian Bazaar

with the classic stereotype of Turk-as-fierce-soldier, it's not the Turks' fault, or the food's; rather, the stereoytpe's.

An interesting link between the two characterizations might be the Janissaries' habit of signalling revolt by overturning the cauldrons which held their dinner of *pilav*. The message from these elite troops to their sovereign might be phrased, 'If you call this food, we have confidence in neither your taste buds nor your leadership'.

Istanbul's inexpensive restaurants are literally every where. Price, by the way, has little to do with quality in Turkish restaurants. In the posh places you will get slightly finer food, elegant presentation and highly polished European-style service. But in the moderate, inexpensive and even very cheap places, the food will be savory and delicious. Little neighbourhood places will charge between $1 (for a simple main-course lunch) to perhaps $3 or $4 for a several-course budget tuck-in. If you order something more expensive, nice portions of meat or fish, and wine, and dessert, etc, expect to pay $5 to a top of $10 per person. After $10, you're definitely in the luxury class.

Types of Restaurants

You can find *hazır yemek* (ha-ZUHR-ye-MEHK) restaurants all over the city. These are the places with a dozen various foods keeping warm on big steam tables right by the front door. The sign may say *lokanta(sı), restaurant,* or *restoran.*

Kebapçı (keh-BAHP-chuh) and *Köfteci* (KURF-teh-jee) restaurants specialize in roast-meat kebabs and *köfte* (ground lamb with savory spices), charcoal-grilled.

A *pideci* (PEE-deh-jee) makes *pide* (PEE-deh), the flat bread called *pita* in Greece, *pizza* in Italy. On top of the bread you will get butter, plus whatever else you order. Ask for it *peynirli* (pey-neer-LEE,

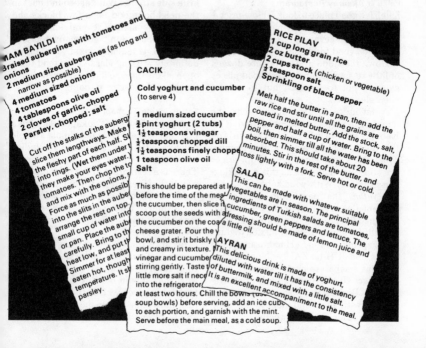

IAM BAYILDI
Braised aubergines with tomatoes and onions
2 medium sized aubergines (as long and narrow as possible)
4 medium sized onions
4 tomatoes
4 tablespoons olive oil
2 cloves of garlic, chopped
Parsley, chopped ; salt

Cut off the stalks of the auberg... slice them lengthways. Make ... the fleshy part of each half. S... into rings. (Wet them under ... they make your eyes water. ... tomatoes. Then chop the to... and mix with the onions, s... Force as much as possib... into the slits in the aube... arrange the rest on top... small cup of water int... or pan. Place the aub... carefully. Bring to th... heat low, and put t... Simmer for at leas... eaten hot, though... temperature. It s... parsley.

CACIK

Cold yoghurt and cucumber
(to serve 4)

1 medium sized cucumber
¾ pint yoghurt (2 tubs)
1½ teaspoons vinegar
½ teaspoon chopped dill
1½ teaspoons finely choppe...
1 teaspoon olive oil
Salt

This should be prepared at l... before the time of the mea... the cucumber, then slice it... scoop out the seeds with a... the cucumber on the coa... cheese grater. Pour the ... bowl, and stir it briskly ... and creamy in texture. ... vinegar and cucumbe... stirring gently. Taste ... little more salt if nece... into the refrigerator... at least two hours. Chill the bowls (... soup bowls) before serving, add an ice cub... to each portion, and garnish with the mint. Serve before the main meal, as a cold soup.

RICE PILAV
1 cup long grain rice
2 oz butter
2 cups stock (chicken or vegetable)
½ teaspoon salt
Sprinkling of black pepper

Melt half the butter in a pan, then add the raw rice and stir until all the grains are coated in melted butter. Add the stock, salt, pepper and half a cup of water. Bring to the boil, then simmer till all the water has been absorbed. This should take about 20 minutes. Stir in the rest of the butter, and toss lightly with a fork. Serve hot or cold.

SALAD
This can be made with whatever suitable vegetables are in season. The principal ingredients of Turkish salads are tomatoes, cucumber, green peppers and lettuce. The dressing should be made of lemon juice and a little oil.

AYRAN
This delicious drink is made of yoghurt, diluted with water till it has the consistency of buttermilk, and mixed with a little salt. It is an excellent accompaniment to the meal.

'with cheese'), or *Kıymalı* (kuy-mah-LUH, ' with ground meat'), or *yumurtalı* (yoo-moor-tah-LUH, 'with eggs'). You can combine these terms, as in *Peynirli yumurtalı bir pide, lütfen* ('A pide with cheese and eggs, please').

If you see a place advertised as an *işkembeci* (eesh-KEHM-beh-jee), it specializes in tripe soup (*işkembe çorbası*). You might not like it. The turks say it cures hangovers. They might mean that if you have one, it'll take your mind off the incredible redolence of this concoction.

Büfe is the Turkish for the French *buffet*. In Istanbul it means a streetside snack or light luch, 'fast food' place. It may be a kiosk on the sidewalk, or a storefront.

Places to Eat
Here are some of the better restaurants to try, grouped according to hotel and sightseeing district.

Laleli & Aksaray Restaurants
Laleli is a good place to look for low-priced eats because Istanbul University is close by. You'll see several places stuffed with students, good food and low prices.

Down the slope in Aksaray are dozens of little restaurants, neighbourhood places catering not to tourists, but to a local clientele.

A favourite in this district has the daunting name of *Hacıbozanoğulları*. It's a Kebapçı at 214 Ordu Caddesi, which is on the north (Laleli) side of the avenue. Though it's somewhat fancied up, prices are still very moderate as this a working-class district. With your kebap you may get *yufka*, the paper-thin unleavened peasant flat bread; or pide, the thicker, leavened flat bread. For a drink, try *ayran*, a healthful and refreshing mix of yoghurt and spring water. Hacıbozanoğulları (that's ha-JUH-bo-ZAHN-oh-ool-lahr-uh) also has a separate pastry shop, called a *baklavacı* (BAHK-lah-vah-juh, 'baklava-maker'). Besides this many-layered pastry stuffed with nuts and honey, the shop features other Turkish sweets.

Restaurants in Sultanahmet
Several little restaurants are open along Divan Yolu, the main street which goes from Sultanahmet Square up the hill toward the university and the Grand Bazaar. Right across Divan Yolu from the Hippodrome is the famous *Pudding Shop*, where the drop-out generation of the 60s kept alive and happy on various nutritious, tasty, inexpensive puddings such as *sütlaç* (SEWT-latch), a milk-and-rice pudding; or its even tastier baked version, *fırın sütlaç* (FUH-ruhn SEWT-latch, baked, but served cold). Today the Pudding Shop serves all sorts of meals. Prices are higher than in the Hippy heyday, but still reasonable. The traffic on busy Divan Yolu, right out front, can be objectionable.

Tourists frequent many of the other little restaurants along Divan Yolu. Although prices aren't bad here, you can do even better by walking up Divan Yolu (east) and turning right, into one of the little side streets. Wander around back in the neighbourhood for a few blocks and you'll come across several small restaurants which don't get many tourists. The food is equally good, the prices definitely working-class. They tend to be open all the time, so if it's very crowded at lunch, come back in an hour.

Eating inside Topkapı Palace
Everyone who visits Topkapı Palace has a problem: since it can take almost a whole day to see the palace properly (including the Harem), where do you eat lunch? There is a restaurant in the palace, all the way at the far end from the main entrance. Tables are both inside and outside under an awning. The outside tables have marvellous views of the Bosphorus and the Asian shore.

Because the restaurant has a captive audience of tourists (not locals, who might complain), food and service are not quite what they should be. But they'll do. The trick is to arrive by 11.30 to beat the lunch rush, or to come later in the afternoon. Tour groups often fill the place. Watch out.

If it's just a nice seat and a cool drink you're looking for, go to the cafe next to the restaurant. Even better views here.

Eating in the Grand Bazaar

On the map of the Grand Bazaar, you will notice a half-dozen little restaurants marked. With one exception, these are tiny, basic places where the workmen of the bazaar eat, or from which prepared meals are taken to their workshops on trays. Turks see no reason why they should eat badly just because they're at work.

Some of these little places rarely see a foreign tourist, some are used to them. All will welcome you and make extra efforts please. The ones that are used to foreigners, where the menus may be in English and where the waiter will know at least a few words of a foreign language, are grouped on Koltuk Kazazlar Sokak and Kahvehane Sokak. Take a seat in the little dining room, or sit at a table set out in one of the little streets. A filling meal will cost around $2.

The exception mentioned above is the *Havuzlu Lakantası*, the only pricey place in the bazaar. Prices here get into the moderate range. The food is about the same as at other places, but at the Havuzlu you get a lofty dining room made of several bazaar streets (walled off for the

purpose long ago), a few tables set out in front of the entrance by a little stone pool (*Havuzlu* means 'with pool'; I suspect it was a deep well centuries ago). Waiter service is much more polite and unhurried. If you want to escape the activity of the bazaar, into a haven of quiet and calm, spend a little more and go to the Havuzlu. It's next to the PTT (peh-teh-TEH, the post office). Follow the yellow-and-black signs, ask for the PTT, or ask for the restaurant.

Grand Bazaar Cafes

You will no doubt pass the *Şark Kahvesi* (SHARK kah-veh-see, the Oriental Cafe), at the end of Fesçiler Caddesi. Always filled with locals and tourists, it can be

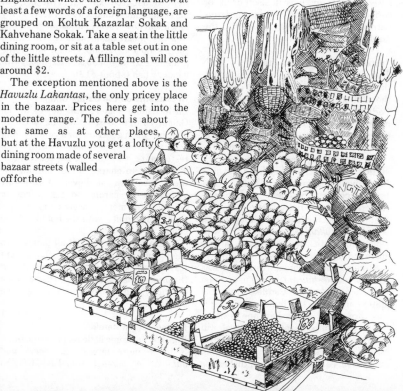

difficult to find a seat. It recently underwent a facelift, and the prices lifted along with it. But this is the real bazaar, and a cup of Turkish coffee, soft drink, or a glass of çay (CHA-ee) will not set you back that much.

In fine weather, head out of the bazaar and next door to the Beyazıt Camii (Mosrque of Beyazıt, between the bazaar and the university gates). You can go through the Sahaflar Çarşısı, the Old Book Bazaar. On the east side of the mosque is a lovely tea garden, a plaza filled with tables, most of them shady. Waiters in traditional coffe-house costumes circulate through the sea of tables carrying trays filled with the pretty little glasses of tea. Signal to the waiter when you see him with a tray and you'll get your tea right away; or order and have it, a soft drink, or coffee, brought to you. As this garden is patronised by university students, the drinks are not expensive.

Restaurants near Sirkeci Station

There are lots of good little restaurants in the Sirkeci area. Turn left as you come out the station door, and head up Ankara Caddesi, turning into the second or third little street on the left. Here is another of those areas of little workshops and offices, with a few little eateries. Take your pick.

For something fancier, go out the station door, turn left, then left again onto Muradiye-Hüdavendigar Caddesi. The first street to the right is Orhaniye (described in the hotel section). Across the street from the Küçük Karadeniz Oteli is the Şehir Lokantası (sheh-HEER), with white tablecloths, waiter service, fancier surroundings, and slightly higher prices.

Sirkeci's most famous restaurant was the Konyalı Restaurant, which used to be right across Ankara Caddesi from the station entrance. The building housing it was torn down, and a new one is being built now. It may be that the Konyalı will have a place in it. If so, you will pay fairly high (for Turkey) prices for unique, innovative, carefully-prepared dishes.

Restaurants in the Spice Bazaar

The Mısır Çarşısı (MUH-suhr char-shuh-suh, 'Egyptian Market') is also called the spice bazaar because of the many spice shops within. A famous old restaurant here has been going for decades.

Quite a while ago, a man named Pandeli opened a modest little restaurant down by the wholesale vegetable and fish markets on the Golden Horn. After gaining a citywide reputation, he moved to the guardroom over the main entrance (facing Galata Bridge) of the Mısır Çarşısı. The small guardroom chambers are covered in beautiful faience, and some of the tables have views out onto the square of Eminönü and the bridge, or inward to the bazaar's main street.

Pandeli Usta ('Chef Pandeli') long ago went to that great kitchen in the sky, but his restaurant remains. It still serves only lunch, but now it serves it to tour groups as well as local businessmen. Go when there's no tour group. You'll enjoy the grilled meats (about $9 for a full meal, with wine) or fish (about $12).

Restaurants on the Galata Bridge

Little fishing smacks still tie up to the Galata Bridge to sell their daily catch. This has been going on for a century, and was the reason numerous little fish restaurants grew up under the bridge. They used to charge almost nothing for the freshest fish you'd ever eaten. Today you must be careful to ask prices in advance, for menus rarely carry them – they change daily, with the bounty of the catch.

These places are not at all fancy, with their formica tables and fluorescent lights. But the fish can be very good, and the prices reasonable (about $6 to $8 for a full meal, with wine or beer) if you ask the prices.

Restaurants in Karaköy

Karaköy has some little restaurants, but it is much more famous for börek and bakava. A börekçi (bur-REK-CHEE) makes various sorts of flaky pastries filled with cheese or chopped parsley. Each type of börek has its own name. *Su böreği* (SOO bur-reh-yee, 'water pastry') is a thick noddle-like affair with sprinklings of white sheep's-milk cheese and chopped parsley. Ask for 200 grams (ee-KEE yewz gram), and the clerk will cut out a square, chop it into manageable bites, and hand it to you on a plastic plate with a fork. It will cost perhaps 40c.

Other sorts of börek are the more familiar flaky pastry-with-stuffing, like *sosisli börek* (soh-sees-LEE), a flaky pastry wrapped around a sausage; or *peynirli*, stuffed with cheese. In Karaköy's many börekçi shops, they're cheap, fresh and good.

The baklava places are also good. The baklava comes with all sorts of stuffings. Prices are marked per kilogram and per portion (usually 150 grams, though you can order as little or as much as you like for a portion). Stuffings include pistachios (ask for *şam Fıstıklı*, SHAHM fuhs-tuhk-luh); walnuts (*cevilzli*, jeh-veez-LEE); even clotted cream (*kaymaklı*, kah-ee-mahk-LUH). Istanbul's most famous *balkavacı* is *Güllüoğlu* (GEWL-loo-oh-loo), in a shop on the street level of the big parking garage which is across from the Yolcu Salonu (International Maritime Passenger Terminal), a hundred yards from the Galata Bridge.

Speaking of the Yolcu Salonu, it contains two of Istanbul's best restaurants. As headquarters for Turkish Maritime Lines, the Yolcu Salonu must have a showplace seafood restaurant. In fact, it has two. Enter on the building's right (west) end and go to either the *Liman Lokantası* or the *Liman Kafeteryası*.

The Kafeterya is a less elegant, less expensive version of the restaurant. You pay a set price (about $6) and help yourself to the various courses at the steam tables.

Upstairs in the Liman Lokantası, a spacious, simple, somewhat old-fashioned dining room overlooks the mouth of the Golden Horn and the Old City. (If there's a cruise ship tied up at the Yolcu Salonu dock, the ship will block the view.) Service is very polite and refined, fish is the speciality, and a full, elegant, delicious lunch from soup to baklava and coffee, with wine, will cost less than $15.

Restaurants near Taksim Square

Taksim has hundreds of restaurants. Every other place you see is a restaurant. The variety is equally vast. It's one of the best areas in the city to find good and inexpensive food.

As Turkish dishes are so varied, and their names so incomprehensible, you might want to start off at the *Selvi Kafeterya*, Sıraselviler Caddesi 40, across from the Kilson and Keban hotels. This big, bright, plain place has the standard cafeteria line, tin trays, steam tables and low prices. They're not as low as they might be however; this is Taksim. Don't over-eat with your eyes. Three selections, plus that good Turkish bread, is plenty for anyone; two usually suffice. You can always go back. Fill up at lunch or dinner for $2 or $3.

İstiklal Caddesi, Beyoğlu's main street, runs (one way to traffic) from Tünel Square to Taksim. Half-way along is Galatasaray, an intersection so named because of the big Galatasaray Lisesi (Lycee) on the southern side of İstiklal, you'll see restaurant after restaurant. Right at the beginning of the street, on the left, is a beer-garden, a new 'import' brought back from Germany with the Turkish workers. Past it are several dependable *hazır yemek* restaurants and *kebapçı* places, also on the left. The *Antep Restaurant* at No 3 has been here for years, and is still going strong. Prices here are moderate ($3 to $5) rather than low.

The *Hacı Baba Restaurant* (ha-JUH bah-bah) at İstiklal Cad. 49 deserves special mention. The tiny, unimpressive doorway you see leads to much better things. Or, continue down İstiklal, turn left at the next corner, and enter the Hacı

Baba from the side street. It's here, on the side street, that you'll see the restaurant's strong-point: a nice little outdoor terrace set with tables overlooking the courtyard of the Aya Triada ('Holy Trinity') Greek Orthodox church next door, a bit of open space, peace and quiet in the midst of the city. Hacı Baba is a full-menu, full-service restaurant with fish, grilled meats, preparing dishes and specialities. Expect to pay $6 to $9 for a full dinner with wine.

Continuing along, İstiklal takes you past numerous little *büfe* places, good for a cheap, quick snack. In many of these you must buy a *fiş* (FEESH), or receipt, from the cashier for the total of your purchases before you order. If you're not sure what things cost, ignore the system, ask for (or point to) what you want, and the cook will shout the total to the cashier. They are very tolerant of foreigners.

After a few blocks you will come to a little mosque, on your right. This is the Ağa Camii (ah-AH jahm-ee). Just beyond it is Sakızağaci Sokak ('pinegumtree street'), turning right off from İstiklal, packed with little restaurants. One of the most long-lived and dependable of these is *Hacı Salih*. Businessmen in the area regularly show up here for lunch because of the good fast service, excellent food, and low prices. It's good for tourists because the steam tables are just past the first little dining room, and you can point to what you want.

Things to See
The first thing you'll see in Istanbul will be the impressive skyline of the Old City. It will take you at least three days to get around and see the major sights. You can easily spend a week at it, for Istanbul offers an awful lot to see.

The sightseeing plan below is organized to show you the most important and accessible sights first, so you can see as much as possible in even a short time. If you have a week, you should be able to see just about everything described here.

Before starting out, remember that museums are closed on Mondays, except for Topkapı Palace, which is closed on Tuesdays instead.

Old Istanbul
In the Old City, Topkapı Palace is right next to Sancta Sophia, which is right next to the Blue Mosque, which is right on the Hippodrome, which is right next to the Cistern Basilica, which is only a few steps from the museum complex, which is right next to Topkapı Palace. You can spend at least two days just completing this loop. Start with the palace, which is among the world's greatest museums.

You can get there from Aksaray and Laleli by dolmuş or bus (or on foot) along Ordu Caddesi, which turns into Yeniçeriler Caddesi, and finally Divan Yolu. Ask the driver if he's going to **Sultanahmet**. From Taksim it's a bit more difficult. Get a dolmuş to **Sirkeci** and walk up the hill for ten minutes (take a short cut to the palace through Gülhane Park); or take a T1 or T4 circle route bus, which stops right in Sultanahmet. The dolmuş is faster.

Topkapı Palace
It will take you the better part of a day to explore Topkapı Palace. Though it's tempting to nip into Sancta Sophia for a look as you go by on your way to Topkapı, I strongly recommend that you resist the urge. Sancta Sophia has been there for 1500 years, and it will be there when you come out of Topkapı. Start on the palace early in the day, before the bus tours get there. If you don't, you'll end up missing something important (like the Harem or the Treasury), or coming back another day.

Topkapı Palace is open from 10 am to 7 pm during July and August; 10 am to 5 pm the rest of the year. Closed Tuesday. When you buy your admission ticket (about $1), remember also to buy a ticket for the Harem tour. If you don't pay the photography fee (less than $1), you'll have to check your camera.

The palace is called the Seraglio by foreigners (including Mozart, in his 'Abduction from the Seraglio'), an Italian word for the Turkish *saray* (palace).

Topkapı Sarayı (TOHP-kahp-uh sah-rah-yuh) was the residence of the sultans for almost three centuries. Mehmet the Conqueror built the first palace here shortly after the Conquest in 1453, and lived here until his death in 1481. Sultan after sultan played out the drama of the Ottoman sovereign here until the 19th century. Mahmut II (1808-1839) was the last emperor to inhabit the palace. After him, the sultans preferred to occupy new European-style palaces – Dolmabahçe, Çırağan, Yıldız – which they built up the Bosphorus. Under the republic, the Saray became Turkey's finest museum. Mozart's famous opera is performed here every year, right in the 'Seraglio', during the Istanbul International Festival.

Church of St Irene Topkapı grew and changed with the centuries, but its basic three-courtyard plan remained the same. As you pass through the great gate behind Sancta Sophia, you enter the first court, the **Court of the Janissaries.** On your left is the former **Church of St Irene**, now a concert hall where recitals are given during the Istanbul International Festival. There was a Christian church here from earliest times, and before that a pagan temple. The early church was replaced by the present one during the reign of the Byzantine emperor Justinian, in the 540s, so the church you see is as old as Sancta Sophia. When Mehmet the Conqueror began building his palace, the church was within the grounds, and thus couldn't be used for worship. It was used as an arsenal for centuries, then as an Artillery Museum (note the rows of cannons outside). In the 1970s, restoration work began, and it was first used as a concert hall.

Topkapı Palace

Court of the Janissaries This was where the sultan's elite corps of guards gathered. It was here that they ate their hearty *pilav*, provided by the sultan. When they were dissatisfied with his rule (which meant his treatment of them), they would overturn the great cauldrons of pilav as a symbol of revolt. After that, the sultan usually didn't last too long. Food was the most important symbol, so important, in fact, that the Janissary corps was organized on commissary lines. Some of the officers had kitchen titles, and the corps was called the *ocak*, 'hearth' or 'cookfire'.

'Janissary' comes from *yeni çeri* (YEHN-ee chehr-ee) 'new levies'. These soldiers were personal servants of the sultan, 'owned' by him, paid regularly and fed by him, and subject to his will. They were full-time soldiers in an age when most soldiers were farmers in spring and fall, homebodies in winter, and warriors only in summer. The Janissaries were mostly recruited as boys of 10 years old, from Christian families in the Balkans. Though Islam forbids the enslavement or forcible conversion of Christians and Jews, the Balkans were looked upon as an exception. Saints Cyril and Methodius, 'Apostles to the Slavs', converted the pagan Slavic peoples to Christianity in the 800s, after the revelation of the Koran to Muhammed. So it was very convenient for the Ottoman religious authorities to rule that Slavic Christians 'had made the wrong choice' in converting to Christianity. Since they had been pagans when the Koran was revealed, they could be enslaved now.

The boys were taught Turkish, and instructed in Islam. The brightest went into the palace service, and many eventually rose to the highest offices, including Grand Vezir. This assured that the top government posts were always held by 'slaves' of the sultan. Those not so bright made up the Janissary corps. Often, in the later years of the empire, they proved that the sultan was their 'slave', and not the other way around.

The end of the Janissary corps started right here. The reforming sultan, Mahmut II, decided to do away with this dangerous and corrupted palace guard in 1826. Risking his throne, his life and his dynasty, he readied a new, loyal European-style army, then provoked a revolt of the Janissaries and wiped them out. But for three and a half centuries before 1826, this courtyard was their headquarters.

Janissaries, merchants and tradesmen could circulate as they wished in the Court of the Janissaries. But the second court was different. The same is true today, in a way, because you must buy your tickets before entering the second court. The ticket booths are on your right as you approach the entrance. Just past them is a little fountain. It's where the Imperial Executioner used to wash the tools of his trade after decapitating a noble or rebel who had displeased the sultan. The head of the unfortunate was put on a pike and exhibited above the gate you're about to enter.

The 'Middle Gate' **Ortakapı**, also called the Gate of Greeting, led to the palace's second court, used for the business of running the empire. Only the sultan was allowed through the Ortakapı on horseback. Everyone else, including the Grand Vezir, had to dismount. The gate you see was constructed by Süleyman the Magnificent in 1524, utilizing architects and workers he had brought back from his conquest of Hungary. That's why it looks more European than oriental.

Within the second court is a beautiful, park-like setting. You'll see at once that Topkapı is not a palace on the European plan, one large building with outlying gardens. Rather, Topkapı is a series of pavilions, kitchens, barracks, audience chambers, kiosks and sleeping quarters built around a central enclosure, much like a fortified camp. It is a delightful castle and palace all in one. As you walk into the second court, the great palace kitchens will be on your right. They now contain a small portion of Topkapı's incredibly large and varied collection of Chinese celadon porcelain. The greater part of the collection, which is quite vast, is in storage. Another room holds a fine collection of European and, especially interesting, Ottoman porcelain and glassware. The last of the kitchens is set up as a kitchen, though, and you can easily imagine what went on in these rooms as the staff prepared food for the 5000 inhabitants of the palace.

On the left side of the second court is the **Kubbealtı**, the ornate Imperial Council Chamber where the Grand Vezir would meet with the Imperial Divan (council) on matters of state. The sultan did not participate in these discussions, but kept track sometimes by sitting behind a screen and listening. *Kubbealtı* means 'beneath the cupola'. The squarish tower which is one of Topkapı's most noticeable features is just above the Council Chamber.

Harem The entrance to the Harem is just behind the Kubbealtı. You will have to take a guided tour; they leave periodically. You will also need a separate ticket for entrance to the Harem. It's a good idea to see the Harem as soon as possible, because it is sometimes closed at lunchtime, and it closes earlier in the day than the rest of the palace. Line up for the Harem tour before you go to the other parts of the palace.

Fraught with legend and wild romance, the Harem is everything that you've imagined, even though the legends and stories are not really quite true.

The usual stereotype shows an army of gorgeous women petting and caressing, amusing and entertaining, and doing their best to exhaust a very pampered man. Well, there's no denying that the sultan had it good. But every detail of Harem life was fraught with tradition, obligation and ceremony. The sultan could not, unfortunately, just leap into a roomful of beauties and go to it.

Every traditional Muslim household had two distinct parts, the *selamlık*, or 'Greeting Room', where the master would greet friends, business associates, and tradesmen; and the *harem* ('private apartments'), reserved for himself and his family. The harem, then, was something akin to the private apartments in Buckingham Palace or the White House. The selamlık was what outsiders saw when they visited.

The Harem of Topkapı was not just a prison full of women kept for the sultan's pleasure. It was his family quarters, and also an important centre of administration for the palace and the empire.

The women of the Harem had to be foreigners, as Islam forbade enslaving Muslims, Christians or Jews (Christians and Jews could be enslaved if taken as war prisoners, or if bought as slaves in a legitimate slave market). Besides war prisoners, girls were bought as slaves (often sold by their parents at a good price), or received as gifts from nobles and potentates. A favourite source of girls for the Harem was Circassia, north of the Caucusus Mountains in Russia, as Circassian women were noted for their beauty, and parents were often glad to sell their ten-year-old girls.

Upon entering the Harem, the girls would be schooled in Islam and Turkish culture and language, plus such arts as make-up and dress, music, reading and writing, embroidery and dancing. They then entered a meritocracy, first as Ladies-in-Waiting to the sultan's concubines and children, then to the sultan's mother, and finally, if they were good enough, to the sultan himself.

Ruler of the Harem was the *Valide Sultan*, or Queen Mother, the mother of the reigning sultan. She often owned large landed estates in her own name, and controlled them through black eunuch servants. She was allowed to give orders directly to the Grand Vezir. Her influence on the sultan, on the selection of his wives and concubines, and on matters of state, was very great.

The sultan was allowed by Islamic law

to have four legitimate wives, who would receive the title of *kadın* (wife). If one bore him a child, she was called *Haseki Sultan* if it was a son, or *Haseki Kadın* if it was a daughter. The ladies of the Harem would do almost anything to get their own son proclaimed heir to the throne, thus assuring their own role as the new Valide Sultan. (The Ottoman dynasty did not observe primogeniture, or succession by the first-born son. The throne was basically up for grabs to any imperial son.)

As for concubines, Islam permits as many as you can support in proper style. The Ottoman sultan could support a lot. Some of the early sultans had as many as 300 concubines, though not all in the Harem at the same time. But actually the domestic thrills of the sultans were usually less spectacular. Mehmet the Conqueror, builder of Topkapı, was the last sultan to have the four official wives. After him, sultans did not officially marry, but instead kept four chosen concubines without the legal encumbrances.

The Harem was much like a small village, with all the necessary services. About 400 or 500 people lived in this distinct section of the palace at any one time. Not many of the ladies stayed in the Harem forever. The sultan would grant them their freedom, and they would be snapped up as wives by powerful men who wanted these supremely graceful and intelligent women, and also their connections with the palace.

The *Kızlaragası* (kuhz-LAHR ah-ah-suh), or Chief Black Eunuch, was the sultan's personal representative in the running of the Harem, and also in other important affairs of state. In fact, he was the third most powerful official in the empire, after the Grand Vezir and the Supreme Islamic Judge.

The imperial princes were brought up in the Harem, taught and cared for by the women. The tradition of the *kafes* (kah-FESS), or 'cage', was one of many things which led to the decline of the great empire. In the early centuries, imperial princes were schooled in combat and statecraft by direct experience: they practised soldiering, they fought in battles, and they were given provinces to administer. In the later centuries, they spent their lives more or less imprisoned in the Harem, where the sultan could keep an eye on them and prevent any move to dethrone him. This meant that the princes were prey to the intrigues of the women and eunuchs; and when one of them did succeed to the throne, he was corrupted by the pleasures of the Harem, and completely ignorant of war and statecraft. Luckily for the empire in this latter period, there were very able generals (pashas) and Grand Vezirs to carry on.

Much of the Harem was constructed during the reign of Süleyman the Magnificent (1520-1566), but a lot was added over the years.

When you enter the Harem, think of it as the family quarters; as a place of art, culture and refinement; and as a political entity subject to intense manoeuvring and intrigue.

The door through which you enter was for tradespeople. Traders who had things necessary to the Harem would bring their wares here and turn them over to the black eunuch guards. The tilework in the second room you enter is some of Turkey's finest. Note the green and yellow colours, unusual in İznik faience. Then a corridor leads past the rooms of the black eunuchs who guarded the sultan's ladies. In the early days, white eunuchs were used, but black eunuchs, sent as presents by the Ottoman governor of Egypt, later took control. As many as 200 lived in the Harem, guarding its doors and waiting on its women.

The sultan, when he walked these corridors, wore slippers with silver soles. They were noisy, and that was the point: no woman in the Harem was allowed to show herself to the Imperial Regard without specific orders. When they heard the clatter of silver on stone, they all ran to hide. This rule no doubt solidifed the

Valide Sultan's control: *she* would choose the girls to be presented to the sultan. There was to be no flirting in the hallways.

You enter a small courtyard, around which were the private apartments of the four *kadıns*, or wives.

A larger courtyard beyond was the domain of the Valide Sultan, or Queen Mother. Besides being the centre of power in the Harem, this was where each new sultan came, after accession to receive the allegiance and congratulations of the people of the Harem.

The sultan's private Turkish bath is next. His mother and his four wives each had their own private bath. Other private baths went to the lady responsible for discipline in the Harem, and to her assistant, the treasurer. After that, all the women shared a common bath. Not with the eunuchs, either.

Next you enter a few of the sultan's private chambers. There is a 17th-century room with a beautifully decorated fireplace, and a reception room with a fountain. Here the sultan would receive the ladies of the Harem, or his married female relatives – sisters, cousins, and aunts. The fountain obscured the sounds of their conversation so that no one – in this hotbed of intrigue – could eavesdrop.

The sultan's private chamber was first built by Sinan, Süleyman the Magnificent's great architect, but the present decor dates from the 18th century.

Sultan Ahmet I (1603-1617), builder of the Blue Mosque, added a nice little library. His successor Ahmet III added the pretty dining room with all the appetizing bowls of fruit painted on the walls, in 1705.

The **Veliaht Dairesi** is the apartment of the Crown Prince, where, in later centuries, he was kept secluded from the world. Note the ingenious little fountains in the windows, and the leather-covered domed ceiling. Next to the Crown Prince's suite are the sumptuous rooms of his mother, the *Haseki Sultan*.

These are the last rooms you see on the tour. You exit into the third, innermost courtyard.

Third Court If you enter the Third Court through the Harem, sort of by the back door, you should head for the main gate into the court. Get the full effect of entering this Holy of Holies by going out through the gate, and back in again.

This gate, the **Bab-i Saadet**, or Gate of Felicity, was the entrance into the sultan's private domain. A new sultan, after girding on the sword which symbolized imperial power, would sit enthroned before this gate and receive the congratulations and allegiance of the empire's high and mighty. Before the annual military campaigns in summertime, the sultan would appear before this gate bearing the standard of the Prophet Muhammed to inspire his pashas (generals) to go out and win for Islam. Today the Bab-i Saadet is the backdrop for the annual performance of Mozart's 'Abduction from the Seraglio', during the Istanbul International Festival in late June and early July.

The Third Court was staffed and guarded by white eunuchs, who allowed only very few, very important people to enter.

Just inside the Bab-i Saadet is the **Arz Odası**, or Audience Chamber. The sultan preserved the imperial mystique by appearing in public very seldom. To conduct official business, important officials and foreign ambassadors would come to this little room. An ambassador, frisked for weapons and held on each arm by a white eunuch, would approach the sultan. At the proper moment, he would kneel and kowtow; if he didn't, the white eunuchs would urge him ever so strongly to do so. After that, he could speak to the sultan through an interpreter.

The sultan, seated on the divans whose cushions are embroidered with over 15,000 seed pearls, would inspect the ambassadors gifts and offerings as they were passed by the small doorway on the left. Even if the sultan and the ambassador could converse in the same language (sultans in the later years knew French, and ambassadors often learned Turkish), all conversation went through an interpreter. One couldn't have just anybody putting words into the Imperial Ear.

During the great days of the empire, foreign ambassadors would be received on days when the Janissaries were to get their pay. Huge sacks of silver coins were brought to the Kubbealtı (Council Chamber). High court officers would dispense them to long lines of the tough, impeccably costumed and faultlessly disciplined troops as the ambassadors looked on in admiration. It all worked for a while.

As you stroll into the Third Court, imagine it alive with the movements of imperial pages and white eunuchs scurrying here and there in their palace costumes. Every now and then the chief white eunuch or the chief black eunuch would appear, and all would deferentially bow. If the sultan walked across the courtyard, all activity stopped until the event was over.

Right behind the Arz Odası is the pretty little **Library of Ahmet III** (1718).

Walk to the right as you leave the Arz Odası, and enter the rooms which were once the Turkish baths of the Third Court staff. They now contain a fascinating collection of imperial robes, caftans and uniforms worked in thread of silver and gold. You'll be surprised at the oriental, almost Chinese design of these garments. Remember that the Turks came originally from the borders of China, and that their cultural history was tied closely with that of the Persian Empire and Central Asia. In fact, tribes in China's westernmost province of Sinkiang still speak a dialect of Turkish.

Next to the baths are the chambers of the **Imperial Treasury**. This you won't believe. After awhile the display cases filled with rubies, emeralds, jade, pearls,

and more diamonds than you ever imagined, will cause you to think, 'These are not all real, they must be plastic'. They're not.

One of my favourite items in the Treasury is the solid gold throne of Shah Ismail, encrusted with tens of thousands of precious stones. It was captured by Sultan Selim I (1512-1520) in a war with the Persians. Other thrones are almost as breathtaking. Look also for the tiny figurine of a sultan sitting under a baldachin. His body is one enormous pearl.

The **Kaşıkçı**, or Spoonmaker's Diamond, is an 86-carat mammoth surrounded by several dozen smaller stones. But the prize for biggest precious stone goes to the uncut emerald which weighs 3.26 kilograms, or almost seven pounds.

In the midst of all this heavy-duty show of wealth, don't lose sight of the fact that the workmanship, design and artistry exhibited in many of these items is extraordinary in itself.

Next door to the Treasury is the **Hayat Balkonu**, or Balcony of Life. Here the breeze is cool, and it offers a marvellous view of the Bosphorus and the Sea of Marmara.

Kiosks To reach the palace restaurant and cafe, walk along the rear side of the Third Court and look for the narrow alley which goes north between the buildings. Down the slope and on the right is the **Mecidiye Köşkü**, or Kiosk of Sultan Abdülmecit. Admire the view, enter the kiosk and go down the stairs to reach the restaurant. Remember, tour groups fill it up around lunchtime, so plan your visit after noon, or at least a half-hour before.

Four imperial pleasure domes occupy the north-easternmost part of the palace, sometimes called the Fourth Court. The Mecidiye, built by Abdülmecit (1839-1861), you've already seen as entrance to the restaurant. In the other direction (north-east) is the **Mustafa Paşa Köşkü**, or Kiosk of Mustafa Pasha also called the *Sofaköskü*.

The gardens around it were once filled with tulips. In fact, the reign of Sultan Ahmet III (1703-1730) is named the Tulip Period because of the craze which spread through the upper classes. Gardens such as this held hundreds of varieties of tulips. Little lamps would be set out among the flowers at night. A new variety of the flower earned its creator fame, entree, and a good deal of money.

Tulips had been grown in Turkey from very early times, having come originally from Persia. Some bulbs made their way to Holland in renaissance times. The Dutch, fascinated by the possibilities in the flower, developed and created many varieties, some of which made their way back to Turkey, and began the tulip craze here.

Up the stairs at the end of the **Tulip Garden** are two of the most enchanting kiosks. Sultan Murat IV (1623-1640) built the **Revan Köşkü**, or Erivan Kiosk, in 1635 after reclaiming the city of Erivan (now in the Soviet Union) from Persia. He also constructed the **Bağdat Köşkü**, Baghdad

Kiosk, in 1638 to commemorate his victory over that city. Notice the İznik tiles, the inlaid and woodwork, and the views from all around.

Just off the open terrace with the wishing well is the **Şunnet Odası**, or Circumcision Room, used for the ritual which admits Muslim boys to manhood. Circumcision is usually performed at the age of nine or ten. Be sure to admire the beautiful tile panels.

Re-enter the Third Court for a look at yet another set of wonders, the **Holy Relics**. On the north-west side of the Third Court are more exhibition rooms. You can sometimes see the Imperial Baldachin, a tent-like shelter of incredibly heavy embroidered cloth. It was the sultan's audience chamber when on military campaign.

Baghdad Kiosk

But the most impressive exhibits are in the **Hırka-i Saadet** suite, the suite of the Felicitous Cloak. These rooms, sumptuously decorated with İznik faience, constituted a Holy of Holy of Holies, in a way. Only the chosen could enter the Third Court, but entry into the Hırka-i Saadet rooms was only for the chosen of the chosen on special ceremonial occasions. For in these rooms reside the cloak of the Prophet Muhammed himself, his battle standard, two of his swords, a hair from his beard, a tooth, his footprint, and a letter in his own handwriting.

The **Felicitous Cloak** itself resides in a golden casket in a special alcove along with the battle standard. This suite of rooms was opened only once a year so that the imperial family could pay homage to the memory of the Prophet on the fifteenth day of the Holy month of Ramazan. Even though anyone, prince or commoner, faithful or infidel, can enter the rooms now, you're supposed to acknowledge the sacred atmosphere by reverent behavior.

Other exhibits in the Third Court include another little library (*Kütüphane*), the mosque of the eunuchs (**Ağalar Camii**), miniature paintings, imperial seals, and arms. These exhibits are sometimes moved around, or closed to make room for special exhibits. In the room with the seals, notice the graceful, elaborate *tuğra* or monogram of the sultans. The tuğra (TOO-rah) was at the top of any imperial proclamation. It actually contains elaborate calligraphic rendering of the names of the sultan and his father. The formula is like this: 'Abdül Hamid Khan, son of Abdül Mecid Khan, Ever Victorious'.

Imperial Stables Enter the Imperial Stables (*Has Ahırları*) from the Second Court, just to the north-east of the main entrance (Ortakapı). Go down the cobbled slope.

The stables are now a museum for the carriages, saddles and other horse-related gear used by the sultans. The usual collection of gold-encrusted coaches, diamond-studded bridles, etc fill the rooms. One gets the impression that the Imperial Lifestyle was at least soft, even though it had its complications.

As you leave the palace proper through the Ortakapı, you can walk to your right and down the slope to the museums (see below), or straight to Sancta Sophia. I'll assume, for the moment, that you're heading to Sancta Sophia.

Just after you leave the tall gate of the Court of the Janissaries, take a look at the ornate little structure on your left. It's the **Fountain of Ahmet III**, the one who liked tulips so much. Built in 1728, it replaced a Byzantine one at the same spring. No water these days, though.

The ornate gate across the road from the fountain was where the Sultan would enter Sancta Sophia for his prayers. It led to a special elevated Imperial Pavilion inside, which you will see. The electric doorbell wasn't the sultan's idea.

Sancta Sophia
The Church of the Holy Wisdom (*Hagia Sofia* in Greek, *Ayasofya* in Turkish) was not named for a saint. Emperor Justinian (527-565) had it built as yet another effort to restore the greatness of the Roman Empire. It was completed in 548, and reigned as the greatest church in Christendom until the conquest of Constantinople in 1453. St Peter's in Rome is larger than Sancta Sophia, but it was built more than a thousand years later.

A lot can happen to a building in 1400 years, especially in an earthquake zone, and a lot has certainly happened to Sancta Sophia. But it is still a wonder and a joy to behold. Ignore the clutter of buttresses and supports, kiosks and tombs and outbuildings which hug its massive walls. Try to see the church as it was meant to be seen by its creators.

You can no longer approach the church exactly as a Byzantine would, walking along a street which lead up a hill and straight to the great main door, but you

Sancta Sophia

can come close. Enter on the side by
Sultanahmet, through what was the Forum
of Augustus (now it's where the buses
park).

Sancta Sophia is open daily except
Mondays, 9.30 am to 5 pm and to 7 pm in
July and August. Entrance to the floor
costs about 40c; to the galleries where the
mosaics are, another 30c (the galleries are
closed for renovations at this writing).

Now, to recapture the feeling that
Justinian had when he first entered his
great creation, walk down to the main
entrance and stop. Here are the sunken
ruins of a Theodosian church (404-415),
and the low original steps.

If you enter the church slowly, one step
at a time you will at first see only darkness
broken by the brilliant colours of stained-
glass windows. As your eyes adjust to the
dark, two more massive doorways appear,
and far beyond them in the dim light, a
semi-dome, blazing with gold mosaics
portraying the Madonna and Child, she as

Queen of Heaven. Just inside the threshold
of the first door, the mosaic is clear and
beautiful, and the apse beneath it makes a
harmonius whole. From where you are
standing now, the mosaic above the third
and largest door, of Christ as Pantocrator
(Ruler of the World), is visible except for
the august expression on the face.

As you approach, the face of the
Pantocrator becomes visible, and you can
also see the apse and lofty semi-dome
above it, which, big as they are, are
dwarfed by by a gigantic dome above
them. At the same time, you are facing the
Pantocrator in all his majesty.

When you walk through the second
door, and toward the immense Imperial
Door the 'gigantic dome' turns out to be
another semi-dome. Halfway to the
Imperial Door, a row of windows peeks out
above the larger semi-dome, and betrays
the secret. As you approach the Imperial
Threshold, the magnificent dome soars
above you like the vault of heaven itself,

and seems to be held up by nothing. Justinian, when he entered his great creation for the first time, came this far and exclaimed, 'Glory to God that I have been judged worthy of such a work. Oh Solomon! I have outdone you!'

During its years as a church (almost a thousand), only imperial processions were permitted to enter through the central, Imperial Door. You can still notice the depressions in the stone by each door just inside the threshold where imperial guards stood.

It was through the Imperial Door that Mehmet the Conqueror rode his horse in 1453 to take possession for Islam of the greatest religious edifice in the world. It remained a mosque for almost 500 years. In 1935, Atatürk proclaimed it a museum. The wisdom in this decision is apparent when you consider that both devout Muslims and Christians would like to have it as a place of worship for their religion.

There are bigger buildings, and also bigger domes, but not without modern construction materials such as reinforced concrete, and steel girders. The achievement of the architects, Anthemius of Tralles and Isidorus of Miletus, is unequalled. The dome, constructed of special hollow bricks made in Rhodes of a unique light, porous clay, was a daring attempt at the impossible. Indeed, it almost was impossible, because the dome lasted only eleven years before an earthquake brought it down (559). Over the centuries it was necessary for succeeding Byzantine emperors and Ottoman sultans to rebuild the dome several times, to add buttresses and other supports, and to steady the foundations. The dome is supported by massive pillars incorporated into the walls. In order to appreciate how this works compare it with the Blue Mosque.

For an acoustic thrill, stand right beneath the centre of the dome and clap your hands.

The Ottoman chandeliers, hanging low above the floor, combined their light with the rows and rows of little oil lamps which lined the balustrades of the gallery and even the walkway at the base of the dome. When all were lit, it must have been an impressive sight.

Justinian ordered the most precious materials for his church. Note the matched marble panels in the walls, the breccia columns. The Byzantine emperor was crowned at the square in the floor, where the large circle with several small circles inside is. The nearby choir gallery is an Ottoman addition, as is the *mihrab*, or prayer niche, which shows the Faithful the direction in which Mecca lies. The large alabaster urns were added by Sultan Murat III (1574-1595) as a place where worshippers could perform their ritual ablutions before prayer. The large medallions inscribed with gilt Arabic letters were added in the 1600s. Calligraphy is a highly-prized art in Islam, and these were done by one of the greatest calligraphers of the 1600s. You'll see these words over and over in Turkish mosques. They are the names of God (*Allah*), Muhammed, and the early caliphs Ali and Abu Bakr.

The curious elevated kiosk, screened from public view, is the **Hünkar Mahfili,** or Sultan's Loge. Ahmet III (1703-1730) had it built so he could come and go unseen.

If you wander around enough, you'll come to the 'weeping column'. A copper facing with a hole in it has been put on a column (to the left after you enter through the Imperial Door). Stick your finger in the hole and make a wish. Legend has it that if the tip of your finger emerges damp, you're supposed to get your wish. Wet or dry, you'll feel slightly silly, but none the worse for that.

Mosaics Justinian filled his church with gorgeous mosaics. The Byzantine church and state later went through a fierce civil war (726-787) over the question of whether images were to be allowed or not. (The debated Biblical passage was Exodus 20:4, 'Thou shalt not make unto thee any graven image, or any likeness of anything

Top: Istanbul as seen from the Süleymaniye minaret
Bottom: Dolmabahçe Palace

Top: The rooftops of the Covered Bazaar
Bottom: Fishing skiffs on the Bosphorus at sunset

that is in heaven above, or that is in the earth beneath, or that is in the water under the earth: Thou shalt not bow down thyself to them, nor serve them ... ') Though the Bible seems clear, the people liked images a lot, and so the iconoclasts ('image-breakers') were defeated.

But when the Turks took Constantinople, there was no controversy. The Koran repeatedly rails against idolatry, as in Sura 16: 'We sent a Messenger into every nation saying, "Serve God and give up idols." Consequently Islamic art is supposed to have no saints' portraits, no pictures of animals, fish or fowl, nor anything else with an immortal soul, and the mosaics had to go. Luckily, they were covered with plaster rather than destroyed. In the 1950s, the American Association for the Preservation of Byzantine Monuments lent the money and expertise to begin restoration of the mosaics. The work is still going on.

From the floor of Sancta Sophia you can see several saints' portraits high up in the semi-circles of the side walls. But the best are in the galleries, reached by a switchback ramp which starts at the northern end of the narthex. The galleries are closed at the time of this writing, but there are plans to open them later.

Some of the work, though partially lost, is superb. Be sure to go all the way to the far ends of the galleries. At the apse end of the south (right-hand) gallery are portraits of emperors, with a difference. The Empress Zoe (1028-1050), for instance, had three husbands. When her portrait was put here in mosaic, her husband was Romanus III Argyrus, but he died in 1034. So when she married Michael IV in that year, she had Romanus's portrait taken out and Michael's put in. But Michael didn't last that long either, and in 1042 his portrait was removed to make way for that of Constantine IX Monomachus. Constantine outlived Zoe, and so it is his portrait that you see today. The inscription reads, 'Constantine, by the Divine Christ, Faithful King of the Romans'.

Leave the galleries. Pass all the way through the corridor-like narthex, and through the door at the end of it. Then turn and look up. Above the door is one of the church's finest mosaics, a Madonna and Child; on the left, Constantine the Great offers her the city of Constantinople; on the right, Justinian offers Sancta Sophia.

A few more steps and you're out of the museum. The fountain to the right was for Muslim ablutions. Immediately to your left is the church's baptistry, converted after the conquest to a tomb for sultans Mustafa and Ibrahim. Other tombs are clustered behind it: those of Murat III, Selim II, Mehmet III, and various princes. By the way, the minarets were added by Mehmet the Conqueror (1451-1481), Beyazit II (1481-1512), and Selim II (1566-1574).

Across the road to the left (east) of the park with the fountain, is a *hammam*, or Turkish bath, now fixed up as a museum. Good Muslims perform ritual ablutions before saying the five daily prayers, which makes cleanliness a tenet of the religion. On Friday, the holy day, it's looked upon as especially good to take a steam bath. Every mosque has a steam bath nearby. This was the one for Sancta Sophia.

Set into Sancta Sophia's enclosing fence, directly across the road from the Turkish bath, is a *sebil*. You'll recognize it as a little cafe, with an ornate kiosk, sidewalk tables and chairs. A sebil was a place where sweet spring water and other refreshing drinks were sold. This one has just been adapted for modern ways. You'll see many others scattered throughout the Old City, mostly closed up, though.

The Blue Mosque

There used to be palaces where the Blue Mosque now stands. The Byzantine emperors built several of them, from near Sancta Sophia, stretching all the way to the site of the mosque. You can see a mosaic from one of these places in the Mosaic Museum (described below).

Sultan Ahmet I (1603-1617) set out to build a mosque that would rival, and even surpass, the achievement of Justinian. He succeeded, but only in part. The *Sultan Ahmet Camii* (Mosque of Sultan Ahmet), or Blue Mosque, is a triumph of harmony, proportion and elegance. But it comes nowhere near the technical achievements of Sancta Sophia.

The mosque is best appreciated if entered, as at Sancta Sophia, by the main gate, slowly. But in this case you can do it right. Don't just walk across the park between the two structures, and in the side door. Rather, go out to the At Meydanı, the Hippodrome, and approach the mosque from the front.

The Blue Mosque is the only one in Turkey with six minarets. When it was built, the sacred mosque of the Kaaba in Mecca had six, and another had to be added so that it would not be outdone. Walk toward the mosque, through the outer gate (the hanging chains prevented men from riding in on horseback). As you walk up the steps to the courtyard door, you will see the domes of the Blue Mosque rise heavenward, one after the other. The effect is marvellous.

The layout of the Blue Mosque is the standard Ottoman design as it evolved over the centuries. The forecourt contains an ablutions fountain in its centre. The portico around three sides could be used for prayer, meditation or study during good weather.

The Blue Mosque is such a popular tourist sight that worshippers were in danger of being lost in the tourist crowds. So you'll be asked to enter from a side door, not through the main door. Turn left, walk through the side gate, then turn right. At the side door, an attendant will take your shoes; if your clothing is unpresentable, he'll lend you a robe to wear while you see the mosque. There's no charge for this, but you may be asked for a donation to the mosque. The money will actually go to the mosque.

Though the stained glass windows are replacements, they still create the marvellous coloured effects of the originals. The semi-domes and the dome are painted in graceful arabesques. The 'blue' of the mosque's name comes from the İznik tiles which line the walls, particularly in the gallery (which is not open to the public). You'll be able to get up close to equally beautiful tiles in the *Rüstem Paşa Camii*, (described below).

You can see immediately why the Blue Mosque, constructed in 1609-1616, over a thousand years after Sancta Sophia, is not as great an architectural triumph as Sancta Sophia. Although the four massive pillars which hold up the dome don't detract from the mosque's breathtaking beauty, they show what an impressive achievement Sancta Sophia is, by showing what's usually needed to hold up a massive dome.

Other things to notice: the imperial loge, covered with marble latticework, to the left; the piece of the sacred Black Stone from the Kaaba in Mecca, embedded in the mihrab; the grandfather clock, to be sure the Faithful know the exact times of the five-times-daily prayers; the elaborate, high chair (*mahfil*) from which the *imam*, or teacher, gives the sermon on Friday; and the *mimber*, or pulpit. The mimber is the structure with a curtained doorway at floor level, a flight of steps, and a small kiosk topped by a spire. This one is particularly notable because of its fine carving (it's all marble), and because it was from here that the destruction of the Janissary corps was proclaimed in 1826 (see above under 'Topkapı').

Mosques built by the great and powerful usually included numerous public service institutions. Clustered around the Sultan Ahmet Camii were a *medrese*, or theological school; an *imaret*, or soup kitchen serving the poor; a *hamam*, or Turkish bath so that the Faithful could wash on Friday, the holy day; and shops, the rent from which went to support the upkeep of the mosque. The tomb of the mosque's great patron, Sultan Ahmet I, is here as well. Buried with Ahmet are his brothers, Sultan Osman II and Sultan Murat IV.

The Textile Museum Parts of the Blue Mosque have been turned into a textile museum officially called the Museum of Kilims and Flat-Woven Rugs (*Kilim ve Düz Dokuma Yaygılar Müzesi*). The cellars, entered from the north side (toward Sancta Sophia), are where you buy your ticket (9 am to 5 pm; closed Monday; about 15c).

On the way into the cellars, you may see a woven nomad's tent, pitched and ready. This was the setting in which many of the kilims were made and used.

Inside the building are impressive stone-vaulted chambers. Huge kilims are stretched on boards, with descriptive tags written in Turkish and English.

Other exhibits are housed upstairs in the Carpet Museum, **Halı Müzesi**, at the end of the stone ramp which you can see from the side door where you entered the mosque. The ramp was for the sultans. They could ride their nobly caparisoned steeds right up and into the shelter of the mosque, dismount, and walk to their loge in safety and imperial privacy.

Turkish oriental carpets are among the finest works of art. The collection here provides a look at some of the best examples.

The Mosaic Museum

Before the Blue Mosque was built, its site was occupied by the palaces of the Byzantine emperors. The Roman art of mosaic work moved, with most other Roman traditions, to Byzantium, and so the palace floors were covered in this beautiful artwork.

Though the palaces have long since disappeared, you can see some of the mosaics, in place, by visiting the **Mozaik Müzesi** (Mosaic Museum), open from 9.30 am to 5 pm, closed Mondays and Tuesdays; admission about 10c; half-price on weekends and holidays.

The museum is directly behind the Blue Mosque at 22 Torun Sokak (follow the signs).

When archaeologists from the University of Ankara and the University of St Andrew's (in Scotland) dug here in the mid-1950s, they uncovered a mosaic pavement dating from early Byzantine times, about 500 AD. The pavement, filled with wonderful scenes of hunting, mythology, and emperors' portraits, was a triumphal way which led from the palace down to the harbour of Boucoleon. Fifteen hundred years' worth of dust and rubble have sunk the pavement considerably below ground level.

Other mosaics in the museum were saved, providentially, when Sultan Ahmet had shops built on top of them. The shops, originally intended to provide rent revenues for the upkeep of the mosque, have been restored, and they still serve to protect these 5th century mosaics.

The Hippodrome

Here was the centre of Byzantium's life for a thousand years, and of Ottoman life for another four hundred. The Hippodrome (*At Meydanı*, 'Horse Grounds' in Turkish) was the scene of countless political and military dramas during the long life of this city. In Byzantine times, the rival chariot teams of 'Greens' and 'Blues' were politically connected. Support for a team was the same as membership in a political party, and a team victory had important effects on policy. A Byzantine emperor might lose his throne as the result of a post-match riot.

Ottoman sultans kept an eye on activities in the Hippodrome. If things were going badly in the empire, a surly crowd gathering here could signal the start of a disturbance, then a riot, then a revolution. In 1826, the slaughter of the debased and unruly Janissary corps was carried out by the reformer-sultan, Mahmut II. Almost a century later, in 1909, there were riots here which caused the downfall of Abdülhamid II and the re-promulgation of the Ottoman constitution.

Though the Hippodrome might be the scene of their downfall, Byzantine emperors and Ottoman sultans outdid one another in beautifying it. Many of the priceless statues carved by ancient masters have disappeared. The soldiers of the Fourth Crusade sacked Constantinople (a Christian ally city!) in 1204, tearing all the bronze plates from the magnificent stone obelisk at the Hippodrome's southern end, in the mistaken belief that they were gold. The crusaders also stole the famous 'quadriga', or team of four horses cast in bronze, which now sits atop the main door to Saint Mark's Church in Venice.

Near the northern end, the little gazebo done in beautiful stonework is actually a fountain (no longer working). Kaiser Wilhelm II of Germany paid a state visit to Abdülhamid II in 1901, and presented this fountain to the sultan and his people as a little token of friendship. According to the Ottoman inscription, the fountain was built in the Hijri (Muslim) year of 1316 (1898/1899 to us). The monograms in the stonework are those of the Ottoman sultan and the German emperor.

The impressive granite obelisk carved with hieroglyphs is called the **Obelisk of Theodosius**, and was carved in Egypt around 1500 BC. According to the hieroglyphs, it was erected in Heliopolis (now a suburb of Cairo) to commemorate the victories of Thutmose III (1504-1450 BC). The Byzantine emperor Theodosius had it brought from Egypt to Constantinople in 390 AD. He then had it erected on a marble pedestal engraved with scenes of himself in the midst of various imperial pastimes. Theodosius's marble billboards have weathered badly over the centuries. The magnificent obelisk, spaced above the pedestal by four bronze blocks, is as crisply-cut and as shiny-bright as when it was cut from the rock in Egypt.

Many obelisks were transported over the centuries to Paris (Place de la Concorde), and London (Cleopatra's Needle), New York, Rome and Florence. A few still remain in Egypt as well.

South of the obelisk is a strange spiral column coming up out of a hole in the ground. It was once much taller, and was topped by three serpents' heads. Originally cast to commemorate a victory of the Hellenic confederation over the Persians, it had stood in front of the temple of Apollo at Delphi from 478 BC, until Constantine the Great had it brought to his new capital city about 330 AD. Though badly bashed up in the Byzantine struggle over the place of images in the church (Iconoclastic Controversy), the serpents' heads survived until the early 1700s. Now all that remains of them is one upper jaw, in the Archaeological Museum.

The level of the Hippodrome rose over the centuries, as civilization piled up its dust and refuse here. The obelisk and serpentine column were cleaned out and tidied up by the English troops who occupied the city after the Ottoman defeat in World War I.

No one is quite sure who built the large rough-stone obelisk at the southern end of the Hippodrome. All we know is that it was repaired by Constantine VII Porphyrogenetus (913-959), and that the bronze plates were ripped off by the Fourth Crusaders.

İbrahim Paşa Sarayı

The Palace of İbrahim Paşa (1524) is on the western side of the Hippodrome. Recently reopened after lengthy restorations, it gives you a glimpse into the opulent life of the Ottoman upper class in the time of Süleyman the Magnificent. İbrahim Paşa was Süleyman's close friend, son-in-law, and Grand Vezir. He was enormously wealthy and so powerful that the sultan finally had him murdered. Roxelana, Süleyman's wife, had convinced the sultan that İbrahim was a rival and a threat.

The buildings behind and beside İbrahim Paşa's palace are Istanbul's law courts, and legal administration buildings.

'Little' Sancta Sophia

This southern end of the Hippodrome is artificially supported by a system of brick arches called the Sphendoneh. Take a detour into Istanbul's lively little back streets for a look at this Byzantine feat of engineering. While you're down there, you can visit the little old Byzantine Church of SS. Sergius and Bacchus (now called the Little Sancta Sophia Mosque, *Küçük Aya Sofya Camii*), and also the Sokollu Mehmet Paşa Camii (mosque).

Facing south, with the Blue Mosque on your left, go to the end of the Hippodrome and turn left, then right, onto Aksakal Sokak. Soon you'll be able to recognize the filled-in arches of the Byzantine Sphendoneh on your right. Follow the curve around to the right and onto Kaleci Sokak. The next intersecting street is Mehmet Paşa Sokak; turn left, and the Küçük Aya Sofya Camii is right there.

If the mosque is not open, just hang around, or signal to a boy on the street, and someone will come with the key.

Justinian and Theodora built this little church sometime between 527 and 536. Inside, the layout and decor are typical of an early Byzantine church, though the building was repaired and expanded several times during its life as a mosque, after the conquest of Constantinople in 1453.

Repairs and enlargements to convert the church to a mosque were added by the Chief White Eunuch Hüseyin Ağa around 1500. His tomb is to the left as you enter.

Go north on Mehmet Paşa Sokak, back up the hill, to the neighbouring mosque of **Sokollu Mehmet Paşa.** This one was built during the height of Ottoman architectural development (1571) by the empire's greatest architect, Mimar Sinan. Though named for the Grand Vezir of the time, it was really built by his wife Esmahan, daughter of Sultan Selim II. Besides its architectural harmony, typical of Sinan's great works, the mosque is unique because the *medrese*, or religious school, is actually

part of the mosque structure, built around the forecourt.

Walk back up the hill on Suterazisi Sokak to get back to the Hippodrome.

Yerebatan Saray

Cross the main road, Divan Yolu, from the Hippodrome. On the north side of the street is a little park with a curious stone tower rising from it. The tower is part of an ancient aqueduct, a segment of this timeless city's elaborate water system. Beneath the park, entered by a little doorway on its north side (on Hilaliahmer Caddesi) is the **Cistern Basilica.**

This 'Sunken Palace' (its Turkish name) is actually a grand Byzantine cistern, 70 metres wide and 140 metres long. The roof is held up by 336 columns. It was built by Justinian the Great (527-565), who was incapable of thinking in small terms.

The city is positively mined with similar cisterns. Many have been discovered, some still hide in the basements of modern construction, still others remain to be discovered.

Gülhane Park & Sublime Porte

Walk down the hill from Yerebatan Saray, along the main street called Alemdar Caddesi. Sancta Sophia will be on your right. Just past a big tree in the middle of the road, the road turns left, but right before you is the arched gateway to Gülhane Park.

Before entering the park peer through the tangle of buses and crowds, looking to your left. That bulbous little kiosk built into the park walls at the next street corner is the **Alay Köşkü,** or 'Parade Kiosk', from whence the sultan would watch the periodic parades of troops and tradesmen's guilds which would commemorate great holidays and military victories.

Across the street from the Alay Köşkü (not quite visible right from the Gülhane gate) is a gate to the Sublime Porte. The gate, not very sublime these days, leads into the precincts of what was once the

Grand Vezirate, or Prime Ministry, of the Ottoman Empire. Westerners called the Ottoman prime ministry the 'Sublime Porte' because of a phrase in Ottoman official documents: 'The Ambassador of (wherever) having come to my Sublime Porte . . . '

In Islamic societies, and in other societies with strong clan roots, it was customary for the chief or ruler to adjudicate disputes and grant favours. To petition the leader, you went to his tent, or house, or palace, stood at the door (hence 'porte'), and waited for a chance to lay it on him. When a western ambassador arrived at the sultan's 'sublime porte', he was looked on as just another petitioner asking favours. In later centuries, ambassadors reported not to the palace but to the Grand Vezirate, which was thus thought to be the Sublime Porte.

Saudi Arabia apparently still carries on the custom, and any Saudi subject, from street sweeper to money magnate, supposedly has the right to a personal hearing by the monarch.

Inside the gates of Gülhane you'll find a shady park, once part of the Topkapı Palace grounds, and a small zoo. There's a minuscule admission charge to enter the park proper.

The Museum Complex

Istanbul's major collection of 'serious' museums is right between Gülhane and Topkapı. As you pass beneath the arched gateway from Alemdar Caddesi, bear right and walk up the slope along a cobbled road, which then turns to the right. After the turn you'll see a gate on the left. Within the gate are the **Archaeological Museum**, the **Çinili Köşk**, and the **Museum of the Ancient Orient**.

You can also reach the museum complex from Topkapı. As you come out the Ortakapı from the palace, walk into the Court of the Janissaries, then turn right and walk down the hill before you get to the Church of St Irene.

The museum complex is open from 9 to 5 every day in summer, closed Mondays off-season. Admission to the complex is about 50c; half-price on Saturday, Sunday, and holidays; 75c for a camera.

These were the palace collections, formed during the 19th century and added to greatly during the republic. While not immediately as dazzling as Topkapı, they contain an incredible wealth of artefacts from the fifty centuries of Anatolia's history.

The **Archaeological Museum** houses a vast collection of statues, sarcophagi, mosaics, coins and jewellery. One of the most beautiful sarcophagi was once thought to be that of Alexander the Great. Today that theory is not held.

Across the court from the Archaeological Museum is the **Çinili Köşk**, or Tiled Kiosk, of Sultan Mehmet the Conqueror. Though once completely covered in fine tilework, you'll see tiles only on the facade these days. Mehmet II had this built not long after the conquest (1472), which makes it the oldest surviving non-religious Turkish building in Istanbul. It now houses an excellent collection of Turkish faience, appropriately enough. You'll see many good examples of fine İznik (Nicaea) tiles from the period in the 1600s and 1700s when that city produced the finest coloured tiles in the world.

Last of the museums in the complex is the **Eski Şark Eserler Müzesi**, or Museum of the Ancient Orient. Go here for a glimpse at the gates of ancient Babylon in the time of Nebuchadnezzar II (604-562 BC), for clay tablets bearing Hammurabi's famous law code (in cuneiform, of course), ancient Egyptian scarabs, and artefacts from the Assyrian and Hittite empires.

Divan Yolu

The main thoroughfare of the Old City stretches between the gate named Topkapı and the palace named Topkapı. Starting from the Hippodrome and Yerebatan Saray, it heads due west, up one of Istanbul's seven hills, past the Grand Bazaar, through Beyazıt Square and the university, to Aksaray Square. Turning north a bit, it continues to the Topkapı (Cannon Gate) in the ancient city walls. In its progress through the city, its name changes from Divan Yolu to Yeniçeriler Caddesi, Ordu Caddesi, Millet Caddesi. At the eastern end, near the Hippodrome, it's Divan Yolu, the Road to the Imperial Council.

The street dates from the early times of Constantinople. Roman engineers laid it out to connect with the great Roman roads heading west. The great milestone from which all distances were measured was right near the tall shaft of stones which rises above Yerebatan Saray. The street held its importance in Ottoman times, as Mehmet the Conqueror's first palace was in Beyazıt Square, and his new one, Topkapı, was under construction.

If you start from Sancta Sophia and the Hippodrome and walk up the slope on Divan Yolu you will see the little **Mosque of Firuz Ağa**, chief treasurer to Beyazit II (1481-1512) on the left. It was built in 1491, in the simple style of the early Ottomans: a dome on a square base, with a simple porch out front. This is the style the Ottomans brought with them from the East or borrowed from the Seljuk Turks. It changed greatly after they conquered Istanbul, inspected Sancta Sophia, and put the great architect Mimar Sinan to work.

Just behind the little mosque of Firuz Ağa are the ruins of the **Palace of Antiochus** (400s), not much to look at these days.

The first major intersection on the right is with Babiali Caddesi. Turn right here and after walking a block you'll be in **Cağaloğlu Square**, once the centre of Istanbul's newspaper publishing. Most of the publishers have moved to large, modern buildings outside the walls. The **Cağaloğlu Hamamı**, a Turkish bath, is just off the square, on the right.

If instead you turn left (south) from Divan Yolu, you'll be on **Klodfarer Caddesi** (not a German word, but a Frenchman's name: Claude Farrere). It leads to a large open area beneath which lies the Byzantine cistern now called **Binbirdirek**, 'A Thousand-and-One Columns'. You'll see the little doorway to the stairs. If the door is locked, call to a child, who will find the guard. Not as large as Yerebatan Saray, Binbirdirek is still very impressive, if a bit neglected these days.

Back on Divan Yolu, the impressive enclosure right at the corner of Babiali Caddesi is filled with tombs of the Ottoman high and mighty. First to be built here was the *türbe*, or mausoleum, of Sultan Mahmut II (1808-1839), the reforming emperor who got rid of the Janissaries and revamped the Ottoman army. After Mahmut, other notables chose to be buried here, including sultans Abdülaziz (1861-1876) and Abdül Hamid II (1876-1909).

Right across Divan Yolu from the tombs is a small stone library built by the Köprülü family in 1659. The Köprülüs rose to prominence in the mid-1600s, furnished the empire with an outstanding succession of Grand Vezirs, generals and Grand Admirals for centuries. They basically ran the empire during a time when the scions of the Ottoman dynasty did not live up to the standards of Mehmet the Conqueror and Süleyman the Magnificent.

Stroll a bit further along Divan Yolu. On the left, the curious *türbe* with wrought iron grillwork on top is that of Köprülü Mehmet Paşa (1575-1661). Across the street, that strange building with a row of streetfront shops is actually an ancient Turkish bath, the **Çemberlitaş Hamamı** (1580).

The derelict, time-worn column rising from a little plaza is one of Istanbul's most ancient and revered monuments. Called **Çemberlitaş** ('The Banded Stone'), or the Burnt Column, it was erected by Constantine the Great (324-337) to celebrate the dedication of Constantinople as capital of the Roman Empire in 330. This area was the grand Forum of Constantine, and the column was topped by a statue of the great emperor himself. In an earthquake zone erecting columns can be a risky business. This one has survived, though it needed iron bands for support within a century after it was built. The statue crashed to the ground almost a thousand years ago.

The little mosque nearby is that of Atik Ali Paşa, a eunuch and Grand Vezir of Beyazıt II.

The Grand Bazaar

Istanbul's *Kapalı Çarşı* ('Covered Market'), the Grand Bazaar – four thousand shops, several kilometres of streets, mosques, banks, police stations, restaurants and workshops.

Starting from a small *bedesten*, or warehouse, the bazaar grew to cover a vast area as neighbouring shopkeepers decided to put up roofs and porches so that commerce could be conducted comfortably in all weather. Great men built *hans*, or caravanserais, at the edges of the bazaar so that caravans could bring wealth from all parts of the empire, unload and trade right in the bazaar's precincts. Finally, a system of locked gates and doors was provided so that the entire mini-city could be closed up tight at the end of the business day.

Though tourist shops are multiplying in the bazaar, it is still a place where an *Istanbullu* (citizen of Istanbul) will come to buy a few metres of printed cloth, a gold bangle for a daughter's birthday gift, an antique carpet, or a fluffy sheepskin.

Whether you want to buy or not, you should see the bazaar. Turn right off Divan Yolu at the Çemberlitaş and walk down Vezir Hanı Caddesi. The big mosque before you is the **Nuruosmaniye** ('Light of Osman'), built between 1748 and 1755 by Mahmut I and his successor Osman III, in the style known as Ottoman Baroque. It's one of the earliest examples of the style.

Turn left through the mosque gate. The courtyard of the mosque is peaceful and green, but with a constant flow of pedestrian traffic heading through it, to and from the bazaar.

Out the other side of the courtyard, you're standing in Çarşıkapı Sokak, Bazaar Gate Street, and before you is one of several doorways into the bazaar. The glorious gold emblem above the doorway is the Ottoman armourial emblem with the sultan's *tuğra* (monogram). While you're here, you might want to see an interesting little street behind the Nuruosmaniye Mosque. If you turn right after leaving the mosque courtyard, then right again, you'll be on **Kılıççılar Sokak**, Swordmakers' Street. The dingy workshops on both sides of the street have fiery forges in the rear. They no longer make swords here, except the miniature ones to be used as letter-openers. Most of the metalwork is brass souvenirs. Once you've taken a look, head back to the doorway with the Ottoman arms above it.

Inside the bazaar, the street you're on is called **Kalpakçılarbaşı Caddesi**. It's the closest thing the bazaar has to a main street. Most of the bazaar is down to your right in the maze of tiny streets and alleys, though you will want to take a left turn up the steps and into the **Kürkçüler Çarşısı**, the Bazaar of the Furriers.

Street names refer to trades and crafts: Jewellers' Street, Pearl-Merchants' Street, Fez-Makers' Street. Though many trades have died out, moved on, or been replaced, there are several areas which you should see. The **Sandal Bedesteni** is the municipal auction hall and pawn shop – take a stroll through. **Kuyumcular Sokak**, the second street on the right as you walk along Kalpakçılarbaşı Caddesi, is Jewellers' Street, aglitter with tons of gold and gems. The Furriers' Bazaar, mentioned above, now houses shops selling leather clothing and other goods, but it's still an interesting corner of the bazaar.

You should of course have a look in the **Old Bedesten** at the centre of the bazaar. This is sometimes called the Cevahir Bedesteni (Jewellery Warehouse), or Old

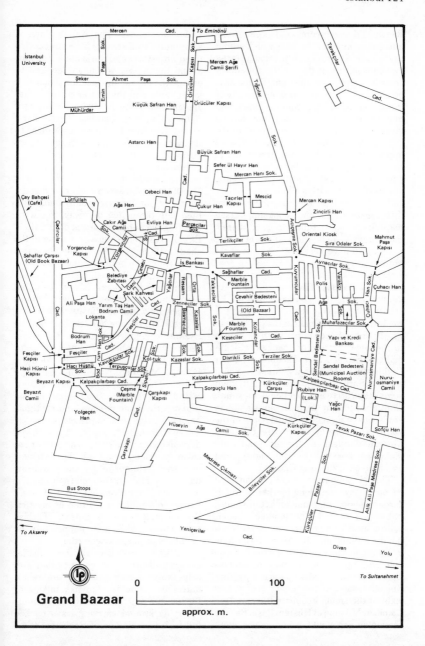

Grand Bazaar

0   100

approx. m.

Bazaar. I'd also recommend explorations into one or more of the hans which adjoin the bazaar. A particularly pretty one is the **Zincirli Han**; it's at the far (north) end of Jewellers' Street, on the right. By the way, no one will mind if you wander into any of these hans for a look around. In fact, you may be invited to rest your feet, have a glass of tea, and exchange a few words.

Don't let the touts get to you. They'll approach you on the main streets and in the tourist-shop areas, but in the bazaar's hans and interesting little back streets, you won't meet with a single one.

The bazaar has numerous inexpensive little restaurants and cookshops (see map). If you need a full restaurant, there's the *Havuzlu Lokantası*; but the little places also have very tasty food at rock-bottom prices.

Uzunçarşı Caddesi There is another very interesting route you can follow by starting from within the bazaar. Near the western end of Kalpakcılarbaşı Caddesi, Sipahi Sokak heads north, changes names to become Feraceciler Sokak (Cloak-makers' Street), then becomes Yağcılar Caddesi (Oil Merchants' Street). You'll see the Şark Kahvesi on your left, then some steps up to a *mescit* (small mosque). Continue straight on, past shops and han entrances to Örücüler Kapısı, Gate of the Darners. Cross a main street named Mercan Caddesi (to the left) and Çak-makçılar Yokuşu (to the right), and continue on Uzunçarşı Caddesi.

This, 'Longmarket Street', is just what its name says: one long market of wood-turners' shops, clog-makers' cubbyholes, bakeries for *simit* (the toasted circular rolls coated with sesame seeds), second-hand clothing merchants, and the like. Follow it all the way down the hill and you will end up in the market district in Eminönü, near the **Mısır Çarşısı** (Egyptian Spice Bazaar) and the Galata Bridge, and right at the small, exquisite **Rüstem Paşa Camii**, or Mosque of Rüstem Paşa. See the section on Eminönü for more information.

Çadırcılar Caddesi The Kapalı Çarşı is surrounded by dozens of little streets also filled with stores and workshops. For your actual purchases, you might do well to escape the bazaar and look for shops with lower rents and thus lower prices. Chief among these, and fascinating in its own right, is Çadırcılar Caddesi, Tentmakers' Street. Exit from the bazaar by walking to the west end of Kalpakçılarbaşı Caddesi. Once outside, turn right, and you'll be on Çadırcılar.

The Old Book Bazaar Just after leaving the bazaar, if you turn right onto Çadırcılar, then left through a doorway, you'll be entering the **Sahaflar Çarşısı**, or Old Book Bazaar. Go up the steps and along to the shady little courtyard. Actually, the wares in the shops are both new and old. Of the new, most are in Turkish. Of the old, many are in other languages. It's unlikely that you'll uncover any treasures here, but you can certainly find a curiosity or two.

The book bazaar here dates from the Byzantine Empire. Many of the book-sellers are members of a dervish order called the *Halveti* after its founder, Hazreti Mehmed Nureddin-i Cerrahi-i Halveti. Their *sema*, or religious ceremony, includes chanting from the Koran, praying, rhythmic dancing and rhythmic breathing to the accompaniment of classical Turkish liturgical music. As with all dervish orders, the *sema* is an attempt at close knowledge of God. The Mevlevi dervishes attempt it by their whirling dance, the Halveti through their circular dance and hyperventilation. But don't expect to wander into a den of mystics. What you'll see are normal Turkish booksellers, who just happen to be members of this dervish order.

Out the north gate of the Sahaflar Çarşısı is a pretty tea-garden filled with cafe tables under colourful umbrellas, university students studying, talking or flirting, and waiters in traditional costume scurrying around carrying trays packed full with tiny glasses of fresh tea. It's a good place for a rest. If you want tea, just signal the waiter when you see him with a full tray. For a soft drink, order anytime.

Beyazıt & Istanbul University

The aforementioned tea-garden is right next to the **Beyazıt Camii**, or Mosque of Sultan Beyazıt II (1481-1512). Beyazıt used an exceptional amount of fine stone in his mosque, which he had built in 1501-1506 on a plan similar to that for Sancta Sophia, but smaller. It's well worth a look.

The main street here, which started out as Divan Yolu, is now called Yeniçeriler Caddesi. It runs past Beyazıt Square, officially called Hürriyet Meydanı (Freedom Square), though everyone knows it simply as Beyazıt. The plaza is backed by the impressive portal of Istanbul University.

Under the Byzantines, this was the largest of the city's many forums, the **Forum of Theodosius**, built by that emperor in 393. Mehmet the Conqueror built his first palace here, a wooden structure which burnt down centuries ago. After Mehmet built Topkapı, he used his wooden palace as a home for aging harem women.

The grand gates, main building and tall tower of the university were originally built as the Ottoman War Ministry, which explains why they are so grandiose and somewhat martial. You used to be allowed up into the tower, which is no doubt still used as a fire lookout post.

Laleli & Aksaray

As you continue west along the main street, now named Ordu Caddesi (Army, or 'Horde', Avenue), notice the huge broken marble columns decorated with peacock-tail designs, on the left-hand side of the roadway. These were part of the decoration in the Forum of Theodosius. There was a monumental arch hereabouts.

A bit further along, on the right, are more university buildings, and beyond them the hotel district of Laleli. Stay on

Ordu Caddesi and you'll soon come to the **Laleli Camii**, an Ottoman baroque mosque built (1759-1763) by Sultan Mustafa III. The ornate baroque architecture houses a sumptuous interior. Underneath it are shops and a plaza with fountain. These were partly to produce rent for the upkeep of the mosque, partly to show off the architect's skill and cunning.

Continue down the hill on Ordu Caddesi and you will enter the confused clamour of Aksaray Square, where there's nothing particularly interesting to see or do. The **Valide Camii** on the square's north-west side is, well, very highly ornamented to say the least. It does not date from any great period of Ottoman architecture, having been built in 1871 by the Valide Sultan Pertevniyal, mother of Sultan Abdülaziz. It used to be attractive, in a way, because it looked like a white wedding cake among the dull, normal structures of Aksaray, but now – with all the exhaust fumes – it's not even white anymore, and traffic flyovers block a good, full view.

Şehzadebaşı & Süleymaniye

The Süleymaniye Camii, or Mosque of Sultan Süleyman the Magnificent, is Istanbul's largest. A few blocks south-west of it, on the other side of the 4th-century **Aqueduct of Valens**, is the pretty Şehzade Camii. To the west is the quaint old Municipal Museum. To get to the Süleymaniye from Beyazıt Square, walk around the university. The mosque is directly north of (behind) the university enclosure. Facing the university portal in Beyazıt, go to the left along Takvimhane Caddesi.

The Süleymaniye crowns one of Istanbul's hills, dominating the Golden Horn and providing a magnificent landmark for all of the city. This, the grandest of all Turkish mosques, had to be built between 1550 and 1557 by the greatest, richest, and most powerful of Ottoman sultans, Süleyman I (1520-1566), 'The Magnificent'. The Turks call this sultan *Kanuni*, 'The Lawgiver', and remember him more for

Süleymaniye Mosque

his codification of the empire's laws than for his magnificent style.

Süleyman was a great builder, who restored the mighty walls of Jerusalem (an Ottoman city since 1516) and built countless other monuments throughout his empire. He was the patron of Mimar Sinan, Turkey's greatest architect. Though the smaller Selimiye Camii in Edirne is generally counted as Sinan's masterpiece, the Süleymaniye is without doubt his grandest work.

Ottoman imperial mosques were instrumental in repopulating the capital after its conquest. In 1453, much of the city had been abandoned, the Byzantine population had shrunk, and huge areas were vacant or derelict. When a sultan built an imperial mosque, it quickly became the centre of a new quarter. Residences and workshops were soon built nearby.

Each imperial mosque had a *külliye*, or collection of public-service institutions, clustered around it. These might include a hospital, insane asylum, orphanage, soup kitchen, hospice for travellers, religious school, library, baths, and a cemetery in which the mosque's imperial patron, his family and other notables could be buried. The *külliye* of the Süleymaniye is particularly elaborate, and includes all of these institutions. Those are the impressive buildings you see surrounding the mosque.

Unfortunately, most visitors enter the mosque precincts by a side door. Though this is the most convenient entrance, coming from Beyazıt, the effect of entering from the north-west side and seeing the four towering minarets and the enormous, billowing domes is better.

Inside, the mosque is breathtaking in its size, and pleasing in its simplicity. There is little in the way of decoration, except for some very fine İznik tiles in the *mihrab* (prayer niche), gorgeous stained glass windows done by one Ibrahim the

Drunkard, and four massive columns, one from Baalbek, one from Alexandria, and two from Byzantine palaces in Istanbul. The painted arabesques on the dome are 19th-century additions, recently renewed.

At the south-east wall of the mosque is the cemetery. Ask for the caretaker (*bekçi*, BEHK-chee) so you can see the tombs (*türbeler*, tewr-beh-LEHR) of Süleyman and his wife Haseki Hürrem Sultan (known in the west as Roxelana), and his architect, the great Mimar Sinan (MEE-mahr see-NAHN). The tombs are high-points of rich, high Ottoman decoration. The İznik tiles in Hürrem's tomb are particularly fine.

By the time you visit, the collections of the Turkish and Islamic Arts Museum may have been moved from the old *imaret* (soup kitchen) on the front, north-west side of the mosque, to the İbrahim Paşa Sarayı on the Hippodrome. Mimar Sinan's tomb is outside the enclosure of the mosque proper, at an intersection of streets just by the north corner of the enclosure.

Aqueduct of Valens Walk along Süleymaniye Caddesi, which goes south-west from the mosque, and turn right on Kovacılar Caddesi. You can see remnants of the high Aqueduct of Valens (*Bozdoğan Kemeri* in Turkish) on the left side of the street. It's not really certain that the aqueduct was constructed by the emperor Valens (364-378), though we do know it was repaired in 1019, and by several sultans in later times. After the reign of Süleyman the Magnificent, parts of it collapsed.

Şehzade Camii On the south side of the aqueduct is the Şehzade Camii, the Mosque of the Prince. Süleyman had it built in 1544-1548 as a memorial to his son Mehmet, who died in 1543. It was the first important work of Mimar Sinan. Among the many important people buried in tile-encrusted türbes here are Prince Mehmet, his brothers and sisters, and Süleyman's Grand Vezirs Rüstem Paşa and İbrahim Paşa.

Municipal Museum If you have a few minutes left, walk west on Şehzadebaşı Caddesi. The dusty modern building on the left is Istanbul's City Hall, or *Belediye Sarayı*. Turn right and pass under the aqueduct, then take your life in your hands and cross Atatürk Bulvarı. Just on the other side of the street is the former *medrese* (religious school) of Gazanfer Ağa (1599), now the **Belediye Müzesi**, or Municipal Museum. It has an odd and eclectic assortment of city memorabilia which you might find interesting.

EMİNÖNÜ

No doubt you've already seen Eminönü. The view of the Galata Bridge, crowded with ferries and dominated by the *Yeni Cami* (YEHN-NEE jahm-mee, 'New Mosque') is a favourite for advertisements and magazine articles about Istanbul. The Yeni Cami sits comfortably and serenely in the midst of bustling Eminönü as the traffic, both vehicular and pedestrian, swirl around it. Anyone who visits Istanbul finds themselves passing through Eminönü time after time.

In a way, Eminönü is the inner city's transportation hub. Not only do the Bosphorus ferries dock here, not only does all Galata Bridge traffic pass through, but Sirkeci Railway Station is just around the corner.

Galata Bridge This dusty bridge may not be very impressive at first glance, but after a little exploration it appears as a microcosm of Istanbul; full of little unexpected suprises.

First of all, the entire bridge is *floating* on pontoons. This is so that the centre section can be removed to allow larger ships to enter the Golden Horn and reach its shipyards. The central section of the bridge, unlatched and driven by small motors, is floated out and to the side each morning at 4.30 am. For a half-hour ships can steam out, then for another half-hour ships can steam in. At 5.30 the centre section is floated back into place.

Underneath the bridge are small fish restaurants which get their provisions directly from the fishmongers who approach the bridge in boats. Itinerant peddlars sell fishing tackle so you can try your luck in the murky waters. There's even a teahouse where you can get tea, Turkish coffee, soft drinks, or a bubbling *nargile* (NAHR-gee-leh, waterpipe).

In Byzantine times, the Golden Horn provided a perfect natural harbour for the city's commerce. Suppliers of fresh vegetables and fruits, grain and staple goods set up shop in the harbour. Today their successors still perform the same services, in the same place: west of the Galata Bridge in Eminönü are Istanbul's *Haller* (hahl-LEHR, from the French *halle*), wholesale vegetable, fruit and fish markets.

Even more picturesque and interesting is the retail market district which surrounds the *Mısır Çarşısı* (MUH-suhr chahr-shuh-suh, the Egyptian, or Spice Bazaar). But before wandering into the maze of market streets, take a look inside the Mosque of the Valide Sultan (1663), the *Yeni Cami*.

Yeni Cami This imperial mosque was begun in 1597, commissioned by Valide Sultan Safiye, the Queen Mother (of Sultan Mehmet III, 1595-1603). The site was earlier occupied by a community of Karaite Jews, radical dissenters from orthodox Judaism. When the Valide Sultan decided to build her grand mosque here, the community was moved to Hasköy, a district further up the Golden Horn, which still bears traces of the Karaite presence.

The Valide Sultan lost her august position when her son the sultan died, and the mosque had to be completed (1663) six sultans later by Valide Sultan Turhan Hatice, mother of Sultan Mehmet IV (1648-1687).

In plan, the Yeni Cami is much like

Istanbul's other imperial mosques which you've seen: the Sultan Ahmet (Blue) mosque, and the Süleymaniye, with a large forecourt and a square sanctuary surmounted by a series of half-domes crowned by a grand dome. The interior is richly decorated with gold, coloured tiles, and carved marble. The mosque and its tiles are 'late', past the period when Ottoman architecture was at its peak. The tilemakers of İznik were turning out slightly inferior products by the late 1600s. Compare these tiles to the ones in the Rüstem Paşa Camii (described below), which are from the high period of İznik tilework.

Mısır Çarşısı (Egyptian Bazaar)

A century or two ago, this fascinating place was twice as fascinating. Its merchants sold such things as cinnamon, gunpowder, rabbit fat, pine gum, peach pit powder, sesame seeds, sarsaparilla root, aloe, saffron, licorice root, donkey's milk, and parsley seeds, all to be used as folk remedies.

Gunpowder, for instance, was prescribed as a remedy for haemorrhoids: you'd boil a little gunpowder with the juice of a whole lemon, strain off the liquid, dry the powder, and swallow it the next morning, with a little water, on an empty stomach. It was also supposed to be a good cure for pimples when mixed with a little crushed garlic. Whatever its values as a pharmaceutical, it was finally banned from the market because the shops in which it was sold kept blowing up.

The market was constructed in the 1660s as part of the Yeni Cami complex, the rents from the shops going to support the upkeep of the mosque and its charitable activities. These included a school, baths, a hospital and public fountains.

Enter the market through the big armoured doors which open onto Eminönü Square. Just inside the doors, to the left, is the little stairway which leads up to the Pandeli restaurant (see the Places to Eat section). Strolling through the market, you can still see numerous shops which sell *baharat* (bah-hah-RAHT, spices), and even a few which specialize in the old-time remedies. Some of the hottest items are bee pollen and royal jelly, used to restore virility. But you'll see also shops selling nuts, candied fruits, chocolate and other snacks. Try some figs (*incir* een-JEER) or Turkish Delight (*lokum* low-KOOM). Fruit pressed into sheets and dried is called *pestil* (pehs-TEEL); often made from apricots (*kayısı*) or mulberries (*dut*), it's delicious and relatively cheap. Buy 50 grams (*elli gram*) or 100 grams (*yüz gram*) to start.

When you come to the crossroads within the market, you have a choice. I'd suggest you turn left, see the rest of the market, then return to the crossroads and take the street to the right.

Turning left will reveal the rest of the market. Many of the shops on this street no longer sell spices or baskets, but instead are packed with toys, clothing and various household goods. You may see a shop which specializes in the white outfits little boys wear on the day of their circumcision (*sünnet*). The white suit is supplemented with a pillbox hat and a red sash which bears the word *Maşallah* (MAH-shah-lah, 'What wonders God has willed!'). When you see a little kid in such an outfit, you'll know that today he's going to get his. He will probably be riding around in the midst of musicians and merrymakers, for a boy's circumcision (at age eight to 10 or so) is his coming of age and an excuse for a tremendous party.

Turn left again at the first opportunity, and you'll leave the bazaar and enter its busy courtyard, backed by the Yeni Cami. This is the city's major market for flowers, plants, seeds and songbirds. There's a WC to your left, down the stairs. To the right, across the courtyard, is the *türbe* (tomb) of Valide Sultan Turhan Hatice, founder of the Yeni Cami. Buried with her are no less than six other sultans, including her son Mehmet IV, plus dozens of imperial princes and princesses.

Now, back at that crossroads within the bazaar, take the right turning and exit through another set of armoured doors. Men especially should watch out for the iron posts set in the doorway, put there to prevent carts from entering. These posts are difficult to see in the press of a crowd, and have resulted in more than one case of emasculation.

Just outside the doors is another crossroads of bustling market streets. You can always smell coffee here, because right across the intersection is the shop of Kurukahveci Mehmet Efendi. Clerks wrap customer's parcels with lightning speed (they take great pride in this), and there always seems to be a line waiting to make a purchase. To the right, down toward the Golden Horn, is a small fish market with a few butchers' shops thrown in for good measure. Up to the left, the shops and street peddlars sell mostly household and kitchen items.

Head out the bazaar doors and straight across the intersection. This is **Hasırcılar Caddesi**, Street of the Mat Makers. Shops along it sell fresh fruits, spices, nuts, condiments, knives and other cutlery, coffee, tea and cocoa, hardware and similar retail necessities. The colours, smells, sights and sounds make this one of the liveliest and most interesting streets in the city.

A few short blocks along Hasırcılar Caddesi, on the right-hand side, you'll come to the **Rüstem Paşa Camii**. Keep your eyes peeled – it's easy to miss as it is not at street level. All you'll see is a tidy stone doorway and a flight of steps leading up; there is also a small marble fountain, and a marble plaque.

This mosque is used heavily by the merchants and artisans of the bazaar. As with most mosques, you should not visit during prayer-time, so if the müezzin has just given the call to prayer, come back in half an hour.

At the top of the steps is an open space, and the mosque's colonnaded porch. You'll notice at once the panels of dazzling

İznik faience set into the mosque's facade. The interior is covered in similarly gorgeous tiles, so take off your shoes (and women should cover heads and shoulders), and venture inside.

This mosque is particularly beautiful. It was built by Sinan, the greatest Ottoman architect, for Rüstem Paşa, son-in-law and Grand Vezir of Süleyman the Magnificent. Ottoman power and glory, Ottoman architecture and tilework were all at their zenith when the mosque was built (1561). You won't forget this one.

After your visit to the mosque, you might want to spend some more time wandering the streets of this fascinating market quarter. If you need a goal, head up the hill (south) on Uzunçarşı Caddesi, which begins right near the Rüstem Paşa Camii and ends at the Kapalı Çarşı (Grand Bazaar; see that section for more details).

THE OUTER CITY

From early times, the heart of this ancient city has been near the tip of Seraglio Point. But as the city grew over the centuries, its boundaries moved westward. That process continues.

There are several points of interest farther out, and if you have at least four days to tour the city, you should be able to see all the essential sights in the centre and still have time for these very impressive ones farther out. They include the mosque of Mehmet the Conqueror, the Kariye Camii (Church of the Holy Saviour in Chora) famous for its Byzantine mosaics, the Palace of Constantine Porphyrogenetus (*Tekfur Saray* in Turkish), several other mosques, the mammoth City Walls, including the Fortress of the Seven Towers, and the village of Eyüp, up the Golden Horn. On you way back downtown, you can stop at the Ecumenical Orthodox Patriarchate and also at a curious Bulgarian church made of cast iron.

A detour to *Yedikule* The Fortress of the Seven Towers, is described at the end of this section.

Fatih Camii

The Mosque of Mehmet the Conqueror, or Fatih Camii is just west of the Aqueduct of Valens, on Fevzi Paşa Caddesi. You can get a dolmuş from Aksaray or Taksim to the City Hall right near the Aqueduct (ask for the *Belediye Sarayı* behl-eh-DEE-yeh sar-rah-yuh) and walk five blocks; or you can catch any bus that has 'Fatih' or 'Edirnekapı' listed on its itinerary board. Buses and trolleybuses going to Edirnekapı pass frequently through Sultanahmet Square.

When Mehmet the Conqueror entered Constantinople in 1453, he found a city depopulated and shrunken in size living within the walls of a once-great city. Large tracts of urban land had reverted to grass and shrubs, and many buildings were in ruins. He sought to repopulate the city with groups from the various nations of his empire, sometimes commanding that they move to Istanbul. A prime method of repopulating a district was to commission the construction of an imperial mosque there. The mosque would become the nucleus of a city quarter, first providing work for construction crews and the merchants and peddlars who served them, then providing a focus of religious and social life. The mosque's *külliye* or complex of charitable buildings such as a hospital, orphanage, soup kitchen, library, bath, insane asylum, etc, would also encourage people to move to the quarter.

The Mosque of the Conqueror was the first great imperial mosque to be built in Istanbul following the conquest. For its site, Fatih Sultan Mehmet (Mehmet the Conqueror) chose the hilltop site of the ruined Church of the Apostles. The mosque complex, finished in 1470, was enormous, and included in its külliye fifteen charitable establishments – religious schools, a hospice for travellers, a caravanserai, etc. But the mosque you see is not the one he built. The original mosque stood for three hundred years before toppling in an earthquake (1766). It was rebuilt, but to a completely

Top: The walls of Ancient Troy
Left: A latter-day Trojan Horse in Troy
Right: The minaret of the Green Mosque in İznik

Top: A burst cannon and a commemorative mural in Çanakkale (Dardanelles)
Bottom: A caravanserai courtyard in Bursa

different plan. The exterior of the mosque still bears some of the mosque's original decoration; the interior is not all that impressive.

While you're here, be sure to visit the türbe (tomb) of Mehmet the Conqueror behind the mosque. His wife Gülbahar, whose türbe is right next to the sultan's, is rumoured to have been a French princess.

When you're finished at the mosque, go back to Fevzi Paşa Caddesi and catch a bus or dolmuş headed north-west toward Edirnekapı. Get off the bus just before the massive city walls. You'll see the Mihrimah Camii, a mosque built by Süleyman the Magnificent's favourite daughter, Mihrimah, in the 1560s. The architect was Sinan, and the mosque marks a departure from his usual style. The inevitable earthquakes worked their inevitable destruction, and the building has been restored several times, the latest being around 1900. Mihrimah married Rüstem Paşa, Süleyman's brilliant and powerful Grand Vezir (you saw his little tile-covered mosque down by the Mısır Çarşısı). You can visit her tomb, and his too, on the south-east side of the mosque.

Take a look at the walls (you can hardly help it!). You'll get a closer look, and even a climb up top, in a little while.

Cross the road from the Mihrimah Camii and, still inside the walls, head north toward the Golden Horn. You'll see signs, and children pointing the way, to the Kariye Camii.

Kariye Camii Mosaics
If we translate the original name for this building, it comes out 'Church of the Holy Saviour Outside the Walls', or 'in the Country', because the original church on this site was indeed outside the walls built by Constantine the Great. But just as London's Church of St Martin in-the-Fields is hardly surrounded by bucolic

Kariye Camii

scenery these days, the Church of the Holy Saviour was soon engulfed by Byzantine urban sprawl. It was enclosed within the walls built by the Emperor Theodosius II in 413, less than a hundred years after Constantine. So the Holy Saviour-in-the-Country has been 'in the country' for about 80 years, and 'in the city' for 1,550 years. The evolution of the church has not ended with its whereabouts: for four centuries it served as a mosque, coming to rest, at last notice, as a museum.

The building you see is not the original church-outside-the-walls. Rather, this one was built in the late 1000s, with lots of repairs and restructuring in the following centuries. Virtually all of the interior decoration – the famous mosaics and the less renowned but equally striking mural paintings – dates from about 1320. Between 1948 and 1959, the decoration was carefully restored under the auspices of the Byzantine Society of America.

The mosaics are breathtaking. There is a definite order to the arrangement of the pictures. The first ones are those of the dedication, to Christ and to the Virgin Mary. Then come the offertory ones: Theodore Metochites, builder of the church, offering it to Christ. The two small domes of the Inner Narthex have portraits of all Christ's ancestors, back to Adam. There's a series outlining the life of the Virgin Mary, and another outlining Christ's early years. Yet another series concentrates on Christ's ministry. There are lots of saints and martyrs everywhere.

In the nave are three mosaics: of Christ, of the Virgin as Teacher, and of the Dormition of the Virgin (turn around to see this one – it's over the main door you just entered). By the way, the baby in the painting is actually Mary's soul, being held by Jesus, while her body lies 'asleep' on its bier.

South of the nave is the Parecclesion, a side chapel also used for the tombs of the church's founder, his relatives, close friends and associates. The frescoes,

appropriately, deal with the theme of death and resurrection. The striking painting in the apse shows Christ breaking down the gates of Hell, raising Adam and Eve, with saints and kings in attendance.

Tekfur Saray

From Kariye, head west to the city walls, then north again, and you'll soon come to the Palace of Constantine Porphyrogenetus, the *Tekfur Saray* (tehk-FOOR sar-rah-yee). Though the building is only a shell these days, it is remarkably preserved for a Byzantine palace built in the 1300s. Sacred buildings often survive the ravages of time because they continue to be used, even though they may be converted for use in another religion. But secular buildings are often torn down and used as quarries for building materials once their owners die. The Byzantine palaces which once crowded Sultanahmet Square are all gone; the great Palace of Blachernae, which adjoined the Tekfur Saray, is gone. Only this one remains.

The caretaker will usually haul out a ladder for you, and you can climb up onto the walls for a view of the palace, the walls, and the entire city. A small tip is proper once you descend.

The City Walls

Since being built in the 400s, the city walls have been breached by hostile forces only twice. The first was in the 1200s, when Byzantium's 'allies', the armies of the Fourth Crusade, broke through and pillaged the town, deposing the emperor and setting up a king of their own. The second was in 1453 under the Mehmet the Conqueror. Even though Mehmet was ultimately successful, he was continually frustrated during the siege as the walls withstood admirably even the heaviest bombardments by the largest cannon in existence at the time. The walls were kept defensible and in good repair until about a century ago, when the development of mighty naval guns made such expense pointless: if Istanbul was going to fall, it would fall to ships firing from the Bosphorus, not to soldiers advancing on the land walls.

For a look at the most spectacular of the defenses in the walls, see *Yedikule* (Fortress of the Seven Towers), below.

At this point, you've seen the high points in this part of the city. But if you've still got time and stamina, take your bearings for these places while you're still up on the walls: outside the walls, on the Golden Horn (which looks anything but golden from this vantage point), is the suburb of Eyüp, with a famous mosque and a famous coffee-house. Inside the walls, near the Golden Horn but back toward the centre, is the *Rum Patrikhanesi*, the seat of the Ecumenical Patriarch of the Orthodox Church. You can't see this, but you'll notice the prominent cupola of a Greek school near it.

Eyüp

This suburb, once a village outside the walls, is named for the standard-bearer of the Prophet Muhammed. Eyüp Ensari (*Ayoub* in Arabic, 'Job' in English) fell in battle here while carrying the banner of Islam during the Arab assault and siege of the city in 674-678. Eyüp had been a friend of the Prophet and a revered member of Islam's early leadership. His tomb is a very sacred place for most Muslims, on a rank (almost) with Mecca, Medina and Jerusalem. Ironically, the tomb even came to be venerated by the Byzantines.

When Mehmet the Conqueror besieged the city in 1453, the tomb was no doubt known to him, and he undertook to build a grander and more fitting structure to commemorate it. But a legend persists that the tomb had been lost, and was miraculously rediscovered by Mehmet's Şeyh-ül-İslam (Supreme Islamic Judge). Perhaps both are true. If the tomb was known to Mehmet Fatih and his leadership, but not generally known by the common soldiers, it could be used for inspiration: have it miraculously 'rediscovered', and

the army would take it as a good omen for the holy war in which they were engaged.

Whatever the truth, the tomb has been a very holy place ever since the Conquest. Mehmet had a mosque built here within five years after the Conquest, and succeeding sultans came to it to be girded with the Sword of Osman, a coronation-like ceremony signifying their supremacy. Levelled by an earthquake in 1766, a new mosque was built on the site by Sultan Selim III in 1800. The Baroque style of the pretty mosque, the tiles, marble, calligraphy and other decoration lavished on it, make this a fine place to see. Be careful to observe the Islamic proprieties when visiting: decent clothing (no shorts), and modest dresses for women, who should also have head, shoulders and arms covered.

As the Eyüp Sultan Camii is such a sacred place, many important people wanted to be buried in its precincts. Many others, particularly the Valide Sultan Mihrişah, mother of Selim III, built important charitable institutions such as schools, baths and soup kitchens.

Pierre Loti Cafe

Up the hill to the north of the mosque is a cafe where 'Pierre Loti' (Louis Marie Julien Viaud, 1850-1923) used to sit and admire the city. Loti's romantic novels about the daily life of Istanbul under the last sultans introduced millions of European readers to Turkish customs and habits. The books, though they romant-icized many subjects and changed them into the sorts of fairy-tales readers wanted, still may have provided a counter-weight to the anti-Turkish propaganda which was (and sometimes still is) broadcast throughout Europe for political purposes.

Loti loved the city, the decadent grandeur of the empire, and the fascinating late-medieval customs of a derelict society in decline. When he sat in this cafe, under a shady grapevine, sipping some *çay* or Turkish coffee, he would have seen a Golden Horn busy with caiques, schooners and a few steam vessels. The water in the Golden Horn was still clean enough for boys to swim in, and the vicinity of the cafe was all pasture land. Not only that, but the cafe owner would have charged him the going rate for his refreshment.

Today it's all different: you pay many times the going rate for a drink, the Golden Horn is not fit to sniff let alone swim in, and buildings crowd the once-bucolic cafe. Still, there is the view. Loti fans will want to come here; others may enjoy the view, but not stay for tea. If you do stay, by all means find out the price of a drink before you sit down and order.

Getting Back to the Centre

There is still ferry service on the Golden Horn, and it will take you from the dock at Eyüp Sultan, not far from the mosque, down to the Galata Bridge at Eminönü. You'll pass shipyards, warehouses, run-down residential and industrial quarters, a government drydock, naval buildings, and the cast-iron Bulgarian church. The trip is no seaborne idyll, mostly because the Golden Horn smells so bad. But it's an adventure.

Otherwise, you can get a bus or dolmuş from Eyüp along the shore of the Golden Horn, or up along the walls and into the city that way. Taking the shore road allows you to stop at the Orthodox Patriarchate, the Mosque of Sultan Selim, and the Bulgarian church, all of which are very interesting sights.

The neighbourhoods along the Golden Horn are picturesque, though pretty rundown; they're not dangerous, just dilapidated.

Balat

The quarter called Balat used to hold a large portion of the city's Jewish population. Spanish Jews driven from their country by the judges of the Spanish Inquisition found refuge in the Ottoman Empire in the late 1400s and early 1500s. As the sultan recognized, they were a boon to his

empire: they brought news of the latest western advances in ballistics and other means of warfare; in medicine; and in clock-making. The refugees from the Inquisition set up the first printing presses in Turkey, almost 500 years ago. Like all other religious 'nations' within the empire, they were under a supreme religious leader, the Chief Rabbi, who oversaw their adherence to Biblical law and who was responsible to the sultan for their good conduct.

Though you can still find a few traces of Jewish life in this quarter, such as inscriptions in Hebrew over doorways, most of the city's Jewish residents have long since moved to more attractive quarters, or emigrated to Europe or Israel. There is still a newspaper published in Ladino Spanish, the language brought by the immigrants in Renaissance times and preserved here in Istanbul.

Church of St Stephen

The Church of St Stephen of the Bulgars, between Balat and Fener on the Golden Horn, is made completely of cast iron. The building is unusual, and its history even more so.

During the 19th century the spirit of ethnic nationalism swept through the Ottoman Empire. Each of the many ethnic groups in the Ottoman Empire wanted to rule its own affairs. Groups identified themselves on the bases of language, religion and racial heritage. This sometimes led to problems, as with the Bulgarians.

The Bulgars, originally a Turkic-speaking people, came from the Volga in about 680 AD and overwhelmed the Slavic peoples living in what is today Bulgaria. They adopted the Slavic language and customs, and founded an empire which threatened the power of Byzantium. In the 800s, they were converted to Christianity.

But the head of the Orthodox church in the Ottoman Empire was an ethnic Greek. In order to retain as much power as possible, the patriarch was opposed to any ethnic divisions within the Orthodox church. He put pressure on the sultan not to allow the Bulgarians, Macedonians and Rumanians to establish their own groups.

But the pressures of nationalism became too great, and the sultan was finally forced to recognize some sort of autonomy for the Bulgars. What he did was to establish not a Bulgarian patriarchate, but an 'exarchate'. The Bulgarian Exarch would be 'less important' than, but independent of, the Greek Orthodox patriarch. In this way, the Bulgarians would get their desired ethnic recognition, and would get out from under the dominance of the Greeks.

St Stephen's is the Bulgarian Exarch's church; the former exarchate headquarters is directly across the street, and still the office of St Stephen's clergy. The Gothic church was cast in Vienna, shipped down the Danube on a hundred barges, and assembled here in 1871. A duplicate church, erected in Vienna, was destroyed by aerial bombing during World War II. The Viennese cast-iron church factory produced no other products, so far as we know.

A number of years ago, St Stephen's was repaired and repainted. The first coat, of course, was metal primer. The whole procedure seemed to fit in well, what with a shipyard on the opposite shore of the Golden Horn.

The priest or sacristan will let you into the church enclosure so you can enjoy the pretty garden, tap a coin on the church wall to verify that it's metal, and admire the interior. Most of the interior decoration is of cast iron as well.

Fener

Next quarter along the Golden Horn is Fener (fehn-EHR, *Phanari* in Greek: lantern or lighthouse), where the Ecumenical Patriarch has his seat. To find the Patriarchate (*patrikhane*, paht-TREEK-hahn-neh), you'll have to head inland from the Fener ferry dock on the Golden Horn, and ask. People will point the way.

Ecumenical Patriarchate

The Ecumenical Patriarch is a ceremonial head of the Orthodox churches, though most of the churches – in Greece, Cyprus, the Soviet Union and other countries – have their own patriarchs who are independent of Istanbul. Nevertheless, the 'sentimental' importance of the patriarchate, here in the city which saw the great era of Byzantine and Orthodox influence, is very great.

These days the patriarch is a Turkish citizen. He is nominated by the church, and appointed by the Turkish government to be an official in the Directorate of Religious Affairs. In this capacity he is the religious leader of the country's Orthodox citizens.

Assuming you don't have any business with the patriarchate, your reason for visiting is to look at the Church of St George, within the patriarchate compound. Like the rest of the buildings here, it is a modest place, built in 1720. The ornate patriarchal throne may date from the last years of Byzantium. The patriarchate itself has been in this spot since about 1600. In 1941 a disastrous fire destroyed many of the buildings, but spared the church.

Selimiye Camii

Only a few blocks south-east of the patriarchate is the mosque of *Yavuz Selim* (Sultan Selim I, 1512-1520), on a hilltop overlooking the Golden Horn. Sultan Selim 'the Grim' laid the foundations of Ottoman greatness for his son and successor, Süleyman the Magnificent. Though he ruled for a very short time, Selim virtually doubled the empire's territory, solidified its institutions, and filled its treasury. He came to power by deposing his father, Beyazıt II (1481-1512), who died 'mysteriously' soon thereafter. To avoid any threat to his power, and thus the sort of disastrous civil war which had torn the empire apart in the days before Mehmet the Conqueror, Selim had all his brothers put to death, and in the eight years of his reign he had eight Grand Vezirs beheaded. So 'Grim' is indeed the word.

But all of this force was in the interests of empire-building, at which he was a master. He doubled the empire's extent during his short reign, conquering part of Persia, and all of Syria and Egypt. He took from Egypt's decadent, defeated Abbasid rulers the title Caliph of Islam, which was borne by his successors until 1924. In his spare time, he liked to write poetry in Persian, the literary language of the time. When he died, the empire was well on the way to becoming the most powerful and brilliant in the world.

The mosque was built mostly during the reign of Selim's son Süleyman. It is especially pretty, with lots of fine, very early İznik tiles (the yellow colour is a clue to their 'earliness'), and a shallow dome similar to that of Sancta Sophia. Selim's türbe, behind the mosque, is also very fine. Among the others buried nearby are several children of Süleyman the Magnificent; and Sultan Abdül Mecit (1839-1861).

To the Galata Bridge You can walk back down the hill to the Fener ferryboat dock, and catch a ferry down to the bridge. They aren't all that frequent, so check the schedule first. Otherwise, catch a bus or dolmuş along the waterfront street, Abdülezel Paşa Caddesi.

Yedikule

The Fortress of the Seven Towers (*Yedikule*) is a long way from most other sights of interest in Istanbul, and involves a special trip. Situated where the great city walls meet the Sea of Marmara, it's accessible by city bus ('Yedikule') from Eminönü, Sultanahmet and Divan Yolu. The ride takes almost a half-hour.

If you arrived in Istanbul by train from Europe, or if you rode in from the airport along the seashore, you've already had a glance of Yedikule towering over the southern approaches to the city.

Theodosius I built a triumphal arch here in the late 300s. When the next Theodosius (408-450) built his great land walls, he incorporated the arch. Four of the fortress's seven towers were built as part of the Emperor Theodosius's walls; the other three, inside the walls, were added by Mehmet the Conqueror. Under the Byzantines, the triumphal arch became known as the Golden Gate, and was used for triumphal state processions into and out of the city. For a time, its gates were indeed plated with gold. The doorway was sealed in the late Byzantine period.

In Ottoman times, the fortress was used for defense, as a repository for the imperial treasury, as a prison, and as a place of execution. Diplomatic practice in Renaissance times included chucking into loathsome prisons the ambassadors of countries with which yours didn't get along. For foreign ambassadors to the Sublime Porte, Yedikule was that prison. It was also here that Sultan Osman II, a seventeen-year-old youth, was executed in 1622 during a revolt of the Janissary corps.

The best view of the city walls and of the fortress is from the Tower of Sultan Ahmet III, near the gate in the city wall.

Beyond the fortress are the city's leather tanning industries. Even in medieval times, the tanners were required to work outside the city walls because their work generated such terrible odours.

Right down at the shoreline, where the land walls meet the Sea of Marmara, is the Marble Tower, once part of a small Byzantine imperial seaside villa.

BEYOĞLU

Often called the New City, Beyoğlu (BEY-oh-loo) is 'new' just in a relative sense. There was a settlement on the northern shore of the Golden Horn, near Karaköy Square, before the birth of Jesus. By the time of Theodosius II (408-450), it was large enough to become an official suburb of Constantinople. Theodosius built a fortress here, no doubt to complete the defense system of his great land walls, and called it *Galata* (gah-LAH-tah), as the suburb was then the home of many Galatians. (The Galatians, by the way, were Gauls who invaded Asia Minor from the west after 300 BC, and settled near Ankara.) During the height of the Byzantine Empire, Galata became a favourite place for foreign trading companies to set up business. To this day, it still harbours the offices of many non-Muslim businessmen and foreign representatives.

The word 'new' actually applies more to Pera, the quarter above Galata, running along the crest of the hill from the Galata Tower to Taksim Square. This was built up only in later Ottoman times. Together, Galata and Pera make up Beyoğlu.

In the 19th century, the European powers were waiting eagerly for the 'Sick Man of Europe' (the decadent Ottoman Empire) to collapse so that they could grab territory and spheres of influence. All the great colonial powers – France, the British Empire, the Russian Empire, the Austro-Hungarian Empire, the German Empire, and the Kingdom of Italy – maintained lavish embassies and tried to cajole and pressure the Sublime Porte into concessions of territory, trade, and influence. The embassy buildings, lavish as ever, still stand in Pera. Ironically, most of the great empires which built them collapsed along with that of the Ottomans. Only the British and French survived to grab any of the spoils. Their occupation of Middle Eastern countries under League of Nations 'mandates' has given us the Middle East we have today.

Beyoğlu is fascinating because it holds the evidence of the Ottoman Empire's frantic attempts to modernize and reform itself; and of the European powers' attempts to undermine and subvert it. The Ottomans were struggling for their very existence as a state; the Europeans were struggling for domination of the entire Middle East, and especially its oil (already important at that time), its holy places, and its sea lanes through the Suez Canal to India.

New ideas walked into Ottoman daily life down the streets of Pera. Europeans brought new fashions, new machines, new arts and manners, and new rules for the diplomatic game, and the Europeans lived in Pera. The Old City across the Golden Horn was content to sit tight and continue living in the Middle Ages with its oriental bazaars, great mosques and palaces, narrow streets, and traditional values. But Pera was to have telephones, underground trains, tramways, electric light, and modern municipal government. Even the sultans got into the act. From the reign of Abdülmecit (1839-1861) onward, no sultan lived in Mehmet the Conqueror's palace at Topkapı. Rather, they built opulent European-style palaces in Pera and along the shores of the Bosphorus to the north.

The easiest way to tour Beyoğlu is to start from its busy nerve-centre: Taksim Square. You can get a dolmuş directly to Taksim from Aksaray or Sirkeci; buses to Taksim are even more plentiful.

Taksim Square

The name could mean 'my taxi' in Turkish, but it doesn't (after a look at the square, you may wonder why not). Rather, it is named after the *taksim* (tahk-SEEM), or distribution point, in the city's water conduit system. The main water line from the Belgrade Forest, north of the city, was laid to this point by Sultan Mahmut I (1730-1754) in 1732, and the branch lines lead from the *taksim* to all parts of the city. You'll get a glance of the *taksim* in a moment.

First thing you'll notice in the elongated 'square' is the Atatürk Cultural Palace (*Atatürk Kültür Sarayı*), sometimes called the Opera House, the large building at the eastern end. In the summertime, during the Istanbul International Festival, tickets for the various concerts are on sale in the ticket kiosks here, and numerous performances are staged in its various halls.

The grassy mall, stretching from the Cultural Palace to the traffic circle, holds a knife-shaped monument to war veterans. To the south is the luxury Etap Marmara Hotel. To the north is the *Taksim Gezi Yeri*, or promenade, with the Istanbul Sheraton at the northern end of it.

In the midst of the roundabout, swirling with traffic, is one of the earliest monuments in the country erected to the Republic and its founders. It was done by an Italian sculptor in 1928. Atatürk, his assistant and successor İsmet İnönü, and other revolutionary leaders are prominent.

From the roundabout, Cumhuriyet Caddesi (Republic Avenue) leads north, past several sidewalk cafes and restaurants, banks, travel agencies, airline offices, nightclubs and the Istanbul Hilton Hotel to the districts called Harbiye and Şişli.

Askeri Müzesi (Military Museum)

A kilometre north of Taksim is the *Askeri Müzesi*, or Military Museum. The small museum, with its exhibits of Ottoman battle dress and relics, is interesting enough. But the best reason to go is for a little concert by the *Mehter*, or Ottoman military band. The Mehter, according to historians, was the first true military band in the world. Its purpose was not to make pretty music for dancing, but to precede the conquering Ottoman pashas into vanquished towns, impressing upon the defeated populace that everything was going to be different now. They would march in with a steady, measured pace, turning all together to face the left side of the line of march, then the right side. With tall Janissary headdresses, fierce moustaches, brilliant instruments, and even kettledrums, they did their job admirably.

The museum is open from 9 am to 5 pm, closed Monday and Tuesday. The Mehter performs each afternoon that the museum is open (if the band is not on tour somewhere) at 3 pm. Check this time at a Tourism Information Office to be sure; there's an office in the Istanbul Hilton Hotel arcade, on the way to the Military Museum.

To reach the museum, walk north out of Taksim Square along Cumhuriyet Caddesi and past the Hilton entrance. Just past the Hilton, on the right side of Cumhuriyet, are the studios of TRT, the Turkish Radio and Television corporation, in a building called Radyo Evi (Radio House). Just past Radyo Evi, turn right. The road curves to the left, passes the Spor ve Sergi Sarayı (Sports and Exhibition Hall), and then the Askeri Müzesi is next, on the left-hand side.

South of Taksim To the south, two streets meet just before the roundabout. Sıraselviler Caddesi goes south, and Istiklal Caddesi goes south-west. The famous *taksim* is to the south-west of the roundabout, just to the right of Istiklal Caddesi. It is a little octagonal building of stone.

Nestled in the little triangle formed by the two mentioned streets, rising above the shops and restaurants which hide its foundations, is the *Aya Triada Kilisesi*, the Greek Orthodox Church of the Holy Trinity. If it's open, as it is often during the day, you can visit: take either street out of Taksim Square, and look for the first possibility to turn toward the church.

Now head down Istiklal Caddesi for a look at the vestiges of 19th-century Ottoman life.

Istiklal Caddesi

Stretching between Taksim Square and Tünel Square, Istiklal Caddesi (ees-teek-LAHL, Independence Avenue) was once known as the Grand Rue de Pera. It was the street with all the smart shops, several large embassies and churches, many impressive office buildings, and a scattering of tea shops and restaurants. Some vignettes of this glory still survive, though Istiklal is now heavy with traffic, and its buildings are cracked and dusty. The smart shops and classy offices have mostly moved farther north. But as you stroll along Istiklal, try to imagine it during its heyday a century ago: frock-coated merchants and Ottoman officials, European officers in colourful uniforms, ladies with parasols, and even some lightly-veiled Turkish ladies.

Just out of Taksim Square, the first building you'll come to on your right is the former French plague hospital (1719), for years used as France's Instanbul Consulate-General. There's a French library here as well.

Istiklal Caddesi is packed with little restaurants and snack shops, bank branches, clothing stores, itinerant pedlars, shoppers and strollers. If you have the time, take a few detours down the narrow sidestreets. Any one will reveal glimpses of Beyoğlu life. The street names alone are fascinating: *Büyükparmakkapı Sokak*, 'The Street of the Gate of the Thumb;' *Sakızağacı Sokak*, 'The Street of the Pine-Gum Tree;' *Kuloğlu Sokak*, 'The Street of the Slave's Son'.

This used to be the cinema centre of Istanbul. With the advent of television, the cinemas found it necessary to appeal to baser appetites, which is what they do now. Baser appetites are also catered for up some of the stairways which lead from the back streets. Though I wouldn't recommend doing a lot of wandering along narrow, dark streets here late at night, the area is perfectly safe during the day and early evening.

A few streets before coming to Galatasaray Square, look on the left for Suterazisi Sokak. Turn into this street, and at its end you'll find the Tarihi Galatasaray Hamamı ('Historical Galatasaray Turkish Bath'). The bath is one of the city's best, with lots of marble decoration, comfy little cubicles for resting and sipping tea after the bath, pretty fountains, and even shoeshine service. However, the staff are very hungry for tips. If you go, you'll enjoy it more if you don't go alone; best of all, go with a Turkish friend. The women's part of the bath, by the way, is not nearly so elegant as the men's.

Galatasaray Square Halfway along the length of Istiklal Caddesi is Galatasaray

(gahl-AH-tah-sah-rah-yee), named for the imperial lycee you can see behind the huge gates on your left. This is the country's most prestigious school, established in its present form by Sultan Abdül Aziz in 1868, who wanted a place where Ottoman youth could hear lectures in both Turkish and French. Across Istiklal from the school is a branch of the PTT (post office).

Çiçek Pasajı But before coming into the square, you'll notice on your right a small street with some flower-sellers' stalls. This is Istanbul's renowned *Çiçek Pasajı* (chee-CHEHK pah-sah-zhuh), or 'Flower Passage'. Besides the flowers, there is a charming market called the *Balık Pazar*, literally the 'fish market', although meats, fruits, vegetables, condiments and kitchen items are sold here as well. You can do a lot of interesting exploring here.

Turn right from Istiklal into the flower-lined street, and then right again into a courtyard. On the lintel of the doorway into the courtyard you can see the legend 'Cite de Pera', for this was at one time the municipal headquarters of the 'modern' European-style city. Today the building is partly in ruins. For years the courtyard has held a dozen little restaurant-taverns. In good weather, beer barrels are rolled out onto the pavement, marble slabs are balanced on top, little stools are put around, and are filled with enthusiastic revellers as soon as they hit the ground. This place is lively and interesting anytime of day, but particularly in the early evening.

Pick a good-looking place, pull up a stool, and order a mug of *bira*: *beyaz* (bey-AHZ) is lager, *siyah* (see-YAH) is dark beer. For something stronger, say *bir kadeh rakı* (BEER kah-deh rah-KUH), 'a shot of rakı'. As for food, it's delicious and not very expensive. Printed menus, even if you can find them, mean little here. If you already know a few Turkish dishes you like, order them. Or, follow the waiter into the kitchen to see what's cooking.

During your supper, strolling musicians will come through (you needn't pay unless you want to, or unless you signal to them that you want a song). Other vendors will pass by with assorted delicacies and treats. A small fight may break out, but will be quickly settled. You may be toasted by the entire multitude. At least three nearby revellers will want to know where you come from; when you tell them, the inevitable response is çok iyi, 'very good!' The Çiçek Pasajı is perhaps the soul of Istanbul, and you shouldn't miss an evening here.

Exploring the Balik Pazar

Walk out of the courtyard to the flower stalls, turn right, then look for a little passage off to the left. This is the *Avrupa Pasajı*, the 'European Passage', a little gallery with marble paving and little shops selling this and that. In Pera's heyday it was undoubtedly very elegant.

Further up the market street, another little street leads off to the left, down to the British Consulate-General (more of that in a moment). Continuing on the same street, though, just past this junction on your right is the entrance to an Armenian church. You can visit if the doors are open; a sacristan will greet you, and will watch to see if you drop a small donation into the box.

Unless you want to continue down the slope among the fishmongers, turn back and then down the little street to the British consulate. You will notice little stands where skewered mussels (*midye*, MEED-yeh) are frying in hot oil, and others where *kokoreç* (koh-koh-RETCH, lamb intestines packed with more lamb intestines) is being grilled over charcoal. I recommend the mussels, but get a skewer that's been freshly cooked, or at least re-cooked.

At the end of the market street you emerge into the light. Right in front of you is Meşrutiyet Caddesi, which makes its way down to the Pera Palas Oteli (see below) and the American Consulate-

General. On the corner here are the huge gates to the British Consulate-General, an Italian palazzo designed by Sir Charles Barry and built in 1845. Sir Charles did the Houses of Parliament as well.

Walk past the British consulate along Meşrutiyet Caddesi. Watch for an iron gate and a small passage on the left, leading into a little courtyard with a derelict lamp-post in the center. Enter the courtyard, turn right up the stairs, and you'll discover the Greek Orthodox Church of Panaya Isodyon. It's quiet and very tidy, hidden away in the midst of other buildings. The doors are open to visitors most of the daytime.

When you've seen the church, go down the stairs *behind* it (not the stairs you came up). Several little streets here are lined with tiny shops, many bearing their Greek proprietors' names. Turn right, and just past the church property on the right-hand side you will see the entrance to the *Yeni Rejans Lokantası*, the 'New Regency Restaurant'. Founded, as legend would have it, by three White Russian dancing girls who fled the Russian Revolution, the restaurant is still operated by their Russian-speaking descendants. This area of Beyoğlu was a favourite with Russian emigres after the revolution. The Yeni Rejans, by the look of it, was a cabaret complete with orchestra loft and grand piano. Lunch and dinner are still served. The food is good, though you pay a certain amount for the seedy nostalgia.

Out the restaurant door, down the steps, turn right, then left along the narrow alley called Olivo Çikmazı, which brings you back to Istiklal Caddesi.

Back on Istiklal Across Istiklal, notice the large Italian Gothic church behind a fence. The Franciscan Church of San Antonio di Padua was founded here in 1725; the brick building dates from 1913.

Cross over to the church, turn right, and head down Istiklal once more. After the church you will pass Eskiçiçekçi Sokak on the left, then Nuriziya Sokak. The third street, a little cul-de-sac, ends at the gates of the *Palais de France*, once the French embassy to the Ottoman sultan. The grounds of the palais are extensive. The buildings include the chapel of St Louis of the French, founded here in 1581, though the present chapel building dates from the 1830s. You can get a better look at the palais and grounds another way: read on.

A few steps along Istiklal brings you to the pretty Netherlands Consulate-General (1855), built by the former architect to the Russian tsar. The first embassy building here dated from 1612.

Past the Dutch consulate, turn left down the hill on Postacılar Sokak. You'll see the Dutch Chapel on the left side of the street. If it's open, take a look inside. The chapel is now the home of the Union Church of Istanbul, a multinational Protestant congregation that holds services in English.

The narrow street jogs right, bringing you face-to-face with the former Spanish embassy. The little chapel, founded in 1670, is still in use though the embassy is not.

The street then jogs left and changes names to become Tomtom Kaptan Sokak. At the foot of the slope, on the right, is the Palazzo di Venezia, once the Venetian embassy, now the Italian consulate. Venice was one of the great Mediterranean maritime powers during Renaissance times, and when Venetian and Ottoman fleets were not madly trading with one another, they were locked in ferocious combat.

To the left across the open space is a side gate to the Palais de France. Peek through the gates for another, better view of the old French embassy grounds. Then you've got to slog back up that hill to Istiklal Caddesi.

Continuing along Istiklal, the Church of St Mary Draperis (1678, 1789) is behind an iron fence and down a flight of steps. It's rarely open to visitors. Past the church, still on the left-hand side, is the

grand Soviet consulate, once the imperial Russian embassy. It is still a busy place as the Soviet Union has a common border with Turkey, and dozens of Soviet ships pass through the Bosphorus and the Dardanelles each day.

Now take a detour: turn right off of Istiklal Caddesi along Asmalı Mescit Sokak, a narrow, typical Beyoğlu street which holds some fusty antique shops, food shops, suspect hotels and little eateries. The street intersects Meşrutiyet Caddesi. To the left of the intersection is the American library and cultural centre, and just beyond it the pretty marble mansion which was first the American embassy, now the Consulate-General. To the right of the intersection is the grand old Pera Palas Oteli (peh-RAH pah-LAHS), the Pera Palace.

Pera Palas Oteli

The Pera Palas was built in the 1890s by Georges Nagelmackers, the Belgian entrepreneur who founded the *Compagnie International des Wagons-Lits et Grands Express Europeens* (1868). Nagelmackers, who had succeeded in linking Paris and Constantinople by luxury train, found that once he got his esteemed passengers to the Ottoman imperial capital there was no suitable place for them to stay. So he built the hotel, here in the section today called Tepebaşı.

It's a grand place, with huge public rooms, a sympathetic bar, a good dining room, and a beautiful birdcage elevator. The guest rooms are enormous – their attached bathrooms are as large as many newer hotels' guest rooms. Once you've taken a turn through the hotel, head back to Istiklal Caddesi.

Crimean Memorial Church

When you reach Istiklal, go straight across it and down the hill on Kumbaracı Yokuşu to reach the Crimean Memorial Church. The Anglican church was built as a memorial to English troops of the Crimean War, and designed by C E Street. Lord

Stratford de Redcliffe, the very influential British ambassador of the time, was instrumental in the church's foundation. The building is not often open to visitors.

Back on Istiklal, you will notice two good bookstores on the left-hand side. *Haşet* (that's *Hachette*) has books, magazines and newspapers in French, English and Turkish; the *Alman Kitabevi* specializes in German books.

Next along the avenue is the Royal Swedish Consulate, once the Swedish embassy, and after that the Four Seasons Restaurant. The road curves to the right; the open space here is known as *Tünel Meydanı*, Tunnel Square.

Tünel

You now have a chance to take a peek at Istanbul's underground railway. Built by French engineers over a century ago (1875), the Tünel provided a means by which the 'modern' citizens of Pera and Galata could negotiate the steep hillside without undue exertion. Up to a few decades ago, the cars were of dark wood with numerous coats of bright lacquer. Signs said, 'It is requested that cigarettes not be smoked'. A modernization program swept away the quaint Swiss-chalet lower station and replaced it with a concrete bunker, and also left us with the present modern rubber-tired French trains, and signs that say 'No Smoking'.

The fare is about that of the bus. Trains run as frequently as necessary during rush hours, about every five or ten minutes other times. Though you may want to use the Tünel later to ascend the hill, right now you should stay on foot. There's a lot to see as you descend slowly toward Karaköy: a whirling dervish convent, the Galata Tower, and fascinating glimpses of Beyoğlu daily life.

Whirling Dervish Convent

Though the main road (Istiklal) bears right as you come into Tünel Square, you should continue walking straight on. The surface turns to paving stones, the street narrows and takes the name of Galip Dede Caddesi, and on your left you'll notice the doorway into the Galata Mevlevi Tekkesi.

The Whirling Dervishes, or *Mevlevi*, took their name from the great Sufi mystic and poet, Jelaleddin Rumi (1207-1273). Rumi was called *Mevlana*, or 'Our Leader', by his disciples. Sufis (Muslim mystics) seek mystical communion with God through various means. For Mevlana, it was through a *sema*, or ceremony, involving chants, prayers, music and a whirling dance. The whirling induced a trance-like state which made it easier for the mystic to 'get close to God'. The Dervish order, founded in Konya during the 1200s, flourished throughout the Ottoman Empire, and survives in Konya even today. The Galata *Mevlevihane* (whirling dervish hall) was open to foreign, non-Muslim visitors, who could witness the *sema*. The dervishes stressed the unity of mankind before God regardless of creed or belief.

Though the dervishes no longer whirl here, you can visit their *tekke* any day except Monday from 9 am to 5 pm; on Sunday and holidays the modest admission charge is even more modest. The dervish orders were banned in the early days of the republic. Though a few still survive unofficially, the hall is now called the Museum of Divan Literature, and holds exhibits of *hattat* (Arabic calligraphy).

The Turks are passionate gardeners, as you'll see when you enter the grounds. In the midst of the city is this oasis of flowers and shady nooks, where you can sit and have a glass of tea. Note the tomb of the sheik, by the entrance passage, and also the *şadırvan* (ablutions fountain).

The modest frame *tekke* was restored in 1967-1972, but the first building here was erected by a high officer in the court of Sultan Beyazıt II in 1491. Its first *şeyh* (sheik, or leader) was *Şeyh Muhammed Şemai Sultan Divani*, a grandson of the great Mevlana. The building burned in 1766, but was repaired that same year by Sultan Mustafa III.

As you approach the building, notice the little graveyard on the left. The stones are very beautiful with their graceful Arabic lettering. The shapes on top of them are those of the hats of the deceased; each hat denotes a different religious rank.

Inside the *tekke*, the central area was where the dervishes whirled. In the galleries above, visitors could sit and watch. Separate areas were set aside for the orchestra, and for female visitors (behind the lattices). Don't neglect the exhibits of calligraphy, writing instruments and other paraphernalia associated with this highly developed Ottoman art.

Galata

Leaving the Whirling Dervish Convent, turn left down Galip Dede Caddesi. The hillside is covered with windy streets, little passageways, alleys of stairs, and European-style houses built mostly in the 19th century. There are some older houses, and if you see them, you'll get a glimpse of what life was like for the European emigres who came to live here and make their fortunes centuries ago. A few minutes' walk along Galip Dede will bring you to Beyoğlu's oldest landmark, the Galata Tower.

Galata Tower

The Galata Tower (*Galata Kulesi*) was the highpoint in the Genoese fortifications of Galata. The tower, rebuilt many times, is ancient. Today it holds an observatory and a restaurant/nightclub. The tower is open to visitors from 10 to 6 every day, for a 50c fee. In the evening, the restaurant, bar and nightclub swing into action.

Daily life in the vicinity of the tower is a fascinating sight. There are woodworking shops, turners' lathes, workshops making veneer and other materials for interior decoration, a few dusty antique stores. This neighbourhood is also one of the last to be inhabited by the city's Spanish-speaking Jewish population. There's a synagogue named Neve Shalom only a

block north-east of the Galata Tower, toward Şişhane Square.

From the Galata Tower, continue downhill on the street called Yüksek Kaldırım to reach Karaköy, once the heart of the Genoese city of Galata.

Karaköy

In order to avoid 'contamination' of their way of life, both the later Byzantine emperors and the Ottoman sultans relegated European traders to Galata. Under the late Byzantines, Genoese traders got such a hold on the town that it was virtually a little Genoa. Though Galata still harbours many shipping and commercial offices, and some large banks, it is also busy with small traders. Approaching the Galata Bridge from Karaköy, the busy ferryboat docks, and also the docks for Mediterranean cruise ships, are to your left. To your right are a few fishmongers' stands, and a warren of little streets filled with hardware stores and plumbing supply houses. Scattered throughout this neighbourhood are Greek and Armenian churches and schools, and a large synagogue, reminders of the time when virtually all of the empire's businessmen were non-Muslims.

At the far end of the square from the Galata Bridge, right at the lower end of Yüksek Kaldırım, Voyvoda Caddesi (also called Bankalar Caddesi) leads up a slope to the right toward Şişhane Square. This street was the banking centre during the days of the empire, and many merchant banks still have headquarters or branches here. The biggest building was that of the Ottoman Bank, now a branch of the Turkish Republic's Central Bank.

Karaköy has busy bus stops, dolmuş queues, and the lower station of the Tünel. To find the Tünel station, descend into the hubbub of the square from Yüksek Kaldırım, and keep to the right. Don't go down the stairs into the pedestrian underpass (subway), squeeze through the narrow passage to the right of the stairway, and then turn right into Tersane

Caddesi. The Tünel is a few steps along, on the right, in what looks like a concrete bunker.

THE BOSPHORUS

The strait which connects the Black Sea and the Marmara, 32 km long, 500 to 3000 metres wide, 50 to 120 metres (average 60 metres) deep, has determined the history not only of Istanbul, but even of the empires governed from this city. In earlier centuries it was one of the city's strongest defenses. Until the age of armoured gunboats, the city was never seriously threatened from the sea.

Greek legend recounts that Zeus, unfaithful to his wife Hera in an affair with Io, tried to make up for it by turning his erstwhile lover into a cow. Hera, for good measure, provided a horsefly to sting Io on the rump and drive her across the strait. In ancient Greek, *bous* is cow, and *poros* is crossing place, giving us Bosphorus: the place where the cow crossed.

In Turkish, the strait is the *Boğaziçi*, from *boğaz*, throat or strait, and *iç*, inside or interior: within the strait.

From the earliest times it has been a maritime road to adventure. It is thought that Ulysses' travels brought him through the Bosphorus. Xenophon, in his *Anabasis*, wrote the history of the ill-fated Greek army of the Ten Thousand who, badly defeated by the Persians, retreated through Anatolia. The end of their tribulations came when they reached the beautiful waters of the Bosphorus.

Byzas, founder of Byzantium, explored these waters before the time of Jesus. Mehmet the Conqueror built two mighty fortresses at the strait's narrowest point so he could close it off to allies of the Byzantines. And each spring, enormous Ottoman armies would take several days to cross the Bosphorus on their way to campaigns in Asia.

At the end of World War I, the defeated Ottoman capital cowered under the guns of Allied frigates anchored in the strait. And when the republic was proclaimed, the last sultan of the Ottoman Empire snuck quietly down to the Bosphorus shore, boarded a launch, and sailed away to exile in a British man-o'-war.

The Bosphorus also provides a convenient boundary for geographers. As it was a military bottleneck, armies marching from the east tended to stop on the eastern side, and those from the west on the western. So the western side was always more like Europe, the eastern more like Asia. Though the modern Turks think of themselves as Europeans, it is still common to say that Europe ends, and Asia begins, at the Bosphorus.

Except for the few occasions when the Bosphorus has frozen solid, crossing it has always meant going by boat – until 1973. Late in that year, the Bosphorus Bridge, fourth longest in the world, was opened to travellers. For the first time in history, there was a firm physical link across the straits from Europe to Asia. (Interestingly, there had been a plan for a bridge during the late years of the Ottoman Empire, but nothing came of it.) Traffic was so heavy over the new bridge that it paid for itself in less than a decade.

How to Tour the Bosphorus

You could spend several days exploring the sights of the Bosphorus. It holds five Ottoman palaces, four castles, the mammoth suburb of Üsküdar, and dozens of interesting little towns. But if you're pressed for time, you can see the main points in a day.

The essential feature of any Bosphorus tour is a cruise along the strait. You just can't appreciate its grandeur and beauty completely if you're in a bus or car. On the other hand, it's time-consuming to take a ferryboat to a certain dock, debark, visit a palace or castle, and return to the dock to wait for the next boat, so a trip combining travel by both land and sea is best.

I've divided the Bosphorus into three regions. First is the European shore very near the city, including the important sights of Dolmabahçe Palace, the Maritime

Museum, and Yıldız Park. Next is the Asian shore near the city, from Haydarpaşa through Üsküdar to Beylerbeyi, including the Asian railway terminal, Çamlıca Hill, and Beylerbeyi Palace. Finally, there is the great length of the Bosphorus north of the bridge, with its castles, villages and verdant slopes, best seen from a boat. For specific boat information, see below under each region.

European Shore, Below the Bridge

Your best bet is to take a bus or dolmuş to reach Dolmabahçe, one km down the hill from Taksim Square. From Taksim, the walk is short and pleasant with views of the Bosphorus and the palace. Walk toward the Cultural Palace. As you stand facing it, the tree-lined, divided street on your right is İnönü Caddesi, formerly called Gümüşsuyu Caddesi. It leads directly to Dolmabahçe. On the right-hand side of İnönü Caddesi, just out of Taksim, you'll see ranks of dolmuşes. Routes are mostly long ones up the European Bosphorus shore, but you may find one going to Beşiktaş/Barbaros Hayrettin Paşa. Take this one to Dolmabahçe if you need to ride.

Coming from other parts of the city, catch a bus that goes via Eminönü and Karaköy to 'B. Hayrettin Paşa'. Any bus heading out of Karaköy along the Bosphorus shore road will take you to Dolmabahçe. Get off at the Kabataş stop. Just north of the stop you will see the Dolmabahçe Camii (mosque), and beyond it the palace.

Dolmabahçe Palace

When you arrive, look for the ornate clock tower between Dolmabahçe Camii and the palace. The gate near the clock tower is the one you enter. The palace is open from 9 to 12 noon and from 1.30 to 4.30 pm, closed Monday and Saturday. Entry costs about 40c; the camera fee is twice as much again. You must take a tour here; it lasts about an hour. Tip the tour leader.

For centuries the *Padişah* (Ottoman

sultan) had been the envy of all other monarchs in the world. Cultured, urbane, sensitive, courageous, controller of vast territories, great wealth, and invincible armies and navies, he was the Grand Turk. The principalities, city-states and small kingdoms of Europe, Africa and the Near East cowered before him, and all stood in fear of a Turkish conquest. Indeed, the Turks conquered all of North Africa, parts of southern Italy, and eastern Europe to the gates of Vienna. The opulent palace of Dolmabahçe might be seen as an apt expression of this Ottoman glory. But it's not.

Dolmabahçe was built in 1840, when the once-mighty Padişah had become 'the Sick Man of Europe'. His many peoples, aroused by a wave of European nationalism, were in revolt; his wealth was mostly mortgaged to, or under the control of, European interests; his armies, while still considerable, were obsolescent and disorganized. The European, western, Christian way of life had triumphed over the Asian, eastern, Muslim one. Attempting to turn the tide, 19th-century sultans 'went European', modernizing the army and civil service, granting autonomy to subject peoples, and adopting – sometimes wholesale – European ways of doing things.

The name *Dolmabahçe*, 'filled-in garden', dates from the reign of Sultan Ahmet I (1607-1617), when a little cove here was filled in and an imperial pleasure kiosk built on it. Other wooden buildings followed, but all burned to the ground in 1814. Sultan Abdülmecit, whose architect was an Armenian named Balyan, wanted a 'European-style' marble palace. What he got is partly European, partly oriental, and certainly sumptuous.

The palace gardens are very pretty. High-stepping guards add a brisk note. The fence along the Bosphorus, and the palace facade, go on for almost half a kilometre. Inside, you'll see opulent public and private rooms, a harem with steel doors, lots of stuff like Sevres vases and Bohemian chandeliers, and also a staircase with a crystal balustrade.

One room was used by Sultan Abdül Aziz (1861-1876), an enormously fat fellow who needed an enormously large bed. You will see just how large.

The magnificent throne room, used in 1877 for the first meeting of the Ottoman Chamber of Deputies, has a chandelier that weighs over 4000 kilograms. The place is awesome.

Don't set your watch by any of the palace clocks, however. They are all stopped at the same time: 9.05. On the morning of November 10, 1938, Kemal Atatürk died in Dolmabahçe. You will be shown the small bedroom which he used during his last days. Each year on November 10, at 9.05 am, Turkey – the entire country – comes to a dead halt in commemoration of the Republic's founder.

Barbaros Hayrettin Paşa

After you've boggled your mind at Dolmabahçe, go back to the vicinity of the clock tower and catch a bus or dolmuş heading north along the palace wall, up the Bosphorus. Your destination is Beşiktaş, now also called Barbaros Hayrettin Paşa. It's not a long walk if you're willing, but the heavy traffic in this corridor between two walls is noisy and smelly. When you emerge from the walls, you'll be in the suburb formerly named Beşiktaş, but now officially called Barbaros Hayrettin Paşa. Most people still call it Beşiktaş.

Naval Museum

The *Deniz Müzesi*, or Naval Museum, is on the Bosphorus shore just south of the flyover in Beşiktaş/Barbaros. Among its exhibits are an outdoor display of cannon and a statue of Barbaros Hayrettin Paşa (1483-1546), the famous Turkish admiral known also as Barbarossa, who conquered North Africa for Süleyman the Magnificent. The admiral's *türbe* (tomb), designed by Sinan, is close by.

Enter the museum from the Bosphorus side. It's open from 9 am to 5 pm, closed Monday and Tuesday. Admission costs about 20c.

Though the Ottoman Empire is most remembered for its conquests on land, its maritime power was equally impressive. During the reign of Süleyman the Magnificent (1520-1566), the eastern Mediterranean was virtually an Ottoman lake. The sultan's navies cut a swath in the Indian Ocean as well. Sea power was instrumental in the conquests of the Aegean coasts and islands, Egypt and North Africa. Discipline, well-organized supply, and good ship design contributed to Ottoman victories. But the navy, like the army and the government, lagged behind the west in modernization during the later centuries. The great battle which broke the spell of Ottoman naval invincibility was fought in 1571 at Lepanto, in the Gulf of Patras off the Greek coast. (Cervantes fought on the Christian side, and was badly wounded.) Though the Turkish fleet was destroyed, the sultan quickly produced another, partly with the help of rich Greek shipowners who were his subjects.

Be sure to see the sleek, swift imperial barges, in which the sultan would shoot up and down the Bosphorus from palace to palace (in those days the roads were not very smooth or very fast). Over 30 metres in length, but only two metres wide, with 13 banks of oars, the barges were obviously the rocket boats of their day. The ones with latticework screens were for the imperial ladies. There's also a war galley with 24 pairs of oars.

You may also be curious to see a copy of the famous Map of Piri Reis, an early Ottoman map (1513) which purports to show the coasts and continents of the New World. It's assumed that Piri Reis ('Captain Piri') got hold of Columbus's work for his map. The original map is in Topkapı; copies of the colourful map are on sale here in the museum.

Top: A driveway to a former mansion in İzmir
Bottom: An antique and carpet shop in Side, Antalya

Top: Ancient columns litter a swimming pool, Pamukkale
Left: Rock tombs at Demre
Right: Distinctive Ottoman gravestone

Yıldız & Çirağan

From the Naval Museum and the flyover in Beşiktaş/Barbaros, you can walk north for ten minutes, or catch a bus or dolmuş heading north along the shore, to reach the entrance to Yıldız Park (bus stop *Yüksek Denizcilik Okulu*). Before you reach the entrance, you'll be passing Çırağan Palace on your right; the ruined palace is hidden from the road by a high wall, though you can get a glimpse of it through its battered gates.

Unsatisfied with the architectural exertions of his predecessor at Dolmabahçe, Sultan Abdül Aziz (1861-1876) had to build his own palace. He built Çırağan on the Bosphorus shore only a kilometre north of Dolmabahçe, replacing an earlier wooden palace. The architect was the selfsame Balyan as for Dolmabahçe. The sultan didn't get to live here much, however. Instead, it served as a detention place for his successor, Sultan Murat V, who was deposed before he had even reigned a year. Later it housed the Ottoman Chamber of Deputies and Senate (1909), but in 1910 it was destroyed by fire under suspicious circumstances. It's still in ruins. Plans for rebuilding it as a luxury hotel have been bruited about for over 30 years.

Sultan Abdülhamid II (1876-1909), who succeeded Murat V, also had to build his own palace. He added considerably to the structures built by earlier sultans in Yıldız Park, on the hillside above Çırağan. Though the largest buildings now house a military academy, and are closed to the public, you can wander in the park and visit several small kiosks, the Şale köşkü, Malta Köşkü, and the Çadır Köşkü; the last was opened only in 1984, after restoration by the Turkish Touring and Automobile Club. The Şale (that's *chalet*) kiosk is fitted out as the Tanzimat Museum, and holds exhibits from the period which followed Abdülmecit's constitutional reforms (Tanzimat) of 1839.

The park, open from 9 am to 6 pm every day for a few pennies' admission, is pleasant enough, though its imperial glamour has faded considerably. Under Abdülhamid it contained exotic and valuable trees, shrubs and flowers, manicured paths, and a superior electric lighting and drainage system. The sultan could reach Çırağan Palace by a private bridge over the roadway from the park. Single women should take an escort.

Onward

After seeing Yıldız, you can take a bus or dolmuş north to Bebek and Rumeli Hisar (see below), or return to Beşiktaş/Barbaros to catch a shuttle ferry over to Üsküdar, on the Asian side, in order to continue your sightseeing. The ferries operate every 15 or 20 minutes in each direction, from 6 am to 12 midnight. There are equally frequent boats between Üsküdar and Eminönü. Ferries to Eminönü may bear the sign *Köprü*, 'bridge', meaning, of course, the Galata Bridge.

If you'd like to pick up the special Bosphorus cruise ferry from Barbaros, catch it heading north at 10.40 am or 1.50 pm (on Sunday and holidays, at 10 and 11 am, 12 noon, 2 and 5 pm). The cruise ferry does not call at Üsküdar.

Üsküdar & Beylerbeyi

Üsküdar is the Turkish form of the name *Scutari*. Legend has it that the first ancient colonists established themselves at Chalcedon, the modern *Kadiköy*, south of Üsküdar. Byzas, bearing the oracle's message to 'Found a colony opposite the blind', thought the Chalcedonites blind to the advantages of Seraglio Point as a townsite, and founded his town on the European shore. Still, people have lived on this, the Asian shore, longer than they've lived on the other.

Today Üsküdar is a busy 'bedroom' community for Istanbul, and you will enjoy an hour's browse through its streets, markets and mosques. You should definitely see the Çinili Cami, with its brilliant tiles, and the attractive little palace of Beylerbeyi.

Getting There

This is easy. The best and most pleasant way is to take a ferryboat from Eminönü (Dock No 2). They run every 20 minutes between 6 am and 12 midnight; even more frequently during rush hours.

A similar, frequent ferry service operates between Üsküdar and Beşiktaş/Barbaros Hayrettin Paşa.

There are also city buses and dolmuşes departing Taksim Square for Üsküdar. The ferryboats are much faster and infinitely more fun, though.

The View from the Ferry

If you take the ferry to Üsküdar, you'll notice **Leander's Tower**, called the *Kız Kulesi* (Maiden's Tower) in Turkish. The tower was a toll booth and defense point in ancient times; the Bosphorus could be closed off by means of a chain stretching from here to Seraglio Point. The tower has really nothing to do with Leander, who was no maiden, and who swam not the Bosphorus but the Hellespont (Dardanelles), 340 km from here. The tower is subject to the usual legends: oracle says maiden will die by snakebite, concerned father puts maiden in snake-proof tower, fruit-vendor comes by in boat, sells basket of fruit (complete with snake) to maiden, maiden gets hers, etc. The legend seems to crop up wherever there are offshore towers. And maidens. Anyway, it's a pretty tower, and an Istanbul landmark.

A landmark for travellers is the German-style **Haydarpaşa Istasyonu**, Istanbul's terminus for Asian trains. During the late 19th century, when Kaiser Wilhelm was trying to charm the sultan into economic and military cooperation, he gave him the station as a little gift.

You will also notice the large **Selimiye Barracks** (*Selimiye Kışlası*), a square building with towers at the corners. It dates from the early 19th century, when Selim III and Mahmut II reorganized the Ottoman armed forces along European lines. Not far away is the Selimiye Mosque (1805). During the Crimean War (1853-56), when England and France fought on the Ottoman side against the Russian Empire, the Selimiye served as a military hospital as well. It was here that the English nurse Florence Nightingale, horrified at the conditions suffered by those wounded in action, established, with 38 companion nurses, the first model military hospital with modern standards of discipline, order, sanitation and care. In effect, her work at the Selimiye established the norms of modern nursing, and turned nursing into a skilled, respected profession.

The highly ornamented building, very storybook Ottoman, is a former harem for aging palace ladies. It's now a school.

Exploring Üsküdar

Hop off the ferry in Üsküdar. The main square is right before you. North of the square, near the ferry landing, is the Mihrimah Camii (1547), built by Sinan for a daughter of Süleyman the Magnificent. To the south of the square is the **Yeni Valide Camii**, or Mosque of the New Queen Mother (1710), built by Sultan Ahmet III for his mother. It resembles the Rüstem Paşa mosque near the Spice Bazaar in Eminönü. Having been built late in the period of classical Ottoman architecture, it is not as fine as earlier works.

West of the square, overlooking the harbour, is the **Şemsi Paşa Camii** (1580), designed by Sinan.

Çinili Cami

Walk out of the busy square along the main road, called Hakimiyeti Milliye Caddesi, or Popular Sovereignty Avenue. (After six centuries of monarchy, the idea of democracy, of the people ruling, is enough to inspire street names.) Watch on the left for Tavukçu Bakkal Sokak, and turn into it. When you reach Çavuşdere Caddesi, turn right and walk less than a kilometre to the little Tiled Mosque (*Çinili Cami*, chee-nee-LEE jahm-mee).

The mosque doesn't look like too much from the outside: just a shady little neighbourhood mosque with the usual collection of nice old men sitting around. But inside it is brilliant with İznik faience (tin-glazed earthenware). It is the work of Mahpeyker Kösem (1640), wife of Sultan Ahmet I (1603-1617) and mother of sultans Murat IV (1623-1640) and Ibrahim (1640-1648).

Çamlıca

From the European shore of the Bosphorus, you may have noticed a hill or two behind Üsküdar, and a television transmission tower. The hills are *Büyük Çamlıca* (bew-YEWK chahm-luh-jah, Big Pine Hill) and *Küçük Çamlıca* (kew-CHEWK, Little Pine Hill). Büyük Çamlıca, especially, has for years been a special picnic place for Istanbullu's. You can get there from the main square in Üsküdar on an Ümraniye bus or dolmuş. Get off at Kısıklı. You can walk to the top on Büyük Çamlıca Caddesi; or take a taxi; or, if it's a busy time (weekend or holiday), take a dolmuş to the top.

Beylerbeyi Palace

Catch a bus or dolmuş north along the shore road from Üsküdar's main square to reach Beylerbeyi, just north of the Asian pylons of the Bosphorus Bridge. Get off at the Çayırbası stop. Beylerbeyi Palace is open from 9 am to 5 pm, closed Monday; small admission fee.

Every emperor needs some little place to get away to, and Beylerbeyi was the place for Abdül Aziz (1861-1876). Mahmut II had built a wooden palace here, but Abdül Aziz wanted stone and marble, so he ordered Serkis Balyan to get to work on Beylerbeyi. The architect came up with an Ottoman gem, complete with fountain in the entrance hall, and two little tent-like kiosks in the sea wall.

One room is panelled in wonderful marquetry (woodwork), all done by the sultan himself. Woodwork was not just a hobby. Under the laws of Islam, every man should have an honest skill with which to make a living. Being a soldier was a duty and an honour, not a living. So was being

king. Thus every sultan had to develop a skill by which, theoretically, he could earn his living. Frequently the sultans chose calligraphy; Abdül Aziz chose woodwork.

Abdül Aziz spent a lot of time here. But so did other monarchs and royal guests, for this was, in effect, the sultan's guest quarters. Empress Eugenie of France stayed here for a long visit in 1869. Other royal guests included Nasruddin, Shah of Persia; Nicholas, Grand Duke of Russia; and Nicholas, King of Montenegro. Another imperial 'guest' was Abdül Hamid II, who lived out his life here from 1913 to 1918, after being deposed by the Young Turks in 1909. He had the dubious honour of watching crumble before his eyes the great empire he had ruled (many would say misruled) for over 30 years.

Küçüksu Kasrı

If Beylerbeyi was a sultan's favourite getaway spot, Küçüksu was for picnics and 'rustic' parties. The Büyük Göksu and Küçük Göksu (Great Heavenly Stream and Lesser Heavenly Stream) were two brooks which descended from the Asian hills into the Bosphorus. Between them was a flat, fertile delta, grassy and shady, just perfect for picnics. The Ottoman upper classes used to get away from the hot city for picnics and rowing here. Foreign residents, referring to the place as 'The Sweet Waters of Asia', would often join them.

Take a bus or dolmuş along the shore road north from Beylerbeyi to reach Küçüksu. The tiny palace here, actually an ornate lodge, was restored and opened to the public in 1983, having been closed for decades. Sultan Abdülmecit was responsible for building this little place, which he did in 1856. Earlier sultans had had wooden kiosks here.

The little palace is open from 9 am to 5 pm, closed Monday.

Onward

If you can get to the ferry dock in Çengelköy, the next village north of

Beylerbeyi, by 10.55 am (except Sunday and holidays), you can catch the special Bosphorus cruise ferry heading north. Otherwise, there are ferries which run on a ring route from Istinye on the European side to Beykoz and Paşabahce on the Asian. Another ring operates from Sarıyer and Rumeli Kavaği in Europe to Anadolu Kavaği, or vice-versa, is less than a dollar. If you can't afford the time for the whole

If the timing's right, you might want to take a bus or dolmuş north all the way to Anadolu Kavaği and catch the Bosphorus cruise ferry as it heads back down toward the city. It departs Anadolu Kavaği at 3.00 and 5.10 pm (1.15, 3.15, 5.15, 6.15 and 7.10 on Sunday and holidays).

A BOSPHORUS CRUISE

Though tour agencies and luxury hotels charter private boats for cruises on the Bosphorus, it's considerably cheaper and much more fun to go the authentic way, on one of the orange-and-white ferries of the Denizyolları (Turkish Maritime Lines). Special Bosphorus cruise trips are operated twice daily on summer weekdays and Saturday, and five times on summer Sundays and holidays. The cost for the 2½ hour cruise from Eminönü to Anadolu Kavaği, or vice-versa, is less than a dollar. If you can't afford the time for the whole trip, you can get off at any of the nine stops en route (six on the European side, three on the Asian). Prices are printed on all tickets. Save your ticket to show the ticket-man when you leave the ferry at your destination.

By tradition, European ports of call are printed on the schedules in black, Asian ports in red.

If you are not visiting Istanbul during the warm months (late spring through early autumn) when the special cruise ferries operate, check the schedules for another likely boat. Read on to discover how.

The special cruise ferries are called *Boğaziçi Özel Gezi Seferleri*. Look for this heading on the schedules, which are posted in the waiting area of each ferry dock. Times will be close to the following, but check to be sure: Eminönü departure at 10.25 am and 1.35 pm; Anadolu Kavaği departure at 3.00 pm and 5.10 pm. On Sundays and holidays, departure times from Eminönü are 9.45, 10.45, 11.45 am; 1.45 and 4.45 pm; from Anadolu Kavaği, Sunday departures are at 1.15, 3.15, 5.15, 6.15, and 7.10 pm.

Special note These special cruise ferries are popular, and fill up quickly, early and often. It's a good idea to get to the dock well ahead of departure (say, a half hour or even more), locate the boat, board, and seize a seat. Keep the sun in mind when you choose your place; you may want some shade as you head north.

If you visit in the cooler months when the special ferries aren't running, look at the schedule for the heading *Boğaz'a Gidiş* (To the Bosphorus), and also *Boğaz'dan Geliş* (From the Bosphorus) for long-distance boats that make good substitutes. Heaviest travel will naturally be down the Bosphorus in the morning rush-hour, and up the Bosphorus in the evening.

Heading Out

As you steam out from the mouth of the Golden Horn, Galata will be on your left and Seraglio Point on your right with the Topkapı Palace rising above it. Down at the water's edge is an Ottoman *tersane* (shipyard). For sights on the Asian shore, refer to the Üsküdar & Berlerbeyi section.

Soon you'll be gliding past the incredible facade and sea-fence of Dolmabahçe Palace on the European side. After that, the main square of Beşiktaş, or Barbaros Hayrettin Paşa, comes into view. Barbaros Bulvarı, a wide highway, cuts a swath up the hill westward. To its right (north) is the green expanse of Yıldız Park. At the waterline is the burned-out hulk of Çirağan Palace. See the European Shore, Below the Bridge section above for more detail.

The handsome Neo-Renaissance mosque nestled at the foot of the Bosphorus

Bridge's European pylons is the **Ortaköy Camii**. Though it has hardly anything to do with Turkish architecture, it's very attractive, and well sited. Within the mosque hang several masterful examples of Arabic calligraphy executed by Sultan Abdülmecit, who was an accomplished calligrapher, and who had the mosque built in 1854.

Above the town you'll notice the New England 19th-century architecture of the Bosphorus University (Boğaziçi Üniversitesi) known as **Bebek** ('baby'). Founded as Robert College in the mid-19th century by the American Board of Foreign Missions, the college had an important influence on the modernization of political, social, economic and scientific thought in Turkey. Though donated to the Turkish nation a decade ago, and now called Bosphorus University, instruction is still in both English and Turkish.

Robert College survives as a special school to prepare bright students for university, having joined forces with the American College for Girls in nearby Arnavutköy.

Just north of Bebek on the European shore is **Rumeli Hisar** (roo-mehl-LEE hee-sahr), the Fortress of Europe. Here at the narrowest part of the Bosphorus, Mehmet the Conqueror had this fortress built in a mere four months (1452), in preparation for his planned siege of Byzantine Constantinople. In concert with Anadolu Hisar on the Asian shore just opposite, the cannon of Rumeli Hisar controlled all traffic on the Bosphorus, and cut the city off from resupply by sea from the north. Built just to serve in the conquest of the city, the mighty citadel served as a glorified toll booth for awhile, and was then more or less abandoned. It has been restored, and is now used for folk dancing, drama, and other performances in the summertime, particularly during the Istanbul International Festival.

Across the strait from Rumeli Hisar is the Fortress of Asia, **Anadolu Hisar** (ahn-nah-doh-LOO hee-sahr). This small castle

had been built by Sultan Beyazıt I in 1391. It was repaired and strengthened by Mehmet the Conqueror in preparation for the great siege. These days a picturesque village snuggles around its foundations.

Each spring a Tulip Festival takes place in **Emirgan**, a well-to-do suburb of Istanbul on the European side. North of Emirgan, at Istinye, is a cove with a drydock. A ring ferry service runs from Istinye to Beykoz and Paşabahçe on the Asian shore. Across on the Asian shore lies **Kanlıca**, a town famous for its yoghurt. The mosque in the town square dates from 1560.

On a point jutting out from the European shore is **Yeniköy**, first settled in classical times. This place later became a favourite summer resort, and preserves that distinction by being the site of the modern Yeniköy Carlton Hotel. Just north of the hotel is the lavish 19th-century Ottoman *yalı* (seaside villa) of one İbrahim Paşa. Not too many of these luxurious villas survive. All were made of wood. Modern economics (and desire for modern conveniences) have caused many to be torn down. Fire has destroyed many others.

Across from Yeniköy are the Asian towns of **Paşabahçe** and **Beykoz**. Much of Turkey's best glassware is produced at the famous Paşabahçe factory – you'll see the name as a brand. In Beykoz, legend says that one of Jason's Argonauts, Pollux by name, had a boxing match with the local king, named Amicus. Pollux was the son of Leda (she of the swan); Amicus was a son of Poseidon. Pollux won.

Originally called Therapeia for its healthful climate, the little cove of **Tarabya** has been a favourite summer watering-place for Istanbul's well-to-do for centuries. Now there is a big hotel, the Grand Tarabya (Büyük Tarabya Oteli) here. Little restaurants, specializing in fish, ring the cove. North of the village are some of the old summer embassies of foreign powers. When the heat and fear of disease increased in the warm months, foreign ambassadors and their staffs would retire to palatial residences, complete with lush gardens, on this shore. The region for such embassy residences extended north to the next village, Büyükdere.

The quaint, pretty town of **Sarıyer** is a logical place to end your cruise up the Bosphorus (or to begin your cruise down). Sarıyer has several good fish restaurants, an interesting little marketplace, and good transportation down the Bosphorus or north to the Black Sea coast at Kilyos.

The far northern port of call for the ferryboats is **Rumeli Kavağı**. From here northward is a military zone. The sleepy little town gets most of its excitement from the arrival and departure of ferries. There is a little public beach named Altınkum (ahl-TUHN-koom) near the village.

Perched above the village of **Anadolu Kavağı** on the Asian side are the ruins of a Genoese castle. As the straits are narrow here, it was a good choice for a defensive site to control traffic. Two more fortresses, put up by Sultan Murat IV, are north of here. But Anadolu Kavağı is the final stop on the special cruise ferry route, and the land to the north is in a military zone.

From Sarıyer you can get a bus or dolmuş to **Kilyos**, on the Black Sea coast. There are some little pensions, hotels and guest houses here, open during the summer, for beach fanciers. If you go to Kilyos for swimming, keep in mind that the waters of the Black Sea are fairly chilly. And, more importantly, that there is a deadly undertow on many beaches. Swim only in protected areas, or where there is an attentive lifeguard. And don't swim alone.

THE PRINCES' ISLANDS

The Turks call these islands, which lie about 20 km south-east of the city in the Sea of Marmara, the *Kızıl Adalar*, 'Red Islands'. Most Istanbullu's get along with *Adalar* (The Islands) however, as there are no other islands nearby.

It's convenient to have islands near a big city. They serve all sorts of useful purposes. In Byzantine times, so the story goes, refractory princes, deposed monarchs, and others who were a threat to the powers-that-be were interned here. A Greek Orthodox monastery and seminary turned out Orthodox priests until only a decade or two ago.

Under the Ottomans, the stray dogs were rounded up from the city's streets and shipped out to *Köpek Adası* (Dog Island), where they were released. After that, their fate was up to God. (Muslim belief holds that animals, too, have immortal souls, and that it is not the business of men to take animal lives needlessly; that is, to kill dogs just to get them off city streets.) From one of the islands, copper was mined. Another was used as a self-contained rabbit farm: bunnies were released on the deserted island to breed, and the 'crop' gathered at leisure.

In the 19th century, the empire's business community of Greeks, Jews and Armenians began to favour the islands as summer resorts. The population was most heavily Greek up to the end of the empire. Many of the pretty Victorian holiday villas and hotels survive, and make the larger islands, Büyükada and Heybeliada, charming places.

If you have the time, and want a leisurely, relaxing outing with no heavy sightseeing or scheduling, by all means cruise out to the islands. If you don't have the time, you still have a chance for a look: if you're heading off to İznik and Bursa, you'll probabaly take a ferry from Kabataş to Yalova. This ferry will pass, and probably call at, both Heybeli and Büyükada.

Getting There

Ferries depart from both Sirkeci (Dock No 5) and Kabataş, but it's Kabataş which has the express ferries. By express, the trip to Heybeli takes 50 minutes; by normal boat it's about one hour, twenty minutes. Büyükada is an additional fifteen minutes' trip beyond Heybeli. Perhaps the best plan for you is to take a boat all the way to Büyükada, see that island, shuttle back to Heybeli, see that one, and then catch a returning ferry to Istanbul.

The summer schedules are heavily in favour of commuters, with frequent morning boats from the islands, and frequent evening boats from the city. But you'll have no trouble getting a convenient boat, if you check the schedules ahead of time. The few morning boats from the city to the islands fill up quickly, and though you'll almost certainly get aboard, you may have to stand the whole way unless you board the boat and seize a seat at least half an hour before departure time.

Here are some convenient times (subject to change, so check): from Sirkeci, normal ferries depart at 6.50 and 10.50 am, 12.50 and 14.50 pm. From Kabataş (near Dolmabahçe), the one morning express ferry departs at 9.45 am. There are many afternoon and evening boats, but these don't leave you much time for sightseeing.

Return trips depart Büyükada at 1.40, 2.40 and 6.40 pm, express to Kabataş; and at 4, 6 and 7.30 pm (plus three more late evening boats) normal to Sirkeci. Departures from Heybeli are 15 minutes later in each case.

Between the islands of Büyükada and Heybeliada there are fairly frequent ferries on the 15-minute trip.

What to See
The ferry steams out of the Golden Horn, with good views all around. To the right is a magnificent panorama of Topkapı Palace, Sancta Sophia and the Blue Mosque; to the left, Üsküdar, Haydarpaşa, and Kadiköy. Along the southern coast of Asia are more suburbs of Istanbul, some of them industrial. Before coming to the bigger islands, you'll pass the small ones named Kınalı and Burgaz. Heybeli is next. Finally, you debark at Büyükada.

Büyükada
The first thing you will notice about this delightful place is that *cars are not allowed*. Except for the necessary police, fire and sanitation vehicles, transportation is by bicycle, horse-drawn carriage, and on foot. It's wonderful!

Something you may not notice, but that you should be aware of, is that there is no fresh water in the islands. Fresh water must be tanked in from the mainland.

Walk from the ferry to the clock tower and the main street. The business district, with some fairly expensive restaurants, are to the left. For a stroll up the hill and through the lovely old houses, bear right. If you need a goal for your wanderings, head for the Greek **Monastery of St George**, in the 'saddle' between Büyükada's two main hills.

Heybeliada
Called Heybeli for short, this small island holds the Turkish Naval Academy. The presidential yacht is often anchored off the academy landing. Within the academy grounds is the grave of Sir Edward Barton (died 1598), ambassador of Queen Elizabeth I to the Sublime Porte.

As soon as you debark from the ferry you'll encounter carriage drivers and their vehicles. Haggle with one for a tour of the island ($5 or $6), or simply for a ride to the other side, where there's a tiny beach for swimming. Otherwise, wander, sip tea or soft drinks, watch the fishermen repair their nets, and generally relax.

ENTERTAINMENT
The name 'Istanbul' often conjurs up thoughts of mysterious intrigues in dusky streets, dens in which sultry belly-dancers do what they do, and who knows what else? As with most aged stereotypes, the reality is very different.

Istanbul International Festival
The most prominent entertainment event in Istanbul is the Istanbul International Festival, which begins in late June and continues through the first half of July. World-class performers – soloists, orchestras, dance companies, etc – give

recitals and performances in numerous concert halls, historic buildings and palaces. The highlight is Mozart's 'Abduction from the Seraglio' performed right in Topkapı Palace, with the Sultan's private Gate of Felicity as backdrop. Don't miss it. Check at the box offices in the Atatürk Cultural Centre (Taksim) for schedules, ticket prices and availability.

Another good bet during the festival, and on other warm summer evenings as well, is a performance of drama or folk dance given in Rumeli Hisar, up the Bosphorus. Several years ago, I saw a fine English company do Shakespeare's 'A Midsummer Night's Dream' here. The performance was excellent, the setting simply spectacular.

There is another open-air theatre (*Açık Hava Tiyatrosu*) just north of the Istanbul Hilton Hotel, off Cumhuriyet Caddesi.

Folklore

Turks are enthusiastic folklore fans, and many are still close enough in tradition to their regional dances to jump in and dance along at a performance. It's usually pretty easy to find a dance performance. University groups, good amateur companies, and professionals all schedule performances throughout the year. The Turkish Folklore Association usually has something going on. For current offerings, ask at a Tourist Information Office, or at one of the larger hotels.

High Culture

There are symphony, opera and ballet seasons, and occasional tour performances by the likes of Jean-Pierre Rampal or Paul Badura-Skoda. Many but not all of these performances are given in the Atatürk Cultural Centre, in Taksim Square. The box offices there will have schedules.

Theatre

The Turks are enthusiastic theatre-goers, and as a people they seem to have a special genius for dramatic art. The problem, of course, is language. If you're a true theatre-buff, you might well enjoy a performance of a familiar classic, provided you know the play well enough to follow the action without benefit of dialogue.

Cinema

Istiklal Caddesi used to be the centre of Istanbul's cinema (*sinema*, SEE-neh-mah) district, with many foreign films being shown. The advent of television changed all that, and now Istiklal's cinemas have mostly porn (light and not so light) and melodrama. Many first-run feature films do make it to Istanbul, however, and you will be able to enjoy them at bargain prices in certain cinemas. Some are along Cumhuriyet Caddesi between Taksim and Harbiye. Others are in the section called Nişantaşı (nee-SHAHN-tah-shuh): head north on Cumhuriyet past the Hilton to Harbiye, and bear right on Valikonağı Caddesi. The cinemas are along this street in the first few blocks.

You may need some words on your cinema outing. Look on the cinema posters for the words *Renkli* and *Türkçe* or *Orijinal* (ohr-zhee-NAHL). If you see '*Renkli Orijinal*', that means the film is in colour, and in the original language, with Turkish subtitles. But if you see '*Renkli Türkçe*', the film is in colour but has been dubbed in Turkish, in which case you may understand nothing.

There are three general seating areas, and you pay according to which you choose: *koltuk* (kohl-TOOK), on the floor in the mid-section to the rear; *birinci* (beer-EEN-jee), on the floor near the screen; and *balkon* (bahl-KOHN), in the balcony where the young lovers congregate. If you're going to the cinema to watch the film, ask for *koltuk*.

When possible, buy your tickets a few hours in advance. Tickets will probably cost under a dollar. Also, the usher will expect a small tip for showing you to your seat.

Nightclubs

Belly-dancers do still perform in Turkey, of course. Many of the nightclubs along Cumhuriyet Caddesi between Taksim and the Hilton feature belly-dancers, folk dance troupes, singers and bands. The usual arrangement is that you pay one price and get dinner and the show; drinks are extra. With Turkish prices being what they are, the price is not all that unreasonable at the independent clubs, perhaps $15 per person. At the large hotels, which also have belly-dancers in their nightclubs, the cost may be twice as high.

The trick is to get a good, legitimate club. The Kervansaray, on the north side of the Hilton, has been catering to both Turks and tourists for years. This is not the cheapest, but it's reasonable, and the show is good. Actually, it may be among the cheaper ones when you remember that at the sleazy ones you may get into quite a tussle over the bill. Istiklal Caddesi and the side streets running from it have many clubs where you can go to watch the show (more or less), meet ladies of the night, and get suckered into paying big money for their drinks.

Gazinos

Turkish gazinos have nothing to do with gambling. Rather, they are open-air nightclubs popular in the summertime. (Some have been built up, and operate in winter, to the point that they are actually nightclubs with a gazino heritage.) The best of these are along the European shore of the Bosphorus. You won't find much belly-dancing here. The shows are mostly Turkish popular singers. Dinner and drinks are served. If the name of the place has the word *aile* (ah-yee-LEH, 'wife' or 'family') in it, as in *Bebek Aile Gazinosu*, it means the proprietor wants to appeal to a respectable, mixed audience, and avoid all-male or heavy-drinking audiences.

Dinner on the Bosphorus

For my money, the most enjoyable thing you can do in Istanbul at night is have a long, leisurely seafood dinner at a little restaurant overlooking the Bosphorus. As Turks very often have the same idea, there are lots of little restaurants to choose from. Most, it must be stated, are in the moderate price range, not extremely cheap. A fish dinner with wine might cost $10 to $15 per person.

Good places to search out a nice restaurant are Arnavutköy and Bebek (the *Kaptan* is an old favourite), Tarabya and Sarıyer. The Asian coast has its share of little places as well.

A Night Cruise

About the cheapest, yet most enjoyable, nighttime activity is to take a Bosphorus ferry somewhere. It doesn't really matter where, as long as you don't end up on the southern coast of the Sea of Marmara or out in the Princes' Islands. Catch one over to Üsküdar, or to any town up the Bosphorus, enjoy the view, the twinkling lights, the fishing boats bobbing in the waves, the powerful searchlights of the ferries sweeping the sea lanes. Have a nice glass of tea (a waiter will bring it round regularly). Get off anywhere, and take a bus or dolmuş home, if you can't catch a ferry back directly.

Perhaps the easiest ferry to catch for this purpose is the Eminönü-Üsküdar. Just go to Eminönü's Dock No 2, buy a ticket to Üsküdar, and walk aboard. (If you want a ticket there and back, say *Üsküdar, gidiş-dönüş* (EW-skew-dahr, gee-DEESH dur-NEWSH). From Üsküdar, just come back; or wait for one of the frequent ferries to Beşiktaş/Barbaros Hayrettin Paşa. From Barbaros you can catch a bus or dolmuş back to your part of town. There are dolmuş ranks right outside the ferry dock.

A fail-safe evening ferry ride is the one to Haydarpaşa or Kadiköy, from Karaköy's Dock No 7 or 8. These two Asian suburbs are the only destinations for ferries from these docks. Return boats bring you back to Karaköy.

Near Istanbul

Thrace

The land to the north of the Aegean Sea was called Thrace by the Romans. Today this ancient Roman province is divided among Turkey, Bulgaria and Greece, with Turkey holding the easternmost part. Turkish Thrace (*Trakya*) is not large, or particularly exciting, except for its major city, Edirne.

EDİRNE

A glance at the map seems to tell you all about Edirne (eh-DEER-neh): it's the first town you come to if you're travelling overland from Europe to Turkey, it's a way-station on the road to Istanbul. It wouldn't be surprising if this had been Edirne's role throughout history, even in the old days when the town was called Adrianople. But there's more to Edirne than this. Because of its history, it holds several of the finest examples, from the greatest periods, of Turkish mosque architecture, and if you have the chance, you should take time for a visit.

If you're coming from Istanbul, you can make the trip to Edirne and back to Istanbul in a day, though a longish one. Get an early morning bus, plan to have lunch and see the sights, and catch a return bus in the late afternoon.

Getting There

The E-5 highway between Europe and Istanbul follows very closely the ancient road which connected Rome and Constantinople. It follows the river valleys past Niš and Sofia, flows comfortably between the mountain ranges of the Stara and Rhodopi to Plovdiv, and cruises along the Maritsa riverbank into Edirne. After Edirne, the road heads out into the rolling, steppe-like terrain of Eastern Thrace toward Istanbul, 225 km further along. The city stands alone on the gently undulating plain, snuggled into a bend of the Tunca (TOON-jah) River.

Border Posts

There are three frontier crossing-points on the outskirts of Edirne. From Bulgaria on the E-5, you come to the busy border post of Kapıkule. After the formalities, you enter the town by crossing the Tunca on the Gazi Mihal bridge (1420) and passing some fragments of Byzantine city walls.

From Greece, the major road goes to Pazarkule; and a sleepy, grass-covered track crosses at Karaağaç. These posts, south of the town on the Maritsa (*Meriç*, mehr-EECH) River, were originally meant to serve the rail line. The frontier, as determined at the Treaty of Lausanne, left the Turkish rail line passing through Greece on its way to Edirne! A bypass line was built in the 1970s, though.

From Pazarkule or Karaağaç, or from the nearby railway station, you will probably have to take a taxi into town, though you may be lucky and find a dolmuş, which would be cheaper.

By Train

You may be coming to Turkey by train, in which case you will probably be ready for a break. Except for the luxurious tour-group re-creation of the Orient Express (Paris-Istanbul, single, $5000), train service is slow and tedious. The international train can take another six to ten hours to reach Istanbul. Get off. Don't miss Edirne.

Three morning trains run from Edirne to Istanbul; three evening trains run in the opposite direction. The schedule says the trip takes 6½ hours; it may take longer.

By Bus

Buses operate very frequently throughout the day – about every 20 minutes or so – and take only four hours. In Edirne, they operate out of the city's Otobüs Garajı, on the outskirts of town. Take a city bus or dolmuş from the *Eski Cami* (see below) to get to the Otobüs Garajı. In Istanbul, the terminus is the Topkapı Otogar, the big bus station just outside the city walls at Topkapı gate, on the E-5 highway (also called the *Londra Asfaltı*).

History

This town was indeed built as a defense post for the larger city on the Bosphorus. The Roman emperor Hadrian founded it in the 2nd century as Hadrianopolis, a name which was later shortened by Europeans to Adrianople, then again by the Turks to Edirne.

The Ottoman Empire grew from the seed of a Turkish emirate in north-western Anatolia. By the mid-1300s, the emirate of the Ottomans with its capital at Bursa had become very powerful, but not powerful enough to threaten the mighty walls of Constantinople. Bent on more conquest, the Ottoman armies crossed the Dardanelles into Thrace, skirting the great capital. Capturing Adrianople in 1363, they made it their new capital and base of operations for military campaigns in Europe.

For almost a hundred years, this was the city from which the Ottoman sultan would set out on his campaigns to Europe and Asia. When the time was finally ripe for the final conquest of the Byzantine Empire, Mehmet the Conqueror set out from Edirne on the road to Constantinople. Even after the great city was captured, Edirne played an important role in Ottoman life and society, for it was still a forward post on the route to conquest in Europe.

When the Ottoman Empire fell apart after World War I, the Allies had decided to grant all of Thrace to the Greek kingdom. Constantinople was to become an international city. In the summer of 1920, Greek armies occupied Edirne. But Atatürk's republican armies were ultimately victorious, and the Treaty of Lausanne left Edirne and Eastern Thrace to the Turks, and Edirne returned to its role as 'the town on the way to Istanbul'.

Orientation

The centre of town is Hürriyet Meydanı (Freedom Square), at the intersection of the two main streets, Saraçlar/Saraçhane Caddesi and Talat Paşa Caddesi. Just west of the square is the Üçşerefeli Cami. North along Talat Paşa Caddesi will bring you to Edirne's masterpiece, the Selimiye Camii. On the way to the Selimiye, you'll pass the Eski Cami. South of Hürriyet Square is the Ali Paşa Çarşısı, Edirne's covered bazaar.

Places To See

The principal reason to stop in Edirne is to see mosques, so start out from Hürriyet Meydanı and go the few steps to the Üçşerefeli Cami.

Üçşerefeli Cami

The name means 'mosque with three galleries (balconies)'. Actually it's one of the mosque's four minarets which has the three balconies. The minarets, built at different times, are all different and wonderfully various.

Enter at the far end of the courtyard rather than through a side gate. That way you can enjoy the full effect of the architect's genius. The courtyard at the Üçşerefeli (EWCH-sheh-reh-feh-LEE) with its *şadırvan* (ablutions fountain) was a prototype for the courtyards of the Ottoman mosques to be built in later centuries.

The mosque was constructed in the mid-1400s, and finished by 1447. It exemplifies a transition from the Seljuk Turkish type of architecture of Konya and Bursa to a truly Ottoman style, which would be perfected later in Istanbul. The Seljuks were greatly influenced by the

Persian and Indian styles prevalent in their empire to the east. The Ottomans learned a great deal from the Byzantines, and for the Byzantines Sancta Sophia was the purest expression of their ideal. Sancta Sophia's outstanding characteristic is its wide, expansive dome covering a great open space. After the Ottomans took Constantinople in 1453, the transition accelerated, as you will see.

In the Seljuk style, smaller domes are mounted on square rooms. But here at the Üçşerefeli, the wide (24 metres) dome is mounted on a hexagonal drum, and supported by two walls and two pillars. Keep this transitional style in mind as you visit Edirne's other mosques, which are either earlier or later in style.

Across the street from the mosque is a *hamam* (hah-MAHM), or Turkish bath, built in the late 1500s and still in use. Designed by the great Mimar Sinan for Grand Vezir Sokullu Mehmet Paşa, it is actually two hamams in one: one for men, one for the ladies. (At most Turkish baths there is only one system of bathing rooms, used by men and women on different days.)

Eski Cami

Now head back to Hürriyet Meydanı, and walk north-east on Talat Paşa Caddesi to the Eski Cami (ehs-KEE jah-mee), or Old Mosque. On your way you'll pass the *bedesten*, another covered market, this one dating from the early 1400s. Behind it to the east is the Rüstem Paşa Hanı, a grand caravanserai which is a hundred years younger than the bedesten.

The Eski Cami (1414) exemplifies one of two principal mosque styles used by the Ottomans in their earlier capital, Bursa. Like Bursa's great Ulu Cami, the Eski Cami has rows of arches and pillars, supporting a series of small domes. Inside, there's a marvellous *mihrab* (prayer niche) and huge calligraphic inscriptions on the walls. The columns at the front were lifted from some Roman building, a common practice over the centuries.

Selimiye Camii

Up the hill past the Eski Cami stands the great Selimiye (seh-LEE-mee-yeh), the finest work of the great Ottoman architect Mimar Sinan – or so the architect himself considered it. Though smaller than Sinan's tremendous Süleymaniye in Istanbul, the Selimiye is wonderfully harmonious and elegant. Crowning its small hill, it can be seen from a good distance across the rolling Thracian steppeland, and makes an impressive sight.

The Selimiye was constructed for Sultan Selim II (1566-1574), and finished just after the sultan's death. Sinan's genius guided him in designing a broad and lofty dome, and supporting it by means of pillars, arches and external buttresses. He did it so well that the interior is very spacious, and the walls can be filled with windows because they don't have to bear all of the weight. The result is a wide, airy, light space for prayer, similar to that of the Süleymaniye.

Part of the Selimiye's excellent effect comes from its four slender, very tall (71 metres) minarets. The fluted drums of the minarets add to the sense of height. You'll notice that each is *üçşerefeli*, or built with three balconies: Sinan's respectful acknowledgement, perhaps, to his predecessor who designed Edirne's Üçşerefeli Cami.

As you might expect, the interior furnishings of the Selimiye are exquisite, from the delicately-carved marble *mimber* (pulpit) to the outstanding İznik faience in and around the *mihrab* (prayer niche).

The Selimiye had its share of supporting buildings – religious schools, libraries, etc. However, all that survive are a *medrese* (theological seminary) and a gallery of shops, called the *Arasta*, beneath the mosque. The shops have been restored and are still in use; rents are dedicated to the upkeep of the mosque, as they have been for over four hundred years.

Beyazıt II Camii

Edirne's last great imperial mosque is that of Sultan Beyazıt II (1481-1512), on the far side (north-west) of the Tunca River. From Hürriyet Meydanı, it will take you about 15 or 20 minutes for the pleasant walk to the mosque, and another 15 or 20 for the return. Walk along Saraçhane Caddesi beside the Üçşerefeli Cami (on your right), and turn left immediately after its Turkish bath, the one built by Sinan. Walk one block and bear right at the ornate little fountain. This street is Horozlu Bayır Caddesi; it changes names later, to İmaret Caddesi, but it will take you right to the bridge (1488) across the Tunca to Sultan Beyazıt's mosque.

The Beyazıt complex (1484-88) was fully restored in the late 1970s, so it now looks good as new. The architect of the complex, a fellow named Hayrettin, didn't have the genius of Mimar Sinan, but did a very creditable job nonetheless.

The mosque lies between the Üçşerefeli and the Selimiye in style, sliding back a bit rather than advancing: the mosque's large prayer hall has one large dome, more like the mosques in Bursa, but it has a courtyard and sadırvan like the Üçşerefeli Cami. Though it's certainly of a high standard, it can't compare to the Selimiye, which was built less than a century later.

The mosque's *külliye* (complex of service buildings) is extensive, including a *tabhane* (hostel for travellers), *medrese* (theological seminary), *imaret* (soup kitchen), and *darüşşifa* (hospital).

Eski Saray and Sarayiçi

Saray means 'palace' in Turkish. Upriver (east) from the Sultan Beyazıt II mosque complex are the ruins of the Eski Saray, or Old Palace. Begun by Sultan Beyazıt II in 1450, the Old Palace once rivalled Istanbul's Topkapı in luxury and size. Today, little is left of it: a few bits of the kitchen buildings. But it's a pleasant walk along the river, less than a half-hour, to reach Eski Saray from the Beyazıt mosque, and

if the day is nice, you might want to do it. From the Eski Saray, Saraçhane Köprüsü (bridge) will take you back across the Tunca; Saraçhane Caddesi then leads directly back to Hürriyet Meydanı.

East of Eski Saray, across a branch of the Tunca (there's a bridge called Fatih Sultan Köprüsü) is Sarayiçi ('within the palace'). This scrub-covered island, once the sultans' hunting preserve, is now the site of the famous annual Kırkpınar Oiled Wrestling Matches (*Tarihi Kırkpınar Yağlı Güreş Festivali*; that's 'yah-LUH gew-RESH', oiled wrestling). In late May and early June, huge wrestlers clad only in leather knickers and slathered with olive oil take part in freestyle matches. An early sultan is said to have invented the sport to keep his troops in shape. Whatever the origin, a *pehlivan* (wrestler) at the Kırkpınar matches is something to behold. Folk dancing exhibitions are organized as part of the wrestling festivities.

If you've made it all the way to Sarayiçi, look for the Kanuni Köprüsü (bridge) to get you back to the south bank of the Tunca. Bear right coming off the bridge, and the road will lead you to Saraçhane Caddesi, and eventually to Hürriyet Meydanı.

The Old Town

While you're here, don't neglect to take a stroll through the old town of Edirne to discover some scenes of Turkish daily life. The Old Town, called *Kale İçi* ('within the fortress') by the locals, was the original medieval town, with streets laid out on a grid plan. Some fragments of Byzantine city walls are still visible at the edges of the grid, down by the Tunca River. The Old Town is bounded by Saraçlar Caddesi and Talat Paşa Caddesi, basically the area behind and to the west of the Ali Paşa Çarşısı.

Places To Stay/Eat

It's relatively easy to find inexpensive pensions and rooming houses in Edirne, as this is the first stop within Turkey on the route from Europe. Travellers who know the route will often push on through northern Greece or Bulgaria in order to get into Turkey so they can enjoy the lower prices and incomparably better food. Edirne is their first night's stay in the country.

However, this route is heavily travelled by Turkish workers on their way to and from Europe, and by international lorry-drivers heading to or from Iran and the Arabic countries. So your companions in the inexpensive hostelries may be mostly bachelors. Also, many places will be filled by crowds of these fellows at holiday time.

You don't really need to spend a night here in order to absorb all the sights, as mentioned above. But should you want to stay, the Tourism Office in Hürriyet Meydanı (tel 1518) can help you locate a room for the night. They're especially good on the cheap little pensions and *otels*.

Edirne's old standard hotel is the *Kervan Oteli* (tel 1382, 1355) on Talat Paşa Caddesi, Kadirhane Sokak 134. They have a private garage for guests' cars, a good restaurant (in which you are required to take breakfast). Rooms cost $9 single, $14 double, plus $1.50 or $2 for breakfast.

Another long-running favourite is the *Sultan Oteli* (tel 1372, 2156), Talat Paşa Caddesi 170, a larger (83-room) place with higher prices: $18 to $20 single, $25 to $27 double. The higher rates are for a room with private bath.

The hotels have the priciest dining rooms in town, but there are plenty of alternatives. A short stroll in the Old Town will reveal any number of tiny hole-in-the-wall *hazır yemek* ('ready food') restaurants, perhaps just bearing the word *lokanta*. For grilled meat rissoles, locate a *köfteci*. A filling lunch at any such place can be had for $2 or less.

Onwards

If you've come from Istanbul, it might make sense to head due south from Edirne directly to the Dardanelles and Troy. By doing this, however, you miss the ferry cruise across the Sea of Marmara, and the delightful cities of İznik, the ancient Nicaea, and Bursa, the first Ottoman capital. So if you've got the time, head back to Istanbul and catch a ferryboat to Yalova, first stop on your explorations of the south Marmara shore.

İznik, Bursa & the South Marmara Shore

The southern shore of the Sea of Marmara is a land of small villages surrounded by olive groves, fruit orchards, rolling hills and rich bottom-land. During the Ottoman Empire, the choice olives for the sultan's table came from here, as did snow to cool his drinks from the slopes of Bursa's *Uludağ* (the Bithynian Mt Olympus). The region's few cities are of moderate size and of significant interest to visitors.

You can enjoy this region and its sights in only only two days: catch an early ferry from Istanbul to Yalova, make a quick tour of İznik (the ancient city of Nicaea), and spend the night in Bursa. After seeing the sights of Bursa the next morning, catch a bus westward to Çanakkale. You'll reach that town on the Dardanelles in time for a late supper.

But if you have another day, you can truly enjoy the Marmara's southern shore. Plan to spend most of your extra time in Bursa, where the mosques and museums are particularly fine (this was the Ottoman's first capital city, before Edirne and Istanbul). You can even bask in hot mineral baths at Çekirge, a spa suburb of Bursa, and take the cablecar to the top of Uludağ, snow-capped for most of the year (skiing in winter).

If you must, you can rocket down to Bursa just for the day. But this means a lot of travel time for only a few hours' sightseeing, and the city really deserves an overnight stay.

Getting There

Bursa is an industrial city of note, and so transport to and from Istanbul is good. However, some of it is meant just for the businessmen. If you go by ferryboat, which is by far the best way to go, you will pass through the town of Yalova on your way to İznik or Bursa.

Express Ferryboats

The best and most enjoyable way to get to Bursa is by express ferryboat across the Sea of Marmara. The ferries depart Kabataş dock, just south of Dolmabahçe, at 9.45 am, 2.15 and 6.10 and 8.15 pm on Monday through Saturday.

Departures from Yalova for the return to Istanbul are at 610, 8.10 and 11.30 am, and 1.30 and 5.30 pm, Monday through Saturday.

On Sunday, the schedules are: from Kabataş at 8.30 and 9.00 am, 12 noon, 2.15, 3.25, 5.35 and 9.15 pm; from Yalova, 6.15 and 10.45 am, 1.00, 3.15, 4.40, 6.35 and 8 pm. The 8 pm boat from Yalova lands you at Sirkeci instead of Kabataş. There are only three boats per day in each direction in the wintertime.

The voyage takes about two hours, depending on stops. Board the boat *at least* a half-hour before departure time (45 minutes or an hour is not too early in summer) if you want to be assured of a seat. The fare, single (one-way), first class (*birinci mevki*), is about $1.50.

Hydrofoil

There's a daily hydrofoil service, for instance, but the outward trip is from Mudanya (a port for Bursa) in the morning, and the return trip is from Istanbul in the evening. You might check to see if they've added a morning departure from Istanbul, and an evening one from Mudanya. The hydrofoil's Istanbul dock is at Kabataş, between Karaköy and Dolmabahçe. On the Bursa side it's at Mudanya, a seacoast town a half-hour by bus or dolmuş (frequent) from Bursa's main bus station, the Otogar.

Bus

There are frequent buses to Bursa from the Harem bus station on the Asian side of the Bosphorus just north of the Haydarpaşa railway station. You can board a ferryboat to Hyadarpaşa, and then walk for 15 minutes or take a taxi. The ferry is preferable to the bus, however, as the bus must drive all the way around the Bay of İzmit to reach Bursa.

There is also dolmuş service to Bursa. You travel in a sedan rather than a minibus, and pay about twice as much for a slightly faster journey.

Those short on time may head straight to Bursa. But they'll be missing a worthwhile detour: the ancient city of Nicaea, today called İznik.

İZNİK

The road from Yalova to İznik (population 14,000) passes among fertile, green hills punctuated by tall, spiky cypress trees, past peach orchards, cornfields and vineyards. The journey of 60 km takes about 1½ hours.

As you approach İznik, you may notice fruit-packing plants among the orchards. You will certainly have admired the vast İznik Gölü, or İznik Lake. Watch for the great Byzantine city walls: the road passes through the old Istanbul Kapısı (Istanbul Gate), and then becomes Atatürk Caddesi, and goes to the ruined Church of Sancta Sophia (now a museum) in the very centre of town. The bus station is a few blocks south-east of the church.

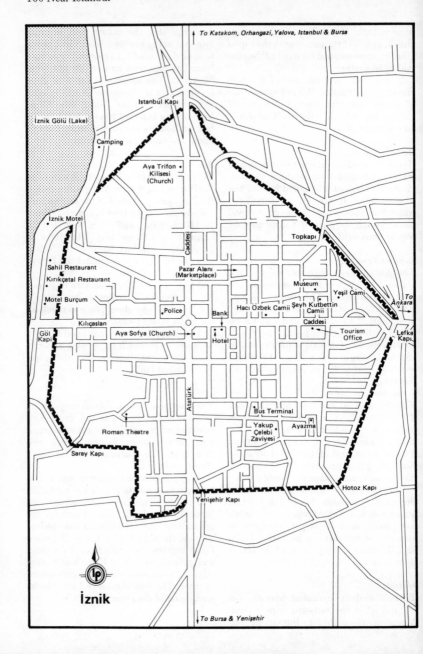

To Katakom, Orhangazi, Yalova, Istanbul & Bursa

İznik Gölü (Lake)

Camping

Istanbul Kapı

Aya Trifon Kilisesi (Church)

İznik Motel

Topkapı

Sahil Restaurant
Kırıkçatal Restaurant

Pazar Alanı (Marketplace)

Museum
Yeşil Cami

Motel Burçum

Caddesi

Hacı Özbek Camii
Şeyh Kutbettin Camii

Police

Bank

To Ankara

Kılıçaslan

Aya Sofya (Church)

Göl Kapı

Hotel

Caddesi

Tourism Office

Lefke Kapı

Atatürk

Bus Terminal

Roman Theatre

Yakup Çelebi Zaviyesi

Ayazma

Saray Kapı

Hotoz Kapı

Yenişehir Kapı

İznik

To Bursa & Yenişehir

Top: Slicing döner to make Bursa Kebabı
Bottom: Turkey's first republican parliament building in Ankara

Top: The Library of Celsus, Ephesus
Bottom: Angelic figure in high relief, Ephesus

History

This ancient city may well have been founded around 1000 BC. We know for sure that it was revitalized by one of Alexander the Great's generals in 316 BC. Another of the generals, Lysimachus, soon got hold of it and named it for his wife *Nikaea*. It became the capital city of the province of Bithynia.

Nicaea lost some of its prominence with the founding of Nicomedia (today's İzmit) in 264 BC, and by 74 BC the entire area had become part of the Roman Empire.

Nicaea flourished under Rome. The emperors built a new system of walls, plus temples, theatres and baths. But invasions of the Goths and the Persians brought ruin by 300 AD.

Ecumenical Councils

With the rise of Constantinople, Nicaea took on a new importance as well. In 325, the First Ecumenical Council was held here for the purpose of condemning the heresy of Arianism. During the great Justinian's reign, Nicaea was grandly refurbished and embellished with new buildings and defenses. They served the city well a few centuries later when the Arabs invaded. Like Constantinople, Nicaea never fell to its Arab besiegers.

In 787 yet another Ecumenical Council, the seventh, was held in Nicaea's Sancta Sophia Church. The deliberations solved the problem of iconoclasm: henceforth it would be church policy not to destroy icons. Theologians who saw icons as 'images', prohibited by the Bible, were dismayed. But Byzantine artists were delighted, and went to work on their art with even more vigor.

Though the city never fell to the Arabs, it did fall to the Crusaders, just like Constantinople. During the period from 1204 to 1261 when a Latin king sat on the throne of Byzantium, the true Byzantine emperor, Theodore Lascaris, reigned over the 'Empire of Nicaea'. When the Crusaders cleared out, Lascaris moved his court back to the traditional capital.

The Turks

The Seljuk Turks had a flourishing empire in Central Anatolia before 1250, and various tribes of nomadic warriors had circulated near the walls of Nicaea during those times. In fact, Turkish soldiers had served as mercenaries in the interminable battles which raged among rival claimants to the Byzantine throne. At one point, a Byzantine battle over Nicaea ended with a Turkish emir as its ruler!

It was Orhan (1326-1361), son of Osman and first true sultan of the Ottoman Empire, who conquered İznik on 2 March, 1331. The city soon had the honour of harbouring the first Ottoman college. Proussa (Bursa) had fallen to the Ottomans on 6 April, 1326, and became their first capital city. In 1337, they took Nicomedia (İzmit), and effectively blocked the Byzantines out of Anatolia.

Sultan Selim I (1512-1520), a mighty conqueror nicknamed 'The Grim', rolled his armies over Azerbaijan in 1514, and took the Persian city of Tabriz. Packing up all of the region's craftsmen, he sent them westward, to be replanted in İznik. They brought with them a high level of expertise in the making of coloured tiles. Soon İznik's kilns were turning out faience which is unequalled even today. The great period of İznik faience continued almost to 1700. At one point, artisans were sent to Tunisia to begin a high-quality faience industry there (Tunisia was then an Ottoman possession).

The art of coloured tiles is being revived in İznik today, and you can buy some good examples at moderate prices in the shops. You should be aware that true İznik tiles from the great period are looked upon as antiquities, and cannot legally be exported from Turkey.

Orientation

İznik's Tourism Office is on the main east-west street, Kilicaslan Caddesi, east of Sancta Sophia; follow the signs. Hours are 8.30 to 12 noon and 2 to 5.30 pm, every day in the warm months; shorter hours off-season.

Sancta Sophia

Start your sightseeing right in the centre of town, and the Church of the Holy Wisdom (Sancta Sophia). This is a good vantage-point from which to consider the layout of the town: two dead-straight boulevards, north-south (Atatürk Caddesi) and east-west (Kılıçaslan Caddesi), leading to the four principal gates in the city walls. North is the Istanbul Kapısı, south is the Yenişehir Kapısı; to the east is Lefke Kapısı, to the west the Göl Kapısı. We'll take a closer look at the walls and gates in a short while.

Sancta Sophia is open from 9 to 12 noon and from 2 to 5 pm daily, closed Monday. Admission costs a few pennies; the camera fee is about 50c. If there's no one about when you visit, continue with your tour. The key is probably at the museum. After you've made your visit there, ask to be let into the church, and a man will come with you and do just that.

The former church is hardly striking in its grandeur, but it has a fascinating past. What you see is the ruin of three different buildings. Inside you can inspect a mosaic floor and a mural of Jesus with Mary and John the Baptist which date from the time of Justinian (500s). That original church was destroyed by earthquake in 1065, but later rebuilt. Mosaics were set into the walls at that time. With the Ottoman conquest (1331), the church became a mosque. A fire in the 1500s ruined everything, but reconstruction was carried out under the expert eye of Mimar Sinan, who added İznik tiles to the decoration.

The Main Street

Now walk east toward Lefke Gate, along İznik's main street, Kılıçaslan Caddesi. On the left is the Belediye Sarayı (Town Hall). The big poplars shade the road from the summer sun. A bit further along on the left is the Hacı Özbek Camii, one of the town's oldest mosques, dating from 1332.

A short detour along the street opposite the Hacı Özbek Camii, to the south, will bring you to the Süleyman Paşa Medresesi. Founded by Sultan Orhan shortly after he captured Nicaea, it has the distinction of being the very first college (actually a theological seminary) founded by a member of the Ottoman dynasty.

Back on the main street, you will soon come to the Tourism Office, on the right-hand side. Soon, to the left, you can see the tile-covered minaret of the Yeşil Cami (Green Mosque). Turn left toward it.

Yeşil Cami

Built in the year that Columbus discovered America (1492), the Yeşil Cami has Seljuk Turkish proportions influenced more by Persia (the Seljuk homeland) than by Istanbul. The green-glazed bricks of the minaret foreshadowed the tile industry that arose a few decades after the mosque's construction. Sultan Selim, impatient to see a tile industry of his own, simply relocated a large number of artisans from Tabriz.

Museum

Across the road from the Yeşil Cami is the Nilüfer Hatun İmareti, or Soup Kitchen of Lady Nilüfer (1388), now set up as the town's museum. Hours are 9 to 12 noon and 1.30 to 5 pm, closed Monday. Entry costs the same as Sancta Sophia.

I'll wager that Lady Nilüfer would be pleased to see her pious gift in its present state. Though intended as a place where the poor could come for free food, it now dispenses culture to the masses. The front court is filled with marble statuary, bits of cornice and column, and similar archaeological flotsam and jetsam. In the lofty, cool halls are exhibits of İznik faience, Ottoman weaponry, embroidery, and calligraphy. Many of the little signs are in French and English, but you'll need to know the word yüzyıl: it's 'century' in Turkish, as XVI. Yüzyıl, '16th Century', (1700s).

While at the museum, inquire about a visit to the **Byzantine tomb** (Yeraltı Mezar or Katakom) on the outskirts of town. You must have a museum official accompany you with the key; there is a small charge for admission, and the official should receive a small tip. Also, you will have to haggle with a taxi-driver for a return-trip price. But once these arrangements have been made, you're in for a treat. The little tomb, discovered by accident in the 1960s, has delightful Byzantine murals covering walls and ceiling. There is another tomb nearby, but it's not really worth the bother or expense to see.

Across the road to the south of the museum is the Şeyh Kutbettin Camii (1492), now in ruins. Sometimes the caretaker will let you climb the stairs in the minaret, up to the stork's nest, for a look at the view.

Lefke Gate

Go back to Kılıçaslan Caddesi, and continue east to the Lefke Kapısı, or Lefke Gate. This charming old monument is actually three gates in a row, all dating from Byzantine times. The middle one has an inscription, which tells us it was built by the Proconsul Plancius Varus in 123 AD. It's possible to clamber up to the top of the gate and the walls here, a good vantage-point for inspection of the ancient walls.

Outside the gate is an aqueduct, still very much in use, and the tomb of Çandarlı Halil Hayrettin Paşa (late 1300s), with the graves of many lesser mortals nearby.

Lefke, by the way, is now called Osmaneli. In Byzantine times it was a city of considerable size, though Osmaneli is just a small town.

Re-enter the city through the Lefke Gate, and turn left. Follow the walls south and west to the Yenişehir Kapısı. On the way you will pass near the ruined Church of the Koimesis which dates from about 800. It's not much to look at, but it is famous as the burial-place of the Byzantine Emperor Theodore I Lascaris. When the Crusaders took Constantinople in 1204, Lascaris fled to Nicaea and established his court here. He never made it back to

his beloved capital. By the way, it was Lascaris who built the outer ring of walls, supported by over 100 towers and protected by a wide moat. No doubt he didn't trust the Crusaders, having lost one city to them.

Near the church is an *Ayazma*, or sacred fountain.

After admiring the Yenişehir Kapısı, start toward the centre along Atatürk Caddesi. Half way to Sancta Sophia, a road on the left leads to the ruins of a Roman theatre (*Roma Tiyatrosu*). Nearby is the Saray Kapısı, or Palace Gate in the city walls. Sultan Orhan had a palace hereabouts in the 1300s.

The Lake

Make your way to the lake shore, where there's a bathing beach (the water tends to be chilly), tea houses and little restaurants. This is the place to rest your feet, have an ice cream, soft drink or glass of tea, and ponder the history of battles which raged around this city. It is obviously much better off as a sleepy fruit-growing centre.

Places To Eat

The lakeside restaurants are the most pleasant for a light meal, if the weather is fine. A snack of white cheese (*beyaz peynir*), bread and a bottle of beer will cost less than $1. Of the restaurants along the lakeshore, the Kırıkçatal ('Broken Fork') is perhaps the most elaborate – and even that is pretty simple.

You'll find a greater selection of hot dishes along the main street in the centre, though, and prices will be lower. Near the Belediye Sarayı, look for the *Balıkçıoğlu* and *İnegöl* restaurants. The latter specializes in İnegöl köftesi, rich grilled rissoles of ground lamb in the style used in the nearby town of İnegöl. There is also a *pastahane* (pastry-shop) hereabouts.

Shopping

Coloured tiles, of course, are the natural souvenir from İznik. Several small shops along the main street sell these. There is also embroidered work, a local cottage industry.

Places To Stay

İznik has a few modest hostelries good for a one-night stay. The *Motel Burcum* (tel 11) has tidy rooms, some with views of the lake, but none with private toilet, for $10 double (lake side) or $6.50 (town side). The *İznik Moteli* (tel 41), on the lake shore, is the town's old standard, but is perhaps a bit expensive for what you get. The 18 rooms cost $7 single, $11 double. There's a restaurant and beach.

In the centre, just across the street from the Belediye Sarayı, is the plain *Hotel Babacan* (tel 211) at Kılıcaslan Caddesi No 104. The simple rooms have no plumbing facilities, and rent for $3 single, $4 double.

Onward to Bursa

Bursa has a much better selection of hotels and restaurants. Unless you are unusually interested in İznik, take one of the hourly buses from İznik's bus station to Bursa. Don't wait until too late in the day, however. The last bus heads out at 6 or 7 pm on the 1½-hour trip. A ticket costs about $1.25.

BURSA

Bursa has a special place in the hearts of the Turks. It was the first capital city of the enormous Ottoman Empire, and in a real sense the birthplace of modern Turkish culture. It's a beautiful city, despite its modern industrial might.

History

Called *Prusa* by the Byzantines, Bursa is a very old and important city. It was founded, according to legend, by Prusias, King of Bithynia, before 200 BC; there may have been an even older settlement on the site. It soon came under the sway of Eumenes II of Pergamum, and soon thereafter under direct Roman control.

Bursa grew to importance in the early centuries of Christianity, when the thermal baths at Çekirge were first developed on a large scale, and when a silk trade was founded here. The importation of silk-worms and the establishment of looms began an industry which survives to this day. It was Justinian (527-565) who really put Bursa on the map. Besides favouring the silk trade, he built a palace for himself, and bathhouses in Çekirge.

With the decline of Byzantium, Bursa's location near Istanbul drew the interest of would-be conquerors, including the Arab armies (circa 700 AD) and the Seljuk Turks. The Seljuks, having conquered much of Anatolia by 1075, took Bursa with ease that same year, and planted the seeds of the great Ottoman empire to come.

With the arrival of the First Crusade in 1097, Bursa reverted to Christian hands, though it was to be conquered and reconquered by both sides for the next hundred years. When the rapacious armies of the Fourth Crusade sacked Constantinople in 1204, the Byzantine emperor fled to İznik and set up his capital there. He succeeded in controlling the hinterland of İznik, including Bursa, until moving back to Constantinople in 1261.

Ever since the Turkish migration into Anatolia during the 11th and 12th centuries, small principalities had risen here and there around Turkish military leaders. A *gazi* (warrior chieftain or 'Hero of the Faith') would rally a group of followers, gain control of a territory, govern it, and seek to expand its borders. One such prince was Ertuğrul Gazi (died 1281), who formed a small state near Bursa. Succeeded by his son Osman Gazi (1281-1326), the small state grew to a nascent empire, and took Osman's name (*Osmanlı*, 'Ottoman'). Bursa was laid siege by Osman's forces in 1317, and was finally starved into submission on 6 April, 1326. It immediately became the Ottoman capital.

After Osman had expanded and enriched his principality, he was succeeded by Orhan Gazi (1326-1361) who, from his base at Bursa, expanded the empire to include everything from Ankara in Central Anatolia to Thrace in Europe. The Byzantine capital at Constantinople was thus surrounded, and the Byzantine Empire had only about a century to live. Orhan took the title of *sultan* (lord), struck the first Ottoman coinage, and near the end of his reign was able to dictate to the Byzantine emperors. One of them, John VI Cantacuzene, was Orhan's close ally and later even his father-in-law (Orhan married the Princess Theodora).

Even though the Ottoman capital would be moved to Edirne (Adrianople) in 1402, Bursa remained an important, even revered, Ottoman city throughout the long history of the empire. Both Osman and Orhan were buried in Bursa, and their tombs are still proud and important monuments in Turkish history.

With the founding of the Turkish Republic, Bursa's industrial development began in earnest. What really brought the boom was the automobile assembly plants, set up in the 1960s and 1970s. Large factories here assemble Renaults, Fiats (called *Murat*) and a Turkish car called the Anadol. Also, Bursa has always been noted for its fruits, and it was logical that a large fruit juice and soft drink industry should be centered here. Tourism is also important.

Information

The Tourism Information Office (tel 12 359) is at Atatürk Caddesi 82, right in the centre of the city, near the Ulu Cami. The staff are helpful, and some speak English.

Getting Around

As Bursa has no rail service, and the small airport has (at this writing) no scheduled air service, you will probably arrive in Bursa by bus or minibus from the ferryboat dock at Yalova, from the hydrofoil dock at Mudanya, or from İznik. All these services come into Bursa's *Otogar* (bus station), sometimes called the *Şehir Garajı*.

Getting Away

When the time comes to leave Bursa, go to the Şehir Garajı. Buses, minibuses and dolmuşes leave frequently for İznik, and for the Istanbul ferryboats at Yalova. If you plan to catch a boat at Yalova, get a bus that departs at least 90 minutes before scheduled ferryboat departure; or a dolmuş which leaves at least 75 minutes before ferry departure, if you plan to catch a boat at Yalova. You can also get a minibus to Mudanya for the morning and late afternoon hydrofoils to Istanbul.

For other destinations, buy your ticket in advance to assure a good seat and good departure time. The bus trip to Ankara takes seven hours; to Izmir, 7½ hours; to Çanakkale (for Troy and Gallipoli), six hours.

Orientation

Out the front door of the Otogar is a big street named Uluyol (oo-LOO yohl, 'Great Road') or Ulu Caddesi. Here you will find dolmuşes, taxis and city buses. For the city buses, you will need to buy a booklet of tickets *before* you board the bus. Look for the ticket kiosk. There's not much in the Otogar area to detain you. The hotels tend to be somewhat rundown, and noisy because of the buses, so, most likely, you will be looking for transport to the centre of town and its hotels, or the hotels along Altıparmak Caddesi, or to the baths and hotels at Çekirge.

Bursa's main plaza is Cumhuriyet Alanı (joom-hoor-ee-YEHT ah-lahn-uh, 'Republic Plaza'), where you will see an equestrian statue of Atatürk. Most people refer to the plaza as *Heykel* (hey-KEHL, statue), and that's what you will see written on a little plastic sign, hung on suction-cup hooks, in the windscreens of dolmuşes waiting just outside the bus station. Hop in a dolmuş to get up the hill to Heykel.

Bursa's main street, Atatürk Caddesi, runs west from Heykel to the Ulu Cami (oo-LOO jah-mee, Great Mosque), a distance of perhaps half a kilometre. This

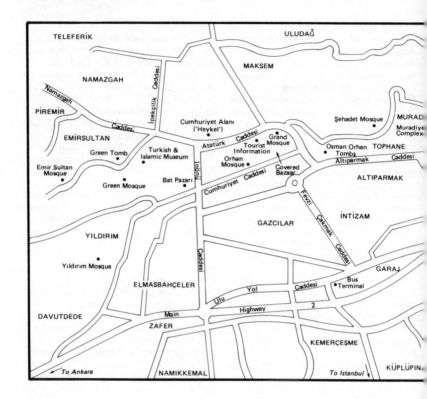

is the downtown business section, the centre of Bursa. The westward continuation of Atatürk Caddesi becomes Cemal Nadir Caddesi, then Altıparmak Caddesi, then Çekirge Caddesi. It leads to the spa suburb of Çekirge, about a ten-minute ride.

From Heykel and Atatürk Caddesi you can get dolmuşes and buses to all other parts of the city, including hotel and sightseeing areas.

Places to Stay

Though there are a few hotels right downtown, Bursa's best selection of lodgings, in terms of both quality and price, is in the western suburb of Çekirge, or nearby. Hotels atop Uludağ are mentioned in the section (below) describing the mountain.

Most Çekirge hotels have their own facilities for 'taking the waters', since that's the reason people come to Çekirge. You may find that the bathtub or shower in your hotel room runs only mineral water, or there may be separate private or public bathing-rooms in the basement of the hotel. One day's dip in the mineral waters is no great thrill. The benefits are acquired over a term of weeks, and are therapeutic. All the same, you may find that a soak in a private tub is included in

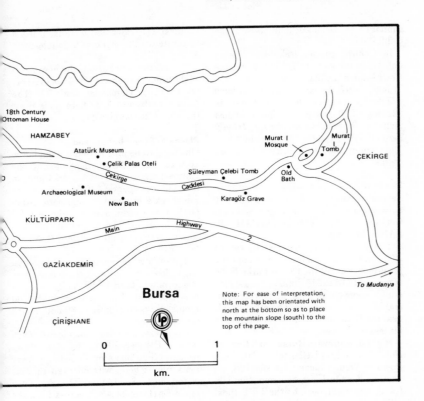

18th Century Ottoman House

HAMZABEY

Atatürk Museum

Çelik Palas Oteli

Çekirge Caddesi

Archaeological Museum

New Bath

KÜLTÜRPARK

Main Highway

Süleyman Çelebi Tomb

Karagöz Grave

Murat I Mosque

Murat I Tomb

ÇEKİRGE

Old Bath

2

GAZİAKDEMİR

To Mudanya

ÇİRİŞHANE

Bursa

Note: For ease of interpretation, this map has been orientated with north at the bottom so as to place the mountain slope (south) to the top of the page.

0   1

km.

the price of the room, even in the very cheapest hotels, so take advantage of it.

For all of these hotels, get a bus or dolmuş from Heykel or along Atatürk Caddesi, and get out at the bus stop mentioned.

Places to Stay – top end

Bursa's most interesting hotel is the old 95-room *Çelik Palas Oteli* (cheh-LEEK pah-lahs, tel 19 600), at Çekirge Caddesi 79, on the road to Çekirge (bus stop Çelik Palas). Built after World War I, it was one of Atatürk's favourites, and hosted many other worthies as well. The late King Idries of Libya used to take the waters

here every year, and he was relaxing in a warm mineral bath when he received word that Colonel Qaddafi had taken over. Facilities at the hotel are, well, ancient and honourable; the musty ambience makes up for a lot. Double rooms cost $22 to $30; the better rooms have nice views. There's a swimming pool, and elaborate facilities for taking the waters rich in minerals (*çelik*).

More modern are the hotels west of the Çelik Palas, closer to Çekirge. The *Hotel Akdoğan* (AHK-doh-ahn, tel 24 755, –6, or –7), Birinci Murat Cad. 5 (bus stop Sigorta), is a modern and comfortable place to stay, though room prices are similar to, or even lower than, those at the Çelik Palas.

In Çekirge proper (take the bus or dolmuş to the end of the line). Here, the *Hotel Dilmen* (DEEL-mehn, tel 21 701, –2) is the most deluxe. Some rooms have wonderful views over the valley. Rates are $22 single, $30 double, $44 triple, breakfast included. Right next door, the *Hotel Gönlü Ferah* (GEWN-lew feh-RAH, tel 17 900, –1) is about the same price for similar rooms.

Places to Stay – mid-range

Several worthy hotels are located half-way between downtown Bursa and Çekirge. Get off at the Yağcılar (YAAH-juh-LAHR) bus stop.

The *Hotel Diyar* (dee-YAHR, tel 19 204, –5), Çekirge Caddesi 17/4, is opposite the green swath of the Kültür Parki. Even at prices of $15 to $18 double, you get nice double rooms with bath or shower, a lift, and other such services. The other hotels near the Diyar are not quite so nice, but a bit less expensive.

Right downtown in Bursa you'll find the *Hotel Artıç* (ahr-TUCH, tel 19 500, –1), Postane Yanı, Ulucami Karşısı 123, on Atatürk Caddesi across from the Ulu Cami, and right next to the PTT (post office). Prices are a bit less than at the Diyar. The location is convenient to downtown activities, but noise may be a problem so select your room carefully.

One of the best choices in this price range is the *Hotel Hünkâr* (hewn-KYAR, tel 17 084, –5), on Acemler Caddesi down the hill from the Sigorta bus stop and the aforementioned Hotel Akdoğan. The hotel's location is quiet and not really inconvenient, it has its own marble mineral baths, and many rooms have pretty views of the valley. A double costs $14.

In Çekirge proper are two more good places to stay. The *Hotel Ada Palas* (ah-DAH pah-lahs, tel 19 200) faces the centre of Çekirge; it's right on Çekirge Caddesi, though its legal address is Birinci Murat

Caddesi 21. Older and well-used, it's a favourite with foreigners. A double costs $12.

Behind the Ada Palas is the newer and slightly more expensive *Hotel Yat* (YAHT, tel 18 695), Hamamlar Cad. 31. The private baths in rooms here have tubs; there's a lift. Doubles go for $16.

Places to Stay – bottom end

One used to be able to find a room in the very centre of Bursa, right next to the Covered Bazaar, just off Atatürk Caddesi, for 85c per person. This was in the ramshackle but very sympathetic Altan Oteli, razed years ago to make way for souvenir shops. The Altan had one cold-water tap to serve all 42 rooms. It was my favourite.

These days one pays more and gets less. Right downtown, or near the bus station, cheap hotels tend to be badly kept, or noisy, or both. But there are still good rooms in this city for $6 to $9 double. All are in Çekirge.

Cheapest are the *Hüsnügüzel Oteli* (hews-NEW-gew-ZEHL, tel 11 640), up past the final bus stop in Çekirge. Very plain rooms here, without even running water, costs $6 double. The *Şifa Oteli* (shee-FAH, tel 11 483), across from the aforementioned Ada Palas, charges the same for rooms within its ramshackle wooden walls. Both have their own mineral baths.

Slightly more expensive ($9 double), but more comfortable, are the *Temizel Oteli* (teh-MEEZ-ehl, tel 11 682), next to the Şifa; the *Yıldız Oteli* (yuhl-DUHZ, tel 23 200, –1), near the Hüsnügüzel; and the *Otel Kılınç* (kuh-LUNCH, tel 12 536), behind the Ada Palas at Birinci Murat Caddesi Arka Sokak 13. The Yıldız and Kılınç have the quietest locations.

Food

Bursa's culinary specialties include fresh fruit, especially peaches (in season), and two types of roast meat. *Bursa kebap* or *İskender kebap* is the most famous, made from döner kebap laid on a bed of fresh pide bread and topped with savoury tomato sauce and browned butter. When I'm in Bursa, I have this every single day. The other specialty is *İnegöl köftesi*, a type of very rich grilled rissole (ground meat patty) which is actually the specialty of the nearby town called İnegöl. You will see several restaurants which specialize in these dishes exclusively, called *Bursa kebapçısı* or *İnegöl köftecisi*.

Places to Eat – Bursa Kebapcıs

My favourite Bursa kebapçı is *Hacı Bey* (hah-JUH bey), on a small street just east of Heykel (ask in the plaza for 'hah-JUH bey BOOR-sah keh-bahp-chuh-suh'). Just a few steps down the street, on the right, you'll recognize it by the döner turning in the window. Simple but neat and tidy, the restaurant serves Bursa kebap in 1, 1½ and 2-portion sizes called *bir porsyon*, *bir buçuk porsyon*, and *duble* (BEER pohr-syohn; BEER boo-CHOOK; DOOB-leh). A single portion with yoghurt (*yoğurtlu*), plus a salad, a bottle of mineral water, and Turkish coffee, tip included, will cost about $3.

Bursa kebap was invented in a small restaurant now called *Kebabcı İskenderoğlu* ('Iskender's Son') at Atatürk Caddesi 60, right in the centre of town. This is another good choice for the famous kebap. Yet another is the *Bursa Kebabcı* at Atatürk Caddesi 86-B, right next to the Romans Çay Bahçesi ('Romance Tea Garden') in the centre of town.

Köfteci

For İnegöl köftesi, try the *İnegöl Köftecisi*, on a little side street right by Atatürk Caddesi 48. On your second visit, you might try the köfte made with onions or cheese as a variation on the basic stuff. A full lunch need cost only $2.50.

Another good köfteci is the *Özömür*, on the western side of the Ulu Cami.

Hazır Yemek

Those marvellously cheap and tasty meals you sampled in Istanbul are readily available in Bursa's many *hazır yemek lokantası*s. Look for ready-food restaurants down sidestreets near Heykel.

In Çekirge

Çekirge has several good restaurants which are especially pleasant because they have delightful views of the green river valley. Both the *Çardak* and the *Papağan* are near the Ada Palas hotel in the centre of Çekirge. A full meal of soup, mixed grill of lamb, salad, dessert, wine or beer, tax and tip might cost $7; you can obviously dine for less if you're not famished.

Places to See

You can see most of Bursa's sights in one full day, though a leisurely tour will take a little more time. Start with the city's most famous architectural monuments, located east of downtown.

The Yeşil Cami Area

Bursa's most famous mosque is the Yeşil Cami, or Green Mosque. Past it, up a hill on the same road, is the Emir Sultan Camii. The way to see these sights is to hop on a bus or dolmuş departing Heykel or Atatürk Caddesi and bound for Emir Sultan. Get off at the end of the line. You'll pass right by the Green Mosque and Green Tomb before coming to the mosque of Emir Sultan, but this way you can walk *down* the hill, not up.

Emir Sultan Camii The Mosque of Emir Sultan is a favourite among Bursa's pious Muslims. Rebuilt by Selim III in 1805, it echoes the romantic decadence of Ottoman Rococo style. The setting, next to a large hillside cemetery, surrounded by huge trees, overlooking the city and the valley, is as nice as the mosque itself. If you have postcards or a diary to write, this is the place to do it. The little tea gardens right next to the mosque provide the necessary table, tea and view.

Yıldırım Beyazıt Camii Gazing across the valley from the Emir Sultan Camii you'll see the two domes of the Yıldırım Beyazıt Camii, the Mosque of Beyazıt the Thunderbolt. It is earlier (1391) than Bursa's famous Yeşil Cami, and takes part in the same architectural evolution (see below). You can walk through the city to this mosque if you like, but go see the Yeşil Cami first.

Next to the Yıldırım Beyazıt Camii is its *medrese*, once a theological seminary, now a public health centre. Here also is the tomb of the mosque's founder, Sultan Beyazit I, and of his son İsa. This peaceful spot gives one no sense of the turbulent times which brought Beyazıt to his death.

Yıldırım Beyazıt (1389-1402) led his Ottoman armies into Yugoslavia and Hungary, and captured even more of Anatolia for the Ottomans. But he was brought down by Tamerlane, who defeated him and took him prisoner at the Battle of Ankara in 1402. Beyazıt died (1403) in captivity, and Tamerlane marched all the way to İzmir and Bursa while Beyazıt's sons argued over the succession to the weakened Ottoman throne. The empire was just about dead. The civil war among Beyazıt's sons lasted for ten years, until 1413, when one of the sons, Mehmet Çelebi, was able to gain supreme power. Six years after becoming sultan, Mehmet I began construction of Bursa's greatest monument, the Green Mosque.

Yeşil Cami The Yeşil Cami, or Green Mosque, is a supremely beautiful building in a fine setting. Built by Sultan Mehmet I Çelebi and finished in 1424, it represents a turning-point in Turkish architectural style. Before this, Turkish mosques echoed the style of the Great Seljuks, which was basically Persian. But in the Yeşil Cami a purely Turkish style emerges. Notice the harmonious facade and the beautiful carved marble work around the central doorway. As you enter, you will pass beneath the sultan's private apart-ments into a domed central hall. The rooms to the left and right, if not being used for prayer, were used by high court officials for transacting government business. The room straight ahead, with the 15-metre-high *mihrab* (prayer niche), is the main prayer room. Greenish-blue tiles on the interior walls gave the mosque its name.

Much of Bursa, including the Green Mosque, was destroyed in an earthquake in 1855. But the mosque was restored, authentically, by 1864.

At some point during your visit, a caretaker is likely to approach you and, with a conspiratorial wink, signal you to follow him up a narrow stairway to the *Hünkâr mahfili*, or sultan's loge, above the main door. The loge is sumptuously tiled and decorated. This is where the sultan actually lived (or at least it was one of his residences), with his harem and household staff in less plush quarters on either side. The caretaker will not take large groups up to the mahfil; he'll choose single travellers or couples. Tip him about 50c.

Yeşil Türbe Walk around the Green Mosque, noticing the slender minarets rising from bulbous bases, across the road and up the steps to the Yeşil Türbe, or Green Tomb. It's not green, of course. The blue exterior tiles were put on during restoration work in the 1800s; the lavish use of tiles inside is original work, however. No need to remove your shoes to enter here. The tomb is open 8.30 to 12 noon, 1 to 5.30 pm, for free.

The most prominent tomb is that of the Green Mosque's founder, Mehmet Çelebi (1413-1421). Others include those of his children. The huge tiled *mihrab* here is very impressive. Take a walk around the outside of the tomb for a look at the tiled calligraphy above several windows.

Museum Down the road a few steps from the Green Mosque is its *medrese*, now used as the **Türk-İslam Eserleri Müzesi**, the Museum of Turkish and Islamic Antiquities.

The building, which is in the Seljuk style for religious schools, and the museum collection, contain a good assortment of local craft items, and are both worth a look. The museum is open 8.30 to 12 noon, 1 to 5.30 pm, closed Monday; admission costs about 6c, cameras about 30c, half-price on Sunday and holidays.

Downtown

Sights downtown in Bursa include the large Ulu Cami (Great Mosque), the Bedesten (Covered Market), and the Bat Pazarı (market section). Start from Heykel.

Bat Pazarı From the plaza at Heykel, walk down the hill on İnönü Caddesi until you come to a small mosque set partly in the roadway. The section to your right – is the Bat Pazarı, or Goose Market. The one thing you won't find here today are geese, but you will find ironmongers' shops, peddlers of old clothes, carpets, rope, utensils, potions, and just about everything else. This market section is lively and colourful, perfect for photographing. When you snap a shot of the blacksmith at his forge, chances are the blacksmith will ask you to send him a copy. It's only fair; you should try to do it.

Bedesten After an hour's stroll through the Bat Pazarı, head back to İnönü Caddesi and ask someone to point out the Bedesten (BEHD-eh-stehn), the Covered Bazaar. Cross İnönü Caddesi and head into the side streets, following their directions.

The Bedesten was originally built in the late 1300s by Yıldırım Beyazıt, but the earthquake of 1855 brought it down. The reconstructed Bedesten retains the look and feel of the original, though it is obviously much tidier. This is not a tourist trap; most of the shoppers are local people. As you wander around, look for the shop called *Karagöz*, run by a man named Şinasi Çelikkol. Şinasi specializes in quality goods (copper and brass,

carpets and kilims, knitted gloves and embroidery, old jewellery, etc) at fair prices, as did his father before him. This is the place to find the delightful Karagöz shadow-play puppets. Cut from flat, dried camel leather, painted in bright colours and oiled to make them translucent, the puppets are an authentic Turkish craft item. The Karagöz shadow play is thought to have originated in Bursa.

Another place you ought to visit in the Bedesten is the **Emirhan**, a caravanserai which is the headquarters of the silk brokers, as it has been for centuries. Just ask directions by saying *Emirhan nerede?* (eh-MEER-hahn neh-reh-deh, 'Where's the Emirhan?'). There's a lovely fountain in the centre of the courtyard, and a tea garden for refreshment. Camels from the silk caravans used to be corralled in the courtyard, while goods were stored in the ground-floor rooms and drovers and merchants slept and did business in the rooms above.

Ulu Cami Next to the Bedesten is Bursa's Great Mosque, the Ulu Cami. This one is completely Seljuk in style, a big rectangular building with immense portals and a forest of supporting columns inside. The roof is a mass of twenty small domes. A *şadırvan* (ablutions fountain) is right within the mosque. It was Yıldırım Beyazıt who put up the money for the building, in 1396. Notice the fine work in the *mimber* (pulpit) and the preacher's chair; also the calligraphy on the walls.

Hisar & Muradiye

From the Ulu Cami, walk west and up a ramp-like street to the section known as **Hisar** (fortress). Coming by bus or dolmuş from Heykel, get a vehicle labelled *Muradiye*.

The main street here is Pınarbaşı Caddesi. This section is among the oldest in Bursa, once enclosed by stone ramparts and walls. Some picturesque old frame houses and neighbourhood quarters survive here.

Tombs of Orhan and Osman In a little park near the edge of the cliff, overlooking the boulevard (Cemal Nadir Caddesi) and the valley, are the tombs (*türbeler*) of sultans Osman and Orhan, founders of the Ottoman Empire. The originals were destroyed in the earthquake of 1855, and rebuilt in Ottoman Baroque style by Sultan Abdül Aziz in 1868. As baroque tombs they make it, but as period reminders of the Founders, they don't. The park is nice, as is the view.

Muradiye Camii The Mosque of Sultan Murat II (1421-1451) is further west, and up the slope, from the tombs. With a shady park in front and a quiet cemetery behind, the mosque is a pretty, peaceful place. The mosque proper dates from 1426, and follows the style of the Yeşil Cami.

Beside the mosque are a dozen tombs dating from the 1400s and 1500s, including those of Sultan Murat himself. Tomb-visiting may not be high on your list of priorities, but you should do it here to see the beautiful decoration, especially in the **Murat II Türbesi**, the **Cem Türbesi**, and the **Mustafa Şehzade Türbesi**.

Murat Evi Across the park from the mosque is an old Ottoman house, the Murat Evi, or House of Murat. It was once rumoured that Sultan Murat lived here, but historians say this could not have been. Even so, the house, now a museum, gives one a fascinating glimpse into the daily life of the Ottoman nobility in the 1600s. Carpets and furnishings are all authentic. Don't miss this one. It's open 8.30 to 12 am, 1 to 5.30 pm, closed Monday, with a small admission charge.

Kültür Parkı
Bursa's Cultural Park (*Kültür Parkı*, kewl-TEWR pahr-kuh) is laid out to the north of the Muradiye complex, down the hill some distance. You can reach it from Heykel by any bus or dolmuş going to Çekirge. Besides a pleasant stroll, the Kültür Parkı is good for its **Arkeoloji Müzesi** (Archaeological Museum). Find the bus stop named 'Arkeoloji Müzesi', enter the park by the gate nearby, and visit the museum from 8.30 to 12 am, 1 to 5.30 pm, any day but Monday; small admission charge. Bursa's history goes back to the time of Hannibal (200 BC). Hellenistic and Roman artifacts are preserved here.

Çekirge and The Baths
The warm mineral-rich waters which spring from the slopes of Uludağ have been famous for their curative powers since ancient times. Today the ailing and the infirm come here for several weeks at a time, taking a daily soak or two in the tub, spending the rest of the time chatting, reading or dining. Most stay in hotels which have their own bathing facilities. But there are independent baths (*kaplıca*) as well, some of historical importance.

The **Yeni Kaplıca** is a bath built in 1522 by Sultan Süleyman the Magnificent's Grand Vezir, Rüstem Paşa, on the site of a much older one built by Justinian. The **Kükürtlü** bath is noted for its high sulphur content. At the **Kaynarca** ('Boiling') bath, it's the extreme heat of the water that is outstanding. Other baths are the **Kara Mustafa** and the **Eski Kaplıca**.

Bathing arrangements vary. Some have private steam rooms, some have rows of tubs, some have a common steam room and pool, some have several of these all under one roof. Bathing fees are low, though tips to the staff can run up the final tab somewhat. Baths will be crowded on Friday, the Muslim sabbath, as local people clean up for the holy day.

The standard Turkish bath has three rooms, as did the ancient Roman bath. The first is cool, the second warm, the third hot. After a soak in the hot room, you retire to the warm one for a wash, then to the cool one for a towelling. A nap, followed by a glass of tea, comes next, if you have the time.

ULUDAĞ

Bursa's Mount Olympus dominates the city. There were numerous mountains named Olympus in the ancient world. This was the one in the Kingdom of Bithynia, later the Roman province of Mysia.

The gods no longer live atop Uludağ, but there is a cable car (*teleferik*), a selection of hotels, a national park, cool forests, and snow. Even if you don't plan to make the hike to the summit (three hours each way), or to go skiing (winter only), you should take the cable car up for the view and the cool, fresh air.

Getting There

Actually there are two ways to ascend Uludağ. Dolmuşes depart from the Şehir Garajı and drive to the top, charging $3 per person, each way. But the cable car is much more fun.

Catch a bus or dolmuş from Heykel going to the Teleferik cable car terminus (tehl-eh-fehr-EEK, tel 13 635) called Teleferuç, a 15-minute ride. Cars run up the mountainside every half hour or so, unless strong winds or bad weather prevent them. A ticket to the top and back down costs $2.50; the trip takes 30 minutes each way.

There is an intermediate stop on the cable car, at a place called Kadıyayla. The upper terminus is called Sarıalan. Get off here, wander among the hotels, marvel at the coolness, and perhaps head for the summit if the weather is good. A dolmuş will take you to a concentration of hotels near the head of the summit trail.

Places to Stay

A dozen inns are scattered about the mountaintop. Many are meant for skiers, so they close for much of the year. A few stay open all the time. Fanciest places to stay are the *Turistik Uludağ Oteli* (tel 13, 59), charging over $30 per night for a double room. The lowest prices are in the *Kar Oberj* (tel 45), about $14 for a double, and the *Ulukardeşler Oberj* (tel 28, 61), for $20. As you can see, the hotels here are priced for vacationers, not travellers. Remember that you will probably have to take all your meals in your hotel, which can double the price.

Gallipoli & Troy

A tremendous amount of world commerce travels by sea. Since commerce means wealth and wealth means power, the people who control the sea have enormous commercial – not to mention military – power. The best place for a small group of people to control an awful lot of sea is at a strait.

The story of the Çanakkale Boğazı (cha-NAH-kah-leh boh-ah-zuh), or Dardanelles, is one of people battling each another for control of this narrow passage which unites the Mediterranean and Aegean seas with the Marmara and Black seas. In ancient times, it was the Achaeans attacking the Trojans; in modern times, the Anzacs facing Atatürk at Gallipoli. The name 'Dardanelles' comes from Dardanus, ruler of a very early city-state at Çanakkale, who controlled the straits.

But the story of the Dardanelles is not all war and commerce; romance, too, has been central to its mythical associations: legends says that the goddess Helle fell from a golden-winged ram into the water here, giving the straits the name Hellespont. And the lovesick Leander, separated from his beloved Hero, swam to her through the fierce currents each night, until one night he didn't make it. 'Swimming the Hellespont' is a challenge for amateur and professional swimmers to this day.

The height of romance is the story of two ancient peoples battling over the love and honour of Helen, most beautiful woman in the world. Historians now tell us that Helen was just a pawn in the fierce commercial and military rivalries between Achaea and Troy. Still, no one says she wasn't beautiful, or that the Trojan horse didn't actually fool the Trojans and lead to their defeat by the Achaeans.

The area of the straits holds these attractions: the town of Çanakkale (population 45,000), a fast-growing agricultural centre on the south-east shore of the straits; the fortifications, ancient and modern, which guarded the straits; the battlefields of Gallipoli, on the north-west side of the straits; and the excavated ruins of ancient Troy, 32 km to the south. For a week in mid-August, the Çanakkale Festival fills the hotels in town. Arrive early in the day, and start your search for a hotel room at once, if you plan to be here around August 10th to 18th.

Getting There & Getting Around

You will probably arrive in Çanakkale by bus. The town has a central bus station (*Otogar*) with several buses a day to Bursa, Istanbul, İzmir and Edirne. You will also find dolmuş-minibuses heading for *Truva* (Troy), less than an hour away; the fare is about 60c each way. If you are here in winter, early spring or late fall, the dolmuşes may not be running all the way to Troy, and you may have to hike and hitch a bit from where the dolmuş drops you. Otherwise, it's a tour by taxi. If you plan to visit Troy and then head south, you should try to buy a ticket on a southbound bus a day in advance, let the ticket seller know you want to be picked up at Troy, then be out on the main highway in plenty of time to catch the bus. Without a ticket you can hitch out to the highway from Troy and hope a bus will come by, and that it will have vacant seats. This often works, though it entails some waiting.

To get from the bus station to the centre of town by the Clock Tower and the car ferry docks, leave the bus station by the front doors, turn left, walk to the first turning to the right, and follow signs straight to the *Feribot* ('ferryboat!'). Just before you come to the docks, you'll see the vaguely Teutonic *Clock Tower* (*Saat Kulesi*, sah-AHT koo-leh-see) on your left. The town's Tourism Information Office (tel 1187) is in a little booth near the quay, between the Clock Tower and the ferry docks.

You may arrive here by ferryboat, also. Two services run across the straits. The northern one is between the towns of Gelibolu and Lapseki. Ferries leave Gelibolu at 1, 6, 7, 8, 9, and 10 am, 12 noon, 2, 4, 5, 6, 7, 8, 9, 10 and 11 pm. From Lapseki, ferries are at 2, 6, 7, 8, 9, 10, 11 am; 1, 3, 5, 6, 7, 8, 9, 10 pm and 12 midnight.

The southern car ferry service runs between Çanakkale and the town of Eceabat (eh-jeh-AH-baht), near the battlefields of Gallipoli. Between 6 am and 11 pm, boats run in each direction every hour on the hour; there are also boats at 12 midnight and 2 am from Eceabat, and at 1 and 3 am from Çanakkale.

Passengers, as well as cars, are carried on the boats, at very low fares (about 11c per person). The crossing from Çanakkale to Eceabat takes about 25 minutes in good weather. Because of the schedules, over-and-back thus takes 1½ hours. You can shorten this time by climbing aboard a *motor* (moh-TOHR, motorboat). These small craft ply between Çanakkale's docks and the village of Kilitbahir, at the foot of the fortress on the opposite shore. The voyage over takes 15 to 20 minutes in a motorboat, which will leave as soon as it has a sufficient number of passengers.

Places to Stay

Çanakkale has several comfortable and more expensive motels on its outskirts. The few downtown hotels range from simple but comfortable and moderately-priced, to rock-bottom.

The downtown hotels are clustered near the Clock Tower. Best is the 35-room *Hotel Bakır* (bah-KUHR, tel 2908, 4088, 9), Rıhtım Caddesi, also called Yalı Caddesi, No 12, where a modern double room , with bath and view of the straits, costs $15. The 66-room *Truva Oteli* (TROO-vah, tel 1024), Kayserili Ahmet Paşa Caddesi, is several blocks from the centre, but charges about the same as the Bakır.

Less expensive hotels include the *Hotel Konak* (koh-NAHK, tel 1150), just behind the Clock Tower, which boasts central heat, constant hot water, and prices of $2.60 single, $3.50 double without private shower, or $4.60 single, $6 double with private shower; and the *Küçük Truva Oteli* (kew-CHEWK TROO-vah, tel 1552), very near the Konak, where the rates are $2.60 per person in a small room with shower, or $2 per bed in a room without. The Küçük Truva has fly screens (*sineklik*) on its windows! The nearby *Hotel Efes* (eh-FEHS, tel 3256) is a similar place.

Only someone with a car would be interested in the motels on the outskirts. If you have a car, look first at the *Tusan Truva Motel* (TOO-sahn TROO-vah, tel İntepe 1), located in the quarter called Karantina. The 64 rooms go for $20 to $23 double, with bath. Rooms at the *Mola Motel* (MOH-lah, tel Guzelyalı 22) are lower, and those at the *İda-Tur Motel* (EE-dah toor, tel Küçükkuyu 56, 102) even lower. The best way to find these motels is to follow the signs along the roads.

Places to Eat

Çanakkale has inexpensive eateries all through town, but the most enjoyable are those right along the quay, to the left of the car ferry docks as you face the water. The *Restaurant Boğaz* (boh-AHZ) is big and lively. The *Rıhtım* is one of my favourites. These, and others, set out tables along the promenade on summer evenings. The *Efes Pilsen* beer garden encourages consumption of the local pilsener, but serves food as well. At the *Yalova Liman Restaurant*, the attraction is a third-floor patio with a fine view of the straits and of Kilitbahir fortress on the opposite shore. A meal of an appetizer, fried or grilled fish, salad, and a bottle of beer may cost $3.

For even cheaper fare, head inland along the main street until you see a *köfteci* or *pideci* shop. At a pideci, fresh flat *pide* (PEE-deh) bread is topped with such things as whole eggs, cheese or ground lamb, dabbed with butter, then baked. It's filling, delicious and very cheap. Price depends on the toppings. Ask for your pide *yumurtalı* (yoo-moor-tah-LUH, with egg), or *peynirli* (pey-neer-LEE, with cheese), or *kıymalı* (kuy-mah-LUH, with ground lamb).

A meal of soup, pide or köfte, bread, and a soft drink should cost about $1.

Places to See

You can walk easily to Çanakkale's interesting sights. To reach the market area, walk behind the Clock Tower and turn into one of the streets on the left-hand side.

There is an interesting **Askeri Müze** (ahs-kehr-EE mew-zeh, Military Museum) in the Military Zone at the southern end of the quay. Start from the ferry docks and walk along the quay to the zone and its fortress.

Within the zone you'll see a mock-up of the old minelayer 'Nusrat', which had a heroic role in the Gallipoli campaign. The day before the Allied fleet was to steam through the straits, Allied minesweepers proclaimed the water cleared. But during the night, the Nusrat went out, picked up loose mines and relaid them, helping to keep the Allies from penetrating the straits the next day.

There's also a small museum with memorabilia of Atatürk and the battles of Gallipoli, and the impressive fortress.

The fortress, built by Mehmet the Conqueror in the mid-1400s, is still considered active in the defense of the straits, so it is forbidden to climb to the top of the walls or the top of the keep. But you're free to examine the wonderful old cannons left from various wars, many made in French, English or German foundries. The keep is a gallery for changing exhibits.

Çanakkale also has a small **Archaeological Museum** (*Arkeoloji Müzesi*, ahr-keh-yohl-oh-JEE mew-zeh-see), in a disused church on an unmarked back street. It holds the flotsam and jetsam of the area's history, which is long and deep.

To Gallipoli

The slender peninsula which forms the north-western side of the straits is called *Gelibolu* (geh-LEE-boh-loo) in Turkish. The fortress on this side, visible from the town, is called *Kilitbahir*, 'Lock on the Sea'. It was built by Mehmet the Conqueror as an aid to cutting off supplies and reinforcements to Constantinople, which Mehmet held under seige in the 1450s. Many foreign naval forces have tried, over the centuries, to force any such 'lock' put on the Dardanelles. Most have had Istanbul as their goal, and most have failed.

On the hillside by Kilitbahir, clearly visible from the far shore, are gigantic letters spelling out the first few words of a poem by Necmettin Halil Onan.

Dur yolcu! Bilmeden gelip bastığın
Bu toprak bir devrin battığı yerdir.
Eğil de kulak ver, bu sessiz yığın
Bir vatan kalbinin attığı yerdir.

('Traveller, halt! The soil you tread
Once witnessed the end of an era.
Listen! In this quiet mound
There once beat the heart of a nation.')

The poem refers to the battles of Gallipoli in World War I. With the intention of capturing the Ottoman capital and the road to eastern Europe, Winston Churchill, First Lord of the Admiralty, organized a naval assault on the straits. A strong Franco-British fleet tried first to force the straits in March, 1915, but failed. Then in April, British, Australian and New Zealand troops were landed on Gallipoli, and French troops near Çanakkale. After nine months of disastrous defeats, the Allied forces were withdrawn.

The Turkish success at Gallipoli was due in part to disorganization in the Allied ranks. Another part was due to reinforcements brought up under the command of General Liman von Sanders. But a crucial element in the defeat was that the Allied troops happened to land in a sector where they faced Lieutenant-Colonel Mustafa Kemal (Atatürk). Though a relatively minor officer, he had Geneneral von Sanders' confidence. He read the Allied battle plan correctly when his commanders did not, and stalled the invasion in bitter fighting which wiped out his division. Though suffering from malaria, he commanded in full view of his troops and of the enemy, and miraculously escaped death several times. At one point a piece of shrapnel tore through the breast pocket of his uniform, but was stopped by his pocket watch. His brilliant performance made him a folk hero, and paved the way for his promotion to general.

The Gallipoli campaign lasted for nine months, until January, 1916, and resulted in huge numbers of casualties. You can visit Turkish, British and French monuments to the war dead at Seddülbahir, as well as Australian and New Zealander cemeteries at Arıburnu. You'll have to negotiate with a taxi driver for a tour of the battlefields and monuments unless you've already made arrangements with the *Troy-Anzac Travel Agency* (tel 1440, 1447), in Çanakkale very near the Clock Tower, which sometimes organizes tours to the battle-grounds.

Troy

The approach to Troy (*Truva*, TROO-vah) is across low, rolling countryside of grain fields, with here and there a small village. This is the Troad of ancient times, all but lost to legend until a German-born California businessman and amateur archaeologist named Heinrich Schliemann (1822-1890) rediscovered it in 1871. The poetry of Homer was assumed, at that time, to be based on legend, not history. But Schliemann got permission from the

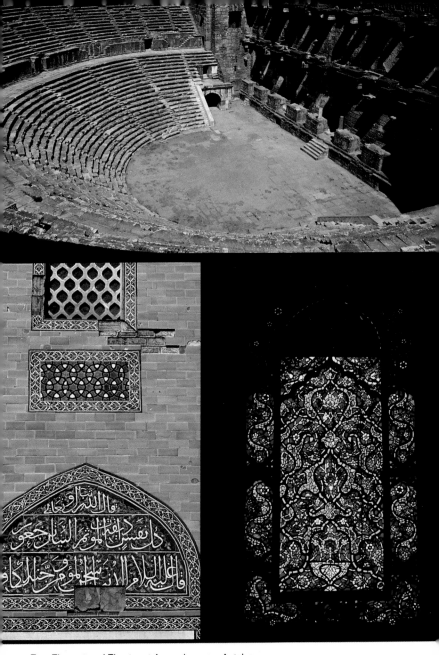

Top: The restored Theatre at Aspendos, near Antalya
Left: Detail from the Green Tomb, Bursa
Right: Stained-glass window in Süleymaniye Mosque

Top: The troglodyte dwellings, Göreme
Bottom: Roman busts and modern syntax in the Ephesus museum

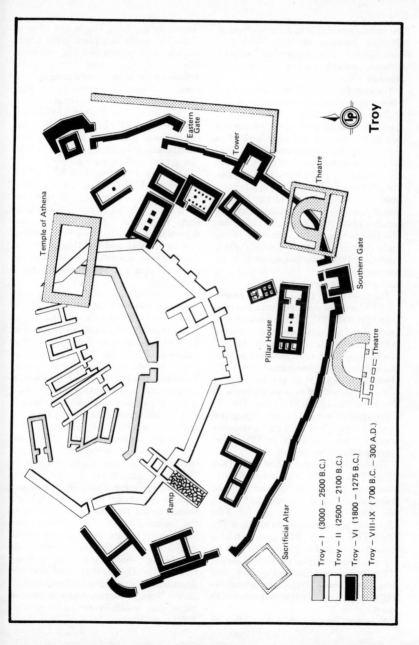

Troy

Temple of Athena

Eastern Gate

Tower

Theatre

Southern Gate

Theatre

Pillar House

Ramp

Sacrificial Altar

Troy – I (3000 – 2500 B.C.)
Troy – II (2500 – 2100 B.C.)
Troy – VI (1800 – 1275 B.C.)
Troy – VIII-IX (700 B.C. – 300 A.D.)

Ottoman government to excavate here at his own expense. He uncovered four superimposed ancient towns, and went on to make notable excavations at other Homeric sites.

Today at Troy you'll find a parking area, a few souvenir and snack stands, a replica of the wooden Trojan horse (children can climb up inside and peer out the windows), a tidy little museum, and Troy itself. The excavations by Schliemann and others have revealed nine ancient cities, one on top of another, going back to 3000 BC. Though there are few thrilling sights here, Troy is exciting because of the Troad's beauty, because of its great antiquity, and because of its semi-legendary character. The first people to live here were of the Early Bronze Age; the last were Turkish soldiers and their families, subjects of the Emir of Karası in the 1300s. After them, the town disappeared.

The cities called Troy I to Troy V (3000-1800 BC) were of similar culture, but with Troy VI (1800-1275 BC) the town took on a new character, with a new population of Indo-European stock related to the Mycenaeans. The town doubled in size, and carried on a prosperous trade with Mycenae. It also held the key, as defender of the straits, to the prosperous trade with Greek colonies on the Black Sea. Troy VI is the city of Priam, the city which engaged in the Trojan War. A bad earthquake brought down the walls in 1275, and hastened the Achaean victory.

The heroic Troy was followed by Troy VII (1275-1100 BC). The Achaeans may have burned the city in 1240; an invading Balkan people moved in around 1190 BC, and Troy sank into torpor for four centuries. It was revived as a Greek city (Troy VIII, 700-300 BC), and then as a Roman one (Troy IX, 300 BC-300 AD). At one point, Constantine the Great thought of building his new eastern Roman capital here, but he chose Byzantium instead. As a Byzantine town, Troy didn't amount to much.

Now for Troy's history according to Homer. In the *Iliad*, this is the town of Ilium. The battle took place in the 1200s BC, with Agamemnon, Achilles, Odysseus (Ulysses), Patroclus and Nestor on the Achaean (Greek) side, and Priam with his sons Hector and Paris on the Trojan side. Homer alludes to no commercial rivalries as cause for the war. Rather, he says that Paris kidnapped the beautiful Helen from her husband Menelaus, King of Sparta, and the king asked the Achaeans to help him get her back.

The war went on for a decade, in which time Hector killed Patroclus, and Achilles killed Hector. When the time came for Paris to kill Achilles, he was up to the task. Paris knew that Achilles' mother had dipped her son in the River Styx, holding him by his heel, and had thus protected Achilles from wounds anywhere that the water had touched. So Paris shot Achilles in the heel.

Even this carnage didn't end the war, so Odysseus came up with the idea of the wooden horse filled with soldiers.

One theory has it that the earthquake of 1275 BC brought down Troy's formidable walls and allowed the Achaeans to battle their way into the city. In gratitude to Poseidon, The Earth-Shaker, they built a monumental wooden statue of Poseidon's horse. Thus there may well have been a real Trojan horse, even though Homer's account is less than fully historical.

The identifiable structures at Troy are well marked. Notice especially the walls from various periods, the Bouleterion, or Council Chamber, built about when Homer was alive (700s BC), and the Temple of Athena, from Troy VIII, but rebuilt by the Romans. Also, don't miss the beautiful views of the Troad, particularly over toward the straits. On a clear day you can see the Gallipoli war memorials on the far shore, and ships passing through the Dardanelles. And you can almost imagine the Achaean fleet beached on the Troad's shores, ready to begin a battle that would be remembered over 3000 years later.

Aegean Turkey

The North Aegean

The North Aegean coast is a beautiful procession of golden wheat fields, fig and olive orchards, fishing villages and holiday resort towns. At Bergama, the ancient Pergamum, you should see the impressive ruins of the Acropolis and the Asclepion, an early medical centre. Many visitors make their base in İzmir, and come north to Bergama for the day. This isn't a bad plan, since Bergama has few hotels, and most of the few are very plain.

Here's what you'll find on the E 24 coastal highway, heading south from Troy.

TROY TO BERGAMA

It's 245 km from Çanakkale to Bergama, a ride of about 3½ hours. For a look at a small archaeological site off the beaten track, turn at Ayvacık for **Behramkale**, called Assos in ancient times. About 20 km from the highway you'll come to the village and the ruins, in a gorgeous setting overlooking the Aegean and the nearby island of Mytileni (Lesvos, *Midilli*, MEE-dee-lee in Turkish). Assos was founded in the 700s BC by colonists from Mytileni. Aristotle stayed here for three years, and St Paul visited briefly. The Turkish artifacts of Behramkale are more interesting than the ruined walls of Assos, however. There's a fine hump-back bridge and a mosque built in the 1300s.

Back on the highway, heading south, you will come round the Bay of Edremit. At the eastern end of the bay are the holiday resorts of Akçay and Ören, with moderately-priced hotels and motels.

AYVALIK

Across a narrow strait from the Greek island of Mytileni, Ayvalık ('EYE'-vah-luhk) is a beach resort, fishing town, olive oil and soap-making centre, and a terminus for boats to and from Mytileni.

Getting Around

Buses along the highway will drop you at the turning for Ayvalık, five km from the centre, unless the bus company specifically designates Ayvalık as a stop. From the highway you must hitchhike into town. If you are dropped in town, it will be at the *Şehirlerarası Otobüs Garajı* ('Intercity Bus Garage'), which is 15 or 20 minutes' walk north of the centre. You can call it the *Otogar*. Ayvalık is spread out, and somewhat difficult to get around on foot.

For information about **boats to Mytileni**, look for the office of Ahmet Cemil Erener, the agent. The office is on the little side street, which begins between the Osmanlı Bankası and the Yapı ve Kredi Bankası, just north of the harbour. (On Mytileni, the agent is Dimitrios Koraka, on Yunani Antonios Picolos.) Both Greek and Turkish boats make trips on Monday, Wednesday and Friday in summer (roughly from late May – early June through September). Thus you can leave from Ayvalık on any of these days at 9 am with the Turkish boat, or 5 pm with the Greek boat. From Mytileni, the weekday times are 8.30 am for the Greek boat and 1.30 pm for the Turkish boat. On weekends the times are different: Saturday at 5.30 am, Sunday at 6 pm from Ayvalık; Saturday at 9 am, Sunday at 8 or 9 pm from Mytileni for the Turkish boat. Off-season, boats operate about once a week, but may halt completely in bad winter weather.

Cost of a single trip is $20, a return trip $36. You must buy your ticket and surrender your passport for paperwork a day in advance of the voyage, whether you are departing from Turkey or from Greece.

Places to Stay

There are numerous beach resort hotels

and motels on Sarmısaklı Plaj (SAHR-muh-sahk-LUH plazh, Garlic Beach), several kilometres south of the centre. You'll also see many pensions and little hotels along the road to Sarmısaklı, at places called Çamlık and Orta Çamlık. The hotels right downtown are convenient, simple, and very cheap.

There's the *Ayvalık Palas* (tel 1064), where rooms without private bath cost $2.30 single, $4 double. You can get breakfast here. The hotel is located just off the main square by the harbour, out along the quay. The *El Otel* (tel 1604) is a block off the main street near the main square, on Talat Paşa Caddesi which leads to a church-like mosque. It is very clean and correct, run by Godfearing types who will rent you a double room with washbasin for $2.75.

Places to Eat

Right on the main square are numerous tea and beer gardens, with a view of the harbour. At the *Efes Birahanesi*, also called *Zekai'nin Yeri* ('Zekai's Place'), you can get a small filet steak called a *bonfile*, salad, puffy *börek* and beer for about $2.50. The clientele is totally male, however.

The tiny streets just north of the harbour, around the Ayvalık Palas hotel, hold several small, simple restaurants with good food and low prices. Try looking on the street which starts between the Osmanlı Bankası and the Yapı ve Kredi Bankası.

Things to See

Ayvalık is about 350 years old. It was inhabited by Ottoman Greeks until after World War I. Then, in the exchange of populations, it was repopulated with Greek-speaking Turks from Crete. A few locals still speak some Greek. Most of the town's mosques are converted Orthodox churches. You can take a look in one of these curiosities as you stroll around town.

Boats depart the harbour for **Ali Bey**

Adası, an island just across the bay, where there are pleasant little seaside restaurants. A causeway links the island to the mainland, so you can go by dolmuş, but this isn't nearly so much fun as the boat. Both are very cheap.

Another goal for excursions is **Şeytan Sofrası** (shey-TAHN soh-frah-suh, Devil's Dinnertable), a hilltop south of the centre from which the view is magnificent. There's a fairly pricey restaurant here. As no bus or dolmuş runs here regularly, you may have to take a taxi.

City buses run through the centre of town and south to Sarmısaklı beach.

Getting Away

It's less than 40 km from Ayvalık to Bergama. Surprisingly, there is not always easy transport between the two. You'll find it easiest to get a bus or dolmuş in the morning and early afternoon, more difficult in late afternoon, and impossible in the evening.

BERGAMA (PERGAMUM)

Modern Bergama (BEHR-gah-mah, population 38,000) is an agricultural market town in the midst of a well-watered plain. There has been a town here since Trojan times, but Pergamum's heyday was during the period after Alexander the Great and before Roman domination of all Asia Minor. At that time, Pergamum was one of the richest and most powerful small kingdoms in the Middle East. Its ruins are very impressive.

Getting There & Getting Around

Two companies run buses between İzmir's *Otobüs Garajı* (central bus terminal) and Bergama every 30 minutes, on the hour and half-hour, for the 100-km, 2-hour trip. A ticket costs about $1. Whether you approach Bergama from the north or south, check to see if your bus actually stops *in* Bergama. Any bus will be glad to drop you along the highway at the turning to Bergama, but you will have to hitchhike seven km into town in this case. The hitch is pretty easy, except in the evening. Better to be on a bus which goes right to Bergama's *Santral Garaj* (central garage). Ask the driver, *Bergama Santral Garajına gidiyor musunuz?* (BEHR-gah-mah sahn-tral gah-rah-zhuh-nah gee-dee-YOHR moo-soo-nooz, Do you go to Bergama's Central Garage?)

The Santral Garaj is on Hükümet Caddesi, the main street, which is also the road from town out to the highway.

Taxi Tours of the Ruins As many tourists come to Bergama from İzmir on day-trips, Bergama doesn't have many hotels. You can easily see the sights of Bergama in a day, and get to İzmir in the evening, especially if you use a taxi to travel among the far-flung ruins. If you plan to walk everywhere (there are no buses to the various ruins), it will be a long, long day. The last bus out of Bergama bound for İzmir leaves around 6 or 7 pm. Check bus departure times as soon as you arrive in town.

You can negotiate with a taxi-driver to get around. The standard rates and times are: up to the Acropolis, $4 per carload; up to the Acropolis, an hour's wait, and back down, $6. To the Asclepion, a half-hour's wait, and back into town, $3. If you're a hiker, walk up to the Acropolis and down in the morning, before it's too hot, and then take a taxi to the Asclepion. If you're a moderately good walker, take a taxi up, but walk down through the hillside ruins, then to the *Kızıl Avlu*, and then take a taxi to the Asclepion. If you want to walk to both sites, stay overnight in Bergama and do one each day.

Places to Stay
Bergama's fanciest place to stay is the 42-room *Tusan Bergama Moteli* (TOO-sahn, tel 173), near the junction of the E 24 highway and the road into town. Doubles with breakfast cost about $20.

Downtown hotels are very basic and plain, and very cheap. The *Park Oteli* (tel 246), closest to the central garage, charges $3 or $4 for a plain double room with cold-water washbasin. Further into town along Hükümet Caddesi, on the left-hand side, are the *Şehir Oteli* and the *Balar Oteli*, next door to one another, with similar rooms at similar prices, but these may be a bit noisier.

Places to Eat
You will pass several restaurants, on the right-hand side, as you come into the centre of town from the central garage. The *Sayın Restaurant* is one with a fancyish sidewalk terrace dining area. Simpler places, with perhaps better food, are further along the main street, on the section named Uzun Çarşı Caddesi. Look for the *Kardeşler Restaurant*. Even cheaper is the *Şehir Restaurant*, and the kebapçi's and snack shops are cheaper still.

On the left-hand side of Hükümet Caddesi, walking into town from the central garage, just before the arch-aeological museum, are tea gardens on a hillside. If the music is not too loud, this is the perfect shady place for a rest and a glass of tea or a cool beer in between sites.

At the ruins, there are soft drinks on sale, but no food.

History
Pergamum owes its prosperity to Lysimachus and to his downfall. Lysimachus, one of Alexander the Great's generals, controlled much of the Aegean region when Alexander's far-flung empire fell apart after his death in 323 BC. In the battles over the spoils, Lysimachus captured a great treasure, which he secured in Pergamum before going off to fight Seleucus for control of all Asia Minor. But Lysimachus lost and was slain (281 BC), so Philetarus, the commander he had posted at Pergamum to protect the treasure, set himself up as governor.

Philetarus was a eunuch, but he was succeeded by his nephew Eumenes I (263-241 BC), and Eumenes was followed by his adopted son Attalus I (241-197 BC). Attalus took the title of king, expanded his power, and made an alliance with Rome. He was succeeded by his son Eumenes II, and that's when the fun began.

Eumenes II (197-159 BC) was the man who really built Pergamum. Rich and powerful, he added the Library and the Altar of Zeus to the hilltop city, and built the 'middle city' on terraces half-way down the hill. The already-famous medical centre of the Asclepion was expanded and beautified as well.

But the Pergamum of Eumenes II is remembered most of all for its library. Said to have held more than 200,000 volumes, it was a symbol of Pergamum's social and cultural climb. Eumenes was a mad book-collector. His library came to challenge the world's greatest, in Alexandria (700,000 books). The Egyptians were afraid Pergamum and its library would attract famous scholars away from Alexandria, so they cut off the supply of papyrus from the Nile. Eumenes set his scientists to work, and they came up with *pergamen* (Latin for 'parchment'), a writing-surface made from animal hides rather than pressed papyrus reeds.

The Egyptians were to have their revenge, however. When Eumenes died, he was succeeded by his brother Attalus II (159-138 BC). Things went pretty well under him. But under Eumenes' son Attalus III (138-133 BC), the kingdom was falling to pieces. Attalus III bore no heir, and so he willed his kingdom to Rome. The Kingdom of Pergamum became the Roman province of Asia in 129 BC.

In the early years of the Christian era, the great library at Alexandria was damaged by fire. Marc Antony, out of devotion to Cleopatra, pillaged the library at Pergamum for books to replace those of the Egyptian queen.

Things to See

Bergama has four sites to visit. The **Arkeoloji Müzesi** is right downtown, next to the hillside tea gardens, not far from the Park Oteli. It has a substantial collection for so small a town. Hours are 8.30 am to 12 noon and 1 to 5.30 pm every day.

The **Kızıl Avlu** (KUH-zuhl ahv-loo, 'Red Courtyard') was originally a temple, built in the 100s AD to Serapis, an Egyptian god. It was converted to a Christian basilica by the Byzantines, and now holds a small mosque, proving the theory that sacred ground tends to remain sacred, even though the religion may change. You'll notice the curious red flat-brick walls of the large, roofless structure if you take the main road to the Acropolis; or, you can see it from atop the Acropolis.

Acropolis

Much of what was built by the ambitious kings of Pergamum did not survive. But what did survive is certainly impressive.

The auto road up to the Acropolis winds around the north side of the hill, and measures several kilometres in length. If you walk up, look for a path just after the entrance gate; this is steeper but more direct.

At the top is a car park, some souvenir and soft-drink stands, and a ticket-seller (23c entry, 25c for a camera). You can visit the Acropolis any day from 8.30 am to 5.30 pm. Head up the stone ramp.

While you're up here on the Acropolis, don't forget to look for the Asclepion, across the valley to the west, on the north edge of town near an army base. You'll also see the ruins of a small theatre, a larger theatre, and a stadium down in the valley.

The outstanding structures on the Acropolis include (of course) the Library, being rebuilt with German aid to its former glory. The great Theatre is impressive (10,000 seats) and unusual. Pergamum borrowed from Hellenistic architecture, but in the case of the theatre it made major modifications. To take advantage of the spectacular view, and to conserve precious building space atop the hill, it was decided to build the theatre into the hillside. Hellenistic theatres are usually more rounded, but because of its location, rounding was impossible, so it was heightened instead. Below the stage of the theatre is the ruined **Temple of Dionysus**.

The **Altar of Zeus**, south of the theatre, shaded by evergreen trees, is in an idyllic setting. Most of the building is now in Berlin, taken there (with the sultan's permission) by the 19th-century German excavators of Pergamum. Only the base remains.

Otherwise, several piles of rubble atop the Acropolis are marked as the palaces of Attalus I and Eumenes II, and there is an Agora as well as fragments of the defensive walls.

Walk down the hill from the Altar of Zeus, through the **Middle City**, and you will pass an **Altar and Temple of Demeter**, the Gymnasium or school, the Lower Agora, and a Roman Bath. The path to the bottom is not well marked.

Asclepion

The road to the Asclepion is at the edge of town on the way to the highway. The ruins are several km from the centre of town.

The Asclepion of Pergamum was not the first nor the only ancient medical centre. In fact, this one was founded by Archias, a citizen of Pergamum who had been treated and cured at the Asclepion of Epidaurus in Greece. But Pergamum's centre came to the fore under Galen (131-210 AD), who was born here, studied in Alexandria and Greece as well as Asia Minor, and set up shop as physician to Pergamum's gladiators. Recognized as perhaps the greatest early physician, Galen added considerably to knowledge of the circulatory and nervous systems, and also systematized medical theory. Under his influence, the medical school at Pergamum became reknown. His work was the basis for all western medicine well into the 1500s. About 162 AD, he moved to Rome and became personal physician to Emperor Marcus Aurelius.

As you walk around the ruins, you'll see bas reliefs or carvings of a snake, the symbol of Aesculapius, god of medicine. Just as the snake shed its skin and gained a 'new life', so the patients at the Asclepion were supposed to 'shed' their illnesses. Diagnosis was often by analysis of dreams. Treatment included massage and mud baths, drinking sacred waters, and the use of herbs and ointments.

There is a **Sacred Way** leading from the car park to the centre. Signs mark a **Temple to Aesculapius**, a Library, and a Roman Theatre. Take a drink of cool water from the Sacred Well, then pass along the vaulted underground corridor to the **Temple of Telesphorus**. It is said that patients slept in the temple, hoping that Telesphorus, another god of medicine, would send a cure, or at least a diagnosis, in a dream. Telesphorus, by the way, had two daughters named Hygeia and Panacea.

BERGAMA TO İZMİR

The coast between Bergama and İzmir was once the Ionian and Aeolian shore, thick with Hellenic cities and busy with trade. But of these ancient cities very few traces remain. Instead what you'll see are farming towns and villages, plus the occasional beach resort.

Due west of Bergama is **Dikili**, four km west of the E 24 highway, on the seacoast. A new wharf capable of serving ocean liners is bringing cruise ships to Dikili; the passengers then bus to Bergama to see the ruins. There are a few small, inexpensive hotels, and some nice waterfront restaurants.

Twenty kilometres south of Dikili along a side road is **Çandarlı**, a farming village with a little restored Genoese fortress of the 1300s.

North of Menemen, a road leads west to **Foça** and **Yenifoça**. Foça is the ancient Phocaea, a town founded before 600 BC (nothing remains). At Yenifoça there's a Club Mediterranee holiday village (*tatil köyü*).

Menemen (MEHN-eh-mehn), 33 km

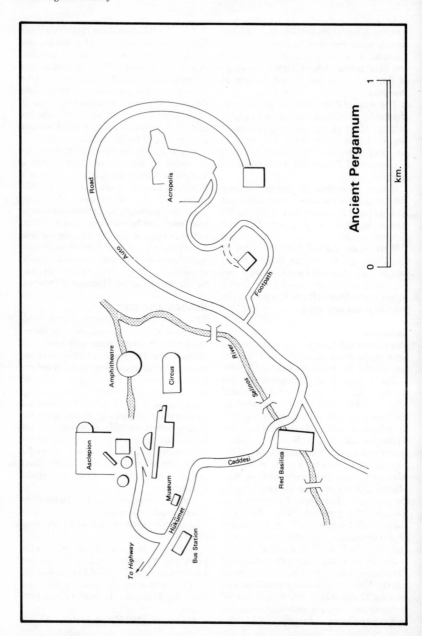

Ancient Pergamum

north of İzmir, is famous for a reactionary riot which took place in 1930. Atatürk's cultural reforms such as abolishing religious law, separating religion from the state, and recognizing the equality of women, were not received well by religious conservatives. A band of fanatical dervishes staged a riot in Menemen's town square. When a young army officer named Mustafa Fehmi Kubilay attempted to quell the disturbance, he was shot and beheaded by the dervishes. The government took immediate action to quash the fanatics' revolt, and proclaimed Kubilay a republican hero. The statue here honours the young officer.

A road goes east 30 km to **Manisa** (mah-NEES-ah, population 100,000), the ancient town of Magnesia ad Sipylus. It is a particularly pleasant little city with an ancient past. An early here was Tantalus, from whom we get the word 'tantalize'. The early, great Ottoman sultans favoured it as a residence, and for a while the province of Manisa was the training-ground for crown princes. As you might expect, it has lots of old mosques, among them the Hatuniye (1490), İlyas Bey (1363), Muradiye (1586), Sultan (1572) and the Ulu Cami (1366). Next to the Muradiye Camii is a small archaeological museum.

During the War of Independence, retreating Greek soldiers wreaked terrible destruction on Manisa. After they passed through, Manisa's 18,000 historic buildings had been reduced to only 500.

Near the end of April each year, Manisa has a special festival celebrating Powergum (*kuvvet macunu*, kew-VEHT mah-joo-noo). Manisa Powergum, a local concoction made from who-knows-what, is distributed. It is supposed to restore health, youth and potency.

Into İzmir

If you approach İzmir from Menemen along the E 24, you will pass a road to Çiğli (CHEE-lee) to İzmir's airport (*havaalanı*, hah-VAH-ah-lahn-uh). Shortly afterward,

the highway passes the suburb of Karşıyaka (KAHR-shuh-YAH-kah), then curves around the end of the bay to the *Otobüs Garaji.*

Coming from Manisa, the road passes through the suburb of Bornova, once the residence of wealthy Levantine businessmen. Some of their mansions are still standing, most now converted to public use such as municipal offices and schools. There's a university here. İzmir city buses run from Bornova to the centre of İzmir.

İZMİR

İzmir (EEZ-meer, population 900,000) is Turkey's third-largest city, and its major port on the Aegean. It's got a different feeling about it, something Mediterranean, something more than just being a large and prosperous Turkish city. The setting is certainly dramatic, for İzmir rings a great bay, and is backed to the east and south by mountains. Most of the city is quite modern and well laid-out, with broad boulevards radiating from a series of hubs. The streets are lined with stucco-and-glass apartment and office blocks, and dotted with shady sidewalk cafes, though here and there the red tile roof and bull's-eye window of a 19th-century warehouse hide in the shadow of an office tower. When you see an old mosque in İzmir, it comes as a surprise, as though it doesn't really fit in.

You will enjoy a short stay in İzmir because it's attractive, friendly and pleasant, with its scents of tobacco and the sea, its bright sun and salt breezes, its palm-lined waterfront promenade and friendly, easy people. It's a wonderful place to live and a nice place to visit.

The city can be explored and enjoyed in a fairly short time because there's not a whole lot to see; most of the remains from its long and eventful history have been swept away by war, fire and earthquake. You can also use İzmir as a base for excursions to a few nearby points: Sardis, for instance. But in most cases you will be ready to move on in a day, perhaps two.

History

İzmir owes its special atmosphere, indeed its entire appearance, to an eventful and turbulent history. What you see today is new because it has risen on the ashes of Ottoman İzmir since 1923, when a Greek invasion and a disastrous fire razed most of the city. Before that year, İzmir was Smyrna, the most western and cosmopolitan of Turkish cities, with more Christian and Jewish citizens than Muslim, and with thousands of foreign diplomats, traders, merchants and seamen. Its connections with Greece and Europe were close and continuous. To the Turks it was 'Infidel Smyrna'.

İzmir's commercial connections with Europe began in 1535, but the city is far, far older than that. The first settlement that we know of, at Bayraklı near the eastern end of the bay, was by Aeolians in the 10th century BC, but there were probably people here as far back as 3000 BC. The city's name comes from the goddess Myrina, prevalent deity before the coming of the Aeolians, who worshipped Nemesis in addition to Myrina. Famous early citizens of Smyrna included the poet Homer, the founder of western literature, who lived before 700 BC.

The city began its history of war and destruction early, for the Aeolians were overcome by the Ionians, and they in turn were conquered by the Lydians, whose capital was at Sardis. Around 600 BC, the Lydians destroyed the city, and it lay in ruins until the coming of Alexander the Great.

Alexander (356-323 BC) re-founded Smyrna on Mount Pagus, now called Kadifekale, in the centre of the modern city. He erected the fortress that you can still see crowning the hill, and made many other improvements.

Smyrna's luck changed during the struggles over the spoils of Alexander's empire. The city sided with Pergamum, the Aegean power-to-be. Later, it welcomed Roman rule and benefitted greatly from it. When an earthquake destroyed the city in

178 AD, Emperor Marcus Aurelius sent money and men to aid in reconstruction. Under Byzantium, the later Roman Empire, it became one of the busiest ports along the coast.

As Byzantium's power declined, various armies marched in, and often out again, including the Arabs, the Seljuk Turks, the Genoese, and the Crusaders. When Tamerlane arrived in 1402, he destroyed the city, true to form, but after he left, the Ottomans took over (1415), and things began to look better.

In 1535, Süleyman the Magnificent signed the Ottomans' first-ever commercial treaty, with Francis I of France, which permitted foreign merchants to reside in the sultan's dominions. After that humble start, İzmir became Turkey's most sophisticated commercial city. Its streets and buildings took on a quasi-European appearance, and a dozen languages were spoken in its cafes. Any merchant worth his salt was expected to be fluent in Turkish, Greek, Italian, German, English and Arabic, and perhaps a few other languages as well.

The Ottoman Empire was defeated along with Germany in World War I, and the victorious Allies sought to carve up the sultan's vast dominions into spheres of influence. Some Greeks have always dreamed of re-creating the long-lost Byzantine Empire. In 1920, with Allied encouragement, they took a gamble, invaded İzmir, seized Bursa, and headed toward Ankara. In fierce fighting on the outskirts of Ankara, where Atatürk's provisional government had its headquarters, the foreign forces were stopped, then turned around and pushed back. The Greek defeat turned to a rout, and the once-powerful army, half its ranks taken prisoner, scorched the earth and fled to ships waiting in İzmir. The day Atatürk took İzmir, 9 September, 1922, was the turning point in the Turkish War of Independence. It's now the big local holiday.

A disastrous fire broke out during the

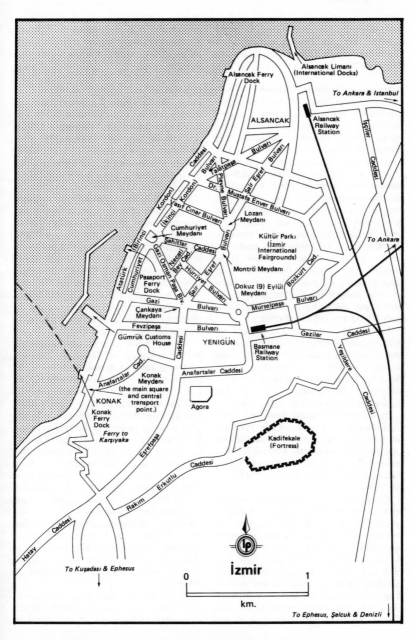

Alsancak Limanı
(International Docks)

Alsancak Ferry
Dock

To Ankara & Istanbul

ALSANCAK

Alsancak
Railway
Station

İşçiler

Caddesi

Caddesi

Bulvarı

Bulvarı

Talâtpaşa

Şair Eşref Bulvarı

Dr. Mustafa Enver Bulvarı

Plevne

Kordon

Yasıf Çınar Bulvarı

(İkinci) Kordon

İrevinç

Lozan
Meydanı

Cumhuriyet
Meydanı

Kültür Parkı
(İzmir
International
Fairgrounds)

To Ankara

(Birinci)

Şehitler

Caddesi

Necati

Bey Cad.

Gazi Osman paşa Blv.

Şair Eşref

Montrö Meydanı

Bozkurt Cad.

Atatürk

Cumhuriyet

Hürriyet Bulvarı

Dokuz (9) Eylül
Meydanı

Pasaport
Ferry
Dock

Gazi

Bulvarı

Mürselpaşa

Bulvarı

Çankaya
Meydanı

Bulvarı

Gaziler

Caddesi

Fevzipaşa

Gümrük Customs
House

Caddesi

YENIGÜN

Basmane
Railway
Station

Yeşildere

Caddesi

Anafartalar Caddesi

Anafartalar

Cad.

Konak
Meydanı
(the main square
and central
transport
point.)

KONAK

Agora

Konak
Ferry
Dock

Ferry to
Karşıyaka

Kadifekale
(Fortress)

Eşrefpaşa

Caddesi

Erkutlu

Caddesi

Rakım

Hatay

Caddesi

To Kuşadası & Ephesus

İzmir

0   1

km.

To Ephesus, Şelcuk & Denizli

final mopping-up operations, and destroyed most of the city. Though a tragedy, it allowed a modern city of wide streets to rise from the ashes.

Getting There & Getting Around

Buses arrive at İzmir's *Otobüs Garajı* (oh-toh-BEWS gah-rah-zhuh, Bus Garage), sometimes called the *Yeni Garaj* (yeh-NEE, New), a mammoth establishment north-east of the city's centre. If you've come on a good line such as Varan, there may be a *servis arabası* (sehr-VEES ah-rah-bah-suh, service car), a minibus shuttle, to take you into town at no extra charge. Otherwise, taxis, dolmuşes and city buses (No 50, 'Yeni Garaj') are available just outside the terminal grounds. For the more expensive and moderate hotels, get something to **Konak** (koh-NAHK), the heart of downtown; your chosen vehicle will probably go fairly close to your chosen hotel. For inexpensive hotels, get something to **Basmane** (bahs-mah-NEH), the railway station.

Arrival by **rail** is even easier. All intercity trains come into *Basmane Garı*, from whence there are buses and dolmuşes to other sections, and numerous hotels close by. İzmir's other railway depot, at *Alsancak* (AHL-sahn-jahk), is for commuter and suburban lines.

By **air**, you will touch down at İzmir's *Çiğli Havaalanı* (CHEE-lee hah-VAH-ah-lah-nuh, Çiğli Airport), a 30-minute bus ride from the city centre. Turkish Airlines buses will trundle you into town for about 75c, right to the THY offices in the Büyük Efes Oteli.

If you are lucky enough to arrive in İzmir by sea, the city will present itself to you wonderfully as you glide by, and your ship will come into the *Yeni Liman* (yeh-NEE lee-mahn, New Harbour), also called *Alsancak Limanı* (AHL-sahn-jahk lee-mah-nuh, Alsancak Harbour), at the northern tip of the city's central section. The harbour is about equidistant from the Otobüs Garajı and the centre of the city, Konak. For transport, turn right as you leave the dock area and walk the block to Alsancak railway station, from which buses, dolmuşes and taxis will take you downtown.

Orientation

İzmir has its wide boulevards and an apparent sense of orderliness, but it is in fact somewhat difficult to negotiate. This is because the numerous roundabouts/traffic circles, with their streets radiating like spokes from a hub, don't give you the sense of direction a street grid does. Here are some tips on getting your bearings.

First of all, the city's two main avenues run parallel to the waterfront, downtown. The waterfront street is officially Atatürk Caddesi, and that is what you will see given in written addresses. But everyone in town calls it the Birinci Kordon (beer-EEN-jee kohr-DOHN, First Cordon); just inland from it is Cumhuriyet Bulvarı (joom-hoor-ee-YEHT bool-vahr-uh, Republic Boulevard), which is called by everyone the İkinci Kordon (ee-KEEN-jee), or Second Cordon.

The city's two main plazas are located along these two parallel avenues. The very centre of town is **Konak Meydanı** (koh-NAHK mey-dah-nuh, Government House Plaza), or simply Konak. Here you will find the municipality buildings, the Ottoman Clock Tower (İzmir's symbol), a little old tiled mosque, pedestrian bridges over the busy roadway, and a dock for ferryboats to Karşıyaka (kahr-shuh-YAH-kah), the suburb across the bay. Konak is the city's bus and dolmuş hub, so you can pick up a vehicle to any part from here. You can also board buses for Selçuk, Ephesus and Kuşadası here as well as at the Otobüs Garajı. Konak also has an entrance to the *çarşı* (CHAR-shuh, bazaar). Anafartalar Caddesi, the bazaar's main street, winds through İzmir's most picturesque quarters all the way to the railway station at Basmane.

The other main plaza holds the equestrian statue of Atatürk and is called Cumhuriyet Meydanı. It is about a kilometre north of Konak along the two Kordons. The PTT, Tourism Information Office, Turkish Airlines office, and Büyük Efes Oteli are here. The 19th-century building right on the quay is called **Pasaport**, and used to be the entry point for foreign ships. It is now a ferryboat dock used during rush hours only. From Pasaport to Konak along the Birinci Kordon is an active shipping centre for local commerce, with colourful *kayık* (kah-YUK) boats moored all along. The offices of the Denizyolları (Turkish Maritime Lines) are here as well.

The section called Çankaya (CHAN-kah-yah) is two long blocks inland, southeast of Cumhuriyet Meydanı.

Another İzmir landmark is the Kültür Park (kewl-TEWR), site of the annual İzmir International Fair, an amusement and industry show extravaganza which takes place from about 20 August to 20 September each year. Hotel space is very hard to find during the fair. When it's not fair time, the grounds provide a pleasant, shady place to walk, sit and rest, with some amusements.

Finally, the hill directly behind the main part of town is impressively crowned by Kadifekale (kah-dee-FEH-kah-leh, Velvet Fortress), a bastion built by Alexander the Great when he moved the city here.

Information

The Ministry of Tourism maintains an information desk (tel 14 21 47) in the Merkez PTT (Central Post Office) in Cumhuriyet Meydanı.

Places to Stay – top end

İzmir's best is the 296-room *Büyük Efes Oteli* (bew-YEWK eh-FEHS, tel 14 43 00, –29), the Grand Ephesus Hotel, located right on Cumhuriyet Meydanı. Though not as luxurious as a Hilton or Sheraton, it is very comfortable and has these advantages: pretty, private gardens with a swimming pool, and some rooms with a view of the bay. Rates are about $80 per

night, double. The 128-room *Etap İzmir* (eh-TAHP, tel 14 42 90, –9) is just around the corner at Cumhuriyet Bulvarı 138. Part of the worldwide French chain, its rooms cost a few dollars less than at the Büyük Efes.

The *Kısmet Oteli* (kuss-MEHT, tel 21 70 50, –2), located behind the Büyük Efes at 1377 Sokak No 9, is comfortable, air conditioned, and costs about $42 for a double room. At the *İzmir Palas* (eez-MEER pah-LAHS, tel 21 55 83), a 148-room place on the waterfront, rooms cost about the same. The İzmir Palas is located on the Birinci Kordon (Atatürk Caddesi) at the intersection of Dr Mustafa Enver Bulvarı and Talat Paşa Bulvarı.

Places to Stay – mid-range

Mid-range prices go from $19 to $30. The *Hotel Anba* (AHN-bah, tel 14 43 80, –4), Cumhuriyet Bulvarı 124, is on the İkinci Kordon just a block south of Cumhuriyet Meydanı and the Büyük Efes; rooms cost $29 double. It's air conditioned. The *Kilim Oteli* (kee-LEEM, tel 14 53 40), right in front of the Anba on Atatürk Bulvarı (Birinci Kordon) is similar, but charges a bit more for sea-view rooms.

Rooms are a bit cheaper at the *Otel Kaya* (KAH-yah, tel 13 97 71, –4), Gazi Osman Paşa Bulvarı 45, and the *Babadan Oteli* (BAH-bah-dahn, tel 13 96 40, –3), on the same street at No 50. These hotels, in the section named Çankaya, are 2½ long blocks from the waterfront, at the intersection of Gazi Osman Paşa Bulvarı and Fevzipaşa Bulvarı, still a convenient location; but both suffer from high traffic noise so choose your room carefully. A double costs $23.

Lowest-priced of the mid-range hotels is the *Billur Oteli* (bee-LOOR, tel 13 62 50, 13 97 32, –5), near Basmane Railway Station at Basmane Meydanı 783. The 70 rooms in this somewhat noisy but convenient location cost $19 to $23 double.

Places to Stay – bottom end

Best of İzmir's budget accommodation is

the wonderful *Pansiyon Fa* (PAHN-see-yohn FAH, tel 21 51 78), quite near the Büyük Efes Oteli, at Kızılay Caddesi, 1375 Sokak No 24/2. The pension, run by Feyyaz and Fatoş Eronat, is homey, very convenient, and inexpensive, but small and thus usually full-up. If you can, write or call ahead for reservations, and then claim them early in the day. Double rooms cost $6, triples $8; meals are served and parking is available. To find the pension, walk north out of Cumhuriyet Meydanı on Cumhuriyet Bulvarı (İkinci Kordon), and look down the first sidestreet on the right; the pension is a few steps up the street, on the left.

İzmir used to have numerous small hotels near Basmane , but these are fast disappearing as the city becomes more sophisticated and land values take off. Still, it's worth a look in the little back streets of the section named Yenigün to see what's still open. Yenigün is bounded by Fevzipaşa Bulvarı, Basmane Meydanı, Anafartalar Caddesi, and Eşrefpaşa Caddesi. The best plan is to walk out the door of the railway station, turn left, cross the road, turn right then left almost immediately: this is Anafartalar Caddesi. It turns right after a block or so, and becomes the main street of the Yenigün section, and (with twists and turns) goes all the way to Konak. As cheap accommodation is difficult to find in İzmir, your reports on good ones are both helpful and appreciated.

Places to Eat – top end

You can dine lavishly in the Büyük Efes Oteli, but I'd recommend more highly the waterfront establishments nearby. From Cumhuriyet Meydanı, walk north along the quay and you'll pass a half-dozen places, more or less fancy, with excellent seafood and genteel service. A full meal need cost only $8 to $10. *Bergama* is one of long standing, and there are others. In good weather, take a sidewalk table to enjoy the harbour view. The *Efes Pilsen* Beer Garden at about No 196, north of the

NATO headquarters, is attractive, not overly expensive, and has a soothing vista.

Places to Eat – mid-range

For medium-priced meals ($2 to $4), perhaps the city's most interesting section is the waterfront between Konak and Cumhuriyet Meydanı. The restaurants named *Express, Mangal,* and *Kazan,* all together at Nos 110 to 112 on the Birinci Kordon, have sidewalk tables, views of the harbour activity, lots of good *meze* (appetizers) and fresh fish prepared various ways. There's even an old-fashioned tea house nearby for a post-prandial coffee and a *nargile* (NAHR-gee-leh, water-pipe). Watch out for the water-pipe. Though it's cheap to rent one, the tobacco is especially powerful. Those not used to it can suffer dizziness, nausea and headaches, so take it easy.

At No 150 on the Birinci Kordon, only a half-block from Cumhuriyet Meydanı, is the *Kordon Kebap Salonu,* flanked by tea houses. This is even cheaper (meals for $1 to $2), though the specialty is kebap, not fish.

A special place for sweets is the *Ali Galip Pastanesi* (ah-LEE gah-LEEP), just a few steps along Anafartalar Caddesi from Konak, on the right-hand side. This is one of the city's oldest and best confectioner's, justly famed for its baklava, helva and other treats.

Places to Eat – bottom end

The lowest-priced meals, and some of the most delightful, are along Anafartalar Caddesi in the bazaar. Start from the Basmane end, and *hazır yemek lokantas*, *kebapçı*s and *köfteci*s will appear all along the way as you wander. A few will have one or two small tables outside. If you begin your wandering along Anafartalar at Konak, you must look down side streets and alleyways. The farther into the bazaar you go from Konak, the more restaurants you will see, and the cheaper they will be. You may also come across a *pideci*, one of the bakeries where flat *pide* bread topped with meat, eggs or cheese is baked. *Pide* is good, nutritious, sanitary (hot from the oven), and very cheap.

You needn't worry about not speaking Turkish. Wander to where the food is being prepared, and sign language will easily get you what you want.

Things to See

Compared to most Turkish towns, İzmir does not have a large number of antiquities. But that doesn't mean its antiquities are uninteresting.

As you make your way around town, you will certainly see the equestrian statue of Atatürk in Cumhuriyet Meydanı. It symbolizes Atatürk's leadership as he began the counter-offensive from Ankara, with the aim of reaching the Aegean.

A few blocks north of the plaza is the South-Eastern Headquarters of NATO, in a building with a long row of flags in front. Here and there along the Birinci Kordon, you can see the few old stone houses which survived the Great Fire of 1922.

Agora

The marketplace built on the orders of Alexander was ruined in an earthquake (178 AD), but there is much remaining from the Agora as it was rebuilt by Marcus Aurelius just after the quake. A few columns, vaulted chambers and statues mark this conspicuously open spot in the midst of the crowded city. To reach it, walk up Eşrefpaşa Caddesi from Fevzipaşa Caddesi to 816 Sokak, on the left. This street leads to the Agora, which is open from 8.30 to 5.30 daily.

Bazaar

İzmir's bazaar, already mentioned, is large and fascinating. A half-day's explorations along Anafartalar Caddesi is a must. You can pick up this street easily, from Eşrefpaşa Caddesi, after your visit to the Agora.

Culture Park & Museum

The Kültür Park is pleasant, and you can see it as you make your way to the *Arkeoloji Müzesi* (Archaeological Museum). The museum is within the park (enter by the Montrö Meydanı gate), open from 8.30 to 12 noon and 1 to 5.30 pm, closed Monday. The collection, from a region so rich in artifacts, is impressive.

Kadifekale

The time to ride up the mountain is an hour before sunset. Catch a dolmuş in Konak (it may say only 'K. Kale' on the sign), and allow 15 or 20 minutes for the ride. The view on all sides is spectacular. Look inside the walls, and even climb up on them if you like. Just at sunset, the muezzins will give the call to prayer from İzmir's minarets. A wave of sound rolls across the city as the lights twinkle on.

Near the gate in the walls are a few little terrace tea houses where you can have a seat and a tea, soft drink, or beer.

Excursions from İzmir

If your goal is Ephesus, consider packing up and moving to Selçuk or Kuşadası, which are delightful places much closer to the ruins. But if you'd like to see Sardis, use İzmir as your base. For beaches and water sports, head west, to Çeşme.

Sardis

The phrase 'rich as Croesus' made its way into language early, in the 6th century BC to be precise. Croesus was the King of Lydia, and Sardis was its capital city. It was here that one of mankind's most popular and valuable inventions was made: coinage. No doubt the Greeks thought Croesus (560-546 BC) rich because he could store so much wealth in such a small place. Rather than having vast estates and far-ranging herds of livestock, Croesus kept his wealth in his pockets.

For all his wealth, Croesus was defeated and captured by Cyrus and his Persians, after which he leapt onto a funeral pyre. Even Croesus couldn't take it with him.

The Lydian kingdom had dominated much of the Aegean area before the Persians came. Besides being the kingdom's wealthy capital, Sardis was a great trading centre as well, obviously because coinage facilitated trade.

After the Persians, Alexander the Great took the city in 334 BC, and embellished it even more. The inevitable earthquake brought its fine buildings down in 17 AD, but the Romans rebuilt.

Sardis (*Sart*) is 90 km east of İzmir along the Ankara road. In high summer, start out early so you're not tramping the ruins in the heat of the day. Buses depart frequently from İzmir's *Otobüs Garajı* on the 1½-hour trip. There are several daily trains from Basmane which stop here; they are slower than the buses. Alternatively, local travel agencies operate full-day tours to Sardis and Manisa for about $20, lunch included.

Get off the bus in the Turkish village of Sart, and you'll see the Acropolis of Sardis to the south. Coming from the train station, you will be north of the highway.

Ruins here include a restored synagogue, a marble street, a gymnasium with palaestra, baths, a theatre and a stadium. The most impressive building was the Temple of Artemis, though it was never completed. Two tall columns serve as a landmark.

Unless you've come by train and have checked the schedules for return trips, the way to get back to İzmir is to wait at a tea house along the highway for a bus to stop. It's pot luck, but this is a busy road.

Çeşme

The name of this village and resort area due west of İzmir means 'fountain' or 'spring' (*çeşme*, CHESH-meh). From the village, it's only about 10 km across the water to the Greek island of Chios. Boats run on Friday in April; Tuesday and Friday in May and October; Tuesday, Friday and Sunday in June till mid-July, and in September; there are daily boats from mid-July through August. At other times, boats may run if there is enough traffic. Contact the *Ertürk Travel Agency* (EHR-tewrk, tel 1768), in Çeşme's main square at Cumhuriyet Meydanı 11/A, for information, reservations and tickets. Buy your ticket at least a day in advance.

The peninsula which guards the Bay of İzmir holds various beach-resort towns. There are hotels and pensions at **Ilıca** (ULL-uh-jah), on the way to Çeşme. Outside of Çeşme village proper is the luxury *Golden Dolphin Holiday Village* (*Altın Yunus Tatilköyü*, tel 1250). But right in the centre of Çeşme is the *Ertan Oteli* (ehr-TAHN, tel 1795, –6), Cumhuriyet Meydanı 12, with 60 rooms priced at $16 to $19 double. Numerous pensions, from cheap to very cheap, accommodate prospective ferryboat passengers.

The Tourism Information Office is right down by the dock at İskele Meydanı No 8 (tel 1653). That little old fortress visible from here was built by the Genoese, but repaired by Beyazıt, son of Sultan Mehmet the Conqueror, to defend the coast from attack by the Knights of St John, based on Rhodes, and from pirates.

The South Aegean

It's often said that Turkey has more ancient cities and classical ruins than does Greece. Well, it's true, and the Aegean coast holds a great number of sites. Even if you are not fascinated by archaeology, there's great pleasure in riding through a countryside rich in fields of tobacco,

passing orchards of fig trees, tramping among verdant fields bright with sunflowers, resting in little village tea houses, and strolling along marble streets which once witnessed the passing of the men who practically invented architecture, philosophy, mathematics and science.

Top: Ishan Paşa Palace, Doğubayazıt
Bottom: Nomad's tent, Doğubayazıt

Top: Jumbled headstones atop Nemrut Daǧi (Mt Nimrod)
Bottom: Mosque inscription, Antalya

And when it gets hot, there's always the beach.

This was Ionia. About 1000 BC, colonists from Greece arrived on these shores, fleeing an invasion by the Dorians. The Ionian culture flourished, and its cities exported these cultural refinements back to Greece.

The history of Ionia is much the same as that of İzmir, with the original Ionian league of cities being conquered by the Lydians of Sardis, then the Persians, then Alexander. They prospered until their harbours silted up, or until the predominance of İzmir siphoned off their local trade. Sometimes a sleepy Turkish village rose among the ruins, sometimes not. Today, several of those once-sleepy villages are bustling seaside resort towns.

This chapter covers the coast from İzmir almost to Bodrum, 265 km due south; the following chapter takes you on a fascinating excursion inland to several ancient cities and a spa. Succeeding chapters cover the south (Mediterranean) coast from Bodrum and Marmaris (opposite Rhodes) eastwards.

Getting Around

İzmir is the transportation hub for the region; the only other airport of any size is at Dalaman, near Fethiye on the Mediterranean coast. İzmir also has the only rail service from Istanbul and Ankara.

By Bus & Dolmuş Buses, of course, go everywhere. Direct service is run from İzmir's *Otobüs Garajı* to Selçuk (for Ephesus; 1½ hours), Kuşadası (for Ephesus and ferryboats to Samos; two hours), Söke (a transfer point; two hours) and Bodrum (for ferryboats to Kos; four hours). You can climb aboard many of these buses at the bus-and-dolmuş loading area in Konak, which is much more convenient than going all the way out to the *Otobüs Garajı*.

In Selçuk, there's a small bus and dolmuş station right in the centre from which you can get minibuses to Ephesus

and Kuşadası. For buses to Bodrum, you wait on the highway for a bus which has empty seats. Most do.

It's a good idea to do your travelling early in the day. Minibus service from Selçuk to Kuşadası, for instance, stops at around 6 or 7 pm. After that time, you pay for a taxi unless you can find enough fellow travellers to hire a whole minibus or car, and share the cost. Should you find yourself in this predicament, look for taxis lurking near the museum in Selçuk. Sometimes there's a driver who lives in Kuşadası, on his way home, looking for some fares so he doesn't travel empty. He'll be amenable to bargaining.

By Train Trains run from İzmir's Basmane station to Selçuk, Söke and Denizli (inland). There are three trains per day in each direction. The trip from İzmir to Selçuk takes about 1-1/2 to 2 hours and costs about 50c.

Rental Cars It's simple, but expensive, to rent a car in İzmir or Kuşadası. You will probably have to return the car to the same city. If you give it up in Antalya or Ankara, you may have to pay a hefty charge to get the car back to its home base. Figure $50 per day, all in, to rent a small Renault or Fiat ('Murat').

SELÇUK & EPHESUS

Ephesus (*Efes*, EFF-ess) was a great trading and religious city, centre for the cult of Cybele, Anatolian fertility goddess. The Ionians replaced Cybele with Artemis, and built a fabulous temple in her honour. When Roman rule made this the province of Asia, Artemis became Diana and Ephesus became the Roman provincial capital. Its Temple of Diana was counted among the Seven Wonders of the World.

As a large and busy Roman town with ships and caravans coming from all over, it had an important Christian congregation very early. St Paul visited Ephesus, and later wrote the most profound of his epistles to the Ephesians.

Ephesus was renowned for its wealth and beauty even before it was pillaged by Gothic invaders in 262 AD, and it was still an important enough place in 431 AD that a church council was held here. There is a lot of the city's glory left for you to see.

Information

Selçuk has a nice little Tourism Information Office (tel 328) in a group of modern shops near the museum, and across the highway from the bus station. It's open every day from 8.30 am to 6.30 or 7 pm. They'll be glad to help you with accommodation here.

Places to Stay

You can make your base in Selçuk, the little town four km from the ruins, or you can stay in the nearby seaside resort of Kuşadası, 17 km away. Selçuk is closer, but Kuşadası has a greater number and variety of lodgings. If you like, stay in Selçuk one night, then move on to Kuşadası.

Selçuk's poshest lodgings are at the *Tusan Efes Moteli* (tel 60), at the turning from the Selçuk-Kuşadası road into the ruins of Ephesus. The location is excellent, a 10-minute walk from the archaeological zone entrance. The 12 rooms cost $17 double.

In the town proper, there's the *Hotel Aksoy* (AHK-soy, tel 40), Atatürk Caddesi No 17, between the main highway and the railway station. The 21 rooms cost $7 or $8 double.

Otherwise, there are small pensions. Rooms in these modest, friendly and very cheap places cost about $2 to $3, double. Try the *Pension Baykal* (bye-KAHL), next to the museum, or the *Pension Kırhan* (KURR-hahn), just up the street from the Baykal, more or less behind the museum; this one has a pretty little front garden with citrus trees. The *Pension Mengi* (MEHN-gee) is a tidy two-storey suburban-type structure, more modern. The *Pension Akbulut* (AHK-boo-loot) is similar, with jasmine and rose bushes in front.

Places to Eat

The place to look for a meal is Cengiz Topal Caddesi (jehn-GEEZ toh-PAHL), between the highway and the railway station. Of the numerous restaurants, the *Yıldız Restaurant* is perhaps best as it has a pleasant outdoor section by the street. A full meal need cost only $1.50. For variety, try the *Girne Köftecisi* (GEER-neh) or the *Lezzet Lokantası* (leh-ZEHT). By the railway station there are some shady tea gardens.

Things to See

Half a day will do you for sightseeing at Ephesus, though you can easily spend more time if you go into detail. In high summer it gets very hot here. Best to start your tramping early in the morning, then retire to a shady restaurant for lunch and your hotel, or the beach, for a siesta.

Selçuk

Before going to Ephesus, take an hour or two to visit the ancient buildings right in Selçuk. The best place to start is the **St John Basilica** atop the hill; look for signs pointing the way to 'St Jean'.

It is said that St John came to Ephesus at the end of his life, and wrote his Gospel here. A tomb built in the 300s was thought to be his, so Justinian erected this magnificent church above it in the 500s. Earthquakes and scavengers for building materials had left the church a heap of rubble until a century ago when restoration began. Virtually all of what you see is restored.

This hill, including the higher peak with the fortress, is called *Ayasoluk*. The view is attractive. Look west: at the foot of the hill is the **İsa Bey Camii**, built in 1307 by the Emir of Aydın in a transitional style which was post-Seljuk and pre-Ottoman. Keep a picture of it in your mind if you plan to venture deep into Anatolia for a look at more Seljuk buildings. There are many in Konya.

Beyond the mosque, you can see how the Aegean once invaded this plain, allowing Ephesus to prosper by maritime commerce. When the harbour silted up, Ephesus began to lose its famous wealth.

Early in the town's existence it had earned money from pilgrims coming to pay homage to Cybele/Artemis. The many-breasted Anatolian fertility goddess had a fabulous temple, the **Artemision**, to the south-west of the St John Basilica. A sign marks the spot today, and you can see the outline of the foundation, but that's all. When you visit Didyma (see below), you can get an idea what the great temple looked like, as the one at Didyma is thought to be very similar. But the cult of the fertility goddess has now moved from Ephesus to men's magazines.

By the way, the citadel atop the hill to the north of the St John Basilica was originally constructed by the Byzantines in the 500s, rebuilt by the Seljuks, and restored in modern times. A small Seljuk mosque and a ruined church are inside.

Selçuk has some tombs and a little mosque dating from the Seljuk period; these are near the bus station. Also, on the streets between the highway and the railway station you can see the remains of a Byzantine aqueduct.

Don't miss Selçuk's pretty little museum in the centre of the town. The statuary, mosaics and artefacts are attractively displayed. Among the prime attractions are several marble statues of Cybele/Artemis, with rows of breasts and elaborate headdress. The museum is open every day from 9.30 am to 6.30 pm; admission 20c, camera 30c extra.

Ephesus

I like to walk the four km from Selçuk to Ephesus, but only at morning or twilight. The walk takes about 45 minutes. But as you'll be doing a lot of walking to get around the large archaeological site, you might want to ride. Dolmuşes headed from Selçuk to Kuşadası will drop you at the Tusan Efes Moteli, from which it's a 10-minute walk to the entrance of the archaeological zone.

As you walk in from the highway, you pass the **Gymnasium of Vedius** (100s AD), which had exercise fields, baths, latrines, covered exercise rooms, a swimming pool and a ceremonial hall. Just south of it is the Stadium, dating from about the same period. Most of its finely cut stones were taken by the Byzantines to build the citadel and walls of Ayasoluk. This 'quarrying' of pre-cut building stone from older, often earthquake-ruined structures, continued through the entire history of Ephesus.

The road comes over a low rise and descends to the parking lot, where there are a few tea houses, restaurants and souvenir shops. To the right (west) of the road are the ruins of the **Church of the Virgin Mary**, also called the Double Church.

Pay the small admission fee and enter the archaeological zone. As you walk down a lane bordered by evergreen trees, a few colossal remains of the **Harbour Gymnasium** are off to the right (west). Then you come to the Arcadian Way.

The marble-paved **Arcadian Way** was the grandest street in Ephesus. With water and sewer lines beneath the paving, street lighting along the colonnades, lined with shops and finished with triumphal columns, it was and still is a grand sight. The builder was the Byzantine emperor Arcadius (395-408). At the far (western) end was the harbour of Ephesus, long since silted up. At the near end is the **Great Theatre**, still used for performances. Its design is Hellenistic; construction was begun in 41 AD and finished in 117. It could - and can - hold almost 25,000 spectators. During the Selçuk Ephesus Festival of Culture and Art, held in the first week of May, performances are given in this dramatic setting. When you visit, no doubt someone will be standing on the orchestra floor of the theatre, speaking to someone seated high up in the *cavea* (auditorium) to demonstrate the fine acoustics.

Behind the Great Theatre is Mount

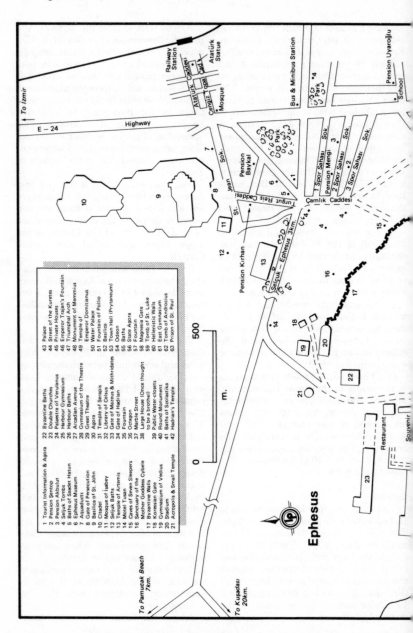

1 Tourist Information & Agora
2 Pension Sentop
3 Pension Akbulut
4 Selçuk Tombs
5 Baths of Saadet Hatun
6 Ephesus Museum
7 Aquaducts
8 Gate of Persecution
9 Basilica of St. John
10 Citadel
11 Mosque of Isabey
12 Selçuk Baths
13 Temple of Artemis
14 Motel Tusan
15 Caves of Seven Sleepers
16 Sanctuary of the
   Mother Goddess Cybele
17 Byzantine Walls
18 Koressian Gate
19 Gymnasium of Vedius
20 Stadium
21 Acropolis & Small Temple

22 Byzantine Baths
23 Double Churches
24 Palaestra of Verulanus
25 Harbour Gymnasium
26 Harbour Baths
27 Arcadian Avenue
28 Gymnasium of the Theatre
29 Great Theatre
30 Agora
31 Temple of Serapis
32 Library of Celsus
33 Gate of Mazeus & Mithridates
34 Gate of Hadrian
35 Fountain
36 Octagon
37 Marble Street
38 Large House (Once thought
   to be a brothel)
39 Public Water-closets
40 Round Monument
41 Baths of Scolastika
42 Hadrian's Temple

43 Palace
44 Street of the Kuretes
45 Private Houses
46 Emperor Trajan's Fountain
47 Triumphal Arch
48 Monument of Memmius
49 Temple of
   Emperor Domitianus
50 Water Palace
51 Fountain of Pollio
52 Basilica
53 Town Hall (Prytaneum)
54 Odeon
55 Baths
56 State Agora
57 Fountain
58 Magnesia Gate
59 Tomb of St. Luke
60 Hellenistic Walls
61 East Gymnasium
62 Tomb of Androclus
63 Prison of St. Paul

Ephesus

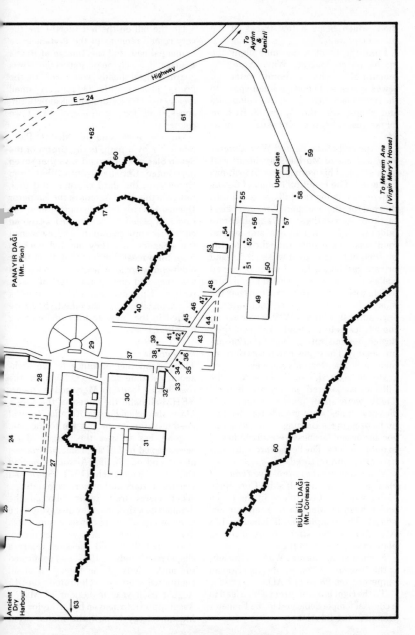

Pion, which bears a few traces of the ruined city walls.

From the theatre, continue along the marble-paved Sacred Way. Note the remains of the city's elaborate water and sewer systems. The large open space to the right, once surrounded by a colonnade and shops, was the Agora (3 BC), or marketplace, heart of Ephesus' business life.

At the end of the Sacred Way, **Curetes Way**, also called Marble Way, heads east up a slope. This corner was 'downtown Ephesus'. The beautiful **Library of Celsus** is here, now being carefully restored with the aid of the German Archaeological Institute. Across the street is an elaborate building with rich mosaics and several fountains. It was once thought to be the brothel, but some say it was just a grand private residence. In the maze of ruined walls you'll come upon a hand pump from which, with a little effort, you can coax the most deliciously refreshing cool water.

Heading up Curetes Way, a passage on the left leads to the **Public Latrines**, their design demonstrating their function unmistakably. These posh premises were for men only. The women's were elsewhere.

On the right side of Curetes Way, the hillside is covered in private houses. These were small places as houses in classical times were mostly for sleeping and dressing. Bathing, amusements, socializing and business were all conducted in public places. The houses are still being excavated and restored.

You can't miss the impressive **Temple of Hadrian**, on the left. It's in Corinthian style, with beautiful reliefs in the porch and a head of Medusa to keep out evil spirits. The temple was finished in 138 AD. Across the street from it is an elaborate house from the same period.

Further along Curetes Way, on the left, is the **Fountain of Trajan**, who was Roman emperor from 98 to 117 AD.

To the right is a side street which lead to a colossal temple dedicated to the Emperor Domitian (81-96 AD).

Up the hill on the left (north) are the very ruined remains of the **Prytaneum**, a municipal hall, and the **Temple of Hestia Boulaea**, in which the perpetual flame was guarded. And finally you come to the pretty little marble Odeum, a small theatre used for lectures, musical performances, and for meetings of the town council.

On the east side of Mount Pion, reachable by a path, is the **Grotto of the Seven Sleepers**. A legend says that seven persecuted Christian youths fled from Ephesus in the third century, and took refuge in this cave. Agents of the Emperor Decius, a terror to Christians, found the cave and sealed it. Two centuries later an earthquake broke down the wall, awakened the sleepers, and they ambled back to town for a meal. Finding that all of their old friends were long dead, they concluded that they had undergone a sort of resurrection. Ephesus was by this time a Christian city. When they died, they were buried in the cave, and a cult following developed.

Meryemana

There is another entrance to the archaeological zone near the Odeum, on the road which leads to Meryemana (mehr-YEHM-ah-nah), the House of the Virgin Mary, also called *Panaya Kapulu*. You will need a taxi to go the five km to the site. Legend has it that the Virgin Mary, accompanied by St Paul, came to Ephesus at the end of her life. A woman named Catherine Emmerich (1774-1824) had visions of Mary and of her surroundings. When clergy from İzmir followed the detailed descriptions, they discovered the foundations of an old house; a tomb, also described by Emmerich, was not found. Pope Paul VI visited the site, where a chapel now stands, in 1967, and confirmed the authenticity of the legend. A small traditional service celebrated on 15 August each year in honour of Mary's Assumption into heaven by Orthodox and Muslim clergy is now the major event here. To Muslims, Mary is *Meryemana*, Mother Mary, who bore *İsa Peygamber*, the Prophet Jesus.

The view from the hilltop is wonderful. A small restaurant provides refreshments.

KUŞADASI

Twenty kilometres from Selçuk, down on the Aegean coast, is Kuşadası (koo-SHAH-dah-suh, Bird Island, population 17,000), a delightful seaside resort town and a perfect base for excursions to the ancient cities of Ephesus, Priene, Miletus and Didyma, and inland to Aphrodisias.

Many Aegean cruise ships on Greek Island tours stop at Kuşadası so that their passengers can take a tour to Ephesus and haggle for trinkets in Kuşadası's shops. For most of these cruise passengers, Kuşadası is all they see of Turkey, which is a shame, but it's much better than nothing. The town's appearance, not to mention its economy, has been affected by this cruise business, of course. But Kuşadası is still a delightful place, a harmonious mixture of hotels and pensions for Turks and foreigners on holiday, of shops for the cruise people, and of businesses serving the farmers, beekeepers and fishermen who make up much of the town's population.

Coming into Kuşadası from Selçuk and Ephesus is a wonderful experience, for the road winds through fields and hills, past olive orchards and a few little houses, then around a turn and down the cliffs, with a splendid view of the Aegean.

Before coming into the town proper, the road from Selçuk passes the *Kuş-Tur Tatil Köyü* (KOOSH-toor tah-TEEL kur-yew, tel 1121, 1734, 2794), a holiday village where double-bedded bungalows rent for about $25 per night. The beach is called Otuzbirler Plajı, and also holds the *Tusan Oteli* (TOO-sahn, tel 1094), on a point of land overlooking the sea, with double rooms priced at $45.

Along the next beach is a *BP Mocamp* and several cheaper camping areas. Then you come into the town, first past the modern yacht marina, then along the seafront to Tayyare Caddesi.

Orientation & Transport

Kuşadası gets its name from a small island, now connected to the mainland by a causeway, called Güvercin Adası (gew-vehr-JEEN ah-dah-suh, Pigeon Island). You can recognize it by the small stone fort, now a supper club, which is the tiny island's most prominent feature. As for downtown landmarks, the biggest is the Ottoman caravanserai, or *Kervansaray* in Turkish, which is now a hotel (see below). It's right at the intersection of the two main streets.

The waterfront road is named Hükümet Caddesi. During high summer, a horse-drawn buggy rolls along this street carrying people from the centre to the northern beach. The main street heading from the wharf into town is Tayyare Caddesi, which changes names to become Kahramanlar Caddesi as it progresses inland. The bus and dolmuş station is on this street, about a kilometre from the sea.

Buses of the Elbirlik company run between İzmir and Kuşadası ten times daily in each direction from about 7 am to 6 or 7 pm, charging 90c for the two-hour trip. Dolmuşes buzz off from Kuşadası to Ephesus and Selçuk every 30 minutes, on the hour and half-hour, charging 45c for the ride. There are dolmuşes to Söke as well; this is what you take if your ultimate destination is Priene, Miletus, Didyma, or Bodrum. Catch another dolmuş, or for Bodrum a bus, in Söke.

Dolmuşes for Kadınlar Plajı, south of town, depart from Tayyare Caddesi next to the Kervansaray.

Boats to Samos

Any travel agency in town will sell you a ticket for a boat to Samos. You can go over for the day and return in the evening, or go there to stay. Boats depart each port, Samos and Kuşadası, at 8.30 am and 5 pm daily in high summer; about four times weekly in spring and autumn. Service is usually suspended in winter except for special excursions. The trip costs $25 one-way, $30 return. You must surrender your passport for immigration processing the evening before you travel; same thing happens if you're coming from Samos to Kuşadası.

Places to Stay

Prices for rooms are highest in July and August, about 20% lower in June and September, and up to 50% lower in other months. Rates quoted below are the high summer rates.

With one exception, the more luxurious hotels are on the outskirts of town, as are the camping areas (see above). In the centre are small attractive moderately-priced hotels, and very cheap pensions.

Places to Stay – top end

Kuşadası's poshest place to stay is a refurbished Ottoman caravanserai called the *Öküz Mehmet Paşa Kervansarayı* (kehr-VAHN-sah-rah-yuh, tel 2457, 2423), sometimes called the Club Caravanserail because of its association with France's Club Mediterranee. It's right in the centre of town at the seaside end of Tayyare Caddesi. Rooms are attractive if small and simple, the courtyard is lush, the ambience superb. A double costs $40 for room alone, but you're usually required to buy 'half-pension' (breakfast and dinner). If you don't stay here, at least come for a meal (expensive), a drink, or a free look around.

The *Tusan*, north of town, is mentioned above. On Kadınlar Plajı south of town are other hotels priced at $25 to $35 double. These include the *İmbat Oteli* (EEM-baht, tel 2000, -1, -2) at the high end, and the *Martı Oteli* (mahr-TUH, tel 1198, 1031) which is lower in price. Unless you have a car, or plan to spend most of your time on the beach, it's more fun to be in town.

The *Hotel Stella* (tel 1632). Bezirgan Sokak 14, overlooks Güvercin Adası, the little island with the small fort, on the southern side of the harbour. Besides the splendid view, this small 15-room place attracts tourists with its moderate prices: $24 double.

Places to Stay – mid-range

Kuşadası has a number of little hotels, and 'pansiyons' which are actually decent little modern hotels, charging $12 to $16 for double rooms; the more expensive ones have private bath or shower.

Town Centre My favourite is the *Hotel Akdeniz* (AHK-deh-neez, tel 1120), up Tayyare Caddesi and then turn right. A double with shower may cost $13 in summer, but usually it's less. North from Tayyare Caddesi opposite the side entrance to the Kervansaray, is the tidy and friendly *Mini Tusan Hotel* (tel 2359), Cephane Sokak 8. The *Otel Karasu* is nearby and similarly good.

North, Near the Sea Try these, along the sea on the north side of town (you'll see signs to them as you come in from Selçuk). The *Günhan Hotel* (GEWN-hahn, tel 1050, 2929) is facing the sea at Hükümet Caddesi 52. Nearby is a group of other good places: the *Yunus Pansiyon* (yoo-NOOS, tel 2268), İstiklal Caddesi 7; *Çidem Pansiyon* (chee-DEHM, tel 1895), next to the Yunus at İstiklal Caddesi 9; and the *Posacı Pansiyon* (POHSS-ah-juh, tel 1151), Leylak Sokak 5, back inland from the shore road a few blocks. Also, the nearby *Hotel Akman* (AHK-mahn, tel 1501, 1502), a neat and modern little place used by Teutonic tour groups; some rooms have bathtubs.

Places to Stay – bottom end

Cheap rooms can be very nice, or pretty basic. Most will have a washbasin, few will have private bath. Prices can be as high as $9 for a double, or as low as $5. Among the nicer, more expensive ones are these:

The *Hotel Alkıs* (ahl-KUSH, tel 1245), Cephane Sokak 4, is very near the aforementioned Mini Tusan Hotel in the centre; tidy and modern, it costs $9 for a double room. Others in this range are the

Neptün, Gürkay, Kuşadası and *Demiroğlu.*
Two right on Tayyare Caddesi charging
about $7 double are the *Otel Atlantik* (aht-
lahn-TEEK, tel 1039), which is the better
one; and the *Pamuk Palas Oteli* (pah-
MOOK pah-lahs, tel 1080).

There are lots of very cheap little
pensions charging around $5 for a double,
$3 single. This buys you a bed in a room
without running water; you may have a
view, and a cheery matron full of homey
advice (all in Turkish). Ask at the Tourism
Information Office for help finding one, or
just head down a little side street. The
farther you get from the beach, the
cheaper the rooms. A good example of this
sort of pension is the *Pansiyon İstanköy*
(ee-STAHN-keuy, tel 1328), in the section
called Türkmen Mahallesi, at Ünlü Sokak
4; make reservations in the shop at
Tayyare Caddesi 83. Simple rooms with
basic cooking facilities, a five-minute walk
from the centre, cost $5 double.

Camping

Besides the BP Mocamp and neighbouring campsites (mentioned above),
there is one opposite the yacht marina,
and others south of the centre, near
Kadınlar Plajı and beyond.

If you have a car, drive to **Pamucak**, a
mostly undeveloped beach several kilometres north of Kuşadası. Coming from
Selçuk, look for a road marked 'Pamucak'
on the right a kilometre or two past the
turning for Ephesus.

Places to Eat

Restaurant prices stretch across the full
range. Most expensive is definitely the
Kervansaray, where a meal can easily set
you back $20. But it's actually more
pleasant to sit at one of the fish restaurants
next to the wharf. This is the town's prime
dining location, and so a full fish dinner
with wine at the *Toros Canlı Balık, Kazım
Usta'nun Yeri* or *Diba* may cost $10 to $12
per person. For cheaper meals of equal
quality, look for a waterfront fish restaurant to the north or south of this area.

As you get away from the sea, prices
drop dramatically, and quality stays high.
The *Çatı* on Tayyare Caddesi is on the
roof of a building, has a fine view of town
life, and costs $5 or $6 for a full fish dinner
with wine.

Go up Tayyare Caddesi past the little
police station, continue on Kahramanlar
Caddesi, and prices drop even more. The
Konya Restoran is a *hazır yemek* place
where you can fill up for $1 or $2. Further
along this street, it won't cost $2, and may
not even cost $1 if you choose carefully.
By the way, the market (*pazar*, pah-
ZAHR) is north off Kahramanlar Caddesi
one block.

Another place to try is the döner kebap
place on the way to Güvercin Adası, next
to the tea houses.

Things to See

You've seen it! Besides a stroll through
the Kervansaray, and out to Güvercin
Adası, and a short ride to the beaches, the
thing to do is take dolmuşes to the nearby
ruined cities. While you're in Kuşadası,
however, you might want to shop for onyx,
meerschaum, leather clothing and acces-
sories, copper and brass, carpets and
jewellery. Don't shop while the cruise
ships are in port, however.

Priene, Miletus & Didyma

South of Kuşadası lie the ruins of three
very ancient and important settlements
well worth a day trip. Priene occupies a
dramatic position, overlooking the plain
of the Meander River. Miletus preserves a
great theatre, and Didyma's Temple of
Apollo is among the world's most impressive.
If you start early in the morning, you can
get to all three by dolmuş, returning to
Kuşadası at night. Tours from Kuşadası
can save you time and uncertainty; one
that covers these three sites will cost
about $12. If you have a car, you can see all
three on your own and be back by mid-
afternoon.

Begin by catching a dolmuş to Söke (15
km), then another to the village of

Güllübahçe (12 km); the driver, suspecting you don't have business in the village, will take you through and a bit farther along, to the ruins of Priene.

Priene

Priene was important around 300 BC because it was where the League of Ionian Cities held its congresses and festivals. Otherwise, the city was smaller and less important than nearby Miletus, which means that its Hellenistic buildings were not buried by Roman buildings. What you see in Priene is mostly what one saw in the city over two thousand years ago.

The setting is dramatic, with steep Mount Mykale rising behind the town, and the broad flood plain of the Meander (*Menderes*) spread out at its feet. As you approach the archaeological zone, you'll come to a shady rest-spot in a romantic setting: water cascades from an old aqueduct, right next to a little tea house-cum-restaurant. This is where you recover from your tramp through the ruins.

Priene was a planned town, with its streets laid out in a grid (the grid system originated in Miletus). Of the buildings which remain, you should see the Bouleterion (City Council meeting place); the Temple of Athena, designed by Pythius of Halicarnassus and looked upon as the epitome of an Ionian temple; the Temple of Demeter; the theatre; ruins of a Byzantine church; and the gymnasium and stadium. As you gaze across the river's flood plain, you will see why the name of this river came to signify a river which twists and turns (meanders) back and forth across its flood plain.

Miletus

When you're done at Priene, wait for a passing dolmuş, or hitchhike, across the flat flood plain 22 km to Miletus. The dolmuş may bear a sign saying 'Balat' (the village next to Miletus) or 'Akköy', a larger village beyond Balat.

Miletus' great theatre rises to greet you as you approach the flood plain's southern boundary. It is the only building remaining of this once-grand city which was an important commercial and governmental centre from about 700 BC till 700 AD. After that time the harbour filled with silt, and Miletus' commerce dwindled. The 15,000-seat theatre was originally a Hellenistic building, but the Romans reconstructed it extensively during the first century AD. It's still in very good condition.

Nearer to the village is the İlyas Bey Camii (1404), a mosque dating from the Emirate period. After the Seljuks, but before the Ottomans, this region was the Emirate of Menteşe. The mosque's doorway, and inside it the mihrab, are nice. There is also a small museum a kilometre south of the theatre.

From Miletus, head south again to Akköy (seven km) and Didim (14 km farther). Transportation may be infrequent in these parts, and it may take some time to reach Akköy. South of Akköy there is more traffic, however, most of it going past Didyma to Altınkum Beach.

Didyma

Called *Didim* in Turkish, this was the site of a stupendous temple to Apollo, where lived an oracle as important as the one at Delphi. The temple and the oracle were important since very early times, but the great temple you see is the one started in the late 300s AD. It replaced the original temple which was destroyed in 494 BC by the Persians, and later construction done by Alexander the Great.

The Temple of Apollo was never finished, though its oracle and its priests were hard at work until Christianity became the state religion of the Byzantines, and they put an end to all such pagan practices. Fourteen hundred years of operation is a pretty good record, however.

When you approach Didyma today, you come into the Turkish village of Yenihisar (YEH-nee-hee-SAHR). A few tea houses and restaurants across the road from the temple provide drinks and meals.

Ancient Didyma was not a town, but the home of a god. People did not live here, only priests. People did not even come here to worship. I assume that the priests, sitting on the temple treasure (which was considerable) had a pretty good life. The priestly family here, which specialized in oracular temple management, had originally come from Delphi.

The temple porch held 120 huge columns, the bases of which are richly carved. Behind the porch is a great doorway, at which the oracular poems were written and presented to petitioners. Beyond the doorway is the *cella* or court, where the oracle sat and prophesied after drinking from the sacred spring. We can only speculate on what that water contained to make someone capable of prophesies. The cella is reached today by a covered ramp on the right side of the porch.

In the temple grounds are fragments of its rich decoration, including a striking head of Medusa (she of the snakes for hair). There used to be a road lined with statuary which led to a small harbour. The statues stood there for 23 centuries, but were then (1858) taken to the British Museum.

Altınkum Plajı (Beach)

Five km south of Didyma is Altınkum Beach (AHL-tuhn-koom, Golden Sand), with little restaurants, pensions and hotels. It's nice, but not as nice, or as convenient for transport, as Kuşadası.

Aphrodisias & Pamukkale

Two hundred and twenty km due east of Kuşadası lies the spa named Pamukkale (pah-MOO-kah-leh, Cotton Fortress), where hot mineral waters burst from the earth to run through a ruined Hellenistic city before cascading over a cliff. The cascades of solidified calcium from the waters form snowy white *travertines*, waterfalls of white stone, which give the spa its name. Nearby are the ruins of Laodicea, one of the Seven Churches of Asia.

On the way to Pamukkale, about 150 km from Kuşadası, you can make a detour to Aphrodisias, one of Turkey's most complete and elaborate archaeological sites, with several buildings exceptionally well preserved.

From Denizli, the city near Pamukkale, you can catch a bus onward to Ankara, Konya or Antalya, but you'll miss the lovely Aegean Coast if you do. Only those pressed for time and anxious to see Central Anatolia should consider such a shortcut. Everyone else should plan to visit Pamukkale as a one or two-night side trip side trip from Selçuk or Kuşadası, before continuing down the coast to Bodrum, Marmaris, Fethiye and Antalya.

Getting There

Bus and train service is good on the route from İzmir through Selçuk, Aydın and Nazilli to Denizli. At Denizli you catch a bus or dolmuş for the 20-km run to Pamukkale.

From Kuşadası, get a dolmuş to Selçuk or Ortaklar, and wait on the road for a bus. If you plan to take the side trip to Aphrodisias, hop on a bus and go as far as Nazilli; otherwise, go all the way to Denizli.

Aphrodisias

The city's name quickly brings to mind 'aphrodisiac'. Both words come from the Greek name for the goddess of love, Aphrodite, called Venus by the Romans. Aphrodite was many things to many people. As Aphrodite Urania she was the goddess of pure, spiritual love; as Aphrodite Pandemos she was the goddess of sensual

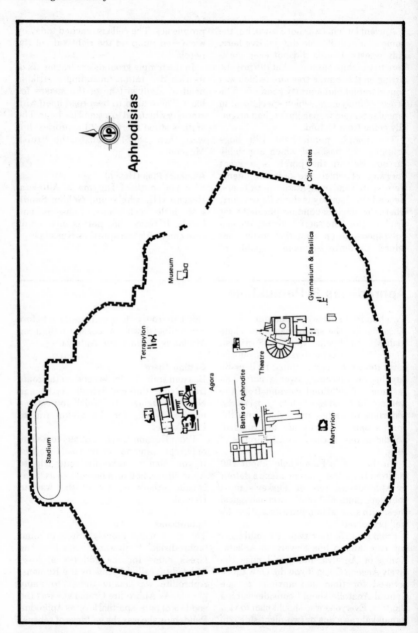

Aphrodisias

love, married to Hephaestus but lover also of Ares, Hermes, Dionysus and Adonis. She got around. Her children included Harmonia, Eros, Hermaphroditus, Aeneas and Priapus, the phallic god. All in all, she was the complete goddess of fertility, fornication and fun.

Her temple at Aphrodisias was famous and a favourite goal of pilgrimages for over a thousand years, beginning in the 700s BC. The city prospered. (How could it not, with such a popular goddess? Just think what worship entailed!) But under the Byzantines the city changed substantially: the steamy Temple of Aphrodite was transformed into a chaste Christian church, and ancient buildings were pulled down to provide building stones for defensive walls (circa 350 AD). The town, diminished from its former glory, was attacked by Tamerlane in his Anatolian rampage (1402), and never recovered.

Ruins lay abandoned and mostly buried until French, Italian, American and Turkish archaeologists began to resurrect them. What they found was a city that held a surprisingly well-preserved stadium, odeum and theatre. The National Geographic Society (USA) supported some of the excavation and restoration. Articles on Aphrodisias are in the August '67, June '72 and October '81 issues of their magazine.

Getting There

Take a bus from İzmir, Selçuk, Ortaklar or Aydın to Nazilli, and from there a dolmuş to Geyre (GEHY-reh), a village 55 km from Nazilli and right next to the ruins. If you can't find a dolmuş to Geyre, take one to Karacasu (KAHR-ah-jah-soo), 45 km from Nazilli, and take a dolmuş (35c), hitch a ride or hire a taxi in Karacasu ($5 one way, $8 return) for the final 12 km to Geyre and the ruins. There are also a few direct buses from İzmir to Karacasu. For those driving, Geyre is 38 km off the E 24 highway. A few small restaurants and snack stands are located at the ruins; there are more in Geyre, and even more in Karacasu. Also in Karacasu, there is a modest hotel right at the bus ticket office (very basic double rooms for $3).

For the onward trip from Geyre, you may be able to get a dolmuş to Tavas, then another to Denizli, which will cut a few kilometres from your trip. Otherwise, get a dolmuş to the E 24 highway and wait for a bus to Denizli.

Museum & Ruins

On the way to the ruins is a tidy modern museum with a good collection of pieces from the ruins. Entry costs 12c, same again for a camera. During Roman times there was a school for sculptors here, which accounts in part for the rich collection. Beds of high-grade marble are nearby. Note especially the 'Cult statue of Aphrodite, second century' and the 'Cuirassed statue of an emperor or high official, second century.'

At the ruins, the dazzling white marble theatre is beautiful, and virtually complete. Behind it, the odeum is more or less the same, in miniature. During your walk around you'll discover the elaborate but well-ruined Baths of Hadrian (circa 200 AD) and the remains of the Temple of Aphrodite. The temple was completely rebuilt when it was converted into a basilica church (circa 500 AD), so it's difficult to picture the place in which orgies to Aphrodite were held. Behind the temple is a monumental gateway which led to a sacred enclosure.

The stadium is wonderfully preserved, and most of its 20,000 seats are usable. Mow the grass in the field, post a ticket-seller, and one could hold chariot races this very afternoon.

DENİZLİ

Denizli (deh-NEEZ-lee, population 150,000) is a prosperous and bustling agricultural city with some light industry as well. It has a number of hotels and restaurants in all price ranges, but little else of direct interest to the tourist. When you arrive at its railway station (*gar* or

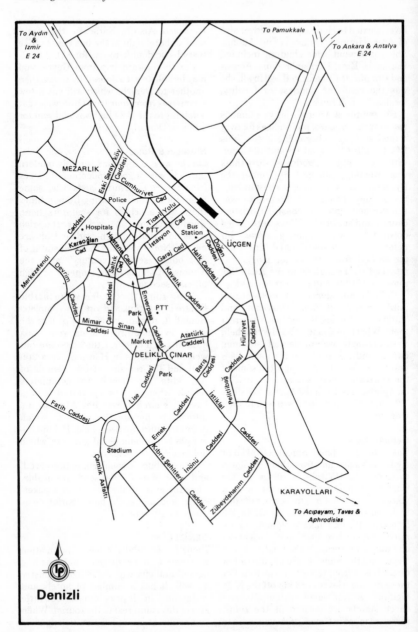

Denizli

istasyon, ees-tahs-SYOHN), or its bus terminal (*otogar*), look for a dolmuş or bus to Pamukkale. Municipal buses make the half-hour trip every hour or so; dolmuşes go more frequently. If you arrive in the evening, you may have to take a taxi, which will cost about $6.

Three trains a day ply between Denizli and İzmir; tickets go on sale an hour before departure. There is also a daily night train hauling couchettes between Denizli and Istanbul called the Pamukkale Ekspresi, which departs Denizli in early evening and arrives in Istanbul 13 or 14 hours later.

Denizli's Tourism Information Office is in the railway station, and this is only one block from the bus terminal.

PAMUKKALE

As you approach Pamukkale from Denizli, the gleaming travertines form a white scar on the side of the ridge. Coming closer, the road winds through the midst of them up to the plateau. It's an unlikely landscape, beautiful and yet somehow unsettling. The travertines form shallow pools supported by stalactites of white and black.

On the plateau are a number of motels lining the ridge, a municipal bathing establishment with various swimming pools and bath houses, and the ruined city of Hierapolis. An overnight stay here is recommended for several reasons; the site is beautiful, the waters deliciously warm and inviting, the accommodation good, and the ruins, especially the restored theatre, worth visiting.

Places to Stay

On weekends you may find the motels at Pamukkale full up, and you may have to seek lodgings in Denizli. But the point of a trip to Pamukkale is to sleep at Pamukkale, so plan to come during the week, or very early in the day on Friday or Saturday.

Of the best motels, several may be filled by tour groups during the summer, so if you plan to live well, reserve in advance.

As there is no town here, just a resort, accommodation on the ridge is in the upper or middle price ranges. At the base of the cliff are several cheap pensions.

Places to Stay – top end

The *Motel Koru* (kohr-OO, tel 5), with a big, beautiful swimming pool, restaurant and gardens is perhaps the best value here; a double costs $13. The *Tusan Moteli* (tel 1) was the first very comfortable motel here, and still commands the top price of $20 per night, double. The *Mistur Moteli* is the third choice in this class. It is at the western end of 'motel row', slightly away from things; its plumbing could be better; its odd beehive rooms produce unnerving echoes (you will scare yourself silly if you snore); and a double costs $13. But it's not bad for all that. At the *İş-Tur* you are in the centre of everything; you have your own individual section of swimming pool right off your room, with a magnificent view of the valley, for $13 double.

Places to Stay – mid-range

My favourite of the motels up here is not at all the most comfortable or eye-catching, but it's very sympathetic. It's the odd *Özel İdare Pamukkale Turizm Moteli* (ur-ZEHL ee-DAH-reh, tel 10), in the midst of the ruins. Operated by the provincial government, it has very simple rooms for $6 single, $11 double, $14 triple and $17 quad, plus a courtyard swimming pool littered with fallen Roman columns.

At the aforementioned *İş-Tur* you can rent a tiny A-frame bungalow without plumbing for $6 double.

Places to Stay – bottom end

Camping is permitted for a small fee at the *Özel İdare*, the *Mistur*, at the *Belediye Tesisleri* (the municipal pools and bath house), and at *Ali's* near the Tusan Moteli.

For beds, walk down the road to the base of the cliff where you'll find the *Konak Sade* (koh-NAHK SAH-deh, tel 7),

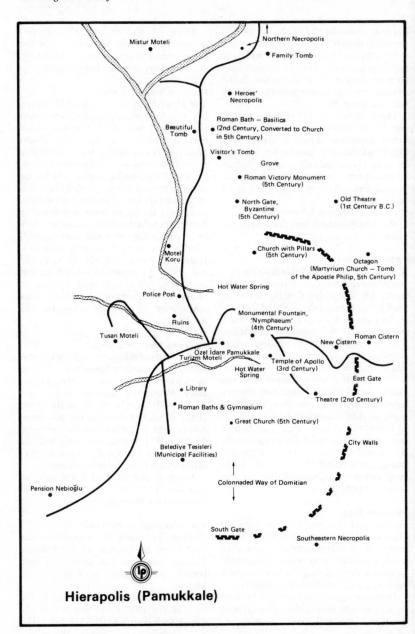

Mistur Moteli

Northern Necropolis

Family Tomb

Heroes'
Necropolis

Roman Bath – Basilica
(2nd Century, Converted to Church
in 5th Century)

Beautiful
Tomb

Visitor's Tomb

Grove

Roman Victory Monument
(5th Century)

North-Gate,
Byzantine
(5th Century)

Old Theatre
(1st Century B.C.)

Motel
Koru

Church with Pillars
(5th Century)

Octagon
(Martyrium Church – Tomb
of the Apostle Philip, 5th Century)

Police Post

Hot Water Spring

Ruins

Monumental Fountain,
'Nymphaeum'
(4th Century)

New Cistern

Roman Cistern

Tusan Moteli

Özel Idare Pamukkale
Turizm Moteli

Temple of Apollo
(3rd Century)

Hot Water
Spring

East Gate

Library

Theatre (2nd Century)

Roman Baths & Gymnasium

Great Church (5th Century)

Belediye Tesisleri
(Municipal Facilities)

City Walls

Pension Nebioğlu

Colonnaded Way of Domitian

South Gate

Southeastern Necropolis

Hierapolis (Pamukkale)

operated by Mehmet Semerci who charges $6 for two people in a marvellous traditional Turkish village house, now a pension. No plumbing in the rooms, beds on the floor village-style; a small swimming pool has the same warm mineral water you pay three times as much for atop the cliff. Down the hill ½ km on the village road past the Sade is the *Pension Nebioğlu*, a more modern building with similar, plain accommodation; and *Ali's Pension*, where beds are very cheap (just over $1), but you have to wash in a nearby stream.

Places to Eat

Eating cheaply at Pamukkale can be a problem. All of the motels have restaurants but the food, while good, tends to be as expensive as the motels. For a special treat, I'd dine at the *Motel Koru*. For a moderately-priced dinner of, say, soup, a mixed grill and beverage, the *Özel İdare* will charge you about $4. At the Belediye Tesisleri you can buy drinks, cheese sandwiches and snacks pretty cheaply. There's even a *pideci* here.

Guests at the Konak Sade can arrange to have reasonably-priced meals here, by the pool.

Also, there are several very cheap *lokantas* serving good food in and near the bus terminal in Denizli.

Still starving for some good Turkish food at moderate prices? Go into Denizli, to Delikli Çinar Meydanı and try the *Çinar Lokantası* or the *Sevimli Kardeşler Döner Kebap Salonu*.

Things to See

Virtually all the lodgings have a place where you can swim. If you want to try some different ones, you can usually do so by paying a small day-use fee. The pool at the Özel İdare is the most charming, and a day pass only costs 40c. Similarly cheap rates are charged at the Belediye baths, but these, though bigger, are hardly as picturesque. Don't have a bathing suit? You can rent one for the day at the Belediye.

After you've sampled the warm mineral waters, tour the **ruins of Hierapolis**. It was a cure centre founded about 190 BC by Eumenes II, King of Pergamum, which prospered under the Romans and even more under the Byzantines. It had a large Jewish community, and therefore an early Christian church. Earthquakes did their worst a few times, and after the one in 1334 the people decided it was actually an unhealthy spot to live, and moved on.

For a health spa, it has a surprisingly large necropolis, or cemetery.

The ancient city's mineral baths are right next to the modern motels, closest to the Özel İdare. Walking toward the prominent theatre, you pass a ruined Byzantine church and a Temple of Apollo. As at Didyma and Delphi, the temple had an oracle attended by eunuch priests. But the source of inspiration was a spring which gave off toxic vapours, potentially lethal, so the priests took it easy on the heavy breathing.

The Theatre dates from Roman times, and, appropriately, has been restored exquisitely by Italian stonecutters. The plan is to hold performances here, and you may find some scheduled.

Laodikya

Three km west of the Denizli–Pamukkale road is the site of Laodicea (*Laodikya*, LAH-oh-DEEK-yah); the turning is marked by the standard yellow sign with black lettering used to indicate archaeological remains. Laodicea was a prosperous commercial city located at the junction of two major trade routes running north-south and east-west. Famed for its black wool, banking and medicines, it had a large Jewish community and a prominent Christian congregation. Cicero lived here a few years before he was put to death at the request of Marc Anthony.

Though the city was a big one, as you see by the ruins spread over a large area, there is not much of interest left for the casual tourist. The stadium is visible, but most of the cut stones were purloined for construction of the railway. One of the two theatres is in better shape, with many of its upper tiers of seats remaining, though the bottom ones have collapsed. Unless you have a car, or are interested in church history, you can bypass Laodicea.

Söke to Bodrum

The south-western corner of Anatolia is mountainous and somewhat isolated. In ancient times this was the Kingdom of Caria, with its own people and customs, who later took on a veneer of Hellenic civilisation. Later, Christian anchorites (hermits) sought out the mountains and lake islands of Caria to be alone, and to escape the invading Arab armies. Ottoman sultans used the mountain region to exile political troublemakers in Bodrum, secure in the belief that they could raise no turmoil from such a remote spot.

Today the region is not at all forbidding, though still remote enough so that development has not ruined the beautiful scenery or polluted the air.

Getting There
Bodrum is 270 km south of İzmir, 150 km south of Kuşadası along a good, fast road (Hwy 30) through lovely country. There is no rail service south of Söke. The nearest airports to Bodrum are at İzmir and Dalaman (near Fethiye).

Buses Three companies operate buses along the route from İzmir: Koç, Karadeveci and Pamukkale. Catch a bus in İzmir, Selçuk, Söke or Milas. There are frequent buses between Bodrum and İzmir (4½ hours), Ankara (14 hours) and Istanbul (15 hours).

The Pamukkale company operates two minibuses daily in each direction on the route Bodrum-Muğla-Marmaris; it's a three hour trip.

Boats to Kos Boats run in the morning on Monday, Wednesday and Friday in summer, and on other days if demand warrants. Make reservations and buy tickets ($21 for the single trip over) at least a day in advance at the *Denizyolları Acentalığı* (deh-NEEZ-yoh-lahr-uh ah-jehn-tah-luh, Maritime Lines Agency) in the plaza just beneath the castle walls, by the dock.

South from Söke
About 35 km south of Söke there is a turning, on the right, for Akköy, Miletus and Didyma, described above in the section on Kuşadası. Soon afterwards, the highway skirts the southern shore of Bafa Gölü (bah-FAH gur-lew, Lake Bafa). The lake was once a gulf of the Aegean Sea. Along the shore are a few isolated little restaurants and tea houses that provide a stopping place for a brief respite.

Ten miles off the highway along a rough road are the ruins of Latmos/Heraclea, near the village of Kapıkırı. If you have a car, it's worth the detour to see the city walls, necropolis, Temple of Athena, agora, bouleterion, and theatre. There's also a shrine thought to be dedicated to Endymion, the legendary shepherd-boy. As the story goes, Endymion was asleep on Mt Latmos (*Beşparmak Dağı*, 1500 metres) when Selene, the moon goddess, fell in love with him. She gave him dreams so wonderful that Endymion begged Zeus to allow him to sleep forever.

This area, ringed by mountains, was one of refuge for Christian hermits during the Arab invasions of the 700s AD. Ruins of monasteries can be seen here and there, including one on a little island in the lake.

About 15 km past the lake, keep your eyes open for the extremely picturesque

Temple of Euromos, on the left-hand side of the road.

MILAS

Another 12 km brings you to Milas (MEE-lahs, population 20,000), a town of very great age. As Mylasa, it was capital of the Kingdom of Caria (except for when Mausolus ruled from Bodrum/Halicarnassus). Today it is an agricultural town, and has many homes in which carpets are woven by hand. You might want to stop and look at some of the 14th-century mosques (*Firuz Bey Camii, Ulu Cami, Orhan Bey Camii*), the Roman gate (*Baltalı Kapı*), but especially the *Gümüskesen Türbe*. This tomb, built in the 1st century AD, is thought to be a smaller copy of the magnificent Mausoleum at Halicarnassus.

Three kilometres south of Milas is an intersection: right to Bodrum, left to Muğla and Marmaris. Turn right and the highway heads west to Güllük, a beach resort with several little pensions, but turns south again before reaching the sea.

Finally, the road climbs a hill, starts down the other side, and the panorama of Bodrum with its striking castle, spreads before you.

BODRUM

It is strange that a town should owe its fame to a man long dead and a building long since disappeared, but that's the way it is with Bodrum (boh-DROOM, population 8,000). Following the Persian invasion, Caria was ruled by a satrap (provincial governor) named Mausolus (circa 376-353 BC), who moved the capital here from Milas, calling this town Halicarnassus. After the satrap's death, his wife undertook construction of a monumental tomb which Mausolus had planned for himself. The Mausoleum, an enormous white marble tomb topped by a stepped pyramid, came to be considered one of the Seven Wonders of the World.

Bodrum's other claim to fame comes from Herodotus (484?-425? BC), the 'Father of History', who was born here.

Herodotus and the Mausoleum are long gone, but Bodrum has many other attractions. Most striking is the fairytale Crusaders' castle right in the middle of town, guarding twin bays now crowded with yachts. Palm-lined streets ring the bays, and white sugar-cube houses are scattered on the hillside. Yachting, boating, swimming, snorkeling and SCUBA diving are prime Bodrum activities. So is just hanging out and enjoying life. Bodrum's economy is now dedicated to tourism, though in winter there is a bounteous citrus crop (especially tangerines), and you will still see a few sponge fishermen's boats. For diversion, you can take boat or jeep trips to nearby secluded beaches and villages, or over to the Greek island of Kos.

Orientation

The bus station is only a block inland from the water, and only three blocks from the castle. Between the bus station and the castle is the market district. Walk from the bus station toward the castle, and you arrive quickly at the Adliye Camii (AHD-lee-yeh jah-mee, Courthouse Mosque). Turn right, and you'll be heading west on Neyzen Tevfik Caddesi toward the *Yat Limanı* (Yacht Marina) and the boatyards; turn right and you will go through a section of market, then pass dozens of hotels and pensions in all price ranges. The array of lodgings continues all the way around the bay, and then along the shore of another bay further on.

The Tourism Information Office (tel 91) is in 12 (Oniki) Eylül Meydanı, the plaza right beneath the castle walls, with yachts moored alongside (most local people call the plaza İskele Meydanı, ees-KEHL-eh). Summer hours are Monday through Friday 8 am to 8 pm, Saturday 9 to 12 noon and 3.30 to 7.30 pm, closed Sunday.

The Bodrum Festival is held annually during the first week in September. Lodgings may be crowded then.

Places to Stay

As mentioned, most of Bodrum's lodgings are on the bay east of the castle, along the street called Cumhuriyet Caddesi. Most people find a room by simply walking along, asking prices, and inspecting rooms. Note that in high summer, especially on weekends, Bodrum can fill up with holiday-makers. Try to arrive early in the day to find a room.

The price range is wide, and you will find double rooms for as little as $5, or as much as $60.

Places to Stay – top end

The fanciest place in Bodrum may or may not be for you: it's the *Halikarnas Motel* (ha-lee-kahr-NAHS, tel 73), well around the eastern bay at Cumhuriyet Caddesi, Kumbahçe Mahallesi. It is 'stylish', with a disco-club for the glitter set that booms and thrums till all hours. The mod customers pay $30 to $60 for one of the 28 double rooms.

The *Baraz Oteli* (bah-RAHZ, tel 57, 714), Cumhuriyet Caddesi 58, is much more normal and standard, with 24 modern, clean doubles priced at $20. Get one with a sea view.

Places to Stay – mid-range

Mid range lodgings are those costing $10 to $20 double. Facing the western bay, along Neyzen Tevfik Caddesi, you'll find the *Herodot Pansiyon* (HEHR-oh-doht, tel 93), with 15 rooms near the marina priced at $14 double: quiet and tidy, but often full up. Also on Neyzen Tevfik Caddesi, at No 164/1, is *Seçkin Konaklar* (sech-KEEN koh-nahk-lahr, tel 351), with four multi-bed rooms priced at $16 double; this is a good choice for families or small groups.

Along Cumhuriyet Caddesi you'll see the *Artemis Pansiyon* (AHR-teh-mees, tel 53), a 16-room place facing the bay and charging $13 double.

Walk all the way out Cumhuriyet Caddesi to the area called Kumbahçe (KOOM-bahh-cheh) to find the *Fesleğen Pansiyon* (fehs-leh-EHN, no tel) at Papatya Sok. 18/1; one of 13 rooms costs $15. At the *Murat Villa* (moo-RAHT, tel 710),

Koyular Sok. 3, one of the 11 rooms costs only $12; same price at the *Evin Pansiyon* (eh-VEEN, tel 312), Ortanca Sok. 7.

Places to Stay – bottom end

In the range of $5 to $10 for a double room are a number of tiny pensions inland from Cumhuriyet Caddesi. The *Kemer* (keh-MEHR, tel 473), for instance, is on a small street called Uslu Çikmazi, at No 30. Rooms have just beds, no plumbing, and cost $2.50 per person. Inland from the Kemer is the *Umut Motel* (oo-MOOT, tel 164), Çukurbahçe Caddesi 23, a collection of bungalows amidst flower gardens only a block from the sea. A double with private shower and breakfast costs $9 to $10.

Pensions charging about $8 double include the *Martı Pansiyon* (mahr-TUH, tel 277), Cumhuriyet Caddesi 84; the *Nereid* (nehr-eh-EED, tel 80), the *Mercan* (mehr-JAHN, tel 111), and the *Balıkçının* (bah-LUHK-chuh-nuhn), all along Cumhuriyet Caddesi.

Camping

Follow signs out of town about three kilometres to several camping spots, including the very pleasant *Ayaz Camping* (ah-YAHZ, tel 174) at Gümbet beach. Charges are $1 for a tent, 75c for a camping vehicle (van, etc.), $2.50 per person; electrical hook-ups, and lots of hot water. They have rooms as well: $13 per person in a room with private shower, breakfast and dinner included.

Places to Eat

Bodrum's most prominent restaurants are those by the sea in the centre of the town, not far from the castle. These are also the more expensive ones. For a good fish dinner with wine and a sea view, you might pay $6 to $11 per person at the *Körfez* (kurr-FEHZ), for example. One of the best fish to try is trança (TRAHN-chah), a tuna of about 10 kilograms , cut into chunks and grilled over charcoal. Ask for *trança şiş* (SHEESH). Always ask the price of fish, and choose those that are in season. When in doubt, ask *Mevsimli mi?* (mehv-seem-LEE mee, Is (it) in season?).

For cheaper food, look for the little eateries in the grid of market streets. The *Kardeşler* (kahr-desh-LEHR) and the *Yıldız* (yuhl-DUHZ), near the Türkiye İş Bankası here have ready food, outdoor tables, and usually a television set, plus low prices. The *Ender Pastanesi* (ehn-DEHR pahs-tah-neh-see) serves breakfast, and pastries the rest of the day.

You will have no trouble finding places to eat, but you may encounter a good deal of mediocre food. Many of the restaurants are seasonal, with part-time staff. In general, these are the pseudo-fancy ones, tarted up with pretentious decoration; avoid them. The centre of town has the best places; the further east along Cumhuriyet Caddesi you go, the more tawdry and undependable the restaurants become.

For very cheap eats, buy a *dönerli sandviç* (dur-nehr-LEE sahn-dveech, sandwich with roast lamb). You may also want to try the ice cream.

Things to See

The castle, of course, is first on anyone's list. When Tamerlane invaded Anatolia in 1402, the Knights Hospitaller of St John of Rhodes took the opportunity to capture Bodrum. They built the **Castle of St Peter**, and it defended Bodrum all the way through World War I. It is now Bodrum's museum and open-air theatre. Hours are 8.30 am to 12 noon and 1 to 5 pm every day.

Perhaps the best plan is to head straight for the French Tower, the castle's highest point. After enjoying the view, descend through the museum exhibit rooms.

Many of the museum's exhibits are the result of underwater archaeology. Numerous ancient coastal cargo ships have been found sunk off Bodrum, and divers have recovered many artifacts. Within the French Tower is the Sub-Mycenaean Archaic Age Hall, with the very oldest finds. The Italian Tower holds the Hellenistic Hall and the Classical Hall.

Then, in descending order, you come to the Medieval Hall, the Hall of Coins and Jewellery, a collection of tombstones (outdoors), and the Snake Tower with a collection of ancient amphorae. The Byzantine Hall has an ingenious model showing how underwater archaeology is conducted; this is a favourite with children. Finally, there is a Bronze Age Hall.

Mausoleum

Though archaeological excavations now mark the spot where this Wonder of the World once stood, you might like to pay a visit. It's located inland from Neyzen Tevfik Caddesi. Turn inland near the little white mosque on the shore, then left onto the road to Karatoprak and Gümüşlük.

Boatyards

By now you must have noticed the quaint, characteristic Bodrum boats. Built at first to haul freight, they are now often seen as plush yachts. To watch the boats abuilding, walk west around the bay, past the marina, and turn left through a stone doorway to the boatyards. No one will mind if you poke around, so long as you avoid getting in the way.

Up on the hill above the boatyards is a curious saint's tomb, with several other headstones around.

Excursions

The beach at Gümbet is only a ten-minute ride from town; or you can walk. It has a few little restaurants to provide sustinence.

You can ride in a dolmuş jeep or minibus to Karatoprak, seven km southwest of Bodrum, where there is a nice beach, and a few little restaurants. Farther along is Gümüşlük, where there is a village with a few little pensions and restaurants, a fine beach, and the ruins of ancient Mindos (some underwater).

Sometimes there are boat excursions to Cnidus, at the tip of the Datça peninsula off Marmaris.

Mediterranean Turkey

The southern coast of Turkey is delightful: a succession of scenic roads, sympathetic villages and picturesque ancient ruins. Only a decade or so ago, one had to explore parts of this coast with a rugged vehicle or a pack animal, or by boat. New highway construction has changed all that, and now you can ride easily from Marmaris, where the Aegean meets the Mediterranean, to Antakya on the Syrian border, enjoying the countryside rather than battling it.

For all its natural beauty, the coast is unspoilt. It looks as though the government will attempt to keep it that way, limiting touristic development to holiday village enclaves. For the moment, congratulate yourself on being one of the early visitors to this pristine area. In years to come, you'll be able to boast that you knew it before it was overrun.

The most idyllic way to explore the coast is by private yacht, and this is not as outrageous as it sounds. While yachts chartered in the Greek islands may charge over $100 per person per day, you can charter a beautiful wooden yacht in Turkey for as little as $25 to $50 per person per day, meals included. The meals, made by the crew, will include fish and octopus pulled fresh from the blue waters, and herbs gathered along the shore. There's more information on yacht chartering in the Marmaris section, below.

You can spend as much or as little time as you like on the coast. Towns such as Marmaris, Kaş and Side are perfect for all-summer idylls lasting from spring to autumn, days in which you swim, sun, dine on seafood, dance, and cruise to islands and secluded coves. The Greek island of Rhodes is close enough for a day trip from Marmaris. Those without a lot of time can see the coast from Marmaris as far as Alanya pretty well in a week.

Getting Around

The airport at Dalaman, near Fethiye, is new and used mostly for charter flights from abroad, though Turkish Airlines may institute regular summer domestic service soon. Otherwise, the south coast's airports are at Antalya and Adana.

There is no rail service south of Söke, Denizli and Isparta; trains do run from Ankara to Adana and Mersin.

Your coastal explorations will be by bus, car or hired yacht. With the yacht and car you can make progress as you like. With the bus you must be aware that traffic is sparse along the coast. There may be only a few buses a day between points. As with most parts of Turkey, service dwindles and disappears in late afternoon or early evening, so do your travelling early in the day, and relax in the evening. With fewer buses it's all the more important to buy your reserved-seat tickets a day or so in advance.

MARMARIS

The fishing village called Marmaris (MAHR-mahr-ees, population 8,000) has in recent years become a busy little holiday resort. Partly this is due to the boat connection with Rhodes; partly to local enthusiasm, because it's now the 'in' place for Turkey's rich and famous.

Why Turkey's movie stars and magnates chose Marmaris is something of a mystery. It is not as charming as Kuşadası, it does not have a fine castle as at Bodrum, nor impressive ruins as does Side. It may have something to do with the yachting trade, as Marmaris has a fine little marina right in its centre, and it is one of Turkey's busiest yacht chartering ports. And Marmaris does have two luxurious 'holiday village' resorts.

Besides the occasional newsworthy Turk, the streets and shores of Marmaris host a varied collection of international

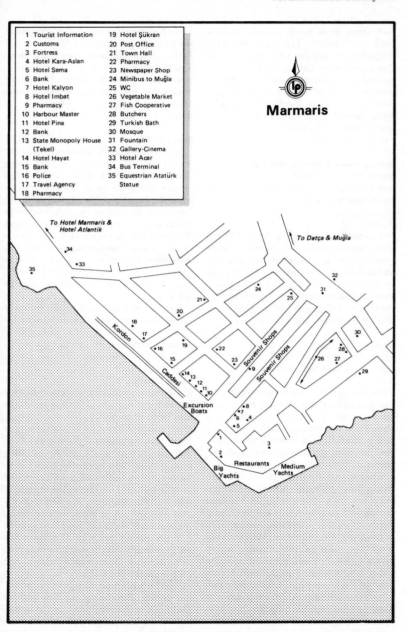

1 Tourist Information	19 Hotel Şükran
2 Customs	20 Post Office
3 Fortress	21 Town Hall
4 Hotel Kara-Aslan	22 Pharmacy
5 Hotel Sema	23 Newspaper Shop
6 Bank	24 Minibus to Muğla
7 Hotel Kalyon	25 WC
8 Hotel Imbat	26 Vegetable Market
9 Pharmacy	27 Fish Cooperative
10 Harbour Master	28 Butchers
11 Hotel Pina	29 Turkish Bath
12 Bank	30 Mosque
13 State Monopoly House	31 Fountain
(Tekel)	32 Gallery-Cinema
14 Hotel Hayat	33 Hotel Acar
15 Bank	34 Bus Terminal
16 Police	35 Equestrian Atatürk
17 Travel Agency	Statue
18 Pharmacy	

Marmaris

To Hotel Marmaris &
Hotel Atlantik

To Datça & Muğla

Kordon Caddesi

Souvenir Shops

Souvenir Shops

Excursion
Boats

Restaurants

Big
Yachts

Medium
Yachts

yachtsmen, from Saudi princes to New York stockbrokers. There are also day-trippers from Rhodes who, ignoring the dire warnings of Greeks that Turkey is expensive, unfriendly and dangerous, come over to find just the opposite. But mostly Marmaris is local village people, some farmers and fishermen, others waiters and shopkeepers. It is definitely not a flashy resort.

Getting There & Getting Around

Marmaris is somewhat remote, but that's part of its charm. Transport by bus is not inconvenient, in any case.

By Air

The airport at Dalaman is about 100 km from Marmaris. As it is charter flights which use this airport, minibuses are often on hand to transport passengers directly to Marmaris for about $10 per person. You can do it much cheaper by getting into the village of Dalaman and catching a bus or dolmuş there, but this takes longer.

By Bus

From İzmir: Direct buses run several times daily from İzmir to Marmaris, a six-hour journey.

From Bodrum: Minibuses operated by the Pamukkale bus company run twice daily (and return) to Marmaris via Muğla, a three-hour, 160-km trip. Catch the minibus next to the PTT in Bodrum. If you miss it, get transport to Muğla, and look for transport to Bodrum from there.

The trip from Bodrum takes you back to Milas, then up into the mountains through the towns of Yatağan and Muğla. The land is rich and heavily cultivated, with vast fields of sunflowers and frequent colonies of beehives. Thirty km from Marmaris the road descends by switchbacks into a fertile valley. You turn right and cross the valley floor through a magnificent double lane of great eucalyptus trees over two kilometres in length. At the other side, the road narrows and ascends into the hills again before coming down into Marmaris.

From Fethiye: Two minibuses daily make the trip each way between Marmaris and Fethiye, in the morning and early afternoon. The distance is 160 km, the time about three hours. If you miss either of the direct minibuses, catch a bus or minibus to Muğla, and find transport to Fethiye from there.

Boats to Rhodes

Boats to and from Rhodes run daily except Sunday in high summer, with Greek and Turkish boats sharing the service. If traffic is heavy, they may put on a Sunday boat. Though you will certainly have difficulty finding the ticket office in Rhodes (because no one will help you find it), you will easily see where to buy tickets in Marmaris: banner signs along the waterfront announce 'Boats to Rhodes' in large letters. Buy your ticket ($12 single trip, $18 return) at least a day in advance.

Every now and then a cruise ship will call at Marmaris on the way to Rhodes (or vice-versa) and will take you across. Travel agents in town can tell you about such infrequent sailings.

Yacht Charters

If you charter a Marmaris yacht through a travel agent outside of Turkey, the cost may be $100 or more per person per day. But if you deal directly with the brokers in Marmaris, the cost can be as low as $25 to $50 per person daily, meals included (booze extra). The larger the yacht (up to 12 berths) and the earlier (in spring) or later (in autumn) the cruise, the cheaper it will be. For instance, an eleven-berth yacht rented for a week in late April, without crew or meals, need cost a mere $12 per person per day. But the same yacht rented in July or August would cost twice as much. If you want a captain, add $5 per person per day.

Smaller boats tend to be more expensive, per person. But even if you hire a larger yacht and cruise with some of the berths empty, the charges are still quite reasonable. A yacht designed to sleep eight people (ten in a pinch) will be all the more comfortable for five or six people. In May or October, with crew and meals included, the charge for such a boat would still be only $50 to $60 daily per person, compared to $40 if there were eight people. Considering that this cost includes lodging, meals, transport and a luxurious, unforgettable experience, the cost is unbeatable.

The trick is to avoid commissions and deal directly with the broker in Marmaris. Write as early as possible to this active and well-established broker: *Yeşil Marmaris Travel Agency*, Kordon Caddesi 37, PO Box 8, Marmaris, Turkey (tel (6121) 1033 or 1559; telex 52 528 gema; cable YESMAR). Or, contact a Turkish travel agency as soon as you arrive in Turkey. You may still find a boat available in spring or autumn.

As for yachting itineraries, virtually eveything described in this book from Bodrum to Antalya is open to you, as well as many secluded coves and islands. Any trip in this area becomes what is called a *Blue Cruise*, which means a cruise along the ancient Carian and Lycian coasts.

Orientation

Marmaris is a small village, and a few minutes' stroll will show you the layout. The Tourism Information Office (tel 1035) is at İskele Meydanı 39, right by the yacht harbour, the wharf for boats to Greece, and the market – in short, right at the centre.

Another landmark is the equestrian statue of Atatürk on Kordon Caddesi. Plaques on the plinth bear the sayings *Türk Ögün Çalış Güven* (Turk! Be Proud. Work. Trust.) and *Ne Mutlu Türküm Diyene* (What joy to him who says, 'I am a Turk'). Both sayings were meant to dispel the Ottoman inferiority complex.

Places to Stay

The more expensive hotels in Marmaris are well around the bay from the town. Transport is easy though: in summer the

municipality operates an open-air 'trailer-train' between the distant hotels and the centre. There is sometimes also a launch running across the bay.

A few moderately-priced hotels are a short walk from town. The cheapest places are very convenient, right in the centre.

Places to Stay – top end

The grand dame here is the *Hotel Lidya* (LEED-yah, tel 1016, 1026, or 1355), a comfortable if not posh place of 220 rooms around the bay from the town in Siteler Mahallesi. Lodgings include rooms looking onto the sea or the gardens, suites, motel-style rooms and apartments. Prices range from $23 to $30 double for rooms, $50 to $60 for an apartment, from mid-June through mid-September. Reductions off-season are about 35%.

Two 'holiday villages' charge more than the Lidya. The *Turban Marmaris Tatil Koyü* (TOOR-bahn, tel 1843), a 250-room place funded by the government, charges only slightly more. The posh *Martı Tatil Köyü* (mahr-TUH, tel 1930) is considerably more expensive, its 213 rooms costing $40 double.

Places to Stay – mid-range

A few lower-priced lodgings exist near the top-price places. Near the Martı is the *Sultansaray Moteli* (sool-TAHN sah-rah-yee, tel İçmeler 1), with 36 rooms at $15. Right next to the Turban is the *Tümer Pansiyon* (tew-MEHR, tel 1447), and a double costs $18.

A modern mid-range favourite is the *Otel Marmaris* (tel 1173, 1308), Atatürk Caddesi 30, on the waterfront street, fifteen minutes' walk from the centre; 63 double rooms for $20. Next door is the older *Otel Atlantik* (aht-lahn-TEEK, tel 1218, 1236), Atatürk Caddesi 34, with 40 doubles priced at $23.

Places to Stay – bottom end

The very cheapest lodgings in Marmaris are called *ev pansiyon* (home pensions),

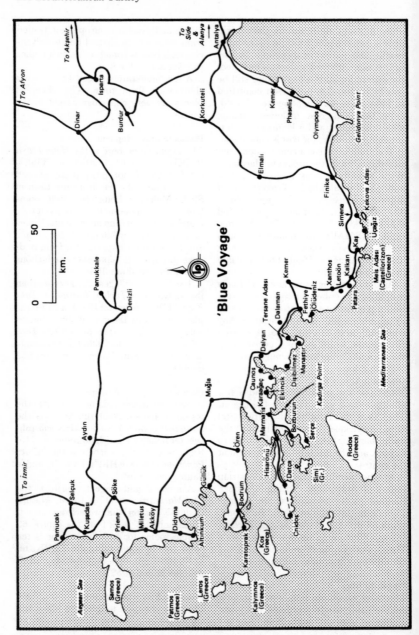

where you rent a room in a private home. The Tourism Office can help you locate one of these. Prices are $4 double, $5.50 triple, $7 for four.

Next cheapest are the small, plain hotels right in the centre such as the *Sema, İmbat, Karaaslan* and *Kalyon*, next to the Tourism Office. These hotels are ranked as Second Class by the Municipality, and charge $4 to $6 double depending on the plumbing in the room. Others are the *Hayat* and the *Pina* on Kordon Caddesi, and the *Şükran* a block inland.

Better, and marginally more expensive, are the Municipality's First Class hotels, of which a good example is the *Hotel Kaptan* (kahp-TAHN, tel 1251), facing the wharf for boats to Rhodes, where a double with breakfast costs $10. The *Hotel Acar* (ah-JAHR) behind the equestrian statue of Atatürk on Kordon Caddesi, charges $6 for doubles at the back, $7 for doubles with little balconies at the front, all with private showers (hot water).

Despite its expensive reputation, the area around the Hotel Lidya has some inexpensive pensions. The *Motel Küçükevler* (kew-CHEWK-ehv-lehr, tel 1857) offers nice little whitewashed, tile-roofed bungalows surrounded by flowers, equipped with toilet and shower, for $8 double, breakfast included. If it's full, try the *Kıvılcım Pansiyon* nearby.

Camping

The most convenient camping areas are the ones near the Hotel Lidya.

Places to Eat

Expensive meals are those served in the top hotels and holiday villages, and even these are not outrageous in price for what you get. Downtown restaurants near the yacht harbour have pleasant outdoor dining areas and moderate prices. The *Birtat* is well established, with a good reputation.

For less expensive fare, head into the market area. The *Ayyıldız Lokantası* has tables set outside beneath the market awnings. A meal of döner kebap, bulgur pilav (cracked wheat pilaff), a salad and beverage might cost $2.

Things to See

Marmaris has a little ruined fortress on the hill just above the yacht harbour, but it holds little to see. Do look at the *Menzilhane*, an Ottoman 'pony express' way-station which now serves as a shopping centre for souvenirs. It's just behind the Tourism Office; look for the Arabic-alphabet Ottoman inscription plaque on the doorway. (It says that the *menzilhane* was built by Sultan Süleyman the Magnificent in 1545.)

Daytime occupations in Marmaris usually have to do with beaches and boats. Besides the beach right in the centre, there are others near the fancy hotels, and still others reached by boat from near the Tourism Office. If you shop for souvenirs, do it before the boats full of day-trippers arrive from Rhodes, or after they leave. Prices are much higher when the trippers are in town. By the way, Marmaris is a honey-producing centre. Those who know honey will want to sample several of the local varieties.

Excursions

Besides the daily boats to Rhodes, there are often boat trips to Datça and Cnidus, well out along the hilly peninsula west of Marmaris. Ask at a travel agency, or haggle with a boatman for a day's excursion to the secluded coves, beaches and ruins which are scattered along the peninsula. You can do the excursion by jeep, but it's fairly long and bumpy. Plan to spend the night at Datça if you like; there are modest pensions there.

At Cnidus are ruins of a prosperous port town dating from about 400 BC. The Dorians who founded it were smart: the winds change as one rounds the peninsula, and ships in ancient times often had to wait at Cnidus for good winds. This happened to the ship carrying St Paul to Rome for trial.

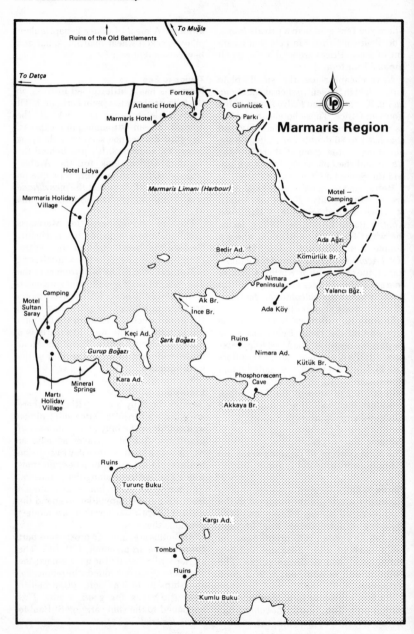

To Muğla

Ruins of the Old Battlements

To Datça

Fortress

Atlantic Hotel
Marmaris Hotel

Günnücek
Parkı

Marmaris Region

Hotel Lidya

Marmaris Limanı (Harbour)

Motel —
Camping

Marmaris Holiday
Village

Ada Ağzi

Bedir Ad.

Kömürlük Br.

Nimara
Peninsula

Camping

Ak Br.

İnce Br.

Yalancı Bğz.

Ada Köy

Motel
Sultan
Saray

Keçi Ad.

Şark Boğazı

Ruins

Nimara Ad.

Gurup Boğazı

Kütük Br.

Phosphorescent
Cave

Mineral
Springs

Kara Ad.

Martı
Holiday
Village

Akkaya Br.

Ruins

Turunç Buku

Kargı Ad.

Tombs

Ruins

Kumlu Buku

Cnidus, being rich, commissioned the great Praxiteles to make a great statue of Aphrodite. They housed it in a circular temple in view of the sea. The statue, said to be the sculptor's masterpiece, has been lost.

MARMARIS TO FETHIYE

Fethiye, 140 km east of Marmaris, is the next good place to spend some time, though there are interesting detours along the road.

Leaving Marmaris, the road climbs into mountains with beautiful panoramas, and fertile valleys in between. Near Köycegiz, a local agricultural centre, is an archaeological site worth a side-trip.

Caunus

About 70 km east of Marmaris, signs point south (right) to 'The Greves (sic) of Likya' and 'The Ruins of Caunus', 15 km down a side road. (Coming by bus, get out at *Ortaca* and catch a dolmuş to *Dalyan*.) The road brings you to the village of Dalyan through lush cotton and vegetable farms, along the winding course of a stream.

Dalyan is tiny, but it has a few very modest pensions, restaurants and tea houses. It's here that you haggle with boatmen for a cruise to the ruins of Caunus. Some of the Lycian tombs, cut high in the rock face on the opposite side of the stream (*Dalyan Çayi*), are visible from the dock. Walk a kilometre along the road past the village for a better view.

The trip to the ruins takes two or three hours. To rent the entire boat (which can take about a dozen people), costs about $9 total. With enough people to share, the price per person is very low.

Caunus was an important Carian city by 400 BC. Right on the border with the kingdom of Lycia, its culture shared aspects of both kingdoms. The tombs, for instance, are in Lycian style (you'll see many more of them at Fethiye, Kaş, and other points east). Though of good size, Caunus suffered from endemic malaria.

Besides the tombs, the theatre is very well preserved; parts of an acropolis and other structures are near the theatre. Those curious wooden structures in the river are fishing weirs (*dalyan*). No doubt the ancient Caunians benefitted from such an industry as well.

Approaching Fethiye

Leaving Dalyan and Ortaca, the next town of note is Dalaman, with its airport; then, 50 km later, Fethiye.

FETHİYE

Fethiye (FEH-tee-yeh, population 15,000) is a very, very old town with few old buildings. An earthquake in 1958 levelled the town, leaving only a few buildings standing. Of these few, most were tombs from the time when Fethiye was called Telmessos (400 BC), but that's good since one of the things Fethiye is famous for is tombs.

The bay of Fethiye is an excellent harbour, well protected from storms. Beaches are good here, and even better at Ölüdeniz, one of Turkey's newly-discovered seaside hot spots. You may want to stop in Fethiye, spend an afternoon or two at Ölüdeniz, climb up to the rock tombs, and then head east.

Fethiye's Tourism Office (tel (6151) 1051) is at İskele Meydanı, right next to the Dedeoğlu hotel, near the yacht harbour, at the end of Atatürk Caddesi right downtown. They will help you with lodgings, and with inexpensive charters of Fethiye's yachts.

Places to Stay

Fethiye has a good selection of lodgings, but you must choose among three areas. For a night or two, stay right in the town. For a beach holiday of three days or more stay at Ölüdeniz. There are also beachfront hotels and pensions out along the beach of Fethiye's bay, called Çalış (chah-LUSH).

First some notes for downtown lodgings, then some for Ölüdeniz.

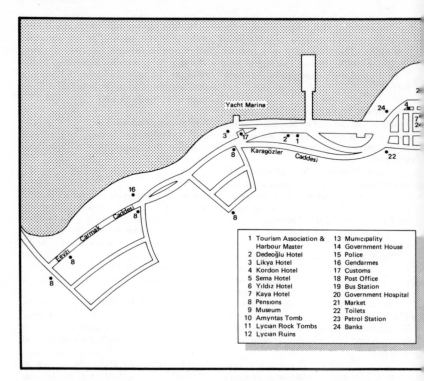

1 Tourism Association &
   Harbour Master
2 Dedeoğlu Hotel
3 Likya Hotel
4 Kordon Hotel
5 Sema Hotel
6 Yıldız Hotel
7 Kaya Hotel
8 Pensions
9 Museum
10 Amyntas Tomb
11 Lycian Rock Tombs
12 Lycian Ruins
13 Municipality
14 Government House
15 Police
16 Gendarmes
17 Customs
18 Post Office
19 Bus Station
20 Government Hospital
21 Market
22 Toilets
23 Petrol Station
24 Banks

Places to Stay – top end

Fethiye's best is the *Hotel Likya* (LEEK-yah, tel 1169, 1690), down by the yacht marina past the Tourism Office. Its 16 modern, tidy rooms open onto the sea and pleasant gardens, and cost $16 double. The *Dedeoğlu Oteli* (DEH-deh-oh-loo, tel 1606, 1707), right next to the Tourism Office, is bigger (41 rooms) and priced about the same, but without the gardens.

Places to Stay – mid-range

Best is perhaps the *Kordon Oteli* (kohr-DOHN, tel 1834), Atatürk Caddesi 8, right where Atatürk Caddesi (the main street) curves to the left in the centre of town. A double with shower costs $8. The 22-room *Sema Oteli* (seh-MAH, tel 1015), Çarşı Caddesi, just off Atatürk Caddesi near the statue of Atatürk, charges $9 for a double with shower; watch out for street noise. The *Yıldız Oteli*, beside the Sema, is cheaper but perhaps noisier.

Places to Stay – bottom end

If you want a downtown hotel, try the little *Hotel Kaya* (KAH-yah), behind the restaurant called 'Oh Yaaa'; graced with a wonderful jasmine vine on its facade, the Kaya charges $4 double for bathless rooms.

For real savings, find a pension. There are lots of them in Fethiye, left from the time before Ölüdeniz was discovered and developed. In those halcyon days, Turks on beach holiday would stay in Fethiye's homes, bringing delightful income to the town's matrons. Since Ölüdeniz, the trade has dropped off, but the pensions remain, and they're better bargains than ever. The

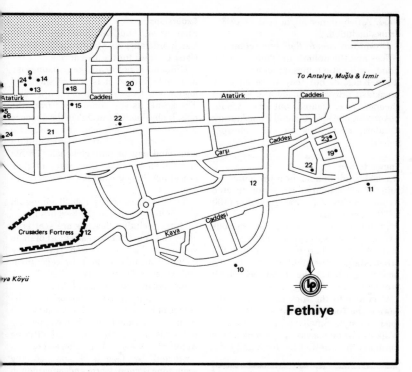

Fethiye

Tourism Office will help you find one, or you can simply walk up the hill behind the Hotel Likya, along Karagözler Caddesi, and look for the little 'pansiyon' signs. The houses are all about the same, as are the rates: about $2.50 per person for a bed and the rights to a shower. Soap and towels are not normally provided.

West of the centre, out along the beach, are more cheap pensions. These are still within walking distance, and they're often more pleasant than the ones on Karagözler Caddesi, if a slight bit more expensive.

Camping
There are numerous camping areas on both Çalış and Ölüdeniz beaches.

Lodgings at Ölüdeniz
Some of the camping areas (Çavuş, Çetin, Deniz, Derya and Belcekız) rent little bungalows as well as camping places, and these are the cheapest lodgings here. Otherwise, there's the *Meri Motel* (meh-REE, tel Ölüdeniz 1), with 75 rooms scattered down a steep hillside amidst pretty gardens. The views from many of the rooms are very fine; the price for a double with bath is $22. The motel has its own beach and seaside restaurant.

Places to Eat
For fancy meals, dine in the Dedeoğlu and Likya hotels. For local colour, the most pleasant place to dine is *Rafet Restoran* (rah-FEHT), just by the Hotel Likya beside the yacht marina. It's not fancy, with fluorescent lights and a noisy television set, but the outdoor tables are very pleasant, the service polite, the food quite

good. A fish dinner might cost $4 or $5, drinks included.

Downtown near the bus company offices and the dolmuş to Ölüdeniz is *Oh Yaaa*, with patio tables under an awning. It's a hangout, but they serve an early breakfast; prices are moderate. For even cheaper fare, search out the *Afrodit Lokantası*, one street inland from Atatürk Caddesi; near it is an even cheaper *pideci*.

Things to See

On the hillside behind the town, notice the ruins of a Crusaders fortress constructed by the Knights of St John on earlier (400 BC?) foundations.

In the town you will notice curious Lycian stone sarcophagi dating from about 450 BC. There is one near the PTT, others stand in the middle of streets or in private gardens; the town was built around them.

Carved into the rock face behind the town is the **Tomb of Amyntas** (350 BC), in the Doric style. Smaller tombs are nearby. Walk up, or take a taxi, for a look at the tomb and fine view of the town and bay.

Ölüdeniz

1 Motel Meri
2 Çavuş Campsite
3 Çetin Campsite
4 Deniz Campsite
5 Derya Campsite
6 Belcekiz Campsite

To Fethiye

Ölüdeniz

Excursions

First of all, Ölüdeniz, the 'Dead Sea'. Catch a dolmuş on Atatürk Caddesi near Çarşı Caddesi for the 15-km ride.

Ölüdeniz is not dead like its namesake in Israel. Rather, it is a very sheltered lagoon not at all visible from the open sea. The scene, as you come down from the hills, is absolutely beautiful: in the distance is open sea, in the foreground a peaceful lagoon bordered by forest, in the middle a long sand spit of perfect beach. Yachts stand at anchor in the blue water, or glide gracefully along the hidden channel out to sea.

You may have to pay a small admission charge to use some of the beaches here.

Other secluded beaches are scattered along this coast, but to reach most of them you must have your own car. These include Katrancı (17 km), Belceğiz (near Ölüdeniz), Günlük (also called Küçük Kargı, north of town), and İnlice.

The old city of Karmylassos, near the village of Kaya, is reached by a road which climbs the hillside behind Fethiye, passing the Crusader castle ruins and offering wonderful views. The shore here is protected by Gemile Island, so the swimming is good, warm and safe, though there's not a lot of sand beach. On Gemile are unexcavated ruins of an ancient city with a large necropolis.

FETHİYE TO KAŞ

This portion of the Lycian coast, sometimes called the Lycian Peninsula because it extends well south into the Mediterranean, is littered with the remains of ancient cities. If you have your own car, you can visit as many as you like by making a few short detours. Without a car, you can still stop at Xanthos, one of the best. The distance from Fethiye to Kaş is 108 km.

Leave Fethiye on Atatürk Caddesi. A few kilometres along, near the town of Kemer, the road forks. Take the right fork, to 'Kaş-Antalya'; the left fork, to 'Korkuteli-Antalya' is the inland route.

The road takes you up into fragrant

evergreen forests, and down to fertile valleys. Herds of sheep and goats (a few cattle) skitter along the roadway near the villages. The road is curvy and somewhat slow. Farm tractors pulling trailers can slow you down as well.

At Kınık, 63 km from Fethiye, the road crosses a river. Up to the left on a rock outcrop is the ruined city of **Xanthos**, once the capital of Lycia, with a fine theatre, Lycian tomb and a monumental stone with Lycian inscriptions. Opposite the theatre is the agora. Though Xanthos was a large and important city, the acropolis is now badly ruined. One does enjoy the

spicy smells of sage and mint which come up while trudging through the ruins, but if you've seen lots of other ancient ruins, you may not want to get off the bus. If you're driving, stop.

Nearby ruined cities include Letoon and Sidyma, Pinara and Patara. Signs on the highway mark the turnings.

About 81 km from Fethiye, the road passes **Kalkan**, an old village with some new touristic installations, which include a yacht marina in the serene, unspoilt bay, and the *Pasha's Inn* (tel Kalkan 77). This small six-room place charges $17 double, and is obviously aimed at the tourist

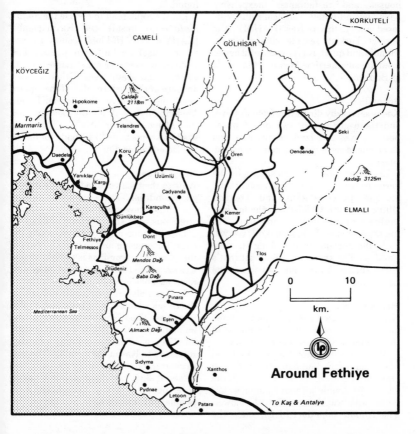

trade. The much more modest *King Pansiyon* is a good deal cheaper.

At 87 km is Kaputaş (or Kapıtaş), a striking mountain gorge crossed by a small highway bridge. The marble plaque on the east side of the bridge, embedded in the rock wall, comemmorates four road workers who were killed during the dangerous construction of this part of the highway. Below the bridge is a perfect little sandy cove.

KAŞ

Fishing boats and a few yachts in the harbour, a sleepy town square with tea houses and restaurants, inexpensive pensions and hotels, classical ruins scattered about: this is Kaş (KAHSH), the perfect Turkish seaside village. Small, friendly and quiet, Kaş is a peaceful haven from the summertime bustle of Marmaris or Bodrum.

Orientation

Kaş is served by direct bus from Fethiye, and there are one or two direct buses between Kaş and İzmir. Otherwise, you catch one of the few buses going along the coast.

Life centres on the town square by the harbour, with its tea houses, restaurants, mosque, police station, and Tourism Office (tel 238). Come down the hill into the town from the highway, and turn left to the town square; if you turn right, you will go to the ancient theatre along Hastane Caddesi. The theatre is about all that's left of ancient Antiphellus, which was the Lycian town.

Places to Stay

Kaş has no fancy lodgings, only simple, modest places at low prices. Ask for any of these, and someone will point the way.

About the best hotel is the *Ali Baba Motel* (ah-LEE bah-bah, tel 126), on Hastane Caddesi in the centre of the village; $4 double without running water, $5.50 with washbasin, $7 with shower. The *Andifli* (ahn-deef-LEE), once the

fanciest (and not fancy at that) is now second, at $4 double without running water. Pensions are everywhere. They charge $4 double. Two of the nicest and quietest are the *Kısmet* (kuss-MEHT) and the *Mini* (MEE-nee).

Camping areas are to be found at the *Ali Baba Motel* and near the ancient theatre.

Places to Eat

The first place you'll notice is the *Eriş*, on the town square, with shady pseudo-rustic tables outside. As this is the first place tourists see, it's the first place they go. Prices are not bad, better food can be found.

Local people tend to choose the *Shady Restaurant*, beside the Kaymakamlık (KAHY-mah-KAHM-luhk, county government house) on the main square. The restaurant takes its English name from its awnings and shade trees. Other restaurants are at the eastern edge of the square near the Belediye (beh-leh-DEE-yah, Municipality); look for the *Belediye* and the *Mercan* (mehr-JAHN). The local wisdom seems to be 'the Shady for lunch, the Belediye for dinner'.

Things to See

Walk to the theatre for a look. It's in very good condition. There are rock tombs in the cliffs above the town, good for a strenuous walk at a cool time of day.

Local boatmen will take you along the coast for cruising and swimming. One of the standard excursions is to Kekova and Üçağız, where there are several interesting ruins, also reachable by road (see below).

You can also go over to Kastellorizon, the Greek island just off the coast, visible from Kaş. The island has no customs and immigration offices, it is not a port of entry into Greece, so you can only go for the day, returning to Kaş in the evening. The cost to charter a fishing boat for the excursion is about $35, which, if divided among seven people, comes to $5 each. Get more people, pay less each.

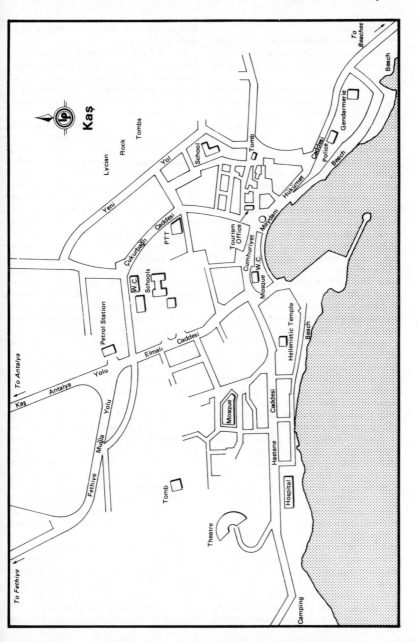

Heading East

From Kaş you climb into the mountains again. You may want to stop to take photos near the top of the hill overlooking the town.

Sixteen kilometres from Kaş you will see signs for a turning (south, right) to Kekova (KEH-koh-vah), or Kale (KAH-leh). Twenty-three km along this side road is the sea, and several ruined cities, including Teimiussa and Simena, across a strait from one another. At Teimiussa the attraction is a necropolis, with many grand tombs. At Kale is a medieval fortress (kale), well preserved, the ancient ruins of Simena, and the little village of Kale. The road to Kale/Simena has only recently been improved, and the site is very attractive. Near the island of Kekova are numerous picturesque, partly-submerged Lycian tombs.

At Demre (DEHM-reh), also called Kale, 37 km east of Kaş, is the Church of St Nicholas. The road descends from the mountains to a very fertile river delta, much of it covered in greenhouses. It is said that the legend of Father Christmas (Santa Claus) began here when a 4th-century Christian bishop gave anonymous gifts to village girls who had no dowry. He would drop bags of coins down the chimneys of their houses, and the 'gift from heaven' would allow them to marry. This is perhaps why he is the patron saint of virgins; he went on to add sailors and children, pawnbrokers and Holy Russia to his conquests. His fame grew, and in 1087 a raiding party from the Italian city of Bari stole his mortal remains from the church. In medieval Europe, relics were hot items. (They missed a few bones, which are now in the Antalya museum.)

The church itself has been restored, and it offers a rare chance to see what a 5th-century Byzantine church looked like. A symposium on St Nicholas is held here each year.

A few kilometres inland from the church are the ruins of Myra, with a striking honeycomb of rock-hewn tombs and a Roman theatre. They're worth a look while you're here.

Demre has several cheap pensions (the Palmiye and the Myra) and very modest restaurants. There are camping places, equally modest, down on the shore. West of the town is a fine beach, with a few more little restaurants.

Thirty km along a twisting mountain road brings you to Finike (FEE-nee-keh, population 5,000), the ancient Phoenicus. Finike has only a few very modest hotels, the best of which is the Hotel Sedir (seh-DEER, tel 183, 256), Cumhuriyet Caddesi 37, where a double room with shower costs $5. The Köşk, behind the Sedir, is older and perhaps noisier, but has sea views. There are very cheap pensions; you'll notice the Kale Pension, a large white building overlooking the docks. As for restaurants, the Fish Restaurant, which bears a giant sign with its name, catches most of the tourists, though townfolk prefer the Lezzet Lokantası or the slightly nicer Deniz Restaurant, right around the corner from the Hotel Sedir.

Leaving Finike, the highway skirts a sand-and-pebble beach which runs for about fifteen kilometres. Signs at intervals read Plaj Sahası Halka Açıktır which means 'The Beach Area is Open to the Public'.

Upon leaving the long beach, the road winds back up into the mountains. You may see crews of wood-cutters, a reclusive people called Tahtacılar who hold to their own unique culture and traditions. About 28 km from Finike there is an especially good panorama. Three km later you enter Beydağları Sahil Milli Parkı, the Bey Mountains Coastal National Park. Another six kilometres and you get splendid views of the mountains.

At 56 km from Finike (13 to Kemer) is a turning for Phaselis, a Lycian city on the shore. The city is now very ruined, and not restored, but its setting is beautiful, and excellent for a picnic or rest stop. Not far along is Olympos, another Lycian city. By walking 1½ hours from Olympos you can see the Chimaera, a perpetual flame issuing from a hole in the rock. Ruins of a temple to Hephaistos (Vulcan) are at the site.

Kemer (keh-MEHR), 42 km from Antalya, is a burgeoning beach holiday village being built under government supervision. Accommodation is in all price ranges, so you should be able to find whatever you like here.

ANTALYA

Antalya (ahn-TAHL-yah, population 175,000) is the chief city of Turkey's eastern Mediterranean coast. Agriculture, light industry and tourism have made Antalya boom during the past few decades, and this attractive Mediterranean city is still growing at a fast pace.

Though Antalya is well worth a visit, one doesn't normally come here for a beach vacation because the city's beaches are out of town. Rather, people come here to see the large museum packed with the archaeological and ethnographic wealth of this deeply historical coast; to see the Old Town and its cosy harbour, which date back several centuries before Christ; and to use this pleasant city as a base for excursions to the dramatic ruins nearby at Termessos, Perge and Aspendos.

History

Antalya is not as old as many other cities which once lined this coast, but it is still prospering while the older cities are dead. Founded by Attalus II of Pergamum in the 100s BC, the city was named Attaleia for its founder. When the Pergamene kingdom was willed to Rome, Attaleia became a Roman city. The Emperor Hadrian visited here in 130 AD, and a triumphal arch (Hadriyanüs Kapısı) was built in his honour.

The Byzantines took over from the Romans. In 1207, the Seljuk Turks based in Konya took the city from the Byzantines, and gave Antalya a new version of its name, and also its symbol, the Yivli Minare (Grooved Minaret). After the

Mongols broke Seljuk power, Antalya was held for awhile by the Turkish Hamidoğulları emirs. It was taken by the Ottomans in 1391.

During World War I, the Allies made plans to divide up the Ottoman Empire, and at the end of the war they parcelled it out. Italy got Antalya in 1918, but by 1921 Atatürk's armies had put an end to all such foreign holdings in Anatolia.

Though always a busy port (trade to Crete, Cyprus and Egypt), Antalya has grown rapidly since the 1960s, and is now Turkey's fifteenth-largest city.

Getting There & Getting Around

Turkish Airlines has direct flights to Ankara, İzmir, Istanbul and Munich.

Being such a popular tourist and commercial city, bus transport to Antalya is frequent and convenient from all points in Turkey. Antalya's bus terminal is on Kazım Özalp/Şarampol Caddesi, several blocks north of Cumhuriyet Caddesi and the Yivli Minare.

There are about a dozen buses a day to Alanya (2 hours), stopping at Manavgat (for Side, 1½ hours); for Perge (15 minutes) and Aspendos (45 minutes), take dolmuşes. Other direct buses go to Adana (12 hours), Denizli (5½ hours) and Konya (7 hours).

Orientation

The city now sprawls well beyond its ancient limits. A çevre yolu (ring road or bypass) carries long-distance traffic around the city. To the west is Konyaaltı Plajı, a pebble beach several kms long, now partly sullied by industrial development. To the east are the sandy bathing beaches, especially Lara Plajı, which has its own hotels, motels and pensions.

In the centre, the main streets have been renamed in recent years, which leads to some confusion as maps and street signs may bear the new names, but citizens may use the old names. The street which has the bus terminal is officially called Kazım Özalp Caddesi, but you may

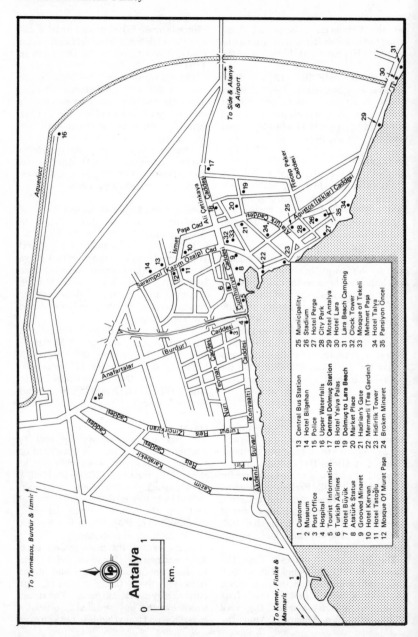

Antalya

0 1
km.

To Termessos, Burdur & Izmir

To Kemer, Finike & Marmaris

To Side & Alanya & Airport

Aqueduct

Paşa Cad Ali Çetinkaya Caddesi

Sarampol

Kazim Özalp) Cad

Ismet

Cumhuriyet Caddesi

(Recep Peker Caddesi)

Agustos (Işıklar) Caddesi

Atatürk Caddesi

(Burdur) Caddesi

Anafartalar

Nurt Teoman Caddesi

(Zincirkiran) Caddesi

Reis

Tuğrul

Pirl

Bulvar

Karabekir Caddesi

Reis Caddesi

Kazim

Akdeniz

(Konyaaltı) Caddesi

1	Customs	
2	Museum	
3	Post Office	
4	Hospital	
5	Tourist Information	
6	Turkish Airlines	
7	Hotel Büyük	
8	Atatürk Statue	
9	Grooved Minaret	
10	Hotel Kervan	
11	Hotel Tatoğlu	
12	Mosque Of Murat Paşa	
13	Central Bus Station	
14	Hotel Bilgehan	
15	Police	
16	Upper Waterfalls	
17	Central Dolmuş Station	
18	Hotel Yalya Palas	
19	Dolmuş to Lara Beach	
20	Market Place	
21	Hadrian's Gate	
22	Mermerli (Tea Garden)	
23	Hidirlik Tower	
24	Broken Minaret	
25	Municipality	
26	Stadium	
27	Hotel Perge	
28	City Park	
29	Motel Antalya	
30	Hotel Lara	
31	Lara Beach Camping	
32	Clock Tower	
33	Mosque of Tekeli	
34	Mehmet Paşa	
35	Hotel Talya	
	Pansiyon Öncel	

also hear Şarampol, the old name. Cumhuriyet Caddesi, the main thoroughfare, used to be called Hastane Caddesi; Ali Çetinkaya Caddesi is the eastern continuation of Cumhuriyet Caddesi. Atatürk Caddesi goes from Cumhuriyet/ Ali Çetinkaya down to the large Karaali Parkı.

Antalya's landmark and symbol is the Yivli Minare, the Grooved Minaret, built in the early 1200s during Seljuk rule. It is on Cumhuriyet Caddesi, next to the plaza which bears the equestrian statue of Atatürk (a very dramatic one), and at the top of the Old Town. The Old Town is called *Kaleiçi* (kah-LEH-ee-chee, within the fortress) or *Eski Antalya* (ehs-KEE, old).

The Tourism Information Office (tel (3111) 11747, 152771) is at Cumhuriyet Caddesi 73, several block west of the Yivli Minare.

Places to Stay – top end

The best is the *Talya Oteli* (TAHL-yah, tel 15600), Fevzi Çakmak Caddesi, a bright and modern 150-room palace overlooking the sea. For the price of $60 to $83 double you get a modern, air-conditioned room, swimming pool, tennis court, restaurant, bar and nightclub, hairdressers and exercise room.

Prices are considerably lower at the *Turban Adalya Oteli* (TOOR-bahn ah-DAHL-yah, tel 18066), by the old harbour in the Old Town, where an air-conditioned double costs $40. After these comes the *Bilgehan Oteli* (BEEL-geh-hahn, tel 15184), Kazım Özalp/Şarampol Caddesi 226, not far from the bus terminal, which charges $24 for an air-conditioned double.

Out at Lara Beach, several km east of the city is the *Lara Oteli* (LAH-rah, tel 15299), Lara Yolu, P. K. 404, with 60 double rooms priced at $24.

Places to Stay – mid-range

Best of the mid-range hotels ($10 to $20 double) is the *Yayla Palas* (YAHY-lah

pah-lahs, tel 11913, –4), Ali Çetinkaya Caddesi 14, not far from the corner of Atatürk Caddesi. Though an older hotel, it is well kept, with an accommodating staff; doubles cost $14.

The *Büyük Otel* (bew-YEWK, tel 11499), Cumhuriyet Caddesi 57, is right in the centre next to the plaza with the equestrian statue of Atatürk and the Yivli Minare (Grooved Minaret). It was once Antalya's premier hotel, but is fairly modest for all that. Doubles now cost $16 to $20, mostly for the location and sea views.

Out by Lara Beach is the *Motel Antalya* (tel 14609), Lara Caddesi 34, a cosy place with 12 rooms priced at $16 double.

Places to Stay – bottom end

The *Otel Tatoğlu* (TAHT-oh-loo, tel 12119) on Şarampol/Kazım Özalp Caddesi 91, is near the bus terminal, has 36 rooms, and costs $8 double. Not far away at No 138 is the *Kervan Oteli* (kehr-VAHN, tel 12044), which is about the same, and charges the same.

The *Atlas Pansiyon* (aht-LAHS, tel 12431) and the *Olimpiyat Pansiyon* (oh-LEEM-pee-yaht, tel 12890) are across from one another on Güllük Caddesi, three and a half blocks west of the Yivli Minare, on the right (north). Both are small (four rooms and eight rooms, respectively), and both charge $9 for a double.

Further from the centre, down near Karaali Parkı and the Talya Oteli, are the *Öncel Pansiyon* (urn-JEHL, tel 12199), Karaalioğlu Sokak 6, and the *Gönen Pansiyon* (gur-NEHN), just down the street. Rooms are quiet unless there's a do in the nearby stadium, and cost just $6 double.

Places to Eat

The top restaurant is in the *Talya Oteli*, of course, and it's very good.

For moderately-priced meals, try the *Antalya Restaurant*, across Cumhuriyet Caddesi from the Yivli Minare; also the *Şehir Restaurant*, directly behind the

Antalya Restaurant, reachable by a passage which goes through the building. The Antalya has a view from its rooftop terrace, and music in the evenings.

Those in search of low-cost meals should go to the intersection of Cumhuriyet and Atatürk caddesis and find the little street (parallel to Atatürk Cad.) called *Eski Sebzeciler İçi Sokak*. The name means 'The Old Inner Street of the Greengrocers' Market', and it is now lined with little restaurants and pastry-shops, many of which have outdoor tables. Most of the food is kebabs, including Antalya's specialty, *tandır kebap* (tahn-DUHR), which is rich but pretty greasy. If there's hash, have it. Other inexpensive restaurants can be found along Kazım Özalp/ Şarampol Caddesi.

Things to See
Start at the **Yivli Minare** (YEEV-lee mee-NAH-reh). The handsome and unique minaret was erected by the Seljuk Sultan Alaeddin Keykubat I in the early 1200s, next to a church which the sultan had converted to a mosque. There is an old stone clock tower in the plaza just above it. The view from the plaza, taking in the Old Town, the bay and the distant ragged summits of the Beydağları (Bey Mountains) is spectacular. Tea houses behind the Büyük Otel offer the opportunity to enjoy the view at leisure.

The Old Town (*Kaleiçi*)
Go down the street at the eastern end of the plaza which descends into the Old Town. Note another old clock tower at the beginning of the street. Just below this is the **Ali Paşa Camii**, the Mosque of Ali Pasha, another Seljuk structure with beautiful Arabic inscriptions above the doors and windows.

Wander down to the harbour, now used for yachts. The harbour had been Antalya's lifeline since the 200 BC, through the Roman, Byzantine, Seljuk and Ottoman empires, up till very recently when a new port was constructed on the outskirts.

The Old Town has been declared a historic zone, and is slated for restoration, which will take some time. The quaint, twisted streets and picturesque Ottoman houses are certainly charming. East of the harbour, you might come across the **Kesik Minare**, or Broken Minaret. Its mosque was once a church, built in the 400s.

The Bazaar
Antalya's tidy bazaar (*çarşı*) is north of Cumhuriyet Caddesi, between Kazım Özalp and Atatürk Caddesis. Don't go in the heat of the afternoon, as many of the shops will be closed.

Hadrian's Gate & Karaali Park
Down Atatürk Caddesi is **Hadriyanüs Kapısı**, Hadrian's Gate, erected during the reign of that Roman emperor (117-138). The monumental marble arch, which now leads to the Old Town, makes a shady little park in the midst of the city.

Farther along Atatürk Caddesi toward the sea is **Karaali Parkı**, a large, attractive, flower-filled park good for a stroll and for views of the sea. Sunset is the time most Turks go; it's the prettiest time. An old stone tower here, the *Hıdırlık Kulesi*, was once a lighthouse and a bastion in the city walls.

The Museum
Antalya's large and rich museum is at the western edge of town, reachable by bus along Cumhuriyet Caddesi (ask the driver: *Müzeye gider mi?*, mew-ZEH-yeh gee-DEHR mee, Does this go to the museum?). The collections include fascinating glimpses into the popular life of the region, with crafts and costume displays, as well as a wealth of ancient artifacts.

Excursions
You can, if you like, use Antalya as a base for excursions to Olympos and Phaselis (see the previous section), Termessos, Perge, Aspendos and Side. But you might find it easier to visit Olympos and Phaselis on your way to or from Kaş, and Perge and

Aspendos on your way to Side. Using the small towns of Kaş and Side as a base is both delightful and less expensive.

With your own car, you can stop at Termessos on your way north or west to Ankara, Istanbul or İzmir. Otherwise, Termessos is the one city you must visit using Antalya as your base.

Travel agencies in Antalya operate tours to all of these sites for a reasonable fee. If you can scrape together a party of four or five people, you can negotiate with a taxi driver for a private excursion. The private taxi method is especially useful for getting to Termessos.

Termessos

High in a rugged mountain valley 34 kms inland from Antalya lies Termessos (tehr-MEH-sohs), a Pisidian city of warlike, spartan people. They lived in their impregnable fortress city and guarded their independence fiercely. Alexander the Great did not attack them, and the Romans accepted them as allies, not as a subject people.

Start early in the day, as you will have to walk and climb a good deal to see the ruins. Though it's cooler up in the mountains than at the shore, the sun is still quite hot. Do this visit in the morning, and spend the afternoon at the beach.

Leave Antalya by the E 24 highway toward Burdur and Isparta, turning after about 12 km onto the road for Korkuteli. Signs mark the entrance to *Termessos Milli Parkı* (National Park). Entry to the park costs 30c for a car, 12c per person. A half-mile into the park is a small museum with photographs and artifacts from the ruins, plus displays touching on the botany and zoology of the park. Near the museum are camping and picnic sites. Continue another 8½ km up the rough dirt road to the ruins.

The road winds up through several gates in the city walls to the agora, the largest flat space in this steep valley. From here you must explore the ruins on foot.

At the agora are the remains of a small

Temple of Hadrian, now little more than a doorway. Head up the path to the city gate, the theatre (best-preserved building here), gymnasium, a Corinthian temple, and the upper city walls.

Your goal is the **necropolis** at the very top of the valley, three km up from the agora. It's a hike, but the necropolis is a fantastic sight, and the mountain vistas are breathtaking. As you toil upward, you'll notice a wire running alongside the path. It goes to a fire tower at the top of the valley, where a man sits, drinks tea, smokes cigarettes, reads newspapers, and keeps a lookout for fires. He has to carry up from the agora all the water he uses.

The necropolis (*mezarlık*) is really something, a vast field of huge stone sarcophagi tumbled about by earthquakes and grave-robbers. The scene is reminiscent of medieval paintings portraying the Judgement Day, when all tombs are to be cast open.

Perge

Perge (PEHR-geh), 15 km east of Antalya, is one of those very ancient towns. Greek colonists came here after the Trojan War and probably displaced even older inhabitants. The city prospered under Alexander the Great and the Romans, but dwindled under the Byzantines. The substantial remains of a great theatre, stadium, huge Hellenistic and Roman gates, and an impressive colonnaded street are worth seeing. The acropolis, on a rise behind the other ruins, has nothing much to see. For a fine view of the site, climb to the top of the theatre.

A visit to Perge can be included in the trip eastward to Aspendos and Side. Leave early in the morning. Ride the 13 km east from Antalya to the turning for Perge, then two km north to the ruins.

Aspendos

The land east of Antalya was called Pamphylia in ancient times. The Taurus Mountains (Toros Dağları) form a beautiful backdrop to the fertile coast, rich with

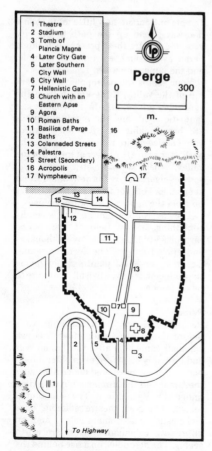

1 Theatre
2 Stadium
3 Tomb of
  Plancia Magna
4 Later City Gate
5 Later Southern
  City Wall
6 City Wall
7 Hellenistic Gate
8 Church with an
  Eastern Apse
9 Agora
10 Roman Baths
11 Basilica of Perge
12 Baths
13 Colonnaded Streets
14 Palestra
15 Street (Secondary)
16 Acropolis
17 Nymphaeum

Perge

0   300

m.

To Highway

goes well back to the Hittite Empire (800 BC). In 468 BC the Greeks and Persians fought a great battle here (the Greeks won, but not for long). Under the Romans, during the reign of Marcus Aurelius (161 – 180 AD), Aspendos gots its theatre.

There are many fine Hellenistic and Roman theatres in Anatolia, but the one at Aspendos is the finest of all. Built by the Romans, maintained by the Byzantines and Seljuks, it was restored after a visit by Atatürk. A plaque by the entrance states that when he saw the theatre, Atatürk declared that it should be restored and used again for performances and sports.

Purists may question the authenticity of the restorations, but more than any other, the theatre at Aspendos allows the modern visitor to see and feel a true classical theatre: its acoustics, its lighting by day and night, and how the audiences moved in and out. Don't miss it.

Other ruins, of a stadium, agora and basilica, offer little to look at. Note however the arches and several towers of a long aqueduct, out in the fields.

SİDE

Cleopatra and Marc Antony chose Side (SEE-deh, population 1200) as the spot for a romantic tryst, and today lots of Turkish couples follow their example. Side has everything: a kilometre of fine sand beach on either side, good Hellenistic ruins, an excellent little museum, and a quaint Turkish village.

It is perhaps too good. In recent years Side has been overrun by tourists in the summer months. During the season even moving down the streets can be difficult. In spring and autumn, the town is delightful, however; and the swimming is still excellent.

The government has a grand scheme for Side. For a decade it has battled in the courts for the right to limit development, and to regulate it according to a master plan for the entire region. It now seems that re-development may begin. This includes the razing of numerous modern

fields of cotton and vegetables. Irrigation troughs of concrete radiate like spiderwebs through the lush agricultural land.

Aspendos (ahs-PEHN-dohs) lies 47 km east of Antalya in the Pamphylian plain. Go as far as the *Köprüçayı* stream, and notice the old Seljuk humpback bridge. Turn left (north) along the western bank of the stream, following the signs to Aspendos. The great theatre is a km from the highway.

What you see here remains from Roman times, though the history of the settlement buildings, the preservation of traditional Turkish stone village houses, the restoration of the classical ruins, and the construction of new hotel complexes away from the historic zone. You may see a lot of such activity when you visit.

If you had seen Side in the 1960s, you'd realize why the government is so anxious to see planned development here. At that time, Side was a tiny, sleepy village (officially named *Selimiye*) scattered quaintly among the ruins. The occasional tourist would wander into town, clamber over the ruins, luxuriate on the perfect beaches, and decide to rent a village house

for a year. It was, in short, a paradise. But within a decade crude discotheques were set up in the temples, restaurants served the same simple food at higher prices, and every inhabitable building had become a pension. Beside the traditional low stone houses rose multi-storey waffle-front structures made of cement block. The modernisation of Side had begun.

Getting There

Side is so popular as a resort that it has its own direct bus service to Ankara, İzmir and Istanbul. The numerous buses which run along the coast between Antalya and

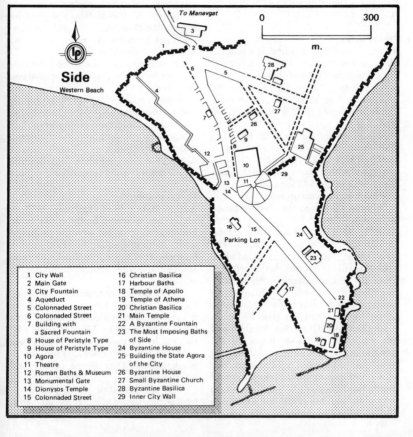

To Manavgat

Side
Western Beach

0   300
m.

Parking Lot

1 City Wall
2 Main Gate
3 City Fountain
4 Aqueduct
5 Colonnaded Street
6 Colonnaded Street
7 Building with
   a Sacred Fountain
8 House of Peristyle Type
9 House of Peristyle Type
10 Agora
11 Theatre
12 Roman Baths & Museum
13 Monumental Gate
14 Dionysos Temple
15 Colonnaded Street
16 Christian Basilica
17 Harbour Baths
18 Temple of Apollo
19 Temple of Athena
20 Christian Basilica
21 Main Temple
22 A Byzantine Fountain
23 The Most Imposing Baths
   of Side
24 Byzantine House
25 Building the State Agora
   of the City
26 Byzantine House
27 Small Byzantine Church
28 Byzantine Basilica
29 Inner City Wall

Alanya will drop you in Side, or in Manavgat, the town on the highway. From Manavgat, dolmuşes travel the few kms down to the shore frequently.

The bus or dolmuş will bring you past ruined aqueducts and city walls, past the museum and theatre, through an ancient stone gate to the town car park. Bus ticket kiosks for the return trip are here as well. Those driving must park their cars here (none are allowed in the town except perhaps to unload luggage), and pay a small fee.

There is no official Tourism Office in Side proper, but there is one in Manavgat (tel (3211) 1645), at Antalya Caddesi 27/B.

Places to Stay

You may have difficulty finding a room in high summer. If you visit then, arrive early in the day. Before mid-June, and after mid-September, you should have no problem finding the lodgings you want. Prices are lower in this off-season, as well.

Side has a few comfortable motels on its western beach, among which the best is the *Motel Side* (tel 22). Close to the village, attractive, with a pretty patio restaurant, the motel charges $30 for a double room, breakfast and dinner included.

Other motels along the western beach include the *Cennet Motel Athena* (jehn-NEHT, tel 17, 167) and the *Turtel* (TOOR-tehl, tel 25), priced at $21 to $23 for a double room (no meals included).

In the village proper, little pensions abound. There are dozens to choose from, and your choice will be dictated by availability as much as price. My favourite is the *Hermes Pansiyon* (HEHR-mess), run by Mrs Ayşe Güzel, her daughter and her son. Ask at the boutique named Hermes in the main square as there may be no sign on the pension. The pension is an old Side house, nothing fancy, but with rooms facing a garden. Only two rooms have plumbing, but all can use a common kitchen, and enjoy the scent of the jasmine

vine in the shady garden. The beach is close by, as is the main square.

Near the Hermes are the *Şen Pansiyon* (SHEN) and the *Huzur Pansiyon* (hoo-ZOOR). A nice one near the eastern beach is the *Martı* (mahr-TUH). As you comb the town for good lodgings, look for little signs which say *Boş oda var* ('Empty room here'). Prices depend on season and facilities, but range from $4 to $10 a double.

Places to Eat

When looking for a pension, ask about cooking facilities. Most have them, and this allows you to save substantial amounts of money. At the motels, you may be required to buy at least two meals a day, so the food problem is solved that way, whether you like it or not.

The restaurants in town, good and not-so-good, tend to be expensive for what you get, except for *Enişte'nin Yeri*, which has reasonably good food at the lowest prices. Service may be inexperienced here, but so may it be in the higher-priced places. The shady terrace is very nice, even with the fluorescent lights.

Ask your pension *hanım* (lady) for tips on the other current favourites.

Things to See

Ancient Side's great wealth was built on piracy and slavery. Many of its great buildings were raised with the profits of such dastardly activities. But slavery flourished only under the Greeks, and was stopped when the city came under Roman control.

No one knows where Side got its name, though it probably means 'pomegranate' in some ancient Anatolian language. The site was colonized by Aeolians about 600 BC, but by the time Alexander the Great swept through, the inhabitants had abandoned much of their Greek culture and language.

After the period of piracy and slave-trading, Side turned to legitimate commerce, and still prospered. Under the Byzantines, it was still large enough to rate a bishop. But the Arab raids of the 600s AD diminished the town, which was dead within two centuries. In the late 1800s, the Ottomans revived it as a town.

Side's impressive ruins are an easy walk from the village. Look first at the Theatre, one of the largest in Anatolia, with 20,000 seats. Originally constructed during Hellenistic times, it was enlarged under the Romans.

Next to the theatre, and across the road from the museum, is the agora. The museum is built on the site of the Roman baths. It has a very fine small collection of statuary and reliefs.

To the east, between these buildings and the **Hellenistic city walls**, lie a Byzantine basilica and some foundations of Byzantine houses. Down at the edge of the eastern beach is another agora.

At the very southern tip of the point of land upon which Side lies are two temples, the **Temple of Athena** and the **Temple of Apollo**, which date from the 100s AD. Who knows that Cleopatra and Marc Antony didn't meet at exactly this spot? Though they met (42 BC) before these great columns were erected, might they not have sat in earlier marble temples to enjoy one of Side's spectacular sunsets? Wandering among these marble remains at dusk is one of the finest things to do here.

To Alanya

You may find it best to take a dolmuş from Side to the highway junction, or to Manavgat, to catch the bus to Alanya.

The journey from Manavgat to Alanya is 60 km, and takes about an hour. About 12 km east of Manavgat, Highway 31 heads north, up to the Anatolian plateau, to Konya.

The coast road (E 24) skirts good sandy beach virtually the whole way to Alanya. Here and there a modern motel or government rest camp has been built to exploit the holiday potential. On the landward side you see the occasional bit of aqueduct, or the foundations of some old

caravanserai or baths. Thirteen kms before Alanya, notice the Şarapsa Hanı, a Seljuk caravanserai. Another one, the Alarahan, is accessible (30 km) by a side road heading north.

ALANYA

The Seljuk Turks built a powerful empire, the Sultanate of Rum (ROOM, Rome), which thrived from 1071 to 1243. Its capital was in Konya, but its prime port was Alanya.

Alanya (ah-LAHN-yah, population 25,000), like Side, occupies a point of land flanked by two great sweeping beaches. A pleasant, small agricultural and tourist town, Alanya has an easy pace, friendly people (many of whom wear the traditional baggy şalvar trousers), and the added attraction of significant Seljuk archaeological remains. It's a delightful place to spend several days before heading east to Silifke or north to Konya.

Getting There & Getting Around

There are ten buses daily to and from Antalya, seven to Adana via Silifke and Mersin, five to Ankara via Konya, two to İzmir, two to Istanbul, and one to Marmaris. Traffic is very sparse around the 'bulge' of Anamur. Seats on buses leaving Alanya can be difficult to find at times, so make your departure arrangements as far in advance as possible.

You can make arrangements in Alanya to catch a ferryboat to northern Cyprus. Boats leave from Taşucu, just west of Silifke, 262 km east of Alanya. At the Tourism Office, you can make a boat reservation and also buy a ticket for the very early morning bus from Alanya to the ferry docks. For more information, see the section on Silifke, below.

In the town, taxis will take you to motels out along the beach, if that's your choice for lodgings. Some motorcycles act as taxis, if you're alone, with little baggage. There are a few city buses, too, but Alanya is not yet large enough for a far-flung system of public transport.

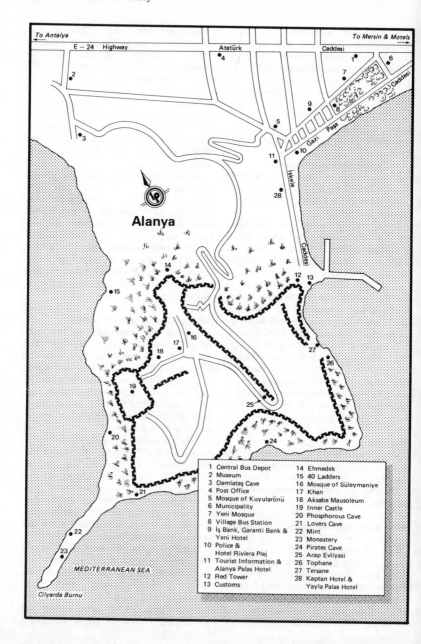

To Antalya

To Mersin & Motels

E – 24 Highway

Atatürk

Caddesi

Alanya

Iskele Caddesi

Gazi Paşa

Caddesi

MEDITERRANEAN SEA

Cilyarda Burnu

1 Central Bus Depot
2 Museum
3 Damlataş Cave
4 Post Office
5 Mosque of Kuyularönü
6 Municipality
7 Yeni Mosque
8 Village Bus Station
9 İş Bank, Garanti Bank &
  Yeni Hotel
10 Police &
   Hotel Riviera Plaj
11 Tourist Information &
   Alanya Palas Hotel
12 Red Tower
13 Customs
14 Ehmedek
15 40 Ladders
16 Mosque of Süleymaniye
17 Khan
18 Aksabe Mausoleum
19 Inner Castle
20 Phosphorous Cave
21 Lovers Cave
22 Mint
23 Monastery
24 Pirates Cave
25 Arap Evliyasi
26 Tophane
27 Tersane
28 Kaptan Hotel &
   Yayla Palas Hotel

Excursions around the rocky promontory crowned by a Seljuk fortress can be made by motorboat. Travel agencies in town sell tickets, or you can make arrangements with the boatmen who gather near the Red Tower, at the harbour.

Orientation

The bus station is on the E 24 highway (Atatürk Caddesi), near the fortress hill. The Tourism Office (tel (3231) 1240) is at İskele Caddesi 56/C, on the way from the highway to the Kızıl Kule. Virtually everything of interest to tourists in Alanya is south of the highway near the fortress hill, or out along the beach.

Places to Stay

The most comfortable and luxurious lodgings are well out on the eastern beach; many of the mid-range places are there as well. Downtown hotels are moderately-priced or quite cheap.

Places to Stay – top end

Alanya's most comfortable rooms are at the 99-room *Alantur Moteli* (ah-LAHN-toor, tel 1224, 1924), also sometimes called the Club Alantur. It is six kilometres east of the centre, a lavish (for Alanya) layout with lawns and gardens, sea views and a swimming pool.

I prefer hotels in the centre of the town, as they allow you easily to walk to restaurants and attractions. If you prefer them too, head for the *Kaptan Otel* (kahp-TAHN, tel 2000, 1094), İskele Cad. 62, very near the Tourism Office. The modern 45-room hotel faces the harbour, the town and the beach; air-conditioned doubles cost $20 to $23.

Places to Stay – mid-range

Several moderately-priced motels are grouped two or three kilometres east of the centre. For an air-conditioned double costing $16 to $21, try the 138-room *Panorama Moteli* (tel 1181) or the 116-room *Banana Moteli* (tel 1548, 3595).

Without air conditioning, double rooms cost $11 or $12 at the *Yeni Motel International* (tel 1195) and the *Merhaba Moteli* (MEHR-hah-bah, tel 1251).

Places to Stay – bottom end

Small hotels and pensions in the town rent rooms for as little as $3.50 or $4 double. The *Yayla Palas* (YAHY-lah pah-LAHS), a converted house on İskele Caddesi, has very low rates; at the nearby *Alanya Palas* (tel 1016) the price for a double without running water is only a few liras more, about $4.

The *Hotel Kent* (tel 1833), İskele Cad. 12, has double rooms with shower for $9. Down in the town on Gazi Paşa Caddesi, the *Hotel Riviera Plaj* (reev-YEH-rah plazh, tel 1953) has cheap waterless doubles, some with a sea view.

Within a 20-minute walk of the centre along the highway to the east are several little pensions. Doubles go for $7 to $8, and may or may not have private shower; usually you get the right to use a communal kitchen. Try the *Gökçe Aile Pansiyon* (GURK-cheh ah-yee-LEH, tel 1191), the *Neslihan* (neh-SLEE-hahn, tel 1922) at Atatürk Cad. 93 (Atatürk Caddesi is the main highway), the *Divan* (dee-VAHN, tel 1201, 1769) at Atatürk Cad. 119, the *Altın* (ahl-TUHN, tel 1451), or the *Pınar* (puh-NAHR, tel 1029).

Camping

Look for camping areas along the beach areas both east and west of town, especially east.

Places to Eat

Though Alanya has several inexpensive *hazır yemek* restaurants, and the good dining room in the Alantur Moteli, you should have at least a few meals at one of the little waterfront restaurants along Gazi Paşa Caddesi in the centre. Walk along the street and you'll see the *Şirin*, the *Yönet*, the *Havuzbaşı*, and the *Mahperi*. There is also a very inexpensive pide and kebap place, the *Konya Etli Pide ve Kebap*

Salonu, as well as an *Efes Pilsen* beergarden.

While you're here, try a few of the local fish: *levrek* (sea bass), *barbunya* (red mullet), or *kuzu balığı* ('muttonfish').

An unusual treat is the local ice cream, made with flavours such as *şeftali* (peach), *kavun* (melon), *dut* (mulberry) and *sakız* (pine resin).

Things to See

Head for the Seljuk sights early in the day, as Alanya gets very hot. Walk down to the harbour for a look at the *Kızıl Kule* (KUH-zuhl koo-leh, Red Tower), constructed in 1226 in the reign of the Seljuk Sultan Alaeddin Keykubad I by a Syrian Arab architect. The five-storey octagonal tower, now restored to its former glory, was the key to Alanya's harbour defenses. Past it, out toward the sea, a path leads to the old Seljuk **Tersane**, or shipyard (1228).

If you hire a boat to take you around the promontory you can see several caves, including those called the **Aşıklar Mağarası** (ah-shuk-LAHR mah-ah-rah-suh, Lovers' Grotto), **Korsanlar Mağarası** (kohr-sahn-LAHR, Pirates' Cave), the **Fosforlu** (fohs-fohr-LOO, Phosphorescent Cave), and **Damlataş** (DAHM-lah tahsh, Cave of Dripping Stones), as well as Cleopatra's Beach, on the west side of the promontory. To hire the entire boat for such a tour might cost $4. By the way, Damlataş is accessible on foot, at the western side of the promontory.

Alanya's most exciting historical site is of course the Kale (KAH-leh, fortress) atop the promontory. You may be lucky enough to find a dolmuş going up. Otherwise it's a very hot hour's walk (three km), or a taxi (about $4); with your own car, you can drive right up to the fort.

The ancient city was enclosed by the rambling wall (1226) which makes its way all around the peninsula. At the top is the **Ehmedek Kalesi**, the inner fortress. From the İç Kale (EECH-kah-leh, inner fort or keep) one gets a dazzling view of the peninsula, the walls, the town, and the great expanses of beautiful coast backed by the blue Taurus Mountains.

Alanya has a tidy little museum on the west side of the peninsula, on the way to Damlataş cave, open daily 8.30 to 12 noon and 1.30 to 5.30, 30c admission. Exhibits span the ages from Old Bronze through Greek and Roman to Ottoman. Don't miss the Ethnology Room at the back, with a fine assortment of kilims (woven mats), cicim (embroidered mats), Turkish carpets, inlaid work of wood and copper, gold and silver, and beautifully written and illuminated religious books.

ALANYA TO SİLİFKE

From Alanya, you will probably want to head north to Konya, Cappadocia and Ankara. The eastern Mediterranean coast has a few sights of interest, but the cities of Mersin, Tarsus, Adana, Iskenderun and Antakya have very little to hold your interest.

Anamur (AH-nah-moor, population 24,000) has a few small hotels and restaurants in the town off the main road. Down by the sea is the Mamure Kalesi, a fortress built by the emirs of Karahan in 1240. About 12 km later are the ruins of another fortress, the Softa Kalesi.

SİLİFKE

Silifke (see-LEEF-keh, population 23,000) is the ancient Seleucia, founded by Seleucus I Nicator in the 290s BC. Seleucus was one of Alexander the Great's most able generals, and founder of the Seleucid dynasty which ruled ancient Syria after Alexander's death.

Silifke's other claim to fame is as the place where Emperor Frederick I Barbarossa (1125-1190), while leading his troops on the Third Crusade, drowned as he crossed the river.

A striking castle dominates the town from a Taurus hillside, and seems to promise good sightseeing. But Silifke, to many people is just a place to catch the boat to Cyprus, or a bus to Mersin, Adana, or Konya.

Silifke's Tourism Information Office (tel 151) is at Atatürk Caddesi 1/2.

Places to Stay

There are very comfortable and rather expensive hotels and motels along the highway at Taşucu (see below) four kilometres west of Silifke. In Silifke proper the hotels are much more modest. As this is a transportation junction, hotels can fill up. Arrive somewhat early in the day or, better yet, make your connection and head out of town.

Boats to Cyprus

Passenger boats to Kyrenia (*Girne*, Turkish Federated Republic of Northern Cyprus) depart from Taşucu, four kilometres west of Silifke. Buy bus tickets to Taşucu at the Tezcanlar bus company ticket desk in the Silifke bus terminal.

In Taşucu, there's a Tourism Office (tel 234) right by the boat dock at Atatürk Caddesi, Gümrük Meydanı 18/A.

You can make your arrangements and buy tickets for the boats in Silifke's bus terminal. Look for the signs for the Uğur company's *Deniz Otobüsü* (deh-NEEZ oh-toh-bew-sew, 'sea bus', hovercraft). The hovercraft departs Monday, Wednesday and Friday at 10 am on the two-hour trip. A single ticket costs $23; twice that amount to go and return.

For the regular boat, tickets cost less, but the trip is longer. The Ertürk company (tel Taşucu 33; Girne 62-308) operates boats on Tuesday, Thursday and Saturday at 10 am on the six-hour trip. Return trips from Girne to Taşucu are made on Wednesday, Friday and Saturday. A single ticket costs $18; to go and return costs $29. The Ertürk boat carries cars as well as passengers. Note that Turkish Maritime Lines operates big, modern car ferries to Cyprus from Mersin (see below).

Buses from Silifke

From Silifke, the bus takes 4½ hours to Konya, 1¼ to mersin, 6½ to Alanya.

SİLİFKE TO ADANA

The distance from Silifke to Adana is 153 km; from Silifke to Mersin, 85 km. Twenty kms east of Silifke you'll notice a romantic castle about 200 metres offshore, and another one (in ruins) right on the shore. This is **Kız Kalesi** (KUHZ kah-leh-see, Maiden's Castle), to which many legends are attached. Historically, they were built by the Byzantines, and later used by the Armenian kings. The castles and good beach are served by a few small restaurants, some pensions, and a motel or two.

Inland from the Kız Kalesi, a road winds two km to **Cennet ve Cehennem**, the caves of Heaven and Hell. This limestone coast is riddled with caverns, but the Cennet (jeh-NEHT) is among the most impressive. Little soft drink and snack stands cluster at the top. Walk down a long path of many steps to reach the cavern mouth. Along the way, notice the strips of cloth and paper tied to twigs and tree branches by those who have come to this 'mystical' place in search of cures.

Near Cennet is Cehennem (jeh-HEHN-nehm), or Hell, a deep gorge entered by a ladder.

The village of Narlıkuyu has a small museum with artifacts collected in the area.

Thirteen km east of Kız Kalesi is a turning to **Kanlıdivane**, the ruins of ancient Elaiussa-Sebaste-Kanytelis. The ancient city occupies a vast site around limestone caverns. As you ride the four km up into the hills, the ruins become thicker.

Eleven km before Mersin, at a place called Mezikli, is a turning on the right (south) to **Viranşehir**, the ancient Soles or Pompeiopolis. Two km down the road is a row of Corinthian columns standing in a field. In the distance is part of an aqueduct, both dating from the 200s AD.

MERSİN (İçel)

Mersin (mehr-SEEN, population 218,000), also called İçel (ee-CHEHL), is a modern city, built to give Anatolia a large port

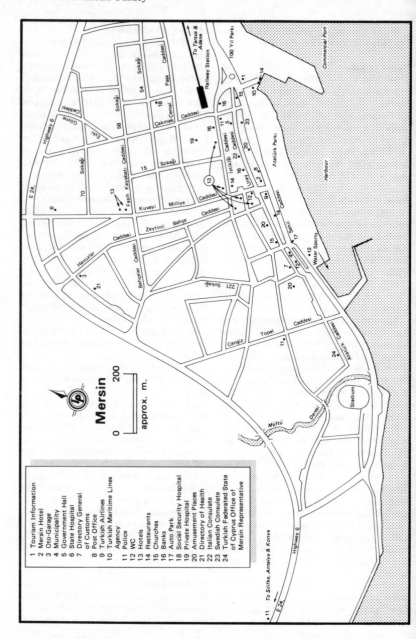

Mersin

0 200

approx. m.

1 Tourism Information
2 Mersin Hotel
3 Oto-Garage
4 Municipality
5 Government Hall
6 State Hospital
7 Directory General
  of Customs
8 Post Office
9 Turkish Airlines
10 Turkish Maritime Lines
   Agency
11 Police
12 WC
13 Hotels
14 Restaurants
15 Churches
16 Banks
17 Auto Park
18 Social Security Hospital
19 Private Hospital
20 Amusement Places
21 Directory of Health
22 Italian Consulate
23 Swedish Consulate
24 Turkish Federated State
   of Cyprus Office of
   Mersin Representative

conveniently close to Adana and its agriculturally-rich hinterland. It has several good hotels in each price range, and can serve as an emergency stop on your way through. The Tourism Information Office is down near the docks, east of the park, at Yenimahalle, İnönü Bulvarı, Liman Giriş Sahası, tel 11265, 12710. Near the office is the stop for buses going out to Viranşehir.

The *Mersin Oteli* (tel 12200), Gümrük Meydanı 112, is down on the waterfront; its 116 rooms are the most comfortable in town, and go for $45 double. The *Toros Oteli* (TOH-rohs, tel 12201, 12580), Atatürk Cad. 33, has 62 comfortable rooms downtown for $22 double.

Rooms are cheaper but still good at the *Hosta Otel* (HOHS-tah, tel 14760), Fasih Kayabalı Cad 4, Yeni Hal Civarı, near the wholesale vegetable markets just a few blocks from the Mersin Oteli.

Ferries to Cyprus Turkish Maritime Lines, down at the docks in Mersin, operates car ferry service to Famagusta (*Magosa*, mah-GOS-sah), Cyprus, and Lattakia (*Lazkiye*), Syria, from Mersin all year. From late April through September ferries depart Mersin at 10 pm on Monday, Wednesday and Friday to arrive the next morning at Famagusta at 8 am. The rest of the year, the ferry departs on Tuesday and Friday. The Friday trip continues to Lattakia, all year.

Onward
Going east, 27 km brings you to **Tarsus**, where St Paul was born almost 2000 years ago. There is very little left of old Tarsus, certainly not enough to stop for.

Three km east of Tarsus, the E 5 highway heads north through the Cilician Gates, a wide gap in the Taurus Mountains, to Ankara.

ADANA
Turkey's fourth-largest city, Adana (AH-dah-nah, population 580,000) is commercial. Its wealth comes from the intensely fertile plain of the Çukurova (CHOO-koor-oh-vah), formed by the rivers Seyhan and Ceyhan, and by the traffic passing through the Cilician Gates.

Passing through Adana, stop to see the marvellous long *Taşköprü*, or **Roman Bridge**, built by Hadrian and repaired by Justinian, which marches for 300 metres across the Seyhan; also the Ulu Cami, dating from 1507, and the good little museum.

Places to Stay
Adana has lots of hotels in all classes. The top place, with 116 doubles priced at $80, is the *Divan Oteli* (dee-VAHN, tel 22701), İnönü Caddesi 142. The *Büyük Sürmeli Oteli* (bew-YEWK sewr-meh-LEE, tel 21944) is the older 80-room hotel with very comfortable rooms going for $52 double.

The 36-room *İnci Oteli* (EEN-jee, tel 226132), Kurtuluş Caddesi, and the 66-room *Koza Oteli* (koh-ZAH, tel 14657), Özler Caddesi 103, both charge about $30 double.

Rooms are moderately-priced at the older, 84-room *İpek Palas Oteli* (ee-PEHK pah-LAHS, tel 18743), İnönü Caddesi 103, and the newer, 36-room *Duygu Oteli* (dooy-GOO, tel 16741), İnönü Caddesi 14/1. Prices range from $18 to $22 double.

Food
While you're here, and if you like spicy food, try *Adana kebap*, the local specialty. Ground lamb is mixed with hot pepper and wrapped around a flat skewer, then grilled over charcoal. You'll find other Arab-inspired dishes as the Syrian influence is strong.

İSKENDERUN & ANTAKYA
The very eastern end of the Turkish Mediterranean coast is at İskenderun and Antakya, in the province of Hatay. Though few tourists go to these cities today, they share a fascinating history.

İskenderun (ees-KEHN-deh-roon, population 125,000) was founded by Alexander the Great, and once bore the name Alexandretta, of which İskenderun is a translation (İskender = Alexander). It was the most important port city on this part of the coast until Mersin was developed (1960s), but has now become less active. It was occupied by the French after World War I, and included under the French Protectorate of Syria as the Sanjak of Alexandretta.

Antakya (ahn-TAHK-yah, population 95,000), also called Hatay (HAH-tahy), is the ancient Antioch, founded by Seleucus I Nicator in 300 BC. Soon it had a population of half a million. Under the Romans it developed an important Christian community (out of its already large Jewish one), which was at one time headed by St Paul.

Persians, Byzantines, Arabs, Armenians and Seljuks all fought for it, and the Crusaders and Saracens battled for it as well. In 1268 the Mamelukes of Egypt took it and wiped it out. It was never to regain its former glory.

The Ottomans held it until Muhammed Ali of Egypt captured the city in his drive for control of the empire (1831). But the Ottomans, with European help, drove their rebellious vassal back. The French held it as part of their Syrian protectorate until 1939. Atatürk saw World War II approaching, and wanted it rejoined to the republic as a defensive measure. He began a campaign to reclaim it, which came to fruition by means of a plebiscite shortly after his death.

Antakya is still rather Arabic in its culture and language. Many people speak Arabic as a first language, Turkish as the second. In the city you can see a Roman bridge built under the reign of Diocletian (200s AD), an aqueduct, the old city walls, several Arab-style mosques (very different from the Turkish), and a museum with many very good Roman mosaics. On the outskirts of town (two km from the centre) is the *Senpiyer Kilisesi*, or Church of St Peter. In this grotto, closed by a wall in Crusader times, it is said that St Peter preached.

Places to Stay

The *Atahan Oteli* (AH-tah-hahn, tel 11036), Hürriyet Caddesi 28, has 28 double rooms for $18. The *Divan Oteli* (tel 11518), İstiklal Caddesi 62, is cheaper, with 23 rooms going for $12. There are also several hotels at Harbiye, the ancient suburb of Daphne. In Seleucid and Roman times the city's residents went to Daphne to indulge in the pleasures of picnics and moonlight strolls, and it is still a resort. Two hotels are the *Hidro* (HEE-droh, tel 6) and the *Çağlıyan* (CHAH-luh-YAHN, tel 11), with doubles priced at $19 and $13 respectively.

INTO SYRIA

From Antakya, you can travel to Aleppo (*Halep* in Turkish) or Lattakia (*Lazkiye*), but only if you already have a Syrian visa. At last report, they are not issued at the border. You'll have to get one in your home country (preferable), or in Ankara. At the border, you must change the equivalent of US$100 into Syrian currency at the official exchange rate.

If you're all set to do this, take a taxi to the border at *Yayladağı* (YAHY-lah-dah) for about $5, cross the border, and take another taxi to Lattakia.

Central Anatolia

When nomadic Turkish herdsmen moved into Anatolia around the year 1100, they found a land which reminded them of Central Asia: semi-arid, rolling steppeland covered with grass, perfect for their flocks. Mountains and great lakes (some of them salt) broke up the vast expanse of steppe. By the numerous streams, marked with rows of tall, spindly cypresses, the nomads finally established villages.

In spring, Central Anatolia is a sea of wildflowers. Great swaths of vivid colour are splashed across the spare landscape in an annual extravagance born of the spring rains. Days are pleasantly warm, nights chilly. In summer the rain and its lushness disappear, and the Anatolian plateau is hotter and drier, but never so humid as the coasts. Riding across Anatolia in summer, the scenery is coloured in delicate pastels: the dark red of newly-ploughed furrows, the straw yellow of grass, grey and green bands of sandstone in a rockface. Winter is cold and rainy, with numerous falls of snow. You shouldn't be surprised at the snow, for the plateau has an average altitude of 1000 metres (3280 ft).

Though Central Anatolia yields a first impression of emptiness, this is deceptive. The armies of a dozen empires have moved back and forth across this 'land bridge' between Europe and Asia; a dozen civilisations have risen and fallen here, including the very earliest established human communities, which date from 7500 BC. Crumbling caravanserais (han) scattered along the modern highways testify to rich trade routes which flourished for several millenia.

Today, Central Anatolia is still flourishing. Wheat and other grains, fruits and vegetables (including delicious melons) are grown in the dry soil, and livestock is still a big concern. Ankara, Turkey's capital city, is a sprawling urban mass in the midst of the semi-desert; Konya and Kayseri, fuelled by the wealth of agriculture and light industry, are growing at a remarkable pace. These cities have a modern aspect made by their wide boulevards, apartment blocks and busy traffic. But at the heart of each is an old town, a fortress dating to Roman times, a few foundations going back to the dawn of civilisation.

ANKARA

Capital of the Turkish Republic, Ankara (AHN-kah-rah, population 3,000,000; altitude 900 metres) was once called Angora. The fine, soft hair (tiftik) on Angora goats became an industry which still thrives. But today Ankara's prime concern is government. It is a city of ministries, embassies, universities, medical centres, gardens and vineyards, and some light industry. Vast suburbs are scattered on the hillsides which surround the centre; most are filled by country people who have moved here in search of work and a better life. Many have found it.

But Ankara has a problem. The principal fuel for heating is a soft brown coal called lignite which produces thick, particle-filled smoke. During the heating season (October 15 to April 15), Ankara's air is badly polluted.

Your stay in Ankara need not be as long as in Istanbul. The city has several significant attractions, but you should be able to tour them all in a day and a half or two days.

History

It was the Hittites who named this place Ankuwash before 1200 BC. The town prospered because it was at the intersection of north-south and east-west trade routes. After the Hittites, it was a Phrygian town, then taken by Alexander, claimed by the Seleucids, and finally occupied by the Galatian tribes of Gaul

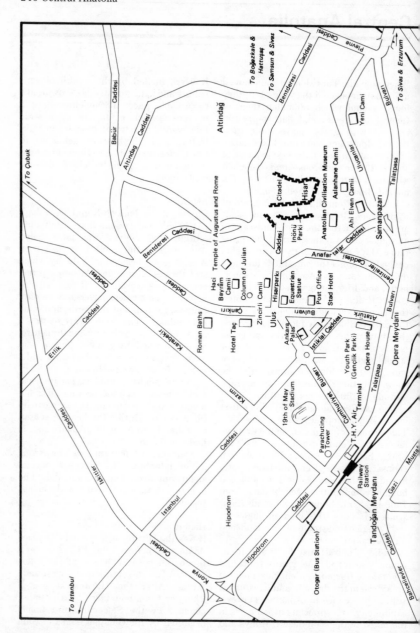

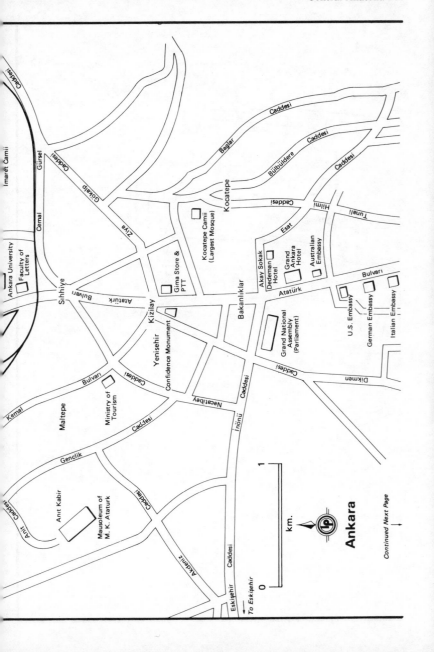

Ankara

To Eskişehir

Continued Next Page

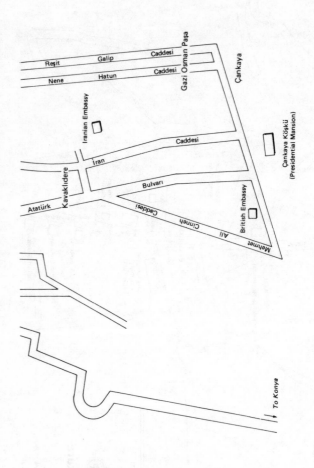

who invaded Anatolia around 250 BC. Augustus Caesar annexed it to Rome in 25 BC as *Ankyra*.

The Byzantines held the town for centuries, with intermittent raids by the Persians and Arabs. When the Seljuk Turks came to Anatolia after 1071, they made Engüriye a Seljuk city, but held it with difficulty. Ottoman possession of Angora did not begin well, for it was near the town that Sultan Yıldırım Beyazıt was captured by Tamerlane, and the sultan later died in captivity. But after the Timurid state collapsed and the Ottoman civil war ended, Angora became merely a quiet town where long-haired goats were raised.

Modern Ankara is a planned city. When Atatürk set up his provisional government here in 1920, it was a small, rather dusty Anatolian town of some 30,000 people, with a strategic position at the heart of the country. After his victory in the War of Independence, Atatürk declared this the new capital of the country (October, 1923), and set about developing it. European urban planners were consulted, and the plan resulted in a city of long, wide boulevards, a large forested park with artificial lake, a cluster of transportation termini, and numerous residential and diplomatic neighbourhoods. From 1919 to 1927, Atatürk did not set foot in the old imperial capital of Istanbul, preferring to work at making Ankara the country's capital city in fact as well as in name.

For republican Turks, Istanbul is their glorious historical city, still the centre of business and finance, but Ankara is their true capital, built on the ashes of the empire with their own blood and sweat. It is modern and forward-looking, and they're proud of it.

Getting There

In Turkey, all roads lead to Ankara. Its role as governmental capital and second-largest city guarantees that transportation will be convenient.

Ankara's *Otogar* (bus terminal) is one block north-west of the *Ankara Garı* (railway station). In a wing of the railway station is the *T.H.Y. Hava Terminali*, the Turkish Airlines Air Terminal. The railway station and the bus terminal are separated, appropriately, by the Ministry of Transportation. This whole transportation complex is about 1¼ km from Ulus, and three km from Kızılay.

By Bus Every city or town of any size will have direct buses to Ankara's huge Otogar. From Istanbul, there is a bus to Ankara at least every 15 minutes throughout the day, and late into the night.

As Ankara has many buses to all parts of the country, it is often sufficient to arrive at the Otogar, baggage in hand, and let a barker lead you to a ticket window for your chosen destination (no charge for the lead). However, it might be well to wander through the rows of ticket kiosks to see if there is a more convenient departure time. If you arrive in Ankara by bus, take a few moments to check on schedules to your onward destination. Buy your ticket, and secure your reserved seat, at the same time if you can.

Numerous bus companies have offices downtown near Kızılay, on Ziya Gökalp Caddesi, Gazi Mustafa Kemal Bulvarı, İzmir Caddesi and Menekşe Sokak.

By Train Train service is fairly convenient, and very comfortable on the top trains. Any train not named *ekspres* or *mototren* will be very cheap, but fantastically slow. Even if you're out to save money, don't take a slow *yolcu* or *posta* train. You may be on it for days (really!).

At present you must make your reservations and buy your train tickets at the station of departure. This means that you cannot reserve a sleeping-car berth on an Ankara-to-Istanbul train while you are in Istanbul. They will tell you to make the reservation when you get to Ankara. As reservations for the best trains should be made several days or more in advance, this can sometimes cause problems, and force you to take a less desirable train, or to hope for a last-minute cancellation.

Ankara – Istanbul Numerous daily express trains run between Ankara and Istanbul. There are two top trains. The *Mavi Tren* (mah-VEE trehn, Blue Train) is an all-reserved 1st class (supplement payable) train with club cars and a dining car, Turkey's version of a Trans-Europe-Express. It departs both Ankara and Istanbul at lunchtime on the 7½-hour trip. Its nighttime equivalent is the *Ankara Ekspresi*, an all-sleeping-car train with 1st and 2nd class berths and a dining car for breakfast only. It departs at 10 pm and arrives at 8.45 am.

Two other express trains take a bit longer, but offer similar comfort and convenience at lower prices. The 1st class *Boğaziçi Ekspresi* (boh-AHZ-ee-chee, Bosphorus), a day train with club cars and a dining car which leaves at breakfast time and arrives at dinnertime, making the run in about nine hours. The *Anadolu Ekspresi* (ah-nah-doh-LOO, Anatolia) is a night train with 1st and 2nd class sleeping cars, club cars and a dining car, which leaves about 9 pm and arrives the next morning about 8 am.

The 'third tier' of express trains are through-trains which stop at Ankara. They are not as dependable or as comfortable as the aforementioned trains, though you may pay as much for a seat. Don't assume these trains will be on time, particularly if you are going from Ankara to Istanbul.

The *Toros Ekspresi* (TOH-rohs, Taurus) is a morning train to and from Istanbul with sleeping cars, 1st and 2nd class coaches. If you catch it from Ankara at dinnertime you can ride it to Adana, an overnight trip.

The *Doğu Ekspresi* (doh-OO, East) goes from Istanbul to Kars; the *Vangölü Ekspresi* goes from Istanbul to Van, and supposedly on to Tabriz and Tehran, though service to Iran is suspended as of this writing. The Istanbul – Ankara

portions of these two trains run together, departing from each city in the evening and arriving the next morning; they haul sleepers, 1st and 2nd class coaches and diners.

Ankara – Izmir Two trains here, one by day, the other by night. The *Ege Ekspresi* (EH-geh, Aegean) departs about 7.30 am and arrives 13½ hours later, hauling 1st class coaches and a diner. The *İzmir Ekspresi* departs just before dinner and arrives just after breakfast, hauling 1st and 2nd class sleepers and coaches, and a dining car.

Other Trains There are daily express services to and from Kayseri (7½ hours; the bus takes about 4½ hours). The *Toros Ekspresi*, mentioned above in the Istanbul – Ankara section, will take you from Ankara to Adana.

By Air Ankara has good international and domestic connections by air. There are non-stop flights between Ankara and the following Turkish cities; unless the number of flights per week is noted, flights are daily: Adana, Antalya (1), Diyarbakır, Elazığ (3), Erzurum, Gaziantep (2), Istanbul, İzmir, Malatya (1), Van (3).

Flights between Ankara and Istanbul are very frequent, every hour or more, but even so they may fill up. Reserve in advance. Flight time is about an hour. As for İzmir, there is one non-stop flight a day; flight time is about 1¼ hours. If you don't get on this flight, you must fly via Istanbul.

The Turkish Airlines Air Terminal at the railway station has these telephone numbers: Reservations, 12 62 00; Information, 12 49 00; Ticket Sales, 12 49 00; at Esenboğa Havaalanı (airport), tel 24 06 50, 24 06 51. The airport is 30 km north of the city. Turkish Airlines buses depart the Air Terminal in Ankara 1½ hours before domestic flight times, 2¼ hours before international flight times. Minimum check-in time for any flight is 45 minutes.

Getting Around
The bad news is that Ankara has elaborate

dolmuş and city bus routes, but many of these vehicles are full most of the time. At rush hours you will see long queues waiting at bus and dolmuş boarding points. At other times, you'll have the best chance of getting a ride by boarding the bus or dolmuş at a major terminus such as Ulus or Kızılay.

The good news is that you can use taxis easily in Ankara because virtually all have meters and drivers use them. Fares are quite low, and most short trips cost only about $1. No need to tip.

If you decide to use dolmuşes, the Ulus-Çankaya ones are most convenient, running the entire length of Atatürk Caddesi.

Orientation

The main boulevard through the city is, of course, Atatürk Bulvarı, which runs from Ulus in the north all the way to the Presidential Mansion in Çankaya, six kms to the south.

The old city of Ankara, dating from the time of Rome and including the Hisar (fortress), is near Ulus Meydanı, called simply Ulus (oo-LOOS), the centre of 'old Ankara'. This is an area with many of Ankara's cheapest hotels, restaurants and markets. The most important museums are near Ulus. You can recognize the square by the large equestrian statue of Atatürk at the south-east corner.

Kızılay (KUH-zuh-lah-yee) is the inter-section of Atatürk Bulvarı and Gazi Mustafa Kemal Bulvarı/Ziya Gökalp Caddesi. Officially called Hürriyet Meydanı, everyone knows it by the name (Kızılay), the 'Red Crescent' (Turkish 'Red Cross') headquarters which used to be here, but was demolished long ago. This is the centre of 'new Ankara', called Yenişehir (yeh-NEE-sheh-heer). It holds several moderate hotel and restaurant choices. There are also bus and airline ticket offices, travel agencies and department stores. On Kocatepe hill in Yenişehir is the Kocatepe Camii, a modern mosque (still abuilding) in Ottoman style, which is among the largest in the world.

At the southern end of Atatürk Caddesi, in the hills overlooking the city, is Çankaya, the residential neighbourhood which holds the Cumhurbaşkanlığı Köşkü, the Presidential Mansion, plus many of the most important ambassadorial resid-ences. Between Kızılay and Çankaya along Atatürk Bulvarı are most of the city's important embassies, and many government ministries, plus the Büyük Millet Meclisi, the Grand National Assembly, parliament of the Turkish Republic.

Places to Stay – top end

Ankara's best is the Büyük Ankara Oteli (bew-YEWK AHN-kah-rah, tel 17 11 06), the Grand Ankara Hotel. Located near the parliament at Atatürk Bulvarı 183, this 180-room air-conditioned high-rise estab-lishment has all the amenities, including a swimming pool and tennis court, and charges $80 a double.

Less dramatic but equally comfortable is the Ankara Dedeman Oteli (DEH-deh-mahn, tel 17 11 00, 13 96 90), Büklüm Sok. 1, a block east of Atatürk Bulvarı at Akay Sokak, also near parliament. The Dedeman has 252 air-conditioned rooms and a swimming pool; doubles cost $43.

The Grand Hotel Balin (BAH-leen, tel 18 41 50), İzmir Caddesi 35, one block west of Atatürk Bulvarı near Kızılay, is fairly modest as top hotels go, despite its grand name. The 91 rooms are not air-conditioned, but comfortable in an old-fashioned way, for $40 double.

Near the Railway Station The Stad Oteli (STAHD, tel 12 42 20), Baruthane Meydanı (also called Müdafaa-i Hukuk Meydanı) near Ulus, is a tall, modern tower with 217 rooms and many services. It's an excellent choice, and only 750 metres from the rail and air termini, one km from the Otogar. Doubles cost $35.

Places to Stay – mid-range

Convenient to Kızılay is the Erşan Oteli (ehr-SHAHN, tel 18 98 75), Meşrutiyet Cad. 13, a block east of Atatürk Bulvarı. The 64 rooms are nothing special, but the location is very convenient; doubles cost $29. This is a favourite with businessmen.

The *Otel Gül Palas* (GEWL pah-lahs, tel 18 21 87), Bayındır Sok. 15, is a quiet place on a pedestrian street, with 41 rooms. Over half are equipped with private baths, but the others are inexpensive bathless singles priced at $11 to $13; with bath, a single is $14 to $18. Doubles with bath cost $23.

A block north of Ulus along Çankırı Caddesi (the northern continuation of Atatürk Bulvarı) is the *Hotel Taç* (TAHCH, tel 24 31 95, 11 16 63) Çankırı Cad. 35, with 35 rooms, over half of them with private bath. A double costs $12 without bath, $16 with. You can walk to many of Ankara's sights from here.

Places to Stay - bottom end

Ulus holds numerous very inexpensive hotels in its back streets. Most are quiet. The *Otel Devran* (dehv-RAHN, tel 24 03 20, –21) has as its official address, Opera Meydanı Tavuz Sokak 8, but you'll find it most easily by looking for Gazi Lisesi (a high school) on Sanayi Caddesi, across Atatürk Bulvarı from the Opera House and Gençlik Parkı. It's an older building, but with those nice touches such as marble staircases, brass trim and little chandeliers. Doubles cost $7 without bath, $9 with shower, $11 with bathtub.

The *Hotel Zümrüt Palas* (zewm-REWT, tel 24 51 65,–66), Posta Cad. 16, is a block east of Atatürk Bulvarı, at the corner of Posta and Sanayi Caddesi (look for the PTT on Atatürk Bulvarı, and go a block behind it). A clean and tidy place popular with Turkish families, they charge $8 for a double with washbasin only, $10 for a double bed with shower, $12 for two beds with shower.

The *Otel Akman* (ahk-MAHN, tel 24 41 40, –41), Tavus Sok. 6, is next to the aforementioned Otel Devran. It's more modern, has a parking lot and a bar with colour TV, and charges $12 for a double with bath.

The *Otel Fuar* (foo-AHR, tel 12 32 88, –

89), Opera Meydanı Kosova Sok. 11, is near the other hotels, and is heavily patronized by men. Rooms are very simple, but clean and undeniably cheap at $5 double with washbasin.

Places to Eat - top end

The restaurant named *RV* (reh-VEH, tel 27 03 76, 27 43 44), İran Caddesi 13, Kavaklıdere, has an elegant but understated decor, very polite service, and an excellent menu (in English) of European and Turkish favourites. A full meal with wine might cost $15 per person. 'RV' is located near Kuğulu Park and Buğday Sokak in the section called Kavaklıdere. İran Caddesi used to be called Reza Şah Pehlevi Caddesi, but the name was changed for the obvious reason.

Near Kızılay is the *Kristal Restoran* (tel 12 19 52), Sakarya Caddesi, Bayındır Sokak 22, where a full-course repast with wine might cost $12. They have a good menu (in English) of the more familiar Turkish specialties. To find the restaurant, walk out of Kızılay along Ziya Gökalp Caddesi, and take the third turning on the left, just by the *Fransız Kültür Merkezi* (French Cultural Centre); this street is Bayındır Sokak.

Places to Eat - mid-range

I keep going back to the *Beyaz Saray*, on Atatürk Bulvarı at Süleyman Sırrı Sokak, near Sıhhiye Meydanı, though the service is terribly inexpert. Perhaps it's the setting: several interior rooms, and a long terrace set back from the boulevard, high up with a view; this building was once the Turkish Airlines Air Terminal. The food is good and varied; the kitchen is just where you'd suppose a restaurant's lobby to be, so you can choose your salads, *meze*, fish and kebabs right there, then take a table. Figure $8 to $10 for a full meal with wine or beer.

Rüyam Lokantası, Yüksel Caddesi 5, near Kızılay, a block east of Atatürk Bulvarı at the corner of Karanfil Sokak, used to be wonderful, and is now good. The shady terrace makes it a good choice for warm summer evenings. The menu is Turkish, and a full meal need cost only $5 to $8, wine included.

For Seafood It's surprising to find good, fresh fish at moderate prices in a land-locked city, but you can at the *Liman Lokantası* (lee-MAHN), just off İzmir Caddesi at Elgün Sokak 3/C, a block west of Atatürk Bulvarı near Kızılay. Decor is non-existent, but service is friendly and efficient, and the food is very good at surprisingly low prices. Try your fish *kiremitte* (KEE-reh-meet-TEH, on a tile); it is served on a clay roofing tile, which keeps it hot throughout the meal. A full meal with wine will cost about $8.

In Ulus Two restaurants just north of Ulus Meydanı on Çankırı Caddesi provide good, full meals in pleasant surroundings at moderate prices. The *Çiçek Lokantası* at Çankırı Cad. 14/C, and the *Ender Lokantası* at 10/A have similar menus and decor; the Çiçek is perhaps the cheaper of the two. A meal with beverage will cost about $4 or $5.

Places to Eat – bottom end
Near Kızılay, try the *Kamil Usta Yeşil Köşe Kebabcı*, Ihlamur Sokak 10, off İzmir Caddesi one-half block. They have good İskender (Bursa) kebap, the döner with savoury tomato sauce and browned butter. The *baklava* (many-layered pastry with honey and nuts) is also delicious. For a drink, try *ayran*, yogurt mixed with spring water. A full meal need cost no more than $2.

Ulus has lots of good, cheap rest-aurants. On Tavus Sokak near several of the hotels mentioned above is the *Özel Urfa Aile Kebap Salonu*, the 'Authentic Urfa Family Kebab Salon'. Urfa is a city near the Turko-Syrian border, and Urfa kebap is doner served with sliced onions and spices. You can get *lahmacun* (LAHH-mah-JOON), a soft 'pizza', grilled chicken

(*piliç*, pee-LEECH), *köfte*, salads and desserts such as *tel kadayıf* (TEHL kah-dah-yuhf, shredded wheat in syrup). They make their own *pide* bread here, so it's fresh and delicious. A full meal will be very tasty, and cost about $1.

An old favourite kebap place is *Hacı Bey*, Devren Sokak 1/B near Tavus Sokak, in this same area. The kebap here is Bursa-style, delicious and cheap. A large meal of kebap, salad, yogurt and dessert, with beverage (no alcohol here) might cost $3.

Right at the centre of Ulus is the *Akman Boza ve Pasta Salonu*, Atatürk Bulvarı 3, in the courtyard of the large building at the south-east corner of the square. Breakfasts, light lunches (sandwiches, omelettes, etc) and pasties are the specialties. *Bozâ*, a fermented millet drink, thick, sweetish and slightly tangy, is a winter favourite. Upstairs and behind the Akman is *9 Kebap Salonu* (doh-KOOZ keh-BAHP), on Yenice Sokak. A standard kebap place with good and varied food, it provides more substantial fare at very low prices (meals for $1).

Things to See
Many of Ankara's important sights are near Ulus, some within an easy walk.

Museum & Hisar
First goal of most sightseers is the **Hisar** (hee-SAHR) or **Kale**, the citadel atop the hill. Near the Hisar, on the south-western slope of the hill, is the important **Anadolu Medeniyetleri Müzesi**, the Museum of Anatolian Civilisations, which is also called the Anadolu Uygarlıkları Müzesi, the Hitit Müzesi or the Arkeoloji Müzesi. On the south-east slope of the hill is the bazaar area, and the **Aslanhane Camii**, one of the city's oldest mosques.

If you're a walker and the day is not too hot, you can climb the hillside to the museum; otherwise, take a taxi. Walk east from Ulus on Hisarparkı Caddesi, and turn right into Anafartalar Caddesi, then bear left along Çıkrıkçılar Sokak to reach the museum. Remember that the museum is closed on Monday.

The museum building is a restored *bedesten*, or covered market, built by order of Grand Vezir Mahmut Paşa in 1471, and the adjoining *Kurşunlu Han*, an Ottoman warehouse. Exhibits here are heavily in favour of the earlier Anatolian civilisations such as the Urartu, Hatti, Hittite, Phrygian and Assyrian. Among the more fascinating items are those brought from Çatal höyük, the earliest known human community. You'll also enjoy the graceful, lively Hittite figures of bulls and stags, and the early water vessels.

As you stroll through the museum's exhibits, you should know that *M. Ö.* is the Turkish abbreviation for BC.

Hisar, the imposing fortress, just up the hill from the museum, took its present form in the 800s with the construction of the outer walls by the Byzantine emperor Michael II. The earlier inner walls date from the 600s. Enter the citadel by the gate called Parmak Kapısı (pahr-MAHK kah-puh-suh), and you're in a Turkish village right at the centre of Ankara! The small mosque here, the Alaettin Camii, dates originally from the 1100s, but has been much rebuilt. Wander into the village, following any path that will take you higher, and soon you'll arrive at the Şark Kulesi (SHARK koo-leh-see, Eastern Tower), from which there's a magnificent view over the entire city, all the way to Yenişehir and Çankaya. The tower at the north, Ak Kale (AHK kah-leh, White Fort), also offers fine views.

Come down from the Hisar, exit by the Parmak Kapısı, and you'll be in the **bazaar**. Warehouses here are filled with *tiftik* (Angora goathair), and merchants busy themselves with its trade. Turn left and walk down through the bazaar area, lined with vegetable stalls, copper and ironmongers' shops, and every variety of household goods shop. Soon you will come to the Aslanhane Camii (ahs-LAHN-hah-neh, Lion House), which dates

from the 1200s and is very Seljuk in aspect. Go inside for a look.

Continue down the hill on Can Sokak, and turn right into Anafartalar Caddesi for Ulus.

Railway Museum

Rail enthusiasts will want to have a look at Atatürk's private white railway coach, on display at the Ankara Railway Station. Enter the station from the street, walk through the main hall and out to the platforms, turn right, and walk along until you come to the coach, on the right. It was constructed in Breslau in 1935, and looks to be very comfy. You can't go inside the coach, but you can tour the Demiryolları Müzesi (deh-MEER-yoh-lah-ruh mew-zeh-see), the Railway Museum, just past the coach. It's open from 8.30 to 12 noon and 1 to 5.30 pm, closed Monday. As there are few visitors, it may be locked. Find an official and request, *Müzeyi âcarmısınız?* (mew-zeh-YEE ah-CHAR-muh-suh-nuhz, Would you open the museum?). If the time is within the hours given, he should oblige.

Roman Ankara

At the north-east corner of the square in Ulus are some buildings; behind them is the first stop on your tour of Roman Ankara. Set in a small park surrounded by provincial government office buildings is the Jülyanüs Sütunu (zhewl-YAH-news sew-too-noo), the **Column of Julian**. The Roman Emperor Julian (the Apostate, 361-363), last of the scions of Constantine the Great, visited Ankara in the middle of his short reign, and the column was erected in his honour. Turkish inhabitants later gave it the name Belkız Minaresi, the 'Queen of Sheba's Minaret.'

Walk east from the park, up the hill; turn right, then left to reach Bayram Caddesi and the **Hacı Bayram Camii** (hah-JUH bahy-RAHM), Ankara's most revered mosque, built on the ruins of the **Temple of Augustus and Rome**. Hacı Bayram Veli was a Muslim saint who founded the

Bayramiye order of dervishes around the year 1400. Ankara was the centre of the order, and Hacı Bayram Veli is still revered by the city's pious Muslims.

The temple walls that you see were once surrounded by a colonnade. Originally built by the kings of Pergamum for the worship of Cybele, the Anatolian fertility goddess, and Men, the Phrygian phallic god, it was later rededicated to the emperor Augustus. The Byzantines converted it to a church, and the Muslims built a mosque and saint's tomb in its precincts. The gods change, the site stays the same.

From Hacı Bayram, walk north on Çiçek Sokak until it meets Çankırı Caddesi. Across this main road, up the hill on the opposite side, is the fenced enclosure of the **Roman Baths** (Roma Hamamları). The layout of the 3rd century baths is clearly visible, as is much of the water system.

Republican Ankara

In the 1920s, at the time of the War of Independence, Ankara consisted of the citadel and a few buildings in Ulus. Atatürk's new city grew with Ulus as its centre, and thus many of the buildings here saw the birth and growing-pains of the Turkish Republic. A short tour through a few of the buildings tells a great deal about how a democratic nation-state grew from the ruins of a vast monarchy.

The museums described below are open from 9 to 12.30 noon and 1.30 to 6 pm, daily.

Kürtülüs Savaşı Müzesi The **War of Salvation Museum** is on Cumhuriyet Bulvarı just at the north-west corner of Ulus. Photographs and displays recount great moments and people in the War of Independence; captions are in Turkish only. This was where the republican Grand National Assembly held its early sessions (earlier called the T.B.B.M. Müzesi for *Türkiye Büyük Millet Meclisi*, Grand National Assembly). Before it was Turkey's first parliament, this building

was the Ankara headquarters of the Committee of Union and Progress, the political party which overthrew Sultan Abdül Hamid in 1909 and attempted to bring democracy to the Ottoman Empire.

Cumhuriyet Müzesi The **Republic Museum** is on Cumhuriyet Bulvarı, just down the hill from Ulus. This was the second headquarters of the Grand National Assembly, the parliament founded by Atatürk in his drive for a national consensus to resist foreign invasion and occupation of the Anatolian homeland. The early history of the assembly is documented in photographs and documents; all captions are in Turkish only, but you can visit the assembly's meeting-room and get a sense of its modest beginnings. The Grand National Assembly is now housed in a vast and imposing building in Yenişehir.

Across Cumhuriyet Caddesi from the museum is the former Ankara Palas hotel, built as the city's first luxury lodging. It has recently been beautifully restored, and now serves as guest quarters for important official visitors.

Gençlik Parkı & Opera House Walk south from Ulus along Atatürk Bulvarı and you'll soon reach the entrance to Gençlik Parkı, the 'Youth Park'. A swamp on this site was converted to an artificial lake on Atatürk's orders, and the park was included in the city's master plan. The park has amusements for children and, in the evening, outdoor cafes with musical performances.

Notice the quaint, small Opera House just past the entrance to the park. Atatürk had become enamoured of opera during a tour of duty as military attache in Sofia (1905), and saw to it that his new capital had a suitable hall for performances as well. The opera has a full season, beginning in autumn.

Etnografya Müzesi The **Ethnography Museum** is perched above Atatürk Bulvarı, to the east of the boulevard and south of

Ulus past Gençlik Parkı. It's an eye-catching white marble Oriental structure (1925), with an equestrian statue of Atatürk in front, reached by walking up Talatpaşa Bulvarı from Atatürk Bulvarı. Recently restored, it has fine collections of Seljuk and Ottoman art, craftwork, musical instruments, weapons, folk costumes, jewellery and household effects. Also on view is a large and elaborately decorated room used by Kemal Atatürk as his office.

Anıt Kabir

Atatürk's mausoleum, called the *Anıt Kabir* (ah-NUHT-kah-beer, Monumental Tomb), stands atop a small hill in a green park about two km west of Kızılay along Gazi Mustafa Kemal Bulvarı. If you saw Ankara from the Hisar or the terrace of the Ethnography Museum, you've already admired from a distance the rectangular mausoleum, with squared columns around its sides, on the hill. A visit to the tomb is essential when you visit Ankara.

Walking along Gazi Mustafa Kemal Bulvarı from Kızılay, you can make a shortcut by turning left onto Maltepe Sokak. This becomes Erdönmez Sokak and then meets Gençlik Caddesi. Turn right onto Gençlik, then left onto Akdeniz Caddesi, and you'll see the back entrance to the park. You may not be allowed to enter by the pedestrian gate, but past it is the auto exit road, and you can enter there.

Should you take a taxi to the Anıt Kabir's main entrance, from Tandoğan Meydani up Anıt Caddesi, you'll see the mausoleum as it is meant to be approached. Up the steps from the car park, you pass between allegorical statues, and two square kiosks; the right-hand one holds a model of the tomb and photoes of its construction. Then you pass down a long monumental avenue flanked by Hittite stone lions to the courtyard.

To the right as you enter the courtyard, beneath the western colonnade, is the sarcophagus of İsmet İnönü (1884-1973),

Atatürk's close friend and chief of staff, an Ottoman pasha, Republican general (hero of the Battle of İnönü, from which he took his surname), diplomat, prime minister, and second president of the republic.

Across the courtyard, on the east side, is a museum which holds memorabilia and personal effects of Atatürk. You can also see his official automobiles, several of which are American-made Lincolns.

Approaching the tomb proper, the high-stepping guards will probably jump to action. Past the colonnade, look to left and right at the gilded inscriptions, which are quotations from Atatürk's speech celebrating the tenth anniversary of the republic (1932). As you enter the tomb past its huge bronze doors, you must remove your hat (if you don't, a guard will remind you that this is correct protocol). The lofty hall is lined in red marble and decorated sparingly with mosaics in timeless Turkish folk designs. At the northern end stands the immense marble sarcophagus, cut from a single piece of stone.

The Anıt Kabir was begun in 1944 and finished in 1953. Its design seeks to capture the spirit of Anatolia: monumental, spare but beautiful. Echoes of several great Anatolian empires, from the Hittites through the Romans and Seljuks, are included in its design, though the final effect is modern, but somehow timeless as well.

Çankaya Köşkü

One last museum in Ankara is well worth a visit. At the far southern end of Atatürk Bulvarı in Çankaya is the Presidential Mansion. Within the mansion's beautiful gardens is the Çankaya Köşkü, or *Çankaya Atatürk Müzesi*. This quaint little chalet was Atatürk's country residence, set amid vineyards and evergreens. In the early days of the republic, it was a retreat from the town, but now the town reaches up to it, and beyond. Visits to the mansion gardens and grounds, and to the museum, are permitted on Sunday afternoons.

The house is preserved as Atatürk used it, with decor and furnishings very much of the 1930s. If you are in Ankara on a Sunday, don't miss it.

Boğazkale & Hattuşaş

Before our own century, very little was known about the Hittites, a people who commanded a vast empire in the Middle East, conquered Babylon, and challenged the Egypt of the pharaohs over three thousand years ago. Though their accomplishments were monumental, time has buried Hittite history as effectively as it has buried the Hittites themselves. Only a few references to them, in the Bible and in Egyptian chronicles, remain.

In 1905 excavations began at the site of the Hittite capital near the Turkish village of Boğazkale (also called Boğazköy), 200 km east of Ankara, off the highway to Samsun. The digging produced notable works of art, most of which are now preserved in Ankara's Museum of Anatolian Civilisations; also brought to light were the Hittite state archives, written in cuneiform (wedge-shaped characters) on thousands of clay tablets. From these tablets, historians and archaeologists were able to construct a history of the Hittite empire.

Getting There

You can make a day's excursion from Ankara to Boğazkale. Ankara travel agents sell bus tours of the ruins, which are a good way to make your visit. With your own car you can stop at Boğazkale on the way to the Black Sea coast at Samsun.

Going by public bus, leave from Ankara's Otogar on a bus for Sungurlu, a town 175 km east of Ankara. At Sungurlu you must wait for a dolmus to Boğazkale (perhaps a long wait), or hire a taxi for the trip. The taxi should cost $12 for the entire car, including the trip to Boğazkale (27 km), a tour of the far-flung ruins, and return to Sungurlu. This is perhaps the best way to do it, as the ruins are spread out on a sprawling hillside, and you will probably want a taxi tour from Boğazkale ($6) anyway; and taxis there may not be readily available. Considering that you will have to pay about $1 per person, each way, for the dolmus ride between Sungurlu and Boğazkale, it is thus only about $2 more expensive to hire a taxi in Sungurlu.

To see the ruins on foot, plan to walk energetically for three or four hours; you may want to spend the night.

Places to Stay

There are several small hotels in Sungurlu, and also the *Turist Oteli* in Boğazkale, where a very simple but clean double room costs $7. Boğazkale also has a small restaurant.

The Hittite Cities

The Hittites spoke an Indo-European language. They swept into Anatolia around 2000 BC and conquered the Hatti, from whom they borrowed both their culture and their name. They established themselves here at *Hattuşaş*, the Hatti capital, and in the course of a millenium enlarged and beautified the city.

Most of the Hittite artifacts are now in Ankara's museum, though there is also a small museum in Boğazkale, open 8 to 12 noon and 1.30 to 5.30 pm. One admission ticket allows you entry to both the ruins and the museum.

The ruins consist of reconstructed foundations, walls, and a few rock carvings. The site itself is strange, almost eerie, exciting for its ruggedness and high antiquity rather than for its buildings or reliefs.

Hattuşaş Walk up from Boğazkale. Part way up the hill is the **Great Temple of the Storm God**, a vast complex, almost a town in itself. High above it is the Fortress, which held the royal palace. Both structures date from the 1300s BC. In the walls are several gates, including the **Sphinx Gate**. One of the sphinxes found here is in Berlin; the other is in Istanbul's Museum of the Ancient Orient. Note the tunnel through the wall: it is topped by a corbelled arch (two flat stones leaned against one another). The Hittites did not know how to make a true arch; their neighbours the Chaldaeans and Assyrians, who built mostly of clay, did develop a true arch made of damp mud bricks. The true masonry arch or vault was not fully developed until Roman times, 1400 years later.

Yazılıkaya The Turkish name (yah-zuh-LUH kah-yah) means 'inscribed rock', and that's what you find at this site about three km from Boğazkale. The low reliefs of gods and goddesses indicate that this was the Hittite's holiest religious sanctuary. The Hittites had 1000 gods, but less than a hundred are represented here. The shrine dates from very late Hittite times, about the 1200s BC.

Alaca Höyük Another great Hittite city, this one is 20 km north of the Sungurlu-Boğazkale road, or about 28 km from Boğazkale. You can haggle with a taxi driver to take you there and back. As at the other sites, moveable monuments have been taken to the museum in Ankara, though there is a small museum on the site, and a few worn sphinxes and low reliefs have been left in place. This is a very old site, settled from about 4000 BC. Time has not been especially kind to it.

Still interested in Hittites? You can visit the very earliest Hittite capital at **Kültepe**, near Kayseri in Cappadocia, but there is even less to see there.

KONYA

Standing alone in the midst of the vast Anatolian steppe, Konya (KOHN-yah, altitude 1030 metres, population 350,000) is like some traditional caravan stopping-place. The windswept landscape gives way to little patches of greenery in the city, and when you're in the town you don't feel the loneliness of the plateau.

The city is true to this feeling, for it has been here a very long time. The Hittites called it *Kuwanna* almost 4000 years ago. Over the years, the name has changed slightly; it was Kowania to the Phrygians, Iconium to the Romans, Konya to the Turks. The city has stood here on its plain longer than human history itself. Neighbouring *Çatal Höyük*, 50 km to the south, is thought to be the oldest known human settlement, dating from 7500 BC.

Under Rome, Iconium was an important provincial town visited on several occasions by the saints Paul and Barnabas, but its early Christian community does not seem to have been very influential.

Konya's heyday was during the 1200s, when it was capital of the Seljuk Sultanate of Rum, the last remnant of an earlier Seljuk empire.

The Seljuk Turks had ruled a powerful state in Iran and Iraq, the Empire of the Great Seljuks, during the 1000s; Omar Khayyam was their most noted poet and mathematician. But Great Seljuk power was fragmented in the early 1100s, and the various parts of the empire set themselves up as independent states. One of these states was the Sultanate of Rum (ROOM, 'Rome'), which encompassed most of Anatolia. Konya was its capital from about 1150 to 1300. In that period, the Seljuk sultans built dozens of fine buildings in an architectural style decidedly Turkish, but with its roots in Persia and Byzantium.

The Sultanate of Rum also produced one of the world's great mystic philosophers. Celaleddin Rumi (jeh-LAH-leh-DEEN roo-MEE), founder of the order of whirling dervishes, was called *Mevlana* (meh-VLAH-nah, Our Guide) by his followers. His poetic and religious work, done mostly in Persian (the literary language of the day), is some of the most beloved and respected in the Islamic world.

When the Ottomans took Konya after invasions by the Mongols and Tamerlane, it returned to its role as a provincial city. In recent years it has been booming, though. The bare-looking steppe is in fact good for

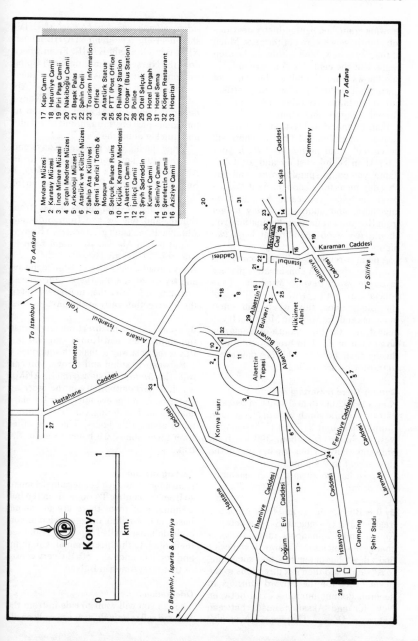

Konya

0   1
km.

1	Mevlana Müzesi
2	Karatay Müzesi
3	İnce Minare Müzesi
4	Sırçalı Medrese Müzesi
5	Arkeoloji Müzesi
6	Atatürk ve Kültür Müzesi
7	Sahip Ata Külliyesi
8	Şemsi Tebrizi Tomb & Mosque
9	Selçuk Palace Ruins
10	Küçük Karatay Medresesi
11	Alaettin Camii
12	İplikçi Camii
13	Şeyh Sadreddin Kunevi Camii
14	Selimiye Camii
15	Şerefettin Camii
16	Aziziye Camii
17	Kapı Camii
18	Hatuniye Camii
19	Piri Paşa Camii
20	Nakiboğlu Camii
21	Başak Palas
22	Şahin Oteli
23	Tourism Information Office
24	Atatürk Statue
25	PTT (Post Office)
26	Railway Station
27	Otogar (Bus Station)
28	Police
29	Otel Selçuk
30	Hotel Dergah
31	Hotel Sema
32	Köşem Restaurant
33	Hospital

growing grain, and light industry provides jobs for those who are not farmers. Much of the city is new, built within the last ten years. But the centre is old, very old. No one knows when the hill at the centre of town, the *Alaettin Tepesi*, was first settled, but it certainly contains the bones of Bronze Age men and women.

Plan to spend at least one full day in Konya (not a Monday! The museums will be closed!), and preferably two. If your interest in Seljuk history and art takes flame, you could spend another half-day or a day pleasantly enough. As it takes a good half-day to reach Konya from anywhere, and another half-day to get from Konya to your next destination, you should figure on spending at least two nights in a hotel here.

A point to remember during your visit is that Konya is a fairly conservative place, a favourite with devout Muslims. Take special care not to jar the sensibilities of the pious; look tidy when you enter mosques and the Mevlana Museum. If you visit during the holy month of Ramazan, do not eat or drink in broad public view during daylight hours; this is a politeness to those who are fasting.

Getting There & Getting Around

Konya is 262 km (5 hrs) south of Ankara, 226 km (4½ hrs) south-west of Nevşehir in Cappadocia, and 218 km (5 hrs) north-west of Silifke. It's about 300 km from Side and Alanya, a long trip because of the slow ascent to the plateau.

Konya has no airport, so access is by road or rail.

By Bus Bus service to and from Ankara is frequent and convenient. Service between Konya and Cappadocia may involve a change of vehicles in Aksaray. If you can't find a direct bus or minibus, take something to Aksaray, and then ask directions to the ticket office for the onward journey. In general, dolmuş minibuses run between Nevşehir and Aksaray; buses between Aksaray and Konya. The phrase is *Nevşehir'e*

giden dolmuş nereden kalkar? (NEHV-sheh-heer-eh gee-dehn DOHL-moosh NEH-reh-dehn kahl-KAHR, From where does the Nevşehir dolmuş depart?) Going to Konya, you must ask *Konya'ya giden otobüs nereden kalkar?* (KOHN-yah-YAH . . . , From where does the bus to Konya depart?) People in Aksaray are used to foreigners passing through, and will gladly and quickly point the way.

Along the highway between Konya and Aksaray (95 km from Konya, 45 from Aksaray) you'll pass the *Sultan Hanı*, a Seljuk caravanserai. Keep an eye open for it.

There are several buses a day from Silifke, and one or two from Side and Antalya. If you can't get a seat on a Konya-bound bus in Alanya, you might want to ride the 50 km to Hwy 31, where the Konya road meets the coastal highway, and try to catch a bus there. More buses originate in Antalya than in Alanya. Get to the intersection early in the day.

By Train There is no direct rail link across the steppe between Konya and Ankara. Bus is the best way to make this journey.

Between Istanbul and Konya, you can ride the *Meram Ekspresi* (mehr-AHM), which departs either city in the morning and arrives in the evening, with 1st class coaches and a dining car. The journey takes about 12½ hours. The only other train takes almost 19 hours to make the trip.

Getting Around

Konya has a modern bus terminal a km or so from the centre. To travel from the bus terminal into town there are municipal buses, and also little three-wheeled motor-cycle dolmuşes called *triportör*. You'll see them outside the bus terminal. Climb in, and you'll bounce along to the very centre of things on Alaettin Bulvarı.

Orientation

Though you will want to ride in from the bus and rail terminals, you can walk easily to most of Konya's attractions. The city's historic axis is Alaettin Bulvarı/Mevlana Caddesi, the main street which runs between the hill called Alaettin Tepesi and the Mevlana Museum. Half-way along this street it broadens into Hükümet Alanı, Government Square. By the way, the Mevlana Museum shelters the tomb of Rumi, and was the first whirling dervish convent. It's the most important building to visit in Konya.

The distance from the hill to the museum is about one km, a 10- to 15-minute walk. Konya's Tourism Information Office (tel (331) 11074) is at Mevlana Caddesi 21, across the square from the Mevlana Museum.

Places to Stay – top end

Konya's nicest hotel is out of town. The *Yeni Sema Oteli* (yeh-NEE seh-MAH) is east of the city on the road to Meram.

Places to Stay – mid-range

Conveniently located right next to the *Otogar* (bus terminal) are the *Özkaymak Park Oteli* (URZ-kahy-mahk, tel 33770, –72), with 90 clean doubles with bath going for $23; and the *Otogar Oteli* (32557, 30138), with 33 rooms priced at $18 double. Most of the moderately-priced hotels are right downtown. The *Başak Palas* (bah-SHAHK pah-LAHS, tel 11338, –9) is right in Hükümet Alanı, facing the provincial government house, midway along Alaettin Bulvarı. An older place with 40 rooms, it's kept brightly painted; doubles with bath cost $16. The *Şahin Oteli* (shah-HEEN, tel 13350, 12376), just out of Hükümet Alanı on the main street, has 44 rooms, some of which can be noisy; check several, take the best, and you'll pay $18 a double. They have also have cheaper rooms without bath, but you may have to ask for these.

The *Otel Selçuk* (SEHL-chook, tel 14161, 11259) is just off Alaettin Bulvarı on Babalık Sokak, near the Alaettin Tepesi. The 52 rooms are priced at $16 double (with washbasin), or $18 (with bath). This one is on a quiet side street near several restaurants.

Very near the Mevlana Museum is the *Hotel Dergah* (dehr-GYAH, tel 11197), across the square from the museum, next to the Tourism Office at Mevlana Caddesi 19. The hotel has its own Turkish bath, and 43 modern-ish rooms with shower priced at $22 double. At Mevlana Caddesi 8 is the *Hotel Sema* (seh-MAH, tel 19212, 13279), with a Turkish bath (*hamam*), and 29 rooms with shower priced at $22 double. The hotel is actually a few steps off the main boulevard, behind the Tourism Office.

Places to Stay – bottom end

Konya has 35 small, bare, local hotels for village folk coming to the city. They are very basic, but very cheap, charging between $4 and $8 for a double rooms, without private bath. If you stay in one, be careful to observe the proprieties: nothing ribald or unkempt from the point of view of a pious Muslim. Konya is a conservative town.

Camping

You can camp at the Şehir Stadı, the sports complex just east of the railway station on İstasyon Caddesi.

Places to Eat

Konya's specialty is *fırın kebap* (fuh-RUHN keh-bahp, Oven Roast), a rich joint of mutton roasted in an oven (*fırın*). It is not normally prepared to order, so you must trust to luck for a taste of it.

Among the favourite restaurants here is *Köşem Restaurant* (kur-SHEHM, tel 11707), Alaettin Bulvarı 26/8, near the Alaettin Tepesi. It's where the city potentates gather for long lunches and dinners, in three large rooms, plus a patio out back. Ask for *meze* (MEH-zeh) and the waiter will bring a large tray of salads and appetizers from which you can choose as few or as many as you like. They bake their own pide (flat bread) here. A full meal can cost as little as $3; liquor is served.

The *Çatal Lokantası* (chah-TAHL) is just behind the Tourism Office, near the Mevlana Museum. This is a simple, tidy kebap place (no booze) next to the Hotel Sema, with good food at low prices.

The *Derya Kebap Salonu* (dehr-YAH) is a good place to look for fırın kebap. It's on Alaettin Bulvarı, behind a little car park, across the boulevard from the small Mevlana Oteli. It's very simple, very cheap, and very crowded with locals at mealtimes.

The *Kenanlar Pasta Salonu* (keh-nahn-LAHR), right across Alaettin Bulvarı from the Şahin Oteli, is good for breakfasts, light meals, snacks, and take-away treats (on long bus journeys, for instance).

Things to See

The centre of Konya is Turkey's best 'outdoor museum' of Seljuk architecture. The Seljuks built doorways. While the buildings themselves are often starkly simple on the outside, the main portal is always grand and imposing, sometimes huge and wildly Baroque in its decoration. The interiors are always very harmonious, and often decorated with blue and white tiles. Coloured tiles are sometimes found, but they rarely have red in them as the fusing of vivid reds on faience was a later, Ottoman accomplishment.

You can walk to all of the buildings described here, but it would be tiring to do so in one day.

Mevlana Museum

First place to visit is the Mevlana Museum, open every day from 9 to 12 noon and 1.30 to 5.30 (admission tickets are sold until 5.10 pm).

The Founder Celaleddin Rumi, or Mevlana (1207-1273), was born in Balkh (near Mazar-i Sharif in present-day Afghanistan), but his family fled the impending Mongol invasion, moving west and south to Mecca, then to the Sultanate of Rum by 1221, reaching Konya by 1228. His father was a noted preacher, and Rumi grew to be a brilliant student of Islamic theology. After his father's death in 1231, Rumi studied in Aleppo and Damascus, but returned to live in Konya by 1240.

In 1244 he met Mehmet Şemseddin Tebrizi, called Şemsi Tebrizi, one of his father's *Sufi* (Muslim mystic) disciples. Tebrizi had a profound effect on Rumi, who became devoted to him. An angry crowd of Rumi's own disciples put Tebrizi to death in 1247, perhaps because of his overwhelming influence on the brilliant Rumi. Stunned by the loss of his spiritual master, Rumi withdrew from the world for meditation, and in this period founded a dervish order. Its members called Rumi *Mevlana* (Our Guide), and the order came to be called *Mevlevi* (Those who Follow the Guide).

Rumi's great poetic work, the *Mesnevi*, has 25,000 verses; it was written in Persian, the literary language of the day. He also wrote many *ruba'i* and *ghazal* poems, collected into his 'Great Opus', the *Divan-i Kebir*.

The Dervishes The way of the Mevlevis spread throughout Anatolia, Syria and Egypt. Wherever there was a branch of the order, there would be a *tekke*, or dervish convent. Their worship ceremony, the *sema*, consisted of a ritual dance representing union with God. The dervishes' long white robes with full skirts represent their shrouds, and the tall conical red hats their tombstones, as they relinquish the earthly life to be reborn in mystical union with God. They pass before the *şeyh* (SHEYHH, Leader), spiritual descendant of Mevlana, with their arms folded. After the şeyh whispers in his ear, each dervish slowly passes on, unfurling his arms and commencing the dance. He holds his right arm upward, palm up to receive the blessings of Heaven, and left downward to communicate them to Earth. Pivoting on the left heel, he whirls ever faster, reaching an ecstatic state with a blissful expression on his face. The dervishes whirling form a 'constellation' on the floor, which itself slowly rotates. All at once the dervishes cease, and kneel to the floor. The dance is repeated three times, with the şeyh joining the third iteration. Musical accompaniment is by an orchestra with small drums, *rebap* (a gourd viol), *kemançe*, and *ney* (an open-tube reed flute), with a male choir. After the whirling, a *hafız* (man who has memorized the entire Kuran) chants poetical passages from the holy book.

The breathy, haunting music of the ney is perhaps the most striking sound during the sema. Each musician 'opens' (makes) his own instrument from a carefully-chosen length of bamboo-like reed, burning the finger-holes according to a mathematical formula. The ney is thought to have its own soul, like that of a man, and 'opening' it liberates the soul, which comes forth in its music.

Rumi's teachings were ecumenical, stressing the universality of God and welcoming any worshipper, of whatever sect or following, to join in worshipping him. Non-Muslims were regularly invited to witness the sema.

The Museum You enter through a courtyard with ablutions fountain and several tombs, then pass into the *Mevlana Türbesi*, or tomb of Rumi. The sarcophagi of Rumi and his most illustrious followers are covered in great velvet shrouds heavy with gold embroidery, giving a powerful impression that this is a sacred place.

The tomb dates from Seljuk times; the mosque and room for the sema were added later by Ottoman sultans (Mehmet the Conqueror was a Mevlevi adherent, and Süleyman the Magnificent made large charitable donations to the order). Selim I, conqueror of Egypt, donated the Mameluke crystal lamps.

In the rooms adjoining the sepulchral chamber are exhibits of Dervish paraphernalia: musical instruments, vestments, illuminated manuscripts and ethnographic artifacts.

What Happened to the Dervishes? Under the Ottoman Empire, dervish orders exerted a great deal of influence in the country's political, social and economic life. Their world-view was monarchist, arch-conservative and xenophobic in most cases. Committed to progress, democracy and separation of religion and state, Atatürk saw the orders as a block to advancement for the Turkish people, so he saw to it that they were proscribed in 1925. Many of the tekkes were converted to museums; the Mevlana tekke opened as a museum in 1927.

Though outlawed, several of the dervish orders survived as fraternal religious brotherhoods, stripped of their influence. The whirling dervishes of Konya are now officially a 'cultural association', which preserves a historical tradition. The annual Festival of Mevlana, held in mid-December, is officially encouraged as a popular – not a religious – event. Groups of dervishes are also sent on cultural exchange tours to other countries, performing the sema from Leningrad to Los Angeles.

The dervishes are no longer interested in politics, but neither are they truly a 'cultural association'. Young novices are recruited as early as grammar school, and devotion to the principles of the order can still be lifelong. Konya's dervishes whirl today to celebrate a great tradition, but also to worship and to seek mystical union with God as Mevlana taught, and as they have been doing for over 700 years.

Near the Museum
Outside the entrance to the Mevlana Museum is the **Selimiye Camii**, endowed by Sultan Selim II (1566-1574). Construction on the Ottoman-style mosque was begun during Selim's term as governor of Konya, before his accession to the throne.

The surrounding streets are a lively market district, and you could do some random exploration of the back streets if you have the time.

Alaettin Tepesi

Except for the Mevlana Museum, many of Konya's principal sights are near the Alaettin Tepesi. One, the ancient Alaettin Camii, is right atop the hill.

Alaettin Camii

The Mosque of Alaeddin Keykubat I (or Alaettin), Seljuk Sultan of Rum, is a great rambling building designed by a Damascene architect in the Arab style and finished in 1221. Over the centuries it was embellished, refurbished, ruined and restored. Recent restoration took place as little as a decade ago. Though hardly as harmonious as an Ottoman work of Sinan, it is very sympathetic and impressive. Notice the forest of old columns surmounted with Roman and Byzantine capitals, the fine carved wood mimber (pulpit, 1156), and the mihrab of marble.

On the north side of the Alaettin Tepesi, the scant ruins of a Seljuk palace are protected by a modern concrete shelter.

Büyük Karatay Medresesi

Now called the Karatay Müzesi (KAH-rah-tah-yee), this Seljuk theological seminary just north of the Alaettin Tepesi houses Konya's outstanding collection of ceramics and tiles. The school was constructed in 1251 by the Emir Celaleddin Karatay, a Seljuk diplomat and statesman. It has a magnificent sculpted marble doorway.

Inside, the central dome is a masterpiece of Seljuk blue tilework with gold accents. The Arabic inscription in Kufic style around the bottom of the dome is the first chapter, or *sura*, of the Kuran. The triangles below the dome are decorated with the names of the first four caliphs who succeeded Muhammed; the Arabic letters are highly stylized.

Note especially the curlicue drain for the central pool: its curved shape gave the sound of running water to the quiet room where students were studying, a pleasant background 'noise'.

As for the museum's collection of tiles, they include interesting coloured ones from Seljuk palaces in Konya and Beyse'hir. Compare these to the later Ottoman tiles from İznik.

İnce Minare Müzesi

Around the Alaettin Tepesi at its west side is the İnce Minare Medresesi (een-JEH mee-NAH-reh), now the museum of wood and stone carving. Don't go right in, for over half of what you came to see is the elaborate doorway, with bands of Arabic inscription running up the sides and looping overhead. As this religious school was built in 1258, it may be that the architect was trying to outdo a rival who had designed the Karatay Medresesi only seven years earlier.

The doorway is far more impressive than the small building behind it. The minaret beside the door is what gave the medrese its popular name of 'slender minaret', though the greater part of the very tall minaret was knocked off by a lightning bolt less than a hundred years ago (having stood here for over 600 years).

The exhibits within the medrese show Seljuk motifs used in wood and stone carving, many of them similar to those used in the tile and ceramic work. In Islam, visual representation of creatures with souls (humans and animals) is forbidden as idolatry, but most great Islamic civilizations had artists who ignored the law from time to time. Though most Islamic art is geometrical or otherwise non-representative, you will still see birds (the Seljuk double-headed eagle, for example), men and women, lions and leopards, etc. Though the Ottomans seem to have observed the law more strictly than the Seljuks, there were some lapses. Mehmet the Conqueror, for instance, had his portrait painted by the great Bellini. But as the finished masterpiece was hung in the palace, the mass of people were none the wiser to this 'sacrilege'.

Sırçalı Medrese Müzesi

Yet another medrese now a museum, this one of

funerary monuments, is the Sırçalı (sirr-chah-LUH), south of the Alaettin Tepesi. As always, the portal is grand and highly decorated. The tiles on the exterior give the medrese its name. Building was finished in 1242, sponsored by a Seljuk *vezir* (prime minister). The inscriptions on the gravestones inside are often very fine, done in a variety of Arabic scripts. Symbols of rank – headgear, usually – served to tell the passer-by of the deceased one's important role in life.

Other Sights

Arkeoloji Müzesi Konya's small **Archaeological Museum** is several blocks south of the Alaettin Tepesi; walk south along Ressam Sami Sokak. Its collection of Greek and Roman artifacts is interesting, but overwhelmed in Konya by the wealth of Seljuk art.

Sahip Ata Külliyesi A *külliye* is a complex of buildings surrounding a mosque. These might include soup kitchens, religious schools, an orphanage or hospital, a library, and other charitable works. Sahip Ata was the man who funded the İnce Minare Medresesi. His mosque and tomb are just east of the Archaeological Museum. There is also a dervish *tekke* and a *hamam*

(Turkish bath). The entire complex was finished in 1283. Note especially the portal to the mosque, and its mihrab (prayer niche). Sahip Ata, by the way, was a Seljuk *vezir*, and obviously very rich.

Other Mosques & Tombs As you wander around town, you will pass other buildings of interest. The mosque and tomb (1300s) of Şemsi Tebrizi, Rumi's spiritual mentor, is just north of Hükümet Alanı, off Alaettin Bulvarı. The **Aziziye Camii** (1874) is a work of Ottoman late Baroque, in the bazaar; it's the one which has twin minarets bearing little sheltered balconies. The **İplikçi Camii** (1202) is perhaps Konya's oldest mosque. The **Şerefettin Camii** was constructed in 1636.

If you have a spare morning or afternoon, take an excursion (less than 10 km) to **Meram**, a pleasant, shady suburb west of the city. It's been a getaway destination for Konya city-dwellers for at least 1000 years.

You can drive, or arrange a taxi excursion, to **Çatal Höyük**, the world's oldest human settlement, 50 km southeast of Konya off Hwy 35, but there is little to see except the setting. The pre-historic artifacts have been removed to museums.

Cappadocia

The region between Ankara and Malatya, between the Black Sea and the Taurus Mountains, with its centre at Kayseri, was once the heart of the Hittite Empire, later an independent kingdom, then a vast Roman province. Cappadocia is mentioned several times in the Bible.

Today the word survives as a name for one of Turkey's most-visited tourist areas, the moon-like landscape around the town of Ürgüp and the Göreme Valley. You won't find the name on an official road map, so you must know that unofficial *Kapadokya* is the area between Kayseri to

the east of Ürgüp, Aksaray to the west, and Niğde to the south.

History

The history of Cappadocia begins with the eruption of two volcanoes, Erciyes Dağı near Kayseri and Melendiz Dağı near Niğde. The eruptions spread a thick layer of hot volcanic ash over the region, and the ash hardened to a soft, porous stone called tuff.

Over the eons of geological time, erosion by wind, water and sand wore away portions of the tuff, carving it into elaborate and unearthly shapes. Boulders of hard stone, caught in the tuff, yet exposed to erosion, would then protect the tuff directly beneath from further erosion. The result was a column or cone of tuff with a boulder perched on top, a formation now whimsically called a *peribaca*, 'fairy chimney'. Entire valleys might be filled with these weird formations.

The tuff was easily worked with primitive tools, and men learned early that sturdy dwellings could be cut from it with a minimum of fuss. One could carve out a cave in a short time, and if the family expanded, more easy carving produced a nursery or storeroom in almost no time!

When invaders flooded across the land-bridge between Europe and Asia, Cappadocians went underground – literally. They carved elaborate multi-level cave cities beneath the surface of the earth, and only came to the surface to tend their fields.

Christianity arrived in Cappadocia, and its adherents found that cave churches, complete with elaborate decoration, could be carved from the rock as easily as dwellings. Large Christian communities throve here, and rock-hewn churches became a unique art form. Arab armies swept through in the 600s, but the Christians retreated into their caves again, rolling stone wheel-doors across the entrances.

For all its apparent barenness, the mineral-laden volcanic tuff is very fertile, and Cappadocia today is a prime agricultural region with many fruit orchards and vineyards. Little wineries experiment with the excellent grapes, sometimes with very gratifying results. Irrigation schemes should greatly increase the productivity of the region.

Another source of wealth is carpet-making, and while the women in Cappadocian villages toil at their looms, Kayseri is a hotbed of persistent rug-dealers. But Cappadocia's new economic dimension is tourism. People come from all over the world to visit the National Park in the Göreme Valley, to explore the rock-hewn churches and dwellings in surrounding valleys, to gaze on the fairy chimneys, and to plumb the depths of the underground cities at Derinkuyu and Kaymaklı, south of Nevşehir.

The most beautiful and artistically significant valleys are national parks, protected from development. Further protection and support are provided by a UNESCO preservation campaign similar to the one launched in Egypt to protect that country's antiquities from the waters of the Aswan High Dam.

Getting There & Getting Around

There are several daily buses from Ankara to Nevşehir and/or Kayseri, and trains and planes to Kayseri. See the Ankara section for details. The trip to or from Konya is described in the Konya section.

Though you could see something of Cappadocia on a lightning day-trip from Ankara, it is far better to stay at least one night in the region. You could easily spend three or four nights if you wanted to explore all there is to see.

Most convenient base for explorations is Ürgüp, a 10-minute ride from the Göreme Valley. When you arrive in Nevşehir or Kayseri, ask for the dolmuş to Ürgüp, and you'll end up at Ürgüp's modern central bus station in the middle of town. There are also hotels and pensions in nearby villages, and several good mid-range hotels in Nevşehir, the provincial capital. Kayseri is separated from Cappadocia by 70 km and a range of hills, and is thus not a convenient base for daily excursions.

While there are convenient dolmuş services between Nevşehir and Ürgüp, public transport to the valleys and villages near Ürgüp is not frequent. If you have more time than money, plan to walk and hitchhike throughout the region, a wonderful way to tour, though tiring.

Otherwise, inquire at the Tourism Information Office in Ürgüp (tel 159), Kayseri Caddesi 37, about taxi tours. The staff will help you find others who want to tour so you can fill a taxi and pay the lowest possible price per person. If you're in a hurry, ask for a tour of all the highlights. If you have more time, get to Göreme and back on your own (Nevşehir dolmuşes will drop you at the Göreme turning, a 15-minute walk to the site). Also, plan to take a dolmuş from Nevşehir to the underground cities at Derinkuyu and Kaymaklı. For the remaining places (Üçhisar, Zelve, Avanos, Sarı Han, Peribacalar Vadisi, etc), arrange a one-day taxi tour.

NEVŞEHİR

Nevşehir (NEHV-sheh-heer, altitude 1260 metres, population 40,000), the provincial capital, is the largest town in the region. The moonlike landscape of Cappadocia is not much in evidence here, but it's very close by.

Buses will drop you in a large square north of the centre. Walk downhill along the highway to reach the business district of banks, shops, restaurants, and the city's hotels. The Tourism Information Office (tel (4851) (1137) is at Lale Caddesi 22.

Places to Stay/Eat

There are small restaurants and snack shops near the bus plaza, and several small places downtown. For fancier dining, go to one of the hotels. This is a farmers' town, not a sophisticated city.

Hotels The best place in town is the *Orsan Kapadokya Oteli* (tel 1035, 2115), on Kayseri Caddesi, the road east to Ürgüp. The 80 doubles-with-bath rent for $23 double; there's a swimming pool. Nearby is the smaller, more modest *Viva Oteli* (tel 1326, 1760), Kayseri Caddesi 111, where the 24 doubles-with-bath are priced at $11.

Right in the centre of Nevşehir, on the main street, the *Hotel Göreme* (GUR-reh-meh, tel 1706) is true to its namesake. Eleven storeys of raw concrete make it look somewhat troglodytic, but it is comfortable with many services; doubles cost $18. The *Lale Oteli* (LAH-leh, tel 1797, 2905), Gazhane Sokak, is right next to the Municipality (*Belediye Sarayı*); all its rooms have bath or shower and rent for $10 or $11.

Camping There are several camping places along the road to Ürgüp. Rates are generally $1.50 per person, another 60c to $1 for tent or caravan.

Follow the signs to Ürgüp, and shortly after leaving Nevşehir you will come to a *BP Mocamp*, behind a BP petrol station. Farther along is the *Koru Mocamp* (tel 2157), with room for 240 persons and hook-ups of water and electricity for camping vehicles. The *Kervansaray Göreme Mokamp* (tel 1428) has room for some 600 persons, and is more elaborate than most. Rates are a bit higher, about $2.50 per adult, $1.50 to $2.50 per tent or vehicle. Less than a km before the Göreme turning is the *Yakut Motel/Camping* (tel Ortahisar 58, 21), a yellow stone structure where double rooms with bath rent for $9, and the camping places have hook-ups and a fine view of the valley.

For other camping areas near Göreme, see the Ürgüp section, below.

Heading East

East out of Nevşehir, the rolling terrain is sandy. After a few kms the panorama of Cappadocia begins to unfold: distant rock formations become visible as fairy chimneys, and valleys with undulating walls of soft volcanic ash fall away from the road. In the far distance, the gigantic snow-capped peak of the volcano, Erciyes Dağı (Mt Aergius), floats above a layer of cloud.

You will pass the Motel Paris on your left, right at the turning for Göreme. The settlement to the right is Ortahisar. Soon afterward, the Turban Ürgüp Moteli will be on your left. Then it's down a long hill (one km) into Ürgüp.

ÜRGÜP

Twenty-three kms east of Nevşehir is the village of Ürgüp (EWR-gewp), at the very heart of the Cappadocian wonderland. Life in Ürgüp is divided between farming and tourism, and a hotel might share a stretch of land with a vineyard or alfalfa field. The main street has a sprinkling of antique and carpet shops, a Tourism Information Office, and some restaurants.

Many of Urgup's citizens still live or work, at least part of the time, in rock houses. Surrounding villages such as Ortahisar and Üçhisar are similarly troglodytic, peopled by cave-dwellers. At Üçhisar there's a rock-dwelling of a different sort, however. The Hotel Kaya, run by Club Mediterranee, is built partially into the rock, but its guests can hardly be said to live the life of cavemen.

Places to Stay

Though Ürgüp is the most convenient place to stay if you don't have a car, there are also lodgings along the Ürgüp-Göreme road, in Ortahisar, Üçhisar and Avanos.

Hotels The old standby is the *Büyük Otel* (bew-YEWK, tel 60, 61), down the hill a bit from the town's main square. Its 54 comfy rooms are often filled by group tours; if not, you can have a double– with–bath for $20. The *Tepe Oteli* (TEH-peh, tel 74, 154) is the one on the hilltop on the outskirts of town, visible from the Büyük Otel. It has a swimming pool, and 36 doubles priced at $21. The *Hotel Pınar* (puh-NAHR, tel 35), down the road from the Büyük, on the way to the Tepe, charges a more modest $9 for its double rooms with shower.

Pensions Ürgüp has numerous little places called *pansiyon* (PAHN-see-YOHN) in which you can get a bed in a clean though spartan room for about $2 per person. The owner (*patron*, pah-TROHN) will be cheerful and helpful. Another bonus is the bath arrangements: you make an appointment for a shower, and a half-hour before the appointed hour the patron builds a fire under the hot water tank. The shower costs an extra 50c or 75c, but you get as much steaming hot water as you like. Any pansiyon in Ürgüp is cheap and satisfactory, but my favourite is the *Erciyes Pansiyon* (EHR-jee-yess, tel 206), Sivritaş Mahallesi, Santral Sokak No 4.

Motels Near Ürgüp Nicest is the new *Turban Ürgüp Moteli* (TOOR-bahn, tel 490), just at the top of the hill as you leave Ürgüp on the road to Nevşehir and Göreme. Operated by the government's Tourism Bank, it's a nice place with comfortable rooms in small bungalows designed in harmony with the landscape and the traditional architecture of Cappadocian villages. Doubles with breakfast cost $18. The motel is walking distance from Ürgüp, a short ride from Göreme.

Across the road from the Turban is the *Çimenli Motel/Camping*, not nearly so fancy, but considerably cheaper, and still within walking distance of the town.

Near Göreme Right at the turning to Göreme, only a km from the entrance to the National Park, is the *Motel Paris/Camping* (PAH-rees, tel Ortahisar 15, 99). It has 24 good (if older) rooms, a swimming pool, and a price of $12 double; in the camping area you'll find room for 600 persons, most services, and the standard low prices.

Down the hill on the Göreme road, ½ km from the park, is the *Kaya Camping*, the perfect place for backpacking tenters. The view of the valley is marvellous.

In Ortahisar In the village opposite the Göreme turning, is the *Hotel Göreme* (tel Ortahisar 5), a very modest place with bathless doubles for $5 and $6. Ortahisar is a 'poor man's' Ürgüp, a farming village with a sleepy ambience except on market day. Stay here if you're adventurous, and you want a true non-tourist, living-with-the-locals experience.

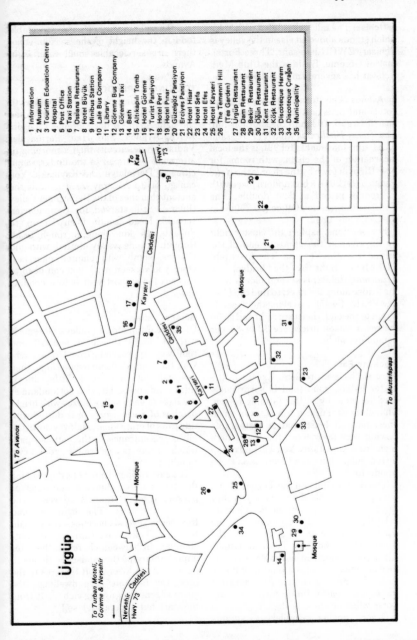

Ürgüp

To Turban Moteli,
Göreme & Nevşehir

Nevşehir Caddesi
Hwy. 73

To Avanos

To Kaş

To Mustafapaşa

1 Information
2 Museum
3 Tourism Education Centre
4 Hospital
5 Post Office
6 Taxi Station
7 Ossiana Restaurant
8 Hotel Büyük
9 Minibus Station
10 Lale Bus Company
11 Library
12 Göreme Bus Company
13 Göreme Taxi
14 Bath
15 Altıkapılı Tomb
16 Hotel Göreme
17 Turist Pansiyon
18 Hotel Peri
19 Hotel Pınar
20 Güzelgöz Pansiyon
21 Erciyes Pansiyon
22 Hotel Hisar
23 Hotel Sefa
24 Hotel Efes
25 Hotel Kayseri
26 The Temenni Hill
   (Tea Garden)
27 Ürgüp Restaurant
28 Dam Restaurant
29 Bekir Restaurant
30 Öğün Restaurant
31 Kent Restaurant
32 Köşk Restaurant
33 Discoteque Harem
34 Discoteque Çırağan
35 Municipality

Kayseri Caddesi

Kayseri Caddesi

Mosque

Mosque

Mosque

In Üçhisar The tall rock riddled with holes which stands above all else in the valley is Üçhisar (EWCH-hee-sahr, Three Forts), east of Göreme. Besides the Club Med, Üçhisar has several small pensions.

In Avanos This town has several good hotels and pensions, and can serve as a base if Ürgüp, 10 km to the south, is full. The *Tusan Kızılırmak Moteli* (TOO-sahn KUH-zuhl-luhr-mahk, tel 99), is the local incarnation of the chain, with rooms for $21. Right in town by the river is the *Hotel Venessa* (tel 201), a big modern place with 72 rooms priced at $20 double. The Tourism Information Office (tel 360) is in the same building.

For pensions, explore the cluster right by the river at the opposite end of the bridge from the Venessa. The *Evim* (eh-VEEM) is right by the bridge; the *Kızılırmak* (tel 92) is several blocks from the bridge along the river; to find the *Üvez* (ew-VEHZ, tel 450), go along the riverside street to the end, then turn right and go 50 metres. Pension prices are $2 or $3 per person per night.

Places to Eat

Here we have a problem. Except in the better hotels, good food is surprisingly hard to come by in this farming region. Though most Turkish towns, even small ones, have at least modest restaurants serving very tasty food, the towns here seem to be exceptions. You will find cheap restaurants, but the food won't be wonderful.

The Büyük Otel and the Turban Motel tend to serve table d'hote meals as they cater to tour groups; try the Büyük first.

Ürgüp's fanciest restaurant is the *Ossiana*, on the main street near the Büyük Otel and the Tourism Office. Attractive enough in a simple way, the food is sometimes disappointing, but give it a try. Everything's better in the height of the tourist season (more turnover), and worse when business is slack.

Other, smaller, simpler restaurants near the main square may serve acceptable food in the height of the season. Also, there are serviceable small eateries in Avanos.

TOURING CAPPADOCIA

Drop in at Ürgüp's Tourism Office to arrange a taxi tour, and then plan to see the sights in this order: Göreme, Çavuşin, Zelve, Avanos, Sarı Han, Peribacalar Vadisi in one circuit; then a morning or afternoon excursion to the underground cities of Derinkuyu and Kaymaklı. You can go on to Aksaray for a look at the ancient churches of the Peristrema Valley (Ihlara). Still starved for Cappadocian scenes? Head south from Ürgüp to Soğanlı, 45 km along a rough road, through a long valley dotted with old villages, some with painted churches. Once you've seen it all, you can head to Kayseri for a short visit before heading onward.

Göreme Valley

Of all the Cappadocian valleys, Göreme is without doubt the most famous, and rightly so. Approaching from Ürgüp (eight km), the road winds up over a ridge, then descends into a maze of little valleys, ridges and cones. The rich bottomland at the base of each valley blazes with bright patches of green crops, or is dotted with tidy rows of grapevines. Halfway down the hill is the entrance to the national park which protects Göreme's rock-hewn wonders.

It's easy to spend most of a day walking the paths here, climbing stairways or passing through tunnels to reach the various churches. The paintings and frescoes in several churches – the Elmalı, Karanlık, Tokalı and Çarıklı – are outstanding. In between churches, the utter improbability of the landscape floods in upon you: the lovely, soft textures in the rock, the fairytale cave dwellings, the spare vegetation growing vigorously from the stark but mineral-rich soil.

Avcılar The village of Göreme (formerly called Avcılar), a mile past the national park, is small but busy with farm wagons and tractors. An occasional souvenir shop serves the travellers who wander through. If you take the time to explore Avcılar's winding streets, you will see many buildings – there's even a flour mill! – carved in the rock.

Çavuşin From Göreme village, the Avanos road leads north to Çavuşin, with its Church of John the Baptist near the top of the cliff which rises behind the village. A half-km north of the village, along the road, is the Çavuşin Church (look for the iron stairway).

A side road from Çavuşin heads up another valley five km to Zelve, which is almost as rich in churches and strange panoramas as Göreme itself. Zelve was a monastic retreat. Besides the rock churches (and a mosque) there is a small restaurant.

Avanos

Four kms past Çavuşin on the main road is Avanos, a town famous for alabaster carving. Workshops turn out ashtrays, lamps, chess sets, and other souvenirs carved from the colourful translucent stone. The town is astride the Kızılırmak, the 'Red River', known for its red dye used in pottery, ancient and modern. If you're not staying here overnight, Avanos is a good place to have lunch, or at least a çay break. Wander around the town a bit, looking in the workshops.

Sarı Han The Yellow Caravanserai (sah-RUH hahn) is six km east of Avanos along the eastern road back to Ürgüp. (There are three roads between Avanos and Ürgüp; be sure you're on the easternmost, which also passes the Peribacalar Vadisi.)

This Seljuk caravanserai looks more ruinous than it is because the finished stones of the walls were taken away for construction of a bridge in Avanos. The elaborate Seljuk portal is still in pretty

good shape, however. Inside, the *han* is on the standard plan with a large court where animals were loaded and unloaded, and a great hall where men and animals could escape the rigours of the weather. Above the portal is a *mescit*, or small mosque, which you can reach by climbing to the top of the walls and walking around. A self-appointed guide will no doubt appear to show you around, and perhaps to sell you an admission ticket.

Peribacalar Vadisi Also along this road is the *Peribacalari Vadisi*, the Valley of the Fairy Chimneys. Though many valleys hold collections of strange cones, these are the best formed and most thickly clustered. Most of the rosy rock cones are topped by flattish stones of a darker colour, which have in fact caused the formation of the cones. Being of a harder rock, the dark cap-stones sheltered the cones from the rains which eroded all the surrounding rock.

After the valley, the road returns to Ürgüp via its southern entrance.

Other Sights

Go to **Üçhisar** with a camera, and bring a lot of film. The place was almost tailor-made for dramatic and folksy photography. **Ortahisar** is not as dramatic, but equally folksy.

The Underground Cities

Göreme and Zelve are where the beauty is. But for sheer fascination and mystery, the places to see are the underground cities at Kaymaklı, 20 km south of Nevşehir along Hwy 41 (the road to Niğde), and at Derinkuyu, seven km further south.

The countryside here is one vast, flat steppe, without enchanting fairy chimneys or sensuously-carved valleys. Yet the stone is the same soft volcanic tuff, and it allowed early residents to develop the real estate cheaply. At Kaymaklı, an unprepossessing farming village of white houses and unpaved streets, an unimpressive little cave in a low mound leads down into a vast maze of tunnels and rooms. To find the entrance, look for signs, or ask for the *Yeraltı Şehri* (YEHR-ahl-tuh shehh-ree, Underground City).

A guide clicks on the electric lights and leads the way into the cool depths, and the feeling is one of entering a huge and very complex Swiss cheese. Holes here, holes there, 'windows' from room to room, paths going this way and that, more levels of rooms above and below. Without the guide and the electric wires, it would be fearfully difficult to find the way out again. If you wander off along another passage, separated from the group by only a few feet, you can hear what they say, you can converse with them, but you can't find your way back to them! Suddenly a foot comes into view, and you realize that they're on the next level, almost above your head!

The guide points out storage jars for oil, wine and water, communal kitchens blackened by smoke, stables with mangers, incredibly deep wells. Soon you no longer find it impossible to believe that tens of thousands of people could have lived here happily year-round, deep within the earth. It's even suspected that there were underground passages which connected Kaymaklı with its sister city of Derinkuyu, seven km away, though the tunnels have yet to be fully excavated.

Having seen Kaymaklı, you can try to catch a vehicle along the highway to Derinkuyu (deh-REEN-koo-yoo, Deep Well) for a look at another such city. It's more of the same.

IHLARA (PERISTREMA)

At the western edge of Cappadocia is the town of Aksaray, on the Konya road. South-east of Aksaray, along a rough road, is Ihlara, at the head of a beautiful valley once called the Peristrema gorge. The churches in this remote monastic area are not carved from the rock, but built of the local stone. Some contain interesting frescoes. The trip along the valley of the *Melendiz Suyu* stream is something of a mini-expedition, somehow wilder and more exciting than touring the beaten track. You can drive in to Ihlara, or take a dolmuş from Aksaray and hike along the valley.

Aksaray has two tourist hotels. The *Orhan Ağaçlı* (tel 4910), at the intersection of the E 5 and Hwy 73 (to Nevşehir), is quite a fancy place where doubles cost $35; and the *Ihlara Oteli* (tel 1842), downtown, has 64 rooms priced at $23 double. There are also the usual very modest lodgings found in Turkish towns.

NİĞDE

The Seljuks built Niğde (NEE-deh, altitude 1208 metres, population 40,000), and if you are passing through you might want to have a look at the Alaeddin Camii (1223), on the hill with the fortress; the Süngür Bey Camii, restored by the Mongols in 1335; the Ak Medrese (1409), now the town's museum; the Hüdavend Hatun Türbesi (1312), a fine example of a Seljuk tomb; and the Dış Cami, an Ottoman mosque with a carved mimber inlaid with mother-of-pearl.

Should you want to stay, Niğde can offer the *Merkez Turistik Oteli* (mehr-KEHZ too-rees-TEEK, tel 860), in the main square called Atatürk Meydanı, with 32 double rooms costing $30. This is the fancy one. There are, alternatively, very simple, cheap places.

KAYSERI

Once the capital of Cappadocia, Kayseri (KAHY-seh-ree, altitude 1068 metres, population 300,000), in the shadow of Erciyes Dağı (Mt Aergius, 3916 metres) is now a booming farm and textile centre. Beside the sleepy old conservative town surrounding the ancient black citadel, a city of modern boulevards lined with apartment blocks has risen in only a few years. These two aspects of Kayseri aren't completely comfortable together, and something remains of old Kayseri's conservative soul.

In Turkish folklore, the people of Kayseri are the crafty dealers. Though every merchant you meet in the bazaar will not fit this image, you are sure to be persecuted by at least one carpet dealer. Kayseri is at the centre of a region which produces many of Turkey's loveliest carpets, and you may do well shopping here. But if you don't buy, the rug merchant who has been following you for days will be there at the bus station, waving and weeping, as you pull out of town.

If you're passing through on your way to Cappadocia, take a few hours to tour Kayseri as it has many Seljuk buildings and a nice bazaar. Those heading east might want to see the sights, spend the night, and get an early start the next morning. Besides the sights in town, there are two superb Seljuk caravanserais north-east of the city, off the Sivas road (Hwy 45). Taxi drivers in Kayseri will quote you a price for a three or four-hour tour including both of them.

History
This was Hittite country, so its history goes way back. The first Hittite capital, Kanesh, was earlier the chief city of the Hatti. It's located at Kültepe, north-east of Kayseri on the Sivas road. There was probably an early settlement on the site of Kayseri as well, though the earliest traces which have come to light are from Hellenistic times.

Under the Roman emperor Tiberius (14-37 AD) the town received its name, Caesarea, and later became famous as the birthplace of St Basil the Great, one of the early Church Fathers. Its early Christian history was interrupted by the Arab invasions of the 600s and later.

The Seljuks took over in 1084, and held the city until the Mongols' arrival in 1243, except for a brief period when the Crusaders captured it on their way to the Holy Land. After almost a hundred years as part of the Mongol Empire, Kayseri's Mongol governor set up his own emirate

(1335) which lasted a mere 45 years. It was succeeded by another emirate, that of Kadı Burhaneddin, was then captured by the Ottomans, seized during the Ottoman interregnum by the Karamanid emirs, later taken by the Mamelukes of Egypt, and finally conquered by the Ottomans again in 1515, all in just over a hundred years. Those were exciting times in Kayseri.

Orientation & Transport
Kayseri receives one flight a week from Istanbul, and several daily trains from Ankara and Adana (see Ankara section for details). You can also take trains eastward to Sivas (3½ hours) and Erzurum (22 hours); the trains are not luxurious. The train between Kayseri and Malatya takes 10 hours, if it's on time; bus is much quicker. There are not good train connections north to the Black Sea; better to take the train to Sivas, then a bus to Samsun.

The railway station is at the end of İstasyon Caddesi, a kilometre from the citadel.

Buses run very frequently – at least every hour – between Kayseri and Ankara, a 4½-hour trip. You can also get convenient buses to Adana, and to Malatya and points east. There are several daily dolmuşes to Ürgüp.

Kayseri's bus terminal is at the western side of the town.

For orientation, use the black-walled citadel at the centre of the old town. The Tourism Information Office (tel (351) 11 190, 19 295) is right beside it at Kağnı Pazarı Honat Camii Yanı No 61.

Places to Stay – top end
The *Hotel Hattat* (hah-TAHT, tel 19 331, 19 829), Istanbul Cad. 1, is the best in town, with 67 doubles priced at $35. This is where the businessmen go. The older *Hotel Turan* (too-RAHN, tel 11 968, 12 506), Turan Cad. 8, is classed higher than the Hattat, but rightly charges less ($23)

for its 70 doubles; it has a roof terrace and a Turkish bath.

Places to Stay – mid-range

Right next to the bus terminal is the *Terminal Oteli* (TEHR-mee-NAHL, tel 15 846), Istanbul Cad. 176, with 21 modernish rooms for $16 double with private shower, $12 double with just a washbasin.

Places to Stay – bottom end

The *Hotel Sur* (SOOR, tel 19 545), Cumhuriyet Mahallesi, Uğur Sokak 12, opened only a few years ago, and offers good value for money. Doubles cost $5 (one large bed), or $6 with a private shower. The hotel is not far from the citadel, behind the city walls off Talas Caddesi. Walk south-east on Talas Caddesi from the citadel, with a remnant of the city walls on your right. Turn right after passing the wall, then right again, and you'll see the hotel. A similarly good choice is the *Hotel Kent* near Düvenönü Meydanı.

The *Hotel Seyhan* (SEHY-hahn, tel 23 489), Mimar Sinan Cad., Seyhan Sokak 6/D, not far from Düvenönü Meydanı, is on a quiet back street, an easy walk from the bazaar and most sights, and charges only $4 for a double room with washbasin.

Places to Eat

Kayseri is noted for a few special dishes, among them *pastırma* (from the same root-word as *pastrami*?), sun-dried beef coated with garlic and savoury spices. It has a very strong flavour, tends to stick in your teeth and despotically rule your breath for hours, but once you acquire the taste, you look forward to a return to Kayseri. Shops in the centre will sell it to you for picnics (try 100 grammes); before you buy, ask for a sample (*Bir tat, lütfen*, beer TAHT lewt-fehn, 'A taste, please').

Other Kayseri specialties include *sucuk* (soo-JOOK), a spicy sausage, *salam* (sah-LAHM), Turkish salami, *tulum peynir* (too-LOOM pehy-neer), hard cheese cured in a goatskin, and *bal* (BAHL),

honey. Few of these things, with the exception of pastırma, will appear on restaurant menus, so you must buy them in food shops for picnics.

The town's best restaurants are in the top hotels, the Hattat and the Turan. For cheaper, less elegant fare, the *İskender Kebap Salonu*, 27 Mayıs Cad. 5, is right by the citadel, one floor above street level; good döner kebap, good view of the busy street, low prices of about $2.50 for a meal.

The *Kardeşler Lokantası* is south of the İskender along 27 Mayıs Caddesi; it, and the nearby *Cumhuriyet Lokantası*, are equally good choices for dining.

The *Hacı Usta Lokanta ve Kebap Salonu*, Serdar Cad. 3 & 7, has two locations in the bazaar. To find them, walk from the citadel on 27 Mayıs Caddesi, pass Vatan Caddesi on the right, and then turn right onto Serdar Caddesi. Both these places are very simple, very cheap, and very tasty.

The *Divan Pastanesi* is a good, serviceable pastry shop on 27 Mayıs Caddesi a block south of the citadel; try it for breakfast or tea.

Things to See

The citadel (*hisar*), which now has a market within it, was built by Emperor Justinian in the 500s, and extensively repaired by the Seljuk Sultan Keykavus I around 1224. In 1486, the Ottoman Sultan Mehmet the Conqueror made major repairs. With Erciyes looming over the town, it's not surprising that the citadel should be made of black volcanic stone.

West of the citadel is Kayseri's tidy, shady bazaar, which you should definitely explore, fending off carpet dealers as you go.

Huant Hatun Camii

East of the citadel is a complex which includes the mosque (1228) of Huant Hatun, wife of the Seljuk Sultan Alaettin Keykubat, a medrese (1237), the tomb of

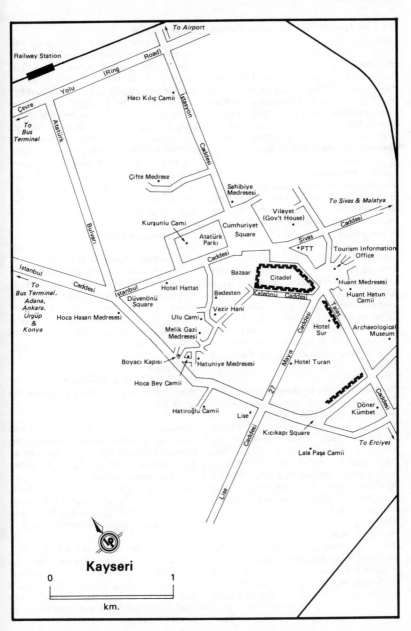

Kayseri

the lady herself, and bits of a Turkish bath.

Ulu Cami

Kayseri's Great Mosque (oo-LOO jah-mee) is near Düvenönü Meydanı. It was begun in 1135 by the Danışmend Turkish emirs, and finished by the Seljuks in 1205. There's been a lot of repair and 'restoration' over the centuries, but it's still a good example of early Seljuk style.

Sahibiye Medresesi

This theological school, now a museum, is at the north side of Cumhuriyet Meydanı, the large square by the citadel. It dates from 1267, and has an especially beautiful Seljuk portal.

Kurşunlu Cami

You can spot this Ottoman-style mosque by its lead-covered dome, unusual in old Kayseri, north of Istanbul Caddesi and west of Cumhuriyet Meydanı and Atatürk Parkı. Also called the Ahmet Paşa Camii after its founder, it was completed in 1585 to plans that may have been drawn, and were certainly influenced, by the great Sinan.

Gıyasiye & Şifaiye Medreseleri

These adjoining religious schools are sometimes called the Çifte Medrese, the Twin Seminary. They're located in a maze of narrow back streets north of the Kurşunlu Cami. Sultan Gıyaseddin Keyhüsrev I ordered the schools built, and they were finished by 1206. For much of their history they functioned as a combined theological school, medical college and clinic.

Hacı Kılıç Camii

North of the aforementioned Çifte Medrese, near İstasyon Caddesi, is the mosque (1249) of the Seljuk vezir Abdül Gazi, with some very fine Seljuk architectural detail, especially in the doorways.

Döner Kümbet

Among Kayseri's other Seljuk archaeological treasures are several türbes, or tombs. The Döner Kümbet (dur-NEHR kewm-beht, Revolving Tomb) is southeast of the citadel along Talas Caddesi about a kilometre. Though it doesn't (and never did) revolve, its cylindrical shape suggests turning, and as you view its marvellous and elaborate Seljuk decoration (1276), you will at least revolve around it. This was a lady's tomb. Nearby is another, the Sırçalı Kum'bet (1300s), which used to be covered in coloured tiles and topped by a pyramidal roof. You may spot other kümbets in and near Kayseri.

Archaeological Museum

The city's archaeological museum is out near the Döner Kümbet, to the east by the railroad tracks. The museum houses the finds from Kültepe, site of ancient Kanesh, including the cuneiform tablets which told historians much about the Hittite Empire. Hittite, Hellenistic and Roman statuary, plus exhibits of local ethnography, help to make it worth a visit.

Excursions

Besides the Seljuk buildings in the city, there are even better ones to see on the outskirts.

Caravanserais Haggle with a taxi-driver for an excursion to the **Sultan Han** and the **Karatay Han**, and you will probably end up with a figure of $10 or $12 for the entire car. If time and money are short, bargain for just the Sultan Han. If only money is short, try to find a bus which will drop you at the *han* (start early in the day!), and then trust luck to catch something back to Kayseri.

Head out on the Sivas road (Hwy 45). Twenty kilometres from Kayseri there is a left turning to **Kültepe**, site of ancient Kanesh. You may want to take a quick look at the site of this incredibly old Hittite city (2000 BC), but there's not a lot to see.

The Sultan Han is on the highway, 45 km north-east of Kayseri. Besides being a fine example of the Seljuk royal caravan lodging, it has been beautifully restored, so it is easy to appreciate the architectural fine points. The *han* was finished in 1236; restoration was carried out only a few decades ago. Don't let the locked gate worry you. Shortly after your car draws up, a boy will come running with the key and a booklet of tickets. Tour the inside, noticing particularly the elegant snake motif on the *mescid* (little mosque) arches; climb up to the roof if you like; but don't neglect a walk around the exterior as well. Note the lion-faced water spouts on the walls, and the plain towers of varying design.

If time is short, the Sultan Han will do nicely as an introduction to Seljuk Turkish caravanserais. But with more time, take your taxi to the Karatay Han, in a Turkish village now well off the beaten track. From the Sultan Han, head back toward Kayseri, and take the turning south or east to

Bünyan (Hwy 60). Pass through Bünyan toward Malatya, and about 30 km along there is a road on the right for Elbaşı. Follow this track five km to Elbaşı, and four km beyond to Karatay, also called Karadayı.

The Karatay Han, built in 1240 for the Seljuk vezir Emir Celaleddin Karatay, was once on the main east-west trade route. It was completely restored in the 1960s, and is yet another fine example of high Seljuk art. A visit to the Karatay Han gives you a glimpse into the life of a Turkish village as well.

Climbing Erciyes Mountaineers may like to know that there is a *Kayak Evi*, or mountain hut of 100 beds, 26 km south of Kayseri on the mountain road. Leave the city by the road to the airport (*havaalanı*) and the village of Hisarcık (14 km), and continue to Kayak Evi. Even if you don't plan to climb, the outing will give you a look at some spectacular scenery.

Black Sea Coast

Turkey's Black Sea coast is a unique area of the country, lush and green throughout the year with plentiful rainfall. Dairy farming, fishing and tea production are big industries, and this coast also produces bumper crops of tobacco (*tütün*), hazelnuts (filberts, *fındık*) and cherries (*kiraz*).

History

The coast was colonized by Milesians and Arcadians in the 700s BC, who founded towns at Sinop, Samsun and Trabzon. Later it became the Kingdom of Pontus. Most of Pontus's kings were named Mithridates, but it was Mithridates IV Eupator who gave the Romans a run for their money in 88-84 BC. Mithridates conquered Cappadocia and other Anatolian kingdoms, finally reaching Nicomedia (İznik), which was an ally of Rome. When Rome came to its defense, Mithridates pushed onward to the Aegean. The Roman response was hampered by civil war at home, but they drove into Cappadocia and Pontus later (83-81 BC), and Mithridates was forced to agree to peace based on pre-war borders.

In 74-64 BC, Mithridates was at it again, encouraging his son-in-law Tigranes I of Armenia to seize Cappadocia from the Romans. He tried, but the Romans conquered Pontus in response, driving Mithridates to flee and later commit suicide. The Romans left a small client kingdom of Pontus at the far eastern end of the coast, based on Trebizond.

The coast was ruled by Byzantium, and Alexius Comnenus, son of Emperor Manuel I, proclaimed himself Emperor of Pontus when the Crusaders sacked Constantinople in 1204. His descendants ruled this small empire until 1461, when it was taken by Mehmet the Conqueror.

While Alexius was in Trabzon, Samsun was under Seljuk rule; the Seljuks granted trading privileges to the Genoese. But when the Ottomans came, the Genoese burned Samsun to the ground before sailing away.

After World War I, the Ottoman Greek citizens of this region attempted to form a new Pontic state with Allied support. Turkish inhabitants, disarmed by the Allied occupation authorities, were persecuted by Greek guerilla bands which had been allowed to keep their arms. It was fertile ground for a revolt. Atatürk used a beaurocratic ruse to escape from the sultan's control in Istanbul, and landed at Samsun on 19 May, 1919. He soon moved to Amasya, and began to organize what would become the battle for independence.

Touring the Coast

Travelling along the coast from Istanbul east to Sinop is not easy by road, but much better by boat (see below), except that you miss Amasya. From Sinop east to the Soviet frontier the road is excellent and very scenic, though with little in the way of historical or artistic interest. The 360-km ride from Samsun to Trabzon can even be done in a day if you wish. You must take a few hours to see the sights in Trabzon, fabled Trebizond, before heading up onto the plateau and Erzurum, or eastward along the coast through the tea plantations to Rize and Hopa.

At Hopa, you can climb into the mountains to Artvin, a ride of exceptional beauty. But roads south and east from Artvin are not good, and may be impassable except in summer; public transport is scarce, as are hotel facilities. Plan to travel from Artvin to Kars or Erzurum only if you have a private car, or can stand long, bumpy bus rides.

Getting There & Getting Around

Among the best ways to explore the Black Sea coast is aboard the steamer which sails weekly, April through October (fortnightly November through March) from Istanbul to Trabzon. Leaving Istanbul at 10 am on Thursday, you steam overnight to Sinop (10 am Friday), onward to Samsun (10 pm Friday), Giresun (7.30 am Saturday) and finally Trabzon (1 pm Saturday); the return trip departs Trabzon at midnight Saturday, arriving Giresun (9 am Sunday), Samsun (12 midnight Sunday), Sinop (11 am Monday) and Istanbul (10 am Tuesday). Accommodation is not luxurious, but sufficient, and fares are moderate. The problem is reserving a place, as this 'mini-cruise' is popular, especially in the summer months. Talk with a Turkish Maritime Lines agency about reserving a bed.

Buses to and along the coast, as usual, are fast, frequent and cheap. Plan to take the bus to Samsun from Ankara (420 km), from Kayseri (450 km), or Sivas (340 km). On the eastern reaches of the coast, the route to take is between Trabzon and Erzurum via Gümüshane.

Turkish Airlines run two flights weekly between Istanbul and Samsun. There are also daily flights between Trabzon, Ankara and Istanbul.

Passenger train service to Samsun, what there is of it, is slow and inconvenient; everybody takes the bus.

AMASYA

On the way to Samsun, you may pass through Amasya (ah-MAHS-yah, altitude 412 metres, population 50,000), capital of the province of the same name, and one-time capital of the Pontic kings. Standing on the banks of the river Yeşilırmak, surrounded by high cliffs, Amasya is an old-time town with a number of things to see. Don't just pass through; stop for a meal or at least a glass of tea. The town can grown on you, and you may find yourself staying the night.

Places to Stay

The *Turban Amasya Oteli* (TOOR-bahn, tel 3134) is the best, with 36 rooms at $14

double. The only other hotel in this class is the *Saraçoğlu* (sah-RACH-oh-loo, tel Suluova 10, 783), 30 km north-west on the Samsun road.

Of the modest places, the *Apaydın Oteli* (AHP-ahy-duhn), on the main street, charges $4 for a double room without bath; the *Şehir* (sheh-HEER) right in the centre charges the same, or $5 double for a room with shower; toilets (the flat kind) down the hall only.

Places to Eat

Look for small restaurants in the narrow market streets off the main square (the one with the statue of Atatürk), such as the Çiçek Lokantası: very basic, but serviceable. For tea, go to the Belediye Parkı (beh-leh-DEE-yeh pahr-kuh, Municipal Park), just across the river from the main square, by the city hall (Belediye Sarayı). It's lovely and shady here.

Things to See

Despite its appearance as a small, sleepy provincial capital, Amasya has seen very exciting times. It was a Hittite town, but came into its own as the capital of Pontus. Several of the Pontic kings are buried in great tombs carved into the rock walls which surround the town. In Ottoman times, it was an important power-base when the sultans led military campaigns into Persia, and a tradition developed that the Ottoman crown prince should be taught statecraft in Amasya, and test his knowledge as governor of the province.

Walk around the town, admiring the old Ottoman houses along the river. There's a tidy little museum on the main street (8 to 12 noon and 1.30 to 5.30 pm, admission 6c), with artifacts from Pontic, Roman, Byzantine, Seljuk and Ottoman times, plus an ethnographic exhibit. In the garden is a Seljuk *türbe*, now containing some fairly disgusting mummies from Seljuk times found beneath the Burmalı Cami.

Nearby is the **Sultan Beyazıt Camii** (1486), Amasya's principal mosque, with its medrese and a nice garden. The **Burmalı Minare Camii** (BOOR-mah-LUH), Mosque of the Spiral Minaret, was built in 1242, a Seljuk construction. Other curious buildings include the **Bimarhane Medrese**, or Insane Asylum Seminary; presumably it was once a place for lunatics, and at another time a place for theological students, and not both at the same time. The **Gök Medrese Camii** (GURK mehdreh-seh), built in 1276, has a wonderfully ornate Seljuk doorway which was once covered in blue tiles. The **Beyazıt Paşa Camii**, finished in 1419, bears many similarities to the famous early-Ottoman Yeşil Cami in Bursa. The **Kapı Ağası Medresesi** (kah-PUH ah-ah-suh), or Seminary of the Chief White Eunuch (1488) is one of the few religious schools built on an octagonal plan.

The Tombs & Citadel You can see the rockhewn tombs from the town. Climb the path toward them and you'll come to the **Kızlar Sarayı** (kuhz-LAHR sah-rah-yuh, Palace of the Maidens). Though there were indeed harems full of girls here, the palace which stood on this rock terrace was that of the kings of Pontus and, later, the Ottoman governors.

Follow the path upward and you will reach the royal tombs of Pontus, cut deep in the rock as early as the 300s BC, and used for cult worship of the deified rulers.

Above the tombs, perched precariously on the cliffs, is the citadel (*hisar*), which can be reached by a path, or by road if you have a car. The remnants of wall date from Pontic times, repaired (of course) by the Ottomans. It's from here that an old Russian cannon is fired to signify the end of the fast-day during Ramazan. The view is magnificent.

SAMSUN

Burned to the ground by the Genoese in the 1400s, Samsun (sahm-SOON, population 200,000) has little to show for its long history. It is a major port and commercial centre, and the largest city on the coast. Your reason to stop here would be for a meal or a bed.

The bus and railway stations are one km east of the centre, about ½ km from one another. Come out of the terminal (either one) and cross the *Sahil Yolu* (Coast Road) so you can catch a bus heading west, into town.

There is a hotel in the bus terminal, called appropriately the *Terminal Oteli* (tel 15 519), with 44 doubles priced at $12. The *Büyük Samsun Oteli* (bew-YEWK, tel 10 750) is the town's status place to stay, right on the shore in the centre with 117 rooms, air conditioning and a swimming pool. Doubles go for $18 to $21, the higher price being for rooms with a sea view.

One block inland from the Büyük Samsun, on Kazım Paşa Caddesi (also called Bankalar Caddesi) is the small, modern *Hotel Burc* (BOORCH, tel 15 479), Kazım Paşa Cad. 36, with 38 rooms priced at $18 double. Nearby at Kazım Paşa Cad. 4 is the *Vidinli Oteli* (vee-deen-LEE, tel 16 050), with 65 rooms for $16 to $18 double. Cheaper hotels are in this district as well.

Kazım Paşa Caddesi is the main business street, with banks, restaurants and kebabci's, and the PTT.

SINOP

West of Samsun 150 km is Sinop (SEE-nohp, population 20,000), which enjoyed a long history as a port, beginning in Hittite times almost 4000 years ago. Successive empires made it a busy trading centre, but the Ottomans preferred to develop Samsun, and under them Sinop became subordinated to its eastern neighbour. Sinop holds memories of its prominence as a Seljuk port in the **Alaettin Camii** (1214), the **Alaiye Medrese** (now the museum), and the **Seyyit Bilal Camii**.

On the road between Samsun and Sinop you pass through Bafra (BAHF-rah), a tobacco-growing centre.

East from Samsun

Two of Anatolia's great rivers, the Kızılırmak and the Yeşilırmak, empty into the sea here, on either side of Samsun. The have built up fertile deltas which are now filled with corn and tobacco amidst Balkan scenes of bucolic contentment. Each house has a lush lawn from its dooryard to the roadway, and each lawn contains a fat cow.

ÜNYE

(EWN-yeh, population 30,000), 95 km east of Samsun, is a small port town. Five kms west of the town are numerous camping places along the beach. The *Belediye Çamlık Motel*, in a pine forest on the shore, is pleasant and inexpensive, with a decent restaurant and obliging service; doubles with bath and a sea view cost $8. There are other small hotels in the town such as the *Otel Ürer* (ew-REHR, tel 1729), with doubles at $9, mostly used by businessmen.

ORDU

(OHR-doo, population 54,000) is another fishing town and port, 70 km east of Ünye, with some nice old houses and the *Turist Oteli* (too-REEST, tel 1466), Sahil Caddesi 4, a bit noisy but not expensive.

GIRESUN

(GEE-reh-soon, population 47,000) was founded 3000 years ago. After the Romans conquered Pontus, they planted cherry trees which made the basis of an important industry which thrives to this day. One theory holds that the ancient name for the town, *Cerasus*, is the root for many of the names for the fruit – *cherry*, *cerise* (French), *kiraz* (Turkish) – as well as for the town's modern name. You can see the ruins of a medieval castle here, and stay overnight in the *Otel Giresun* (tel 2469, 3017), a modern hotel on the shore one block from the town hall (*Belediye Sarayı*), where doubles cost $11.

From Giresun, it's another 150 km to Trabzon.

TRABZON

Trabzon (TRAHB-zohn, population 110,000), earlier called Trebizond, and even earlier Trapezus, is an ancient town with a modern purpose. Iran's oil wealth has led to massive purchases of western goods, and many of these goods come to Trabzon by sea, continuing overland by lorry.

Though it is the 20th century oil boom which has given Trabzon new life, it actually performed a similar role in the 1800s; the trade at that time was mostly British. The English-speaking world still thinks of 'Trebizond' as some remote and romantic outpost, though its cosmopolitan days of traders, consulates and international agents are long past.

The main reasons for visiting Trabzon are to see the church of Aya Sofya (1200s), to poke around the old town, to visit Atatürk's lovely villa on the outskirts, and to make an excursion through the gorgeous alpine scenery to Sumela, a dramatic Byzantine monastery carved out of a sheer rock cliff.

Orientation

Trabzon's airport and bus terminal are east of town. The commercial and governmental centre is at Taksim Meydanı, on a hill above the port; go here to find hotels and restaurants, and the Tourism Information Office (tel (031) 12 722), Taksim Caddesi 31.

Places to Stay

Trabzon's hotels are in or near *Taksim Meydanı*, looming over the port. The best in town is the *Hotel Usta* (OOS-tah, tel 12 843), İskele Caddesi, Telgrafhane Sokak 1. Its 72 rooms cost $13 to $18 double. The nearby *Hotel Özgur* (urz-GEWR, tel 11 319) has 45 modern-ish rooms priced at $19 double. The *Horon Oteli* (hoh-ROHN, tel 11 199) is a 41-room place also on the square which charges $13 double.

Slightly cheaper, if not quite as fancy, are the other hotels around Taksim. The *Otel Kalfa* (KAHL-fah, tel 12 690),

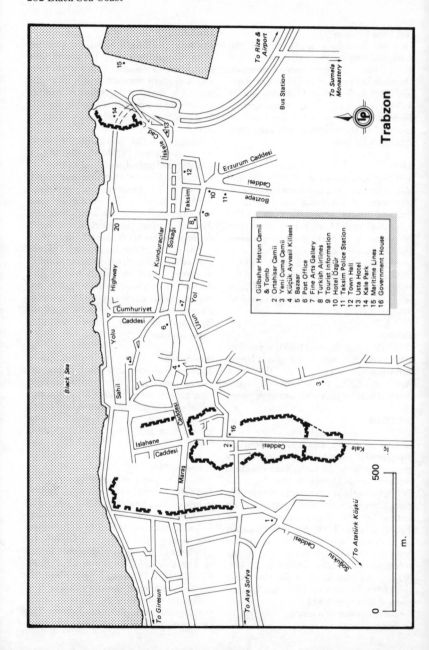

Trabzon

1 Gülbahar Hatun Camii
  & Tomb
2 Ortahisar Camii
3 Yeni Cuma Camii
4 Küçük Ayvasil Kilisesi
5 Bazaar
6 Post Office
7 Fine Arts Gallery
8 Turkish Airlines
9 Tourist Information
10 Hotel Özgür
11 Taksim Police Station
12 Town Hall
13 Usta Hotel
14 Kale Park
15 Maritime Lines
16 Government House

Belediye Karşısı (beh-leh-DEE-yeh kahr-shuh-suh, 'across from Town Hall'), is simpler and considerably cheaper at $7 double, yet it is only a few steps from the western end of the square. Even cheaper is the *Otel Benli* (behn-LEE), up the hill off the western end of the square behind the İskander Paşa Camii; a double room with washbasin and cold water costs $6.

Places to Eat

Look around Taksim, and you'll find this: the rooftop restaurant in the *Hotel Özgur* is nice, but don't eat there if it's not busy. The *Kuyu Restaurant* serves liquor, but tends to be a bit noisy (all men) in the evenings. The *Gaziantep Kebabcısı & Baklavacısı* has good, cheap kebaps and sweets.

Things to See

Trabzon has lots of old churches, many of which were converted to mosques after the Ottoman conquest of the city. If you stroll along the *Uzun Yolu* (oo-ZOON yoh-loo, Long Road) west from Taksim, you'll pass the remains of the **Küçük Ayvasıl Kilisesi**, the 9th-century basilica Church of St Anna. Then you cross the gorge of the Tabakhane Deresi (stream), turn left onto Kale Sokak, and enter the *Kale*, or citadel, centre of the old town. Within the ancient walls is the **Ortahisar Camii**, which began life in the 900s as the Panaghia Chrysokephalos church, Trebizond's chief place of worship (Aya Sofya was built later, and as a monastery church).

Aya Sofya

This church, named for the Holy Wisdom, is three km west of the centre on a terrace above the shore road, reachable by city bus or dolmuş. It's now a museum.

Built in the 1200s, its design was influenced by eastern Anatolian and Seljuk motifs, though the excellent wall paintings and mosaic floors follow the style of Constantinople. Tombs were built into the north and south walls of the church. Near the church is its bell tower.

Atatürk Villa

The **Atatürk Köşkü**, accessible by city bus or dolmuş, is south-west of the Kale, above the town with a fine view and lovely gardens. The white villa is built in a Black Sea style seen more in the Crimea. It's now a museum with various bits of Atatürk memorabilia.

Sumela Monastery

You can't miss this, as it is among the most impressive and fascinating sights in Turkey. You may have to hire a taxi to take you there, as dolmuşes are infrequent. With your own car, head out of Trabzon on the Erzurum road (E 100, or Hwy 65). At Maçka (31 km), turn left to Sumela (also called *Meryem Ana*, as the monastery was dedicated to the Virgin Mary). For the next 23 km, until you reach the monastery, you won't believe you're in Turkey. The road winds into dense evergreen forests, following the sinuous course of a rushing mountain stream. Mists may hang about the tops of the trees, and the air becomes much cooler. Peasant houses look like something out of central Europe.

At the end of the road is a small park, picnic and camping area, and the start of the trail up to the monastery. The trail which starts here is steep, but easy to follow, and is the one most people use. There is another trail further up the valley. Follow the unpaved road, then cross the stream and head upward. Climb through forests and alpine meadows, ascending 250 metres in 30 to 45 minutes. You get glimpses of the monastery as you climb, and finally arrive at the entrance where a guard will sell you a ticket.

Sumela was founded in Byzantine times (500s), and was abandoned (1923) after hopes were dashed of creating a new Greek Pontic state. The various chapels and rooms here are mere shells, or just facades, but with a good deal of fine fresco painting, some of it with gilt. It is a mysterious, eerie place, especially when mists swirl among the tops of the trees in the valley below.

East to Hopa

Frequent dolmuşes run along the coast, connecting the various towns and villages. You may find this method of transport more fun than the bus as it allows you to break your journey for a look around whenever you like.

RIZE

(REE-zeh, population 45,000), 75 km east of Trabzon, is at the heart of Turkey's tea plantation area. The steep hillsides which swoop upward from the coast are thickly planted with tea bushes. Local men and women bear large baskets on their backs, taking the leaves to the processing plants. The tea is cured, dried and blended here, then shipped throughout the country. A few years ago there was a shortage of processed tea (due, some say, to bad industry planning), and all Turkish eyes were on Rize. In this country, a shortage of tea could spell imminent social collapse.

HOPA

(HOH-pah, population 11,000) is the easternmost Turkish port on the Black Sea coast. It's a small town with friendly people, curious about the few tourists who pass through. The Soviet frontier is 30 km farther east; no reason to go there as you can't continue to Batum, a pretty seaside resort which was once an Ottoman town.

The *Hotel Papila* (PAH-pee-lah, tel 1440) is right on the shore, a surprisingly modern and comfortable lodging to discover in remote Hopa. Double rooms with bath cost $9 to $12.

ARTVİN

Hopa is in the province of Artvin (ahrt-VEEN), the capital of which is the town of that name (altitude 600 metres, population 15,000) high in the mountains south of the coast.

The ride to Artvin is wonderfully scenic

though something of a dead end: there is not much to see in the town, few tourist facilities, and infrequent and uncomfortable transport to any place except Hopa.

If you're up to it, take the 70-km ride into the mountains. As you approach Artvin you'll notice medieval castles guarding the steep mountain passes.

The bus station is at Çarşı, the market district at the foot of the hill which bears the town; you must take a dolmuş or taxi up five km to reach the centre, which is called Hükümet Konağı (hew-kew-MEHT koh-nah-uh, Government House). The Hükümet Konağı is a very modern building with a statue of Atatürk, and the PTT nearby.

Also near it is the *Otel Genye* (GEHN-yeh), Artvin's best – and an extremely modest – place to stay. The obliging staff will rent you a small, simple but tidy double room with washbasin for $3; shower and flat toilet are down the hall.

Beneath the hotel is the *Piknik Restaurant* (peek-NEEK), the local eating and drinking place. It's not great, it's what there is. Dine early. Most of the food is gone by 8 pm, as everyone in Artvin goes to bed early.

Onward

You can get to Erzurum from Artvin, bashing over the mountains for 215 km. The scenery is extremely beautiful, and even makes up for much of the discomfort.

As for getting to Kars, that's far more difficult, with infrequent dolmuşes, several stretches of execrable road, and very few services. By private car, fill your fuel tank in Artvin, pack some food, and start early in the day. By dolmuş, start early for Şavşat, then onward to Ardahan, 120 km from Artvin, where there is a hotel and restaurant. By private car you can make this by lunchtime, and Kars (another 110 km) by evening.

Eastern Anatolia

Eastern Turkey is a land of adventure, almost a magical place where each event of the day seems to take on the character of some fabled happening. You might go to bed at night disappointed because Mt Ararat was covered in cloud. But early next morning, the mountain will take you by surprise, intruding into your consciousness, shining in the sun outside your hotel window. Or you might be riding along a rough road and suddenly come upon the ruins of a medieval castle, not marked on any map, not described in any guidebook. Every day reveals some new notion of epic events.

The east is not as well-developed as western Turkey. You will see fewer tractors in the fields, more draught animals. Instead of machinery, you might come across farmers threshing and winnowing in the ancient manner.

The people are no less friendly than in other parts of Turkey. But they are not, generally speaking, used to seeing and dealing with foreigners (except in the hotels and tourist offices). It may take a little more time for the friendliness of the adults to emerge. Not so the children. Every single one will simply *have* to find out where you come from, and what language you speak.

Be prepared for the distances. You may ride for hours to get from one town to the next. And when you get to that town, there may not be many hotels to choose from. Travelling in eastern Turkey is certainly not as comfortable as in the west. But if you are adaptable and out for adventure, this is the place to find it.

Touring the Region

The eastern mountains and high plateaux are subject to long and severe winters. I don't recommend travel out east except from May through September, and preferably in July and August. If you go in May or September, be prepared for some quite chilly nights.

Most visitors touring this part of the country make a loop through it. Such a trip might follow this itinerary: from Kayseri or Adana, head for Adıyaman, then Kâhta, to see Nemrut Dağı, then to Diyarbakır for its ancient walls and mosques. Head east through Bitlis and around the southern shore of Van Gölü (Lake Van), stopping to see the Church of the Holy Cross on the island of Akdamar, before reaching the city of Van. Then head north to Ağrı, and east to Doğubayazıt to see Mt Ararat and also the İşak Paşa Sarayı, the dramatic Palace of Ishak Pasha. From Doğubayazıt head north to Kars to see the ruins of Ani, then to Erzurum. At Erzurum you can catch a plane westward, or toil through the mountains to Artvin, or head for the Black Sea coast at Trabzon, or start the return journey westward to Sivas and Ankara. This itinerary, from Kayseri to Van to Kars to Erzurum to Sivas, is about 2500 km, and would take a minimum of one week to complete; better, two weeks.

Getting There

If you're touring by public transport, you may want to consider flying to or from the eastern region. Buses, as always, go everywhere; there are even direct Istanbul-Erzurum buses. Though there are some trains, they're not usually preferable to the bus.

By Air Turkish Airlines has these flights to the east (per week): between Istanbul/Ankara and Diyarbakır (8), Elazığ (3), Erzurum (7), Gaziantep (4), Malatya (2), Trabzon (14), Van (3). Make your flight reservations as early as possible.

By Bus Services to and from Ankara are frequent. Routes running east-west are generally not a problem, but service north-south can be infrequent, so allow time and check departures early on.

By Train From Ankara via Kayseri, there are two major eastern rail destinations: Erzurum and Van. The Erzurum line goes on to Kars and the Soviet frontier, with a connecting train to Moscow. The Van line goes on to Iran, with a connection (sometimes) to Tabriz and Tehran. South of Elazığ, this line branches for Diyarbakır and Kurtalan. The far southern line along the Syrian frontier to Nusaybin is not of much use to tourists.

Don't expect any of these trains to be on time; they may be hours late.

To Sivas & Malatya The journey from Kayseri to Sivas is not bad, taking about 4½ hours. It's another 5½ hours from Sivas to Malatya, and the trains either depart Sivas before dawn, or arrive in Malatya around midnight, so it's not convenient service.

To Erzurum From Istanbul and Ankara, trains include the *Doğu Expresi* (doh-OO), which hauls sleeping cars, a diner and regular coaches, and takes about 20 hours, overnight, between Kayseri and Erzurum. Several trains without sleeping cars, the *Mehmetçik Expresi* among them, make the trip in the same amount of time. The portion from Erzurum to Kars takes about seven hours by train; it's about four hours by bus.

To Van The best train on this route is the *Vangölü Ekspresi* (VAHN-gur-lew) which, at the best of times, connects Istanbul and Tehran. From Kayseri it proceeds, daily, to Sivas, Malatya, Elazığ and Tatvan, hauling couchette cars, coaches and a dining car. At Tatvan, 2nd class passengers walk aboard a lake steamer; those in 1st class seats or couchettes can stay in their coach as the whole thing is taken aboard the boat for the trip to Van, at the eastern end of the lake. The journey from Kayseri to Malatya takes 9½ hours, from Malatya to Tatvan another 9½ hours. The steamer-cruise across the lake is yet another four hours.

To Diyarbakır The railway branches south of Elazığ, with the southern line going to Diyarbakır and Kurtalan. The *Güney Ekspresi* runs from Istanbul, Ankara, Kayseri and Malatya to Diyarbakır, and will carry you from Malatya to Diyarbakır in six hours, from about 2 am to 8 am; there is a more convenient afternoon train, however.

SİVAS

The highway comes through Sivas, the railway comes through Sivas, and over the centuries the dozens of invading armies have come through Sivas, often leaving the town in ruins when they left. It started life, so far as we know, in Roman times under the name Megalopolis, later changed to Sebastea, which the Turks shortened to Sivas. Today it is a fairly modern and unexciting place, full of farmers, yet at its centre are some of the finest Seljuk buildings ever erected. And outside Sivas, deep in the countryside, is a Seljuk masterpiece hidden among the hills.

In recent times, Sivas (SEE-vahss, altitude 1300 metres, population 175,000) gained fame as the location for the Sivas Congress, which opened on September 4, 1919. Atatürk came here from Samsun and Amasya, seeking to consolidate the Turkish resistance to Allied occupation and partition of the country. He gathered as many delegates, from as many parts of the country as possible, and confirmed decisions which had been made at a congress held earlier in Erzurum. These two congresses were the first breath of the revolution, and heralded the War of Independence.

Orientation

The centre of town is Konak Meydanı; near it are most of Sivas's important sights, and also the Tourism Information Office (tel (4771) 3535, 2850), in the Vilayet Konağı (vee-lah-YEHT koh-nah-uh), the provincial Government House.

Places to Stay

Not much fancy in town, just the *Köşk Oteli* (KURSHK, tel 1150), Atatürk Caddesi 11, with 44 doubles-with-bath priced at $19 to $21. The *Sultan Oteli* (sool-TAHN, tel 2986), Belediye Sokak, has 30 double rooms which cost $12 with shower, $11 without. There are cheaper places, but they're pretty basic.

Things to See

The Çifte Minare Medrese has, as its name explains, a pair (*çift*) of minarets. Today, that's about all it has, the medrese building itself being long ruined. It was commissioned by the Mongol vezir who ruled here, and finished in 1271. It is among the greatest monuments of the Seljuk architectural style.

Near the Çifte Minare is the Mehmet Paşa Camii (1580), an Ottoman work.

Across the street from the Çifte Minare is the Darüşşifa, or Şifaiye Medresesi, a hospital medical school built in the same year as the Çifte Minare, by Sultan Keykavus I of the Seljuks, who chose to be buried here. His tomb is just to the right of the entrance. Inside, the court has four *eyvans*, or niche-like rooms; note the remnants of tilework.

Across the square is the Bürüciye Medresesi, built in 1271 (a busy year in Sivas!) by Muzaffer Bürücirdi, who is entombed in it (inside, to the left, with the fine tilework).

Sivas's other sights are south-east of Konak Meydanı along Cumhuriyet Caddesi.

The Ulu Cami, or Great Mosque (1197) is Sivas's oldest building of significance, a large room with a forest of fifty columns. The brick minaret was added later.

Further along Cumhuriyet Caddesi is the Gök Medrese, or Blue Seminary, built in that bumper year of 1271 at the behest of Sahip Ata, the same fellow who funded the Sahip Ata mosque complex in Konya. Although built to the traditional Seljuk medrese plan, in this one the fancy embellishments of tiles, brickwork designs and carving are not just on the doorway,

but on windows and walls as well. The blue tilework gave the school its name, *gök* (sky) being an old Turkish word for 'blue'.

DIVRIĞI

South-east of Sivas, 170 km over rough roads (but also on the rail line) lies Divriği (DEEV-ree, population 15,000), a town hidden away in a fertile valley and very rarely visited by foreign tourists. Above the town, a ruined castle stands guard over two magnificent Seljuk buildings, the Ulu Cami, or Great Mosque, and the Darüşşifa, or hospital. Both were built in 1228 by Ahmet Şah, the local emir, and his wife, the lady Fatma Turan Melik. They've been beautifully restored and preserved, and there they sit, miles from anywhere, a wonderful work of art hidden away in the boondocks.

Getting There

With your own car, you can drive in and out; there is no road through. Otherwise, inquire about buses and dolmuşes along the route from Sivas to Kangal (kahn-GAHL), Çetinkaya (chet-EEN-kah-yah) and Divriği.

The rail line from Sivas to Erzurum passes through Divriği, and if you catch the morning Mehmetçik Ekspresi you should arrive at a reasonable hour. Another train, which runs four days a week, departs Sivas before dawn. But as both these trains may be late, you may in fact have a pleasant day trip, with return trains to Sivas coming through in the late afternoon and evening. You may, of course, continue eastward by train from Divriği, to Erzurum, about 6½ hours away.

The Divriği railway station is about two kms from the Ulu Cami.

Things to See

The portal of the Ulu Cami is simply incredible, with geometric patterns, medallions, luxuriant stone foliage and intricate Arabic-letter inscriptions in a richness that simply astonishes. It is the sort of doorway which only a provincial emir, with more money than restraint, would ever conceive of building. In a large Seljuk city, this sort of extravagance would have been ridiculed as lacking in taste. Here in Divriği, it's the wonderful, fanciful whim of a petty potentate shaped in stone.

Adjoining the Ulu Cami is the hospital, plainer and simpler except for its requisite elaborate portal. The octagonal pool in the court has a spiral run-off, similar to the one in Konya's Karatay Medresesi, which allowed the soothing tinkle of running water to break the silence of the room.

Ahmet Şah's tomb is near the Ulu Cami, as are several earlier ones from 1196, and another dating from 1240.

The town is nice, and old-fashioned, its houses still uncrowded by modern construction.

NEMRUT DAĞI

The temples atop 2000-metre-high Nemrut Dağı (NEHM-root dah-uh) are certainly unique. Though the world has many larger and more elaborate temples, none is quite like Nemrut in its megalomania. On a bare mountaintop in south-eastern Anatolia, a petty pre-Roman king cut two ledges in the rock, filled them with colossal statues of himself and the gods (his 'relatives'), then ordered an artificial mountain peak of crushed rock fifty metres high to be piled between them. The king's tomb may well lie beneath those tons of rock. Nobody knows.

In fact, nobody knew anything about Nemrut Dağı until 1881, when a geologist making a survey was amazed to come across a remote mountaintop full of statues. Archaeological work didn't begin until 1953, when the American School of Oriental Research undertook the project.

The story they read in the inscriptions is this: in 80 BC, Mithridates Callinicus proclaimed himself King of Commagene and set up his capital at Arsameia, near what is now the village of Eski Kâhta.

The Seleucid successors of Alexander the Great, who once ruled south-eastern Anatolia, were on the decline. But to solidify his legitimacy, Mithridates (himself of Persian royal ancestry) married a Seleucid princess. Their son, Antiochus I Epiphanes (64-32 BC), ruled his small but rich principality in grand style, signing a non-aggression treaty with Rome, and acting as a buffer state at the edge of the empire. It was Antiochus who ordered the building of the artificial mountaintop and the temples. Along with statues of himself and his father, Antiochus commissioned colossal statues of the Hellenistic and Persian gods who were his 'ancestors'. Earthquakes have toppled the heads from most of the statues, but many of the colossal bodies sit silently in rows, and the two-metre-high heads watch from the ground. It's something to see.

Getting There

The nearest city of any size is Malatya (mah-LAHT-yah, altitude 900 metres, population 180,000), which has rail, air and bus connections (see above). A road is being cut through the mountains directly from Malatya to Nemrut Dağı, but until it is finished the easiest access is via Adıyaman, Kâhta and Eski Kâhta. If you can get a bus from Malatya directly to Kâhta, do so; otherwise, change buses or stay the night in Adıyaman (ah-DUH-yah-mahn, altitude 725 metres, population 55,000) There are several motels: see below. There is also a Tourism Information Office (tel (8781) 1008) in the Hükümet Konağı (hew-kew-MEHT koh-nah-uh, Government House), on the ground floor.

Minibus tours run to Nemrut Dağı from Adıyaman and Kâhta (ky-YAH-tah, population 17,000), and you will have no trouble finding out about them. Every citizen of these two towns knows that the Nemrut tours are the reason any foreigner is in town. To hire a minibus from Kâhta for the ride to the top of Nemrut will cost about $40; for the complete tour including Nemrut, Arsameia and Yeni Kale, figure

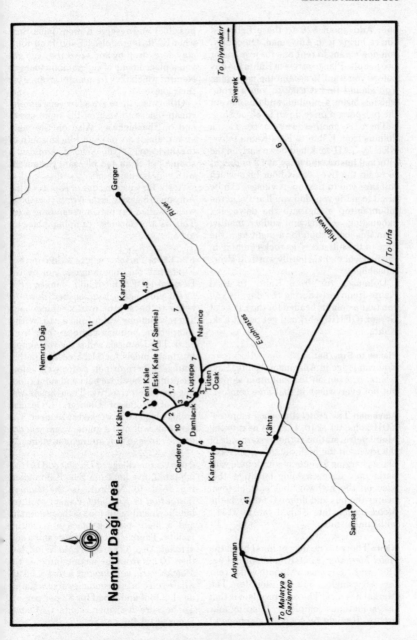

Nemrut Dağı Area

To Diyarbakır

Siverek

Highway

6

To Urfa

Gerger

River

Karadut

4.5

Nemrut Dağı

11

7

Narince

Euphrates

Eski Kähta

Yeni Kale

Eski Kale (Ar Sameia)

1.7

3

7 Kustepe 7

Tüten Ocak

3

2

10 Damlacık

Cendere

4

Karakuş

10

Kähta

41

Adıyaman

Samsat

To Malatya & Gaziantep

$58. Add about $20 to these figures if you're hiring it in Adıyaman. Obviously, you don't want to rent one for just one or two people. Plan to arrive in Kâhta the day before you want to ascend the mountain. You should find it easy to join a group which is hiring a minibus, and this can cut the per-person price down to $3 or $5.

There is another way to go. Get a dolmuş from Kâhta to Eski Kâhta (ehss-KEE ky-YAH-tah), bed down early in the informal hostel, and arise at 12 midnight to begin the five– or six-hour hike which will take you to the top. A villager can be hired to guide you, and you'll arrive at the mountaintop along with the dawn. It's exhausting, exciting, and wildly romantic. Plan this expedition for a night near the time of the full moon, as rock-climbing in the black of night is hardly worth it. Bring a flashlight.

Dolmuşes run from Kâhta to Eski Kâhta frequently during the day; or you can take a dolmuş headed for the village of Gerger (GEHR-gehr) and get out at Eski Kâhta.

Places to Stay/Eat

You can lodge in Adıyaman, Kâhta, Eski Kâhta, or even on the mountain slope – but not everywhere in the same comfort.

Adıyaman The *Motel Antiochos* (ahn-tee-YOH-kohs, tel 1240, 1184) is next to the Mobil petrol station at the western side of the town, on the highway. It's a 43-room place charging $18 per night, double with bath; they have camping facilities, too. Also on the highway, but east of town nearer the bus and dolmuş station, is the *Motel Arsemia* (ahr-SEEM-yah, tel 3131), with similar rates.

Kâhta There is one decent hotel here, the *Hotel Merhaba* (MEHR-hah-bah, tel 98, 139), with 28 rooms-with-bath which rent for $6 single, $12 a double. The Merhaba is nice. The only problem is that it is sometimes completely filled by tour groups. It might be good to telephone (if possible) and reserve a room for a time when Kâhta is groupless. Even if you don't stay here, drop by and see if they can get you a place in one of the minibus tours to Nemrut which they frequently arrange for their guests.

Otherwise, there are a few very simple, cheap places to stay on the main street and on the highway. Also on the main street, about six or eight blocks south of the highway, is the *Şehir Lokantası*, a simple but clean and pleasant restaurant with very friendly staff.

At the far western edge of Kâhta, on the Adıyaman highway, is the *Nemrut Camping*, with a walled car park and camping area. This is the fanciest camping place in town.

Eski Kâhta This tiny village 25 km north of Kâhta has one lodging, run by the Demiral (DEH-meer-ahl) family. For $2.50 per person you can bed down (it helps to have your own sleeping bag). There's running water from a can. With a campervan, you can camp in their front yard. The Demirals will serve you simple but tasty meals for $1.25 each, whether you sleep here or not; order well before mealtime. They have beer and soft drinks, but no wine or spirits. Their house was that of Professor Doerfer, a German archaeologist who worked at Nemrut. The Demirals will find a guide whom you can employ to lead you up the mountain.

Other At the village of Damlacık (DAHM-lah-juhk), five km from Eski Kâhta along the road to Nemrut, is the *Bahçeli Restaurant ve Kamping*. Expect good tea but rough-and-ready food in the restaurant, and a mere parking place as camping facility. There is running water and a sort of toilet. Also, 35 km from Eski Kâhta, less than 10 km from the mountaintop, is the *Motel Nemrut ve Camping*, a sort of hostel where you can find running water, a simple meal, a roof and a bed for $2 per person. To be sure it's open, contact Mustafa Deniz at tel 459 in Kâhta.

Things to See

If you take a minibus tour to Nemrut, everything will be taken care of. But some tips are in order for those who intend to drive their own car, or to hike from Eski Kâhta.

To Eski Kâhta

Rumour has it that the minibus tour people in Kâhta have tried to make it difficult for people to see the mountain on their own by removing some highway signs. For instance, you won't see any signs marking the way to Eski Kâhta; you must follow the ones which point to Nemrut and Gerger. Rest assured that you can easily do it on your own.

Dolmuşes from Kâhta to Gerger usually pass by Eski Kâhta. The dolmuş garage is at the western end of Kâhta, at the base of the hill; look for the sign reading 'Kâhta – Gerger'.

If you are driving, fill your fuel tank in Kâhta. There are no fuel stations after this. In emergencies, villagers may be able to sell you a few litres. It's a good idea to have some snacks – biscuits, dried fruits and nuts – and a bottle of water. Tramping around ruins is hot work, and you'll be very grateful for these simple supplies.

It's 24 km from Kâhta to Eski Kâhta. After 15 km you come to a fork in the road, with no sign ! Take the right fork.

The road from Kâhta passes through the villages of Karakuş and Cendere, and the sights begin 10 km after leaving Kâhta. A mound by the roadside, marked with columns, holds the graves of royal ladies from the Kingdom of Commagene.

Nineteen km from Kâhta, five km before Eski Kâhta you'll cross a Roman bridge built in honour of Emperor Septimius Severus (194-211 AD), his wife and sons. Of the four original columns (two at either end), three are still standing.

As you leave the bridge, a sign points to the right for *Nemrut Dağı* and *Gerger*. Even though there's no mention of Eski Kâhta, this road to the right is the one you want.

Yeni Kale You approach Eski Kâhta along the valley of a stream called the Kâhta Çayı. Opposite the town are the ruins of a Mameluke castle (1300s), now called **Yeni Kale** (yeh-NEE kah-leh, New Fortress) which you can explore. It bears some Arabic inscriptions; the Mamelukes were originally a Turkic people, but they were assimilated into Egyptian society.

Eski Kâhta to Nemrut

Seeing Nemrut in the early morning is a thrill, and you should plan your visit for that time if you visit in July or August, as it will be blazing hot during most of the day. At other times of year, be advised that it can be chilly and gusty at the very top in the early morning. It would be a shame to make your way up, and then not be able to spend some time at the summit due to insufficient clothing.

Those planning to ascend on foot at night should have warm clothing at any time of year.

The 45-km ride from Eski Kâhta to the summit takes about 1½ hours (about two hours if you leave from Kâhta). Road crews are working to smooth the path, and your time may well be faster. Along the way are several interesting places to stop.

Just after leaving Eski Kâhta, the road passes through a dramatic, beautiful gorge spanned by an ancient bridge which appears to be Seljuk in design.

Eski Kale About a km up the road from Eski Kâhta, a turnoff to the left takes you (two km) to Eski Kale, the ancient Commagene capital of Arsameia. Walk up the path from the car park, and you'll come to a large stela with a female (?) figure on it; further along are two more stelae, a monumental staircase, and behind them an opening in the rock leading down to a cistern.

Another path leads from the first path to the striking stone relief which portrays the founder of Commagene, Mithridates I Callinicus, shaking hands with the god

Heracles. Next to it is a long inscription in Greek, and to the right is a tunnel descending through the rock. The locals will tell you the tunnel goes all the way to the valley floor below, though it has not been cleared of the centuries of rubble yet.

Above the relief on the level top of the hill are the foundations of Mithridates' capital city. The view is magnificent from here. If you stop at Arsameia on your way down from Nemrut, this is the perfect site for a picnic.

Along the Road Driving upward from Eski Kale, you pass through **Damlacık** (three km), with its humble restaurant and camping place, then **Kuştepe** (seven km), then **Tüten Ocak** (three km). Near here a road goes right (south), back to Hwy 59 and Kâhta.

Seven km east of this junction is the hamlet of **Narince**, and another seven km east of Narince is a turning to the left marked for Nemrut, which you want to take; were you to continue straight on, you'd end up in the village of Gerger.

Continue on up the mountain through the hamlet of **Karadut**, five km from the last turning. This length of the road is being paved in stone blocks, and it's a welcome change from the bone-jangling rough stretch. On the far (north) side of Karadut is the *Motel Nemrut* (see above) and its camping area, and three km beyond the village is a tea house. From here it is less than eight km to the summit. You're well above treeline when you climb the final ridge and pull into the car park at the summit.

Just up from the car park is a ruined stone house where a man sells hot tea, soft drinks and souvenir booklets. Beyond him is the pyramid of stones; it's a hike of less than a kilometre (15 or 20 minutes) over the broken rock to the western temple. Sometimes donkeys are on hand to carry you, but this is not much help since staying on the donkey is almost as difficult as negotiating the rocks on your own.

At the Top At the western temple, note the bas reliefs as well as the colossal statues. On the west side the bodies have mostly been tumbled down along with the heads. But on the eastern terrace the bodies are largely intact, except for the fallen heads, which seem more badly weathered than the heads at the west; on the backs of the eastern statues are inscriptions in Greek.

That flat space with an 'H' at its centre is a helipad, which accepts the arrival of the wealthy, the important and the fortunate.

Onward to Diyarbakır

From Kâhta your next destination may be Diyarbakır, the most important city in south-eastern Turkey. On this ride you will enter that fabled cradle of civilisation, the watershed of the Tigris (*Dicle*, DEEJ-leh) and the Euphrates (*Fırat*, fuh-RAHT) rivers. The shortest route is east from Kâhta to Çaylarbaşı (29 km), and then 11 km more to Hwy 6. Turn left (east) at the highway, and travel 23 km to Siverek, and another 90 km to Diyarbakır, a total distance of 153 km.

There are other routes. It's 265 km between Malatya and Diyarbakır, On the way between these two cities you will pass by the modern town of Elazığ (EHL-lah-zuh).

Should you take the southern route, stops along the way include Gaziantep – without any significant 'tourist attractions' – and Urfa (OOR-fah), onetime capital of the Crusader Principality of Edessa. If you go this way, stop in Urfa for a look at the pretty **Abdürrahman Medresesi** with its ancient pool full of fish, and the **Halil Medresesi**, also by the pool.

DİYARBAKIR

The Tigris (*Dicle*) flows by the mighty black walls of Diyarbakır (dee-YAHR-bah-kuhr, altitude 660 metres, population 240,000). As with many Turkish cities, this one has grown beyond its ancient walls only in the last few decades.

Farming, stock-raising, some oil prospecting and light industry provide Diyarbakır with its income.

The city prides itself especially on its watermelons. 'In olden times', states a brochure printed up for the annual Watermelon Festival (held in late September), 'our watermelons had to be transported by camel as they weighed 90 or 100 kilograms. They were carved with a sword and sold in the market'. The brochure goes on to say that these days the prize-winning melons at the festival weigh a 'mere' 40 to 60 kilograms!

Today this city, lying in the midst of a vast, lonely plain, is like a desert oasis full of traders. Many of the men wear the traditional baggy trousers called *salvar* (SHAHL-vahr), and older women have black head coverings which often serve unofficially as veils. Visiting men from Syria and Iraq have the long robes (*jallabiya*) and headscarves (*keffiye*) of Arab lands, and the women may even be in purdah, wearing the black *chadoor*.

The tawdry chaos of signs at the city's centre, the narrow alleys, the mosques in the Arab style with black-and-white banding in the stone – all these serve to give Diyarbakır a foreign, frontier feeling.

History

Considering that Mesopotamia, the land between the Tigris and Euphrates valleys, saw the dawn of the world's first great empires, it's no surprise that Diyarbakır's history begins with the Hurrian Kingdom of Mitanni (circa 1500 BC), and proceeds through domination by the civilisations of Urartu (circa 900 BC), Assyria (1356-612 BC), Persia (600-330 BC), Alexander the Great and his successors the Seleucids. The Romans took over in 115 AD, but because of its strategic position the city changed hands numerous times until it was conquered by the Arabs in 639. Until then it had been known as Amida, but the Arabs settled it with the tribe of *Beni Bakr*, who named their new home *Dıyar Bakr*, 'The Realm of Bakr'.

I'd like to make this city's history simple for you, and say that when it was conquered by the Seljuks (1085) or the Ottomans (1515) it became a peaceful place, but this isn't so. Because it stands right in the way of invading armies from Anatolia, Persia and Syria, it got clobbered a lot more. It is still a bit unsettled, for south-eastern Turkey has a large Kurdish population. The authorities in Ankara want the Kurds, who are Muslims, to assimilate, and will not permit any talk of secession. Among the Kurds there are nationalists who dream of a Kurdish state encompassing the areas in Turkey, Syria, Iraq and Iran where there are large populations of Kurds.

Orientation

Though the city has grown, your concern is with the old part within the walls, except for the bus and rail stations west of the old city.

Old Diyarbakır has a standard Roman town plan, with the rough circle of walls pierced by four gates at the north, south, east and west. From the gates, avenues travel to the centre, where they all meet. Since Roman times, several sections of wall have been razed, and a few new gates opened.

The railway station (*Gar*) is at the western end of İstasyon Caddesi. From the station, this street travels east to the Urfa Kapısı (OOR-fah kah-puh-suh, Edessa Gate), the city's eastern gate. Inside the walls, the continuation of İstasyon Caddesi is named Melek Ahmet Caddesi, or sometimes Urfa Caddesi.

The bus station (*Otogar*) is north-east of the city where Elazığ Caddesi (also called Ziya Gökalp Bulvarı) intersects the highway. Travel along Elazığ Caddesi to the centre and you will pass the *Turist Oteli* just before penetrating the walls at the Dağ Kapısı (DAAH kah-puh-suh, Mountain Gate), the northern gate, sometimes also called the *Harput Kapısı*. From this gate, Gazi Caddesi leads to the centre.

The Tourism Information Office (tel

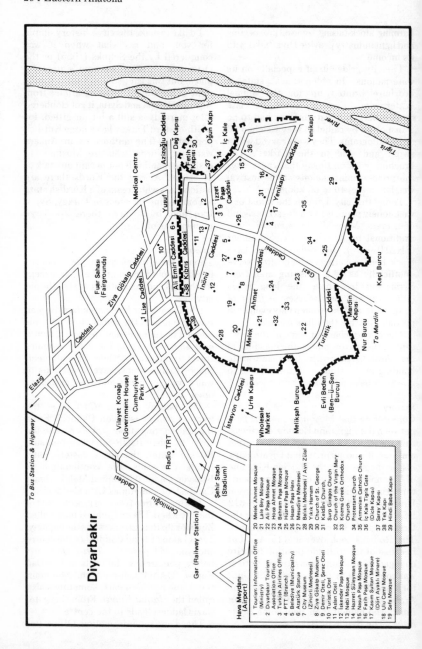

Diyarbakır

1 Tourism Information Office (Ministry)
2 Diyarbakir Tourism Association Office
3 Turkish Airlines Office
4 PTT (Branch)
5 Belediye (Municipality)
6 Hasan Paşa Hanı
7 Atatürk Statue
8 City Museum
9 Ziya Gökalp Museum
10 Demir Otel, Saraç Oteli, Turistik Otel
11 Aslan Oteli
12 İskender Paşa Mosque
13 Nebi Mosque
14 Hazreti Süleyman Mosque
15 Nasuh Paşa Mosque
16 Fatih Paşa Mosque
17 Kasim Sultan Mosque (Dört Ayaklı Minare)
18 Ulu Cami Mosque
19 Safa Mosque
20 Melek Ahmet Mosque
21 Lale Bey Mosque
22 Ali Paşa Mosque
23 Hoca Ahmet Mosque
24 Behram Paşa Mosque
25 Hüzrev Paşa Mosque
26 Mesudiye Medresesi
27 Mesudiye Medresesi (Zinciri Medresesi)
28 Balikli Medresesi / Ayn Zilal
29 Yikik Hamam
30 Church of St. George
31 Keldari Church, Suru Giragos Church
32 Church of the Virgin Mary
33 Kozma Greek Orthodox Church
34 Protestant Church
35 Armenian Catholic Church
36 İç Kale Tigris Gate (Dicle Kapisi)
37 Saray Kapisi
38 Tek Kapi
39 Hindi Baba Kapisi

(8311) 12 173, 17 840) is in the new city north of the walls at Lise Caddesi 24, Onur Ap. Ask for 'LEE-seh jah-deh-see', which runs west from Elazığ Caddesi about three blocks north of the Dağ Kapısı. The office is about 3½ blocks along.

Places to Stay

Diyarbakır's hotels are fairly simple, with no truly luxurious places. The best in town is the *Demir Oteli* (deh-MEER, tel 12 315), İzzet Paşa Caddesi 8, at the intersection with Gazi Caddesi a short distance south of Dağ Kapısı. The 39-room Demir rents its rooms for $18 single, $26 double. Next in line is the *Saraç Oteli* (sah-RAHCH, tel 12 365), İzzet Paşa Caddesi 16, almost next door to the aforementioned Demir. Here, the 35 rooms are quite simple, but cost only $11 or $12 with shower.

Two hotels nearby charge a bit more ($13) for a double with shower: the 75-room *Kentim Oteli* (kehn-TEEM, tel 11 827), İnönü Caddesi 4/H, and the *Saruhan Oteli* (SAH-roo-HAHN, tel 12 470), İnönü Caddesi 7.

The *Hotel Ertem* (ehr-TEHM, tel 12 972), just across from the Saraç, is very modest, with beds and nothing else in the rooms, but the price for a double is only $3 – in the centre of town!

Just outside the Dağ Kapısı is the veteran 39-room *Turistik Oteli* (too-rees-TEEK, tel 12 662), Ziya Gökalp Bulvarı 7, older but well-kept, with doubles at $18.

Places to Eat

In Diyarbakır, kebab places are everywhere, and they solve the dining problem easily and cheaply most of the time. Many are near the junction of İnönü/İzzet Paşa and Gazi caddesi's, near the aforementioned hotels. Look for *Hacı Baba* (hah-JUH bah-bah). Other restaurants to try are *Lokanta 77* ('77' is said 'yeht-MEESH yeh-DEE'), and *Beşkardeş* (BEHSH-kahr-desh, Five Brothers). For slightly fancier meals, head for the hotel restaurants in the Demir (a rooftop place) and the Turistik. There are also some *pastane*'s in the centre, good for breakfast or a snack.

Things to See

As the old walls are so extensive (almost six km long), perhaps the most delightful way to tour them is in a horse-drawn carriage, called a *fayton* (FAH-yee-tohn, Phaeton). The going rate is about $6, but you may have to haggle for this. Your driver may be able to explain a few things to you in English.

The Walls

The historic names for the gates in the walls are the *Harput Kapısı* (north), *Mardin Kapısı* (south), *Yenikapı* (east), and *Urfa Kapısı* (west). The massive black basalt walls are defended by 72 bastions and towers, many of them gathered around the *İç Kale* (EECH-kaleh, Citadel or Keep) at the north-east corner, overlooking the Tigris. Of the gates, the Harput Kapısı (Dağ Kapısı) is in the best condition. Perhaps the most rewarding area of the walls to explore for inscriptions and decoration is the portion between the İç Kale and the Mardin Kapısı, going westward (away from the river).

Though there were Roman and probably earlier walls here, the present ones date from early Byzantine times (330-500 AD).

Diyarbakır has many mosques, but the most interesting one is the **Ulu Cami**, built in 1091 and extensively restored in 1155 after having been damaged by fire. The mosque is rectangular in plan – an Arab-style mosque, not an Ottoman mosque. Its founder was Malik Şah, an early sultan of the Seljuks. Across the courtyard from the Ulu Cami is the **Mesudiye Medresesi**, now used as offices.

On the south-west side of the Ulu Cami, only a few steps out of the courtyard, is the **Zincirli Medresesi** (1100s), a seminary which now serves as the city's museum. Visit for the building, if not for the exhibits. You may notice that the museum director has chosen the nicest room to be his office.

EXCURSION TO MARDÌN

A hundred kms south of Diyarbakır is Mardin (mahr-DEEN, altitude 1325, population 40,000), an odd antique of a town overlooking the vast, roasted Syrian plains. The history of Mardin, like that of Diyarbakır, involves disputes by rival armies over dozens and dozens of centuries, though now nobody cares. There is a certain amount of smuggling trade with Syria (sheep for instance, which are much more expensive in Syria than in Turkey), but other than that, Mardin sizzles and sleeps.

This town had a large Christian community, and there are still a few Syriac Christian families, and their churches, here. On the outskirts, in the hilly region known as Tur Abdin, are several monasteries (visitors welcome) in which Aramaic – the language of Jesus – is still used as the liturgical tongue. The monastery named **Der Zaferan** is the seat of the Syriac patriarch.

In Mardin proper are numerous Muslim buildings such as the **Sultan İsa Medresesi** (1385), the **Kasım Paşa Medresesi** (1400s), and the ancient **Ulu Cami** (1000s), an Iraqi Seljuk structure.

If you're travelling on a few dollars a day, you'll find suitable hotels in Mardin. Anyone looking for luxury or comfort rather than just the necessities had better make Mardin a day-trip from Diyarbakır.

BÌTLÌS

Travelling eastward from Diyarbakır along Highway 6, 88 km brings you to the town of Silvan, and another 22 km to Malabadi. Just east of the latter town is the *Batman Suyu*, a stream which is spanned by a beautiful hump-backed stone bridge built by the Artukid Turks in 1146. It is thought to have the longest span (37 metres) of any such bridge in existence. With that engaging bend in the middle, it's truly a work of art.

Another 235 km brings you to Bitlis (BEET-lees, altitude 1570 metres, population 28,000), an interesting old town squeezed into the narrow valley of a stream. A castle dominates the town; a nice hump-backed bridge, and another old bridge, span the stream. The **Ulu Cami** here was built in 1126, the **Şerefiye Camii** and **Saraf Han** (a caravanserai) in the 1500s. The town was the capital of a semi-autonomous Kurdish principality in late Ottoman times.

Should you need to stay here, the *Hotel Turist*, on the highway in the centre of town, is very plain but clean.

Walnut trees surround the town, and in autumn children stand by the highway with bags of nuts for sale. Up the hill at the eastern side of the town, on the left (north) side of the road, is an old caravanserai, the Pabsin Hanı, built by the Seljuks in the 1200s. Feel free to stop and have a look around.

It's only 26 km to Tatvan, railhead and western port for lake steamers. From here you can board a steamer to Van (four hours), or make the journey more quickly by bus around the southern shore. Though the church at Akdamar is the most important sight on the lake, there are things to see along the northern shore. Refer to the Van section, below, for details.

AKDAMAR

On the 156-km journey along the southern shore from Tatvan to Van, the scenery is beautiful, but there is no reason to stop except at a point two km east of Gevaş, and there you *must* stop. Motorboats ferry sightseers over to an island in the lake which bears the 10th century **Church of the Holy Cross**, called the *Akdamar Kilisesi* in Turkish. The boats run about every 30 minutes if traffic warrants, which usually does in the warm months. (If it doesn't, you may have to charter one.) The trip takes about 20 minutes.

In 921, Gagik Artzruni, King of Vaspurakan, built a palace, church and monastery here on the island of Akdamar (or Akhtamar), three km out in the lake. Little remains of the palace and monastery, but the church walls are in superb condition, and the wonderful relief carvings on them are among the masterworks of Armenian art. If you are familiar with the Bible stories, you'll immediately recognize Adam and Eve, Jonah and the Whale, David and Goliath, Abraham about to sacrifice Isaac (but he sees the heaven-sent ram, with its horns caught in a bush, just in time!), Daniel in the Lions' Den, Sampson, etc. The paintings inside the church are not in the best of shape, but their vagueness and frailty seems in keeping with the shaded, partly ruined interior. The church and its setting are incomparable – don't miss this place. It's one of the major reasons you've come to eastern Turkey.

VAN

At the south-eastern edge of the vast *Van Gölü* (VAHN gur-lew), almost 100 km across the water from Tatvan, lies Van (altitude 1725 metres, population 94,000), eastern railhead on the line to Iran and the largest Turkish city east of Diyarbakır and south of Erzurum. Van has several claims to fame. It was the Urartian capital city, and at the Rock of Van near the lakeshore are long cuneiform inscriptions and the skeletal outlines of an ancient city. Van is also the market centre for the Kurdish tribes who live in the mountain fastnesses of extreme south-eastern Turkey.

Orientation

The very centre of Van is the junction of Cumhuriyet Caddesi and Alpaslan/Çavuştepe Caddesi. The bus terminal is here, at the very northern end of Cumhuriyet Caddesi. The Tourism Information Office (tel (0611) 2018) is at the opposite, southern end of this thoroughfare, at Cumhuriyet Caddesi 127. Between the bus terminal and the Tourism Office is the commercial district, with hotels in the streets running west.

There are two railway stations, the İskele İstasyon, or lakeside Dock Station, and the Şehir İstasyon, or City Station. The city station is due north of the centre; the dock station is two km north-east. The Rock of Van (*Van Kalesi*), the only significant sight, is just over a km west of the centre.

Places to Stay

Van has a decent, modern, comfortable hotel, and a good selection of cheaper places. Best is the 75-room *Hotel Akdamar* (AHK-dah-mahr, tel 3036), Kazım Karabekir Cad. 22; this street runs west from Cumhuriyet Caddesi near the Tourist Office. The Akdamar's 75 rooms rent for $19 double. Next best is the *Tekin Oteli* (teh-KEEN, tel 3010), Küçük Cami Civarı ('near the Little Mosque') west of Cumhuriyet Caddesi – you can identify the hotel easily by the sign on its roof. Fifty-two rooms here, in a quietish place, renting for $11 double with shower. The *Bayram Oteli* (BAH-yee-RAHM, tel 1136), Cumhuriyet Cad. 1/A, is very near the bus terminal. Its 68 rooms with bath go for $13 double. A similar, but slightly cheaper, place is the *Beşkardeşler Oteli* (BEHSH-kahr-desh-LEHR, tel 1116), Cumhuriyet Cad. 34, with 50 rooms for $9 double.

Cheapest of the modernish hotels are the *Kent Oteli* (tel 2404), behind the Türkiye İş Bankası (63 rooms) and the *Çaldiran Oteli* (CHAHL-duh-RAHN, tel 2718), on Sıhke Caddesi near the Yeni Cami ('New Mosque'), with 48 rooms. Both offer doubles with shower for $8. The Kent has bathless doubles ($6) as well.

Places to Eat

The fanciest, and probably the best food is at the Hotel Akdamar. Cumhuriyet Caddesi has numerous kebabci's, cheap and good as always. A good, cheap, general-purpose restaurant is the *Birkoç* (BEER-kohch), off Cumhuriyet Caddesi at Yedinci Sokak (go to Cumhuriyet Cad. 79, and then make your way around to the

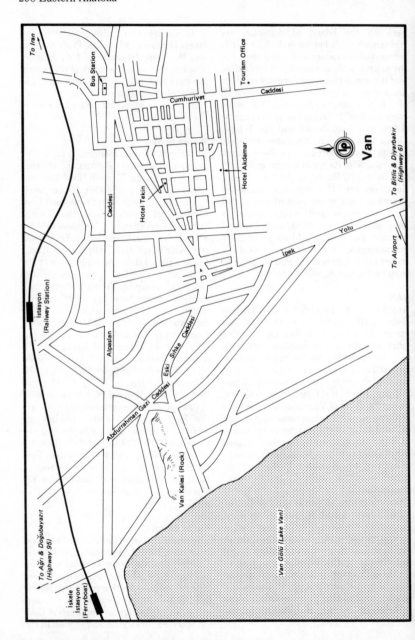

back of this address to find the Birkoç). The *Köşk* restaurant, which you'll see, is a popular community place. The food is too expensive for what you get.

For breakfast, try the *Seval Kahvaltı Salonu* (seh-VAHL).

Things to See

There are only two things to see in Van, but they are fascinating and very, very old.

Museum

Off Cumhuriyet Caddesi not far from the Bayram Oteli is the museum (müze), with some exhibits dating back *before* Urartian times. Other exhibits include some beautiful Urartian gold jewellery, some with amber and coloured glass; Urartian cylindrical seals; pots from the Old Bronze Age (circa 5000 BC); the Urartu Süsleme Plakaları (Jewellery Breastplates) from the 800s to 600s BC are particularly fine, as are the bronze belts. Another exhibit has *At Gemleri* (horse-bits) from the 800s and 700s BC.

In the ethnographic exhibits upstairs are countless *kilims*, the flat-woven rugs which are superbly made by the Kurdish and Turkoman tribes who live in the mountains. At the far end of the room is a *sedir*, or low couch, such as is found in village houses, covered with traditional crafts.

Rock of Van

Ask for directions to *Van Kalesi* (VAHN kah-leh-see, Van Castle), and you'll be pointed toward the Rock of Van.

On the north side of the rock is the tomb of a Muslim saint, visited frequently by pilgrims. A stairway from the car park at the north-western corner leads to the top, where you can see the fortifications and several cuneiform inscriptions dating from about 800 BC. On the south side is a narrow walkway (now with an iron railing) leading to several funeral chambers cut from the rock. Before reaching them you pass a long cuneiform inscription.

The view south of the rock reveals a flat space broken by the grass-covered foundations of numerous buildings. This was Tushpa, an Urartian city which flourished almost 3000 years ago. The sight is stunning: a dead city, buried as though in a grave, seemingly untouched for 30 centuries.

Shopping

In the shops of Van you will see hand-woven craft items – kilims, saddlebags, etc – finer than you've ever seen before. The dealers, however, realize that these finely-made things will fetch high prices in Paris, London and New York, so they seem to have decided to save you the trouble of buying there: they'll charge you the high prices right here! Perhaps a paucity of buyers at such prices will moderate their expectations. Go shopping anyway. Even if you don't buy (and there is no obligation – don't feel pressured!), looking at these crafts is a wonderful experience. Some of the dealers speak English.

TO HÂKKARI

The absolute, positive dead-end of Turkey is Hâkkari (hah-KYAH-ree, altitude 1700 metres, population 19,000), 210 km south of Van over torturous zigzagging mountain roads. But the scenery is spectacular, both here and at **Yüksekova** on the road to Iran. Those with their own camping equipment or a van might want to give it a try.

Around Lake Van

Lake Van is highly alkaline. It was formed when the volcano named Nemrut Dağı (not the one with the statues!) blocked its natural outflow; the water level is now maintained by evaporation, which results in a high mineral concentration in the water. It's not good to drink, but it's fine to swim in, and if you wash your clothes in it, you need no soap!

If you circle the lake, you will pass through Erciş, a modern town which covers settlements that date from Urartian times. Continuing west brings you past Süphan Dağı (4430 metres high) to **Adilcevaz**, another onetime Urartian town with a ruined castle. At **Ahlat** are numerous *türbes* (tombs), of which the largest is the Ulu Türbe. The castle dates from the reign of Süleyman the Magnificent (mid-1500s).

North of Ahlat some 60 km is **Malazgirt**, the ancient Manzikert, which is hugely important in Turkish history. On 26 August, 1071, the Seljuk Turkish Sultan Alp Arslan and his armies decisively defeated the Byzantine emperor, Romanus Diogenes, and took him prisoner. The Byzantine defeat effectively opened Anatolia to Turkish migration and conquest. The Seljuks established themselves in the Sultanate of Rum, and other nomadic Turkish tribes came from Central Asia and Iran to settle here. A band of border warriors following a leader named Osman later spread its influence, and founded a state which would become the vast Ottoman Turkish Empire. It all started here, in 1071, when the heir of the Caesars lost to a Turkish emir.

South-east of Ahlat, near Tatvan, is Nemrut Dağı (3050 metres, not to be confused with the Nemrut of the statues, near Adıyaman). This mountain is the volcano which dammed up the outflow of the lake, causing it to take its present vast size of 3750 square km. The crater has a lake in it, and some hot springs.

North from Van

Having come this far, your next goal must be Doğubayazıt, the town in the shadow of Mt Ararat, at the Iranian frontier on the E 23 highway. There are two routes you can follow.

If you go by bus, it will undoubtedly go via the town of Ağrı, where you must change for a bus eastward to Doğubayazıt. This route, 227 km from Van to Doğubayazıt, is the easiest. Driving a private car, you have an alternative. Where the lake ring road turns westward at the town of

Bendimahi, you can, if you like, continue north toward Muradiye, Çaldıran and Ortadirek. The road is unpaved after Çaldıran, badly marked, has no regular public transport, and is extremely rough for the 60 km between Çaldıran and Ortadirek, but it's usually passable and wonderfully scenic. You save a few kms, as this route is only 184 km long, but you should not drive on this road after 5 pm. It is officially closed after that hour, and Turkish army patrols are on duty to stop smugglers. They are very friendly if you obey the regulations, but will be uncomfortably strict after 5 pm.

AĞRI

The Turkish name for Mt Ararat is Ağrı Dağı, and the town of Ağrı (ah-RUH, altitude 1640, population 42,000) is 100 km west of the snow-capped peak. There is nothing to hold you here except the few small, very modest hotels (if you arrive at night). Otherwise, head onward, to Doğubayazıt to the east, or Erzurum to the west.

DOĞUBAYAZIT

It's only 35 km between the Iranian frontier and Doğubayazıt (doh-OO-bah-yah-zuht, population 25,000), a town that is dusty in summer, muddy in winter. The town seems to be made of the dun-coloured earth on which it rests. Behind the town is a range of bare, jagged mountains, before it a table-flat expanse of wheatfield and grazing land. But on the far northern side of this flatness rises **Mount Ararat** (*Ağri Dağı*, 5165 metres), an enormous volcano capped with ice and often shrouded in dark clouds.

The name *Ararat* is derived from *Urartu*. The mountain has figured in legends since time began, most notably as the supposed resting-place of Noah's Ark. But more of that later.

Doğubayazıt's other attraction is the İşak Paşa Sarayı, a castle/fortress/palace/mosque complex perched on a terrace seven km east of town.

Places to Stay/Eat

Rising above the mud-brick roofs and television aerials of Doğubayazıt is the *Hotel Ararat* (tel 139, 159), Emniyet Cad. 48, with 60 double rooms priced at $15, with shower. It's modern and comfortable (comparatively speaking), with its own car park and Turkish baths. The restaurant is the best in town, and not overly expensive.

The only other place in this class is the *Sim-Er Moteli* (SEEM-ehr, tel 601), P K 13, a modern 38-room establishment located on the eastern edge of town on the E 23 highway to Iran. Views of Ararat are very fine, and a double costs about the same as at the Hotel Ararat.

After that, there's not much. The *Hotel Gül* (tel 176), or the *Hotel Beyazıt* would be next choice. The several little places along the main street of the town, used mostly by lorry-drivers travelling to and from Iran, are for emergencies, especially dire ones. In fact, the hotel rooms may inspire thoughts of emergency.

The main street also holds three or four kebabci's, one of which advertises (in English) 'All Kinds of Meals Found Here'.

Things to See

Head east for the İşak Paşa Sarayı (ee-SHAHK pah-shah sah-rah-yuh), seven km from town. There are dolmuşes that pass nearby, especially on weekends.

Though ruined, the fortress-like palace has many elements which are in good shape; the mosque is still used for prayers. The building was begun in 1685 by Çolak Abdi Paşa and completed in 1784 by his son, a Kurdish chieftain named İşak ('Isaac'). The architecture is an amalgam of Seljuk, Ottoman, Georgian, Persian and Armenian styles. A grand main portal leads to a large courtyard. The magnificent gold-plated doors which once hung on the portal were removed by the Russians, who invaded in 1917 and took the doors to a museum in Moscow.

The palace was equipped with a central heating system, running water and a sewerage system. You can visit the mosque and the various palace rooms, as well as the minaret (claustrophobic on the way up, but with a wonderful view). Note especially the little türbe in a corner of the court, with very fine relief work on it.

Across the valley are a mosque and the ruins of a fortress. The fortress foundations may date from Urartian times, though the walls will have been rebuilt by whoever needed to control this mountain pass. The mosque is thought to date from the reign of the Ottoman Sultan Selim the Grim (1512-1520), who defeated the Persians decisively near the town of Çaldıran, 70 km south of Doğubayazıt, in 1514. Selim thus added all of eastern Anatolia to his burgeoning empire, and went on to conquer Syria and Palestine.

The ruined foundations you see rising in low relief from the dusty plain are of Eski Bayazıt, the old city, which was probably founded in Urartian times (circa 800 BC).

Mt Ararat

The mountain has two peaks when seen from Doğubayazıt. The right-hand peak, called Great Ararat (*Büyük Ağrı*) is 5165 metres high; Little Ararat (*Küçük Ağrı*) rises to about 3925 metres. Best time to view the mountain is at sunrise or early in the morning, before the clouds obscure it.

You can climb Ararat, but you need *written* permission from the authorities in Ankara, and then you must have an approved guide. The mountain is dangerous: severe weather, ferocious sheepdogs, rock and ice-slides, smugglers and outlaws can turn an adventure into a disaster.

The easiest way to go up the mountain is with an organized group, which will already have made the necessary official arrangements. *Mountain Travel* of Albany, California (tel 415-527-8100) operates such trips, as do two Turkish agencies: *Trek Travel*, Taksim Meydanı 10/6, Istanbul; and *Metro Tourism*, Cumhuriyet

Cad. 43/5, Platin Ap., Taksim, Istanbul.

Once you have your written permission, you'll need a guide. Get in contact with Ahmet Çöktin (tel 314, 410) in Doğubayazıt. Ahmet Ağa *owns* the southern slope of Mount Ararat, and will take you to Eli, a hamlet at 2100 metres, which is the starting point for the trek. You stay at two more camps before the final ascent, for which you should have ice-climbing gear.

Over the years, several people have reported sighting a 'boat shape' high on the mountain, and in 1951 an expedition brought back what was presumed to be a piece of wood from the ark, which had been found in a frozen lake. But so far no one, not even American astronaut James Irwin, who climbed in 1982, has brought back a full report. If it's there, it will be found, for the activity nowadays is intense, with scientists, archaeologists, Fundamentalist Christian sects, the Turkish Mountaineering Federation and various universities all sending expeditions.

Getting Away

From Doğubayazıt, you can go west to Erzurum, a distance of 284 km.

If you want to see Kars and the ruins of Ani, you can go north via Iğdır (UH-duhr), Tuzluca and Kağızman, a distance of 236 km. At Tuzluca there are salt caves you can visit. North of Kağızman, above the village of Çamuşlu Köyü (chah-moosh-LOO kur-yew) are pre-historic rock carvings (*kaya resimleri*, kah-YAH reh-seem-leh-ree) which the villagers can show you.

As this route passes very close to the Soviet frontier between Iğdır and Tuzluca, it's important for you to know that the border zone is a no-man's-land 700 metres deep on each side of the frontier line, and that the Soviet border guards will *shoot to kill* anyone who enters that 700-metres strip, on either the Turkish or the Russian side. This is no joke. Don't attempt to approach the border. The Turkish army guards wont appreciate any provocative action either.

ERZURUM

Erzurum (EHR-zoo-room, altitude 1950, population 192,000) is the largest city on the high plateau of Eastern Anatolia. It has always been a transportation centre and military headquarters, the command-post for the defense of Anatolia from Russian invasion, and in the days of the empires, from Persian invasion as well. Under the republic, it is assuming a new role as an eastern cultural and commercial city. There is a university here.

The Byzantines called the city Theodosiopolis, and they had their hands full defending it from Arab attack on several occasions. The Seljuks took it after the Battle of Manzikert (1071) opened Anatolia to Turkish settlement. As for the Ottomans, it was Selim the Grim who conquered the city in 1515.

Erzurum lacks the colour and grace of Istanbul or Izmir. The severe climate and the spare landscape make one think that this is the beginning of the vast, high steppe of Central Asia. The people, too, reflect the severity of the climate and sparseness of refinements.

For tourists, Erzurum is a transfer point, with air, rail and bus connections. But when you stay the night here, you will be able to occupy your free time with visits to some very fine Turkish buildings.

The local Tourism Information Office (tel (011) 15 697, 19 127) is on Cemal Gürsel Caddesi.

Places to Stay

Though there are no hotels in the luxury class, there are plenty of sufficient, comfortable places.

Places to Stay – mid-range

About the most comfortable place in town is the *Oral Oteli* (oh-RAHL, tel 19 740), Terminal Caddesi, with 90 rooms going for $16 double. Next is the *Efes Oteli* (eh-FESS, tel 17 081), Tahtacılar Cad. 36, with 46 rooms priced at $11. The *Buhara Oteli* (boo-HAH-rah, tel 15 096), Kazım Karabekir Caddesi, has 44 rooms which cost $9 with shower. Other hotels in this range of comfort and price are the nearby *Polat Oteli* (poh-LAHT, tel 11 623), Kazım Karabekir Caddesi, with 60 rooms; and the *Kral Oteli* (KRAHL, tel 11 930), Erzincan Kapı, with 51 rooms.

Places to Stay – bottom end

Make your choice between rooms with or without shower at the *Hotel Çinar* (chuh-NAHR, tel 13 580), Ayazpaşa Caddesi 18. The 36 rooms cost $4.50 double without shower, $7 with.

Things to See

Right downtown is the **Çifte Minareli Medrese** (1253), now the museum, and next to it the **Ulu Cami** (1179). The contrast between the two buildings is interesting: the Ulu Cami, built by the Saltuklu Turkish emir of Erzurum, is very restrained; the Twin Minaret Seminary has more elaborate decoration, as it was built by Alaettin Keykubat II, son of the Seljuk sultan known for his many great building projects. In the Çifte Minareli is the tomb (*Hatuniye Türbesi*) of Huant Hatun, the sultan's daughter. Behind the Ulu Cami down Gürcü Mehmet Sokak are three more tombs with good decoration, the best being the octagonal **Emir Sultan Türbesi** (1100s).

Erzurum castle, erected by Theodosius (400s), was across from the Çifte Minareli and the Ulu Cami. Only a few bits of wall remain. The tomb nearby, the **Gümüşlü Türbe**, dates from Seljuk times. To the west, along the way to Trabzon and Sivas, is the **Yakutiye Medresesi**, a Mongol theological seminary dating from 1310. It's now in a military zone, so you can't go inside.

The other old structures you'll see are mostly Ottoman mosques. The **Lala Mustafa Paşa Camii** (1563) is thought to have been designed by Sinan. Other mosques in this style are the **Kuyucu Murat Paşa Camii** and the **İbrahim Paşa Camii**.

KARS

Kars (KAHRSS, altitude 1750 metres, population 60,000) is an odd place. It is chilly and drab most of the time. There are lots of police and soldiers, and every single one of them can tell you without hesitation the precise number of days he has yet to serve in Kars, before he can go west 'to civilization'. And they will want to talk to you. As a foreigner, you bring them a breath of culture. As for the locals, a harsh climate and a rough history has made them, for the most part, dour and sombre, though not unpolite. The children, as always, are friendly and inquisitive, anxious to try out their ten words of English on you.

Kars doesn't look at all like a Turkish town. It is dominated by a stark, no-nonsense medieval fortress (rebuilt in 1855) which is still used as part of the city's defenses. Many of the public buildings, and even some of the residences, look Russian, not Turkish. The school gymnasium was obviously built as a Russian Orthodox church.

Kars was indeed held by the Russians for a time (1878-1920), which accounts for the 19th-century Russian aspect of the town. And the mood of the inhabitants comes from the fact that Kars, though set in the midst of fertile agricultural land, is a garrison town. What people do here is grow wheat, make carpets, and watch out for the Russians.

Getting There

The train from Erzurum takes seven hours to reach Kars. In the switching yard you might see some marvellous old steam locomotives.

There is direct bus service between Kars and Adana, Ankara, Ardahan, Bursa, Denizli, Diyarbakır, Erzurum, Iğdır, Istanbul, İzmir, Kayseri, Konya, Malatya and Sivas. For Doğubayazıt, change buses at Iğdır.

Buses take about four hours to cover the 200 km between Erzurum and Kars.

The Tourism Information Office (tel

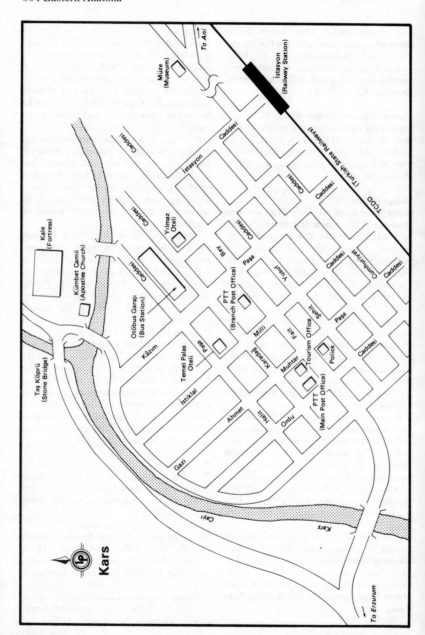

(0211) 2724) is on Faik Bey Caddesi; walk through the garden of the building, to the left, and up the stairs to the upper floor. Hours are (more or less) 8 to 12 noon and 1.30 to 5.30 pm; on Saturday and Sunday 8.30 am to 4 pm.

Places to Stay

There is no hotel in Kars worth the money charged. This is one of those places in which you have to pay what is asked in order to get what is available. Choice doesn't really come into it.

The *Temel Palas Oteli* (teh-MEHL pah-LAHS, tel 1376), Kazım Paşa Caddesi 41, with 20 rooms, and the *Yılmaz Oteli* (yuhl-MAHZ, tel 1074, 2387), 36 rooms, right next to the bus terminal, both charge $12 for a double with shower. They are rated by the Ministry of Culture and Tourism as Fourth Class; heaven knows why. Look at the Yılmaz first.

The *Hotel Bal* (BAHL, tel 1108, 1933), Atatürk Cad. 12, charges only $4 for a double. Baths in the rooms are only Turkish splash baths; for a shower you must walk down the hallway, so why not just rent a bathless room ($3) in the first place? The sheets are as clean (?) as any in town.

There are other small, inexpensive hotels like the Bal, though they're not as good. You may find this difficult to believe.

Places to Eat

The best restaurant in town is in the *Yılmaz hotel*. They serve alcoholic beverages, which is not the case in most places. The next-best restaurant is in the other 'top' hotel, the Temel Palas. The other small restaurants in Kars are much cheaper, much more modest, but offer better value-for-money. The *Manolya Pastanesi* (mah-NOHL-yah), two blocks from the Belediye Sarayı and the Temel Palas, is okay for dessert, tea and pastries.

All the food in Kars is very basic, though they do have excellent honey (*bal*) here.

Things to See

You have come to Kars with the intention of visiting Ani. Without that intention, it doesn't make much sense to come here. But while in Kars, there are a few things well worth seeing.

Kars Müzesi First of all is the fine, new little museum, open from 8 to 12 noon and 1.30 to 5.30 pm, closed Monday. Oldest exhibits date from Old Bronze Age times. The Roman and Greek periods are represented, as are the Seljuks and Ottomans. Several photo exhibits show the excavations at Ani; there are shots of Armenian churches in Kars, as well. The chief exhibit is a pair of carved doors from an orthodox church, and a Russian church bell from the time of Tsar Nicholas II (1894-1917).

You should not miss the ethnographic exhibits upstairs, as this area produces some very fine kilims, carpets and *cicims* (embroidered kilims). Costumes, saddle-bags, jewellery, samovars, and a home carpet loom complete the exhibit.

Kümbet Camii Though called the 'Drum-Dome Mosque' in Turkish, this building down by the river was built as the Church of the Apostles by the Bagratid King Abas in 938. The relief carvings on the drum are of the apostles; the porches were added to the ancient structure in the 1800s. As of this writing, the church awaits restoration; you can't see the interior.

Not far from the church is an old bridge, the Taş Köprü, which dates from the 1400s. Ruins of the Ulu Cami and a palace called the **Beylerbey Sarayı** are beneath the Kale (fortress). The fortress is not open to visitors.

Carpet Buying

When I was in Kars, I bought several of the local carpets. The weave of the modern rugs is coarse, the local wool is used undyed, in its natural earthy colours. Any dealer in town can show you some *Kars halıları* (KAHRSS hah-luh-lah-ruh, Kars carpets), and will quote you a price of so-many-liras per square metre. There are several grades of carpets, and thus several different price ranges. Once you've found a carpet you like, and have agreed on a price per square metre (Haggle! You must!), the carpet is measured, yielding the final, exact price.

These are not fine Turkish carpets, but they are very earthy, attractive, and sturdy – and not expensive, though heavy and bulky to carry home. I'm not sure I'd trust having them shipped.

Though there are numerous carpet merchants, the best I found was Mr. Memduh Yıldız (mehm-DOOH yuhl-DUHZ); just ask, and somebody will point the way to his shop.

Ani

The ruined city at Ani (AH-nee), 44 km east of Kars, is striking. It's a medieval ghost town set in grassy fields overlooking the Arpaçay stream, which forms the boundary between the Turkish Republic and the Soviet Armenian Republic. On the far side, sinister-looking Soviet watchtowers shelter border guards who will shoot to kill if you show an intention of violating their border. The border no-man's-land extends to a distance of 700 metres on either side of the Arpaçay, and the Russians will shoot whether you're within 700 metres on the Russian side, or 700 metres on the Turkish side.

Getting There

To visit Ani, you must have permission from the authorities. The Turks want no trouble with the Russians, so everyone going into the no-man's-land must be accounted for. Ani lies so close to the border that under normal conditions anyone spotted there would be gunned down. The Russians make an exception for the ruins, but there are some rules you must follow.

There is no regular transport out to Ani Köyü, the hamlet near the ruins. The road, being a dead-end, has little regular traffic good for hitchhiking, so you must arrange for transport yourself. Unless you have a car, or can locate other tourists (Turkish or foreign) in Kars who do have a car, you must arrange with a local dolmuş or taxi driver to take you out and back. The Tourism Office may help you find others to share the trip. Begin making your arrangements as soon as you arrive in Kars.

The Formalities Once you've arranged transport, head for the Tourism Office to begin formalities for the visit. Have your passport with you. A sign in front of the Tourism Office says, 'No visits to Ani arranged on Sunday'! But as with many things in Turkey, I arranged a visit on Sunday with no problems.

After they take down the necessary information, you'll be referred to the Emniyet Müdürlüğü (ehm-nee-YEHT mew-dewr-lew, Security Headquarters) across the street, where police officials in green uniforms will approve your application. Usually, the approval is routine. Then you set out on the road, and when you reach Ani you report to the soldiers at the *Jandarma* (zhahn-DAHR-mah, Gendarmerie) post. A soldier will be assigned to guide you around the ruins. If you stay with the soldier, and obey the regulations, you will have no trouble from the Russians.

The regulations include these: no staring or pointing toward the Russian side; no use of binoculars or cameras whatsoever; no taking notes; no picnicking or remaining in one spot for too long; stay together in the group. All this is very scary, but there will be no trouble so long as you scrupuously observe the rules.

The Ruins The walls of Ani, over a kilometre in length, will impress you as you drive across the wheat-covered plains toward the border. Your soldier-guide will take you through the Alp Arslan Kapısı, a double gate. Your first view of Ani is stunning, the wrecks of buildings in a ghost city, where once hundreds of thousands lived. This was the capital of an Urartian state, and later of an Armenian Bagratid kingdom from 953 to 1045, when it was taken by the Byzantines. After the short-lived Armenian kingdom, the city was taken from the Byzantines by the Great Seljuks of Iran, then by the king of Georgia, then by Kurdish emirs. The struggle for the city went on among these groups until the Mongols arrived in 1239 and cleared everybody else out. The Mongols, who were nomads, had no use for city life, and Ani became a ghost city after their victory.

Within the walls are the ruins of eight churches, a convent, and the citadel (*İç Kale*). The cathedral is the most impressive of the churches. Ani became the seat of the Armenian Catholics in 993; this church was built between 989 and 1010. As the grandest religious edifice in the

city, it was transformed into a mosque whenever Muslims held Ani, and back to a church when the Christians took over.

Other than the cathedral, the most interesting churches are the **Church of the Holy Saviour** (1036), and the Church of St Gregory of Tigran Honentz (1215).

You won't be allowed to visit the citadel. As you walk back toward the Alp Arslan Kapısı, take a good look around and fix it in your memory, for this is the only 'photograph' of Ani you'll take. If you find it constricting to be so limited in your examination of these magnificent remnants, keep in mind that you can look, point, photograph and picnic to your heart's content on the island of Akdamar near Van, where the Church of the Holy Cross is much better preserved, with much more that is worthy of close examination.

Turkish Language Guide

HISTORY

From the time when Turks first encountered Islam about the year 670, Turkish had been written in the Arabic alphabet, the letters of the Kuran. But the Arabic letters did not suit the sounds of Turkish well, and made the task of literacy very difficult.

Even under the empire, alphabet reform had been proposed in order to promote literacy and progress. But it was Atatürk, of course, who did it, in 1928. The story is typical of him: when told that it would take several years of expert consultation to devise a suitable Latin alphabet for Turkish, and then about five years at the least to implement it, he replied, 'The change will be carried out in three months, or not at all'. Needless to say, the new alphabet was ready in six weeks, and three months later the old alphabet was forbidden in public use. And it worked! The president of the republic himself got a slate and chalk, went into the public parks, and held informal classes to teach the citizenry the new letters.

SYNTAX & PRONUNCIATION

Despite daunting oddities such as the soft 'g' (ğ) and undotted 'i' (ı), Turkish is phonetic and simple to pronounce. In a few minutes you can learn to pronounce the sounds reasonably well. The guide below will show you how.

As for grammar, that's another matter entirely. Though supremely logical and unencumbered by genders and mountains of exceptions, Turkish structure is so different from that of the Indo-European languages that it is completely unfamiliar at first. A few hints will help you comprehend road and shop signs, schedules and menus.

Suffixes

A Turkish word consists of a root and one or more suffixes added to it. Though in English we have only a few suffixes (-'s for possessive, –s or –es for plural), Turkish has lots and lots of suffixes. Not only that, these suffixes are subject to an unusual system of 'vowel harmony' whereby most of the vowel sounds in a word are made in a similar manner. What this means is that the suffix might be –lar when attached to one word, but – ler when attached to another; it's the same suffix, though.

Sometimes these suffixes are preceded by a 'buffer letter', a 'y' or an 'n'.

Here are some of the suffixes you'll encounter most frequently.

Noun suffixes

–a, –e	to
–dan, –den	from
–dır, –dir, –dur, –dür	emphatic (ignore it!)
–(s)ı, –(s)i, –(s)u, –(s)ü	for object-nouns (ignore it!)
–(n)ın, –(n)in	possessive
–lar, –ler	plural
–lı, –li, –lu, –lü	with
–sız, –siz, –suz, –süz	without

Verb suffixes

–ar, –er, –ır, –ir, –ur, –ür	simple present tense

−acak, −ecek, −acağ-, −eceğ-	future tense
−dı, −di, −du, −dü	simple past tense
−ıyor-, −iyor-	continuous (like our '-ing')
−mak, −mek	infinitive ending

Nouns

Suffixes can be added to nouns to modify them. The two you will come across most frequently are −ler and −lar, which form the plural: *otel*, hotel; *oteller*, hotels; *araba*, car; *arabalar*, cars.

Other suffixes modify in other ways: *ev*, house; *Ahmet*, Ahmet; but *Ahmet'in evi*, Ahmet's house. Similarly, *Istanbul*, *banka*, but *Istanbul Bankası* when the two are used together. You may see −i, −ı, −u, or −ü; −si, −sı, −su, or −sü added to any noun. A *cami* is a mosque; but the *cami* built by Mehmet Pasha is the *Mehmet Paşa Camii*, with two i's. Ask for a *bira* and the waiter will bring you a bottle of whatever type he has; ask for an *Efes Birası* and that's what you'll get.

Yet other suffixes on nouns tell you about direction: −a or −e means 'to', as in *otobüs*, 'bus', but *otobüse* (oh-toh-bews-EH), to the bus; *Bodrum'a* (boh-droom-AH), to Bodrum. The suffix −dan or −den means 'from': *Ankara'dan*, from Ankara; *köprüden*, from the bridge. Stress is on these final syllables (-a or −dan) whenever they are used.

Verbs

The infinitive form is with −mak or −mek, as in *gitmek*, to go; *almak*, to take. The stress in the infinitive is always on the last syllable, 'geet-MEHK', 'ahl-MAHK'.

The simple present form is with −r, as in *gider*, 'he/she/it goes', *giderim*, 'I go'. The suffix −iyor means about the same, gidiyorum, 'I'm going'. For the future, there's −ecek or −acak, as in *alacak*, (ah-lah-JAHK) 'he will take (it)'.

Word Order

The nouns and adjectives usually come first, then the verb; the final suffix on the verb is the subject of the sentence: *Istanbul'a gideceğim*, I'll go to Istanbul; *Halı almak istiyorum*, I want to buy (take) a carpet (literally 'carpet to buy want I').

Pronunciation Key

Most letters are pronounced as they appear. Here are the tricky ones, the vowels and the exceptions.

A, a short 'a' as in *art* or *bar*

â very faint 'y' sound in preceding consonant, e.g. Lâleli is lyaah-leh-LEE

E, e 'eh' as the first vowel in *ever* or *fell*

İ, i as 'ee' in *see*

I, ı 'uh' or the vowel sound in *were* or *sir*

O, o same as in English

Ö, ö same sound as in German, or like English 'ur', as in *fur*

U, u 'oo', like the vowel in *moo* or *blue*

Ü, ü same as in German, or 'ew' in *few*

C, c pronounced like English 'j' as in *jet*

Ç, ç 'ch' as in *church*

G, g always hard like *get*, not soft like *gentle*

ğ not pronounced; lengthens preceding vowel; ignore it!
H, h never silent, always unvoiced, as in *half*
J, j like French 'j', English 'zh', or the 'z' in *azure*
S, s always 'sss' as in *stress*, not 'zzz' as in *ease*
Ş, ş 'sh' as in *show*
V, v soft, almost like a 'w'
W, w exists only in foreign words; not really Turkish
X, x only in foreign words; Turks use 'ks' instead

An important point for English speakers to remember is that each Turkish letter is pronounced; there are no diphthongs as in English. Thus the name *Mithat* is pronounced 'meet-HOT', not like the English word 'methought', and Turkish *meshut* is 'mess-HOOT', not 'meh-SHOOT'. Watch out for this! Your eye, used to English double-letter sounds, will keep trying to find them in Turkish, where they don't exist.

These examples also demonstrate that the 'h' is pronounced as an unvoiced aspiration (like the first sound in 'have' or 'heart', the sound a Cockney drops), and it is pronounced every time it occurs; it is never combined to make a diphthong. So your Turkish friend is named not 'aa-meht' but 'ahh-MEHT'; the word *rehber*, 'guide', is not 're-ber' but 'rehh-BEHR'. In the old days, English writers used to spell the name *Achmet* just to get people to breathe that 'h', but it didn't work: people said 'otch-met'. You can't do it? Nonsense! Say, 'a HALF'. You just did it! Now say 'Ah MEHT' the same way. Easy!

Common Words & Phrases

Cardinal Numbers

¼	*Çeyrek*	chehy-REHK
½	*Yarım*	YAH-ruhm (used alone, as 'I want half')
½	*Buçuk*	boo-CHOOK (always used with a whole number, as '1½', *bir buçuk*)
1	*Bir*	BEER
2	*İki*	ee-KEE
3	*Üç*	EWCH
4	*Dört*	DURRT
5	*Beş*	BEHSH
6	*Altı*	ahl-TUH
7	*Yedi*	yeh-DEE
8	*Sekiz*	seh-KEEZ
9	*Dokuz*	doh-KOOZ
10	*On*	OHN
11	*On bir*	ohn BEER
12	*On iki*	ohn ee-KEE
13	*On üç*	ohn EWCH
20	*Yirmi*	yeer-MEE
30	*Otuz*	oh-TOOZ
40	*Kırk*	KUHRK
50	*Elli*	ehl-LEE

60	*Altmış*	ahlt-MUSH
70	*Yetmiş*	yeht-MEESH
80	*Seksen*	sehk-SEHN
90	*Doksan*	dohk-SAHN
100	*Yüz*	YEWZ
200	*İki yüz*	ee-KEE yewz
1000	*Bin*	BEEN
2000	*İki bin*	ee-KEE been
10,000	*On bin*	OHN been
1,000,000	*Milyon*	meel-YOHN

Ordinal Numbers

Ordinal numbers consist of the number plus the suffix –inci, –ıncı, –uncu, or –üncü, depending upon 'vowel harmony'.

First	*Birinci*	beer-EEN-jee
Second	*İkinci*	ee-KEEN-jee
Sixth	*Altıncı*	ahl-TUHN-juh
Thirteenth	*Onüçüncü*	ohn-ew-CHEWN-jew
Hundredth	*Yüzüncü*	yewz-EWN-jew

Days of the Week

Day	*Gün*	GEWN
Week	*Hafta*	hahf-TAH
Sunday	*Pazar*	pah-ZAHR
Monday	*Pazartesi*	pah-ZAHR-teh-see
Tuesday	*Salı*	sah-LUH
Wednesday	*Çarşamba*	char-shahm-BAH
Thursday	*Perşembe*	pehr-shehm-BEH
Friday	*Cuma*	joo-MAH
Saturday	*Cumartesi*	joo-MAHR-teh-see

Months of the Year

Month	*Ay*	AHY
Year	*Sene*	SEH-neh
Year	*Yıl*	YUHL
January	*Ocak*	oh-JAHK
February	*Şubat*	shoo-BAHT
March	*Mart*	MAHRT
April	*Nisan*	nee-SAHN
May	*Mayıs*	mah-YUSS
June	*Haziran*	HAH-zee-RAHN
July	*Temmuz*	teh-MOOZ
August	*Ağustos*	AH-oo-STOHSS
September	*Eylül*	ehy-LEWL
October	*Ekim*	eh-KEEM
November	*Kasım*	kah-SUHM
December	*Aralık*	AH-rah-LUHK

The Basics

English	Turkish	Pronunciation
Yes	*Evet*	eh-VEHT
No	*Hayır*	HAH-yuhr
Not	.... *değil*	deh-YEEL
None	*Yok*	YOHK
And	*Ve*	VEH
Or	*Veya*	veh-YAH
Good	*İyi*	EE
Bad	*Fenah*	feh-NAH
Beautiful	*Güzel*	gew-ZEHL
Please	*Lütfen*	LEWT-fehn
Pardon me	*Affedersiniz*	AHF-feh-DEHR-see-neez
Pardon	*Pardon*	pahr-DOHN
Help yourself	*Buyurun(uz)*	BOOY-roon-(ooz)
Thank you	*Teşekkür ederim*	teh-sheh-KEWR eh-deh-reem
very much	*Çok teşekkür ederim*	CHOHK ...
Thanks	*Teşekkürler*	teh-sheh-kewr-LEHR
Thanks	*Mersi*	mehr-SEE
You're welcome	*Bir Şey değil*	beer SHEHY deh-YEEL
What?	*Ne?*	NEH
How?	*Nasıl?*	NAH-suhl
Who?	*Kim?*	KEEM
Why?	*Niçin, neden?*	NEE-cheen, NEH-dehn
Which one?	*Hangisi?*	HAHN-gee-see
What's this?	*Bu ne?*	BOO neh
Where is ....?	.... *nerede?*	NEH-reh-deh
When?	*Ne zaman?*	NEH zah-mahn
At what time?	*Saat kaçta?*	saht-KAHCH-tah
How much/many?	*Kaç/tane?*	KAHCH/tah-neh
How many liras?	*Kaç lira?*	KAHCH lee-rah
How many hours?	*Kaç saat?*	KAHCH sah-aht
How many minutes?	*Kaç dakika?*	KAHCH dahk-kah
What does it mean?	*Ne demek?*	NEH deh-mehk
This	*Bu(nu)*	boo(NOO)
That	*Şu(nu)*	shoo(NOO)
The other	*o(nu)*	oh(NOO)
Give me	.... *bana verin*	bah-NAH veh-reen
I want	.... *istiyorum*	ees-tee-YOH-room
Hot/cold	*Sıcak/soğuk*	suh-JAHK/soh-OOK
Big/small	*Büyük/küçük*	bew-YEWK/kew-CHEWK
New/old	*Yeni/eski*	yeh-NEE/ehss-KEE
Open/closed	*Açık/kapalı*	ah-CHUHK/kah-pah-LUH

Greetings & Polite Phrases

English	Turkish	Pronunciation
Hello	*Merhaba*	MEHR-hah-bah
Good morning,	*Günaydın*	gew-nahy-DUHN
Good day	*Günaydın*	gew-nahy-DUHN
Good evening	*İyi akşamlar*	EE ahk-shahm-LAHR
Good night	*İyi geceler*	EE geh-jeh-LEHR

Good-bye	*Allaha ısmarladık*	ah-LAHS-mahr-lah-duhk (said only by the person who is departing to go somewhere – see *Güle Güle*)
Bon Voyage	*Güle güle*	gew-LEH gew-LEH
How are you?	*Nasılsınız?*	NAHS-suhl-suh-nuhz (see *İyiyim, teşekkür ederim*)
Very well	*Çok iyiyim*	CHOHK ee-YEE-yeem
Pardon me	*Affedersiniz*	af-feh-DEHR-see-neez
May it contribute to your health	*Afiyet olsun!*	ah-fee-EHT ohl-soon (said to someone sitting down to a meal)
May your life be spared	*Basınız sağ olsun!*	bah-shuh-nuhz SAAH ohl-soon (said to someone who has just experienced a death in the family)
May your soul be safe from harm	*Canınız sağ olsun!*	jah-nuh-nuhz SAAH ohl-soon (said to someone who has just accidentally broken something)
May it be in your past	*Geçmiş olsun!*	gech-MEESH ohl-soon (said to someone who is ill or injured, or otherwise distressed)
Good-bye	*Güle güle*	gew-LEH gew-leh (said only by the person who is staying behind; literally, 'Go smiling' – see *Allah ısmarladık*)
Good morning/Good day	*Günaydın*	gew-nah-yee-DUHN
I'm fine, thank you	*İyiyim, teşekkür ederim*	ee-YEE-yihm, tesh-ek-KEWR eh-dehr-eem
Please	*Lütfen*	LEWT-fehn (see *Teşekkür ederim*)
May it last for hours	*Saatler olsun!*	saaht-LEHR ohl-soon (said to someone who just emerged from a bath or shower, a shave or a hair cut. It's a corruption of *sihhatler olsun*)
'In your honour' or 'To your health'	*Şerefinize!*	sheh-rehf-ee-neez-EH

Getting Around
Requests

Where is a/the	.... *nerede?*	NEH-reh-deh
.... railway station?	*Gar/İstasyon*	GAHR, ees-tah-SYOHN
.... bus station?	*Otogar*	OH-toh-gahr
.... cheap hotel?	*Ucuz bir otel*	oo-JOOZ beer oh-TEHL
.... toilet?	*Tuvalet*	too-vah-LEHT
.... restaurant?	*Lokanta*	loh-KAHN-tah
.... post office?	*Postane*	POHSS-tah-neh
.... policeman?	*Polis memuru*	poh-LEES meh-moo-roo
.... checkroom?	*Emanetçi*	EH-mah-NEHT-chee
Left	*Sol*	SOHL
Right	*Sağ*	SAH
Straight on	*Doğru*	doh-ROO
Here	*Burada*	BOO-rah-dah

There	Şurada	SHOO-rah-dah
Over there	Orada	OH-rah-dah
Near	Yakın	yah-KUHN
Far	Uzak	oo-ZAHK
A ticket to	.... bir bilet	BEER bee-LEHT
A ticket to Istanbul	İstanbul'a bir bilet	uh-STAHN-bool-AH
Map	Harita	HAH-ree-TAH
Timetable	Tarife	tah-ree-FEH
Ticket	Bilet	bee-LEHT
Reserved seat	Numaralı yer	noo-MAH-rah-LUH yehr
First class	Birinci mevki	beer-EEN-jee mehv-kee
Second class	İkinci mevki	ee-KEEN-jee mehv-kee
For today	Bugün için	BOO-gewn ee-cheen
For tomorrow	Yarın için	Yah-ruhn ee-cheen
For Friday	Cuma günü için	joo-MAH gew-new ee-cheen
Single/one-way	Gidiş	gee-DEESH
Return/round-trip	Gidiş-Dönüş	gee-DEESH-dew-NURSH

Time

When does it	Ne zaman	NEH zah-mahn
.... depart?	.... kalkar?	kahl-KAHR
.... arrive?	.... gelir?	geh-LEER
Eight o'clock	Saat sekiz	sah-AHT seh-KEEZ
At nine-thirty	Saat dokuz buçukta	sah-AHT doh-KOOZ boo-chook-TAH
In 20 minutes	Yirmi dakikada	yeer-MEE dahk-kah-dah
How many hours does it take?	Kaç saat sürer?	KAHCH sah-aht sew-REHR
.... hours,	.... saat	sah-AHT
.... minutes	.... dakika	dahk-KAH
Early/late	Erken/geç	ehr-KEHN/GECH
Fast/slow	Çabuk/yavaş	chah-BOOK/yah-VAHSH
Upper/lower	Yukarı/aşaği	yoo-kah-RUH/ah-shah-UH

Trains

Railway	Demiryolu	deh-MEER-yoh-loo
Train	Tren	tee-REHN
Railway station	Gar, İstasyon	GAHR, ees-tahs-YOHN
Sleeping car	Yataklı vagon	yah-tahk-LUH vah-gohn
Dining car	Yemekli vagon	yeh-mehk-LEE vah-gohn
Couchette	Kuşet	koo-SHEHT

Buses

| Bus | Otobüs | oh-toh-BEWSS |
| Bus terminal | Otogar | OH-toh-gahr |

Airlines

| Airplane | Uçak | oo-CHAHK |
| Airport | Havaalanı | hah-VAH-ah-lah-nuh |

| Flight | *Uçuş* | oo-CHOOSH |
| Gate | *Kapı* | kah-PUH |

Ships

Ship	*Gemi*	geh-MEE
Ferryboat	*Feribot*	FEH-ree-boht
Dock	*İskele*	ees-KEH-leh
Cabin	*Kamara*	KAH-mah-rah
Berth	*Yatak*	yah-TAHK

Accommodation

Where is	*....... nerede?*	NEH-reh-deh
Where is a hotel?	*Bir otel nerede?*	BEER oh-TEHL NEH-reh-deh?
Where is the toilet?	*Tuvalet nerede?*	too-vah-LEHT NEH-reh-deh?
Where is the manager?	*Patron nerede?*	pah-TROHN NEH-reh-deh?
Where is someone who knows English?	*İngilizce bilen bir kimse nerede?*	EEN-geh-LEEZ-jeh bee-lehn beer KEEM-seh NEH-reh-deh?
Room	*Oda*	OH-dah
Single room	*Bir kişilik oda*	BEER kee-shee-leek OH-dah
Double room	*İki kişilik oda*	ee-KEE kee-shee-leek OH-dah
Triple room	*Üç kişilik oda*	EWCH kee-shee-leek OH-dah
Room with one bed	*Tek yataklı oda*	TEHK yah-tahk-LUH OH-dah
Room with two beds	*İki yataklı oda*	ee-KEE yah-tahk-LUH OH-dahh
Room with twin beds	*Çift yataklı oda*	CHEEFT yah-tahk-LUH OH-dah
Double bed	*Geniş yatak*	geh-NEESH yah-tahk
Room with bath	*Banyolu oda*	BAHN-yoh-LOO OH-dah
Room without bath	*Banyosuz oda*	BAHN-yoh-SOOZ OH-dah
Room with shower	*Duşlu oda*	doosh-LOO OH-dah
A quiet room	*Sakin bir oda*	sah-KEEN beer oh-dah
It's very noisy	*Çok gürültülü*	CHOHK gew-rewl-tew-lew
What does it cost?	*Kaç lira?*	KAHCH lee-rah
Cheaper	*Daha ucuz*	dah-HAH oo-jooz
Better	*Daha iyi*	dah-HAH ee
Very expensive	*Çok pahalı*	CHOHK pah-hah-luh
Bath	*Banyo*	BAHN-yoh
Turkish bath	*Hamam*	hah-MAHM
Shower	*Duş*	DOOSH
Soap	*Sabun*	sah-BOON
Towel	*Havlu*	hahv-LOO
Toilet paper	*Tuvalet kağıdı*	too-vah-LEHT kyah-uh-duh
Hot water	*Sıcak su*	suh-JAHK soo
Cold water	*Soğuk su*	soh-OOH soo
Clean	*Temiz*	teh-MEEZ
Not clean	*Temiz değil*	teh-MEEZ deh-YEEL
Laundry	*Çamaşır*	chah-mah-SHUHR
Dry cleaning	*Kuru temizleme*	koo-ROO teh-meez-leh-meh
Central heating	*Kalorifer*	kah-LOH-ree-FEHR
Air conditioning	*Klima*	KLEE-mah
Light(s)	*Işık(lar)*	uh-SHUHK(-LAHR)
Light bulb	*Ampül*	ahm-PEWL

Shopping

Do you have .... ?	.... *var mı?*	VAHR muh
We don't have	.... *yok*	YOHK
Cheap/expensive	*Ucuz/pahalı*	oo-JOOZ/pah-hah-LUH
Price	*Fiyat*	fee-YAHT
Which?	*Hangi?*	HAHN-gee
This one	*Bunu*	boo-NOO
Money	*Para*	PAH-rah
Small change	*Bozuk para*	boh-ZOOK pah-rah
Turkish liras	*Lira*	LEE-rah
Dollars	*Dolar*	doh-LAHR
Very expensive	*Çok pahalı*	CHOHK pah-hah-luh
I'll give you	.... *vereceğim*	VEH-reh-JEH-yeem
Shop	*Dükkan*	dyook-KAHN
Market	*Çarşı*	chahr-SHUH
This much	*Bu kadar*	BOO kah-dahr
Service charge	*Servis ücreti*	sehr-VEES ewj-reh-tee
Tax	*Vergi*	VEHR-gee

Post Office

I wonder, where's the post office?	*Acaba, postane nerede?*	AH-jah-bah POHS-tah-neh NEH-reh-deh
Open	*Açık*	ah-CHUHK
Express Mail, Special Delivery	*Ekspres*	ehks-PRESS
Customs	*Gümrük*	gewm-REWK
Money Order	*Havale*	hah-vah-LEH
Telephone token (large, small)	*Jeton (Büyük, Küçük)*	kew-CHEWK pah-keht
Closed	*Kapali*	kah-pah-LUH
Postcard	*Kartpostal*	kahrt-pohs-TAHL
Parcel	*Koli*	KOH-lee
Inspection (prior to mailing)	*Kontrol*	kohn-TROHL
'Small Packet' (a mail category)	*Küçük Paket*	kew-CHEWK pah-keht
Printed Matter	*Matbua*	MAHT-boo-ah
Letter	*Mektup*	meht-TOOP
Parcel	*Paket*	pah-KEHT
Poste Restante, General Delivery	*Postrestant*	pohst-rehs-TAHNT
Postage Stamp	*Pul*	POOL
Registered Mail	*Taahhütlü*	TAA-hewt-LEW
'By Plane' (Airmail)	*Uçakla* or *Uçak İle*	oo-CHAHK-lah, oo-CHAHK-ee-leh

Menu Translator

Except in the fanciest restaurants, Turks don't have much use for menus. This is a society in which the waiter (*garson*, gahr-SOHN) is supposed to know his business and to help you order. Nonetheless, the waiter will bring a menu (*menü*, meh-NEW, or *yemek listesi*, yeh-MEHK lees-teh-see) if you ask for one. The menu will at least give you some prices so you'll know what you will be asked to pay.

Otherwise, you may choose from the menu several times only to get the response *Yok!* (YOHK, None!). The menu, as I said, is not much use. Instead, the waiter will probably say *Gel! Gel!* (Come, come!) and lead you into the kitchen for a look. In the glass-fronted refrigerator cabinets you'll see the shish kebabs, *köfte, bonfile* steaks, lamb chops, liver, kidneys and fish which are in supply. Also in the cabinet may be the cheeses, salads and vegetable dishes, if meant to be served cold. Then he'll lead you right to the fire for a look at the stews, soups, pastas and pilavs. With sign language, you'll have everything you want in no time. It's a good idea to ask prices for a few items, though cheating on price has not been much of a problem in Turkey in the past.

Some general words to know are:

Lokanta	loh-KAHN-tah	Restaurant
Pastane	PAHSS-tah-neh	Pastry-shop
Fırın	FUH-ruhn	'Oven' (bakery)
Pideci	PEE-deh-jee	'Pizza' place
Köfteci	KURF-teh-jee	Köfte restaurant
Kebapçı	keh-BAHP-chuh	Kebap restaurant
Büfe	bew-FEH	Snack shop
Kahvahltı	KAHH-vahl-TUH	Breakfast
Öğle yemeği	ury-LEH yeh-meh-yee	Lunch
Akşam yemeği	ahk-SHAHM yeh-meh-yee	Supper
Yemek	yeh-MEHK	To eat; meal, dish
Porsyon	pohr-SYOHN	Portion, serving
Çatal	chah-TAHL	Fork
Bıçak	buh-CHAHK	Knife
Kaşık	kah-SHUHK	Spoon
Tabak	tah-BAHK	Plate
Bardak	bahr-DAHK	Glass
Hesap	heh-SAHP	Bill, check
Servis ücreti	sehr-VEES ewj-reh-tee	Service charge
Vergi	VEHR-gee	Tax
Bahşiş	bah-SHEESH	Tip
Yanlış	yahn-LUSH	Error
Bozuk para	boh-ZOOK pah-rah	Small change

Here is a guide to restaurant words, arranged (more or less) in the order of a Turkish menu and a Turkish meal. I've given the names of the corses (*çorba, et*, etc) in the singular form; you may see them in the plural (*çorbalar, etler*, etc).

Çorba (CHOHR-bah, Soup)

Balık Çorbası	bah-LUHK	Fish soup
Domates Çorbası	doh-MAH-tess	Tomato soup
Düğün Çorbası	dew-EWN	Egg-and-lemon soup
Et suyu (yumurtalı)	EHT soo-yoo, yoo-moor-tah-LUH	Mutton broth with egg
Ezo Gelin çorbası	EH-zoh GEH-leen	Lentil & rice soup
Haşlama	hahsh-lah-MAH	Broth with mutton
İşkembe çorbası	eesh-KEHM-beh	Tripe soup
Mercimek çorbası	mehr-jee-MEHK	Lentil soup
Paça	PAH-chah	Trotter soup
Sebze çorbası	SEHB-zeh	Vegetable soup
Şehriye çorbası	shehh-ree-YEH	Vermicelli soup
Tavuk çorbası	tah-VOOK	Chicken soup
Yayla çorbası	YAHY-lah	Yogurt & barley soup

Meze (MEH-zeh, Hors d'Oeuvres)

Note: *Meze* can include almost anything, and you can easily – and delightfully – make an entire meal of *meze*. Often you will be brought a tray from which you can choose those you want.

Beyaz peynir	bey-AHZ pehy-neer	White cheese
Börek	bur-REHK	Flaky pastry
Kabak dolması	kah-BAHK	Stuffed squash/marrow
Patlıcan salatası	paht-luh-JAHN	Aubergine/eggplant puree
Pilaki, Piyaz	pee-LAH-kee	Cold white beans vinaigrette
Tarama salatası	tah-rah-MAH	Red caviar in mayonnaise
Yalancı dolması	yah-LAHN-juh	See *Yaprak dolması*
Yaprak dolması	yah-PRAHK dohl-mah-suh	Stuffed vine leaves
(etli)	eht-LEE	with lamb (hot)
(zeytinyağlı)	zehy-teen-yah-LUH	with rice (cold)

Balık (bah-LUHK, Fish)

Note: A menu is no use in ordering fish. You must ask the waiter what's fresh, and then ask the approximate price. The fish will be weighed, and the price computed at the day's per-kilo rate. Sometimes you can haggle. Buy fish in season (*mevsimli*), mehv– seem-LEE , as fish out of season are very expensive.

Alabalık	ah-LAH-bah-luhk	Trout
Barbunya	bahr-BOON-yah	Red mullet
Dil balığı	DEEL bah-luh	Sole
Hamsi	HAHM-see	Anchovy (fresh)
Havyar	hahv-YAHR	Caviar
Istakoz	uhss-tah-KOHZ	Lobster

Kalkan	kahl-KAHN	Turbot
Karagöz	kah-rah-GURZ	Black bream
Karides	kah-REE-dess	Shrimp
Kefal	keh-FAHL	Grey mullet
Kılıç	kuh-LUHCH	Swordfish
Levrek	lehv-REHK	Sea bass
Lüfer	lew-FEHR	Bluefish
Mercan	mehr-JAHN	Red coralfish
Midye	MEED-yeh	Mussels
Palamut	PAH-lah-moot	Tunny, bonito
Pisi	PEE-see	Plaice
Sardalya	sahr-DAHL-yah	Sardine (fresh)
Tarama	tah-rah-MAH	Roe, red caviar
Trança	TRAHN-chah	Aegean tuna
Uskumru	oos-KOOM-roo	Mackerel
Yengeç	yehn-GECH	Crab

Et ve Kebap (EHT veh keh-BAHP, Meat and Kebab)

Note: In *kebap* (keh-BAHP) the meat is always lamb, ground or in chunks; preparation, spices and extras (onions, peppers, *pide*) make the difference among the kebaps. Some may be ordered *yoğurtlu* (yoh-oort-LOO) , with a side-serving of yogurt.

Adana kebap	ah-DAH-nah	Spicy-hot roast köfte
Böbrek	bur-BREHK	Kidney
Bonfile	bohn-fee-LEH	Small filet beefsteak
Bursa kebap	BOOR-sah	Döner with tomato sauce
Çerkez tavuğu	cher-KEHZ tah-voo	Chicken in walnut sauce
Çöp kebap	CHURP	Tiny bits of skewered lamb
Ciğer	jee-EHR	Liver
Dana	DAH-nah	Veal
Döner kebap	dur-NEHR	Spit-roasted lamb slices
Domuz	doh-MOOZ	Pork (forbidden to Muslims)
Güveç	gew-VECH	Meat & vegetable stew
Kağıt kebap	kyah-UHT	Lamb & vegetables in paper
Karışık ızgara	kah-ruh-shuk uhz-gah-rah	Mixed grill (lamb)
Koç yumurtası	KOHCH yoo-moor-tah-suh	Ram's 'eggs' (testicles)
Köfte	KURF-teh	Grilled ground lamb patties
Kuzu (süt)	koo-ZOO (SEWT)	Milk-fed lamb
Orman kebap	ohr-MAHN	Roast lamb with onions
Pastırma	pahss-TUHR-mah	Sun-dried, spiced beef
Patlıcan kebap	paht-luh-JAHN	Aubergine/eggplant & meat
Pilic	pee-LEECH	Roasting chicken
Pirzola	peer-ZOH-lah	Cutlet (usually lamb)
Şatobriyan	sha-TOH-bree-YAHN	Chateaubriand
Sığır	suh-UHR	Beef
Şinitzel	shee-NEET-zehl	Wienerschnitzel

Şiş kebap	SHEESH	Roast skewered lamb
Tandır kebap	tahn-DUHR	Pit-roasted lamb
Tas kebap	TAHSS	Lamb stew
Tavuk	tah-VOOK	Boiling chicken

Salata (sah-LAH-tah, Salad)

Note: Each one of the names below would be followed by the word *salata* or *salatası*. You may be asked if you prefer it *sirkeli* (SEER-keh-LEE), with vinegar or *limonlu* (LEE-mohn-LOO), with lemon juice ; most salads (except söğüş) come with olive oil. If you don't like hot peppers, say *bibersiz* (BEE-behr-SEEZ), though this often doesn't work.

Amerikan	ah-meh-ree-KAHN	Mayonnaise, peas, carrots
Beyin	behy-EEN	Sheep's brain
Çoban	choh-BAHN	Chopped mixed salad
Domates salatalık	doh-MAH-tess sah-LAH-tah-luhk	Tomato & cucumber salad
Karışık	kah-ruh-SHUHK	Chopped mixed salad
Marul	mah-ROOL	Romaine lettuce
Patlıcan	paht-luh-JAHN	Roast aubergine/eggplant puree
Rus	ROOSS	Mayonnaise, peas, carrots
Söğüş	sur-EWSH	Plain sliced vegetables
Turşu	toor-SHOO	Pickled vegetables
Yeşil	yeh-SHEEL	Green salad

Sebze (sehb-ZEH, Vegetable)

Bamya	BAHM-yah	Okra
Barbunye	bahr-BOON-yeh	Red beans
Bezelye	beh-ZEHL-yeh	Peas
Biber	bee-BEHR	Peppers
Domates	doh-MAH-tess	Tomato
Havuç	hah-VOOCH	Carrot
Hıyar	huh-YAHR	Cucumber
Ispınak	uhs-spuh-NAHK	Spinach
Kabak	kah-BAHK	Marrow/squash
Karnabahar	kahr-NAH-bah-hahr	Cauliflower
Kuru fasulye	koo-ROO fah-sool-yah	White beans
Lahana	lah-HAH-nah	Cabbage
Patates	pah-TAH-tess	Potato
Salatalık	sah-LAH-tah-luhk	Cucumber
Soğan	soh-AHN	Onion
Taze fasulye	tah-ZEH fah-sool-yah	Green beans
Turp	TOORP	Radish

Meyva (mehy-VAH, Fruit)

Armut	ahr-MOOT	Pear
Ayva	ahy-VAH	Quince
Çilek	chee-LEHK	Strawberries
Elma	ehl-MAH	Apple
Greyfurut	GREY-foo-root	Grapefruit
İncir	een-JEER	Fig
Karpuz	kahr-POOZ	Watermelon
Kavun	kah-VOON	Yellow melon
Kayısı	kahy-SUH	Apricot
Kiraz	kee-RAHZ	Cherry
Mandalin	mahn-dah-LEEN	Tangerine, Mandarin
Muz	MOOZ	Banana
Nar	NAHR	Pomegranate
Portakal	pohr-tah-KAHL	Orange
Şeftali	shef-tah-LEE	Peach
Üzüm	ew-ZEWM	Grapes
Vişne	VEESH-neh	Morello (sour cherry)

Tatlı (taht-LUH, Sweets/Desserts)

Aşure	ah-shoo-REH	Walnut, raisin, pea pudding
Baklava	bahk-lah-VAH	Many-layer pie, honey, nuts
Burma kadayıf	boor-MAH kah-dah-yuhf	Shredded wheat with pistachios & honey
Dondurma	dohn-DOOR-mah	Ice cream
Ekmek kadayıf	ehk-MEHK kah-dah-yuhf	Crumpet in syrup
Fırın sütlaç	foo-roon SEWT-lach	Baked rice pudding (cold)
Güllaç	gewl-LACH	Flaky pastry, nuts, milk
Helva	hehl-VAH	Semolina sweet
Hurma tatlısı	hoor-MAH	Semolina cake in syrup
Kabak tatlısı	kah-BAHK	Candied marrow/squash
Kadin göbeği	kah-DEEN gur-beh-yee	'Lady's navel', doughnut in syrup
Kazandibi	kah-ZAHN-dee-bee	'Bottom of the pot', baked pudding (cold)
Kek	KEHK	Cake
Keşkül	kehsh-KEWL	Milk & nut pudding
Komposto	kohm-POHSS-toh	Stewed fruit
Krem karamel	KREHM kah-rah-MEHL	Baked caramel custard
Krem şokolada	KREHM shoh-koh-LAH-dah	Chocolate pudding
Lokum	loh-KOOM	Turkish Delight
Meyve	mehy-VEH	Fruit
Muhallebi	moo-HAH-leh-bee	Rice flour & rosewater pudding
Pasta	PAHSS-tah	Pastry

Peynir tatlısı	pehy-NEER TAHT-luh-suh	Cheese cake
Sütlaç	sewt-LAHCH	Rice pudding
Tavuk göğsü	tah-VOOK gur-sew	Sweet of milk, rice, chicken
Tel kadayıf	TEHL kah-dah-yuhf	Shredded wheat in syrup
Yoğurt tatlısı	yoh-OORT taht-luh-suh	Yogurt & egg pudding
Zerde	zehr-DEH	Saffron & rice sweet

Other Dishes and Condiments

Bal	BAHL	Honey
Beyaz peynir	bey-AHZ pey-neer	White (sheep's cheese)
Bisküvi	BEES-koo-VEE	Biscuits
Börek (-ği)	bur-REHK	Flaky or fried pastry
Kıymalı	kuhy-mah-LUH	With ground lamb
Peynirli	pehy-neer-LEE	With white cheese
Sigara	see-GAH-rah	'Cigarette' fritters
Su	SOO	Noodle pie
Buz	BOOZ	Ice
Cacık	jah-JUHK	Yogurt & grated cucumber
Dolma(sı)	DOHL-mah(-suh)	Stuffed (vegetable)
Biber	bee-BEHR	Green pepper
Kabak	kah-BAHK	Marrow/squash
Lahana	lah-HAH-nah	Cabbage leaves
Yalancı	yah-LAHN-juh	Vine leaves
Yaprak	yah-PRAHK	Vine leaves
Ekmek	ehk-MEHK	Bread
Hardal	hahr-DAHL	Mustard
İmam bayıldı	ee-MAHM bah-yuhl-duh	Aubergine/eggplant baked with onions & tomatoes
Kara biber	kah-RAH bee-behr	Black pepper
Karnıyarık	KAHR-nuh-yah-RUHK	Aubergine & lamb (hot)
Kaşar peynir	kah-SHAHR pey-neer	Mild yellow cheese
Limon	lee-MOHN	Lemon
Makarna	mah-KAHR-nah	Macaroni, noodles
Musakka	moo-sah-KAH	Aubergine & lamb pie
Pasta	PAHSS-tah	Pastry (not noodles)
Peynir	pehy-NEER	Cheese
Pide	PEE-deh	Pizza; flat bread
Reçel	reh-CHEHL	Fruit jam
Sarmısak	SAHR-muh-SAHK	Garlic
Şeker	sheh-KEHR	Sugar; candy; sweets
Sirke	SEER-keh	Vinegar
Siyah biber	see-YAH bee-behr	Black pepper
Spaket	spah-KEHT	Spaghetti
Tereyağı	TEH-reh-yah	Butter
Tuz	TOOZ	Salt
Yağ	YAH	Oil, fat
Yoğurt	yoh-OORT	Yogurt

| Zeytin | zehy-TEEN | Olives |
| Zeytinyaği | zehy-TEEN-yah-uh | Olive oil |

İcki, Meşrubat (eech-KEE, mehsh-roo-BAHT, Drinks)

Note: *İcki* usually refers to alcoholic beverages, *meşrubat* to soft drinks. If your waiter says *İçecek?* or *Ne içeceksiniz?*, he's asking what you'd like to drink.

As for Turkish coffee, you must order it by sweetness; the sugar is mixed in during the brewing, not afterwards. When the waiter asks *Kahve?* (kahh-VEH), say *sade* (sah-DEH) if you want no sugar; *az* (AHZ) if you want just a bit; *orta* (ohr-TAH) for a middling amount; *çok* or *şekerli* or even *çok şekerli* (CHOHK sheh-kehr-LEE) if you want lots of sugar. When the coffee arrives, the waiter may well have confused the cups, and you may find yourself exchanging with your dinner-mates.

Aslan sütü	ahs-LAHN sew-tew	'Lion's milk' (*rakı*)
Ayran	AH-yee-RAHN	Yogurt drink
Bira	BEE-rah	Beer
Beyaz	bey-AHZ	Light
Siyah	see-YAH	Dark
Boza	BOH-zah	Thick millet drink
Buz	BOOZ	Ice
Çay	CHAH-yee	Tea
Cin	JEEN	Gin
Kahve(si)	kah-VEH(-see)	Coffee
Türk	TEWRK	Turkish
Fransız	frahn-SUHZ	Coffee & milk
Amerikan	ah-meh-ree-KAHN	American coffee
Limonata	lee-moh-NAH-tah	Lemonade
Maden sodası	mah-DEHN soh-dah-suh	Fizzy mineral water
Maden suyu	mah-DEHN soo-yoo	Mineral water
Rakı	rah-KUH	Anise-flavoured brandy
Sahlep	sah-LEHP	Hot milk & tapioca root
Şarap	shah-RAHP	Wine
Beyaz	bey-AHZ	White
Kırmızı	kuhr-muh-ZUH	Red
Köpüklü	kur-pewk-LEW	Sparkling
Roze	roh-ZEH	Rose
Su	SOO	Water
Süt	SEWT	Milk
Vermut	vehr-MOOT	Vermouth
Viski	VEE-skee	Whisky
Votka	VOHT-kah	Vodka

Cooking Terms

Buğlama	BOO-lah-MAH	Steamed
Etli	eht-LEE0	With meat
Ezme(si)	ehz-MEH(-see)	Puree
Fırın	fuh-RUHN	Baked, oven-roasted

Haşlama	hahsh-lah-MAH	Boiled, stewed
İyi pişmiş	ee-YEE peesh-meesh	Well-done, –cooked
Izgara	uhz-GAH-rah	Charcoal grilled
Kıymalı	kuhy-mah-LUH	With ground lamb
Kızartma	kuh-ZAHRT-mah	Broiled
Peynirli	pehy-neer-LEE	With cheese
Pişkin	peesh-KEEN	Well-done, –cooked
Rosto	ROHSS-toh	Roasted
Salçalı	sahl-chah-LUH	With savoury tomato sauce
Sıcak	suh-JAHK	Hot, warm
Soğuk	soh-OOK	Cold
Soslu	sohss-LOO	With sauce
Terbiyeli	TEHR-bee-yeh-LEE	With sauce
Yoğurtlu	YOH-oort-LOO	With yogurt
Yumurtali	yoo-moor-tah-LUH	With egg

Index

LONELY PLANET NEWSLETTER

We collect an enormous amount of information here at Lonely Planet. Apart from our research we also get a steady stream of letters from people out on the road – some of them are just one line on a postcard, others go on for pages. Plus we always have an ear to the ground for the latest on cheap airfares, new visa regulations, borders opening and closing. A lot of this information goes into our new editions or 'update supplements' in reprints. But we want to make better use of this information so, we also produce a quarterly newsletter packed full of the latest news from out on the road. It appears in January, April, July and October of each year. If you'd like an airmailed copy of the most recent newsletter just send us $7.50 for a years subscription, or for $2 each for single issues. That's US$ in the US or A$ for Australia, write to:

Lonely Planet Publications

PO Box 88, Sth Yarra, VIC., 3141 Australia
or
Lonely Planet Publications

PO Box 2001A, Berkeley, CA 94702 USA

Contents

Ruins: Troy   Med. Cente Galen Asclepion

· pg 191 → Pergamum (Bergama Taxi from Izmir)

Tour#12

Ephesus

pg 202 # Miletus & Priene Didymos. day trip

Helicarassus

Side   Bodrum from Kusadasi

(Mausoleum)

Izmir = Ionia

(Smyrna) Ionic columns

no mosques on Fridays
Cover Arms/head "long" skirt

Lonely Planet travel guides

Africa on a Shoestring
Australia – a travel survival kit
Alaska – a travel survival kit
Bali & Lombok – a travel survival kit
Burma – a travel survival kit
Bushwalking in Papua New Guinea
Canada – a travel survival kit
China – a travel survival kit
Hong Kong, Macau & Canton
India – a travel survival kit
Japan – a travel survival kit
Kashmir, Ladakh & Zanskar
Kathmandu & the Kingdom of Nepal
Korea & Taiwan – a travel survival kit
Malaysia, Singapore & Brunei – a travel survival kit
Mexico – a travel survival kit
New Zealand – a travel survival kit
Pakistan – a travel survival kit
Papua New Guinea – a travel survival kit
The Philippines – a travel survival kit
South America on a Shoestring
South-East Asia on a Shoestring
Sri Lanka – a travel survival kit
Thailand – a travel survival kit
Tramping in New Zealand
Trekking in the Himalayas
USA West
West Asia on a Shoestring

Lonely Planet phrasebooks

Indonesia Phrasebook
Nepal Phrasebook
Thailand Phrasebook

Lonely Planet travel guides are available around the world. If you can't find them, ask your bookshop to order them from one of the distributors listed below. For countries not listed or if you would like a free copy of our latest booklist write to Lonely Planet in Australia.

Australia
Lonely Planet Publications, PO Box 88, South Yarra, Victoria 3141.

Canada see USA

Denmark
Scanvik Books aps, Store Kongensgade 59 A, DK-1264 Copenhagen K.

Hong Kong
The Book Society, GPO Box 7804.

India & Nepal
UBS Distributors, 5 Ansari Rd, New Delhi.

Israel
Geographical Tours Ltd, 8 Tverya St, Tel Aviv 63144.

Japan
Intercontinental Marketing Corp, IPO Box 5056, Tokyo 100-31.

Malaysia
MPH Distributors, 13 Jalan 13/6, Petaling Jaya, Selangor.

Netherlands
Nilsson & Lamm bv, Postbus 195, Pampuslaan 212, 1380 AD Weesp.

New Zealand
Roulston Greene Publishing Associates Ltd, Box 33850, Takapuna, Auckland 9.

Pakistan
London Book House, 281/C Tariq Rd, PECHS Karachi 29, Pakistan

Papua New Guinea
Gordon & Gotch (PNG), PO Box 3395, Port Moresby.

Singapore
MPH Distributors, 3rd Storey, 601 Sims Drive #03-21, Singapore 1438

Sweden
Esselte Kartcentrum AB, Vasagatan 16, S-111 20 Stockholm.

Thailand
Chalermnit, 1-2 Erawan Arcade, Bangkok.

UK
Roger Lascelles, 47 York Rd, Brentford, Middlesex, TW8 0QP.

USA
Lonely Planet Publications, PO Box 2001A, Berkeley, CA 94702.

West Germany
Buchvertrieb Gerda Schettler, Postfach 64, D3415 Hattorf a H.

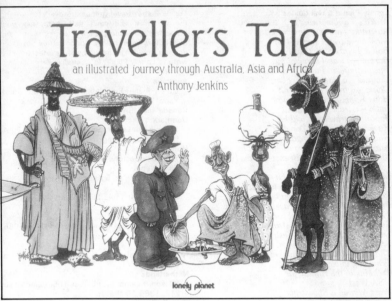

Traveller's Tales

an illustrated journey through Australia, Asia and Africa

Anthony Jenkins

lonely planet

Cartoonist Anthony Jenkins has spent several years on the road, travelling in 55 countries around the world. Along the way he has filled numerous sketchbooks with his drawings of the people he met.

This is a book of people, not places. A tattooed Iban tribesman in Sarawak, a mango seller in Cameroon, fellow travellers in Nepal . . . all are drawn with perception and (in most cases) affection.

Equally perceptive are Jenkins' written comments and descriptions of incidents during his travels. The combined result is like a series of personal illustrated letters.

. This is a traveller's travel book. If you have ever endured an Indian train, watched the world go by in Kathmandu's Durbar Square or tried to post a letter in southern Africa, then opening these pages will be like meeting old friends and will probably give you itchy feet to be on the road once more.